Keltie (ed.)

A history of the Scottish Highlands,
- ?... clans and Highland Regiments

vol 2.²

Hill pushed forward from Alava to attack the left. The enemy dreading the consequences of an attack on his centre, which he had weakened to strengthen his posts on the heights, abandoned his position, and commenced a rapid retreat to Vittoria.

Whilst these combined movements of the right and centre were in progress, the left wing, under Sir Thomas Graham, drove the enemy's right from the hills above Abechuco and Gamarra. To preserve their communication with Bayonne, which was nearly cut off by this movement, the enemy had occupied the villages of Gamarra, Mayor, and Menor, near which the great road touches the banks of the Zadorra. They were, however, driven from these positions by a Spanish division under Colonel Longa, and another of Portuguese under General Pack, supported by General Anson's cavalry brigade and the fifth division of infantry under General Oswald. General Graham, at the same time, attacked and obtained possession of the village of Abechuco.

Thus cut off from retreat by the great road to France, the enemy, as soon as the centre of the allies had penetrated to Vittoria, retreated with great precipitation towards Pampluna, the only other road left open, and on which they had no fortified positions to cover their retrograde movement. The enemy left behind them all their stores and baggage, and out of 152 pieces of cannon, they carried off only one howitzer. General Hill, with his division, continued to pursue the panic-stricken French from one position to another till the 7th of July, when he took post on the summit of the pass of Maya, beyond the Pyrenees, "those lofty heights which," as Marshal Soult lamented, in a proclamation he issued, "enabled him proudly to survey our fertile valleys."

With the exception of Pampluna and St Sebastian, the whole of this part of the north of Spain was now cleared of the enemy. To reduce these places was the next object. It was resolved to blockade the former and lay siege to the latter, which last-mentioned service was intrusted to General Graham. This was a most arduous task, as St Sebastian was, in point of strength, next to Gibraltar. After an unsuccessful assault, however, the attention of the commander-in-chief being directed to the movements of Marshal Soult, who was advancing with a large army, the siege of St Sebastian was suspended for a time.

At this time the allied army occupied a range of mountain passes between the valley of Roncesvalles, celebrated as the field of Charlemagne's defeat, and St Sebastian, but as the distance between these stations was sixty miles, it was found impossible so to guard all these passes as to prevent the entrance of an army. The passes occupied by the allies were defended by the following troops:—Major General Byng's brigade and a division of Spanish infantry held the valley of Roncesvalles, to support which General Cole's division was posted at Piscarret, with General Picton's in reserve at Olaque, the valley of Bastan and the pass of Maya was occupied by Sir Rowland Hill, with Lieutenant-general William Stewart's and Silviera's Portuguese divisions, and the Spanish corps under the Conde de Amaran; the Portuguese brigade of Brigadier-general Archibald Campbell was detached to Los Alduidos; the heights of St Barbara, the town of Pera, and the Puerto de Echelar, were protected by Lord Dalhousie and Baron Alten's light division, Brigadier-general Pack's being in reserve at Estevan. The communication between Lord Dalhousie and General Graham was kept up by General Longa's Spanish division, and the Conde de Abisbal blockaded Pampluna.

Such were the positions of the allied army when Marshal Soult, who had been lately appointed to the command of a numerous French army, recently collected, having formed a plan of operations for a general attack on the allied army, advanced on the 25th of July at the head of a division of 36,000 men against Roncesvalles, whilst General Count d'Erlon, with another division of 13,000 men, moved towards the pass of Maya. Pressed by this overwhelming force, General Byng was obliged, though supported by part of Sir Lowry Cole's division, to descend from the heights that commanded the pass, in order to preserve his communication, in which situation he was attacked by Soult and driven back to the top of the mountain whilst the troops on the ridge of Arola, part of Cole's division, were forced to retire with considerable loss, and to take up a position in the rear   General Cole was again obliged to retire, and fell back on Lizoain   Next day General Picton moved forward to support General Cole, but both were obliged to retire in consequence of Soult's advance

Meanwhile Count d'Erlon forced the battalions occupying the narrow ridges near the pass of Maya to give way, but these being quickly supported by Brigadier-general Barnes's brigade, a series of spirited actions ensued, and the advance of the enemy was arrested   General Hill hearing of the retrograde movement from Roncesvalles, retired behind the Irurita, and took up a strong position   On the 27th Sir Thomas Picton resumed his retreat   The troops were greatly dejected at this temporary reverse, but the arrival of Lord Wellington, who had been with the army before St Sebastian, revived their drooping spirits   Immediately on his arrival he directed the troops in reserve to move forward to support the division opposed to the enemy, formed General Picton's division on a ridge on the left bank of the Argua, and General Cole's on the high grounds between that river and the Lanz.   To support the positions in front, General Hill was posted behind the Lizasso, but, on the arrival of General Pakenham on the 28th, he took post on the left of General Cole, facing the village of Sourarom, but before the British divisions had fully occupied the ground, they were vigorously attacked by the enemy from the village   The enemy were, however, driven back with great loss

Soult next brought forward a strong column, and advancing up the hill against the centre of the allies, on the left of General Cole's line, obtained possession of that post, but he was almost immediately driven back at the point of the bayonet by the Fusiliers   The French renewed the attack, but were again quickly repulsed   About the same time another attack was made on the right of the centre, where a Spanish brigade, supported by the 40th, was posted   The Spaniards gave way, the 40th not only keeping their ground, but driving the enemy down the hill with great loss

The enemy pushing forward in separate bodies with great vigour, the battle now became general along the whole front of the heights occupied by the fourth division, but they were repulsed at all points, except one occupied by a Portuguese battalion, which was overpowered and obliged to give way   The occupation of this post by the enemy exposed the flank of Major-General Ross's brigade, immediately on the right, to a destructive fire, which forced him to retire.   The enemy were, however, soon dispossessed of this post by Colonel John Maclean, who, advancing with the 27th and 48th regiments, charged and drove them from it, and immediately afterwards attacked and charged another body of the enemy who were advancing from the left   The enemy persevered in his attacks several times, but was as often repulsed, principally by the bayonet   Several regiments charged four different times

After various successful attacks, the enemy, on the 30th, to use the words of Lord Wellington, "abandoned a position which is one of the strongest and most difficult of access that I have yet seen occupied by troops"   The enemy were now pursued beyond Olaque, in the vicinity of which General Hill, who had been engaged the whole day, had repulsed all the attacks of Count d'Erlon.

The enemy endeavoured to rally in their retreat, but were driven from one position to another till the 2d of August, when the allies had regained all the posts they had occupied on the 25th of July, when Soult made his first attack.   As the 92d or Gordon Highlanders was the Highland regiment which had the good fortune to be engaged in these brilliant attacks, in which they particularly distinguished themselves, the account of these operations might have been deferred till we come to give an account of the services of that excellent regiment, but as the omission of these details in this place would have broken the continuity of the narrative, it was deemed proper to insert them here

After this second expulsion of the French beyond the Pyrenees, the siege of St Sebastian was resumed with redoubled energy   A continued fire was kept up from eighty pieces of cannon, which the enemy withstood with surprising courage and perseverance   At length a practicable breach was made, and on the morning of the 31st of August the troops advanced to the assault. The breach was extensive, but there was only one point at which it was possible to enter, and this could only be done by single files. All the inside of the wall to the height of the curtain formed a perpendicular scarp of twenty feet. The troops made the most persevering exertions to force the breach, and everything that bravery could attempt was repeatedly tried by the men, who were brought forward in succession from the trenches; but each time, on attaining the summit, all who attempted to remain were destroyed by a heavy fire from the entrenched ruins within, so that "no man outlived the attempt to gain the ridge."[4] The moment was critical; but General Graham, with great presence of mind, directed his artillery to play against the curtain, so as to pass a few feet over the heads of the troops in the breach. The fire was directed with admirable precision, and the troops advanced with perfect confidence. They struggled unremittingly for two hours to force the breach, and, taking advantage of some confusion occasioned by an explosion of ammunition within the ramparts, they redoubled their efforts, and by assisting each other got over the walls and ruins. After struggling about an hour among their works, the French retreated with great loss to the castle, leaving the town, which was now reduced to a heap of ruins, in the possession of the assailants. This success was dearly purchased,—the loss of the allies, in killed and wounded, being upwards of 2000 men. Soult made an attempt to raise the siege, by crossing the Bidassoa on the very day the assault was made with a force of nearly 40,000 men; but he was obliged, after repeated attacks, to repass the river.

Having determined to carry the war into France, Lord Wellington crossed the Bidassoa at low water, near its mouth, on the 7th of October. After a series of successful operations, the allied army was established in the French territories; but as Pampluna still held out, the commander-in-chief delayed his advance for a time. Pampluna surrendered on the 31st of October, after a blockade of four months. Lord Wellington having now the whole allied force, amounting to upwards of

4 General Graham's Despatches.

85,000 men, at his disposal, resolved to commence operations.

Since the battle of the Pyrenees, the French had occupied a position with their right towards the sea, at a short distance from St Jean de Luz, their centre on a village in Sare, and on the heights behind it, with their left resting on a stony height in the rear of Ainhoe. This position, strong by nature, had been rendered still stronger by art. The attack on the French lines was to be made in columns of divisions. In consequence of heavy falls of snow and rain, Lord Wellington was obliged to defer his attack till the 10th of November, on the morning of which day the allies moved forward against the enemy.

The attack was begun by General Cole's division, which attacked and carried the principal redoubt in front of Sare with such rapidity, that several of the enemy were taken in it before it could be evacuated. Another redoubt on the left was carried in the same rapid manner by Lord Dalhousie's division, commanded in his absence by Colonel Le Cor. General Cole's division thereupon took possession of the village. General Alten having carried La Petite Rhune, the whole centre divisions united, and made a joint attack on the enemy's principal position behind the village. Sir Thomas Picton's division (now commanded in his absence by General Colville), and that of Le Cor, carried the redoubt on the left of the enemy's centre. The light division advancing from La Petite Rhune, attacked the works in their front, supported by the 52d regiment, which, crossing with great rapidity a narrow neck of land, was here exposed to the fire of two flanking batteries, rushed up the hill with such impetuosity, that the enemy grew alarmed, and fled with precipitation.

Meanwhile the right, under General Hill, attacked the heights of Ainhoe. The attack was led by General Clinton's division, which, marching on the left of five redoubts, forded the Nivelle, the banks of which were steep and difficult, and attacked the troops in front of the works. These were immediately driven back with loss, and General Hamilton joining in the attack on the other redoubt, the enemy hastily retired. The brigade of General Stewart's division, under General Pringle, drove in the enemy's picquets in front of Ainhoe, whilst General Byng's brigade attacked and drove the enemy from the entrenchments, and from a redoubt farther to the left.

The enemy at length seeing further resistance hopeless, abandoned all their positions and works in front of St Jean de Luz and retired upon Bidart, after destroying all the bridges on the Lower Nivelle. In these successful and complicated movements, the allies had 21 officers and 244 soldiers killed, and 120 officers and 1657 soldiers wounded. Of the 42d regiment, Captain Mungo Macpherson and Lieutenant Kenneth Macdougall were wounded, one private only killed, and 2 sergeants and 23 rank and file wounded. The French lost 31 pieces of cannon, 1300 prisoners, and had a proportional number killed and wounded.

In consequence of the heavy rains and the destruction of the bridges, the allies were prevented from pursuing the enemy, who retired to an entrenched camp near Bayonne. The allied troops were cantoned between the Nivelle and the sea, and made preparations for dislodging the French from their new position; but the incessant rains, which continued till December, put an entire stop to all active movements. Having thrown bridges over the Nive in the beginning of December, Lord Wellington commenced operations on the 9th for the passage of that river. As the position of the enemy was considered too strong to be attacked in front, the commander-in-chief determined to make a movement to the right, and by thus threatening Soult's rear, he hoped to induce him to abandon his position. Accordingly the allied army crossed the Nive at different points on the 9th. General Hope met with little opposition, and General Hill, who crossed by the ford of Cambo, was scarcely opposed. In danger of being intercepted by General Clinton's division, which had crossed at Ustariz, the enemy retired in great haste, and assembled in considerable numbers at Villefranche, but they were driven from this post by the light infantry and two Portuguese regiments, under Colonels Douglas and Browne. General Hill next day took up a position with his division, with his left on Villefranche and his right on the Adour, in consequence of which he cut off the communication between Bayonne and St Jean Pied de Port. In this situation the French troops stationed at the latter place were forced to retire on St Palais.

Leaving a force to keep General Hill in check, Marshal Soult left his entrenched camp on the morning of the 10th, and making an impetuous attack on the light division of General Hope's wing, drove back his out-posts. Then establishing himself on a ridge between the corps of Baron Alten and Major-General Andrew Hay's fifth division, he turned upon the latter, and attacked it with a determined bravery which it was almost impossible to withstand; but after an arduous struggle the enemy were repulsed by Brigadier-general Robinson's brigade of the fifth division, and Brigadier-general Archibald Campbell's Portuguese brigade. The enemy, no way discouraged by these repulses, renewed the attack about three o'clock, but with the same want of success.

During the night, Soult made dispositions for attacking the light division at Arcangues; but Sir John Hope perceiving his intention, moved towards the threatened point. Anticipated in this movement, the experienced Marshal again changed his dispositions to the left, but General Hope, equally on the alert, met him also in that direction. With the exception of some partial skirmishing between the out posts, no occurrence of any importance took place on the following day; but on the 12th the enemy renewed the attack on the left without success.

Thus foiled in all his attempts, Soult resolved to change entirely his plan of operations, and accordingly, during the night of the 12th, he drew his army through Bayonne, and on the morning of the 13th attempted to force his way between the centre and right of the British position, at the head of 30,000 men. Advancing with great vigour and celerity, he might have succeeded, had not General Hill, with his usual promptitude and decision, ordered his troops on the flanks to support the centre. The enemy, after a violent struggle, were repulsed with great loss, and retired with such precipitation that they were out of reach before the arrival of the sixth division, which had been ordered up to support General Hill.

Whilst this contest was going on, General

Byng's brigade, supported by the Portuguese brigade under General Buchan, carried an important height, from which the enemy made several attempts to dislodge them, but being unsuccessful at all points, they at length retired to their entrenchments, whither they were followed by General Hill, who took up a parallel position. At the passage of the Nive the 42d had Captain George Stewart and Lieutenant James Stewart killed, and 11 rank and file wounded.

The inclemency of the weather, and a succession of heavy rains which had swelled the rivers and destroyed the roads, rendering farther movements impracticable for a time, Marshal Soult availed himself of the interruption thus given to the progress of the allied army to strengthen his position. The weather becoming favourable about the middle of February 1814, Lord Wellington began a series of movements with the view of inducing Soult to withdraw from his strong position, or, should he decline, to cut off his communication with France, by marching the allied army into the heart of that country. By these movements the British general obtained the command of the Adour, which obliged Soult, who obtained his supplies down that river from the interior, to withdraw from Bayonne in the direction of Daxe. He left, however, a strong garrison in the place.

Leaving General Hope to blockade Bayonne, Lord Wellington made a general movement with the right and centre of the army on the 24th of February. Next day they marched forward to dislodge the enemy from a position they had taken up on the Gave de Pau at Orthés. Between the extreme points of this position ran a chain of heights receding in a line, bending inwards, the centre of which was so retired as to be protected by the guns of both wings. On his left, Soult was supported in this strong position by the town and the river; his right rested on a commanding height in rear of the village of St Bois; whilst the centre, accommodating itself to the incurvation of the heights, described a horizontal reversed segment of a circle protected by the strong position of both wings.

In a short time every point was carried, but the enemy retired in a very orderly manner, firing by echelons of divisions, each covering the other as they retreated. Observing General Hill, who had just crossed the river, advancing upon their left flank, on the road from Orthés to St Sever, the enemy became at once apprehensive that they would be intercepted, and, instead of continuing their masterly retreat, they ran off at full speed, followed by their pursuers. The latter continued the chase for nearly three miles at a full trot, and the French at length breaking their lines, threw away their arms, and fled in all directions. The pursuit was continued however as far as Sault de Navailles, on reaching which the remains even of an army were no longer to be seen. The loss of the enemy was estimated at 8000 men in killed, wounded, and prisoners. The loss of the allies in killed and wounded amounted to about 1600. Of the 42d, Lieutenant John Innes was the only officer killed, besides 1 sergeant, and 3 rank and file. Major William Cowell, Captain James Walker, Lieutenants Duncan Stewart and James Brander, 5 sergeants, and 85 rank and file were wounded.

The French army, lately so formidable, was now broken and dispersed, and many of the soldiers, dispirited by their reverses, returned to their homes; others, for the first time, abandoned their standards, and went over to the allies. Soult, however, undismayed by these difficulties, collected the remains of that part of his army which still remained faithful, and exerted all his energies to arrest the progress of the victors, but his efforts were unavailing; and after sustaining a defeat at Ayre, where he attempted to cover the removal of considerable magazines, he retreated to Tarbes. All the western part of Gascony being thus left exposed to the operations of the allied army, Lord Wellington detached Marshal Beresford and Lord Dalhousie, with three divisions, to Bordeaux, which they entered amidst the acclamations of the inhabitants.

Having obtained reinforcements from Spain and England, Lord Wellington, after leaving 4000 men at Bordeaux under Lord Dalhousie, again put his army in motion. Soult attempted to make a stand at Vicq with two divisions, but he was driven from this position by General Picton with the third division, and forced to retire beyond Tarbes. With the apparent intention of disputing the farther advance of the allies, the Marshal concentrated his whole force at this point, but he was dislodged from this position by a series of combined movements. It was now discovered that the enemy were drawn up on two hills running parallel to those from which their advance had been driven, and it was farther ascertained that this commanding position could not be gained by an advance in front without a great sacrifice of men, reinforced as it had been by the troops driven from the heights in front. It was therefore determined to attack it on flank, but, before the necessary arrangements could be completed, night came on, and Soult taking advantage of the darkness, moved off towards Toulouse, whither he was followed next morning by the allies, who reached the banks of the Garonne on the 27th of March.

This river was much swollen by recent rains and the melting of the snow on the Pyrenees. There being only one bridge at Toulouse, and that being in possession of the enemy, it became necessary to procure pontoons to enable the army to pass. Whilst the necessary preparations were going on for this purpose, Marshal Soult made the most extraordinary exertions to put himself in a proper posture of defence. He was not even yet without hopes of success, and although it is generally believed that he was now aware of the abdication of Buonaparte, an event which, he must have known, would put an immediate end to the war, he was unwilling to let slip the only opportunity he now had of wiping off the disgrace of his recent defeats.

The city of Toulouse is defended by an ancient wall, flanked with towers. On three sides it is surrounded by the great canal of Languedoc and by the Garonne, and on the fourth side it is flanked by a range of hills close to the canal, over which pass all the roads on that side the town. On the summit of the nearest of these hills the French had erected a chain of five redoubts, between which and the defences of the town they formed entrenchments and lines of connection. These defences consisted of extensive field-works, and of some of the ancient buildings in the suburbs well fortified. At the foot of the height, and along one-half its length, ran the small river Ers, the bridges of which had all been destroyed; on the top of the height was an elevated and elongated plain in a state of cultivation, and towards the end next the town there stood a farmhouse and offices. Some trenches had been cut around this house, and three redoubts raised on its front and left. Such was the field selected by Soult to redeem, if possible, by a last effort, his fallen reputation, and to vindicate the tarnished honour of the French arms.

Pontoons having been procured, part of the allied army crossed the Garonne on the 4th of April; but the melting of the snow on the Pyrenees, owing to a few days of hot weather, swelled the river so much that it became necessary to remove the pontoons, and it was not till the 8th that they could be replaced. On that day the whole army crossed the river, except General Hill's division, which remained opposite the town in front of the great bridge, to keep the enemy in check on that side. From the insulated nature of the town, no mode of attack was left to Lord Wellington but to attempt the works in front.

Accordingly, on the 10th of April, he made the following dispositions:—The Spaniards under Don Manuel Freyre were to attack the redoubts fronting the town; General Picton and the light division were to keep the enemy in check on the great road to Paris, but not to attack; and Marshal Beresford, with General Clinton and the sixth division, was to attack the centre of the entrenchments, whilst General Cole with the fourth marched against the right. The part taken by the 42d in this struggle is so well and fully described by Mr Malcolm, formerly of the 42d, in his *Reminiscence of a Campaign in* 1814, that we shall quote his description here:—

"Early on Sunday morning, the 10th of April, our tents were struck, and we moved with the other regiments of the sixth division towards the neighbourhood of Toulouse, until ordered to halt on a level ground, from whence we had a distinct view of the enemy's position on the ridge of hills already mentioned. At the same time we saw Lord Wellington, accompanied by his staff, riding back from the front at a hard trot. Some of the men called out. 'There goes Wellington, my lads; we shall have some hot work presently.'

"At that moment Major General Pack, who commanded our brigade, came up, and calling its officers and non-commissioned officers round him, addressed them to the following effect:—'We are this day to attack the enemy; your business will be to take possession of those fortified heights, which you see towards the front. I have only to warn you to be prepared to form close column in case of a charge of cavalry; to restrain the impetuosity of the men; and to prevent them from wasting their ammunition.' The drums then beat to arms, and we received orders to move towards the enemy's position.

"Our division (the sixth) approached the foot of the ridge of heights on the enemy's right and moved in a direction parallel to them, until we reached the point of attack. We advanced under a heavy cannonade, and arrived in front of a redoubt, which protected the right of the enemy's position, where we were formed in two lines,—the first, consisting of some Portuguese regiments,—and the reserve, of the Highland Brigade.

"Darkening the whole hill, flanked by clouds of cavalry, and covered by the fire of their redoubt, the enemy came down upon us like a torrent. Their generals and field-officers riding in front, and waving their hats amidst shouts of the multitude, resembling the roar of an ocean. Our Highlanders, as if actuated by one instinctive impulse, took off their bonnets, and waving them in the air, returned their greeting with three cheers.

"A deathlike silence ensued for some moments, and we could observe a visible pause in the advance of the enemy. At that moment the light company of the Forty-second Regiment, by a well-directed fire, brought down some of the French officers of distinction, as they rode in front of their respective corps. The enemy immediately fired a volley into our lines, and advanced upon us amidst a deafening roar of musketry and artillery. Our troops answered their fire only once, and unappalled by their furious onset, advanced up the hill, and met them at the charge. Upon reaching the summit of the ridge of heights, the redoubt, which had covered their advance, fell into our possession; but they still retained four others, with their connecting lines of intrenchments, upon the level of the same heights on which we were now established, and into which they had retired.

"Meantime, our troops were drawn up along a road, which passed over the hill, and which having a high bank at each side, protected us in some measure from the general fire of their last line of redoubts. Here our brigade remained until Marshal Beresford's Artillery, which, in consequence of the badness of the roads, had been left in the village of Mont Blanc, could be brought up, and until the Spaniards under General Don Manuel Freyre, who, in proceeding along the left of the Ers, had been repulsed, could be reformed, and brought back to the attack. Marshal Beresford's artillery having arrived, and the Spanish troops being once more brought forward, Major-General Pack rode up in front of our brigade, and made the following announcement:—'I have just now been with General Clinton, and he has been pleased to grant my request, that in the charge which we are now to make upon the enemy's redoubts, the Forty-second regiment shall have the honour of leading on the attack; the Forty-second will advance.'

"We immediately began to form for the charge upon the redoubts, which were about two or three hundred yards distant, and to which we had to pass over some ploughed fields. The grenadiers of the Forty-second regiment followed by the other companies, led the way, and began to ascend from the road; but no sooner were the feathers of their bonnets seen rising over the embankment, than such a tremendous fire was opened from the redoubts and intrenchments, as in a very short time would have annihilated them. The right wing, therefore, hastily formed into line, and without waiting for the left, which was ascending by companies from the road, rushed upon the batteries, which vomited forth a most furious and terrific storm of fire, grape-shot, and musketry.

"The redoubts were erected along the side of a road, and defended by broad ditches filled with water. Just before our troops reached the obstruction, however, the enemy deserted them and fled in all directions, leaving their last line of strongholds in our possession, but they still possessed two fortified houses close by, from which they kept up a galling and destructive fire. Out of about 500 men, which the Forty-second brought into action, scarcely 90 reached the fatal redoubt from which the enemy had fled.

"Our colonel was a brave man, but there are moments when a well-timed manœuvre is of more advantage than courage. The regiment stood on the road with its front exactly to the enemy, and if the left wing had been ordered forward, it could have sprung up the bank in line and dashed forward on the enemy at once. Instead of this, the colonel faced the right wing to its right, counter-marched in rear of the left, and when the leading rank cleared the left flank it was made to file up the bank, and as soon as it made its appearance the shot, shell, and musketry poured in with deadly destruction; and in this exposed position we had to make a second countermarch on purpose to bring our front to the enemy. These movements consumed much time, and by this unnecessary exposure exasperated the men to madness. The word 'Forward—double-quick!' dispelled the gloom, and forward we drove, in the face of apparent destruction. The field had been lately rough ploughed or under fallow, and when a man fell he tripped the one behind, thus the ranks were opening as we approached the point whence all this hostile vengeance proceeded; but the rush forward had received an impulse from desperation, 'the spring of the men's patience had been strained until ready to snap, and when left to the freedom of its own extension, ceased not to act until the point to which it was directed was attained.' In a minute every obstacle was surmounted, the enemy fled as we leaped over the trenches and mounds like a pack of noisy hounds in pursuit, frightening them more by our wild hurrahs than actually hurting them by ball or bayonet.

"Two officers (Captain Campbell and Lieutenant Young) and about 60 of inferior rank were all that now remained without a wound of the right wing of the regiment that entered the field in the morning. The flag was hanging in tatters, and stained with the blood of those who had fallen over it. The standard, cut in two, had been successively placed in the hands of three officers, who fell as we advanced, it was now borne by a sergeant, while the few remaining soldiers who rallied around it, defiled with mire, sweat, smoke, and blood, stood ready to oppose with the bayonet the advancing column, the front files of which were pouring in destructive showers of musketry among our confused ranks. To have disputed the post with such overwhelming numbers, would have been hazarding the loss of our colours, and could serve no general interest to our army, as we stood between the front of our advancing support and the enemy, we were therefore ordered to retire. The greater number passed through the cottage, now filled with wounded and dying, and leaped from the door that was over the road into the trench of the redoubt among the killed and wounded.

"We were now between two fires of musketry, the enemy to our left and rear, the 79th and left wing of our own regiment in our front. Fortunately the intermediate space did not exceed a hundred paces, and our safe retreat depended upon the speed with which we could perform it. We rushed along like a crowd of boys pursuing the bounding ball to its distant limit, and in an instant plunged into a trench that had been cut across the road; the balls were whistling amongst us and over us, while those in front were struggling to get out, those behind were holding them fast for assistance, and we became firmly wedged together, until a horse without a rider came plunging down on the heads and bayonets of those in his way; they on whom he fell were drowned or smothered, and the gap thus made gave way for the rest to get out.

"The right wing of the regiment, thus broken down and in disorder, was rallied by Captain Campbell (afterwards brevet lieutenant-colonel) and the adjutant (Lieutenant Young) on a narrow road, the steep banks of which served as a cover from the showers of grape that swept over our heads.

"As soon as the smoke began to clear away, the enemy made a last attempt to retake their redoubts, and for this purpose advanced in great force; they were a second time repulsed with great loss, and their whole army was driven into Toulouse."[5]

Finding the city, which was now within reach of the guns of the allies, quite untenable, Soult evacuated it the same evening, and was allowed to retire without molestation. Even had he been able to have withstood a siege, he must have soon surrendered for want of the provisions necessary for the support of a population of 60,000 inhabitants, and of his own army, which was now reduced by the casualties of war and recent desertions to 30,000 men.

The loss of the 42d in the battle of Toulouse, was 4 officers, 3 sergeants, and 47 rank and file killed; and 21 officers, 14 sergeants, 1 drummer, and 231 rank and file wounded. The names of the officers killed were Captain John Swanson, Lieutenant William Gordon, Ensigns John Latta and Donald Maccrummen; the wounded were Lieutenant-colonel Robert Macara, Captains James Walker, John Henderson (who died of his wounds), Alexander Mackenzie, and Lieutenants Donald Mackenzie, Thomas Munro, Hugh Angus Fraser, James Robertson, R. A. Mackinnon, Roger Stewart Robert Gordon, Charles Maclaren, Alexander Strange, Donald Farquharson (who died of his wounds), James Watson, William Urquhart; Ensigns Thomas Macniven, Colin Walker,

James Geddes, John Malcolm, and Mungo Macpherson.

The allies entered Toulouse on the morning after the battle, and were received with enthusiasm by the inhabitants, who, doubtless, considered themselves extremely fortunate in being relieved from the presence of the French army, whose retention of the city a few hours longer would have exposed it to all the horrors of a bombardment. By a singular coincidence, official accounts reached Toulouse in the course of the day of the abdication of Buonaparte, and the restoration of Louis XVIII.; but it is said that these despatches had been kept back on the road.

At this time the clothing of the army at large, but the Highland brigade in particular, was in a very tattered state. The clothing of the 91st regiment had been two years in wear; the men were thus under the necessity of repairing their old garments in the best manner they could: some had the elbows of the coats mended with gray cloth, others had the one-half of the sleeves of a different colour from the body; and their trousers were in as bad a condition as their coats.

The 42d, which was the only corps in the brigade that wore the *kilt*, was beginning to lose it by degrees; men falling sick and left in the rear frequently got the kilt made into trousers, and on joining the regiment again no plaid could be furnished to supply the loss; thus a great want of uniformity prevailed; but this was of minor importance when compared to the want of shoes. As the march continued daily, no time was to be found to repair them, until completely worn out; this left a number to march with bare feet. These men being occasionally permitted to straggle out of the ranks to select the soft part of the roads or fields adjoining, others who had not the same reason to offer for this indulgence followed the example, until each regiment marched regardless of rank, and sometimes mixed with other corps in front and rear.[6]

In consequence of the cessation of hostilities, the British troops removed without delay to their appointed destinations, and the three Highland regiments were embarked for Ireland,

---

[5] In a conversation between General Hill and Major-General Stewart (Garth), a few days after the battle, the former, alluding to the attempt of the enemy to take the redoubt, said to General Stewart, "I saw your old friends the Highlanders in a most perilous situation; and had I not known their firmness I should have trembled for the result. As it was, they could not have resisted the force brought against them if they had not been so instantaneously supported." Being asked by General Stewart what was the amount at which he calculated the strength of the enemy's column of attack, he replied, "Not less than 6000 men." In passing soon afterwards through Languedoc, Stewart stopped to view a brigade of French infantry exercising. The French commanding officer rode up to him, and invited him, with great politeness, to accompany him through the ranks. Talking of the recent battles, the French general concluded his observations thus,— "Well, we are quite satisfied if the English army think we fought bravely, and did our duty well." General Stewart mentioning the Highland corps, "Ah!" said the Frenchman, "these are brave soldiers. If they had good officers, I should not like to meet them unless I was well supported. I put them to the proof on that day." Being asked in what manner, he answered "that he led the division which attempted to retake the redoubt;" and on a further question as to the strength of the column, he replied, "More than 6000 men." As General Hill was more than two miles from the field of action, the accuracy of his calculation is remarkable.

[6] Anton's *Military Life*, p. 120.

where they remained till May 1815, when they were shipped for Flanders, on the return of Buonaparte from Elba   In Ireland the 1st battalion was joined by the effective men of the 2d, which had been disbanded at Aberdeen in October 1814

The intelligence of Buonaparte's advance reached Brussels on the evening of the 15th of June, when orders were immediately issued by the Duke of Wellington for the assembling of the troops   The men of the 42d and 92d regiments had become great favourites in Brussels, and were on such terms of friendly intercourse with the inhabitants in whose houses they were quartered, that it was no uncommon thing to see a Highland soldier taking care of the children, and even keeping the shop of his host,—an instance of confidence perhaps unexampled   These two regiments were the first to muster [7]   "They assembled with the utmost alacrity to the sound of the well-known pibroch, *Come to me and I will give you flesh*,[8]—an invitation to the wolf and the raven, for which the next day did, in fact, spread an ample banquet at the expense of our brave countrymen, as well as of their enemies   About four o'clock in the morning of the 16th of June, the 42d and 92d Highland regiments marched through the Place Royal and the Parc   One could not but admire their fine appearance, their firm, collected, steady, military demeanour, as they went rejoicing to battle, with their bagpipes playing before them, and the beams of the rising sun shining upon their glittering arms   Before that sun had set in the night, how many of that gallant band were laid low !   The kind and generous inhabitants assembled in crowds to witness the departure of their gallant friends, and as the Highlanders marched onward with a steady and collected air, the people breathed many a fervent expression for their safety "

The important part taken in the action of Quatre Bras by the Black Watch could not be told better than in the simple words of one who was present, and did his own share of the work, Sergeant Anton [9] of the 42d —

" On the morning of the 16th June, before the sun rose over the dark forest of Soignes, our brigade, consisting of the 1st, 44th, and 92d regiments, stood in column, Sir Denis Pack at its head, waiting impatiently for the 42d, the commanding-officer of which was chidden severely by Sir Denis for being so dilatory   We took our place in the column, and the whole marched off to the strains of martial music, and amidst the shouts of the surrounding multitude   As we entered the forest of Soignes, our stream of ranks following ranks, in successive sections, moved on in silent but speedy course, like some river confined between two equal banks

"The forest is of immense extent, and we continued to move on under its welcome shade until we came to a small hamlet, or auberge, imbosomed in the wood to the right of the road   Here we turned to our left, halted, and were in the act of lighting fires, on purpose to set about cooking   We were flattering ourselves that we were to rest there until next day, for whatever reports had reached the ears of our commanders, no alarm had yet rung on ours   Some were stretched under the shade to rest, others sat in groups draining the cup, and we always loved a large one, and it was now almost emptied of three days' allowance [1] of spirits, a greater quantity than was usually served at once to us on a campaign , others were busily occupied in bringing water and preparing the camp-kettles, for we were of the opinion, as I have already said, that we were to halt there for the day   But, "hark ! a gun '" one exclaims , every ear is set to catch the sound, and every mouth seems half opened, as if to supersede the faithless ear that doubts of hearing   Again another and another feebly floats through the forest   Every ear now catches the sound, and every man grasps his musket.   No pensive looks are seen , our generals' weather-beaten, war-worn countenances are all well known to the old soldiers, and no throb of fear palpitates in a single breast , all are again ready in column, and again we tread the wood-lined road.

"The distant report of the guns becomes more

---

[7] Cannon's *Historical Records of the 42d*, p 141
[8] For music of this see end of the history of this regiment
[9] Anton's *Military Life*, p 188

[1] One English pint   There were four days' allowance of bread, and three days' of beef and spirits, issued before leaving Brussels for each man

loud, and our march is urged on with greater speed We pass through Waterloo, and leave behind the bright fields of Wellington's fame, —our army's future glory and England's pride Quatre Bras appears in view, the frightened peasantry come running breathless and panting along the way We move off to the left of the road, behind a gently rising eminence, form column of companies, regardless of the growing crop, and ascend the rising ground a beautiful plain appears in view, surrounded with belts of wood, and the main road from Brussels runs through it. We now descend to the plain by an echelon movement towards our right, halted on the road (from which we had lately diverged to the left), formed in line, fronting a bank on the right side, whilst the other regiments took up their position to right and left, as directed by our general A luxuriant crop of grain hid from our view the contending skirmishers beyond, and presented a considerable obstacle to our advance We were in the act of lying down by the side of the road, in our usual careless manner, as we were wont when enjoying a rest on the line of march, some throwing back their heads on their knapsacks, intending to take a sleep, when General Pack came galloping up, and chid the colonel for not having the bayonets fixed This roused our attention, and the bayonets were instantly on the pieces

"Our pieces were loaded, and perhaps never did a regiment in the field seem so short taken We had the name of a crack corps, but certainly it was not then in that state of discipline which it could justly boast of a few years afterwards Yet notwithstanding this disadvantage, none could be animated with a fitter feeling for the work before us than prevailed at that moment.

"We were all ready and in line,—"*Forward!*" was the word of command, and forward we hastened, though we saw no enemy in front. The stalks of the rye, like the reeds that grow on the margin of some swamp, opposed our advance, the tops were up to our bonnets, and we strode and groped our way through as fast as we could By the time we reached a field of clover on the other side, we were very much straggled, however, we united in line as fast as time and our speedy advance would permit The Belgic skirmishers retired through our ranks, and in an instant we were on their victorious pursuers Our sudden appearance seemed to paralyse their advance. The singular appearance of our dress, combined no doubt with our sudden debut, tended to stagger their resolution we were on them, our pieces were loaded, and our bayonets glittered, impatient to drink their blood Those who had so proudly driven the Belgians before them, turned now to fly, whilst our loud cheers made the fields echo to our wild hurrahs France fled or fell before us, and we thought the field our own. We had not yet lost a man, for the victors seldom lose many, except in protracted hard contested struggles with one's face to the enemy, he may shun the deadly thrust or stroke, it is the retreating soldier that destruction pursues

"We drove on so fast that we almost appeared like a mob following the rout of some defeated faction. Marshal Ney, who commanded the enemy, observed our wild unguarded zeal, and ordered a regiment of lancers to bear down upon us We saw their approach at a distance, as they issued from a wood, and took them for Brunswickers coming to cut up the flying infantry, and as cavalry on all occasions have the advantage of retreating foot, on a fair field, we were halted in order to let them take their way they were approaching our right flank, from which our skirmishers were extended, and we were far from being in a formation fit to repel an attack, if intended, or to afford regular support to our friends if requiring our aid I think we stood with too much confidence, gazing towards them as if they had been our friends, anticipating the gallant charge they would make on the flying foe, and we were making no preparative movement to receive them as enemies, further than the reloading of the muskets, until a German orderly dragoon galloped up, exclaiming, "Franchee ! Franchee !" and, wheeling about, galloped off We instantly formed a rallying square, no time for particularity ; every man's piece was loaded, and our enemies approached at full charge, the feet of their horses seemed to tear up the ground Our skirmishers having been impressed with the same opinion, that these were Brunswick cavalry, fell beneath their lances, and few escaped death or wounds; our brave colonel fell at this time, pierced through the chin until the point of the lance reached the brain. Captain (now major) Menzies fell, covered with wounds, and a momentary conflict took place over him; he was a powerful man, and, hand to hand, more than a match for six ordinary men. The grenadiers, whom he commanded, pressed round to save or avenge him, but fell beneath the enemy's lances.

"Of all descriptions of cavalry, certainly the lancers seem the most formidable to infantry, as the lance can be projected with considerable precision, and with deadly effect, without bringing the horse to the point of the bayonet; and it was only by the rapid and well-directed fire of musketry that these formidable assailants were repulsed.

Colonel (afterwards Sir) R. H. Dick. From Miniature (painted about four years after Waterloo) in possession of William Dick, Esq. of Tullymet.

"Colonel Dick assumed the command on the fall of Sir Robert Macara, and was severely wounded. Brevet-major Davidson succeeded, and was mortally wounded; to him succeeded Brevet-major Campbell. Thus, in a few minutes

we had been placed under four different commanding-officers.

"An attempt was now made to form us in line; for we stood mixed in one irregular mass, —grenadier, light, and battalion companies,—a noisy group; such is the inevitable consequence of a rapid succession of commanders. Our covering sergeants were called out on purpose that each company might form on the right of its sergeants; an excellent plan had it been adopted, but a cry arose that another charge of cavalry was approaching, and this plan was abandoned. We now formed a line on the left of the grenadiers, while the cavalry that had been announced were cutting through the ranks of the 69th regiment. Meantime the other regiments, to our right and left, suffered no less than we; the superiority of the enemy in cavalry afforded him a decided advantage on the open plain, for our British cavalry and artillery had not yet reached the field. We were at this time about two furlongs past the farm of Quatre Bras, as I suppose, and a line of French infantry was about the same distance from us in front, and we had commenced firing at that line, when we were ordered to form square to oppose cavalry. General Pack was at our head, and Major Campbell commanded the regiment. We formed square in an instant, in the centre were several wounded French soldiers witnessing our formation round them; they doubtless considered themselves devoted to certain death among us seeming barbarians; but they had no occasion to speak ill of us afterwards; for as they were already incapable of injuring us, we moved about them regardful of their wounds and suffering.

"Our last file had got into square, and into its proper place, so far as unequalised companies could form a square, when the cuirassiers dashed full on two of its faces: their heavy horses and steel armour seemed sufficient to bury us under them, had they been pushed forward on our bayonets.

"A moment's pause ensued; it was the pause of death. General Pack was on the right angle of the front face of the square, and he lifted his hat towards the French officer as he was wont to do when returning a salute. I suppose our assailants construed our forbearance as an indication of surrendering: a false idea; not a blow had been struck nor a musket levelled; but when the general raised his hat, it served as a signal, though not a preconcerted one, but entirely accidental; for we were doubtful whether our officer commanding was protracting the order, waiting for the general's command, as he was present. Be this as it may, a most destructive fire was opened; riders, cased in heavy armour, fell tumbling from their horses; the horses reared, plunged, and fell on the dismounted riders; steel helmets and cuirasses rung against unsheathed sabres, as they fell to the ground; shrieks and groans of men, the neighing of horses, and the discharge of musketry, rent the air, as men and horses mixed together in one heap of indiscriminate slaughter. Those who were able to fly, fled towards a wood on our right, whence they had issued to the attack, and which seemed to afford an extensive cover to an immense reserve not yet brought into action.

"Once more clear of those formidable and daring assailants, we formed line, examined our ammunition boxes, and found them getting empty. Our officer commanding pointed towards the pouches of our dead and dying comrades, and from them a sufficient supply was obtained.

"We lay down behind the gentle rise of a trodden down field of grain, and enjoyed a few minutes' rest to our wearied limbs; but not in safety from the flying messengers of death, the whistling music of which was far from lulling us to sleep.

"Afternoon was now far spent, and we were resting in line, without having equalized the companies, for this would have been extremely dangerous in so exposed a position; for the field afforded no cover, and we were in advance of the other regiments. The enemy were at no great distance, and, I may add, firing very actively upon us.

"Our position being, as I have already observed, without any cover from the fire of the enemy, we were commanded to retire to the rear of the farm, where we took up our bivouac on the field for the night.

"Six privates fell into the enemy's hands; among these was a little lad (Smith Fyfe) about five feet high. The French general, on seeing this diminutive looking lad, is said to have lifted him up by the collar or breech and exclaimed to the soldiers who were near him, "Behold the sample of the men of whom you seem afraid." This lad returned a few days afterwards, dressed in the clothing of a French grenadier, and was saluted by the name of Napoleon, which he retained until he was discharged.

"The night passed off in silence: no fires were lit; every man lay down in rear of his arms, and silence was enjoined for the night. Round us lay the dying and the dead, the latter not yet interred, and many of the former, wishing to breathe their last where they fell, slept to death with their heads on the same pillow on which those who had to toil through the future fortunes of the field reposed."

The principal loss sustained by the Highlanders was at the first onset; yet it was by no means so severe as might have been expected. Lieutenant-colonel Sir Robert Macara, Lieutenant Robert Gordon, and Ensign William Gerrard, 2 sergeants, and 40 rank and file were killed. Including officers, there were 243 wounded.

In the battle of Waterloo, in which the regiment was partially engaged, the 42d had only 5 men killed and 45 wounded. In these last are included the following officers, viz.: Captain Mungo Macpherson, Lieutenants John Orr, George Gunn Munro, Hugh Angus Fraser, and James Brander, and Quarter-master Donald Mackintosh. "They fought like heroes, and like heroes they fell—an honour to their country. On many a Highland hill, and through many a Lowland valley, long will the deeds of these brave men be fondly remembered, and their fate deeply deplored. Never did a finer body of men take the field, never did men march to battle that were destined to perform such services to their country, and to obtain such immortal renown."

The Duke of Wellington in his public despatches concerning Quatre Bras and Waterloo paid a high compliment to the 42d. "Among other regiments, I must particularly mention the 28th, 42d, 79th, and 92d, and the battalion of Hanoverians."

The word "Waterloo," borne on the colours of the regiment, by royal authority, commemorates the gallantry displayed by the regiment on this occasion; a medal was conferred on each officer and soldier; and the privilege of reckoning two years' service, towards additional pay and pension on discharge, was also granted to the men. It may not be uninteresting to give here a list of the officers of the regiment who were present at the battle of Quatre Bras and Waterloo It will be seen that while only 3 were killed, few escaped without a wound.

OFFICERS AT WATERLOO—1815.

Lieut.-Col. Sir Robert Macara,	Killed.
Major Robert Henry Dick,	Wounded.
Capt. Archibald Menzies,	Wounded.
,, George Davidson,	Died of Wounds.
,, John Campbell,	
,, Mungo Macpherson,	Wounded.
,, Donald M'Donald,	Wounded.
,, Daniel M'Intosh,	Wounded.
,, Robert Boyle,	Wounded.
Lieut. Donald Chisholm,	Wounded.
,, Duncan Stewart,	Wounded.
,, Donald M'Kenzie,	Wounded.
,, James Young, Adjutant,	Wounded.
,, Hugh A. Fraser,	Wounded.
,, John Malcolm,	Wounded.
,, Alexander Dunbar,	Wounded.
,, James Brander,	Wounded.
,, Roger Stewart,	
,, Robert Gordon,	Killed.
,, James Robertson,	
,, Kenneth M'Dougal,	
,, Donald M'Kay,	
,, Alexander Innes,[2]	
,, John Grant,	
,, John Orr,[2]	Wounded.
,, George Gunn Munro,	Wounded.
,, William Fraser,	Wounded.
Ensign George Gerard,	Killed.
,, Andrew L. Fraser,	
,, Alexander Brown,	Wounded.
,, Alexander Cumming,	
Adjutant James Young, Lieut.,	Wounded.
Quarter-Master Don. M'Intosh,	Wounded.
Surgeon Swinton Macleod,	
Assistant Surgeon Donald M'Pherson,	
Assistant Surgeon John Stewart,	

It has been observed, as a remarkable circumstance in the history of the Royal Highlanders, that on every occasion when they fired a shot at an enemy (except at Ticonderoga,

[2] These are the only officers of the regiment now (1873) alive who served in the Peninsula and at Waterloo; the former being now Captain Innes, and a military knight of Windsor, and the latter, Captain Orr, residing in Edinburgh.

where success was almost impossible), they were successful to such an extent at least, that whatever the general issue of the battle might be, that part of the enemy opposed to them never stood their ground, unless the Highlanders were by insurmountable obstacles prevented from closing upon them. Fontenoy even does not form an exception; for although the allies were defeated, the Highlanders carried the points assigned them, and then, as at Ticonderoga, they were the last to leave the field.[3]

As the battle of Waterloo terminates a period of active service and hard fighting in the case of the 42d, as well as of other regiments, and as it had a rest of many years during the long peace, we shall here give a summary of the number of men that entered the regiment, from its formation down to the battle of Waterloo, and the number of those who were killed, wounded, died of sickness, or were discharged during that period.

The grand total of men embodied in the Black Watch and 42d or Royal Highland regiment, from its origin at Tay Bridge in April 1740, to 24th June 1815, exclusive of the second battalion of 1780[4] and that of 1803,[5] was	. 8792
Of these there were killed, during that period, exclusive of 35 officers,	816
Wounded during the same period, exclusive of 133 officers,	. 2413
Died by sickness, wounds, and various casualties, including those who were discharged and those who volunteered into other regiments, when the 42d left America in 1767, up to 25th June 1793,	. 2275
Died by sickness, wounds, and various casualties, from 25th June 1793 to 24th June 1815,	. 1135[6]
Discharged during same period,	. 1485
Unaccounted for during same period, having been left sick in an enemy's country, prisoners, &c.	. 138
	—— 8262
Number remaining in the first battalion on 24th June 1815,	530

When it is considered that out of seventy-five year's service, forty-five were spent in active warfare, the trifling loss of the regiment

[3] Stewart's *Sketches.*
[4] There were no exchange of men and officers between this and the first battalion.
[5] The number of men who died in this battalion from December 1803, to 24th October 1814, was 322. The number discharged and transferred to the first battalion and to other regiments, from 1803 till the reduction in 1814, was 965 men.
[6] The deaths by sickness in the second battalion are not included. This battalion sustained very little loss in war.

by the enemy will appear extraordinary; and the smallness of that loss can only be accounted for by the determined bravery and firmness of the men, it being now the opinion of military men that troops, who act vigorously, suffer less than those who are slow and cautious in their operations.

After spending several months in the vicinity of Paris, the regiment marched to Calais and embarked for England, arriving at Ramsgate, December 19th 1815. The regiment proceeded by Deal and Dover to Hythe, where it lay two weeks, when it marched to Chelmsford.

After staying two weeks in Chelmsford Barracks, the regiment proceeded northwards to Scotland by easy stages, and was everywhere received with overwhelming enthusiasm and lavish hospitality. At Cambridge, for example, Sergeant Anton, in his *Military Life*, tells us, the bells welcomed the Royal Highlanders with joy; every table smoked with savoury viands for their entertainment, and every cellar contributed a liberal supply of its best October for their refreshment. The same thing occurred at Huntingdon and other towns, and at several places the men received a donation equal to two day's pay. And so it was at every town through which the regiment had to pass; the men were feted and petted as if they had saved their country from destruction.

As they approached Edinburgh, the whole population seemed to have poured to welcome them to its arms. Preceded by a guard of cavalry, with its band of music, they entered the city amidst the loud cheering and congratulatory acclamations of friends; while over their heads, "from a thousand windows, waved as many banners, plaided scarfs, or other symbols of courtly greetings."[7] At Edinburgh they were entertained in a manner that would have made the men of any regiment but a "crack" one completely lose their heads; but the self-possessed Royal Highlanders, while heartily enjoying the many good things provided for them, and grateful for their hearty welcome, seem never to have forgotten the high reputation they had to maintain.[8]

[7] Anton's *Military Life*, p. 247.
[8] The following is an extract from the account pub-

After this, for many years, the Royal Highlanders had a rest from active service.

V.

1816—1854.

The Highland Society's Vase—Ireland—The Whiteboys—Critical Service—Anecdotes—Old Manoeuvres—Bad Management—The Dublin Medal—Gibraltar—Innovations—Regimental Library—Malta—Ionian Islands—Lieutenant-Colonel Middleton's Farewell Order—Scotland—Ireland—Malta—Corfu—Death of Major-General Sir R. H. Dick—Bermuda—Halifax—Home.

WE have already narrated (p. 374, vol. ii.) the proceedings at the meeting of the Highland Society, after the Egyptian campaign, with reference to the 42d. From 1811 to 1817, endeavours had been frequently made to establish a better feeling between the officers and the Highland Society, but in vain: the *Egyptians* would not yield, and in the meantime the vase remained at the makers.

After the return of the regiment from the Waterloo Campaign in 1816, H.R.H. The Duke of York became the mediator, and arranged that the vase should be accepted on the 21st March 1817, the anniversary of the battle of Alexandria. By this time only two of the officers who had served in Egypt were in the regiment, therefore the amicable arrangement was more easily arrived at.

It was at Armagh barracks, on Wednesday the 18th of June 1817, that the vase was presented to the regiment. At the time 5

lished at the time; "Tuesday, the first division of the 42d regiment, under the command of Lieutenant-Colonel Robert Henry Dick (who succeeded to the command of the regiment, on the death of Lieutenant-Colonel Sir Robert Macara, killed at Quatre Bras), marched into the Castle. Major-General Hope, commander of the district, and Colonel David Stewart of Garth, accompanied the Lieutenant-Colonel at the head of the regiment. Not only the streets of the city were crowded beyond all former precedent with spectators, but the windows, and even the house-tops, were occupied. The road from Musselburgh, a distance of six miles, was filled with relations and friends; and so great was the crowd, that it was after four o'clock before they arrived at the Castle Hill, although they passed through Portobello about two o'clock. It was almost impossible for these gallant men to get through the people, particularly in the city. All the bells were rung, and they were everywhere received with the loudest acclamations."

companies were detached to Newry, and several other detachments were absent from Armagh; therefore not more than about 3 companies were present at the ceremony. The parade was in review order, in side arms, and a square of two deep was formed. On a table in the centre was the vase, covered, and several small kegs of Highland whisky, brought over from Scotland for the express purpose. A portion of the correspondence with the Highland Society was read by the Adjutant: Lieutenant-Colonel Robert Henry Dick addressed the regiment: the casks of whisky were broached, and the cup filled. The Colonel drank to the officers and men, the staff officers followed, and afterwards the captains and officers drank to the health of their respective companies, and the cup, held by both hands, and kept well replenished, went three times down the ranks. All was happiness and hilarity, not only on the parade, but for the remainder of the day.

Thus was introduced to the regiment the

Vase presented to 42d Royal Highlanders by the Highland Society of London.

beautiful vase, which, for elegance and design, is hardly to be surpassed.

Of the officers and men present on the occasion, Lieutenant-Colonel Wheatley cannot bring to his recollection any now alive but himself and another, viz., Alexander Grant, a pensioner, living at Granton, Inverness-shire (in 1873). Of the officers in the regiment at the time, the last of them, Captain Donald M'Donald, died at Musselburgh, on the 24th September 1865, aged 82.

The day of "the Cup" was long remembered amongst the men, and it was always enthusiastically spoken of as to the quality and quantity of the whisky. The vase has lately (1869) been renovated, and placed on an ebony stand, which has given additional grandeur to its elegance.

The regiment left Glasgow in April of this year, and proceeded to Ireland, landing at Donaghadee, marching thence to Armagh, and detaching parties to all the adjacent towns. The regiment remained in Ireland till 1825, moving about from place to place, and occasionally taking part in the duties to which the troops were liable, on account of the disturbed state of the country   Many of these duties were far from pleasant, yet the 42d discharged them in such a manner as to gain the respect and goodwill of the natives among whom they sojourned

In June 1818, the regiment marched to Dundalk, and in May 1819, to Dublin, where it remained upwards of twelve months, receiving highly commendatory notices in orders, from Major-General White, Major General Bulwer, and Major-General Sir Colquhoun Grant

On the 29th of January 1820, the colonelcy of the regiment was conferred on Lieutenant-General John Earl of Hopetoun, G C B, from the 92d Highlanders, in succession to General the Marquis of Huntly

From Dublin the regiment marched, in August, to Kilkenny and Clonmel, and while at these stations its appearance and discipline were commended in orders by Major-General Sir Thomas Brisbane, and Major-General Egerton

The regiment marched, in October 1821, to Rathkeale, and took part in the harassing duties to which the troops in the county of Limerick were exposed during the disturbed state of the country, and its conduct procured the unqualified approbation of the general officers under whom it served

In July 1822, the regiment marched to Limerick, and the orders issued after the usual half yearly inspections, by Major-General Sir John Lambert, and Major General Sir John Elley, were highly commendatory.

From Limerick the regiment proceeded to Buttevant, in July 1823, and afterwards occupied many detached stations in the county of Cork where it preserved its high reputation for correct discipline, and for general efficiency, which procured for it the encomiums of the inspecting generals.

On the death of General the Earl of Hopetoun, G C B, the colonelcy was conferred on Major-General Sir George Murray, G C B, G C H (see portrait in steel plate of Colonels of 42d), from the 72d, or the Duke of Albany's Own Highlanders, by commission, dated the 6th of September 1823

The following details, for which we are indebted to Lieutenant-Colonel Wheatley, will give the reader a vivid idea of the state of Ireland at this time, as well as of the critical

nature of the duties which the 42d had to perform —

The 42d, which was quartered at Rathkeale, were joined in these duties by the 79th and 93d, the former quartered at Limerick, and the latter at Ennis, County Clare   All three regiments were highly and deservedly popular with the inhabitants

Detachments were posted all over the country in every village or hamlet, where a house could be hired to hold from 12 to 30 men   But little could be done towards putting the Whiteboys down, as the only offence against the law was being caught in arms   But as soon as the Parliament met, the "Insurrection Act" was hurried through both houses, and became law on the night of the 28th February 1822   By the Act transportation for seven years was the punishment awarded to any one found out of his dwelling place any time between one hour after sunset and sunrise   It was harassing duty patrolling over the country, sometimes all night, calling the rolls, and apprehending such as had been found absent on former occasions.   The law was carried out by what was called a "Bench of Magistrates," two or more, with a Sergeant-at-Law as president   All field officers and captains were magistrates and seven years' transportation was the only sentence the bench could give   the prisoner had either to be let off with an admonition or transported.   When the prisoner was brought in, evidence was simply taken that he was found out of his dwelling-place at an unlawful hour, or that he was absent from his habitation on such a night when the roll was called   The local magistrates knew the character he bore, a few minutes consultation was held, when sentence was given, and an escort being already at the court-house door, the prisoner was handcuffed and put on a cart   The words were given "with cartridge prime and load, quick march," and off to the Cove of Cork, where a ship was at anchor to receive them   This summary procedure soon put an end to the nightly depredations which had kept the country in terror and alarm for months previous   The convicted were at once sent off to Sydney,—"Botany Bay" at this time.   Here is one instance of how the act was put in force

Every rail going out of Italy also had a

guard or outpost to prevent a surprise, and near to the Askeaton-road guard lived a character known as "the red haired man," a noted White-boy (so named from wearing shirts over their clothes when on their nocturnal excursions), who had taken care of himself from the pass-ing of the Insurrection Act, although still a leader and director of their doings. His house was close to the guard, and there were special orders to watch him, and at uncertain hours to visit the house, to find him absent, if possible. On an evening in June, the sentry called to the sergeant of the guard that "the red haired man," half an hour back, had gone into a house where he was still." The sergeant walked about, the retreat beat, and watch in hand, he kept his look-out ; one hour after sunset "the red haired man" came out without his hat, and laughing heartily : he was taken prisoner, and next day was on his way to the Cove of Cork ! !

Pages could be filled with anecdotes con-nected with the doings of the several portions of the regiment in their various quarters. One more, to show the natural inborn Irish inclina-tion for fighting.—The major commanding at Shannogalden, while standing on the street on a fair-day, was thus accosted by a tall, gaunt, wiry man, of some 60 years of age. "Good morning to your honour." "Good morning, Mr Sullivan." "I've a favour to ask of you, Major." "Well, Mr Sullivan, what can I do for you ?" "Well, your honour knows that I've been a loyal man, that during them dis-turbed times I always advised the boys to give up the foolish night-work ; that I've caused a great many arms to be given up to yourself, Major." Mr Sullivan's detail of his services and his appreciation of them being much too long to go over, it ended in :—"It's a long time, Major, since the boys have had a fight, and all that I want is, that yourself and your men will just keep out of sight, and remain at this end of the town, till me and my boys go up to the fair, and stretch a few of the Whichgeralds." (Fitzgeralds, the opposite fac-tion.) "Oh, then, Major, we'll not be long about it, just to stretch a dozen or two of them Whichgeralds, and then I'll engage we'll go home quietly." Much to Mr Sullivan's dis-appointment, the Major replied that he could

not allow the peace to be broken, and grievously crest-fallen, Mr S. went to report the failure of his request to the fine set of young Sul-livans who were in sight, waiting the issue of the singular application, and ready to be let loose on the Fitzgeralds. A Mr V——, a local magistrate, who was standing with the Major, said that it would tend much to break up the combination of Whiteboyism to let the factions fight among themselves, and that he could not do better than to wink at the Sullivans having a turn with their opponents ; but the Major would not entertain the idea of having, possibly, half-a-dozen murders to think of.

In 1821, on the day the head-quarters division marched out of the city of Limerick for Rathkeale, a man dropped out of the ranks without leave, to take leave of some friends belonging to the 79th (quartered at Limerick), when the roar guard came up; poor David Hill was found senseless on the road, with a deep cut on the back of his head, and his musket gone. On reaching Rathkeale, he was tried by a Court Martial held in a square, formed there and then, before the regiment was dismissed. He was sentenced to 300 lashes, and to pay for his musket. It was what would rightly now be considered an unnecessarily cruel individual suffering, though the most stringent discipline was required, as the regiment was virtually in an enemy's country.

About three months afterwards an officer of the 79th was out snipe shooting, near to the scene of poor Hill's misfortune. A country-man entered into conversation with the officer, watched his opportunity, knocked him over, and was off with the gun. Two of the 3d light dragoons on dispatch duty, from Rathkeale for Limerick, saw it ; one of them leaped wall after wall, and apprehended the culprit. A special commission was at the time sitting in Limerick, by which he was tried next day, and hanged a day or two after. On the scaffold he confessed that it was he who had knocked over the Highlander, and told the priest where the gun was to be found. When it was recovered it was found cut down to make it a "handy gun." It was given over to Hill.

Lieutenant-Colonel Wheatley, who was with the 42d at this time, was himself an ear-witness to the following :—About ten minutes after he and his comrade reached their billets at Rathkeale, the man of the house came in from his work, evidently not aware of the soldiers' presence. From the kitchen and stable, one apartment, the latter overheard the following catechism between the father and a child about four years old :—" Well Dan, have you been a good boy all day?" " Yes, father." " Come to my knee, Dan ; now tell me, what will you do to the peeler, Dan ?" " I'll shoot him, father, I will." " You'll shoot him, will you ?" " Yes, father, when I'm big like brother Phill." " Ah, you're a fine fellow, Dan ; there's a penny for you to buy bread." Comment is unnecessary.[1]

In September 1823 the 42d, along with the other regiments in the Munster district, was taught the "Torrance" system of drill, which this year superseded the cumbrous old " Dundas." This system effected an entire change in the drill, particularly in the field movements and the platoon exercise. Before this the wheeling or counter-marching of a column was unknown. He was a rash commanding officer who attempted an echelon movement in quick time, and it was not to be presumed upon before a general officer. The marching past in slow time was such a curiosity, that it is worthy of record. At every angle, the command "Halt, left wheel, halt, dress, march," was given, and such work it was again to step off in time with the preceding company ; about one in twenty could do it. Altogether, a drill book of " Dundas's 18 manœuvres" would be a curious study for the present day ; and that corps was to be admired whose Colonel could put them through "the 18 manœuvres." At present the whole could be done in 20 minutes, and as to skirmishing it was almost unknown, except in rifle and light infantry corps.

Long marshes were common in those days. The following account of a long march while in Ireland, illustrates well the sad want of system at this time in connection with the army, and the little attention paid to the men's welfare. In the month of May 1819, the regiment

was ordered from Dundalk to Dublin. The detachment (of one subaltern and twenty men) at Cootehill, in County Cavan, was ordered, when relieved, to march to Ardee, and thence to Drogheda, to join a division under a field officer for Dublin. The relieving party of the 3d Buffs did not arrive until after mid-day on the 21st of May, when the detachment of the 42d marched by Shercock under the belief that they would halt at Kingscourt for the night, 18 miles from Cootehill. But, alas ! they marched on amidst pelting rain, and reached Ardee between 11 and 12 o'clock at night, 13 miles from Kingscourt, with the pipe-clay so thoroughly washed from their belts (cross in those days), that they were quite brown. The question will naturally arise, why did they not stop at Kingscourt ? even that distance being a long day's march. There was a reason. The end of the month was the 24th day at this time, and from some neglect or mistake the officer was short of money to keep the men all night at Kingscourt. But 42d soldiers made no complaints, on any occasion, in those days. With the consolatory saying, " what we march to-day we will not have to march to-morrow," the march was, with few exceptions, made cheerfully, although every man carried his full kit.

At this period there was a lamentable want of organisation and good management in many particulars. For instance, there was a garrison field day every Thursday (in Dublin 1819–20), and the guards who went on at ten o'clock the previous day had nothing served to them in the way of food from the scanty dinner of Wednesday, till they reached their barracks about seven or eight the following evening.

Pay-sergeants were always consulted in all matters of interior economy, whether it regarded the supply of necessaries or improvements in messing, and they looked upon it as an innovation on their *rights* to propose any plan for the good of the soldiers, by which the smallest portion of the pay would have been diverted from passing through their (the pay sergeants') hands ; and thus a great portion of the men were always in debt. A baneful system it was, when men were allowed to be in debt to the sergeant to the extent of several pounds.

[1] Peelers and Bobbies are names by which the police are sometimes, even yet, referred to. They were embodied under an Act brought in by Sir Robert Peel about 1820. In 1823 it was extended to all Ireland.

During the time the regiment was quartered in Dublin in 1819, a breakfast mess was established, much to the benefit of the soldier, who until this time had pleased himself regarding that meal. Bread and water satisfied some, while others indulged themselves according to their taste or ability to procure what was agreeable to them.

In 1819 a regimental medal (bearing on one side the names Corunna, Fuentes D'Onor, Pyrenees, Nevelle, Nive, Orthés, Toulouse, Peninsula) was struck in Dublin, and issued to those entitled to wear it—at their own expense. The authority of His Royal Highness the Duke of York, at the time commander-in-chief, was obtained for the wearing of it. Many good and gallant soldiers wore them in the regiment for years, but they quickly disappeared, although few of them were discharged under 19 and 20 years' service. The last of them were discharged between 1830 and 1834. Many inquiries have been made concerning this medal, which has puzzled collectors, but on the authority of Lieutenant-Colonel Wheatley, the above is a correct account of its origin and history.

Leaving the province of Munster, in June 1825, the regiment received a highly commendatory communication from Lieutenant-General Sir John Lambert, expressing the high sense he entertained of the discipline and conduct of the corps. It afterwards marched to Dublin, where it was stationed three months.

The regiment was divided into six service and four depôt companies, and the service companies received orders to proceed to the celebrated fortress of Gibraltar. They accordingly marched from Dublin, for embarkation at the Cove of Cork, on board His Majesty's ship "Albion," and the "Sovereign" and "Numa" transports : the last division arrived at Gibraltar in the middle of December. The depôt companies were removed from Ireland to Scotland.

On arrival at Gibraltar, the regiment occupied Windmill-hill Barracks, and was afterwards removed to Rosia, where it was stationed during the year 1827.

In February 1828, the regiment took possession of a wing of the grand casemates. As an epidemic fever prevailed in the garrison, from which the regiment suffered severely, it encamped, in September, on the neutral ground. Its loss from the fever was, Ensign Charles Stewart, 6 sergeants, and 53 rank and file.

The regiment returned to the grand casemates on the 9th of January 1829 ; again encamped in the neutral ground in July, leaving in barracks the men who had recovered from the fever. It returned within the fortress in October.

As there is little or nothing to record with regard to the doings of the regiment during the six years it was at Gibraltar, where it took its share of the usual garrison work, we shall again recur to Lieutenant-Colonel Wheatley's memoranda, and present the reader with some interesting notes on the manners, customs, &c., of the regiment about this time. Let us, however, note here, that in 1825, the regiment was armed with "The Long Land Tower" musket, being the only corps of the line to which it was issued ; and again, in 1840, it was the first corps to receive the percussion musket, in both cases, through the interest of Sir George Murray, its colonel.

The bugle, for barrack duty, was introduced in 1828, whilst the 42d was encamped on the neutral ground, Gibraltar, during the epidemic fever. Before this the solitary bugler of the regiment sounded part of "quick march" for the guard, and had about half-a-dozen calls for the light company, whose knowledge of skirmishing barely extended to the covering of an advance in line. In the following year, and 1830, it was taken up in reality, and the corps soon became famous for their skirmishing: not that either the bugle calls for barracks or the light infantry drill was without its enemies. Indeed, in general, the officers were averse to the "new fangled innovations," and, in some instances, complained that they could not understand the bugle even for the men's breakfast, dinner, &c., and wished a return to the drum ! However, the innovations, with numerous others, were supported by the commanding officers, and in due time the 42d became equal to its neighbours.

While at Gibraltar, in 1830, a regimental library was started, and continued in a flourishing condition for many years. Its history, as told by one of its originators, Lieutenant-

Colonel Wheatley, is extremely interesting. It deserves to be recorded, as it was creditable to the corps, and equally so to the men who so nobly supported it. At this time, such institutions were unknown in the army; indeed, if anything, they were discouraged.

The regiment was quartered with the 43d in the grand casemates, in February 1830. The sergeant-major of that corps had a small library, his private property, collected at sales of books from time to time, from the famous garrison library; he from that formed a circulating library, lending books at a certain rate per month. It was spoken of in the orderly-room one day, after the finish of the morning's duty, and Sir Charles Gordon expressed his surprise that in a Scotch regiment nothing of the kind had been instituted. As soon as he left, the pay sergeants were called, and desired, by nine o'clock the following morning, to give a return of the number of subscribers willing to pay six days' pay of their rank, to be levied in three monthly instalments, and after the third month, to pay a subscription of sixpence a month. A return of 224 was given in, and it having willingly been approved of by Sir Charles, immediate steps were taken to establish the library. A large order was sent off to the Messrs Tegg, of London, and within a month, what from a purchase of cast works from the garrison library, and donations of books from the officers, the regiment was in good reading order. The officers were most liberal in their donations. The members continued to increase, and various alterations were made from time to time, and in 1836 the subscriptions were reduced to fourpence. The funds were always fully able to meet any charge of conveyance whilst at home, from 1836 to 1841, and again from 1852 to 1854. On being ordered to Turkey in 1854, the whole of the books were disposed of, because the Government reading-rooms and libraries had been in force some time before this, and some corps had been ordered to do away with the regimental ones. At the time of its being broken up, it contained nearly 3000 volumes, and during its existence was highly creditable to the regiment.

In 1832, the regiment received orders to leave Gibraltar and proceed to Malta, embarking on the 13th January, when the governor,

Sir William Houston, expressed in garrison orders "that the 42d Royal Highlanders had embarked in a manner fully supporting their high character for discipline and good conduct, and he regretted their departure." After remaining at Malta till December 1834, the regiment was removed to the Ionian Islands, where it stayed till June 1836, having by that time completed a period of ten years and six months' service in the Mediterranean.

The 42d left Corfu for Britain on the 30th of June, and was accompanied to the place of embarkation by the Lord High Commissioner, Major-General Sir Howard Douglas, who, on its being formed on the esplanade, addressed it in the following terms:—

"*Colonel Middleton, Officers, Non-Commissioned Officers, and Soldiers of the Royal-Highlanders,*

"I have come hither to assure you, that the conduct of the Forty-second has given me the highest degree of satisfaction during the time it has been under my orders, and I wish to express to you the deep regret I feel at the departure of this gallant and distinguished corps from the station under my command.

"The highest professional obligation of a regiment, is so to act as to render itself dreaded as well as respected by enemies. This the Forty-second has hitherto nobly and effectually done; and that power, though it exists unimpaired in the condition of this regiment, reposes for the present happily in peace.

"It is peculiarly the duty of a British soldier to conciliate, by personal demeanour and individual conduct, the esteem and regard of his fellow-subjects at home, and wherever he may be serving abroad, to cultivate the best terms, and gain the respect and good will of all classes of persons in the community of the place where he may be quartered. This, too, Forty-second, you have well done! The good terms which so happily subsist between the protector and the protected here, have not only been undisturbed, but cemented by your good conduct; and it affords me the greatest pleasure to have heard it declared by the highest authorities here, that you take with you the regard, respect, and good wishes of this population. As I was honoured by having this regiment placed under my orders, and I am highly satisfied with the conduct of the corps to the moment of its departure, so should I feel gratified if I should have the good fortune to have you again under my command. If this should be in peace, I shall have the pleasure of renewing the agreeable intercourse I have had with the officers, and the pleasing duties I have had to discharge with you. Should a renewal of the connection take place in war, it will afford me much delight and satisfaction, and I shall feel great honour conferred upon me by being again associated with a corps, which, I well know, would acquire fresh inscriptions to its own renown, and to the honour of our country, on the banners which have braved many a hard-fought battle-field, and which have waved triumphantly over many a victory! Forty-second, *farewell!*"

The regiment, on landing at Leith, on the 7th September 1836, was joined by the depôt companies waiting it in Edinburgh Castle. It remained in Scotland till the spring of 1838, when it embarked from Glasgow for Dublin, where it remained until the beginning of 1841. While in Ireland, new colours were presented to the regiment on March 7th, 1839.

While in Ireland, Lieutenant-Colonel Middleton was reluctantly compelled to resign his command, on doing which he issued the following pathetic farewell order:—

"NEW BARRACKS, LIMERICK,
12th August, 1839.

" *Regimental Order.*

"The Lieutenant-Colonel is persuaded that the officers, non-commissioned officers, and the soldiers of the regiment will enter into his feelings, and easily believe that it caused him many a heart-rending struggle before he brought himself to the sad conclusion of severing ties which connected his destiny for thirty-six years with that of the 42d, and which, but for one consideration, nothing on this side the grave could have induced him to do. That consideration they cannot be ignorant of, and which he is sure they will duly appreciate.

"It remains with him, therefore, only to return them, collectively and individually, the warmest expression of his thanks for the cordial and unremitting manner with which they co-operated with him in the various duties connected with his command, which made his situation

truly an envious one; indeed, he may with truth assert without alloy, until now, when bidding the regiment farewell. In his sorrow, however, it affords him consolation to think that he resigns his proud and enviable charge into the hands of Major Johnstone, so capable in every way of maintaining their discipline, and watching over the best interest of the regiment. The Lieutenant-Colonel hopes the officers, non-commissioned officers, and soldiers, will give the same undeviating support to him that they have on every occasion given the Lieutenant-Colonel, the recollection of which can never be banished from his mind; and wherever his future lot may be cast, his heart will always be with the Royal Highlanders; in saying which, should a tablet be over his tomb, the only epitaph he would wish engraved upon it would be, that he once belonged to the 42d."

In January 1841, the six service companies left Ireland for the Ionian Islands, and in May following, the depôt companies left Dublin for Scotland, being stationed at Stirling, which they quitted in March 1842, for Aberdeen.

The 42d and eight other regiments[1] having been augmented to an establishment of 1 lieutenant-colonel, 2 majors, 12 captains, 14 lieutenants, 10 ensigns, 6 staff officers, 67 sergeants, 25 drummers, and 1200 rank and file; the Royal Highlanders received upwards of 400 Scots volunteers from other corps (180 of whom were furnished by the 72d, 79th, 92d, and 93d Highland regiments), towards the completion of their new establishment; and the depôt was moved to Aberdeen in May, where it was formed into 6 companies, to be termed the *Reserve Battalion,* and its organisation rapidly proceeded.

In August 1842, when her Majesty the Queen Victoria visited Scotland, the reserve battalion of the Royal Highlanders furnished a guard of honour for Her Majesty at Dupplin, Taymouth, Drummond, and Stirling Castles, and the brevet rank of lieutenant-colonel was conferred on the commanding officer, Major James Macdougall.

In November 1842, the reserve battalion embarked from Gosport for Malta, to be joined by the first battalion from the Ionian Islands.

[1] The 12th, 20th, 23d, 45th, 71st, 91st, 97th, and second battalion Rifle Brigade.

The head-quarters and three companies of the first battalion, under the command of Lieutenant-Colonel Johnstone, embarked at Cephalonia, and landed at Malta on the 20th February ; the other three companies arrived at Malta from Zante on the 27th March.

When the regiment embarked at Cephalonia, the Regent, the Bishop, and all the dignitaries saw Colonel Johnstone, the officers and men to the boats, and the leave-taking was nearly as touching as the one at Corfu in 1841. The Regent of the Island and the Civil authorities subsequently sent a large gold medal to Colonel Johnstone, with Cephalos and his dog on one side of it, and the Colonel's name on the other.[3]

On the 29th of December 1843, General the Right Honourable Sir George Murray, G.C.B., was removed to the 1st, or the Royal Regiment of Foot, in succession to General Lord Lynedoch, deceased ; and the colonelcy of the 42d Royal Highlanders was conferred on Lieutenant-General Sir John Macdonald, K.C.B. (Adjutant-General of the Forces), from the 67th regiment. Sir George Murray on his removal, addressed a letter to Lieutenant-Colonel Cameron, commanding the regiment, from which the following are extracts :—

Colonel Johnstone's Medal.

"I cannot leave the command of the Forty-second Royal Highlanders without requesting you to express to them, in the strongest terms, how high an honour I shall always esteem it to have been for upwards of twenty years the colonel of a regiment, which, by its exemplary conduct in every situation, and by its distinguished valour in many a well-fought field, has earned for itself so large a share of esteem and of renown as that which belongs to the FORTY-SECOND regiment.

"Wherever the military service of our country may hereafter require the presence of the Royal Highlanders, my most friendly wishes and best hopes will always accompany them, and it will afford me the greatest pleasure to learn that harmony and mutual goodwill continue, as heretofore, to prevail throughout their ranks ; and that discipline, so essential to the honour and success of every military body, is upheld amongst them, not more by the vigilance and the good example of those in command,

[3] Lieutenant-Colonel Johnstone appropriately acknowledged the honour thus conferred upon him by his Cephalonian friends :—

"Farewell to Cephalonia, 1843.

"GENTLEMEN,

"Nobili e cari Signori.

"I hardly know how to express my sense of your kindness, or how much I feel honoured by the announcement you have just made me of the intention of my friends in Cephalonia to present me with a medal, on my departure from this Island. As a proof of yours and their esteem, I cannot value it too highly, nor can I fail, however poor my merits may have been, to appreciate the generosity of feeling which has actuated you on this occasion.

Your allusions to the 42d and my family have been most gratifying to me, and one and all desire to join me in every good wish for your prosperity and happiness. May this happiness be long continued to you ; and may the zeal and ability for which so many of you are distinguished be honourably and usefully employed in promoting the best interests of your country."

"Dear Friends, farewell,
"Cari Cefeleni Amici, Addio."

than by the desire of all to discharge regularly, faithfully, and zealously, the several duties which it belongs to each respectively to perform. Whilst the Royal Highlanders persevere (as I feel confident, by my long acquaintance with them, both before and during the period of my having the honour to command them, that they always will) in the same path of duty which they have hitherto followed, they will never cease to add to that high reputation which they have already achieved for themselves, and for their native land."

Until the 42d went to Corfu, in December 1834, according to Lieutenant-Colonel Wheatley, no Highland regiment had ever been seen there, and the natives flocked from all parts of the island to see the wonderful soldiers. Many of the natives, no doubt, had heard something of the dress, but could only think of it as being like the Albanian kilt, nor would they believe that the knees were bare. The Greeks, says the Colonel, are very stoical, but at the parade next day (Sunday), on the esplanade, they could not conceal their excitement. Both the officers and men of the 42d were very popular at Corfu; and when, after an absence of four years and a-half on home service, the regiment returned to the island in 1841, the islanders regarded it as a compliment, and declared that "the regiment had only been sent to England to get percussion muskets."

On February 10th, 1846, was killed in action at Sobraon in India, Major-General Sir R. H. Dick, who had entered the 42d as ensign in 1800. He served with the second battalion of the 78th in Sicily in 1806; was wounded at the battle of Maida; was in Calabria and Egypt, in 1807; and was severely wounded at Rosetta. He was in the Peninsula from 1809, and was wounded at Waterloo. In the entrance of St Giles' Church, Edinburgh, is a tablet to his memory, erected by the officers of the 42d in 1846.

The two battalions remained at Malta until 1847, when both were ordered to Bermuda. The first sailed on the 27th February, and landed three companies (head-quarters) at Hamilton, and three companies at Ireland Island on the 16th April. The reserve battalion embarked in March, and landed at St. George's Island on the 24th of April.

On the 1st April 1850, the reserve battalion was consolidated into the first, forming a regiment of ten companies of 1000 rank and file. In May 1851, three companies were separated from the regiment to be sent to Scotland, to be joined by the depôt company from the Isle of Wight, and on 4th June, the six service companies embarked on board the "Resistance," and on the following day sailed for Halifax, where they arrived on the 12th, sending out detachments to Prince Edward's Island, Cape Breton, and Annapolis, in all 200 men.

The regiment was relieved by the 56th at Bermuda, and replaced the 88th at Halifax, ordered home. The depôt left Bermuda for Aberdeen on 13th July.

Before leaving, a letter, complimenting the regiment highly on its commendable conduct while in Bermuda, was forwarded to Colonel Cameron by his Excellency the governor. We give the following address from "the Corporation and other inhabitants of the town and parish of St. George," which was presented to Colonel Cameron on June 3d, 1851.

" To Lieutenant-Colonel D. A. Cameron,

42d R. H. Commandant, &c., &c., &c.

"SIR,—As Her Majesty's 42d regiment under your command is about to leave these Islands, we cannot allow its departure without expressing our esteem for the kindly feelings which have existed between the inhabitants and the 42d, during the four years' residence in this garrison. The urbanity and affability of the officers, the steady and upright conduct of the non-commissioned officers and men, have been eminently conspicuous. To our knowledge, not a man of your gallant and distinguished corps has been convicted of any crime before the civil authorities of this colony; a very gratifying circumstance, and bespeaking the high state of discipline of the regiment.

"To yourself, Sir, officers, and men, we sincerely tender our best wishes for your future welfare; and assured are we, that should the time arrive for the 'Forty-second' to be called into active service, they will display that loyalty and valour for which they are so justly renowned. Wishing you a safe and pleasant passage,—We have the honour to be, Sir, your obedient, humble servants :—

"(Signed by the Mayor, Corporation, and other Inhabitants of the town and parish of St George.)"

To this Colonel Cameron made a suitable reply.

This shows the esteem in which the regiment was held by the inhabitants of Bermuda, and it was well deserved. Not a man had been convicted before the civil authorities; it was something new to the Bermudans, and a subject which they often dwelt upon.

The mean strength of the regiment in the Islands for four years and two months, viz:— April 1847 to June 1857, was 1090 ; and the deaths, including accidents, &c., were only 31, being much less than the usual mortality at home. The regiment that the 42d had relieved (1st and reserve battalions of the 20th) sustained a heavy loss—several hundreds—from cholera ; and the 56th, which replaced it, lost 6 officers and 224 men, in the autumn of 1853.

Early in 1852, the several detachments rejoined at Halifax, and on the 29th May the regiment (again in the "Resistance") embarked to return home, and on July 16th anchored at Greenock. They landed on the 19th, and proceeded by rail to Stirling, three companies going to Perth, and two to Dundee. The depôt was waiting the arrival of the service companies in Stirling Castle. The regiment had been absent from Scotland upwards of 14 years, viz., since embarking at Glasgow for Dublin in 1838.

Early in April 1853, the regiment was ordered to be in readiness to proceed to England. On the 22d headquarters left Stirling, and proceeded to Weedon, detaching two companies to Northampton. On the 14th of June left Weedon for Chobham. It was there encamped with the 1st Life Guards ; 6th Dragoon Guards; 13th Light Dragoons, 17th Lancers ; 1st Battalion Grenadier Guards ; 1st Battalion Scots Fusiliers ; 1st Battalion Coldstreams; 38th, 50th, 93d, and 95th regiments ; and 2d Battalion Rifle Brigade, &c., &c.

On the 14th July, the whole of the troops were replaced, and the regiment proceeded to Haslar and Gosport (Fort Monckton), detaching three companies, under Major Cumberland, to Weymouth.

VI.
1854—1856.

Regiment Embarks for Crimea—Landing at Kalamita Bay—March to the Alma—Russian Position—Battle of the Alma—The Highland Brigade—Sir Colin Campbell — Work done by the 42d — Sir Colin's Bonnet—Work of the 42d before Sebastopol—Sir Colin Campbell's Addresses—The Kertch Expedition—Return Home.

EARLY in 1854, the regiment was removed to Portsea, preparatory to embarking for Turkey, in consequence of hostilities with Russia.

About 200 Volunteers were received from depôts in Ireland, and for the first time for upwards of 45 years, without regard to country. The ten service companies embarked in the hired screw ship the "Hydaspes," Captain John Baker, on the 20th May, and sailed next morning. They consisted of 32 officers, 45 sergeants, 20 Drummers and Pipers, and 850 Rank and File. On 1st June they went into Malta, and on the 7th anchored off Scutari. They landed and encamped on the 9th, joining in Brigade with the 79th and 93d.

On the 13th the division, consisting of the Brigade of Guards and the Highlanders, embarked and reached Varna next day, and disembarked on 15th, encamping near to Varna. On the 1st of July they moved to Aladyne; on the 28th to Gevrekler ("The there springs") ; and on 16th August repassed Varna to Galatabourna,[1] where the regiment was in camp until the embarkation of the army on the 29th, on which day it went on board the ss. "Emeu," and sailed with the expedition on the 5th September.

The British force consisted of 27,000 men of all arms ; the French about 30,000; and the Turks 7000 ; making a total of 63,000 men, with 128 guns. Lord Raglan was the chief of the British forces, while Marshal St Arnaud commanded the army of France. The English infantry consisted of four divisions ; the Light, First, Second, and Third Divisions. The First Division, under the command of H. R. H. the Duke of Cambridge, consisted of the third battalion of the Grenadier Guards, and the first battalions of the Coldstream and Scotch Fusilier Guards, commanded by Major-General Bentinck. Major-General Sir Colin Campbell (Lord Clyde, of whom we give a steel

[1] Galatabourna, close to the Black Sea, about five miles to the south-west of Varna.

portrait) was commander of the other half of this division (the Highland Brigade), composed of the 42d, 79th, and 93d Highlanders. The 42d was commanded by Colonel Cameron, who had joined the regiment in 1825, and was made lieutenant-general in 1868.

On the 14th of September 1854, the allied armies of England and France, landed unopposed at Old Fort, Kalameta Bay, about 30 miles north of Sebastopol.

"The seamen knew," says Kinglake,[2] the fascinating historian of the Crimean War, "that it concerned the health and comfort of the soldiers to be landed dry, so they lifted or handed the men ashore with an almost tender care : yet not without mirth—nay, not without laughter far heard—when, as though they were giant maidens, THE TALL HIGHLANDERS OF THE FORTY-SECOND, placed their hands in the hands of the sailor, and sprang, by his aid, to the shore, their kilts floating out wide while they leapt." It was not until the 18th that all the soldiers and their accompaniments were landed, and not until the 19th that the march southwards on Sebastopol commenced. On the first night of their march, the allies bivouacked on the banks of the stream of the Bulganak, six miles from their landing place.

"During the march, the foot-soldiers of the Allied armies suffered thirst ; but early in the afternoon the troops in advance reached the long-desired stream of the Bulganak ; and as soon as a division came in sight of the water, the men broke from their ranks, and ran forward that they might plunge their lips deep in the cool, turbid, grateful stream. In one brigade a stronger governance was maintained. Sir Colin Campbell would not allow that even the rage of thirst should loosen the discipline of his grand Highland regiments. He halted them a little before they reached the stream, and so ordered it that, by being saved from the confusion that would have been wrought by their own wild haste, they gained in comfort, and knew that they were gainers. When men toil in organised masses, they owe what well being they have to wise and firm commanders."[3]

When the allied forces came in sight of the Alma, they found the Russians intrenched in what looked a very formidable position, on the hills which rise from its left or southern bank. For a short distance from the mouth of the river, the banks rise precipitously from the river and form a table-land above, accessible by several gorges or passes. Further up the river the banks rise more gently, and the slope of the hills southwards is more gradual ; everywhere are the heights cut up by passes or ravines into knolls and separate rounded heights. "From the sea-shore to the easternmost spot occupied by Russian troops, the distance for a man going straight was nearly five miles and a-half ; but if he were to go all the way on the Russian bank of the river, he would have to pass over more ground, for the Alma here makes a strong bend and leaves open the chord of the arc to invaders who come from the north."[4] All over the heights extending from near the sea to this distance eastwards along the south-side of the river, the Russian force, amounting to 39,000 men and 106 guns, was massed on the side of the various slopes, in formidable looking columns. On the right of the Russian position rose gradually from the banks of the river a gentle slope, which terminated in a large rounded knoll, known as the Kourganè-hill. At about 300 yards from the river, the Russians had thrown up a large breastwork armed with fourteen heavy guns ; this was known as the Great Redoubt. With this work Prince Mentschikoff, the Russian commander, was delighted ; indeed, he fancied his position so impregnable, that he expected to hold out for three days, by which time he was confident the allies would be utterly exhausted, and fall an easy prey to his northern legions. On the same hill, but higher up, and more to his right, the Prince threw up another slight breast-work, which he armed with a battery of field guns. This was the Lesser Redoubt. At many other points which commanded the approaches to his position he had large batteries planted, and the vineyards which skirted the north bank of the river were marked and cleared, so as to give effect to the action of the artillery.

As it would be out of place here to give a

[2] Whose kindness in allowing us to make these extracts we have pleasure in acknowledging.
[3] Kinglake's Crimea, vol. ii. pp 186, 216.
[4] Ibid. vol. ii. p. 204.

general account of the battle of the Alma, we shall content ourselves mainly with setting forth the part taken in it by the 42d Royal Highlanders, the actual strength of which regiment going into action was 27 officers, 40 sergeants, 20 pipers and drummers, and 703 rank and file The work done by the other Highland regiments will be told in the proper place. The French and Turks, who formed the right of the allied army, were appointed to attack the left of the Russian position, while the British had to bear the brunt of the battle, and engage the enemy in front and on the right, being thus exposed to the full force of the murderous fire from the above mentioned batteries [5]

"The right wing of the Russian army was the force destined to confront, first our Light Division, and then the Guards and the Highlanders. It was posted on the slopes of the Kourganè Hill. Here was the Great Redoubt, armed with its fourteen heavy guns, and Prince Mentschikoff was so keen to defend this part of the ground, that he gathered round the work, on the slopes of the hill, a force of no less than sixteen battalions of regular infantry, besides the two battalions of Sailors, and four batteries of field-artillery The right of the forces on the Kourganè Hill rested on a slope to the east of the Lesser Redoubt, and the left on the great road Twelve of the battalions of regular infantry were disposed into battalion-columns posted at intervals and checkerwise on the flanks of the Great Redoubt, the other four battalions, drawn up in one massive column, were held as a reserve for the right wing on the higher slope of the hill. Of the four field-batteries, one armed the Lesser Redoubt, another was on the high ground commanding and supporting the Great Redoubt, and the remaining two were held in reserve General Kvetzinski commanded the troops in this part of the field On his extreme right, and posted at intervals along a curve drawn from his right front to his centre rear, Prince Mentschikoff placed his cavalry,—a force comprising 3400 lances, with three batteries of horse-artillery.

"Each of these bodies of horse, when brought within sight of the Allies, was always massed in column

"Thus, then, it was to bar the Pass and the great road, to defend the Kourganè Hill and to cover his right flank, that the Russian General gathered his main strength, and this was the part of the field destined to be assailed by our troops That portion of the Russian force which directly confronted the English army, consisted of 3400 cavalry, twenty-four battalions of infantry, and seven batteries of field-artillery, besides the fourteen heavy guns in the Great Redoubt, making together 23,400 men and eighty-six guns "[6]

In the march from its bivouac on the night of the 19th there were two or three protracted halts, one caused by a slight brush with some Cossack cavalry and artillery The rest we must relate mainly in the charming words of Kinglake, after whose narrative all others are stale

"The last of these took place at a distance of about a mile and a half from the banks of the Alma. From the spot where the forces were halted the ground sloped gently down to the river's side, and though some men lay prostrate under the burning sun, with little thought except of fatigue, there were others who keenly scanned the ground before them, well knowing that now at last the long-expected conflict would begin They could make out the course of the river from the dark belt of gardens and vineyards which marked its banks , and men with good eyes could descry a slight seam running across a rising-ground beyond the river, and could see, too, some dark squares or oblongs, encroaching like small patches of culture upon the broad downs. The seam was the Great Redoubt; the square-looking marks that stained the green sides of the hills were an army in order of battle.

"That 20th of September on the Alma was like some remembered day of June in England, for the sun was unclouded, and the soft breeze of the morning had lulled to a breath at noon-tide, and was creeping faintly along the hills. It was then that in the Allied armies there occurred a singular pause of sound—a pause so general as to have been observed and remembered by many in remote parts of the ground, and so marked that its interruption by the mere neighing of an angry horse seized the attention of thousands; and although this strange silence was the mere result of weariness and chance, it seemed to carry a meaning; for it was now that, after near forty years of peace, the great nations of Europe were once more meeting for battle.

"Even after the sailing of the expedition, the troops had been followed by reports that the war, after all, would be stayed; and the long frequent halts, and the quiet of the armies on the sunny slope, seemed to harmonise with the idea of disbelief in the coming of the long promised fight. But in the midst of this repose Sir Colin Campbell said to one of his officers, 'This will be a good time for the men to get loose half their cartridges;' and when the command travelled on along the ranks of the Highlanders, it lit up the faces of the men one after another, assuring them that now at length, and after long expectance, they indeed would go into action. They began obeying the order, and with beaming joy, for they came of a warlike race; yet not without emotion of a graver kind—they were young soldiers, new to battle." [7]

The Light Division formed the right of the British army, and the duty of the Highland Brigade and the Guards was to support this division in its attack on the right of the Russian position. The 42d formed the right of the Highland Brigade, the 93d the centre, and the 79th the left. The Kourganè hill, which had to be assailed by the Light Division, supported by the Highlanders and Guards, was defended by two redoubts, by 42 guns, and by a force of some 17,000 men.

The battle commenced about half-past one P.M., and lasted a little over two hours. The French attack on the left was comparatively a failure, and their losses small, for they had but little of the fighting to sustain. The battle on the part of the English was commenced by the Light and Second Divisions crossing the Alma, the former getting first to the other or Russian side, driving the Russian skirmishers and riflemen before them at the point of the bayonet. As soon as they got out of the vineyards, double the number of guns opened upon them with grape and canister, still they moved on, keeping up a telling fire against the Russian gunners. By the time they reached the great redoubt they were terribly shattered, but, nevertheless, successfully carried it and captured two guns. Being, however, now comparatively few in number, and unsupported, they were compelled to leave the redoubt by a huge body of Russian infantry, upon whom, they never turned their backs. Other operations, with more or less success, were going on in other parts of the hillside, but our place is with the Highlanders of the First Division, who, along with the Guards, were now advancing to support the Light Division, so sore bestead. "This magnificent division, the flower of the British army, had crossed the river rather higher up than the Light Division, and consequently were on its left. . . . The First Division formed-up after crossing the Alma, and although they incurred considerable loss in so doing, they nevertheless advanced in most beautiful order—really as if on parade. I shall never forget that sight—one felt so proud of them." [8] Lord Raglan had been looking on all this time from some high ground, where he and his staff were posted, and where he obtained a comprehensive view of the battle-field. When he saw the First Division coming up in support, he said, "Look how well the Guards and Highlanders advance!" [9] We must allow Mr Kinglake to tell the rest.

"Further to the left (of the Guards), and in the same formation (of line), the three battalions of the Highland Brigade were extended. But the 42d had found less difficulty than the 93d in getting through the thick ground and the river, and again the 93d had found less difficulty than the 79th; so, as each regiment had been formed and moved forward with all the speed it could command, the brigade fell naturally into direct échelon of regiments, the 42d in front.

```
                                    |
                                   42d.

                    |
                   93d.

     |
    79th.
```

[7] Kinglake's Crimea, v. ii. p. 257.
[8] Letters from H———.
[9] Kinglake's Crimea, v. ii. p. 443.

And although this order was occasioned by the nature of the ground traversed and not by design, it was so well suited to the work in hand that Sir Colin Campbell did not for a moment seek to change it.

"These young soldiers, distinguished to the vulgar eye by their tall stature, their tartan uniforms, and the plumes of their Highland bonnets, were yet more marked in the eyes of those who know what soldiers are by the warlike carriage of the men, and their strong, lithesome, resolute step. And Sir Colin Campbell was known to be so proud of them, that already, like the Guards, they had a kind of prominence in the army, which was sure to make their bearing in action a broad mark for blame or for praise."[1]

[1] We shall take the liberty of quoting here the same author's sketch of Campbell's career:—

"Whilst Ensign Campbell was passing from boyhood to man's estate, he was made partaker in the great transactions which were then beginning to work out the liberation of Europe. In the May of 1808 he received his first commission—a commission in the 9th Foot; and a few weeks afterwards—then too young to carry the colours—he was serving with his regiment upon the heights of Vimieira. There the lad saw the turning of a tide in human affairs; saw the opening of the mighty strife between 'Column' and 'Line;' saw France, long unmatched upon the Continent, retreat before British infantry; saw the first of Napoleon's stumbles, and the fame of Sir Arthur Wellesley beginning to dawn over Europe.

"He was in Sir John Moore's campaign, and at its closing scene—Corunna. He was with the Walcheren expedition; and afterwards, returning to the Peninsula, he was at the battle of Barossa, the defence of Tarifa, the relief of Taragona, and the combats at Malaga and Osma. He led a forlorn hope at the storming of St Sebastian, and was there wounded twice; he was at Vittoria; he was at the passage of the Bidassoa; he took part in the American war of 1814; he served in the West Indies; he served in the Chinese war of 1842. These occasions he had so well used that his quality as a soldier was perfectly well known. He had been praised and praised again and again; but since he was not so connected as to be able to move the dispensers of military rank, he gained promotion slowly, and it was not until the second Sikh war that he had a command as a general: even then he had no rank in the army above that of a colonel. At Chilianwalla he commanded a division. Marching in person with one of his two brigades, he had gained the heights on the extreme right of the Sikh position, and then bringing round the left shoulder, he had rolled up the enemy's line and won the day; but since his other brigade (being separated from him by a long distance) had wanted his personal control, and fallen into trouble, the brilliancy of the general result which he had achieved did not save him altogether from criticism. That day he was wounded for the fourth time. He commanded a division at the great battle of Gujerat; and, being charged to press the enemy's retreat, he had so executed his task that 158 guns and the ruin of the foe were the fruit of the victory. In 1851 the following year he commanded against the hill-tribes. It was he who forced the Kohat Pass. It was he who, with only a few men and some guns, at Punj Pao,

"The other battalions of the Highland Brigade were approaching; but the 42d—the far-famed 'Black Watch'—had already come up. It was ranged in line. The ancient glory of the corps was a treasure now committed to the charge of young soldiers new to battle; but Campbell knew them—was sure of their excellence—and was sure, too, of Colonel Cameron, their commanding officer. Very eager—for the Guards were now engaged with the enemy's columns—very eager, yet silent and majestic, the battalion stood ready.

"Before the action had begun, and whilst his men were still in column, Campbell had spoken to his brigade a few words—words simple, and, for the most part, workmanlike, yet touched with the fire of war-like sentiment. 'Now, men, you are going into action. Remember this: whoever is wounded—I don't care what his rank is—whoever is wounded must lie where he falls till the bandsmen come to attend to him. No soldiers must go carrying off wounded men. If any soldier does such a thing, his name shall be stuck up in his parish church. Don't be in a hurry about firing. Your officers will tell you when it is time to open fire. Be steady. Keep silence.

compelled the submission of the combined tribes then acting against him with a force of 8000 men. It was he who, at Ishakote, with a force of less than 3000 men, was able to end the strife; and when he had brought to submission all those beyond the Indus who were in arms against the Government, he instantly gave proof of the breadth and scope of his mind as well as of the force of his character; for he withstood the angry impatience of men in authority over him, and insisted that he must be suffered to deal with the conquered people in the spirit of a politic and merciful ruler.

"After serving with all this glory for some forty-four years, he came back to England; but between the Queen and him there stood a dense crowd of families—men, women, and children—extending further than the eye could reach, and armed with strange precedents which made it out to be right that people who had seen no service should be invested with high command, and that Sir Colin Campbell should be only a colonel. Yet he was of so fine a nature that, although he did not always avoid great bursts of anger, there was no ignoble bitterness in his sense of wrong. He awaited the time when perhaps he might have high command, and be able to serve his country in a sphere proportioned to his strength. His friends, however, were angry for his sake; and along with their strong devotion towards him there was bred a fierce hatred of a system of military dispensation which could keep in the background a man thus tried and thus known.

"Upon the breaking-out of the war with Russia, Sir Colin was appointed—not to the command of a division, but of a brigade. It was not till the June of 1854 that his rank in the army became higher than that of a colonel.'"

Fire low. Now, men'—those who know the old soldier can tell how his voice would falter the while his features were kindling—' Now, men, the army will watch us; make me proud of the Highland Brigade!'

"It was before the battle that this, or the like of this, was addressed to the brigade; and now, when Sir Colin rode up to the corps which awaited his signal, he only gave it two words. But because of his accustomed manner of utterance, and because he was a true, faithful lover of war, the two words he spoke were as the roll of the drum: 'Forward, 42d!' This was all he then said; and, 'as a steed that knows his rider,' the great heart of the battalion bounded proudly to his touch.

"Sir Colin Campbell went forward in front of the 42d; but before he had ridden far, he saw that his reckoning was already made good by the event, and that the column which had engaged the Coldstream was moving off obliquely towards its right rear. Then with his Staff he rode up a good way in advance, for he was swift to hope that the withdrawal of the column from the line of the redoubt might give him the means of learning the ground before him, and seeing how the enemy's strength was disposed in this part of the field. In a few moments he was abreast of the redoubt, and upon the ridge or crest which divided the slope he had just ascended from the broad and rather deep hollow which lay before him. On his right he had the now empty redoubt, on his right front the higher slopes of the Kourganè Hill. Straight before him there was the hollow, or basin, just spoken of, bounded on its farther side by a swelling wave or ridge of ground which he called the 'inner crest.' Beyond that, whilst he looked straight before him, he could see that the ground fell off into a valley; but when he glanced towards his left front he observed that the hollow which lay on his front was, so to speak, bridged over by a bending rib which connected the inner with the outer crest—bridged over in such a way that a column on his left front might march to the spot where he stood without having first to descend into the lower ground. More towards his left, the ground was high, but so undulating and varied that it would not necessarily disclose any troops

which might be posted in that part of the field.

"Confronting Sir Colin Campbell from the other side of the hollow, the enemy had a strong column—the two right battalions of the Kazan corps—and it was towards this body that the Vladimir column, moving off from the line of the redoubt, was all this time making its way. The Russians saw that they were the subject of a general officer's studies; and Campbell's horse at this time was twice struck by shot, but not disabled. When the retiring column came abreast of the right Kazan column it faced about to the front, and, striving to recover its formation, took part with the Kazan column in opposing a strength of four battalions—four battalions hard-worked and much thinned —to the one which, eager and fresh, was following the steps of the Highland General.

"Few were the moments that Campbell took to learn the ground before him, and to read the enemy's mind; but, few though they were, they were all but enough to bring the 42d to the crest where their General stood. The ground they had to ascend was a good deal more steep and more broken than the slope close beneath the redoubt. In the land where those Scots were bred, there are shadows of sailing clouds skimming straight up the mountain's side, and their paths are rugged, are steep, yet their course is smooth, easy, and swift. Smoothly, easily, swiftly; the ' Black Watch' seemed to glide up the hill. A few instants before, and their tartans ranged dark in the valley—now, their plumes were on the crest. The small knot of horsemen who had ridden on before them were still there. Any stranger looking into the group might almost be able to know—might know by the mere carriage of the head—that he in the plain, dark-coloured frock, he whose sword-belt hung crosswise from his shoulder, was the man there charged with command; for in battle, men who have to obey sit erect in their saddles; he who has on him the care of the fight seems always to fall into the pensive yet eager bend which the Greeks—keen perceivers of truth— used to join with their conception of Mind brought to bear upon War. It is on board ship, perhaps, more commonly than ashore, that people in peace-time have been used to

see their fate hanging upon the skill of one
man. Often, landsmen at sea have watched the
skilled, weather-worn sailor when he seems to
look through the gale, and search deep into the
home of the storm. He sees what they cannot
see; he knows what, except from his lips,
they never will be able to learn. They stand
silent, but they question him with their eyes.
So men new to war gaze upon the veteran
commander, when, with knitted brow and
steady eyes, he measures the enemy's power,
and draws near to his final resolve. Campbell,
fastening his eyes on the two columns standing
before him, and on the heavier and more
distant column on his left front, seemed not to
think lightly of the enemy's strength; but in
another instant (for his mind was made up,
and his Highland blood took fire at the coming
array of the tartans) his features put on that
glow which, seen in men of his race—race
known by the kindling grey eye, and the light,
stubborn crisping hair—discloses the rapture
of instant fight. Although at that moment
the 42d was alone, and was confronted by the
two columns on the farther side of the hollow,
yet Campbell, having a steadfast faith in
Colonel Cameron and in the regiment he commanded, resolved to go straight on, and at once,
with his forward movement. He allowed the
battalion to descend alone into the hollow,
marching straight against the two columns.
Moreover, he suffered it to undertake a
manœuvre which (except with troops of great
steadiness and highly instructed) can hardly be
tried with safety against regiments still un-
shaken. The 'Black watch' 'advanced firing.'

"But whilst this fight was going on between
the 42d and the two Russian columns, grave
danger from another quarter seemed to threaten
the Highland battalion; for, before it had
gone many paces, Campbell saw that the
column which had appeared on his left front
was boldly marching forward; and such was
the direction it took, and such the nature of
the ground, that the column, if it were suffered
to go on with this movement, would be able to
strike at the flank of the 42d without having
first to descend into lower ground.

"Halting the 42d in the hollow, Campbell
swiftly measured the strength of the approaching
column, and he reckoned it so strong that he

resolved to prepare for it a front of no less
than five companies. He was upon the point
of giving the order for effecting this bend in the
line of the 42d, when looking to his left rear, he
saw his centre battalion springing up to the
outer crest."[2] This was the 93d.

"Campbell's charger, twice wounded already,
but hitherto not much hurt, was now struck by
a shot in the heart. Without a stumble or a
plunge the horse sank down gently to the
earth, and was dead. Campbell took his aide-
de-camp's charger; but he had not been long
in Shadwell's saddle when up came Sir Colin's
groom with his second horse. The man, perhaps,
under some former master, had been used to be
charged with the 'second horse' in the hunting-
field. At all events, here he was; and if Sir
Colin was angered by the apparition, he could
not deny that it was opportune. The man
touched his cap, and excused himself for being
where he was. In the dry, terse way of those
Englishmen who are much accustomed to
horses, he explained that towards the rear the
balls had been dropping about very thick, and
that, fearing some harm might come to his
master's second horse, he had thought it best
to bring him up to the front.

"When the 93d had recovered the perfect-
ness of its array, it again moved forward, but
at the steady pace imposed upon it by the chief.
The 42d had already resumed its forward
movement; it still advanced firing.

"The turning moment of a fight is a moment
of trial for the soul, and not for the body; and
it is, therefore, that such courage as men are
able to gather from being gross in numbers,
can be easily outweighed by the warlike virtue
of a few. To the stately 'Black Watch' and
the hot 93d, with Campbell leading them on,
there was vouchsafed that stronger heart for
which the brave pious Muscovites had prayed.
Over the souls of the men in the columns there
was spread, first the gloom, then the swarm of
vain delusions, and at last the sheer horror
which might be the work of the Angel of
Darkness. The two lines marched straight on.
The three columns shook. They were not yet
subdued. They were stubborn; but every
moment the two advancing battalions grew
nearer and nearer, and although—dimly mask-

[2] Kinglake, *Crimea*, vol. ii. pp. 474–79.

ing the scant numbers of the Highlanders—there was still the white curtain of smoke which always rolled on before them, yet, fitfully, and from moment to moment, the signs of them could be traced on the right hand and on the left in a long, shadowy line, and their coming was ceaseless.

" But moreover, the Highlanders being men of great stature, and in strange garb, their plumes being tall, and the view of them being broken and distorted by the wreaths of the smoke, and there being, too, an ominous silence in their ranks, there were men among the Russians who began to conceive a vague terror—the terror of things unearthly; and some, they say, imagined that they were charged by horsemen strange, silent, monstrous, bestriding giant chargers. Unless help should come from elsewhere, the three columns would have to give way; but help came. From the high ground on our left another heavy column—the column composed of the two right Sousdal battalions—was seen coming down. It moved straight at the flank of the 93d."[3] This was met by the 79th.

" Without a halt, or with only the halt that was needed for dressing the ranks, it sprang at the flank of the right Sousdal column, and caught it in its sin—caught it daring to march across the front of a battalion advancing in line. Wrapped in the fire thus poured upon its flank, the hapless column could not march, could not live. It broke, and began to fall back in great confusion; and the left Sousdal column being almost at the same time overthrown by the 93d, and the two columns which had engaged the 'Black Watch' being now in full retreat, the spurs of the hill and the winding dale beyond became thronged with the enemy's disordered masses.

" Then again, they say, there was heard the sorrowful wail that bursts from the heart of the brave Russian infantry when they have to suffer defeat; but this time the wail was the wail of eight battalions; and the warlike grief of the soldiery could no longer kindle the fierce intent which, only a little before, had spurred forward the Vladimir column. Hope had fled.

" After having been parted from one another

by the nature of the ground, and thus thrown for some time into échelon, the battalions of Sir Colin's brigade were now once more close abreast ; and since the men looked upon ground where the grey remains of the enemy's broken strength were mournfully rolling away, they could not but see that this, the revoir of the Highlanders, had chanced in a moment of glory. Knowing their hearts, and deeming that the time was one when the voice of his people might fitly enough be heard, the Chief touched or half lifted his hat in the way of a man assenting. Then along the Kourgané slopes, and thence west almost home to the Causeway, the hill-sides were made to resound with that joyous, assuring cry, which is the natural utterance of a northern people so long as it is warlike and free.[4]

" The three Highland regiments were now re-formed, and Sir Colin Campbell, careful in the midst of victory, looked to see whether the supports were near enough to warrant him in pressing the enemy's retreat with his Highland Brigade. He judged that, since Cathcart was still a good way off, the Highlanders ought to be established on the ground which they had already won ; and, never forgetting that, all this while, he was on the extreme left of the whole infantry array of the Allies, he made a a bend in his line, which caused it to show a front towards the south-east as well as towards the south.

" This achievement of the Guards and the Highland Brigade was so rapid, and was executed with so steadfast a faith in the prowess of our soldiery and the ascendancy of Line over Column, that in vanquishing great masses of infantry 12,000 strong, and in going straight through with an onset which tore open the Russian position, the six battalions together did not lose 500 men."[5]

The British loss was 25 officers and 19 sergeants killed, and 81 officers and 102 sergeants wounded; 318 rank and file killed, and 1438 wounded, making, with 19 missing, a total loss of 2002. The French loss was probably

[3] Kinglake's Crimea, vol. ii. p. 481.

[4] Many of our people who had heard the cheers of the Highlanders were hindered from seeing them by the bend of the ground, and they supposed that the cheers were uttered in charging. It was not so. The Highlanders advanced in silence.

[5] Ibid. vol. ii. pp. 483, 484.

not more than 60 killed and 500 wounded, while the Russian killed and wounded amounted to considerably above 6000. The 42d in killed and wounded lost only 37 men.

After the battle, it was a touching sight to see the meeting between Lord Raglan and Sir Colin Campbell. The latter was on foot, as his horse had been killed in the earlier period of the action. Lord Raglan rode up, and highly complimented Campbell and his brigade. Sir Colin, with tears in his eyes,[6] said it was not the first battle-field they had won together, and that, now that the battle was over, he had a favour to ask his lordship, which he hoped he would not refuse—to wear a bonnet with his brigade while he had the honour to command it.

The request was at once granted, and the making up of the bonnet was intrusted secretly to Lieutenant and Adjutant Drysdale of the 42d. There was a difficulty next morning as to the description of heckle to combine the three regiments of the Brigade. It was at last decided to have one-third of it red, to represent the 42d, and the remaining two-thirds white at the bottom, for the 79th and 93d. Not more than half a dozen knew about the preparation of the bonnet, and these were confined to the 42d. A brigade parade was ordered on the morning of 22d September on the field of Alma, "as the General was desirous of thanking them for their conduct on the 20th." The square was formed in readiness for his arrival, and he rode into it with the bonnet on. No order or signal was given for it, but he was greeted with such a succession of cheers, again and again, that both the French and English armies were startled into a perfect state of wonder as to what had taken place. Such is the history of "the bonnet gained."

The 42d had its own share in the harassing and tedious work which devolved on the British soldiers while lying before Sebastopol, although it so happened that it took no part in any of the important actions which followed Alma. Here, as elsewhere, the men supported the well-known character of the regiment in all respects. On the first anniversary of the battle of the Alma, September 20, 1855, the

first distribution of medals was made to the soldiers in the Crimea, on which occasion Lieutenant-General Sir Colin Campbell issued the following stirring address, duty preventing him from being present :—

"*Highland Brigade,*

"On the first anniversary of the glorious battle of the Alma, our gracious Sovereign has commanded the Crimean medal to be presented to her gallant soldiers, who were the first to meet the Russians and defeat them on their own territory. The fatigues and hardships of last year are well known, and have greatly thinned our ranks since we scaled the Alma heights together; but happy am I to see so many faces around me, who, on that day, by their courage, steadiness, and discipline, so materially assisted in routing the Russian hordes from their vaunted impregnable position. To that day Scotchmen can look with pride, (and Scotchmen are everywhere). For your deeds upon that day you received the marked encomiums of Lord Raglan, the thanks of the Queen, and admiration of all. Scotchmen are proud of you! I, too, am a Scotchman, and proud of the honour of commanding so distinguished a Brigade; and still prouder, that through all the trying severities of the winter, its incessant labours, and decimating disease, you have still maintained the same unflinching courage and energy with which your discipline, obedience, and steadiness, in whatever circumstances you have been placed, make you so unrivalled (and none more so than the oldest regiment of the brigade), and your commander confident of success, however numerous and determined your foe. The young soldiers who have not this day been presented with a medal, nor shared in the glories of the Alma, may soon win equal honours, for many an Alma will yet be fought, when I hope they will prove themselves worthy comrades of those who have struck home for Scotland, and for honours for their breast.

"Many have shared the greatest portion of the hardships of this campaign, and were ready upon the 8th (September) to do their duty, and eager for the morning of the 9th, when if we had been required I am positive would have gained renown.

"The honour of these last days all are equally entitled to, and I hope soon again to be presenting the young soldiers with their medals.

"I cannot conclude without bringing to your minds, that the eyes of your countrymen are upon you. I know you think of it, and will endeavour by every effort to maintain your famed and admirable discipline; also that your conduct in private equals your prowess in the field; and when the day arrives that your services are no longer required in the field, welcome arms will be ready to meet you with pride, and give you the blessings your deeds have so materially aided to bring to your country. And in after years, when recalling the scenes of the Crimea by your ingle side, your greatest pride will be that you too were there, and proved yourself a worthy son of sires who, in by-gone days, on many a field added lustre to their country's fame."

The brave Sir Colin seems to have been particularly fond of the old Black Watch, "the senior regiment" of the Highland Brigade, as will be seen from the above address, as well as from the following, in which, after regretting he was not present at the distribution of medals and clasps on the 20th September, he proceeds:—

"Your steadiness and gallantry at the battle of Alma were most conspicuous and most gratifying to me, whilst your intrepidity, when before the enemy, has been equalled by the discipline which you have invariably preserved.

"Remember never to lose sight of the circumstance, that you are natives of Scotland; that your country admires you for your bravery; that it still expects much from you; and, as Scotchmen, strive to maintain the name and fame of our countrymen, who are everywhere, and who have nobly fought and bled in all quarters of the globe. In short, let every one consider himself an hero of Scotland. It is my pride, and shall also be my boast amongst the few friends which Providence has left me, and those which I have acquired, that this decoration of the order of the Bath, which I now wear, has been conferred upon me on account of the distinguished gallantry you have displayed. Long may you wear your medals, for you well deserve them! And now for a word to the younger officers and soldiers. It is not

only by bravery in action that you can anticipate success; much depends upon steadiness and discipline. Remember this, for it is owing to the high state of discipline heretofore maintained in the Highland Brigade, *and in the senior regiment thereof in particular*, that such results have been obtained as to warrant the highest degree of confidence in you, in whatever position the fortune of war may place you.

"Endeavour, therefore, to maintain steadiness and discipline, by which you will be able to emulate the deeds of your older comrades in arms, for we may yet have many Almas to fight, where you will have the opportunity of acquiring such distinction as now adorn your comrades."

From the 19th of October, the Highland Brigade was commanded by Colonel Cameron of the 42d, Sir Colin having been appointed to command the forces in and about Balaclava. In January 1855, the establishment was increased to 16 companies, and on the 3d of May, the regiment was embarked to take part in the Kertch expedition, but was recalled on the 6th. It again embarked on the 2d May, and landed at Kertch on the 24th, whence it marched to Yenikale. Two of the 42d men, while the regiment was at the last-mentioned place, were shot in rather an extraordinary manner. They were standing in a crowd which had assembled round a house for the purpose of "looting" it, when a Frenchman, having struck at the door with the butt of his musket, the piece went off, killing one 42d man on the spot and wounding the other. These, so far as we can ascertain, were the only casualties suffered by the regiment in this expedition. The 42d returned to Balaclava on the 9th of June, and on the 16th of the same month, took up its position in front of Sebastopol. On June 18th it formed one of the regiments of reserve in the assault of the outworks of Sebastopol, and was engaged in siege operations until August 24th, when the regiment marched to Kamara, in consequence of the Russians having again appeared in force on the flank of the allied armies. On September 8th, it marched to Sebastopol, took part in the assault and capture, returned to Kamara the following day, and remained there until the peace, 30th March 1856.

On June 15th, the regiment embarked at Kameish for England, landed at Portsmouth on the 24th of July, proceeded by rail to Aldershott, and was reviewed by Her Majesty Queen Victoria, after which it proceeded by rail to Dover, in garrison with the 41st, 44th, 79th, and 93d regiments.

The actual losses of the regiment in the Crimea from actual contact with the enemy, were nothing compared with the sad ravages made upon it, along with the rest of the army, by disease and privation, and want of the actual necessaries of life. During the campaign only 1 officer and 38 men were killed in action, while there died of wounds and disease, 1 officer and 226 men, 140 men having had to be sent to England on account of wounds and ill-health.

VII.

1856—1869.

The 42d proceeds to India—Cawnpore—Seria-Ghat—Marches and Skirmishes—Lucknow—42d Storms La Martiniere—The Begum Kootee—Fort Ruhya—Bareilly—Rohilkund—Maylah Ghaut—Khyrugher Jungles—Presentation of Colours—Title of "Black Watch" restored—Cholera—Embarks for England—Reception at Edinburgh—Leave Edinburgh for Aldershot.

On December 1856, the establishment was reduced to 12 companies. On July 31st 1857, the regiment proceeded to Portsmouth, and on the 4th of August following it was reviewed by Her Majesty the Queen, who expressed herself highly satisfied with the fine appearance of the regiment. Between this date and the 14th the corps embarked in six different ships for the east, to assist in putting down the Indian Mutiny, and arrived at Calcutta in the October and November following.

The headquarters, with five companies of the 42d Royal Highlanders, had orders to march for Cawnpore on the night of the 28th November; but the news of the state of affairs at Cawnpore having reached Allahabad, the column was recalled, and ordered to form an intrenched camp at Cheemea. Next morning the work was begun, and progressed favourably until the 1st of December. Meanwhile the party was reinforced by a wing of Her Majesty's 38th Regiment, a wing of the 3d battalion Rifle Brigade, a party of Sappers and Artillery,

making in all a force of 1050 men, with two 8-inch howitzers and four field-pieces.

At 5 A.M. on the 2d December, a messenger arrived in camp with a despatch from the Commander-in-chief, ordering the column to make forced marches to Cawnpore. It marched accordingly at 8 P.M. on the same day, and reached Cawnpore about noon on the 5th, having marched a distance of 78 miles in three days, though the men were fairly exhausted through fatigue and want of sleep.

The position which the rebels held at Cawnpore was one of great strength. Their left was posted amongst the wooded high grounds, intersected with nullahs, and thickly sprinkled with ruined bungalows and public buildings, which lie between the town and the Ganges. Their centre occupied the town itself, which was of great extent, and traversed only by narrow winding streets, singularly susceptible of defence. The position facing the intrenchment was uncovered; but from the British camp it was separated by the Ganges canal, which, descending through the centre of the Doab, falls into that river below Cawnpore. Their right stretched out behind this canal into the plain, and they held a bridge over it, and some lime-kilns and mounds of brick in front of it.

The camp of the Gwalior contingent of 10,000 was situated in this plain, about two miles in rear of the right, at the point where the Calpee road comes in. The united force, amounting now, with reinforcements which had arrived, to about 25,000 men, with 40 guns, consisted of two distinct bodies, having two distinct lines of operation and retreat;—that of the Nana Sahib (and under the command of his brothers), whose line of retreat was in rear of the left on Bithoor; and that of the Gwalior contingent, whose retreat lay from the right upon Calpee.

General Windham, commanding in the fort, opened a heavy fire from every available gun and mortar from the intrenchment upon the hostile left and their centre in the town, so as to draw their attention entirely to that side and lead them to accumulate their troops there. Brigadier Greathed, with his brigade of 8th, 64th, and 2d Punjaub infantry, held the line of intrenchment, and engaged the enemy by a brisk attack. To the left, Brigadier Walpole, with the 2d and 3d battalion Rifle brigade and a wing of 38th foot, crossed the canal just above the town, and advancing, skirted its walls, marking as he reached them every gate leading into the country, and throwing back the head of every column which tried to debouch thence to the aid of the right; whilst to the left, Brigadier Hope, with his Sikhs, and Highlanders, the 42d and 93d, and the 53d foot, and Brigadier Inglis, with the 23d, 32d, and 82d, moved into the plain, in front of the brickmound, covering the enemy's bridge on the road to Calpee. Meanwhile the whole cavalry and horse artillery made a wide sweep to the left, and crossed the canal by a bridge two miles farther up, in order to turn the flank of the rebels.

The battle commenced on the morning of the 6th with the roar of Windham's guns from the intrenchment. After a few hours this tremendous cannonade slackened, and the rattle of Greathed's musketry was heard closing rapidly on the side of the canal. Walpole's riflemen pushed on in haste; and Hope and Inglis's brigades, in parallel lines, advanced directly against the high brick mound, behind which the enemy were formed in great masses, and their guns, worked with great precision, sent a shower of shot and shell upon the plain. The field batteries on the British side opened briskly, whilst the cavalry were seen moving on the left. The 42d skirmishers now rushed on and closed upon the mound, from which the enemy fell back to the bridge. Lieutenant-Colonel Thorold, commanding, riding in front of the centre of the regiment, here had his horse shot under him by a round shot, which swept through the line and killed private Mark Grant. The gallant old Colonel sprung to his feet, and with his drawn sword in hand, marched in front of the regiment during the remainder of the action, and the pursuit of the flying enemy.

After a moment's pause, the infantry again pushed on, and rushed upon the bridge. The fire was heavy in the extreme, when the sound of heavy guns was heard, and Peel's noble sailors, dragging with them their heavy 24-pounders, came up to the bridge, and brought them into action. The enthusiasm of the men was now indescribable; they rushed on, either

crossing the bridge or fording the canal, came upon the enemy's camp, and took some guns at the point of the bayonet. A Bengal field-battery galloped up and opened fire at easy range, sending volleys of grape through the tents. The enemy, completely surprised at the onslaught, fled in great haste, leaving everything in their camp as it stood;—the rout was complete. The cavalry and horse artillery coming down on the flank of the flying enemy, cut up great numbers of them, and pursued along the Calpee road, followed by the 42d, 53d, and Sikhs, for 14 miles. The slaughter was great, till at last, the rebels despairing of effecting their retreat by the road, threw away their arms and accoutrements, dispersed over the country into the jungle, and hid themselves from the sabres and lances of the horsemen. Night coming on, the wearied forces returned to Cawnpore, carrying with them 17 captured guns. The strength and courage of the young men of the Royal Highlanders was remarkable. Many of them were mere lads, and had never seen a shot fired before, yet during the whole of this day's action and long march, not a single man fell out, or complained of his hardships.

As soon as the Gwalior contingent was routed on the right, a severe contest took place with the Nana Sahib's men in the town, at a place called the Sonbadar's Tank, but before nightfall all Cawnpore was in our possession.

The Nana's men fled in great confusion along the road to Bithoor, whither they were pursued on the 8th by Brigadier-General Hope Grant, at the head of the cavalry, light artillery, and Hope's brigade of infantry (42d and 93d Highlanders, 53d, and 4th Punjaub rifles). Bithoor was evacuated, but the force pushed on, marching all night, and came upon the enemy at the ferry of Seria-Ghat on the Ganges, 25 miles from Cawnpore, at daylight on the 9th. The rebels had reached the ferry, but had not time to cross. They received the British force with a heavy cannonade, and tried to capture the guns with a charge of cavalry, but the horsemen of the British drove them away. Their infantry got amongst the enclosures and trees; but the whole of the guns, amounting to 15 pieces, were captured, together with a large quantity of provisions, camp equipage, and ammunition. Lieutenant-Colonel Thorold, commanding the regiment, and Captain J. C. M'Leod, commanding the rear guard, are honourably mentioned by Brigadier-General Hope Grant, in his despatch dated 11th December 1857.

The grenadier company, when destroying some baggage-carts, &c., found a very large gong, which was kept as a trophy by the regiment. The troops encamped near the Ghat on the 9th and 10th, and on the 11th marched back to Bithoor, where they were employed till the 28th December, destroying the palace of the Nana Sahib, and searching for treasure,—a great quantity of which was found in a tank,—with a considerable amount of labour, the flow of water being so great that 200 men were employed night and day baling it out, so as to keep it sufficiently low to enable the sappers to work.

The remainder of the regiment—Nos. 2, 4, 5, 6, and 7 companies—under the command of Major Wilkinson, joined at Bithoor on the 22d December 1857. Lieutenant-Colonel Cameron and Major Priestley, who had been left at Calcutta, joined head-quarters on the 12th December.

The Commander-in-chief with the forces at Cawnpore, marched towards Futteghur on the 25th December, and the column at Bithoor followed on the 28th, overtaking the head-quarter's column on the 29th at Merukie Serai. The regiment marched from the latter place, and at 1 o'clock, P.M. joined the head-quarters camp at Jooshia-Gunge—the whole force a few days after proceeding to Futteghur. After various skirmishes with the enemy during January 1858, about Futteghur, the force on the 1st February commenced a retrograde march on Cawnpore, which it reached on the 7th. On the 10th the 42d and 93d Highlanders crossed the Ganges into Oudh, as a guard on the immense siege-train which had been collected in Cawnpore for service at Lucknow. On the 11th they marched to Onao, where, with other troops the regiment remained, acting as convoy escort to the immense train of provisions and military materials being sent forward towards Lucknow.

On the 21st the regiment moved forward, and on the morning of the 26th, met their old companions in arms, the 79th Highlanders, at Camp Purneah. A cordial greeting took place between old comrades, after which the regiments proceeded together to Bunteerah the same morning. Here the whole of the Commander-in-chief's force assembled. The siege train, &c., was gradually brought forward, and all necessary preparations made for the attack on Lucknow.

The force marched from Bunteerah on the 1st March, and passing through Alum Bagh (the post held by Major-General Sir George Outram) and by the old fort of Jellalahabad on the left, soon met the enemy's outposts, which, after a few rounds from their field-guns, retired to the city. The palace of Dalkoosha was seized without opposition, and being close to the river Goomptee, formed the right of the British position. The intervening space between this and the Alum Bagh on the left was held by strong bodies of troops posted under cover, for the hour of action had not yet arrived.

Lucknow had been fortified by every means that native art could devise to make a strong defence. The canal was scarped, and an immense parapet of earth raised on the inner side, which was loop-holed in all directions. Every street was barricaded, and every house loop-holed. The Kazerbagh was so strengthened as to form a kind of citadel, and the place was alive with its 50,000 mutinous sepoys, besides a population in arms of one kind or other of double that number.

Brigadier Franks, who had marched from Benares with a column, by way of Sultanpore, having been joined by the Nepaulese contingent under General Jung Bahadoor, reached Lucknow on the 5th March; and on the 6th a division, under command of Sir James Outram, crossed the Goomptee, opposite the Dalkoosha park, and moved round towards the old Presidency, driving in the enemy's posts. Sir James Outram, from his position on the opposite bank of the river, was enabled to enfilade, and take in reverse a great portion of the great canal embankment, and effectually to shell the enemy within his works.

The enemy's most advanced position was La Martiniere, a large public building surrounded on three sides by high walls and ruined houses, and its front covered by the river.

The plan of attack having been arranged,

the 42d Highlanders were ordered to storm the Martiniere, which they did in gallant style on the 9th Four companies, under Major E R Priestley, advanced in extended order, the remaining five advanced in line under Lieutenant-Colonel Cameron The Highlanders went steadily on until within two hundred yards of the place, when, giving three cheers, they rushed on in double time, the pipers playing "The Campbells are coming" The enemy became so alarmed, that they bolted from their trenches without waiting to fire more than their first round Thus, the first position in Lucknow was gained without the loss of a single man

Till the flying enemy, having been joined by reinforcements at their second line of intrenchment, summoned fresh courage, and showed battle to the four skirmishing companies who had followed up, a very smart affair ensued, in which the regiment suffered several calamities The enemy from behind their works were enabled to do this without themselves being seen

The five companies under Lieutenant-Colonel Cameron were ordered to take position in an old village to the right of La Martiniere about 300 yards, in passing to which they were exposed to a heavy fire upon the great parapet of the canal, but on reaching the village it was observed that the parapet near the river was undefended, having at that end been enfiladed by General Outram's guns The 42d, with the 4th Punjaub rifles, under Major Wyld, making steps in the face of the parapet with bayonets, &c, scrambled up, and taking ground to the left, cleared the line of work as far nearly as Bank's bungalow Reinforcements were brought up, and the position was held for the night Early next morning, the several companies of the regiment were collected together, and the order was given to occupy Bank's bungalow and the houses and gardens adjacent These points were also carried with little opposition, the enemy nowhere attempting to stand, but keeping up a constant fire of all kind of missiles from the tops of houses, loop holes, and other points

The regiment was now close under the Begum Kootee, an extensive mass of solid buildings, comprising several courts a mosque, bazar,

&c This place was strongly fortified, and became an important post Two 68-pound naval guns were at once brought up and commenced breaching, within Bank's bungalow were placed 16 mortars and cohorns, from which shells were pitched at the Kootee that day, and all night, until the following day about 2 o'clock (March 11th), when the 93d Highlanders stormed the breach, and carried the place in gallant style Upwards of 500 corpses told the slaughter which took place within those princely courts During the attack, the 42d grenadier and light companies were ordered to protect the left flank of the 93d, in doing which several casualties took place, caused by the fire of the enemy from a loop holed gateway near which the light company had to pass After occupying Bank's bungalow, two companies of the 42d were sent under Major Priestley to clear and occupy some ruined houses on the left front This party, having advanced rather farther than this point, got hotly engaged with the enemy, but held their original ground

A large section of the city being now in possession of the British, operations were commenced against the Kaizer Bagh, from the direction of the Begum Kootee, as well as from Sir James Outram's side. He took the Messhouse by storm, and other outworks in that direction, and on the morning of the 14th got into this great palace The place was now almost wholly in possession of the British forces, at no one point did the enemy attempt to make a stand, but fled in every direction

By the 20th the rebels had been everywhere put down, and peace partially restored On the 22d the 42d Royal Highlanders were moved to the Observatory Mess-house and old Presidency, where they remained doing duty until the 2d April. During this time the men suffered greatly from fever, brought on by hardship and exposure to the sun They had now been a whole month constantly on duty, their uniform and accoutrements never off their backs, and the effluvium arising from the many putrid half-buried carcases in the city, especially about the Presidency, rendered the air very impure Notwithstanding the hard work performed by the regiment at Lucknow, only 5 rank and file were killed, and Lieutenant F. E. H. Farquharson and 41 non-commissioned officers and privates wounded. Lieutenant Farquharson was awarded the Victoria Cross "for a distinguished act of bravery at Lucknow, 9th March 1858."

On the evening of the 2d April, the regiment marched to camp at the Dalkoosha, having been ordered to form part of the Rohilcund field force under Brigadier Walpole. On the morning of the 8th the regiment marched from camp, accompanied by the 79th and 93d Highlanders, to the Moosha Bagh, a short distance beyond which the brigade encamped; and having been joined by the remainder of the force and the new Brigadier, commenced a march through Oudh, keeping the line of the Ganges. Nothing of note occurred until the 15th. On reaching Rhoadamow, Nurpert Sing, a celebrated rebel chief, shut up in Fort Ruhya, refused to give his submission. The fort was situated in a dense jungle, which almost completely hid it from view. Four companies of the 42d, with the 4th Punjaub rifles, were sent forward in extended order, to cover the guns and reconnoitre, and were brought so much under the enemy's fire from the parapet and the tops of trees, that a great many casualties occurred in a very short time. Brigadier Adrian Hope and Lieutenants Douglas and Bramley here received their death wounds. After remaining in this exposed condition for six hours, and after losing so many men, the Brigadier withdrew his force about sunset, and encamped about two miles off. During the night, the rebel chief retired quietly with all his men and material. Besides the two officers above mentioned, 1 sergeant and 6 privates were killed, and 3 sergeants and 34 privates wounded. Quarter-Master Sergeant John Simpson, Lance-Corporal Alexander Thompson, and Private James Davis were awarded the Victoria Cross.

Nothing of importance occurred till the force reached Bareilly, when they came up with the enemy's outposts at daybreak on the 5th May. After a short cannonade for about half-an-hour, the enemy fell back from the bridge and nullah, and occupied the topes (clumps of trees) and ruined houses in the cantonments. In this position it was necessary to shell every tope and house before advancing, which caused considerable delay: all the time the sun was shining on the troops with full force. About 10 A.M. the enemy made a bold attempt to turn the British left flank, and the 42d were ordered forward in support of the 4th Punjaub rifles, who had been sent to occupy the old cavalry lines, but were there surprised by the enemy in great numbers. Just as the 42d reached the old lines, they were met by the Punjabees in full flight, followed by a lot of Gazees carrying tulwars and shields. These rushed furiously on, and the men for a moment were undecided whether they should fire on them or not, their friends the Punjabees being mixed up with them when, as if by magic, the Commander-in-chief appeared behind the line, and his familiar voice, loud and clear, was heard calling out, "Fire away, men; shoot them down, every man jack of them!" Then the line opened fire upon them; but in the meantime, some of these Gazees had even reached the line, and cut at the men, wounding several. Four of them seized Colonel Cameron in rear of the line, and would have dragged him off his horse, when Colour-Sergeant Gardner stepped from the ranks and bayoneted them, the Colonel escaping with only a slight wound on his wrist. For this act of bravery Gardner was awarded the Victoria Cross. In this affair 1 private was killed, and 2 officers, 1 sergeant, and 12 privates wounded. No. 5 company 42d took possession of the fort which was abandoned, and a line of piquets of the 42d and 79th Highlanders was posted from the fort to the extreme right of the Commander-in-chief's camp. Next day the place was cleared of rebels.

The regiment was told off as a part of the Bareilly brigade, and on the 5th June detached a wing to Mooradabad under command of Lieutenant Colonel Wilkinson. This wing marched to Bedaon with a squadron of carbineers, and joined Brigadier Coke's force, but received orders to leave the carbineers with Brigadier Coke, and proceed to Mooradabad. On this march the men suffered from exhaustion and the heat. Indeed, the men who were still under canvas now began to suffer very much from sun-stroke, fevers, diarrhœa, &c. Every exertion was made to get them into temporary barracks, but this was not effected until the middle of July, just in time to escape the rains.

Lieutenant Colonel Alexander Cameron died of fever on the 9th August, and Lieutenant Colonel F. G. Wilkinson succeeded to the command of the regiment.

The headquarters and left wing were ordered to Peeleebheet on the 14th October, where it remained encamped till the 24th November, when, in order the better to guard against the rebels crossing from Oudh into Rohilkund, Colonel Smyth, Bengal Artillery, in command of a small column, was ordered to take up a position on the banks of the Sarda, to watch the Ghauts. No 6, Captain Lawson's company, joined Colonel Smyth's column. At the same time, Major M'Leod was ordered, with the troops under his command, viz., 4 companies 42d Royal Highlanders, 2 squadrons Punjaub cavalry, 1 company Kumaon levies, and 2 guns, to proceed to Madho-Tanda, being a central position whence support might be sent in any direction required. This force subsequently moved close to the Sarda, in consequence of the numerous reports of the approach of the enemy, but all remained quiet until the morning of the 15th January 1859. The enemy having been pursued in the Khyrugher district by a force under command of Colonel Dennis, attempted to force his way into Rohilkund, with the view, as was supposed, of getting into Rampore. Early on the morning of the 15th the enemy, about 2000 strong, effected the passage of the Sarda, at Maylah Ghaut, about three miles above Colonel Smyth's camp, at daylight. The alarm having been given, the whole of the troops in camp moved out with all speed, and attacked the rebels in the dense jungle, close to the river. Ensign Coleridge, 42d, was detached in command of a piquet of 40 men of Captain Lawson's company, and 40 men Kumaon levies, and was so placed as to be cut off from the remainder of the force. The jungle was so dense, that the cavalry could not act; the Kumaon levies were all raw recruits, who were with difficulty kept to their posts, so the fighting fell almost wholly to the lot of the 37 men under command of Captain Lawson. The enemy, desperate, and emboldened by the appearance of so small a force before them, made repeated attempts to break through the thin line of skirmishers, but the latter nobly held their ground. Captain Lawson received

a gun-shot wound in his left knee, early in the day; Colour Sergeant Landles was shot and cut to pieces, two corporals—Ritchie and Thompson—were also killed, and several other casualties had greatly weakened them. The company now without either officers or non-commissioned officers, yet bravely held on their ground, and, cheered on by the old soldiers, kept the enemy at bay from sunrise to sunset. Privates Walter Cook and Duncan Miller, for their conspicuous bravery during this affair were awarded the Victoria Cross.

Major M'Leod's force was then at a place called Sunguree on the Sarda, 22 miles from Colonel Smyth's force. About 8 A.M. when the numbers and nature of the enemy's attack were discovered, a Sowar was despatched to Major M'Leod (in temporary command) for a reinforcement of two companies, and ordering the remainder of the force to proceed with all speed to Madho-Tanda to await the result of the battle. No. 7 and 8 companies were dispatched from Sunguree about noon, but did not reach the scene of action till after 5 P.M. Their arrival turned the tide of battle altogether. Such of the enemy as could recrossed the river in the dark, and next morning nothing remained on the field, but the dead and dying, 2 small guns, and some cattle belonging to the rebels. Lord Clyde complimented the regiment very highly on this occasion, and in particular, spoke of Captain Lawson's company as a pattern of valour and discipline.

General Walpole having received intelligence about the 22d that a body of rebels were hovering about, under Goolah Sing, in the Khyrugher jungles, two companies of the 42d Royal Highlanders at Colonel Smyth's camp, a squadron of the Punjaub cavalry, a squadron of Crossman's Horse, and three companies of Ghoorkhas, under command of Colonel Wilkinson, were ordered to cross the river at the spot where the rebels came over, and march to Gulori, 40 miles in the interior, under the Nepaul hills. Gulori was reached in 4 days, but Goolah Sing had secured himself in a fort under Nepauleese protection. Colonel Dennis, with a force from Sultanpore had orders to march on a village 20 miles from Gulori, and also sweep the jungles and communicate with Colonel Wilkinson. As he never arrived, and the jungles being free from rebels, the force recrossed the river and returned to camp.

The left wing of the 42d remained on the Sarda until the 14th of March, when it returned to Bareilly, and joined the right wing, which had returned from Mooradabad on the 18th February, having been relieved by a wing of the 82d regiment; but information having been received that the rebels were again appearing in force in the Khyrugher districts, the right wing, under command of Lieutenant-Colonel Priestley, was sent to the Sarda to join Colonel Smyth on the 13th March, where it remained until the 15th May 1859, when it returned to Bareilly, the weather being by this time very hot and the district perfectly quiet. About this time, Lieutenant-Colonel Wilkinson went on leave to England, and was appointed to a depot battalion, and on the 27th September Lieutenant-Colonel Priestley succeeded to the command of the regiment.

The regiment occupied the temporary barracks at the old Kutchery, Berkley's House, and the Jail, during the hot and rainy seasons. The men were remarkably healthy, and very few casualties occurred.

His Excellency, Sir Hugh Rose, Commander-in-chief in India having been invited on the 18th September, by Lieutenant-Colonel Priestley in the name of the officers and soldiers of the 42d Royal Highlanders, to present new colours to the regiment, arrived in Bareilly for that purpose on the 1st of January 1861. After the old colours had been lodged, and the new been presented by His Excellency, and trooped with the usual ceremonies, Sir Hugh Rose addressed the regiment in the following speech :—

"42d *Royal Highlanders*,

"I do not ask you to defend the colours I have presented to you this day. It would be superfluous: you have defended them for nearly 150 years with the best blood of Scotland.

"I do not ask you to carry these colours to the front should you again be called into the field; you have borne them round the world with success. But I do ask the officers and soldiers of this gallant and devoted regiment not to forget, because they are of ancient date, but to treasure in their memories the recol-

lection of the brilliant deeds of arms of their forefathers and kinsmen, the scenes of which are inscribed on these colours. There is not a name on them which is not a study; there is not a name on them which is not connected with the most important events of the world's history, or with the pages of the military annals of England.

"The soldiers of the 42d cannot have a better or more instructive history than their regimental records. They tell how, 100 years ago, the 42d won the honoured name of 'Royal' at Ticonderoga in America, losing, although one battalion, 647 killed and wounded. How the 42d gained the 'Red Heckle' in Flanders. How Abercromby and Moore in Egypt and in Spain, dying in the arms of victory, thanked, with parting breath, the 42d. Well might the heroes do so! The fields of honour on which they were expiring were strewed with the dead and wounded soldiers of the 42d.

"The 42d enjoy the greatest distinction to which British regiments can aspire. They have been led and commanded by the great Master in War, the Duke of Wellington. Look at your colours: their badges will tell you how often—and this distinction is the more to be valued, because his Grace, so soldierlike and just was he, never would sanction a regiment's wearing a badge, if the battle in which they had been engaged, no matter how bravely they may have fought in it, was not only an important one, but a victory.

"In the Crimea, in the late campaign in this country, the 42d again did excellent service under my very gallant and distinguished predecessor, Lord Clyde. The last entry in the regimental records shews that the spirit of the 'Black Watch' of 1729 was the same in 1859, when No. 6 company of the 42d, aided only by a company of the Kumaon levy, four guns, and a squadron of irregular cavalry, under Sir Robert Walpole, beat back, after several hours obstinate fighting, and with severe loss, 2000 rebels of all arms, and gained the day. Lord Clyde bestowed the highest praise on the company that a general can do,—His Lordship thanked them for their valour and their discipline.

"I am sincerely obliged to Lieutenant-Colonel Priestley for having, on the part of the

42d Royal Highlanders, requested me to present them with their new colours. It is an honour and a favour which I highly prize, the more so, because I am of Highland origin, and have worn for many years the tartan of another regiment which does undying honour to Scotland— the 92d Highlanders.

" I have chosen this day—New Year's day— for the presentation of colours, because on New Year's day in 1785 the colours were given to the 42d under which they won their red plume. Besides, New Year's day, all over the world, particularly in Scotland, is a happy day. Heaven grant that it may be a fortunate one for this regiment !"

On the 3d, after inspecting the regiment, His Excellency desired Lieutenant-Colonel Priestley to thank them for the admirable condition in which he found them, and for their regularity and good conduct. His Excellency further called several officers and soldiers to the front of the battalion and thanked them for their gallant conduct on various occasions, and No. 6 company for the valour and discipline evinced by them on the occasion alluded to in His Excellency's speech.

On the 8th of March three companies were detached to Futteghur. On 23d March headquarters moved from Bareilly to Agra, where they arrived on the 8th of April, and were garrisoned along with the 107th regiment. On 27th July the regiment moved into camp, on account of cholera having broken out, and returned to barracks on 12th August, having lost from cholera 1 officer and 40 non-commissioned officers and men. After returning to barracks, the regiment was prostrated by fever and ague, so many as 450 men having been at one time unfit for duty out of seven companies.

On 12th September the regiment was delighted by having its old name reconferred upon it, as a distinguished mark of honour. A notification was received that on 8th July 1861 Her Majesty had been pleased graciously to authorise The Royal Highland Regiment to be distinguished, in addition to that title, by the name by which it was first known— "The Black Watch."

In March 1862, Lieutenant-General, the Marquis of Tweeddale, was appointed Colonel

in place of the deceased Sir James Douglas. The Marquis, however, in September of the following year, removed to the 2d Lifeguards, and was succeeded by the regiment's former commander, who led them up the slopes of Alma—Major-General Sir Duncan Cameron.

On 6th December 1863, the Black Watch marched by forced marches from Lahore to Rawal Pundee, on account of active operations having been commenced against some of the hill tribes. It arrived at the latter place on December 19. Affairs on the frontier having, however, assumed a favourable aspect, the regiment returned to Dugshai, which it reached on the 13th February 1864, but returned to Rawal Pundee, where on 14th December it was put into garrison with the 79th. It left the latter place in October 1865, and proceeded to Peshawur, where it was in garrison with the first battalion of the 19th regiment, and subsequently with the 77th. In 1867, while at Peshawur, cholera broke out in the cantonments, and on the 21st of May five companies, under Major Macpherson, were removed to camp ; these were followed on the 25th by headquarters and the other five companies. From the 20th to the 31st May, 66 men, 1 woman, and 4 children died of cholera. On the 1st of June the regiment commenced its march to Cheroat, a mountain of the Kultoch range, where headquarters was established on the 15th. The health of the regiment was not, however, immediately restored, and the number of deaths at Cheroat were 1 officer, 15 non-commissioned officers and men, 2 women, and 1 child. The total deaths in the regiment, from 20th May to 17th October, including casualties at depot, were 2 officers, 86 non-commissioned officers and men, 5 women, and 9 children ;— altogether 102, or nearly one-sixth of the whole regiment.

On 17th October was commenced the march towards Kurrachee, preparatory to embarkation for England. On January 17, 1868, the regiment embarked at Kurrachee for Bombay, and on the 21st was trans-shipped to the Indian troopship "Euphrates," which landed it at Suez on 15th February. On the 18th it embarked at Alexandria on board the "Serapis," which reached Portsmouth on the 4th of March, when the regiment immediately left by sea for Scotland and landed at Burntisland on the 7th, headquarters and 1 company proceeding to Stirling Castle, 5 companies to Perth, and 4 to Dundee. Colonel Priestley came home with the regiment from India, and carried on his duties till the 24th of March, the day before his death. He was succeeded by Brevet Lieutenant-Colonel M'Leod, who joined the regiment in 1846. On 12th October headquarters moved by rail from Stirling to Edinburgh Castle, and the detachments from Perth and Dundee followed soon after. The reception accorded to Scotland's favourite and oldest regiment, on its arrival in Edinburgh, was as overwhelmingly enthusiastic as in the days of old, when the military spirit was in its glory. The reader will have an idea of the enthusiasm with which this regiment is still regarded, and will be so so long as its ranks are mainly recruited from Scotland, by the following account of its reception, for which we are indebted to the *Scotsman* newspaper of the day following the regiment's arrival :—" The train arrived at the station about 10 minutes past 1 P.M., but long before that hour large and anxious crowds had collected on the Waverley Bridge, in Princes Street Garden, on the Mound, the Calton Hill, the Castle, and every other point from which a view of the passing regiment could be obtained. The crowd collected on the Waverley Bridge above must have numbered several thousands. The scene altogether was very imposing and animated. Such a turn-out of spectators has not been witnessed on the occasion of the arrival of any regiment here since the 78th Highlanders came from India, nearly ten years ago. Immediately after the train entered the station, the bugle sounded, and the men were arranged in companies, under the command of their respective captains. The regiment was under the command of Lieutenant-Colonel J. C. M'Leod, assisted by Major Cluny M'Pherson, Major F. C. Scott, and Adjutant J. E. Christie, and was drawn up in 8 companies. On emerging from the station the band struck up 'Scotland yet,' and the appearance of the regiment was hailed with hearty cheers from the spectators. The crowd in Canal Street was so great that it was with some difficulty the soldiers managed to keep their ranks. Their line of march lay along Princes Street, and every window and housetop from which a view of the gallant 42d could be obtained was crowded with spectators. The regiment proceeded by the Mound, Bank Street, and Lawnmarket, and was loudly cheered at every turn. On the Castle esplanade the crowd was, if possible, more dense than anywhere else. A large number of people had taken up their position on the top of the Reservoir, while every staircase from which a view could be obtained was thronged with anxious spectators. Large numbers had also gained admission to the Castle, and all the parapets and embrasures commanding a view of the route were crowded with people.

" On the regiment arriving at this point, loud cheers were raised by the immense crowd assembled on the esplanade, which were immediately taken up by those in the Castle, and enthusiastically continued. On arriving at the Castle gate, the band ceased playing, and the pipes struck up a merry tune. Even after the regiment had passed into the Castle, large numbers of people, including many relatives of the soldiers, continued to linger about the esplanade. It is now thirty-two years since the regiment was in Edinburgh, and certainly the reception which they received yesterday was a very enthusiastic one. Four companies came from Perth, and joined the headquarters at Stirling, and the whole regiment proceeded from thence to Edinburgh."

We cannot refrain here from quoting some verses of a short poem on the Black Watch, which appeared about this time, so happy and spirited that it deserves a more permanent resting-place than a newspaper.

THE BLACK WATCH.

A HISTORIC ODE, BY DUGALD DHU.

Written for Waterloo Day, 1868.

Hail, gallant regiment ! Freiceadan Dubh !
  Whenever Albion needs thine aid,
" Aye ready" for whatever foe,
  Shall dare to meet "the black brigade !"
Witness disastrous Fontenoy,
  When all seemed lost, who brought us through ?
Who saved defeat ? secured retreat ?
  And bore the brunt ?—the " Forty-Two !"

So, at Corunna's grand retreat,
  When, far outnumbered by the foe,
The patriot Moore made glorious halt,
  Like setting sun in fiery glow.

Before us foam'd the rolling sea,
Behind, the carrion eagles flew ;
But Scotland's "Watch" proved Gallia's match,
And won the game by "Forty-Two !"

The last time France stood British fire
"The Watch" gained glory at its cost ;
At Quatre Bras and Hugomont,
Three dreadful days they kept their post.
Ten hundred there, who form'd in square,
Before the close a handful grew ;
The little phalanx never flinched,
Till "Boney" ran from Waterloo !

The "Forty-Second" never dies—
It hath a regimental soul ;
Fond Scotia, weeping, fill'd the blanks
Which Quatre Bras left in its roll.
At Alma, at Sevastopol,
At Lucknow, waved its bonnets blue !
Its dark green tartan, who but knows!
What heart but warms to "Forty-Two !"

But while we glory in the corps,
We'll mind their martial brethren too ;
The Ninety-Second, Seventy-Ninth,
And Seventy-First—all Waterloo !
The Seventy-Second, Seventy-Fourth—
The Ninety-Third—all tried and true !
The Seventy-Eighth, real, "men of Ross ;"
Come, count their honours, "Forty-Two!"

Eight noble regiments of the Queen,
God grant they long support her crown !
"Shoulder to shoulder," Hielandmen !
United rivals in renown!
We'll wreath the rose with heath that blows
Where barley-rigs yield mountain dew ;
And pledge the Celt, in trews or kilt,
Whence Scotland drafts her "Forty-Two !"

It is worthy of remark, that from the time that the regiment embarked at Leith for England in May 1803, until October 1868, a period of upwards of 65 years, it was quartered in Edinburgh only 15 months—6 months in 1816, and 9 months in 1836-7. At its last visit it remained only about a year, taking its departure on November 9, 1869, when it embarked at Granton in the troop-ship "Orontes," for Portsmouth, en route for the camp at Aldershot, where it arrived on the 12th. The enthusiasm of the inhabitants of Edinburgh appears to have been even far greater to the Black Watch on its departure than on its entry into the northern metropolis. During their residence in Edinburgh the Highlanders conducted themselves in such a manner as to win the favourable opinions of all classes of the community, and to keep up the ancient prestige and unbroken good name of the regiment. The following is the *Scotsman's* account of its departure :

"After a sojourn in Scotland of eighteen months, twelve of which have been passed in Edinburgh, the 42d Royal Highlanders departed yesterday from the city, taking with them the best wishes of the inhabitants. Since the arrival of the 78th Highlanders, immediately after the close of the Indian mutiny, such a degree of excitement as was displayed yesterday has not been witnessed in connection with any military event in the metropolis. It was generally known that 9 A.M. had been fixed for the evacuation of the Castle by the Highlanders, and long before that hour the Lawnmarket and the esplanade were crowded with an eager and excited multitude. At 9 o'clock the crowd increased fourfold, by the thousands of workpeople, who, set free at that time, determined to spend their breakfast-hour in witnessing the departure of the gallant 'Black Watch.' At half-past nine, the regiment, which had assembled in heavy marching order in the Castle Square, began to move off under the command of Colonel M'Leod, the band playing 'Scotland Yet,' and afterwards 'Bonnets o' Blue.' As the waving plumes were seen slowly wending down the serpentine path which leads to the esplanade, an enthusiastic and prolonged cheer burst from the spectators. As soon as the regiment had passed the drawbridge, a rush was made by the onlookers to get clear of the Esplanade. The narrow opening leading to the Lawnmarket was speedily blocked, and the manner in which the living mass swayed to and fro was most alarming—the din created by the crowd completely drowning the music of the band. The pressure of the crowd was so great that for a time the ranks of the regiment were broken, and a word of praise is due to the Highlanders for their forbearance under the jostling which they received from their perhaps too demonstratively affectionate friends. The line of route taken was Lawnmarket, Bank Street, the Mound, Hanover Street, Pitt Street, Brandon Street, to Inverleith Row, and thence by the highway to Granton. The whole way to the port of embarkation the regiment had literally to force its passage through the dense masses which blocked the streets, and every now and again a parting cheer was raised by the spectators. The crowd, as has already been mentioned, was the largest that has been seen in Edinburgh for many years, and has been roughly estimated as numbering from fifty to sixty thousand persons.

During the march to Inverleith toll, the band played 'Scotland for Ever,' the 'Red, White, and Blue,' 'Home, sweet Home,' and 'Loudon's bonnie Woods and Braes.' Shortly after passing through the toll, and when within a mile of Granton, the Highlanders were met by the 90th Regiment of Foot (Perthshire Volunteers), who were *en route* to Edinburgh to succeed the 'Black Watch' as the garrison of the Castle. According to military custom, the junior regiment drew up alongside the roadway, and presented arms to the Highlanders, who fixed bayonets and brought their rifles to the shoulder as they marched past. At this interesting ceremony the band of the Highlanders played 'Blue Bonnets over the Border,' while that of the 90th struck up the 'Gathering of the Grahams.' Granton was reached about 11 o'clock, and as the Highlanders marched along the pier, 'Auld Langsyne' was appropriately played by the band. The slopes leading down to the harbour and the wharfs were thickly covered with spectators, who lustily cheered the Highlanders, and who showed the liveliest interest in the process of embarkation."

VIII.

1817—1873.

Account of Variations in Dress of the Black Watch—Regimental Pets—"Pincher"—"Donald the Deer"—"The Grenadiers' Cat"—Monument to Black Watch in Dunkeld Cathedral—Conclusion.

BEFORE concluding our history of this, the oldest Highland regiment, we shall present a brief account of the variations which have from time to time taken place in the dress of the regiment, and wind up with short biographies of the regimental pets. For our information on both these matters, as well as for the greater part of the modern history of the regiment, we must again express our large indebtedness to the manuscript memorials of Lieutenant-Colonel Wheatley.

It is a curious study to note the many alterations that have taken place in the uniform of officers and men since 1817. In 1817 the officers had a short-skirted coatee, elaborately covered with rich gold lace, about nine bars

on the breast over blue lappels, hooked in the centre. It was also thickly covered with lace on the collar, cuffs, and skirts. All ranks wore two heavy epaulets of rich bullion. The field officers only wore scarves, which were their distinguishing mark of rank. All the officers wore richly braided scarlet waistcoats, and frills plaited very small, the shirt collar well exposed above the black silk stock. Sky-blue cloth trousers, with a broad stripe of gold lace edged with scarlet was the usual parade uniform; and parade invariably took place morning and afternoon, every officer present, and in the above-mentioned uniform, and with feathered bonnet. The gold-laced trousers were abolished in 1823, and blue-gray substituted without lace, which was continued until 1829, when Sir Charles Gordon introduced the trews of regimental tartan, which were fringed round the bottom, and up the outer seams. The fringe system was continued for some years, when it was also done away with.

The undress in barracks was in general a light gray long frock coat; but leaving the barracks, the officers invariably appeared in the coatee and a tartan bonnet without feathers, with a short red heckle in front, confined by a gold ring about one-third up. This handy bonnet was also worn on the line of march with the coatee. It was replaced in 1824 by a tartan shako, with black silk cord ornaments and a heavy red ostrich plume, which again gave way to the regular forage cap in 1826, first introduced with a broad top, and stiff in appearance, with a small gold embroidered thistle in front. Before 1830, when the single-breasted blue frock-coat, without any shoulder ornaments, was introduced into the army, a richly braided blue frock-coat was worn; but it was optional. White Cashmere trousers, narrow at the ankles with a gold stripe edged with scarlet, silk socks, and long quartered shoes with buckles, was also permitted for the evening (about 1819-20).

Before the adoption of the tartan trousers, the officers' dress was a strange mixture of Highland and line. For instance, at the guard mounting parade in Dublin in 1819-20, could anything, in the way of dress, be more absurd in a Highland regiment than to see the officers for the Castle guards in full Highland dress, and the five or six for other guards, the field officer, adjutant, quarter-master, and medical officer, in white Cashmere pantaloons, and short (under the knee) Hessian tasseled boots, and that with a feathered bonnet? All officers for guard ought to have been in the full dress of the regiment, but it was put on by them with the greatest reluctance, and so seldom, that the officers could not dress themselves, and their remarks reached the barrack rooms, through their servants, which caused the dislike to the dress to descend to the men, and for years had the direct effect of causing the men to rail much against it Since 1843, officers and men alike wear it on duty and on parade, which ought always to have been the case In 1823-24 the officers all wore wings, rich and heavy, which were discontinued in 1830, by order, and epaulets, with bullion according to rank (for the first time) substituted, and it is a singular fact that the men were authorised to wear wings, by regulation, the same year, and still more singular, until the epaulets were abolished 25 years afterwards, the non commissioned officers and men wore wings, and the officers epaulets The laced lappels and braided waistcoats disappeared in 1830, when lace was generally done away with on the breast of the coat in the army When the regiment returned from the Peninsula in 1814, from being so long in the field, the feathers had disappeared from the bonnet, and a little red feather on the front, the same as on a shako, had been adopted When the bonnets were renewed, the rank and file were not allowed to have foxtails, under the impression that it caused an unsteady appearance in the ranks Why not the officers and sergeants cause an unsteady appearance? Be that as it may, to the disgust of the men, and a source of amusement to all the other Highland regiments, was our "craw's wing," a wirework 8 inches above the cloth, covered with flats (almost free of anything like ostrich feathers) having a large unmeaning open gap at the right side, famous for catching the wind, which was ornamented with a large loose worsted tuft of white for the grenadiers, green for the light company and red for the others Yet this hideous thing was continued until the summer

of 1821, when most willingly the men paid about thirty shillings each to have the addition of "foxtails," yet these were a draw back, as the tails were not to hang lower than the top of the dice of the tartan The grand point was, however, gained in getting rid of the frightful "craw's wing," and by degrees the tails descended to a proper length At this time there were a variety of heckles worn in the bonnet, another piece of bad taste—white for the grenadiers, green for the light company, the band white, and the drummers yellow, with each of them two inches of red at the top, and the other eight companies (called battalion companies) red On going to Dublin in 1825, from Buttevant, the colonel of the regiment, Sir George Murray, was the commander of the forces, and at the first garrison parade, noticing the extraordinary variety of heckles, asked an explanation as to the reason of any heckle being worn in the regiment other than the red, it being "a special mark of distinction," and desired that all other colours should disappear The next day every officer and man was in possession of a red heckle

The white jacket was first worn with the kilt in 1821, which was considered at first to be very odd Up to 1819, it was sometimes served out without sleeves, and when sleeves became general, the soldiers were charged 1s 3d for them, "for the colonel's credit" Until 1821 it was used as a waistcoat, or for barrack-room wear. It is still in use in the Guards and Highland regiments, notwithstanding its being a most useless article to the soldier Instead of being used, it has to be carefully put up ready for the next parade Moreover, why were the Guards and Highlanders left to suffer under it, when the reason for doing away with it in 1830 was—"It having been represented to the general commanding-in-chief, that the frequent use of dry pipe-clay, in the cleaning of the white jacket, is prejudicial to the health of the soldiers?" Surely the lungs of the Guards and Highlanders were as vulnerable as those of the rest of the army, and their health and lives equally precious Many a time it was brought to notice, but "to be like the Guards" was sufficient to continue it Yet there is no doubt the hon ui would be willingly dispensed with, and the getting rid of it would be much to the men's comfort. Let us hope it will soon disappear, as well as the white coats of the band, still in use for all the army in 1873.

Until about 1840, never more than 4 yards of tartan were put into the kilt, and until lately, it never exceeded 4½ to 5. The plaid up to 1830 contained about 2½ yards, for no use or purpose but to be pushed up under the waist of the coat, taking from the figure of the man.

Until 1822, to have trousers was optional, even on guard at night. Many men were without them, and cloth of all colours, and fustian, was to be seen. From soon after the return of the regiment to Edinburgh after Waterloo, long-quartered shoes and buckles were worn on all occasions. The shoes were deserving of the name given to them —"toe cases." To such a ridiculous extent was the use of shoes and buckles carried, that after a marching order parade, the spats had to be taken off, and buckles put on before being permitted to leave the barracks. The red and white hose cloth up to 1819 was of a warm, woolly, genial stuff; but, for appearance, a hard cold thin article was encouraged, and soon became so general, that it was finally adopted, and the warm articles put out of use. At this time the regiment was in Richmond Barracks, Dublin (1819–20), and, consequently had to go to the Royal Barracks for guard mounting, and often from a mile or two farther to the guard, in the shoe already described. In rainy weather, it was quite a common occurrence to see men reach the guard almost shoeless, with the hose entirely spoiled, and no change for twenty-four hours; yet, bad as this was, it had its consolation, that "it was better than breeches and leggings," the guard and review dress for the infantry at this time. Had gaiters been taken into use, even in winter, and the strong shoe, it would have added much to the comfort of the men. The hose being made out of the piece, with coarse seams, were also badly adapted for the march, and not a man in twenty had half hose and socks. The soldier in general is thoughtless, and at this time no consideration for his comfort was taken by those whose duty it was do so, either in eating or clothing. As a proof of it, we have seen

that no breakfast mess was established until 1819.

It was at Gibraltar, in the beginning of 1826, that the gaiters were taken into daily wear and for guard; and the frill, the pest of the men (because of the care that had to be taken of it), and the soldiers' wives who did the washing. There were individuals who rejoiced in these frills, and to excel, paid from 2s. 6d. to 4s. for them. White leather pipeclayed gloves were also part of the soldier's dress at all parades, and "gloves off" became a regular word of command before "the manual and platoon." In short, what with shoes and buckles, frills, a stock up to the ears, about six yards of garters on each leg, muskets with clear locks (burnished in many cases), and well bees-waxed stocks and barrels, they were a most singularly equipped set of soldiers. Yet such was the force of habit, and what the eye had been accustomed to, when the frills and buckles disappeared, many (officers) considered it as an unwarrantable innovation; but not so the soldiers, who derived more comfort from the change than can well be imagined.

In 1820, shoulder tufts, about four inches, were substituted for the smaller ones hitherto worn by the battalion companies. The following year they became a little longer. In 1824, though still short of a regular wing, a shell was added, but without lace, stiffened with pasteboard. In 1827 a little lace was added, and in 1830 the ambition of having wings was consummated, as it became regulation for the non-commissioned officers and men of Highland regiments to wear wings, although, as already mentioned, the officers continued to wear epaulets.

Patent leather chin straps were first used in 1822. Before that a few only had narrow tape, which was not always approved of, it resting upon the whim of the officers or sergeant-major.

Until about 1840, the lace on the coats of both cavalry and infantry was of great variety, a few corps having it all white, but, in general with a "worm" of one or two colours of from one-fifth to one-third of the breadth of the lace. The 42d wore white lace, with a red "worm" three-fourths of the white on one side of the red, and one-fourth on the other. The 73d had the same lace, continued from the time it was the 2d battalion of the regiment.

The breast, cuffs, collars, and skirts were covered with lace, the cause of much dry pipe-claying. Some corps had it with square bars, others in "frogs." The 42d had the latter. Its abolition about 1830 was regretted by many, because it was an old-established custom, and also that it added much to the appearance of the sergeants' uniform; but when it came to be worn at a cost of from six to seven pounds for lace and fringe, it was, without doubt, a hardship, and Sir Charles Gordon did well in abolishing it.[1]

All the staff-sergeants wore the turned-back blue lappels, barred with square lace, and hooked in the middle, which was particularly handsome, and much admired. They ceased to wear the silver at the same time as the others, more to their regret, as a coat served many of them for years. The sergeant-major and quarter-sergeant only continued it, being furnished to them, with handsome bullion wings, along with their clothing.

The only changes of late years have been the Highland jacket and dark hose, both for the better, and the bonnet much reduced in size, also a decided improvement, all introduced after the Crimean war. The kilt is also more ample, and better made, adding to the better figure and appearance of the men, who are in all better dressed at present (1873) than at any previous period. May they always continue to be the pattern, as they ought to be, to all the Highland regiments, and that not only in dress, but also in all the qualities of good soldiers.

Out of the many pets of the regiment, we present our readers with the lives of these three, as being on the whole most worthy of

[1] We omitted to notice the death of this excellent officer in the proper place. It occurred while the regiment was at Vido in 1835. Sir Charles had gone on leave to Switzerland, with unaccountable reluctance it is said, though he was in apparently perfect health, and died at Geneva, after a short illness, on 30th September. His loss was deeply lamented by all ranks. The announcement of his unexpected death cast a gloom over the regiment, which was long felt. His gentlemanly bearing and kindly disposition made him universally loved and respected both by officers and men. The regiment was fortunate in his successor—Major William Middleton, who had served in the corps from 1803.

record,—the dog "Pincher," "Donald" the Deer, and the "Grenadiers' Cat."

"Pincher" was a small smooth-skinned terrier that attached himself to the regiment on the march in Ireland, at some stage near to Naas, its destination on coming home after the Peninsular war in 1814. Pincher was truly a regimental dog. If he had any partiality, it was slightly towards the light company. He marched to Kilkenny with the regiment, back from Naas, remained with it during the winter, and embarked for Flanders in the spring; went into action with it at Quatre Bras, and was wounded somewhat severely in the neck and shoulder, but, like a good soldier, would not quit the field. He was again in action at Waterloo, accompanied his regiment to Paris, and, amidst armies of all nations, Pincher never lost himself, came home, kept to his post, and went over to his native country in 1817. Late in that year, or early in 1818, he went with some men going on furlough to Scotland, who were landed at Irvine. Poor Pincher ran after some rabbits in an open warren, and was shot by a keeper, to the general grief of the regiment, when the intelligence reached it, which was not until one of the men returned from Scotland to join. In the meantime, Pincher had hardly been missed. There was some wonder at Armagh, and remarks made that Pincher was long on his rounds, but no anxiety regarding him, because it was well known, that from the time of his joining the regiment in 1814, it mattered not how many detachments were out from head-quarters, in turn he visited them all; and it was often a matter of wonder how he arrived, and by what instinct he found them out. Poor Pincher was a good and faithful soldier's dog, and, like many a good soldier, died an inglorious death. His memory was respected while his generation existed in the regiment.

"Donald" the Deer was with the depot which awaited the regiment when it went into Edinburgh Castle in September 1836 after landing at Granton from Corfu. He was a youth at the time, and not so formidable as to cause his antlers to be cut, which had to be done afterwards. He marched the three days to Glasgow in June 1837. He was somewhat mischievous that year, sometimes stopping the way when he chose to make his lair, or with the meddlers and intruders on the Green when the regiment was out at exercise. But it was in Dublin, in the summer of 1838, that Donald came out. Without any training, he took his place at the head of the regiment alongside of the sergeant-major. Whether marching to and from the Phœnix Park for exercise, marching out in winter, or at guard mounting on the day the 42d furnished the band and staff, Donald was never absent. He accompanied the regiment to all garrison field-days, went to feed until the time came for going home, was often a mile from them, but always at his post when the time came. With one exception, about the third-field day, the 79th were there for the first time, and Donald trotted up to them when marching off. He somehow discovered his mistake, and became uneasy and bumptious, and on reaching Island Bridge, when the 79th had to turn off to Richmond Barracks, declined to accompany his new friends any farther. Colonel Ferguson desired half a dozen men to hand over their muskets to their comrades, and to drive Donald towards the Royal Barracks. He went willingly, and happened to rejoin his own corps at the Park gate, evidently delighted. He never committed a similar mistake. When the regiment had the duty, he invariably went with the guard to the Castle; and whether going or coming, the crowd was always dense, although a daily occurrence, but Donald made his way, and kept it clear too, and the roughs knew better than to attempt to annoy him. Indeed, he has been known to single out an individual who did so, and give chase after him through the crowd. There was never any concern about him, as he could well defend himself. The Greys were in the Royal Barracks with the 42d, and permitted Donald to make his bed, even by tossing down their litter, fed him with oats daily, &c. But early in 1839 the Greys left, and the Bays' succeeded them. It was very soon evident that Donald and the new comers did not understand each other. The Bays would not allow him to make his bed, nor did they give oats, and Donald declared war against all Bays, when and wherever they came near him, till at last

a Bay man could hardly venture to cross the Royal square, without looking out that Donald was out of the way. It gave rise to a clever sketch made on the wall of the officers' room at the Bank guard of the "Stag at Bay," where Donald was represented as having one of them up against a wall. In May 1839, he made nine days' march to Limerick, although very foot-sore and out of temper, and woe to the ostlers in the hotel-yard who interfered with him after a day's march. Donald had another failing, which his countrymen are accused of, which was a great liking for whisky or sherry. He suffered after a debauch, and it was forbidden to indulge Donald in his liking in that way. At Limerick, as soon as the officers' dinner pipe went, he made his way to the mess-room windows, which were on the ground floor, to look for sherry, until a high fine had to be made on any one who gave it to him. Donald afterwards marched to Templemore, and finally to Cork. He had by this time become so formidable in his temper, particularly to strangers, that it was clear he could not be taken on board a ship to Corfu, even if the captain of the troopship would permit it; and, to the regret of all, it was decided that Donald must be transferred to strangers. Colonel Johnstone arranged with Lord Bandon, who promised that Donald should have the run of his fine park at Bandon Castle while he lived, and it was Donald's own fault that it was not so. It was really an effecting sight to see poor Donald thrown over and tied with ropes by those he loved so well, and put into a cart to be carried off. His cries were pitiful, and he actually shed tears, and so did some of his friends, for Donald was a universal favourite. Thus the regiment parted with dear old Donald, and nothing more was heard of him for many years.

In 1862, nearly 22 years afterwards, Lieu-tenant-Colonel Wheatley being appointed to the Cork district, soon after arriving at Cork, took steps to ascertain the subsequent history of Donald. The reply was, "That from the day he was set at liberty in the park, he declined having any intercourse with either man or beast. That summer and winter he kept in out-of-the-way places to which no one could approach; and that they had been so many complaints against him, that about the end of two years his lordship reluctantly sanctioned his being shot." Poor Donald! the regiment and its ways was the only home he ever knew, and his happiness left him when separated from it. So has it been with many others besides Donald.

The "Grenadier's Cat" was picked up by the company in one of the encampments in Bulgaria, probably in Gevreeklar, and was embarked at Varna for the Crimea. Having seen it at the bivouac at Lake Touzla, Lieutenant-Colonel Wheatley was induced, after the action at Alma had commenced, to ask what had become of poor puss, when one of No. 1 company called, "It is here, sir," and opening his haversack, the animal looked out quite contented. It was shut up again, and on making inquiry next morning, it was found that "Bell" had escaped both death and wounds, and was amongst them in the bivouac, well taken care of in so far as having an ample share of the rations. It appears that the man who carried the cat and took care of it, was exempted by the company from fatigue duties, or his turn of carrying the cooking-kettles, &c. Like all the pets, it did not come to a peaceful end. It finally became an inmate of the regimental hospital, being the only quiet place to be found for it, got worried, and died at Balaclava. Such was the end of Bulgarian "Bell," the only instance, probably, of a cat going into action.

On 2d April 1872 took place one of the most interesting events in connection with the history of the Black Watch, viz., the unveiling in Dunkeld Cathedral of a magnificent monument (a plate of which we give) to the memory of the officers, non-commissioned officers, and men of the regiment, who fell in war from the creation of the regiment to the close of the Indian mutiny. The monument, which had been in preparation for several years, was subscribed for by the officers of the regiment, and was executed by Mr John Steell, R.S.A., the celebrated Scottish sculptor. It is placed in the vestibule of the cathedral, at the east end of the choir, and is the largest and one of the finest mural monuments ever erected in Scotland.

The monument, as we have intimated, is a mural one, having for its principal feature a beautiful piece of sculpture in *alto relievo*. As originally designed by the artist, this composition was on a comparatively small scale. When, however, the sketch came to be submitted to the officers of the regiment, they were so much pleased with the idea embodied in it that they resolved to have the figures executed of life size, and increased their contributions accordingly. Standing out against a large pointed panel of white marble, the sculptured group, which is worked out in the same material as the background, represents an officer of the 42d visiting a battle-field at the close of an engagment to look for some missing comrade. The point of time selected is the moment in which the searcher, having just discovered the body of his friend, stands with uncovered head, paying mute homage to departed valour. The central figure of the composition is admirably modelled, the expression of the soldier's countenance being in fine keeping with the calm and subdued tone which pervades the whole work. On the left, beneath the remains of a shattered gun-carriage, lies the body of a young ensign, his hand still grasping the flag he had stoutly defended, and his face wearing a peaceful expression, as befitted a man who had died at his post. Other accessories combine with those just mentioned to suggest the grim realities of war; but the artist has so toned his composition that the mind is insensibly led to dwell on that other aspect of the battlefield in which it speaks of danger braved and duty nobly done. A slab underneath the sculpture bears the following inscription:—

IN MEMORY OF
THE OFFICERS, NON-COMMISSIONED OFFICERS,
AND
PRIVATE SOLDIERS
OF THE
42d ROYAL HIGHLANDERS—THE BLACK WATCH
WHO FELL IN WAR
FROM
THE CREATION OF THE REGIMENT
TO
THE CLOSE OF THE INDIAN MUTINY,
1859.
THE TEN INDEPENDENT COMPANIES OF THE FREACADAN DUBH, OR BLACK WATCH, WERE FORMED INTO A REGIMENT ON THE 25TH OCTOBER 1739, AND THE FIRST MUSTER TOOK PLACE IN MAY 1740, IN A FIELD BETWEEN TAYBRIDGE AND ABERFELDY.

Here, 'mong the hills that nursed each hardy Gael,
Our votive marble tells the soldier's tale;
Art's magic power each perished friend recalls,
And bids us gaze on Glencoe's bloody walls.

J. H. G. Fecit.   Sc. Eng.

MONUMENT IN DUNKELD CATHEDRAL.

On either side of the above inscription are recorded the names of the hard-fought fields in which the regiment gained its enviable reputation. How many memories are recalled as one reads the long roll of historic battle-grounds—"Fontenoy, Flanders, Ticonderoga, Martinique, Guadaloupe, Havannah, Egypt, Corunna, Fuentes D'Onor, Pyrenees, Nivelle, Nive, Orthes, Toulouse, Peninsula, Waterloo, Alma, Sebastopol, Lucknow!" The selection of a site for the monument was determined by considerations connected with the history of the regiment. The gallant 42d having been originally drawn chiefly from Perthshire, it was felt to be appropriate that the memorial intended to commemorate its fallen heroes should be erected in that county; and all will concur in the propriety of the arrangement by which a shrine has been found for it within the venerable Cathedral of Dunkeld.

For the following account of the ceremony we are indebted to the *Scotsman* of 3d April 1872 :—

A detachment of the 42d, under the command of Major Macpherson, had been sent down from Devonport to perform the ceremony of handing over the monument to the custody of the Duke of Athole, and also to place over it the colours under which the regiment had fought on many a bloody field. In the vestibule of the cathedral were the Duke and Duchess of Athole, the Duchess Dowager of Athole, and many other distinguished persons.

Upon entering the vestibule, Major Macpherson, younger of Cluny, placed the old colours of the regiment over the monument. He then requested the Duchess-Dowager to unveil the monument; which having been done,

Major Macpherson said—May it please your Grace, ladies, and gentlemen—We, a detachment of the 42d Royal Highlanders, have come here to deposit the old colours of the regiment in Dunkeld Cathedral—a place which has been selected by the regiment as the most fitting receptacle for the colours of the 42d—a regiment which has been essentially connected with Perthshire. In the name of the officers of the regiment, I have to express to his Grace the Duke of Athole our kindest thanks for the great interest he has taken in this memorial,

which I have had the too great honour to ask the Duchess-Dowager to unveil; and if I may be allowed, I would express to your Grace the kindest thanks of the regiment for the great interest the late Duke of Athole took in this monument.

The Duke of Athole then said—You have this day paid a great compliment to the county of Perth, and to this district in particular. By the placing of this beautiful monument in our cathedral you have enhanced its value, and by placing over it your time and battle-worn colours. I can assure you we shall value the possession of this monument excessively, and do our utmost to preserve it from all harm. I trust that the cloud which is now hanging over the connection between the 42d and Perthshire will yet be dispelled, and that the old ties may not be broken, and that we may yet see the 'Freiceadan Dubh' localised in Perth.[2] I need not allude to the services of the 42d—they are far too well known to require comment on my part. One of the earliest colonels of the regiment was one of my own family—Lord John Murray; and at different times a great many men from Athole have served in your ranks. Members of almost every large family in Athole have at one time or other been officers in the corps. Many relatives and friends of my own have likewise served with the regiment. His Grace concluded by asking Major Macpherson to convey to the officers of the 42d the thanks of the county of Perth for the honour they had done to the county.

At the close of the proceedings a salute of 21 guns was fired from a battery placed on Stanley Hill.

After the ceremony the Duchess-Dowager entertained a select party at her residence to lunch. The detachment of the 42d and the Athole Highlanders at the same time partook of dinner in the Servants' Hall. When the dinner had been concluded, the Duchess-Dowager, the Duke and Duchess of Athole, and party, entered the Servants' Hall, where the Dowager-Duchess proposed the health of the 42d, a detachment of which regiment had come such a long dis-

<hr/>

[2] Alluding to the Brigade Centre for the 42d and 79th being told off for Dundee, which was subsequently altered to Perth.

tance in order to place their beautiful colours in the Cathedral of Dunkeld. Her Grace having made a touching allusion to the various battles in which the colours had been borne, remarked that there was no better place where the regiment could lodge them than the old historical cathedral of the city where the corps was chiefly raised. The colours had been given in charge to the Athole Highlanders, and she was sure that they would be as proud to look upon them hanging on the walls of the Cathedral as the 42d themselves would be to see them in the midst of battle, and she might assure the detachment that the utmost care would be taken of them.

Major Macpherson returned thanks on behalf of the officers and men of the 42d. He stated that the officers had taken a vote as to where the colours should be lodged, and the majority were in favour of having them placed over this monument in Dunkeld Cathedral, on the banks of the Tay, where the regiment was originally formed. He begged, on behalf of the officers and men, to thank her Grace for the exceedingly kind reception which had been accorded to them during their stay in Dunkeld, and concluded by calling upon the men to drink to the health of the Duchess-Dowager of Athole. The original colours of the 42d are in the Tower of London.

The colours placed in Dunkeld Cathedral were carried through the Crimean campaign and the Indian Mutiny. The colours which the regiment presently possesses were presented by the Commander-in-Chief at Aldershot in 1871.

In the autumnal manœuvres of 1871, the Black Watch, as might be surmised, performed their part brilliantly, and to the satisfaction and gratification of all present, the foreign officers especially awarding them the palm as models in every respect of what soldiers ought to be ; indeed, their praises were in the mouths of all.

In September 1871 the regiment went to Devonport ; and when, in February 1873, in accordance with the scheme for the establishment of military centres, the 42d were allocated to Perth in conjunction with the 79th, we believe both corps felt the greatest gratification, as they had stood "shoulder to shoulder" in many a hard-fought field, always indeed in the same brigade—in Egypt, the Peninsula, Waterloo, the Crimea, and last of all in the Indian Mutiny.

We cannot help expressing our gratification at being able to present our readers with a group of authentic steel portraits of four of the most eminent Colonels of the Black Watch. That of the first Colonel, John, Earl of Crawford, is from the original in the possession of the Earl of Crawford and Balcarres, at Haigh Hall, Wigan. The Earl is represented in a Russian or Hungarian dress. That of Sir George Murray, so long and intimately associated with the regiment, is from an original painting by H. W. Pickersgill, R.A. The portrait of Sir John Macdonald, his successor, is taken from the original in possession of Mrs Burt, Edinburgh : And that of the present brave and much respected Colonel, Sir Duncan Alexander Cameron, from a photograph taken expressly for this work ; and Sir Duncan's modest reluctance, we ought to say, to allow his portrait to be published, was not easily overcome.

Here may we fitly end the story of the brave Black Watch, which nearly a century and a half ago was originated not far from Perth by the chivalry of the North. In these later days of rapid advance in military science, when the blind enthusiasm of our forefathers is spoken lightly of, have the highest military authorities come to the conclusion, after much discussion and cogitation, that it is wise after all to give way occasionally to sentiment ; and thus have they been led to assign to the old Black Watch, after a glorious but chequered career, a permanent recruiting home in the country of its birth, not many miles from the spot where it was first embodied.

SUCCESSION LISTS OF COLONELS, FIELD AND STAFF OFFICERS, &c.

COLONELS.

John, Earl of Crawford, 25th October 1739.

Hugh Lord Sempill, 14th January 1741.

Lord John Murray, 25th April 1745.

Sir Hector Munro, K.B., 1st June 1787

George, Marquis of Huntly, 3d January 1806

John, Earl of Hopetoun, G.C.B., 29th January 1820.

The Right Hon. Sir George Murray, G.C.B., G.C.H. 6th September 1823.

Removed to the First, or the Royal Regiment of Foot, on the 29th December 1843.

Sir John Macdonald, K.C.B., 15th January 1844.

Died 28th March 1850.

Sir James Douglas, K.C.B., 10th April 1850.

Died 6th March 1862.

George, Marquis of Tweeddale, K.T., 7th March 1862.

Removed to 2d Life Guards 9th September 1863.

Major General Sir Duncan Alexander Cameron, K.C.B., 9th September 1863.

Sir Duncan Alexander Cameron, K.C.B , joined the Regiment in 1825 as Ensign, and has never served in any other.—He was appointed Brigadier in Turkey, (local rank) on the . 24th October 1854.

Major-General, (local) . .	5th October 1855.
Major-General, (local) in England,	24th July 1856.
Major-General, . . .	25th March 1859.
Colonel of the 42d, . . .	9th Sept. 1863.
Lieutenant-General, . .	1st May 1868.

He served throughout the Eastern campaign of 1854–1855 ; commanded the regiment at the battle of Alma, and the Highland Brigade at the battle of Balaklava, on the expedition to Kertch—Siege and fall of Sebastopol and assault on the outworks 18th June—Was appointed president of the Council of Education in 1857—Commander-in-chief in Scotland in 1860—Commander of the forces in New Zealand, with the local rank of Lieut.-General 1861, and of the Australian Colonies and New Zealand in 1863—Governor of The Royal Military College at Sandhurst in 1865, which he still holds (1873).

LIEUTENANT-COLONELS.

Sir Robert Munro, 25th October 1739.

Promoted to Colonelcy Ponsonby's Regiment, 17th June 1745.

John Monroe, 17th July 1745.

Died in 1749.

John Campbell, 24th May 1749.

Promoted to Colonelcy of 36th Foot, 23d December 1755.

Francis Grant, 17th December 1755.

Promoted to be Colonel-Commandant of 90th Regiment, 19th February 1762.

Gordon Graham, 9th July 1762.

Retired 12th December 1770.

Thomas Graeme, 12th December 1770.

Retired 7th September 1771.

Thomas Stirling, 7th September 1771.

Promoted to 71st Regiment, 13th February 1782.

Norman Macleod, 21st March 1780.

Removed to 73d in 1786, which regiment was formed from second battalion of the 42d Regiment.

Charles Graham, 28th April 1782.

Promoted to a regiment serving in the West Indies, 30th November 1796.

William Dickson, 1st September 1795.

Retired 23 March 1808.

James Stewart, 14th December 1796.

Retired 19th September 1804.

James Stirling, 7th September 1804.

Promoted to rank of Major-General, 4th June 1814.

Robert Lord Blantyre, 19th September 1804.

Exchanged to half-pay, late Eighth Garrison Battalion, 6th May 1813.

John Farquharson, 3d March 1808.

Retired 16th April 1812

Robert Macara, 16th April 1812.

Killed in action, 16th June 1815.

Sir George Leith, Bart, 6th May 1813.

Placed on Half-pay, 26th December 1814.

Robert Henry Dick, 18th June 1815.

Exchanged to Half-pay, 26th November 1828.

Honourable Sir Charles Gordon, 26th November 1828.

William Middleton, 23d October 1835.

George Johnstone, 23d August 1839.

Henry Earl of Uxbridge, 5th September 1842.

Duncan Alexander Cameron, 5th September 1843.

James Macdougall, 14th April 1846.

Charles Dunsmure, 15th February 1850.

Thomas Tulloch, 9th March 1855.

Alexander Cameron, 9th October 1855.

George Edward Thorold, 28th July 1857.

Frederick Green Wilkinson, 5th March 1858.

Edward Ramsden Priestley, 10th August 1858

John Chetham M'Leod, 26th March 1868.

The Lieut.-Colonels from 1815 are also included in the general alphabetical list.

MAJORS.

George Grant, 25th October 1739.

Died in 1742.

James Colquhon, 24th June 1742.

Retired in 1745.

Francis Grant, 1st October 1745.

Promoted December 17, 1755.

Duncan Campbell, 17th December 1755.

Killed at Ticonderago.

Gordon Graham, 17th July 1758.

Promoted July 9, 1762.

John Reid, 1st August 1759.

Exchanged to half-pay, February 10, 1770.

John M'Neil, 9th July 1762.

Died in 1762.

Allan Campbell, 15th August 1762.

Placed on half-pay on the reduction of the regiment, March 18, 1763.

John Murray, 10th February 1770.

Retired March 31, 1776.

Thomas Graeme, 31st March 1770.

Promoted December 12, 1770.

Thomas Stirling, 12th December 1770.
  Promoted September 7, 1771.
William Murray, 7th September 1771.
  Promoted to Twenty-seventh Regiment, October 5, 1777.
William Grant, 5th October 1777.
  Retired August 25, 1778.
Charles Graham, 25th August 1778.
  Promoted April 28, 1782.
Patrick Graham, 21st March 1780.
  Died October 22, 1793.
Walter Home, 28th April 1782.
  Retired March 16, 1791.
John Campbell, 23d October 1784.
  Died March 23, 1784.
Hay Macdowall, 24th March 1784.
  Removed in 1786 to Seventy-third, which corps was formed from second battalion Forty-second Regiment.
George Dalrymple, 16th March 1791.
  Promoted to Nineteenth Foot, December 31, 1794.
William Dickson, 14th January 1795.
  Promoted September 1, 1795.
Robert Pigot Christie, 1st September 1795.
  Died June 23, 1796.
William Munro, 2d September 1795.
  Promoted to Caithness Legion Fencibles, October 21, 1795.
James Stewart, 21st October 1795.
  Promoted December 14, 1796.
Alexander Stewart, 24th June 1796.
  Retired September 7, 1804.
James Stirling, 14th December 1796.
  Promoted September 7, 1804.
John Farquharson, 9th July 1803.
  Promoted March 3, 1808.
Archibald Argyll Campbell, 9th July 1803.
  Died in February 1899.
Charles Macquarie, 7th September 1804.
  Retired May 2, 1811.
James Grant, 7th September 1804.
  Retired November 14, 1805.
Robert Macara, 14th November 1805.
  Promoted April 16, 1812.

Thomas Johnston, 3d March 1808.
  Exchanged to half-pay, Bradshaw's Levy, July 14, 1808.
Robert Henry Dick, 14th July 1808.
  Promoted June 18, 1815.
Hamilton Rose, 9th February 1809.
  Died in October 1811.
William Munro, 2d May 1811.
  Exchanged to half-pay, Royal Regiment of Malta, May 30, 1811.
William Cowell, 30th May 1811.
  Retired April 8, 1826.
Maxwell Grant, 10th October 1811.
  Placed on half-pay, December 28, 1814.
Robert Anstruther, 16th April 1812.
  Placed on half-pay, December 28, 1814.
Archibald Menzies, 18th June 1815.
James Brander, 8th April 1826.
William Middleton, 15th August 1826.
John Malcolm, 25th December 1828.
Hugh Andrew Fraser, 3d December 1829.
George Johnstone, 4th May 1832.
James Macdougall, 23d October 1835.
Duncan Alexander Cameron, 23d August 1839.
Charles Dunsmure, 5th September 1843.
Daniel Frazer, 14th April 1846.
George Burell Cumberland, 15th February 1850.
Thomas Tulloch, 20th May 1853.
John Cameron Macpherson, 29th December 1854.
The Honourable Robert Rollo, 5th January 1855.
Alexander Cameron, 24th April 1855.
Charles Murray, 10th August 1855.
Frederick Green Wilkinson, 9th October 1855.
Andrew Pitcairn, 12th September 1856.
Edward Ramsden Priestley, 17th July 1857.
John Chetham M'Leod, 18th March 1858.
John Drysdale, 10th August 1858.
Duncan Macpherson, 5th July 1865.
Francis Cunningham Scott, 26th March 1868.

The Majors from 1815 are also included in the alphabetical list.

PAYMASTERS.

John Home, 21st March 1800 — the first appointment of that rank to the Regiment.
Alexander Aitken, 25th December 1818.
Charles Wardell, 23d February 1821.
Stephen Blake, 3d July 1823.

William A. M'Dougall, 23d August 1833.
John Wheatley, 12th October 1828.
James A. Bazalgette, 24th April 1855.
Frank Samwell, 15th Dec. 1869.

ADJUTANTS.

Gilbert Stewart, 25th October 1739.
Lieut. James Grant, 26th June 1751.
  ,, Alexander Donaldson, 20th March 1759.
  ,, John Gregor, 27th August 1760.
  ,, William Gregor, 22d October 1761.
  ,, Duncan Cameron, 6th October 1762.
  ,, John M'Intosh, 1st November 1768.
  ,, Hugh Fraser, 29th March 1776.
  ,, Robert Leslie (2d Battalion), 21st March 1780.
  ,, John Farquharson, 6th April 1791.
  ,, John Fraser, 5th October 1795.
  ,, Simon Fraser, 21st March 1800.
  ,, James Walker, 5th April 1801.
  ,, Archibald Menzies, 9th July 1803.
  ,, James Hunter, 28th September 1804.
  ,, James Swanson, 6th June 1805.
  ,, John Innes (Killed at Orthes), 8th December 1808.
  ,, James White, 8th June 1809.
  ,, Colin M'Dougall, 13th February 1812.

Lieutenant James Young, from 13th March 1814.
Lieutenant James Robertson, 14th September 1815.
Ensign (from Sergeant Major) William Duff, 14th April 1825.
Lieutenant William Dick Macfarlane, 16th July 1829.
Ensign (from Acting Sergeant-Major) John Wheatley, 20th July 1832.
Ensign Duncan Cameron, 30th October 1838.
Lieut. Athole Wentworth Macdonald, 8th May 1840.
Lieut. Archibald Colin Campbell, 31st March 1843.
Lieut. Thomas Robert Drummond Hay, 24th January 1845.
Lieutenant Andrew Pitcairn, 28th August 1846.
Lieut. William John Cunninghame, 9th March 1849.
Ensign John Drysdale, 25th June 1852.
Ensign (from Quarter-Master) William Wood, 16th February 1855.
Lieutenant James Edmund Christie, 4th May 1863.
Andrew Gilbert Wauchope, 5th April 1870.

The Adjutants from 1814 are also included in the alphabetical list.

QUARTERMASTERS FROM 1795.

David Rawlins, 5th October 1795.
Donald M'Intosh, 9th July 1803.
Finlay King, from Sergt. Major, 31st December 1818.
Edward Paton, from Quarter-Master Sergt., 19th June 1840.
Charles Fraser, from Ensign, 28th August 1846.

William Wood, from Sergeant-Major, 5th May 1854.
Alexander M'Gregor, from Quarter-Master Sergeant, 25th May 1855.
John Simpson, V.C. from Quarter-Master-Sergeant, 7th October 1859.

All, with the exception of the first, are included in the general alphabetical list.

SUCCESSION OF SURGEONS FROM 1800.

Alexander Grant, 26th September 1795.
Swinton Macleod, 9th July 1803.
Brinsley Nicholson, M.D., 15th November 1829.
James Paterson, M.D. 19th June 1835.

James M'Gregor, 26th February 1841.
John Gillespie Wood, M.D. 12th March 1852.
John Sheldon Furlong, M.D. 9th February 1855.
James Edmund Clutterbuck, M.D. 14th June 1864.

All, with the exception of the first, are included in the general alphabetical list.

SUCCESSION OF SERGEANT-MAJORS.

Sergeant-Major James, was killed in action at Toulouse, 10th April 1814.
Sergeant-Major Perie, was killed in action at Quatre Bras (Waterloo), on the 16th June 1815.
Finlay King, 16th June 1815, to Quarter-Master, 1818.
William Duff, 31st December 1818, to Adjutant, 1825.
John Macdonald, 14th April 1825. Discharged to pension, 10th December 1834. Died the following year.
John Wheatley, appointed Acting, on the 15th November 1827; at the regiment (the Sergeant-Major being at the Depot), to Adjutant, 1832.
Thomas Penny, acting with service companies, from 20th July 1832—Sergeant-Major, 11th December 1834. Discharged to Pension 1839. Died at Glasgow 15th February 1865.
Charles Fraser, 12th December 1839, to Ensign, 1843.

Alexander Geddes, appointed to Reserve Battalion 1st April 1843. Discharged to Pension 22d October 1851—appointed Quarter-Master of the Perth Militia 22d November 1856.
John Drysdale, 5th September 1843, to Ensign, 1847.
James Ranken, 22d June 1847. Discharged to Pension 10th November 1853. Quarter-Master Argyll Militia 14th April 1869.
William Wood, 11th November 1853, to Quarter-Master, 1854.
John Wilson, 5th May 1854, to Ensign, 1854.
William Lawson, 10th August 1854, to Ensign, 1854.
John Granger, 18th January 1855, to Lieutenant Land Transport Corps, 1855.
Peter White, 7th September 1855. Discharged to Pension 25th July 1865.
John Forbes, 26th July 1865.

The Sergeant-Majors who were promoted to be Officers are included in the general alphabetical list.

LIST OF OFFICERS

Who have served in the 42d Royal Highlanders, "The Black Watch," from the date of the Muster taken at Armagh on the 28th of May 1817, the day of marching in from Glasgow, for the period ended on the 24th of May up to the 31st of December 1872.[1] From Lieut.-Colonel Wheatley's MS.

Abercromby, Samuel Douglas, Lieut.—3d June 1842, Ensign. Died at Bermuda 16th May 1847.
Ainslie, Montague, Ensign, 20th May 1843. Died at Gosport, 18th Oct. 1853.
Aitken, Alex., Paymaster, 25th Dec. 1818.—Half-pay 7th February 1821. Died at Brighton, 13th May 1871.

Aitken, Walker, Lieut.—3d Dec. 1861, Ensign—Lieut. 19th Dec. 1865.
Alexander, Sir James Edward, Major-General.—9th March 1832, Captain—Half-Pay 14th April 1838.
Allan, Fife, Ensign 23d Sept. 1855. Retired 12th Dec. 1856.
Baird, William, Bt.-Major.—17th Nov. 1854, Ensign—Captain 22d May 1857—Bt.-Major 5th July 1872.
Balfour, James William, Captain.—2nd March 1847, Ensign. On Reduction to 89th, Lieut. Retired Captain from 7th Dragoon Guards 16th June 1857.
Balguy, Charles Yelverton.—24th Feb. 1854, Captain from 41st Retired 24th April 1855.

[1] The rank after the name is that held in December 1872, or the one attained before death. The first date is that of joining the regiment, followed by the rank at the time. Field and staff officers since 1817 are included in the general list, as well as in the separate succession lists of those officers. Those left unfinished were alive, or still serving in the regiment, on the 1st January 1873.

Barnett, John Osborne, Lieut.—16th Nov. 1841, Ensign. Retired 12th Nov. 1847.

Bayly, Richard Kerr, Captain.—16th Mar. 1855, Ensign—Captain 5th July 1865.

Bazalgette, James Arnold.—24th April 1855, Paymaster.—Half-pay 1859.

Beales, William, Lieut.-Colonel.—24th April 1838, Captain.—To Half-Pay 30th August 1844, Captain. Died at St Heliers, Jersey, on retired full pay, 25th April 1868.

Bedingfield, William.—9th Dec. 1862, Ensign from 58th Regiment—To 7th Hussars, Cornet, 22d Nov. 1864.

Bennett, William Henry.—27th May 1853, Lieut. from 20th Regiment. Retired 11th May 1855.

Berwick, William Alex., Lieut.—17th Feb. 1862, Ensign from 16th Foot.—Lieut. 28th Oct. 1871.

Bethune, Alex. (of Blebo), Lieut.—29th May 1842, Ensign. Retired 2d March 1847.

Black, Wilsone, Major.—11th August 1854, Ensign—Half-pay on reduction, 9th Jan. 1857—To 6th Foot 17th Nov. 1857—Brevet-Major 14th April 1873.

Blake, Stephen, Paymaster.—3d July 1828, Paymaster—Exchanged to 7th Fusiliers 23d Aug. 1833. Died Paymaster of the 93d at Dublin, 5th Oct. 1848.

Borrowes, Peter Robert.—2d Sept. 1845, Lieut. from 15th Foot. Retired 16th June 1848. Died in Dublin 1854.

Bosworth, Percie Mackie, Lieut.—23d March 1855, Ensign—Lieut. 2d Oct. 1855. Died at Nynee, India, 19th June 1858.

Boyle, Robert, Captain.—5th April 1806, Ensign—Half-Pay 31st May 1821. Died in London 11th July 1847.

Brandy, Alfred Jennings, Lieut.—15th March 1855, Ensign—Lieut. 2d Oct. 1855. Killed in action at Roorah, India, 15th April 1858.

Brandy, Henry Jennings, Lieut.—30th Dec. 1859, Ensign. Retired Lieut. 3d March 1865. Died at Tunbridge Wells 19th Feb. 1870.

Braniger, James, Major.—14th Dec. 1809, Ensign—To Half-pay, Lieut.-Colonel, 15th Aug. 1826. Died at Pitgaveny House, Elgin, 23d March 1854.

Brereton, Robert, Captain.—8th Dec. 1825, Captain, to Half-pay 9th March 1833. Retired 12th May 1842.—Dead.

Prickenden, Richard H. Lambert, Lieut.—18th July 1865, Ensign—Lieut. 11th Jan. 1867.

Brooke, Henry, Ensign.—5th Aug. 1859. Retired 9th Dec. 1862.

Brophy, N. Winsland, Lieut.—30th Jan. 1866, Ensign from 6th Regiment—Lieut. 17th March 1869.

Cameron, Alexander, Lieut.-Colonel.—24th Feb. 1832, Ensign. Died Lieut.-Colonel Commanding at Bareilly, India, 9th Aug. 1858.

Cameron, Duncan (of Inverailort), Lieut.—28d Oct. 1835, Ensign. Retired 8th May 1840.

Cameron, Sir Duncan Alexander, Lieut.-General—8th April 1825, Ensign—In the Regiment until promoted to Major-General in 1855—Colonel of the Regiment 9th Sept. 1863.

Cameron, Wm. Gordon, C.B., Colonel.—24th May 1844, Ensign—To Grenadier Guards, Lieut. 12th May 1847—4th Foot, Major, 23d Oct. 1857—Lieut.-Colonel 1st April 1873.

Campbell, Archibald (of Glendarnel), Captain.—26th Nov. 1825, Ensign. Retired Captain 6th March 1840.

Campbell, Arch. Colin (Renton), Brevet-Major.—24th Feb. 1827, Ensign. Retired Captain and Brevet-Major 7th Sept. 1855. Died at Mordington House, Berwickshire, 23d Nov. 1866.

Campbell, Colin (Southhall family), Lieut.—8th April 1826, Ensign. Retired Lieut. 27th Sept. 1859. Died at Anchan, Isle of Man, 19th Oct. 1859.

Campbell, Colin George (of Stonefield), Lieut.—31st Dec. 1829, Ensign. Retired Lieut. 24th April 1838.

Campbell, Farquhar (of Aros), Captain.—30th Nov 1835, Ensign. Retired Captain 26th Oct. 1849.

Campbell, George Frederick, Lieut.—11th Jan. 1867, Ensign—Lieut. 25th March 1871, to 51st Regiment 31st Oct. 1871.

Campbell, John, Colonel.—3d Dec. 1807, Captain from 35th—Half-pay Major and Brevet Lieut.-Colonel 22d April 1826. Died at Marseilles, 31st March 1841.

Campbell, John Charles, M.B.—29th March 1861, Assistant-Surgeon, from 4th Hussars—To Half-pay 2d July 1861.

Campbell, John Gordon, Captain.—17th Nov. 1848. Ensign. Retired 9th May 1856. Died at Peebles 30th Nov. 1865.

Campbell, Patrick, Captain.—24th Aug. 1815, Ensign—To Half-pay 3d Sept. 1829. Died at Ford near Dalkeith, 24th Feb. 1856.

Ceely, Arthur James, Lieut.—16th Aug. 1855, Ensign—Lieut. 30th June 1858. Died at Point de Galle, Ceylon, Sick from India, 29th Dec. 1866.

Chawner, Edward Hoare, Captain.—9th June 1825, Ensign—Exchanged to 4th Dragoon Guards, Lieut.—Half-pay, Captain, 7th Sept. 1832. Died 23d Nov. 1858.

Childers, William, Captain.—8th June 1826, Captain. Retired 14th Sept. 1832. Died at St Heliers, Jersey, 28th Feb. 1861.

Chisholm, Arch. Macra, Captain.—17th April 1842, Ensign. Retired Captain 6th April 1855.

Chisholm, Donald, Captain.—10th Oct. 1805, Lieut. from 39th—To 4th Veteran Battalion, Captain, 24th Feb. 1820. Died at Portobello, Edinburgh, 21st Aug. 1853.

Christie, James Edmund, Captain.—10th Aug. 1855, Ensign—Captain, Half-pay 1st April 1870.

Clark, James, Ensign.—26th Aug. 1819, Ensign—To Half-Pay 2d Sept. 1824. Died 12th Dec. 1838.

Clarke, Alfred T. Stafford, M.D. 8th Aug. 1862, Assistant-Surgeon, from Staff—To Royal Artillery, 20th Sept. 1864.

Clarke, Charles Christopher, Lieut.—2d Aug. 1815, Ensign—To Half-Pay 1st Nov. 1827. Died in the 33d Regiment in Jamaica, 23d Sept. 1831.

Clavering, Ernest, F.G. Lieut.—15th April 1842, Ensign. Retired 6th July 1849. Died in Edinburgh 9th Aug. 1852.

Clutterbuck, James Edward, M.D.—14th June 1864, Surgeon from Staff—Surgeon-Major, 22d Dec. 1868.

Cockburn, George William, Captain.—23d Feb. 1855, Ensign—Captain 24th March 1863—Exchanged to 83d, 28th Jan. 1870. Retired 30th Nov. 1870.

Cockburn, Thomas Hugh, Lieut.-Colonel.—6th March 1840, Ensign—Exchanged Captain to 43d—Half-Pay Major 29th May 1863. Retired with rank of Lieut.-Colonel 18th April 1865.

Coleridge, Francis George, Captain.—11th Jan. 1856. Ensign—Lieut. in 25th 13th Dec. 1859. Retired as Captain 28th June 1871.

Colquhoun, Alan John, Lieut.—15th Oct. 1861.—Ensign, from Cornet 16th Lancers—Lieut. 13th Nov. 1865. Retired 23d Jan. 1869.

Cooper, Egbert William, Captain.—From 2d West India Regiment, 30th July 1869.

Coveny, Robert Charles, Lieut.—2d Sept. 1862, Ensign—from 23d Regiment, Lieut. 30th Jan. 1866.

Cowell, William, Major from H. P., and Brevet Lieut.-Colonel—30th May 1811, Major. Retired 8th April 1826. Died at Portarlington, Ireland, 29th May 1847.

Creagh, A. Michael, Lieut.—16th April 1861, Ensign from 58th—Lieut. 3d March 1865.

Crompton, William Henry, (Now Crompton-Stansfield), Lieut.-Colonel.—17th Aug. 1854, Ensign—

To Half-Pay Captain on reduction 7th Nov. 1856
—11th Foot 9th Jan. 1858—Lieut.-Colonel, 22d
July 1871.

Crosse, Robert Legh, 18th June 1861, Ensign. —To 52d,
3d Dec. 1861.

Cumberland, George Bentinck Macleod, Lieut. —22d
Nov. 1854, Ensign—Lieut. 29th Dec. 1856.

Cumberland, George Burrel, Major.—28th May 1829,
Lieut. Retired Major 5th Jan. 1855. Died at
Wolvers Dean, Andover, 22d May 1865.

Cumming, Alex. Ensign.—17th July 1814, Ensign
—To Half-Pay, 26th Aug. 1819. Died Jan. 1853.

Cunninghame, Robert Campbell, Captain.—29th Aug.
1846, Ensign. Sent from the Crimea. Died at
Malta, 5th Sept. 1855.

Cunninghame, William John, Lieut.—25th Oct. 1844,
Ensign. Died at Halifax on sick leave from Bermuda, 21st June 1850.

Daniel, John Hinton—22d May 1846, Captain from
49th. Retired 23d July 1852. Died in London 8th
May 1862.

Davidson, Wm. Alex., M.D., Surgeon.—28th March
1854, Assistant Surgeon—To 1st Royal Dragoons
31st July 1855.

Dawson, Charles, M.D.—9th Oct. 1840, Assistant-
Surgeon—To Surgeon into the 54th, 9th Oct. 1846.
Died at Antigua, West Indies, 13th Nov. 1849.

Dempster, James, M.D., Surgeon.—14th April 1825,
Assistant Surgeon—To 94th Surgeon 27th Sept.
1827.

Dick, Sir Robert Henry, Major-General.—22d Nov.
1800, Ensign—Half-Pay Colonel, 25th Nov. 1828
—Killed in action at Sobraon, 10th Feb. 1846.

Douglas, Arthur Henry Johnstone—27th Nov. 1866,
Ensign. Retired 23d July 1869.

Douglas, Charles.—23d March 1855, Lieutenant from
Canadian Rifles. Died of wounds at Rooyah, India,
17th April 1858.

Douglas, Henry Sholto, Captain.—31st May 1839, Ensign. Retired Captain 17th Nov. 1838.

Douglas, Sir James, General.—10th April 1850, Colonel. Died at Clifton, 6th March 1862.

Douglas, William, Lieut.—1st Nov. 1827, Lieut.—Retired 20th July 1832.—Dead.

Drake, John Allat, 18th July 1865, Lieut.—from
Bengal Staff Corps. Retired 9th Nov. 1866.

Drummond, Henry Maurice, Colonel, (now Drummond Hay) of Seggieden.—4th Dec. 1832, Ensign.
—Retired Captain, 8th June 1852.—Lieut.-Colonel,
Royal Perth Rifles, 5th Nov. 1855. Retired with
the rank of Colonel, 21st Nov. 1870.

Drummond, Malcolm, (Viscount Forth), 4th Nov.
1853, Ensign. Retired 17th Nov. 1854. Died at
Gloucester 8th Oct. 1861.

Drysdale, John, Brevet Lieut.-Colonel.—Joined the
Regiment 28th June 1836—Ensign from Sergeant-
Major, 22d June 1847—Major 10th Aug. 1858.
—Brevet Lieut.-Colonel on the day that he died,
viz, 4th July 1865, at Uphall, near Edinburgh, on
sick leave from India.

Duff, William, Lieut.—Joined the Regiment 16th
Aug. 1806—Ensign and Adjutant from Sergeant-
Major 14th April 1825.—To Half-pay 16th July 1829.
Died at Ayr 8th Oct. 1832.

Dunbar, Alex., Lieut.—25th July 1807, Ensign,
—To Half-pay 3d March 1825. Died at Inverness,
15th Feb. 1832.

Dunbar, Sir Frederick Wm., Bart.—24th April 1838,
Ensign. Retired 19th Jan. 1840. Died Dec. 1841

Dunbar, Rothes Lennox, Captain.—13th May 1854,
Ensign. Retired Captain 7th Sept. 1856. Died in
London, 31st Jan. 1857.

Dunsmure, Charles, Lieut.-Colonel.—9th April 1825,
Ensign—Reduced Lieut.-Colonel 1st April 1850,
with the Reserve battalion. Retired 8th June 1852.

Dundas, Charles Whitely Dean, Lieut.—25th Dec.
1823, Ensign—To Coldstream Guards, 3d Aug. 1830.
Retired 21st April 1837. Died at Edinburgh, 11th
April 1856.

Eden, Charles John, Lieut.—20th Oct. 1865, Ensign
from the 39th—Lieut. 23d March 1867.

Elgin, Edward Arthur, Lieut.—from 17th Foot, 10th
July 1860. Died at Agra, 28th July 1861.

Fairlie, William, Lieut.—22d June 1815, Ensign
—Half-pay 19th Sept. 1819. Died 18th May 1824.

Farquharson, Francis Edward Henry, V.C. Captain.
—19th Jan. 1855, Ensign—Captain 28th June 1862.

Feilden, Henry Wemys, Lieut.—1st Feb. 1856, Ensign. Retired Lieut. 27th Sept. 1861.

Ferguson, Adam, Captain.—18th Aug. 1854, Ensign.
- Captain 1st May 1857. Died in India, 11th Sept.
1865.

Fergusson, James Muir (of Middlehaugh), Lieut.—9th
Nov. 1826, Ensign. Retired Lieut. 29th May 1839.
Died at Perth, 20th May 1867.

Fletcher, Duncan Downie—2d April 1851, Ensign.
Retired 6th May 1853. Died at Killarney, 20th
May 1855.

Foley, H.P. Stanhope, Lieut.—14th June 1864, Ensign—Lieut. 9th Nov. 1866. Retired 16th March
1869.

Fraser, Alex., Captain.—26th May 1863, Ensign—
Half-Pay 8th Dec. 1825. Died in Edinburgh, 24th
June 1835.

Fraser, Charles, Captain.—Joined the Regiment 21st
April 1813—From Sergeant-Major, Ensign 5th Sept.
1843—Quarter-Master, 28th Aug. 1846—Reduced
with Reserve Battalion, 1st April 1850, appointed
to 49th—To Half-Pay with the rank of Captain.
—30th June 1854.

Fraser, George, Captain.—6th July 1849, Ensign.
Died in India, Captain 27th June 1862.

Fraser, The Hon. Henry Thomas, Lieut.-Colonel.—
10th April 1858, Ensign—To Scots Fusilier Guards,
24th June 1859.

Fraser, Hugh Andrew, Major.— 25th April 1806,
Ensign—Half-pay, 4th May 1852. Died at Maid-
stone, Kent, 3d May 1855.

Fraser, William Thomas, Lieut.—1st May 1855, Ensign—Lieut. 14th Dec. 1855. Retired 9th April
1861.

Frazer, Daniel, Colonel.—27th Dec. 1827, Captain
from H. P. Retired on full-pay, Major and Brevet
Lieut.-Colonel. Died Colonel at Feversham Rec-
tory, Newport, Pagnel-Bucks, 12th July 1868.

Frazer, Rowland Aynsworth (son of Col. Daniel
Frazer). Captain—14th April 1846, Ensign. Killed
before Sebastopol, 17th July 1855.

Furlong, John Sheldon, M.D. Surgeon-Major.—9th
Feb. 1855, Surgeon from 39th—To 6th Dragoons,
14th June 1864.

Furse, George Armand, Captain.—29th March 1855,
Ensign.—Captain 12th Sept. 1865.

Fyfe, Laurence, Captain.—10th Oct. 1817, Ensign—
Exchanged to 17th Foot, 10th Aug. 1838. Retired
from Half-pay 22d Nov. 1842.

Gartshore, John Murray, (of Ravelston), Captain—
7th Dec. 1826. Retired 30th March 1838.

Gisborne, Henry Francis, Assistant-Surgeon—15th Jan.
1827, Assistant-Surgeon. Resigned 27th Nov. 1828.

Goldie, Mark Wilkes.—27th Aug. 1844, Captain from
22d. Retired 3d Nov. 1854.

Gordon, Lord Cecil, Captain.—10th Aug. 1838, Captain from 17th. Retired 4th Nov. 1841.

Gordon, The Hon. Sir Charles, Lieut.-Colonel.—From
H. P. 93d, 25th Nov. 1828. Died at Geneva, when
on leave from Corfu, 30th Sept. 1835.

Gordon, George, Lieut.—20 Feb. 1812, Ensign—Half-
pay 30th Dec. 1819. Died at Glasgow, 31st March
1861.

Gordon, Hamilton Douglas.—2d May 1851, Captain from 78th. Died at Cairo, on his way to join from India, 9th Sept. 1851.

Gordon, Rowland Hill, Captain from Coldstream Guards, 7th Sept. 1855. Retired 30th June 1860.

Graham, Charles Campbell, (now Graham Stirling, of Craigbarnet), Brevet-Major.—30th Aug. 1844, Ensign. Retired 1st May 1847.

Graham, Thomas, Lieut.-Colonel.—30th April 1827, Lieut.—Half-Pay, Captain, 9th Aug. 1833. Died Lieut.-Colonel 1st Royal Scots at Haslar, Gosport, from the Crimea, 29th Oct. 1855.

[1]Granger, John, Captain—Joined the Regiment 21st Dec. 1837.—Promoted from Sergeant-Major to Lieut. in Land Transport Corps, 1st Oct. 1855.—Captain, 1st Feb. 1856, Half-pay, 1st April 1857. Retired in 1860.

Grant, Alexander, Lieut.—16th Oct. 1866, Ensign from 15th Foot.—Lieut. 22d Oct. 1870. Retired 24th March 1871.

Grant, Edward Birkett, Captain.—14th Nov. 1826, Ensign—To 92d, 22d March 1827. Retired Captain from 4th Light Dragoons, 13th May 1829. Died at Hill, near Carlisle, 25th Sep. 1852.

Grant, The Hon. George Henry Essex, Captain.—5th Nov. 1841, Ensign. Retired Captain, 6th April 1865. Died at Crieff, 31st May 1873.

Grant, The Hon. James, Lieut.—30th March 1838, Ensign. Retired 26th October 1841.

Grant, John, Lieut.—20th May 1811, Ensign—To Half-pay 24th Aug. 1821. Died 18th June 1827.

Grant, John, (of Glenmoriston), Captain.—8th May 1840, Lieut. from 62d—Exchanged Captain, to 49th 22d May 1846. Retired 23d May 1848. Died at Moy House, Forres, 17th Aug. 1867.

Grant, William Oliver, Lieut.—29th March 1827, Ensign. Retired Lieut. 25th Sept. 1835. Died in 1839.

Green, William, Bt.-Major.—16th Jan. 1855, Ensign—Captain 19th Aug. 1859.—Bt.-Major 5th July 1872.

Grogan, Edward George, Lieut.—24th July 1869, Ensign—Lieut. 28th Oct. 1871.

Grove, J. Charles Ross, Captain.—9th Sept. 1851, Ensign—Half-pay Captain, 14th June 1864. Retired 16th Oct. 1866.

Guthrie, John (of Guthrie), Lieut.—16th July 1829, Lieut.—Half-pay 15th June 1832. Retired 19th July 1836.

Guthrie, William, Captain.—21st March 1827, Lieut.—To Half-pay Captain, 10th August 1847.

Haldane, Edward, Orlando.—30th June 1863, Lieut. from H. P. 14th Hussars. Retired 23d Nov. 1865.

Halkett, Sir P. Arthur, of Pitfirrane, Bart., Captain.—20th May 1853, Ensign from 71st, exchanged Captain to 3d Light Dragoons 8th Jan. 1856. Retired 21st May 1858.

Hamilton, Alex. Thomas, Lieut.—18th August 1869, Ensign—Lieut. 28th October 1871. Retired 26th March 1873.

Harrison, James Compson, Lieut.—23d Nov. 1867, Ensign from 73d—Lieut. 28th Oct. 1871. Retired 22d April 1873.

Harvey, John, E. A.—31st Oct. 1871, Lieut. from 51st.

Hay, T. R. Drummond, Lieut.-Colonel.—2d August 1839, Ensign—Exchanged Captain to 78th—To Half-pay 2d Feb. 1864.

Haynes, Jonathan Wynyard, Captain.—25th May 1855, Ensign—Captain 19th July 1866—Exchanged to 2d West India Regiment, 30th July 1869.

Hesketh, Wm. Pemberton, Lieut.—9th March 1855, Ensign—Lieut. 6th Sept. 1855—To 18th Hussars 16th March 1858. Retired 7th Nov. 1862.

Hicks, Edward Percy, Lieut.—24th May 1861—Ensign 12th Sept. 1865.

[1] Never served in the regiment as an officer.

Hill, Harcourt, Lieut.—10th Feb. 1825, Ensign—Half-pay 25th May 1829. Dead.

Hill, Marcus, Lieut.—7th June 1854, Ensign—Resigned 23d March 1855.

Hogarth, George, Lieut.-Colonel.—4th Nov. 1819, Ensign—Lieut. H. P. 13th Sept. 1821. Died Major and Brevet. Lieut.-Colonel in the 26th Regiment at Quebec, 25th July 1854.

Home, John, Paymaster.—21st March 1800, Paymaster—Half-pay 26th December 1818. Died at Eskbank, near Dalkeith, 14th April 1849.

Hooper, Alfred, Surgeon.—31st July 1857, Assistant Surgeon from Staff—To Staff Corps in India, 1st Sept. 1865—Surgeon 13th July 1866.

Hopetoun, John, Earl of, General.—29th Jan. 1820, Colonel. Died 27th August 1823.

Hulse, Samuel George.—3d March 1865, Ensign. Retired 11th Dec. 1866.

Hunter, James, Captain.—17th Nov. 1837, Ensign—Exchanged to 18th Foot, Lieut., 2d Sept. 1845. Died Staff Officer of Pensioners at Chester, 26th March 1860.

Inglis, Abraham, Lieut.—15th August 1826, Ensign—Retired Lieut. 15th Jan. 1833.

Jackson, Adam Thomas, M.D., Surgeon Major.—15th Feb. 1833, Assistant-Surgeon—To Staff 5th May 1837. Died at Athlone, Surgeon-Major Depot Battalion, 1st May 1860.

James, Thomas Mansfield, Lieut.—11th May 1855, Ensign—Lieut. 22d Nov. 1855. Died at Almorah, India, 26th Sept. 1860.

James, William, Lieut.—30th March 1855, Ensign.—Lieut. 16th April 1858. Retired 19th Dec. 1865.

Jervoise, Henry Clark, Lieut.-Colonel.—8th April 1853, Lieut. from 23d—Exchanged to Coldstream Guards Captain, 7th Sept. 1855.

Johnstone, George, Lieut.-Colonel.—From H. P. late of the Grenadier Guards—4th May 1832, Major—To Half-pay from Lieut.-Colonel Commanding, 5th Sept. 1843.

Johnstone, Wm. James Hope (Yr. of Annandale), Lieut.—16th March 1838, Ensign. Retired 16th May 1840. Died at Annandale, 17th March 1850.

Kauntze, George, E. F. Major.—8th June 1856 Captain from 3d Light Dragoons—To Half-pay on reduction 7th Nov. 1856.—To 7th Dragoon Guards. Retired Major 1867.

Kellet, Robert J. Napier, Captain.—3d Sept. 1829, Captain—To Half-pay 24th Feb. 1837. Retired 19th Oct. 1838. Died at Florence 2d Nov. 1858.

Kerr, Lord Charles Lennox, Captain.—1st Sept. 1837, Lieut.—Half-pay Captain 23d August 1844. Retired 19th Dec. 1848.

Kidston, Alex. Ferrier, Captain—9th Nov. 1858, Ensign—Captain 12th Feb. 1873.

King, Finlay. Joined the Regiment in 1803.—31st Dec. 1818, from Sergeant-Major promoted to Quarter-Master—Half-pay 19th June 1840. Died at Guernsey, 7th November 1842.

King, Robert Henry (son of the Quarter-Master).—18th August 1848, Assistant-Surgeon—To Staff 16th July 1852. Died in Canada 31st July 1853.

Kinloch, Thomas, Captain.—14th Sept. 1832, Ensign—Retired 25th Oct. 1844. Died at Logie, Perthshire, 6th Dec. 1848.

Lawson, William, Captain.—Joined the Regiment 29th Sept. 1837—Promoted to Ensign from Sergeant-Major, 5th Nov. 1854—Captain 19th August 1858. Died from wounds received in action, 19th August 1858.

Leith, T. Augustus Forbes.—18th Nov. 1854. Resigned 23d March 1855.

Leslie, John, Captain.—29th July 1815, Ensign—To Half-pay 9th March 1838. Died at Aberdeen 25th Dec. 1845.

M'Dakin, S. Gordon, Lieut.—23d Oct. 1855, Ensign —Lieut. 24th May 1861—To 19th Foot 5th Nov. 1861—Half-pay 22d Dec. 1863.

Macdonald, Atholl Wentworth, Captain.—9th August 1843, Ensign. Retired Captain 6th Dec. 1844. Died in the Pavilion Floriana Malta, with the Regiment, 27th February 1845.

Macdonald, Charles Kerr, Brevet-Major.—15th May 1823, Ensign—Half-pay Captain, 7th Nov. 1826. Died at Alexandria in Egypt, 17th Oct. 1867.

M'Donald, Donald, Captain.—16th August 1803, Ensign—Half-pay 27th May 1819. Died at Musselburgh 24th Sept. 1865.

Macdonald, Sir John, Lieut.-General.—15th Jan. 1844, Colonel. Died in London 28th March 1850.

M'Donald, Ranald, Ensign.—10th August 1815— Half-pay 8th July 1819. Cashiered from 3d Foot 31st July 1828.

Macdonald, Robert Douglas, Captain.—11th July 1822, Ensign. Exchanged to 94th 15th June 1838. Died Barrack-Master at Dover, 9th Feb. 1860.

Macdougall, James, Lieut.-Colonel.—From H. P. 23d, 30th Dec. 1819, Lieut. Retired from Lieut.-Colonel Commanding the Reserve Battalion, 15th Feb. 1850.

M'Dougall, Kenneth, Lieut.—6th March 1809, Ensign. Retired 9th Nov. 1826. Died in the Island of Skye, 1827.

M'Dougall, William Adair, Paymaster—23d August 1838.—To Half-pay 1st Oct. 1838. Died at Guernsey 27th Jan. 1841.

M'Duff, John, Major-General.—7th April 1825, Ensign—from Half-pay; Lieut. 40th Regiment 26th June 1827—Major-General 23d Oct. 1863. Died at New-mills Stanley, Perthshire, 25th September 1865.

Macfarlane, Victor, Ensign.—2d October 1855.—Superseded for absence without leave, 29th July 1856.

Macfarlane, Wm. Dick (of Donavourd), Captain.— 10th Sept. 1825, Ensign—Half-pay Captain 16th Nov. 1832. Retired from 92d 15th Jan. 1836. Died at Perth 3d Feb. 1838.

M'Gregor, Alexander.—Joined the Regiment 13th March 1833.—Promoted to Quarter-Master from Quarter-Master Sergeant 25th May 1855—To a Depot Battalion, 30th August 1859—To Half-pay with rank of Captain, from 93th Regiment 1st August 1868.

M'Gregor, Alex. Edgar, Captain.—18th June 1852 Lieut. from 93d. Died Captain in the 31st at Hong-Kong, 12th August 1860.

M'Gregor, James (of Fonab), Dep. Inspector General. —12th April 1826, Assistant-Surgeon—To Staff Surgeon 1st class 12th March 1852—To Half-pay, 7th Dec. 1858.

M'Gregor, James, M.D.—12th March 1841, Assistant-Surgeon—To Staff 22d Nov. 1842.

M'Intosh, Daniel, Captain.—4th June 1815, Lieut. Retired 24th October 1821. Died at Hamilton 13th March 1830.

M'Intosh, Donald, Quarter-Master.— Joined the Regiment, not known—9th July 1803, Quarter-Master—Half-pay 30th Dec. 1818. Died at Perth 30th July 1829.

M'Intosh, William Henry.—27th Oct. 1846, Assistant-Surgeon.—Resigned 18th August 1848.

M'Iver, George, Captain.—31st March 1814, Ensign —To Half-pay 5th April 1839. Died July 1845.

M'Kay, Donald, Captain.—25th Jan. 1810, Ensign. Died at the Regimental Depot, Stirling, 13th Feb. 1832.

Mackie, Hugh, 7th August 1846, Surgeon.—To Staff 1st April 1850. Died at Halifax, Nova Scotia, 10th April 1858.

M'Kenzie, Donald, Captain.—23d July 1807, Lieut. Retired 19th Sept. 1821. Died in Edinburgh 5th Dec. 1860.

M'Kenzie, Thomas, Captain.—8th Feb. 1856, Ensign. Exchanged to 78th 23d Oct. 1857.

M'Kinnon, Wm. Alex., C. B., Surgeon-Major.—24th March 1854, Assistant-Surgeon from the Staff—To 57th Surgeon 28th Jan. 1862.

Maclachlan, James.—16th April 1842, Ensign. Resigned 24th May 1844.

M'Laine, Murdoch, Brevet-Major.—18th Jan. 1800, Ensign. Died 12th Dec. 1822.

M'Laren, Charles, Lieut.—2d June 1808, Lieut.— Half-pay 25th June 1817. Died in London 18th March 1818.

M'Lean, Alex., Surgeon.—7th Sept. 1854, Assistant-Surgeon—To Royal Artillery 8th Nov. 1861.

Macleod, Arthur Lyttleton, Captain.—12th Dec. 1822, Ensign—Half-pay Lieut. 9th June 1825. Retired from 86th 12th March 1841. Nothing more known of him.

M'Leod, John Chetham, C.B., Colonel.—21st April 1846, Ensign—now (1873) in command of the Regiment.

M'Leod, Murdoch, Captain.—20th Feb. 1855, Ensign —Captain 24th May 1861. Retired 17th August 1869.

Macleod, Swinton, Dep.-Inspec.-General.—25th June 1801, Assistant-Surgeon—Half-pay 5th Nov. 1829. Died in London 27th Dec. 1847.

Macnish, Wm. Lear, Lieut.—28th August 1846, Ensign—Exchanged to 93d, Lieut. 18th June 1852. Drowned at Scutari, Turkey, 19th May 1854.

Macpherson, Andrew Kennedy, Lieut.—19th Dec. 1865, Ensign—To 17th Foot 16th Feb. 1869. Lieut. Bengal Staff Corps 14th Dec. 1869.

Macpherson, Donald, Surgeon.—1st June 1809, Assistant-Surgeon—To half-pay from 62d 24th July 1835. Died at Chatham, 25th June 1829.

Macpherson, Duncan (Younger of Cluny), Major.— 25th June 1852, Ensign—Major 5th July 1865.

Macpherson, Ewen (of Cluny), 15th June 1830, Captain.—Half-pay 14th June 1833. Retired 16th July 1841.

Macpherson, John Cameron, Lieut.-Colonel.—10th September 1830, Ensign—To full-pay Major, with rank of Lieut.-Colonel 24th April 1855. Died at Stirling, 23d April 1873.

Macpherson, Mungo, Major.—4th Nov. 1800, Ensign—Half-pay Major 18th May 1826. Died at Hastings 26th Nov. 1844.

Macquarie, George W., Captain.—25th Sept., Ensign —Exchanged to 63d—Captain 21st Jan. 1853. Retired 7th Sept. 1855.

Maginn, Daniel Wedgworth, Assistant-Surgeon 27th Nov. 1828. Exchanged to Staff 15th Feb. 1833. Died at Chatham 20th March 1834.

Maitland, Charles.—12th Nov. 1847, Ensign. Died at Bermuda 21st April 1851.

Maitland, George Thomas, Lieut.—9th April 1861, Ensign—Lieut. 5th July 1865—To Bengal Staff Corps 2d March 1866.

Malcolm, John, Major.—19th Feb. 1807, Ensign. Died at Cork, returning home on sick leave from Gibraltar 14th Nov. 1829.

Malcolm, John, Ensign.—6th Jan. 1814, Ensign—To Half-pay 4th Nov. 1819. Died 8th Sept. 1835.

Menzies, Archd., Major.—25th September 1800, Ensign—Retired Major 25th Dec. 1828. Died at Avondale, near Falkirk, 11th July 1854.

Menzies, Gilbert Innes, Lieut.—18th April 1842, Ensign. Retired 20th May 1853.

Middleton, William, Lieut.-Colonel.—9th July 1803, Ensign. Retired from command of the Regiment 23d August 1839. Died at Woolwich 18th Feb. 1843.

Mitchel, James William.—5th March 1858, Lieut. from St Helena Regiment- To 17th Foot 19th July 1860. Retired 2d July 1861.

Montague, George, Brevet-Major.—5th April 1839.
—From H. P. 52d, 3d June 1842.
Montgomery, Thos. Henry (of Hattonburn), Captain.
—3d March 1847, Ensign. Retired 22d May 1847.
Moore, George T. Carus, Captain.—12th Dec. 1856,
Ensign—Captain 23d Nov. 1872.
Moseley, Herbert Henry, Captain.—3d June 1853,
Ensign—Retired 24th March 1863. Died at Cal-
cutta 19th May 1863.
Moubray, William Henry H. C., Lieut.—22d Oct.
1870, Ensign—Lieut. 28th Oct. 1871.
Muir, Sir Wm., K.C.B., M.D. and C.B.—22d Nov. 1842,
Assistant-Surgeon—Promoted Surgeon 33d Regi-
ment 24th Feb. 1854—Inspector-General 15th Feb.
1861.
Munro, George Montgomery, Sub-Lieut.—11th Dec.
1872.
Murray, Charles, Lieut.-Colonel.—21st June 1833,
Ensign—To Half-pay Major 12th Sept. 1856. Re-
tired 21st Sept. 1860 with rank of Lieut.-Colonel.
Murray, The Hon. David Henry, Brevet-Major.—6th
April 1828, Ensign—To Lieut. 7th Fusiliers 9th
Nov. 1830. Retired from Scots Fusilier Guards 4th
Feb. 1848. Died at Taymount, Perthshire, 5th
Sept. 1862.
Murray, Sir George, General.—6th Sept. 1823,
Colonel—Removed to the 1st Royal Scots 29th
Dec. 1843. Died in London 28th July 1846.
Murray, Henry Dundas.—30th Jan. 1835, Ensign.
Retired 17th Nov. 1837.
Murray, James Wolfe (of Cringletie).—25th Jan. 1853,
Ensign. Retired 24th June 1853.
Murray, Sir Robert, Bart.—15th Dec. 1837, Ensign.
Retired 2d August 1839.
Murray, Sir William Keith, Bart.—Captain 1st
Oct. 1825.—Half-pay 16th June 1830. Retired
16th March 1838. Died 16th Oct. 1861.
Nicholson, Brinsley, M.D., Dep.-Inspector-General.
—15th Nov. 1829, Surgeon—Staff-Surgeon to the
Forces 19th June 1835—Half-pay 30th Dec. 1845.
Died at Red Hill, Surrey, 15th March 1857.
Orde, John W. Powlett, Captain (yr. of Kilmory).—
6th Dec. 1844, Ensign. Retired 9th Jan. 1857.
Paterson, Augustus, Captain.—10th Jan. 1840, En-
sign—To 68th Captain on reduction 24th Sept. 1850.
Retired from 41st on the 24th Nov. 1854.
Paterson, James, M.D., Surgeon.—19th June 1835,
Surgeon—To Half-pay 26th Feb. 1841. Died in
Edinburgh 26th August 1866.
Paterson, James Erskine, Lieut. (now Erskine Erskine
of Linlathen).—3d Nov. 1846, Ensign. Retired
12th Oct. 1852.
Paton, Edward, Captain.—Joined the Regiment as
Armourer-Serjeant 24th August 1814.—Quarter-
Master-Serjeant 15th Nov. 1838—Quarter-Master
19th June 1840—To Half-pay 5th May 1854.
Died at Southsea, Portsmouth, 2d May 1863.
Peter, James John, Lieut.—16th April 1861, Ensign
from 5th foot—Lieut. 14th June 1864. Died in
India, 11th Nov. 1865.
Pitcairn, Andrew, Lieut.-Colonel.—15th May 1840,
Ensign—Exchanged Major to 26th, 17th July 1857
To Half-pay Lieut.-Colonel on reduction of a Depot
Battalion—1st April 1870. Retired 21st August
1871.
Priestly, Edward Ramsden, Colonel.—17th July 1857,
Major from 25th Regiment. Died in command of
the Regiment at Stirling, 25th March 1868.
Ramsay, Alexander, Captain.—16th May 1840, En-
sign—Exchanged to 68th Captain 27th Sept. 1853.
Retired 26th Jan. 1854.
Ramsay, Robert Williamson, Captain.—15th June
1832, Lieut. from 62d. Retired 16th Nov. 1841.
Raynes, Thomas, Captain.—2d Sept. 1824, Ensign.
Retired 30th Jan. 1835.

Robertson, George Duncan (of Struan), Lieut.—14th
June, 1833, Ensign. Retired 10th May 1840.
Died at Beachurch, Isle of Wight, 3d April 1864.
Robertson, James, Captain.—1st Dec. 1808, En-
sign—to Half-pay Captain 13th Feb. 1827. Died
in the 48th Regiment, at Chatham, 20th April
1833.
Robertson, Wm. James (younger of Kinlochmoidart),
Captain.—16th June 1848, Ensign—Exchanged
Lieut. to 30th Regiment. Retired 4th Dec. 1857.
Died at Kinlochmoidart, 26th June 1869.
Rollo, The Hon. Robert, C.B., Major-General.—10th
Aug. 1832, Ensign—To Half-pay Lieut.-Colonel
17th July 1855.
Rose, Eustace, Henry.—21st Jan. 1833, Captain from
60th Rifles—Exchanged to 71st Fusiliers 27th May
1853. Retired 3d June 1856.
Ross, Gilian M'Lean, Brevet-Major.—17th Nov. 1841
—Lieut. from 57th—To Half-pay as Captain 4th
Sept. 1849—To 3d W. I. Regiment—and To Half-
pay from it 6th March 1863. Died in London
23d May 1866.
Ross, James Kerr, Lieut.-General.—31st May 1821,
Captain—Half-pay 27th Dec. 1827. Died at Edin-
burgh, 26th April 1872.
St John, George Frederick Berkeley, Major.—25th
Nov. 1819, Lieut.—To Half-pay Captain 25th Oct.
1821—To H. P. Major from the 52d, 31st May 1839.
Died a Knight of Windsor, 23d July 1866.
Samwell, Frank, Captain.—Paymaster from Half-pay
102d 15th Dec. 1869.
Sandeman, Thos. Fraser, Captain.—24th Dec. 1848,
Ensign—Half-pay Lieut. 10th Aug. 1832. Retired
from 73d Captain 31st May 1844.
Sandilands, E. Nimmo, Lieut.-Colonel.—21st May
1842, Ensign—Promoted to Lieut. 8th Foot 3d
April 1846—Lieut.-Colonel Bengal Staff Corps.
Scobie, Mackay John, Lieut.—12th Jan. 1867, En-
sign—Lieut. 28th Oct. 1871.
Scott, Francis Cunningham (younger of Malleny),
Major.—24th Nov. 1852, Ensign—Major 26th
March 1868.
Scott, James Rattray, Lieut.—4th July 1819, Ensign
—To 47th 11th July 1822. Resigned 6th Dec.
1826.
Shuttleworth, Charles, Captain.—23d April 1855,
Ensign—To Bengal Staff Corps, Lieut. 27th Oct.
1865—Captain 23d April 1867.
Simpson, John, V.C.—Joined the Regiment 8th
June 1843—From Quarter-Master Sergeant pro-
moted to Quarter-Master 7th Oct. 1859.
Sinclair, Robert Bligh, Captain.—27th Sept. 1839,
Ensign.—To Half-pay Captain on reduction 15th
Nov. 1850. Retired from 66th Captain 3d Nov.
1854—Was Adjutant-General of Militia for Nova
Scotia, and went to the Danish Island of Santa
Cruz for the benefit of his health, where he died on
the 28th of June 1872.
Spens, Colin, Lieut.—2d Dec. 1862, Ensign—Lieut.
2d March 1866. Died in India 22d June 1867.
Spooner, Wm. Henry, Lieut.—9th Oct. 1855, Ensign
—To 9th Foot Lieut. 16th April 1861—To 90th
11th April 1862—Half-pay 27th Feb. 1867. Died
at Bingen on the Rhine, 29th Nov. 1870.
Stevenson, A. Scott, Lieut.—17th March 1869, En-
sign—Lieut. 28th Oct. 1871.
Stevenson, George Milne, Lieut.-Colonel.—10th Sept.
1818, Lieut.—To Half-pay Captain 19th June 1840
—To H. P. Lieut.-Colonel from Rifle Brigade 19th
June 1846. Retired 7th August 1846. Nothing
more known of him.
Stewart, Andrew David Alston, Captain.—26th Sept.
1851, Ensign—Exchanged to 6th Foot Lieut. 1st
Sept 1857. Died in India, Captain 61st, 18th May
1848.

Stewart, Charles Edward, Ensign.—8th June 1826, Ensign. Died at Gibraltar, 3d Nov. 1828.

Stewart, The Hon. Randolph Henry. Captain.—2d March 1855, Ensign—Captain 14th June 1864.—To Half-pay 23d March 1867.

Stewart, John, Assistant-Surgeon.—4th May 1809.—To Half-pay 25th Dec. 1818. Died at Perth, 2d Jan. 1837.

Stewart, Roger, Captain.—28th June 1810, Ensign—To Half-pay Captain 13th Feb. 1827. Died in the Royal African Corps, on the West Coast, 15th July 1833.

Stirling, James, Captain.—13th August 1805, Ensign. Retired 25th Sept. 1817. Died at Musselburgh 20th Jan. 1818.

Stirling, Thos. Jas. Graham (of Strowan), Lieut.—8th Nov. 1827, Ensign. Retired 15th Dec. 1837.

Strange, Alex., Lieut.—8th Feb. 1809, Ensign. Died 15th May 1823.

Stuart, J. G. Gordon, Lieut.—1st June 1855, Ensign—Lieut. 1st May 1857—Exchanged to St Helena Regiment 5th March 1858. Retired 23d Sept. 1862.

[2] Stuart, John Patrick, Brevet-Major.—Joined the Regiment 18th May 1825—Promoted from Colour-Serjeant to 2d Lieut. in the 21st Fusiliers, 30th Dec. 1838—To Staff-Officer of Pensioners, 1st Jan. 1855, from 43d Light Infantry.

Suther, William King, Lieut.—13th Feb. 1866, Ensign from 99th—Lieut. 18th August 1869.

Thompson, William Kerr, Lieut.—7th April 1825, Ensign from Half-pay, Lieut. 26th Regiment, 26th April 1823. Died on Half-pay 27th May 1833.

Thompson, William Thomas, Captain from 83d, 28th Jan. 1870. Retired 19th Oct. 1872.

Thornhill, T. Allen, M.B.—24th July 1867, Assistant-Surgeon to 7th Hussars 25th March 1859.

Thorold, George Edward, Colonel.—28th July 1857, Lieut.-Colonel from H. P. 92d. Retired on Full-pay, with rank of Colonel, 16th March 1858.

Tinnie, William Thomas, Captain.—26th June 1827, Ensign—To 86th Lieut. 20th Dec. 1827. Retired Captain from 8th Hussars 15th Nov. 1839. Died 21st March 1848.

Troup, Robert William, M.B.—1st Sept. 1865, Assistant-Surgeon from the Staff.

Tulloch, Thomas, Colonel.—15th June 1838, Captain from 94th—To Half-pay Lieut.-Colonel 9th Oct. 1855. Retired with the rank of Colonel 21st Oct. 1859. Died in London 3d Jan. 1866.

Tulloch, James Tulloch, M.D., Assistant-Surgeon.—2d July 1861, from Rifle Brigade. Died in India 16th July 1867.

Underwood, William, Captain.—5th June 1855, Ensign—Captain 11th Jan. 1867. Retired 12th Feb. 1873.

Wade, Thos. Francis, Colonel.—13th July 1809, Captain from 20th—Half-pay Major 4th May 1826. Died at Haverford West, 3d Dec. 1846.

Never served in the Regiment as an Officer.

Wade, Thomas Francis (son of the Colonel), Lieut.—23d August 1839, Ensign—Promoted in 98th, Lieut. 16 Nov. 1841. Retired 22d June 1847. Now British Minister at Pekin.

Walter, William Sanders, Captain.—25th Jan. 1856, Ensign—Captain 23d March 1867. Retired 23d Nov. 1872.

Ward, William Crofton, Captain.—18th August 1848, Ensign—Retired 24th May 1861.

Wardell, Charles, Paymaster.—22d Feb. 1821.—Half-pay 25th Jan. 1828. Died 29th July 1862.

Warner, Chas. W. Pole.—28th Dec. 1860, Ensign from 43d. Resigned 16th April 1861.

Warraud, Arthur Wellesley, Lieut. 24th March 1863, Ensign—Lieut. 10th July 1866. Retired 21st Oct. 1870. Died at Cape of Good Hope 1st June 1871.

Wauchope, Andrew Gilbert, Lieut. and Adjutant.—21st Nov. 1865, Ensign—Lieut. 23d June 1867—Adjutant 5th April 1870.

Webber, W. G. Everard, Captain.—23d Nov. 1852, Ensign. Died in India, 9th July 1866.

Wedderburn, John Walter, Lieut.-Colonel.—26th Oct. 1841, Ensign. Retired Captain 12th May 1854—Major, Royal Perth Rifles, 5th Nov. 1855. Retired with rank of Lieut.-Colonel 10th Dec. 1869.

Wheatley, John, Lieut.-Colonel.—Joined the Regiment 1st May 1817—Ensign and Adjutant from Acting Serjeant-Major 20th July 1832—To a Depot Battalion, 26th Jan. 1855. Retired on Half-pay 27th June 1866.

Whigham, Robert, Major.—6th June 1854, Ensign To Half-pay Captain on reduction 1st Jan. 1857—7th Fusiliers 31st Dec. 1857—16th Lancers 9th Oct. 1863.

Whitehead, Edmund, Captain.—22d May 1857, Ensign.—Captain 17th August 1869.

Whitehead, Frederick G. I.—27th May 1853, Captain from 7th Fusiliers. Retired 27th July 1854.

Wilkes, Edwin.—10th July 1860, Assistant-Surgeon from Staff—To Staff Corps in India, 8th Aug. 1862.

Wilkinson, Frederick Green, Colonel.—28th Nov. 1851, Captain from 43d—Lieut.-Colonel, exchanged to a Depot Battalion 27th Sept. 1861.

Wilson, John, Bt.-Major.—Joined the Regiment 22d Oct. 1844—Promoted Ensign from Sergeant-Major 10th August 1854—Captain 16th March 1858—Bt.-Major 5th July 1872.

Wood, John Gillespie, M.D.—12th March 1852, Surgeon—To Staff Surgeon-Major 9th Feb. 1855—To Half-pay Dep.-Inspec.-General, 8th June 1867.

Wood, William, Major—Joined the Regiment 27th July 1843—Promoted to Quarter-Master from Sergeant-Major, 5th May 1854—Adjutant 16th Feb. 1855—To Half-pay Captain 17th March 1863—Major 1st April 1870.

Young, James, Lieut.—22d Oct. 1805, Ensign—Half-pay 25th Nov. 1819. Died in Edinburgh, 15th June 1846

HIGHLAND PIBROCH:

Composed by one of the MacCrummens in the midst of the Battle of Inverlochy, 1427, wherein
Donald Balloch of the Isles was victorious over the Royal Forces.

ARRANGED FOR THE BAGPIPES.

VARIATION 1st.
Slow.

VARIATION 2nd. *Slow and pointed.*

VARIATION 3rd. *A little lively.*

DOUBLING OF VARIATION 3rd.

VARIATION 4th. *Livelier.*

Doubling of VARIATION 4th.
Lively.

Trebling of VARIATION 4th.
Livelier still.

CREANLUIDH, OR ROUND MOVEMENT.
Brisk.

Doubling of CREANLUIDH.
Very brisk.

Trebling of CREANLUIDH.

As lively as can be played distinctly.

The ground of this Piobaireachd may be played after the Doubling of each VARIATION.

NOTE.—This HIGHLAND PIBROCH was played by the 42nd Royal Highlanders while marching to Quatre Bras.   See page

LOUDON'S HIGHLANDERS.

1745—1748.

Raising of Regiment—Rebellion of 1745—Flanders—
Bergen-op-Zoom——Reduction of Regiment.

THE bravery displayed by Lord John Murray's
Highlanders at Fontenoy opened the eyes of
Government to the importance of securing the
military services of the clans. It was therefore
determined to repair, in part, the loss sustained
in that well-fought action, by raising a second
regiment in the Highlands, and authority to
that effect was granted to the Earl of Loudon.
By the influence of the noblemen, chiefs, and
gentlemen of the country, whose sons and
connexions were to be appointed officers, a
body of 1250 men was raised, of whom 750
assembled at Inverness, and the remainder at
Perth. The whole were formed into a battalion
of twelve companies, under the following
officers, their commissions being dated June 8th
1745 :—

Colonel.—John Campbell, Earl of Loudon, who
died in 1782, a general in the army.
Lieutenant-Colonel.—John Campbell (afterwards
Duke of Argyll), who died a field-marshal in 1806

Captains.

John Murray (afterwards Duke of Athole), son of
Lord George Murray.
Alexander Livingstone Campbell, son of Ardkinglass.
John Macleod, younger of Macleod.
Henry Munro, son of Colonel Sir Robert Munro of
Fowlis.
Lord Charles Gordon, brother of the Duke of Gordon.
John Stewart, son of the Earl of Moray.
Alexander Mackay, son of Lord Reay
Ewen Macpherson of Clunie.
John Sutherland of Forse.
Colin Campbell of Ballimore, killed at Culloden.
Archibald Macnab, who died a lieutenant-general in
1791, son of the laird of Macnab.

Lieutenants.

Colin Campbell of Kilberrie.
Alexander Maclean.
John Campbell of Strachur, who died in 1806, a
general in the army, and colonel of the 57th regi-
ment.
Duncan Robertson of Drumachuine, afterwards of
Strowan.
Patrick Campbell, son of Achallader.
Donald Macdonald.
James Macpherson of Killihuntly.
John Robertson or Reid, of Straloch, who died in
1806, at the age of eighty-five, a general in the
army, and colonel of the 88th or Connaught
Rangers.[1]
Patrick Grant, younger of Rothiemurchus.
John Campbell of Ardeliginish.

[1] For details as to General Reid, see account of
Clan Robertson and the 42d Regiment.

Alexander Campbell, brother to Barcaldine.
Donald Macdonell of Lochgarry.
Colin Campbell of Glenure.

Ensigns.

James Stewart of Urrard.
John Martin of Inch.
George Munroe of Novar.
Malcolm Ross, younger of Pitcalnie.
Hugh Mackay.
James Fraser.
David Spalding of Ashintully.
Archibald Campbell.
Donald Macneil.
Alexander Maclagan, son of the minister of Little
Dunkeld.
Robert Bisset of Glenelbert, afterwards commissary-
general of Great Britain.
John Grant, younger of Dalrachnie.

Before the regiment was disciplined, the
rebellion broke out, and so rapid were the
movements of the rebels, that the communication between the two divisions, at Perth and
Inverness, was cut off. They were therefore
obliged to act separately. The formation of
the regiment at the time was considered a
fortunate circumstance, as many of the men
would certainly have joined in the insurrection;
and indeed several of the officers and men went
over to the rebels. Four companies were
employed in the central and southern Highlands, whilst the rest were occupied in the
northern Highlands, under Lord Loudon.
Three companies under the Hon. Captains
Stewart and Mackay, and Captain Munro of
Fowlis, were, with all their officers, taken
prisoners at the battle of Gladsmuir. Three
other companies were also at the battle of
Culloden, where Captain Campbell and six
men were killed and two soldiers wounded.

On the 30th of May 1747, the regiment
embarked at Burntisland for Flanders, but it
did not join the Duke of Cumberland's army
till after the battle of Lafeldt, on the 2d of
July. Though disappointed of the opportunity
which this battle would have given them of
distinguishing themselves, another soon offered
for the display of their gallantry. Marshal
Saxe having determined to attack the strong
fortress of Bergen-op-Zoom, with an army of
25,000 men under General Count Lowendahl,
all the disposable forces in Brabant, including
Loudon's Highlanders, were sent to defend
the lines, which were strongly fortified. To
relieve the garrison, consisting of six battalions,
and to preserve a communication with the

country, eighteen battalions occupied the lines. The fortress, which was considered impregnable, was defended by 250 pieces of cannon. The siege was carried on unremittingly from the 15th of July till the 17th of September, during which time many sorties were made. In the *Hague Gazette*, an account is given of one of these, which took place on the 25th of July, in which it is stated " that the Highlanders, who were posted in Fort Rouro, which covers the lines of Bergen-op-Zoom, made a sally, sword in hand, in which they were so successful as to destroy the enemy's grand battery, and to kill so many of their men, that Count Lowendahl beat a parley, in order to bury the dead. To this it was answered, that had he attacked the place agreeably to the rules of war, his demand would certainly have been granted; but as he had begun the siege like an incendiary, by setting fire to the city with red-hot balls, a resolution had been taken neither to ask or grant any suspension of arms."

Having made breaches in a ravelin and two bastions, the besiegers made an unexpected assault on the night of the 16th of September, and throwing themselves into the fosse, mounted the breaches, forced open a sally port, and, entering the place, ranged themselves along the ramparts, almost before the garrison had assembled. Cronstrun, the old governor, and many of his officers, were asleep, and so sudden and unexpected was the attack, that several of them flew to the ranks in their shirts. Though the possession of the ramparts sealed the fate of the town, the Scottish troops were not disposed to surrender it without a struggle. The French were opposed by two regiments of the Scotch brigade, in the pay of the States-general, who, by their firmness, checked the progress of the enemy, and enabled the governor and garrison to recover from their surprise. The Scotch assembled in the market-place, and attacked the French with such vigour that they drove them from street to street, till, fresh reinforcements pouring in, they were compelled to retreat in their turn,—disputing every inch as they retired, and fighting till two-thirds of their number fell on the spot, killed or severely wounded,—when the remainder brought off the old governor and joined the troops in the lines.

The troops in the lines, most unaccountably, retreated immediately, and the enemy thus became masters of the whole navigation of the Scheldt. "Two battalions," says an account of the assault published in the *Hague Gazette*, "of the Scotch brigade have, as usual, done honour to their country,—which is all we have to comfort us for the loss of such brave men, who, from 1450, are now reduced to 330 men —and those have valiantly brought their colours with them, which the grenadiers twice recovered from the midst of the French at the point of the bayonet. The Swiss have also suffered, while others took a more *speedy way to escape* danger." In a history of this memorable siege the brave conduct of the Scotch is also thus noticed: "It appears that more than 300 of the Scotch brigade fought their way through the enemy, and that they have had 19 officers killed and 18 wounded. Lieutenants Francis and Allan Maclean of the brigade were taken prisoners, and carried before General Lowendahl, who thus addressed them: ' Gentlemen, consider yourselves on parole. If all had conducted themselves as you and your brave corps have done, I should not now be master of Bergen-op-Zoom.' " [2]

The loss of a fortress hitherto deemed impregnable was deeply felt by the allies. The eyes of all Europe had been fixed upon this important siege, and when the place fell strong suspicions were entertained of treachery in the garrison. Every thing had been done by the people of the United Provinces to enable the soldiers to hold out: they were allowed additional provisions of the best quality; and cordials were furnished for the sick and dying. Large sums of money were collected to be presented to the soldiers, if they made a brave defence; and £17,000 were collected in one

[2] Lieutenant Allan Maclean was son of Maclean of Torloisk. He left the Dutch and entered the British service. He was a captain in Montgomery's Highlanders in 1757; raised the 114th Highland regiment in 1759; and, in 1775, raised a battalion of the 84th, a Highland Emigrant regiment; and, by his unwearied zeal and abilities, was the principal cause of the defeat of the Americans at the attack on Quebec in 1775-6. Lieutenant Francis Maclean also entered the British service, and rose to the rank of Major-general. In the year 1777 he was appointed colonel of the 82d regiment, and, in 1779 commanded an expedition to the Penobscot in Nova Scotia, in which he succeeded.——*Stewart's Sketches.*

day in Amsterdam, to be applied in the same way, if the soldiers compelled the enemy to raise the siege. Every soldier who carried away a gabion from the enemy was paid a crown, and such was the activity of the Scotch, that some of them gained ten crowns a-day in this kind of service. Those who ventured to take the burning fuse out of the bombs of the enemy (and there were several who did so), received ten or twelve ducats. In this remarkable siege the French sustained an enormous loss, exceeding 22,000 men; that of the garrison did not exceed 4000.[3]

After the loss of Bergen-op-Zoom, Loudon's Highlanders joined the Duke of Cumberland's army, and at the peace of 1748 returned to Scotland, and was reduced at Perth in June of the same year.

MONTGOMERY'S HIGHLANDERS,
OR
SEVENTY-SEVENTH REGIMENT.
1757—1763.

Lord Chatham and the Highlanders—Raising of the Regiment—America—Fort du Quèsne—Ticonderoga—Cherokees—Dominique—West Indies—Newfoundland—Fort Pitt.

WE have already quoted 'Lord Chatham's eloquent statement with regard to the Highland Regiments, in his celebrated speech on the differences with America in 1766. The only way by which the Highlanders could be gained over was by adopting a liberal course of policy, the leading features of which should embrace the employment of the chiefs, or their connections, in the military service of the government. It was reserved to the sagacity of Chatham to trace to its source the cause of the disaffection of the Highlanders, and, by suggesting a remedy, to give to their military virtue a safe direction.

Acting upon the liberal plan he had devised, Lord Chatham (then Mr Pitt), in the year 1757 recommended to his Majesty George II. to employ the Highlanders in his service, as the best means of attaching them to his person. The king approved of the plan of the minister, and letters of service were immediately issued for raising several Highland regiments. This call to arms was responded to by the clans, and "battalions on battalions," to borrow the words of an anonymous author, "were raised in the remotest part of the Highlands, among those who a few years before were devoted to, and too long had followed the fate of the race of Stuarts. Frasers, Macdonalds, Camerons, Macleans, Macphersons, and others of disaffected names and clans, were enrolled; their chiefs or connections obtained commissions; the lower class, always ready to follow, with eagerness endeavoured who should be first listed."

This regiment was called Montgomerie's Highlanders, from the name of its colonel, the Hon. Archibald Montgomerie, son of the Earl of Eglinton, to whom, when major, letters of service were issued for recruiting it. Being popular among the Highlanders, Major Montgomerie soon raised the requisite body of men, who were formed into a regiment of thirteen companies of 105 rank and file each; making in all 1460 effective men, including 65 sergeants, and 30 pipers and drummers.

The colonel's commission was dated the 4th of January 1757. The commissions of the

[3] The following anecdote of faithful attachment is told by Mrs Grant, in her *Superstitions of the Highlanders*. Captain Fraser of Culduthel, an officer of the Black Watch, was a volunteer at this celebrated siege, as was likewise his colonel, Lord John Murray. Captain Fraser was accompanied by his servant, who was also his foster-brother. A party from the lines was ordered to attack and destroy a battery raised by the enemy. Captain Fraser accompanied this party, directing his servant to remain in the garrison. "The night was pitch dark, and the party had such difficulty in proceeding that they were forced to halt for a short time. As they moved forward Captain Fraser felt his path impeded, and putting down his hand to discover the cause, he caught hold of a plaid, and seized the owner, who seemed to grovel on the ground. He held the caitiff with one hand, and drew his dirk with the other, when he heard the imploring voice of his foster-brother. 'What the devil brought you here?' 'Just love of you and care of your person.' 'Why so, when your love can do me no good; and why encumber yourself with a plaid?' 'Alas! how could I ever see my mother had you been killed or wounded, and I not been there to carry you to the surgeon, or to Christian burial? and how could I do either without any plaid to wrap you in?' Upon inquiry it was found that the poor man had crawled out on his knees and hands between the sentinels, then follow the party to the

distance, till he thought they were approaching the place of assault, and then again crept in the same manner on the ground, beside his master, that he might be near him unobserved."

Captain Fraser was unfortunately killed a few days thereafter, by a random shot, while looking over the ramparts.

[4] Vol. ii. p 343.

other officers were dated each a day later than his senior in the same rank.

Lieutenant-Colonel Commanding.

The Hon. Archibald Montgomerie, afterwards Earl of Eglinton, died a general in the army, and colonel of the Scots Greys, in 1796.

Majors.

James Grant of Ballindalloch, died a general in the army in 1806.
Alexander Campbell.

Captains.

John Sinclair.
Hugh Mackenzie.
John Gordon.
Alexander Mackenzie, killed at St John's, 1761.
William Macdonald, killed at Fort du Quèsne, 1759.
George Munro, killed at Fort du Quèsne, 1759.
Robert Mackenzie.
Allan Maclean, from the Dutch brigade, colonel of the 84th Highland Emigrants; died Major-general, 1784.
James Robertson.
Allan Cameron.
Captain-lieutenant Alexander Mackintosh.

Lieutenants.

Charles Farquharson.
Alexander Mackenzie, killed at Fort du Quèsne, 1759.
Nichol Sutherland, died Lieutenant-colonel of the 47th regiment, 1780.
Donald Macdonald.
William Mackenzie, killed at Fort du Quèsne.
Robert Mackenzie, killed at Fort du Quèsne.
Henry Munro.
Archibald Robertson.
Duncan Bayne.
James Duff.
Colin Campbell, killed at Fort du Quèsne, 1759.
James Grant.
Alexander Macdonald.
Joseph Grant.
Robert Grant.
Cosmo Martin.
John Macnab.
Hugh Gordon, killed in Martinique, 1762.
Alexander Macdonald, killed at Fort du Quèsne.
Donald Campbell.
Hugh Montgomerie, late Earl of Eglinton.
James Maclean, killed in the West Indies, 1761.
Alexander Campbell.
John Campbell of Melford.
James Macpherson.
Archibald Macvicar, killed at the Havannah, 1762.

Ensigns.

Alexander Grant.	William Maclean.
William Haggart.	James Grant.
Lewis Houston.	John Macdonald.
Ronald Mackinnon.	Archibald Crawford.
George Munro.	James Bain.
Alexander Mackenzie.	Allan Stewart.
John Maclachlane.	

Chaplain.——Henry Munro.
Adjutant.——Donald Stewart.
Quarter-master.——Alex. Montgomerie.
Surgeon.——Allan Stewart.

The regiment embarked at Greenock for Halifax, and on the commencement of hostilities in 1758 was attached to the corps under Brigadier-general Forbes in the expedition against Fort du Quèsne, one of the three great enterprises undertaken that year against the French possessions in North America. Although the point of attack was not so formidable, nor the number of the enemy so great, as in the cases of Ticonderoga and Crown Point; yet the great extent of country which the troops had to traverse covered with woods, morasses, and mountains, made the expedition as difficult as the other two. The army of General Forbes was 6238 men strong.

The brigadier reached Raystown, about 90 miles from the Fort, in September, having apparently stayed some time in Philadelphia.[5] Having sent Colonel Boquet forward to Loyal Henning, 40 miles nearer, with 2000 men, this officer rashly despatched Major Grant of Montgomery's with 400 Highlanders and 500 provincials to reconnoitre. When near the garrison Major Grant imprudently advanced with pipes playing and drums beating, as if entering a friendly town. The enemy instantly marched out, and a warm contest took place. Major Grant ordered his men to throw off their coats and advance sword in hand. The enemy fled on the first charge, and spread themselves among the woods; but being afterwards joined by a body of Indians, they rallied and surrounded the detachment on all sides. Protected by a thick foliage, they opened a destructive fire upon the British. Major Grant then endeavoured to force his way into the wood, but was taken in the attempt, on seeing which his troops dispersed. Only 150 of the Highlanders returned to Loyal Henning.

In this unfortunate affair 231 soldiers of the regiment were killed and wounded. The names of the officers killed on this occasion have already been mentioned; the following were wounded: viz. Captain Hugh Mackenzie; Lieutenants Alexander Macdonald, junior, Archibald Robertson, Henry Munro; and Ensigns John Macdonald and Alexander Grant. The enemy did not venture to oppose the main body, but retired from Fort du Quèsne on its approach, leaving their ammunition, stores, and provisions untouched. General Forbes took possession of the Fort on the 24th of November, and, in honour of Mr Pitt, gave it the name of Pittsburgh.

⁵ vol. ii. p. 153, 154

VIEW OF THE CITY OF PHILADELPHIA

AS IN 1758 A.D.,

TAKEN FROM THE JERSEY SIDE OF THE DELAWARE,

1. Christ Church.
2. State House
3. Academy.
4. Wesleyan Church.
5. Dutch Calvinist Church.
6. The Court House.
7. Corn Mill.
8. Quaker Meeting House

From a rare print, the drawing of which was made under the direction of Nicholas Scull, Surveyor-General of Pennsylvania

The regiment passed the winter of 1758 in Pittsburgh, and in May following they joined part of the army under General Amherst in his proceedings at Ticonderoga, Crown Point, and the Lakes,—a detail of which has been given in the history of the service of the 42d regiment.

In consequence of the renewed cruelties committed by the Cherokees, in the spring of 1760, the commander-in-chief detached Colonel Montgomery with 700 Highlanders of his own regiment, 400 of the Royals, and a body of provincials, to chastise these savages. The colonel arrived in the neighbourhood of the Indian town Little Keowee in the middle of June, having, on his route, detached the light companies of Royals and Highlanders to destroy the place. This service was performed with the loss of a few men killed and two officers of the Royals wounded. Finding, on reaching Estatoe, that the enemy had fled, Colonel Montgomery retired to Fort Prince George. The Cherokees still proving refractory, he paid a second visit to the middle settlement, where he met with some resistance. He had 2 officers and 20 men killed, and 26 officers and 68 men wounded.[*] Of these, the Highlanders had 1 ser-

[*] "Several soldiers of this and other regiments fell into the hands of the Indians, being taken in an ambush. Allan Macpherson, one of these soldiers, witnessing the miserable fate of several of his fellow-prisoners, who had been tortured to death by the Indians, and seeing them preparing to commence some operations upon himself, made signs that he had something to communicate. An interpreter was brought. Macpherson told them, that, provided his life was spared for a few minutes, he would communicate the secret of an extraordinary medicine, which, if applied to the skin, would cause it to resist the strongest blow of a tomahawk or sword; and that, if they would allow him to go to the woods with a guard to collect the proper plants for this medicine, he would prepare it, and allow the experiment to be tried on his own neck by the strongest and most expert warrior amongst them. This story easily gained upon the superstitious credulity of the Indians, and the request of the Highlander was instantly complied with. Being sent into the woods, he soon returned with such plants as he chose to pick up. Having boiled the herbs, he rubbed his neck with their juice, and laying his head upon a log of wood, desired the strongest man amongst them to strike at his neck with his tomahawk, when he would find he could not make the smallest impression. An Indian, levelling a blow with all his might, cut with such force, that the head flew off at the distance of several yards. The Indians were fixed in amazement at their own credulity, and the address with which the prisoner had escaped the lingering death prepared for him; but, instead of being enraged at this escape of their victim, they were so pleased with his ingenuity that they refrained from inflicting farther cruelties on the remaining pri..." Stew..t's Ske...

geant and 6 privates killed, and Captain Sutherland, Lieutenants Macmaster and Mackinnon, and Assistant-surgeon Monro, and 1 sergeant, 1 piper, and 24 rank and file wounded. The detachment took Fort Loudon, —a small fort on the confines of Virginia,— which was defended by 200 men.

The next service in which Montgomery's Highlanders were employed was in an expedition against Dominique, consisting of a small land force, which included six companies of Montgomery's Highlanders and four ships of war, under Colonel Lord Rollo and Commodore Sir James Douglas. The transports from New York were scattered in a gale of wind, when a small transport, with a company of the Highlanders on board, being attacked by a French privateer, was beaten off by the Highlanders, with the loss of Lieutenant Maclean and 6 men killed, and Captain Robertson and 11 men wounded. The expedition arrived off Dominique on the 6th of June 1761. The troops immediately landed, and marched with little opposition to the town of Roseau. Lord Rollo without delay attacked the entrenchments, and, though the enemy kept up a galling fire, they were driven, in succession, from all their works by the grenadiers, light infantry, and Highlanders. This service was executed with such vigour and rapidity that few of the British suffered. The governor and his staff being made prisoners, surrendered the island without further opposition.

In the following year Montgomery's Highlanders joined the expeditions against Martinique and the Havannah, of which an account will be found in the narrative of the service of the 42d regiment. In the enterprise against Martinique, Lieutenant Hugh Gordon and 4 rank and file were killed, and Captain Alexander Mackenzie, 1 sergeant, and 26 rank and file file, were wounded. Montgomery's Highlanders suffered still less in the conquest of the Havannah, Lieutenant Macvicar and 2 privates only having been killed, and 6 privates wounded. Lieutenants Grant and Macnab and 6 privates died of the fever. After this last enterprise Montgomery's Highlanders returned to New York, where they landed in the end of October.

Before the return of the six companies to

New York, the two companies that had been sent against the Indians in the autumn of 1716, had embarked with a small force, under Colonel Amherst, destined to retake St John's, Newfoundland, which was occupied by a French force. The British force, which consisted of the flank companies of the Royals, a detachment of the 45th, two companies of Fraser's and Montgomery's Highlanders, and a small party of provincials, landed on the 12th of September, seven miles to the northward of St John's. A mortar battery having been completed on the 17th, and ready to open on the garrison, the French commander surrendered by capitulation to an inferior force. Of Montgomery's Highlanders, Captain Mackenzie and 4 privates were killed, and 2 privates wounded.

After this service the two companies joined the regiment at New York, where they passed the ensuing winter. In the summer of 1763 a detachment accompanied the expedition sent to the relief of Fort Pitt under Colonel Bouquet, the details of which have been already given in the account of the 42d regiment. In this enterprise 1 drummer and 5 privates of Montgomery's Highlanders were killed, and Lieutenant Donald Campbell, and Volunteer John Peebles, 3 sergeants, and 7 privates were wounded.

After the termination of hostilities an offer was made to the officers and men either to settle in America or return to their own country. Those who remained obtained a grant of land in proportion to their rank. On the breaking out of the American war a number of these, as well as officers and men of the 78th regiment, joined the royal standard in 1775, and formed a corps along with the Highland Emigrants in the 84th regiment.

FRASER'S HIGHLANDERS,
OR
OLD SEVENTY-EIGHTH AND SEVENTY-FIRST REGIMENTS.

I.
78TH REGIMENT.
1757—1763.

Raising of the Regiment——Uniform——North America—— Louisburg——Quebec——General Wolfe——Newfoundland——Reduction of the Regiment——Its descendants.

FOLLOWING up the liberal policy which Lord

Chatham had resolved to pursue in relation to the Highlanders, he prevailed upon George II. to appoint the Hon. Simon Fraser, son of the unfortunate Lord Lovat, and who had himself, when a youth, been forced into the rebellion by his father, Lieutenant-colonel commandant of a regiment to be raised among his own kinsmen and clan. Though not possessed of an inch of land, yet, such was the influence of clanship, that young Lovat in a few weeks raised a corps of 800 men, to whom were added upwards of 600 more by the gentlemen of the country and those who had obtained commission. The battalion was, in point of the number of companies and men, precisely the same as Montgomery's Highlanders.

The following is a list of the officers whose commissions were dated the 5th January 1757 :——

Lieutenant-Colonel Commandant.
The Hon. Simon Fraser, died a Lieutenant-general in 1782.

Majors.
James Clephane.
John Campbell of Duneon, afterwards Lieutenant-colonel commandant of the Campbell Highlanders in Germany.

Captains.
John Macpherson, brother of Cluny.
John Campbell of Ballimore.
Simon Fraser of Inverallochy, killed on the heights of Abraham, 1759.
Donald Macdonald, brother to Clanranald, killed at Quebec in 1760.
John Macdonell of Lochgarry, afterwards colonel of the 76th, or Macdonald's regiment, died in 1789 colonel.
Alexander Cameron of Dungallon.
Thomas Ross of Culrossie, killed on the heights of Abraham, 1759.
Thomas Fraser of Strui.
Alexander Fraser of Culduthel.
Sir Henry Seton of Abercorn and Culbeg.
James Fraser of Belladrum.
Captain-Lieutenant——Simon Fraser, died Lieutenant-general in 1812.

Lieutenants,
Alexander Macleod.
Hugh Cameron.
Ronald Macdonell, son of Keppoch.
Charles Macdonell from Glengarry, killed at St John's.
Roderick Macneil of Barra, killed on the heights of Abraham, 1759.
William Macdonell.
Archibald Campbell, son of Glenlyon.
John Fraser of Balnain.
Hector Macdonald, brother to Boisdale, killed 1759.
Allan Stewart, son of Innernaheil.
John Fraser.
Alexander Macdonald, son of Barisdale, killed on the heights of Abraham, 1759.
Alexander Fraser, killed at Louisburg.
Alexander Campbell of Aross.
John Douglas.

II.   3 M

John Nairn.
Arthur Rose, of the family of Kilravock.
Alexander Fraser.
John Macdonell of Leeks, died in Berwick, 1818.
Cosmo Gordon, killed at Quebec, 1760.
David Baillie, killed at Louisburg.
Charles Stewart, son of Colonel John Roy Stewart.
Ewen Cameron, of the family of Glennevis.
Allan Cameron.
John Cuthbert, killed at Louisburg.
Simon Fraser.
Archibald Macallister, of the family of Loup.
James Murray, killed at Louisburg.
Alexander Fraser.
Donald Cameron, son of Fassifern, died Lieutenant on
    half-pay, 1817.

Ensigns.

John Chisolm.
Simon Fraser.
Malcolm Fraser, afterwards captain 84th regiment.
Hugh Fraser, afterwards captain 84th or Highland
    Emigrants.
Robert Menzies.
John Fraser of Errogie.
James Mackenzie.
Donald Macneil.
Henry Munro.
Alexander Gregorson, Ardtornish.
James Henderson.
John Campbell.

Chaplain.—Robert Macpherson.
Adjutant.—Hugh Fraser.
Quarter-master.—John Fraser.
Surgeon.—John Maclean.

The uniform of the regiment " was the full
Highland dress with musket and broad-sword,
to which many of the soldiers added the dirk
at their own expense, and a purse of badger's
or otter's skin. The bonnet was raised or
cocked on one side, with a slight bend inclin-
ing down to the right ear, over which were
suspended two or more black feathers. Eagle's
or hawk's feathers were usually worn by the
gentlemen, in the Highlands, while the bonnets
of the common people were ornamented with
a bunch of the distinguishing mark of the
clan or district. The ostrich feather in the
bonnets of the soldiers was a modern addition
of that period, as the present load of plumage
on the bonnet is a still more recent introduction, forming, however, in hot climates, an
excellent defence against a vertical sun."

The regiment embarked in company with
Montgomery's Highlanders at Greenock, and
landed at Halifax in June 1757. They were
intended to be employed in an expedition
against Louisburg, which, however, after
the necessary preparations, was abandoned.
About this time it was proposed to change the

uniform of the regiment, as the Highland garb
was judged unfit for the severe winters and
the hot summers of North America ; but the
officers and soldiers having set themselves in
opposition to the plan, and being warmly supported by Colonel Fraser, who represented to
the commander-in-chief the bad consequences
that might follow if it were persisted in, the
plan was relinquished. " Thanks to our
gracious chief," said a veteran of the regiment,
" we were allowed to wear the garb of our
fathers, and, in the course of six winters,
showed the doctors that they did not understand our constitution ; for, in the coldest
winters, our men were more healthy than
those regiments who wore breeches and warm
clothing."

Amongst other enterprises projected for the
campaign of 1758, the design of attacking
Louisburg was renewed. Accordingly, on
the 28th of May, a formidable armament sailed
from Halifax, under the command of Admiral
Boscawen and Major-general Amherst, and
Brigadier-generals Wolfe, Laurence, Monckton,
and Whitmore. This armament, consisting
of 25 sail of the line, 18 frigates, and a number
of bombs and fire-ships, with 13,000 troops
including the 78th Highlanders, anchored, on
the 2d of June, in Gabarus Bay, seven miles
from Louisburg. In consequence of a heavy
surf no boat could approach the shore, and it
was not till the 8th of June that a landing
could be effected. The garrison of Louisburg
consisted of 2500 regulars 600 militia, and
400 Canadians and Indians. For more than
seven miles along the beach a chain of posts
had been established by the enemy, with
entrenchments and batteries ; and, to protect
the harbour, there were six ships of the line
and five frigates placed at its mouth, of which
frigates three were sunk.

The disposition being made for landing, a
detachment of several sloops, under convoy,
passed the mouth of the harbour towards
Lorembec, in order to draw the enemy's
attention that way, whilst the landing should
really be on the other side of the town. On
the 8th of June, the troops being assembled in
the boats before day-break in three divisions,
several sloops and frigates, that were stationed
along shore in the bay of Gabarus, began to

scour the beach with their shot. The division on the left, which was destined for the real attack, consisted of the grenadiers and light infantry of the army, and Fraser's Highlanders, and was commanded by Brigadier-general Wolfe. After the fire from the sloops and frigates had continued about a quarter of an hour, the boats containing this division were rowed towards the shore; and, at the same time, the other two divisions on the right and in the centre, commanded by Brigadiers-general Whitmore and Laurence, made a show of landing, in order to divide and distract the enemy. The landing-place was occupied by 2000 men entrenched behind a battery of eight pieces of cannon and ten swivels. The enemy reserved their fire till the boats were near the beach, when they opened a discharge of cannon and musketry which did considerable execution. A considerable surf aided the enemy's fire, and numbers of the men were drowned by the upsetting of the boats. Captain Baillie and Lieutenant Cuthbert of the Highlanders, Lieutenant Nicholson of Amherst's, and 38 men were killed; but, notwithstanding these disadvantages, General Wolfe pursued his point with admirable courage and deliberation: "and nothing could stop our troops, when headed by such a general. Some of the light infantry and Highlanders got first ashore, and drove all before them. The rest followed; and, being encouraged by the example of their heroic commander, soon pursued the enemy to the distance of two miles, where they were checked by a cannonading from the town."

The town of Louisburg was immediately invested; but the difficulty of landing stores and implements in boisterous weather, and the nature of the ground, which, being marshy, was unfit for the conveyance of heavy cannon, retarded the operations of the siege. The governor of Louisburg, having destroyed the grand battery which was detached from the body of the place, recalled his outposts, and prepared for a vigorous defence. He opened a fire against the besiegers and their work from the town, the island battery, and the ships in the harbour, but without much effect. Meanwhile General Wolfe, with a strong detachment, marched round the north-east part of the harbour to secure a point called the

Light-house Battery, from which the guns could play on the ships and on the batteries on the opposite side of the harbour. This service was performed on the 12th by General Wolfe with great ability, who, "with his Highlanders and flankers," took possession of this and all the other posts in that quarter with very trifling loss. On the 25th the inland battery immediately opposite was silenced from this post. The enemy however, kept up an incessant fire from their other batteries and the shipping in the harbour. On the 9th of July they made a sortie on Brigadier-general Lawrence's brigade, but were quickly repulsed. In this affair Captain, the Earl of Dundonald, was killed. On the 16th General Wolfe pushed forward some grenadiers and Highlanders, and took possession of the hills in front of the Light Horse battery, where a lodgement was made under a fire from the town and the ships. On the 21st one of the enemy's line-of-battle ships was set on fire by a bombshell and blew up, and the fire being communicated to two others, they were burned to the water's edge. The fate of the town was now nearly decided, the enemy's fire being almost totally silenced and their fortifications shattered to the ground. To reduce the place nothing now remained but to get possession of the harbour, by taking or burning the two ships of the line which remained. For this purpose, in the night between the 25th and 26th, the admiral sent a detachment of 600 men in the boats of the squadron, in two divisions, into the harbour, under the command of Captains Laforey and Balfour. This enterprise was gallantly executed, in the face of a terrible fire of cannon and musketry, the seamen boarding the enemy sword in hand. One of the ships was set on fire and destroyed, and the other towed off. The town surrendered on the 26th, and was taken possession of by Colonel Lord Rollo the following day; the garrison and seamen, amounting together to 5637 men, were made prisoners of war. Besides Captain Baillie and Lieutenant Cuthbert, the Highlanders lost Lieutenants Fraser and Murray, killed; Captain Donald M'Donald, Lieutenants Alexander Campbell (Barcaldine), and John M'Donald, wounded; and 67 rank and file killed and wounded.

In consequence of the treaty of peace between Great Britain and the several nations of Indians between the Apalachian mountains and the Lakes, the British government was enabled to carry into effect those operations which had been projected against the French settlements in Canada. The plan and partial progress of these combined operations have been already detailed in the service of the 42d regiment. The enterprise against Quebec, the most important by far of the three expeditions planned in 1759, falls now to be noticed from the share which Fraser's Highlanders had in it.

According to the plan fixed upon for the conquest of Canada, Major-general Wolfe, who had given promise of great military talents at Louisburg, was to proceed up the river St Lawrence and attack Quebec, whilst General Amherst, after reducing Ticonderoga and Crown Point, was to descend the St Lawrence and co-operate with General Wolfe in the conquest of Quebec. Though the enterprise against this place was the main undertaking, the force under General Wolfe did not exceed 7000 effective men, whilst that under General Amherst amounted to more than twice that number; but the commander-in-chief seems to have calculated upon a junction with General Wolfe in sufficient time for the siege of Quebec.

The forces under General Wolfe comprehended the following regiments,—15th, 28th, 35th, 43d, 47th, 48th, 58th, Fraser's Highlanders, the Rangers, and the grenadiers of Louisburg. The fleet, under the command of Admirals Saunders and Holmes, with the transports, proceeded up the St Lawrence, and reached the island of Orleans, a little below Quebec, in the end of June, where the troops were disembarked without opposition. The Marquis de Montcalm who commanded the French troops, which were greatly superior in number to the invaders, resolved rather to depend upon the natural strength of his position than his numbers, and took his measures accordingly. The city of Quebec was tolerably well fortified, defended by a numerous garrison, and abundantly supplied with provisions and ammunition. This able, and hitherto fortunate leader had reinforced the troops of the line, with five regular bat-

talions, formed of the best of the inhabitants, and he had, besides, completely disciplined all the Canadians of the neighbourhood capable of bearing arms, and several tribes of Indians. He had posted his army on a piece of ground along the shore of Beaufort, from the river St Charles to the falls of Montmorency,—a position rendered strong by precipices, woods, and rivers, and defended by intrenchments where the ground appeared the weakest. To undertake the siege of Quebec under the disadvantages which presented themselves, seemed a rash enterprise; but, although General Wolfe was completely aware of these difficulties, a thirst for glory, and the workings of a vigorous mind, which set every obstacle at defiance, impelled him to make the hazardous attempt. His maxim was, that "a brave and victorious army finds no difficulties,"[3] and he was anxious to verify the truth of the adage in the present instance.

Having ascertained that, to reduce the place, it was necessary to erect batteries on the north of the St Lawrence, the British general endeavoured, by a series of manœuvres, to draw Montcalm from his position; but the French commander was too prudent to risk a battle. With the view of attacking the enemy's intrenchments, General Wolfe sent a small armament up the river above the city, and, having personally surveyed the banks on the side of the enemy from one of the ships, he resolved to cross the river Montmorency and make the attack. He therefore ordered six companies of grenadiers and part of the Royal Americans to cross the river and land near the mouth of the Montmorency, and at the same time directed the two brigades commanded by Generals Murray and Townshend to pass a ford higher up. Close to the water's edge there was a detached redoubt, which the grenadiers were ordered to attack, in the expectation that the enemy would descend from the hill in its defence, and thus bring on a general engagement. At all events the possession of this post was of importance, as from it the British commander could obtain a better view of the enemy's intrenchments than he had yet been able to accomplish. The grenadiers and Royal Americans were the first who landed. They had received orders to form in four distinct bodies, but not to begin the attack till the first brigade should have passed the ford, and be near enough to support them. No attention, however, was paid to these instructions. Before even the first brigade had crossed, the grenadiers, ere they were regularly formed, rushed forward with impetuosity and considerable confusion to attack the enemy's intrenchments. They were received with a well-directed fire, which effectually checked them and threw them into disorder. They endeavoured to form under the redoubt, but being unable to rally, they retreated and formed behind the first brigade, which had by this time landed, and was drawn up on the beach in good order. The plan of attack being thus totally disconcerted, General Wolfe repassed the river and returned to the isle of Orleans. In this unfortunate attempt the British lost 543 of all ranks killed, wounded, and missing. Of the Highlanders, up to the 2d of September, the loss was 18 rank and file killed, Colonel Fraser, Captains Macpherson and Simon Fraser, and Lieutenants Cameron of Glenaves, Ewen Macdonald, and H. Macdonald, and 85 rank and file, wounded. In the general orders which were issued the following morning, General Wolfe complained bitterly of the conduct of the grenadiers: "The check which the grenadiers met with yesterday will, it is hoped, be a lesson to them for the time to come. Such impetuous, irregular, and unsoldier-like proceedings, destroy all order, make it impossible for the commanders to form any disposition for attack, and put it out of the general's power to execute his plan. The grenadiers could not suppose that they alone could beat the French army; and therefore it was necessary that the corps under brigadiers Monckton and Townshend should have time to join, that the attack might be general. The very first fire of the enemy was sufficient to repulse men who had lost all sense of order and military discipline. Amherst's (15th regiment) and the Highlanders alone, by the soldier-like and cool manner they were formed in, would undoubtedly have beaten back the whole Canadian army if they had ventured to attack them."

General Wolfe now changed his plan of operations. Leaving his position at Mont-

moreney, he re-embarked his troops and artillery, and landed at Point Levi, whence he passed up the river in transports; but finding no opportunity of annoying the enemy above the town, he resolved to convey his troops farther down, in boats, and land them by night within a league of Cape Diamond, with the view of ascending the heights of Abraham, —which rise abruptly, with steep ascent, from the banks of the river,—and thus gain possession of the ground on the back of the city, where the fortifications were less strong. A plan more replete with dangers and difficulties could scarcely have been devised; but, from the advanced period of the season, it was necessary either to abandon the enterprise altogether, or to make an attempt upon the city, whatever might be the result. The troops, notwithstanding the recent disaster, were in high spirits, and ready to follow their general wherever he might lead them. The commander, on the other hand, though afflicted with a severe dysentery and fever, which had debilitated his frame, resolved to avail himself of the readiness of his men, and to conduct the hazardous enterprise in which they were about to engage in person. In order to deceive the enemy, Admiral Holmes was directed to move farther up the river on the 12th of September, but to sail down in the night time, so as to protect the landing of the forces. These orders were punctually obeyed. About an hour after midnight of the same day four regiments, the light infantry, with the Highlanders and grenadiers, were embarked in flat-bottomed boats, under the command of Brigadiers Monckton and Murray. They were accompanied by General Wolfe, who was among the first that landed. The boats fell down with the tide, keeping close to the north shore in the best order; but, owing to the rapidity of the current, and the darkness of the night, most of the boats landed a little below the intended place of disembarkation.[a] When the troops were landed the boats

[a] "The French had posted sentries along shore to challenge boats and vessels, and give the alarm occasionally. The first boat that contained the English troops being questioned accordingly, a captain of Fraser's regiment, who had served in Holland, and who was perfectly well acquainted with the French language and customs, answered without hesitation to Qui vive?—which is their challenging word,—la France; and being asked, by the second

were sent back for the other division, which was under the command of Brigadier-general Townshend. The ascent to the heights was by a narrow path, that slanted up the precipice from the landing-place; this path the enemy had broken up, and rendered almost impassable, by cross ditches, and they had made an intrenchment at the top of the hill. Notwithstanding these difficulties, Colonel Howe, who was the first to land, ascended the woody precipices, with the light infantry and the Highlanders, and dislodged a captain's guard which defended the narrow path. They then mounted without further molestation, and General Wolfe, who was among the first to gain the summit of the hill, formed the troops on the heights as they arrived. In the ascent the precipice was found to be so steep and dangerous, that the troops were obliged to climb the rugged projections of the rocks, pulling themselves up by aid of the branches of the trees and shrubs growing on both sides of the path. Though much time was thus necessarily occupied in the ascent, yet such was the perseverance of the troops, that they all gained the summit in time to enable the general to form in order of battle before daybreak. M. de Montcalm had now no means left of saving Quebec but by risking a battle, and he therefore determined to leave his stronghold and meet the British in the open field. Leaving his camp at Montmorency, he crossed the river St Charles, and, forming his line with great skill, advanced forward to attack his opponents. His right was composed of half the provincial troops, two battalions of regulars, and a body of Canadians and Indians; his centre, of a column of two battalions of Europeans, with two field-pieces; and his left of one battalion of regulars, and the remainder of the colonial troops. In his front, among brushwood and corn-fields, 1500 of his best marksmen were posted to gall the British as they approached. The British were drawn up in two lines: the first, consisting of the grenadiers, 15th, 28th, 35th Highlanders, and 58th; the 47th regiment formed the second line, or reserve. The Canadians and the Indians, who were posted among the brushwood, kept up an irregular galling fire, which proved fatal to many officers, who, from their dress, were singled out by these marksmen. The fire of this body was, in some measure, checked by the advanced posts of the British, who returned the fire; and a small gun, which was dragged up by the seamen from the landing-place, was brought forward, and did considerable execution. The French now advanced to the charge with great spirit, firing as they advanced; but, in consequence of orders they received, the British troops reserved their fire till the main body of the enemy had approached within forty yards of their line. When the enemy had come within that distance, the whole British line poured in a general and destructive discharge of musketry. Another discharge followed, which had such an effect upon the enemy, that they stopped short, and after making an ineffectual attempt upon the left of the British line, they began to give way. At this time General Wolfe, who had already received two wounds which he had concealed, was mortally wounded whilst advancing at the head of the grenadiers with fixed bayonets. At this instant every separate corps of the British army exerted itself, as if the contest were for its own peculiar honour. Whilst the right pressed on with their bayonets, Brigadier-general Murray briskly advanced with the troops under his command, and soon broke the centre of the enemy, "when the Highlanders, taking to their broad-swords, fell in among them with irresistible impetuosity, and drove them back with great slaughter."[1] The action on the left of the British was not so warm. A smart contest, however, took place between part of the enemy's right and some light infantry, who had thrown themselves into houses, which they defended with great courage.

question, which was much more particular and difficult. When the sentinel demanded, *à quel régiment ?* the captain replied, *de la reine,* which he knew, by accident, to be one of those that composed the body commanded by Bougainville. The soldier took it for granted this was the expected convoy (a convoy of provisions expected that night for the garrison of Quebec), and, saying *passe,* allowed all the boats to proceed without further question. In the same manner the other sentries were deceived; though one, more wary than the rest, came running down to the water's edge, and called, *Pour quoi est ce que vous ne parlez pas haut ?* 'Why don't you speak with an audible voice?' To this interrogation, which implied doubt, the captain answered with admirable presence of mind, in a soft tone of voice, *Tai toi nous serons entendues !* 'hush! we shall be overheard and discovered.' Thus cautioned, the sentry retired without further altercation." *N. o.*

[1] — account of the battle.

During this attack, Colonel Howe, who had taken post with two companies behind a copse, frequently sallied out on the flanks of the enemy, whilst General Townshend advanced in platoons against their front. Observing the left and centre of the French giving way, this officer, on whom the command had just devolved in consequence of General Monckton, the second in command, having been dangerously wounded, hastened to the centre, and finding that the troops had got into disorder in the pursuit, formed them again in line. At this moment, Monsieur de Bougainville, who had marched from Cape Rouge as soon as he heard that the British troops had gained the heights, appeared in their rear at the head of 2000 fresh men. General Townshend immediately ordered two regiments, with two pieces of artillery, to advance against this body; but Bougainville retired on their approach. The wreck of the French army retreated to Quebec and Point Levi.

The loss sustained by the enemy was considerable. About 1000 were made prisoners, including a number of officers, and about 500 died on the field of battle. The death of their brave commander, Montcalm, who was mortally wounded almost at the same instant with General Wolfe, was a serious calamity to the French arms. When informed that his wound was mortal,—"So much the better," said he, "I shall not live to see the surrender of Quebec." Before his death he wrote a letter to General Townshend, recommending the prisoners to the generous humanity of the British. The death of the two commanders in-chief, and the disasters which befell Generals Monckton and Severergues, the two seconds in command, who were carried wounded from the field, are remarkable circumstances in the events of this day. This important victory was not gained without considerable loss on the part of the British, who, besides the commander-in-chief, had 8 officers and 48 men killed; and 43 officers and 435 men wounded. Of these, the Highlanders had Captain Thomas Ross of Culrossie, Lieutenant Roderick Macneil of Barra, Alexander Macdonell, son of Barrisdale, 1 sergeant and 14 rank and file killed; and Captains John Macdonell of Lochgarry, Simon Fraser of Inverallochy; Lieutenants Macdonell, son

of Keppoch, Archibald Campbell, Alexander Campbell, son of Barcaldine, John Douglas, Alexander Fraser, senior; and Ensigns James Mackenzie, Malcolm Fraser, and Alexander Gregorson; 7 sergeants and 131 rank and file, wounded. The death of General Wolfe was a national loss. When the fatal ball pierced the breast of the young hero, he found himself unable to stand, and leaned upon the shoulder of a lieutenant who sat down on the ground. This officer, observing the French give way, exclaimed,—"They run! they run!" "Who run!" inquired the gallant Wolfe with great earnestness. When told that it was the French who were flying: "What," said he, "do the cowards run already? Then I die happy!" and instantly expired.[2]

On the 18th of September the town surrendered, and a great part of the surrounding country being reduced, General Townshend embarked for England, leaving a garrison of 5000 effective men in Quebec, under the Hon. General James Murray. Apprehensive of a visit from a considerable French army stationed in Montreal and the neighbouring country, General Murray repaired the fortifications, and put the town in a proper posture of defence; but his troops suffered so much from the rigours of winter, and the want of vegetables and fresh provisions, that, before the end of April, 1760, the garrison was reduced, by death and disease, to about 3000 effective men. Such was the situation of affairs when the general received intelligence that General de Levi, who succeeded the Marquis de Montcalm, had reached Point au Tremble with a force of 10,000 French and Canadians, and 500 Indians. It was the intention of the French commander to cut off the posts which the British had established; but General Murray defeated this scheme, by ordering the bridges over the river Rouge to be broken down, and the landing-places at Sylleri and Foulon to be secured. Next day, the 27th of April, he marched in person with a strong detachment and two field-pieces, and took possession of an advantageous position, which he retained till the afternoon, when the outposts were withdrawn, after which he returned to Quebec with very little loss, although the enemy pressed closely on his rear.

[2] Smollett

General Murray was now reduced to the necessity of withstanding a siege, or risking a battle. He chose the latter alternative, a resolution which was deemed by some military men as savouring more of youthful impatience and overstrained courage, than of judgment ; but the dangers with which he was beset, in the midst of a hostile population, and the difficulties incident to a protracted siege, seem to afford some justification for that step. In pursuance of his resolution, the general marched out on the 28th of April, at half-past six o'clock in the morning, and formed his little army on the heights of Abraham. The right wing, commanded by Colonel Burton, consisted of the 15th, 48th, 58th, and second battalion of the 60th, or Royal Americans : the left under Colonel Simon Fraser, was formed of the 43d, 23d Welsh fusiliers, and the Highlanders. The 35th, and the third battalion of the 60th, constituted the reserve. The right was covered by Major Dalling's corps of light infantry ; and the left by Captain Huzzen's company of rangers, and 100 volunteers, under the command of Captain Macdonald of Fraser's regiment. Observing the enemy in full march in one column, General Murray advanced quickly forward to meet them before they should form their line. His light infantry coming in contact with Levi's advance, drove them back on their main body ; but pursuing too far, they were furiously attacked and repulsed in their turn. They fell back in such disorder on the line, as to impede their fire, and in passing round by the right flank to the rear, they suffered much from the fire of a party who were endeavouring to turn that flank. The enemy having made two desperate attempts to penetrate the right wing, the 35th regiment was called up from the reserve, to its support. Meanwhile the British left was struggling with the enemy, who succeeded so far, from their superior numbers, in their attempt to turn that flank, that they obtained possession of two redoubts, but were driven out from both by the Highlanders, sword in hand. By pushing forward fresh numbers, however, the enemy at last succeeded in forcing the left wing to retire, the right giving way about the same time. The French did not attempt to pursue, but allowed the British to retire quietly within the

walls of the city, and to carry away their wounded. The British had 6 officers, and 251 rank and file killed ; and 82 officers, and 679 non-commissioned officers and privates, wounded. Among the killed, the Highlanders had Captain Donald Macdonald,[3] Lieutenant Cosmo Gordon and 55 non-commissioned officers, pipers, and privates ; their wounded were Colonel Fraser, Captains John Campbell of Dunoon, Alexander Fraser, Alexander Macleod, Charles Macdonell; Lieutenants Archibald Campbell, son of Glenlyon, Charles Stewart,[4] Hector Macdonald, John Machean, Alexander Fraser, senior, Alexander Campbell, John Nairn, Arthur Rose, Alexander Fraser, junior, Simon Fraser, senior, Archibald M'Alister, Alexander Fraser, John Chisholm, Simon Fraser, junior, Malcolm Fraser, and Donald M'Neil ; Ensigns Henry Monro, Robert Menzies, Duncan Cameron (Fassifern), William Robertson, Alexander

[3] "Captain Macdonald was an accomplished high-spirited officer. He was a second son of Clanranald. He entered early in life into the French service, and following Prince Charles Edward to Scotland, in 1745, he was taken prisoner, and along with O'Neil, afterwards a lieutenant-general in the service of Spain, and commander of the expedition against Algiers in 1775, was confined in the castle of Edinburgh ; but being liberated without trial, he returned to France, where he remained till 1756, when he came back to Scotland, and was appointed to a company in Fraser's Highlanders. On the expeditions against Louisburg and Quebec he was much in the confidence of Generals Amherst, Wolfe, and Murray, by whom he was employed on all duties where more than usual difficulty and danger was to be encountered, and where more than common talent, address, and spirited example were required. Of this several instances occurred at Louisburg and Quebec." —Stewart's Sketches.

[4] "This officer engaged in the Rebellion of 1745, and was in Stewart of Appin's regiment, which had seventeen officers and gentlemen of the name of Stewart killed, and ten wounded, at Culloden. He was severely wounded on that occasion, as he was on this. As he lay in his quarters some days afterwards, speaking to some brother officers on the recent battles, he exclaimed, 'From April battles and Murray generals, good Lord, deliver me !' alluding to his wound at Culloden, where the vanquished blamed Lord George Murray, the commander-in-chief of the rebel army, for fighting on the best field in the country for regular troops, artillery, and cavalry ; and likewise alluding to his present wound, and to General Murray's conduct in marching out of a garrison to attack an enemy, more than treble his numbers, in an open field, where their whole strength could be brought to act. One of those story retailers who are sometimes about headquarters, lost no time in communicating this disrespectful prayer of the rebellious clansman ; General Murray, who was a man of honour and of a generous mind, called on the wounded officer the following morning, and heartily wished him better deliverance in the next battle, when he hoped to give him occasion to pray in a different manner."— Stewart, Sketches.

Gregorson, and Malcolm Fraser,[5] and 129 non-commissioned officers and privates. The enemy lost twice the number of men.

Shortly after the British had retired, General Levi moved forward on Quebec, and having taken up a position close to it, opened a fire at five o'clock. He then proceeded to besiege the city in form, and General Murray made the necessary dispositions to defend the place. The siege was continued till the 10th of May, when it was suddenly raised; the enemy retreating with great precipitation, leaving all their artillery implements and stores behind. This unexpected event was occasioned by the destruction or capture of all the enemy's ships above Quebec, by an English squadron which had arrived in the river, and the advance of General Amherst on Montreal. General Murray left Quebec in pursuit of the enemy, but was unable to overtake them. The junction of General Murray with General Amherst, in the neighbourhood of Montreal, in the month of September, and the surrender of that last stronghold of the French in Canada, have been already mentioned in the history of the service of the 42d regiment.

Fraser's Highlanders were not called again into active service till the summer of 1762, when they were, on the expedition under Colonel William Amherst, sent to retake St John's, Newfoundland, a detailed account of which has been given in the notice of Montgomery's Highlanders. In this service Captain Macdonell of Fraser's regiment, was mortally wounded, 3 rank and file killed, and 7 wounded.

At the conclusion of the war, a number of the officers and men having expressed a desire to settle in North America, had their wishes granted, and an allowance of land given them. The rest returned to Scotland, and were discharged. When the war of the American revolution broke out, upwards of 300 of those men who had remained in the country, enlisted in the 84th regiment, in 1775, and formed

part of two fine battalions embodied under the name of the Royal Highland Emigrants.

Many of the hundreds of Frasers who now form so important a part of the population of Canada claim descent from these Fraser Highlanders who settled in America. Full details concerning the Canadian branch of the great clan Fraser have already been given at the conclusion of our history of that clan.

The loss of this regiment during four years' active service was—

	KILLED.
In officers,	14
Non-commissioned officers and privates,	109
Total,	123

	WOUNDED.
In officers,	46
Non-commissioned officers and privates,	400
Total,	446
Grand Total,	569

II.

OLD SEVENTY-FIRST REGIMENT.

1775—1783.

Raising of the Regiment—American Revolutionary War—Honourable place assigned to the regiment—Brooklyn—Various expeditions—Savannah—Boston Creek—Defence of Savannah—Stony Point and Verplanks—Cambden—Catawba River—South Carolina—Guilford Court-house—York River—Reduction of Regiment.

THE American revolutionary war requiring extraordinary exertions on the part of the Government, it was resolved in 1775 to revive Fraser's Highlanders, by raising two battalions, under the auspices of Colonel Fraser, who, for his services, had been rewarded by King George III. with a grant of the family estates of Lovat, which had been forfeited in 1746. In his exertions to raise the battalions, Colonel Fraser was warmly assisted by his officers, of whom no less than six, besides himself, were chiefs of clans, and within a few months after the letters of service were issued, two battalions of 2340 Highlanders were raised, and assembled first at Stirling, and afterwards at Glasgow, in April 1776. The following were the names of the officers :—

FIRST BATTALION.

Colonel.—The Honourable Simon Fraser of Lovat, died in 1782, a lieutenant-general.
Lieutenant-Colonel.—Sir William Erskine of Torry, died in 1795, a lieutenant-general.

---

[5] In a journal kept by this officer, lent to the editor by the Hon. John Fraser de Berry, "Chief of the Frasers of the Province of Quebec," Member of the Legislative Council of Canada, &c., it is stated that the 78th had about 400 men in the field on this occasion, half of whom had of their own accord left the hospital to take part in the fight.

Majors.

John Macdonell of Lochgarry, died in 1789, colonel.
Duncan Macpherson of Cluny, retired from the foot-
guards in 1791, died in 1820.

Captains.

Simon Fraser, died lieutenant-general in 1812.
Duncan Chisholm of Chisholm.
Colin Mackenzie, died general in 1818.
Francis Skelly, died in India, lieutenant-colonel of the
94th regiment.
Hamilton Maxwell, brother of Monreith, died in
India lieutenant-colonel of the 74th regiment, 1794.
John Campbell, son of Lord Stonefield, died lieu-
tenant-colonel of the 2d battalion of 42d regiment
at Madras, 1784.
Norman Macleod of Macleod, died lieutenant-general,
1796.
Sir James Baird of Saughtonhall.
Charles Cameron of Lochiel, died 1776.

Lieutenants.

Charles Campbell, son of Ardchattan,
killed at Catauba.
John Macdougall.
Colin Mackenzie.
John Nairne, son of Lord Nairne.
William Nairne, afterwards Lord Nairne.
Charles Gordon.
David Kinloch.
Thomas Tanse, killed at Savannah.
William Sinclair.
Hugh Fraser.
Alexander Fraser.
Thomas Fraser, son of Leadclune.
Dougald Campbell, son of Craignish.
Robert Macdonald, son of Sanda.
Alexander Fraser.
Roderick Macleod.
John Ross.
Patrick Cumming.
Thomas Hamilton.

Ensigns.

Archibald Campbell.
Henry Macpherson.
John Grant.
Robert Campbell, son of Ederline.
Allan Malcolm.
John Murchison.
Angus Macdonell.
Peter Fraser.

Chaplain.—Hugh Blair, D.D., Professor of Rhetoric
in the University of Edinburgh.
Adjutant.—Donald Cameron.
Quarter-master.—David Campbell.
Surgeon.—William Fraser.

SECOND BATTALION.

Colonel.—Simon Fraser.

Lieutenant-Colonel.

Archibald Campbell, died lieutenant-general, 1792.

Majors.

Norman Lamont, son of the Laird of Lamont.
Robert Menzies, killed in Boston harbour, 1776.

Captains.

Angus Mackintosh of Kellachy, formerly Captain in
Keith's Highlanders, died in South Carolina, 1780.
Patrick Campbell, son of Glenure.
Andrew Lowrie.

Æneas Mackintosh of Mackintosh.
Charles Cameron, son of Fassifern, killed at
Savannah, 1779.
George Munro, son of Culcairn.
Boyd Porterfield.
Law Robert Campbell.

Lieutenants.

Robert Hutchison.
Alexander Sutherland.
Archibald Campbell.
Hugh Lamont.
Robert Duncanson.
George Stewart.
Charles Barrington Mackenzie.
James Christie.
James Fraser.
Dougald Campbell, son of Achnaba.
Lodovick Colquhoun, son of Luss.
John Mackenzie.
Hugh Campbell, son of Glenure.
John Campbell.
Arthur Forbes.
Patrick Campbell.
Archibald Maclean.
David Ross.
Thomas Fraser.
Archibald Baluevis, son of Edradour.
Robert Grant.
Thomas Fraser.

Ensigns.

William Gordon.
Charles Main.
Archibald Campbell.
Donald Cameron.
Smollett Campbell, son of Craignish.
Gilbert Waugh.
William Bain.
John Grant.

Chaplain.—Malcolm Nicholson.
Adjutant.—Archibald Campbell.
Quarter-master.—J. Ogilvie.
Surgeon.—Colin Chisholm, afterwards physician in
Bristol.

At the time when the regiment was mustered
in Glasgow, there were nearly 6000 Highlanders
in that city, of whom 3000 belonging to the
42d and 71st regiments were raised and brought
from the North in ten weeks. A finer and a
more healthy and robust body of men could
not have been anywhere selected; and their
conduct was so laudable and exemplary as to
gain the affections of the inhabitants, between
whom and the soldiers the greatest cordiality
prevailed. So great was the desire of the
Highlanders to enlist into this new regiment,
that before leaving Glasgow for embarkation,
it was found that more men had arrived than
were required, and it became necessary, therefore, to leave some of them behind; but unwilling to remain, several of these stole on board
the transports, and were not discovered till
the fleet was at sea. There were others,

however, who did not evince the same ardour to accompany their countrymen. A body of 120 men had been raised on the forfeited estate of Captain Cameron of Lochiel, by the ancient tenants, with the view of securing him a company. Lochiel was at the time in London, and being indisposed, was unable to join the regiment. His men were exceedingly disappointed at not meeting their chief and captain at Glasgow, and when they received orders to embark, they hesitated, as they believed that some misfortune had befallen him ; but General Fraser, with a persuasive eloquence, in which he was well skilled, removed their scruples ; and as Captain Cameron of Fassifern, a friend and near relation of Lochiel, was appointed to the company, they cheerfully consented to embark.[6] When Lochiel heard of the conduct of his men he hastened to Glasgow, though he had not recovered from the severe illness which had detained him in London ; but the fatigue of the journey brought on a return of his complaint, to which he fell a victim in a few weeks. His death was greatly lamented, as he was universally respected.

Some time after the sailing of the fleet, it was scattered in a violent gale, and several of the ships were attacked singly by American privateers. One of these, with eight guns, attacked a transport with two six pounders only, having Captain (afterwards Sir Æneas) Macintosh and his company on board. Having spent all their ammunition, the transport bore down upon the privateer to board her ; but the latter sheered off, and the transport proceeded on her voyage.

Another transport, having Colonel Archibald Campbell and Major Menzies on board, was not so fortunate. Ignorant of the evacuation of Boston by General Howe, they sailed into Boston harbour, and were instantly attacked by three privateers full of men. The transport beat off her antagonists, but expended all her ammunition, and getting her rudder disabled by a shot, she grounded under a battery, and was forced to surrender. Major Menzies and seven men were killed, and Colonel Campbell and the rest were made prisoners. The death of Major Menzies was a great loss, as from his great military experience he was particularly well qualified to discipline the corps which had not yet undergone the process of drilling.

The regiment joined the army under General Howe in Staten island, and though totally undisciplined, the 71st was immediately put in front, the general judging well from the experience he had had of Fraser's Highlanders in the seven years' war, that their bravery, if engaged before being disciplined, would make up for their want of discipline. The regiment was divided, the grenadiers being placed in the battalion under the Hon. Lieutenant-Colonel Charles Stewart, and the other companies, which were formed into three small battalions, formed a brigade under Sir William Erskine.

The first affair in which they were engaged was the battle of Brooklyn, referred to in the notice of the 42d. In this action they fully justified the expectations of the commander. They displayed, in common with the other troops, great eagerness to push the enemy to extremities, and compel them to abandon the strong position they had taken up ; but from a desire to save the lives of his troops, General Howe restrained their ardour by recalling the right wing, in which the grenadiers were, from the attack. The loss sustained on this occasion by the 71st was 3 rank and file killed, and 2 sergeants and 9 rank and file wounded.

The regiment passed the winter at Amboy. The next campaign was spent in skirmishes, in some of which the regiment was engaged. They were also employed in the expeditions against Willsborough and Westfield, at the commencement of the campaign of 1777. They afterwards embarked for the Chesapeake, and part of them were engaged in the battle of Brandywine. They embarked for New York in November, where they received an accession of 200 recruits from Scotland. Along with 100 more from the hospital, they were formed

---

[6] "While General Fraser was speaking in Gaelic to the men, an old Highlander, who had accompanied his son to Glasgow, was leaning on his staff gazing at the general with great earnestness. When he had finished, the old man walked up to him, and with that easy familiar intercourse which in those days subsisted between the Highlanders and their superiors, shook him by the hand, exclaiming, 'Simon, you are a good soldier, and speak like a man ; as long as you live, Simon of Lovat will never die ;' alluding to the general's address and manner, which, as was said, resembled much that of his father, Lord Lovat, whom the old Highlanders knew perfectly. The late General Sir George Beckwith witnessed the above scene, and often spoke of it with much interest." Stewart's Sketches.

into a corps under Captain Colin (afterwards General) Mackenzie. This small corps acted as light infantry, and formed part of an expedition sent up the New River to make a diversion in favour of General Burgoyne's movements. This corps led a successful assault on Fort Montgomery on the 6th of October, in which they displayed great courage. In the year 1778 the 71st regiment was employed in the Jerseys, under Lord Cornwallis, in which excursion on occasion occurred for distinguishing themselves.

On the 29th of November 1777, an expedition, of which the 71st formed a part, destined against Savannah, the capital of Georgia, sailed from Sandy Hook, and reached the river of that name about the end of December, under Lieutenant-Colonel Archibald Campbell, who had been exchanged this year. The 1st battalion and the light infantry, having landed a little below the town, Captain Cameron, an "officer of high spirit and great promise," instantly pushed forward to attack the advanced post of the enemy, when he and three men were killed by a volley. The remainder advancing, charged the enemy and drove them back on the main body drawn up in line in an open plain behind the town. As soon as the disembarkation was finished, Colonel Campbell formed his army in line, and whilst he detached Sir James Baird with the light infantry, to get round the right flank of the enemy by a narrow path, he sent the corps, lately Captain Cameron's, to get round the left. The attention of the enemy being occupied by the army in front, they neglected to watch the motions of the flanking parties, who, on reaching their ground, made signals to the front to advance. These being instantly answered, the enemy now perceived they were nearly surrounded, and turning their backs fled in great disorder. They suffered severely from the light infantry, who closed in upon their flanks; they had 100 men killed, and 500 wounded or taken prisoners. The British had only 4 soldiers killed and 5 wounded. The town then surrendered, and the British took possession of all the shipping and stores and 45 pieces of cannon.

Colonel Campbell now advanced into the interior, and entered Augusta, a town 150 miles distant from Savannah, where he established

himself. Meanwhile General Prevost, having arrived at Savannah from Florida, assumed the command. Judging the ground occupied too extensive, he evacuated Augusta. The Americans, taking courage from this retrograde movement, assembled in considerable numbers, and harassed the rear of the British. The Loyalists in the interior were greatly dispirited, and, being left unprotected, suffered much from the disaffected. The winter was spent in making some inroads into the interior, to keep the Americans in check. About this time Lieutenant-Colonel Maitland succeeded to the command of the regiment, in consequence of the return of Colonel Campbell to England, on leave of absence.

The regiment remained almost inactive till the month of February 1779, when it was employed in an enterprise against Boston Creek, a strong position defended by upwards of 2000 men, besides 1000 occupied in detached stations. The front of this position was protected by a deep swamp, and the only approach in that way was by a narrow causeway ; on each flank were thick woods nearly impenetrable, except by the drier parts of the swamps which intersected them ; but the position was more open in the rear. To dislodge the enemy from this stronghold, which caused considerable annoyance, Lieutenant-Colonel Duncan Macpherson,[7] with the first battalion of the 71st, was directed to march upon the front of the position ; whilst Colonel Prevost, and Lieutenant-Colonels Maitland and Macdonald, with the 2d battalion, the light infantry, and a party of provincials, were ordered to attempt the rear by a circuitous route of many miles. These combined movements were executed with such precision, that, in ten minutes after Colonel Macpherson appeared at the head of the causeway in front, the fire of the body in the rear was heard. Sir James Baird, with the light infantry, rushing through the openings in the swamps on the left flank, the enemy were overpowered after a short resistance. In this affair the Highlanders had 3 soldiers killed, and 1 officer and 12 rank and file wounded.

[7] This officer was called *Duncan of the Kiln*, from the circumstance of his being born in an old malt-kiln, which was fitted up as a temporary residence for his mother, after the destruction of his father's castle of Cluny, in 1745.

General Prevost next determined to dislodge a considerable force under General Lincoln, stationed on the South Carolina side of the river. With the troops lately so successful at Brien's Creek, he crossed the river ten miles below the enemy's position. Whilst the general advanced on their front, he ordered the 71st to attack their rear by a circuitous march of several miles. Guided by a party of Creek Indians, the Highlanders entered a woody swamp at eleven o'clock at night, in traversing which they were frequently up to the shoulders in the swamp. They cleared the woods at eight o'clock in the morning, with their ammunition destroyed. They were now within half a mile of the enemy's rear, and although General Prevost had not yet moved from his position, the Highlanders instantly attacked and drove the enemy from their position without sustaining any loss.

Emboldened by this partial success, the general made an attempt upon Charleston; but after summoning the town to surrender, he was induced, by the approach of the American general, Lincoln, with a large force, to desist, and determined to return to his former quarters in Georgia. As the Americans were in arms, and had possessed themselves of the principal pass on the route, he was forced to return by the sea-coast, a course very injurious to the troops, as they had to march through unfrequented woods, and salt water marshes and swamps, where they could not obtain fresh water. In this retreat, the British force was separated in consequence of Lieutenant-Colonel Prevost, the Quarter-master-general, who had gone with a party on a foraging excursion, having removed part of a bridge of boats leading to John's Island. The enemy, who had 5000 men in the neighbourhood, endeavoured to avail themselves of this circumstance, and pushed forward 2000 men with some artillery, to attack a battalion of the Highlanders and some Hessians under Colonel Maitland, who were placed in a redoubt at Stone Ferry, for the purpose of protecting the foraging party. Hearing of the advance of the enemy, Colonel Maitland sent out Captain Colin Campbell,[8] with 4 officers and 56 men, to reconnoitre.

Whilst this small party was standing on an open field, the enemy emerged from a thick wood. Regardless of the inequality of numbers, Captain Campbell attacked the enemy with great vivacity; and a desperate contest took place, in which all the Highlanders and officers, except 7 of the soldiers, fell. When Captain Campbell was struck, he desired such of his men as were able to retire to the redoubt; but they refused to obey, as they considered that if they left their officers behind in the field, they would bring a lasting disgrace on themselves. The enemy, unexpectedly, ceased firing, and the 7 men, availing themselves of the respite, retired, carrying their wounded officers along with them, followed by such of the soldiers as were able to walk. The enemy then advanced on the redoubt, and the Hessians having got into confusion, they forced an entrance; but they were driven out by the Highlanders, at the point of the bayonet. The enemy were preparing for another attack, but the second battalion of the Highlanders having come up, the Americans retired with considerable loss.

After this affair, General Prevost retired with the main body towards Savannah, leaving behind him 700 men under Colonel Maitland, who took up a position in the island of Port Royal. In the month of September 1779, the Count D'Estaing arrived on the coast of Georgia with a large fleet, with troops on board, for the purpose of retaking Savannah, then garrisoned by 1100 effective men, including one battalion of the 71st. The town, situated on a sandy plain, gently declining towards the south, had few natural or artificial means of defence, and as the force about to attack it was said to exceed 12,000 men, the British general had nothing to rely upon but the energy and firmness of his troops. The Count, on landing, made regular approaches, and summoned the town to surrender. In the absence of Colonel Maitland's detachment in Port Royal, time was of importance, and being demanded, was granted. Colonel Maitland, on hearing of the arrival of the enemy, instantly set out for Savannah; but finding the principal passes and fords in possession of the enemy, he made a wide circuit; and after a most tedious march through marshes and woods hitherto considered impassable, he

[8] He was son of Campbell of Glendaruel, in Argyleshire.

reached Savannah before General Prevost had returned a definitive answer to D'Estaing's summons.

Having thus accomplished his object, General Prevost made immediate preparations to defend the place to the last extremity, and being seconded by the zeal and abilities of Captain Moncrieff, the chief engineer, and the exertions of the officers and soldiers, assisted by the Negro population, the town was put in a good state of defence before the enemy had completed their approaches. During these operations, several sorties were made by the garrison. On the morning of the 24th of September, Major Colin Graham sallied out with the light company of the 16th and the Highlanders, and drove the enemy from their outworks, with the loss of 14 officers, and 145 men killed, wounded, and prisoners. In this affair, Lieutenant Henry Macpherson of the 71st and 3 privates were killed, and 15 wounded. In another sortie, Major Macarthur with the piquets of the Highlanders advanced with such caution, that, after a few rounds, the Americans and French, mistaking their object, fired on each other, and killed 50 men, during which encounter he retired without loss.

Having completed his arrangements, D'Estaing made an assault, on the 9th of October, before day-break, with all his forces. Owing to a thick fog, and the darkness of the morning, it was some time before the besieged could ascertain in what direction the principal attack was to be made. As soon as daylight appeared, the French and American forces were seen advancing in three columns, D'Estaing leading the right in person. By taking too large a circuit, the left column got entangled in a swamp, and being exposed to the guns of the garrison, fell into confusion, and was unable to advance. The heads of the right and centre columns suffered greatly, from a well-directed fire from the batteries; but they still persevered in advancing; the men in the rear supplying the place of those who fell in front. When the enemy reached the first redoubt, the contest became furious; many of them entered the ditch, and some of them even ascended and planted the colours on the parapet, where they were killed. The first man who mounted was stabbed by Captain Tawse of the 71st, who

commanded the redoubt, and the Captain himself was shot dead by the man who followed. The grenadiers of the 60th came up to the support of Captain Archibald Campbell, who had assumed the command of the redoubt, and the enemy's column, being attacked on both sides, was broken and driven back with precipitation.

In this enterprise the enemy are supposed to have lost 1500 men killed, wounded, and prisoners. The British had only 3 officers and 36 soldiers killed, and 2 officers and 60 men wounded. The Americans retired to South Carolina, and the French to their ships. The garrison before the siege was sickly, but during active operations, the disease was in a manner suspended, an affect which has been often observed in the army. After the cause of excitement was over, by the raising of the siege, the men relapsed, and one-fourth of them were sent to the hospital.[a]

The grenadiers of the 71st were not employed in Georgia, but were posted at Stony Point and Verplanks, in the state of New York, which places had been recently taken from the enemy. Wishing to make amends for allowing his post to be surprised by Major-General Sir Charles Grey, the American general, Wayne, was sent to retake the posts of Stony Point and Verplanks. Accordingly, with a body of troops, he proceeded at eight o'clock in the evening of the 15th of July 1779, and taking post in a hollow within two miles of the fort, advanced unperceived, about midnight, in two columns. One of these gained the summit, on which the fort stood, without being observed, and the garrison being surprised, surrendered after a short resistance, with the loss of 17 soldiers

[a] One of the first who died was the Honourable Lieutenant-Colonel Maitland, son of the Earl of Lauderdale. He was an able and an enterprising officer, and attracted the particular notice of General Washington, with whom he was personally acquainted. During some of the operations, which brought them into occasional collision, Colonel Maitland jocularly notified to the American general, that, to enable him to distinguish the Highlanders, so that he might do justice to their exploits, in annoying his posts, and obstructing his convoys and detachments, they would in future wear a red feather in their bonnets. Fraser's Highlanders accordingly put the red feather in their bonnets, which they wore till the conclusion of the war. This must not be confounded with the red feather of the 42d, the origin of which has been given in the history of that regiment.

killed, and 3 officers and 72 privates wounded. The piquet, which was commanded by Lieutenant Cumming of the 71st, resisted one of the columns till almost all the men composing it were killed or wounded. Lieutenant Cumming was among the latter.

After the surrender of Charleston on the 12th of May 1780, to the forces under Sir Henry Clinton, Lord Cornwallis was appointed to the command of the southern provinces. Having projected an excursion into the interior, he was joined by the 71st, which had remained at Savannah in quarters during the winter. In the beginning of June, the army, amounting to 2500, reached Cambden, and encamped in the neighbourhood, the general making that place his head quarters. The American general, Gates, having, in July, assembled a force of 7000 men, took up a position at Rugley's Mill, nearly twelve miles from Cambden. Determined to surprise and attack the enemy, the British general moved forward on the night of the 15th of August; whilst, by a singular coincidence, the American commander left his position at the very same hour, with the same intention. It was full moon, and the sky was unclouded. Before three o'clock in the morning, the advanced guards met halfway, and exchanged some shots; but both generals, ignorant of each other's strength, declined a general action, and lay on their arms till morning. The ground on which the armies lay was a sandy plain, with straggling trees, but a part on the left of the British was soft and boggy. Each army prepared for battle, by forming line. The British right consisted of the light infantry and the Welsh fusileers; the 33d regiment and the volunteers of Ireland formed the centre; and the provincials composed the left, having the marshy ground in their front. Whilst this formation was going on, Captain Charles Campbell, who commanded the Highland light companies on the right, mounted the stump of an old tree to reconnoitre, and perceiving the enemy in motion, as if they intended to turn his flank, he leaped down, muttering to himself, "I'll see you damned first," and calling to his men, said, "Remember you are light infantry; remember you are Highlanders:—charge?" The Highlanders instantly rushed forward, and such was the

impetuosity of the attack, that the division of the enemy which was to have surrounded the right of the British was completely broken, and driven from the field before the battle commenced in the other parts of the line. In the contest which took place between these, the centre of the enemy gained ground; but neither party seeming disposed to advance, a pause of a few minutes took place, as if by mutual consent, during which both parties remained stationary without firing a shot. Whilst matters were in this state Lord Cornwallis ordered the corps in the centre to open their right and left; and when a considerable space intervened, he directed the Highlanders, who were getting impatient at being left in the rear, whilst their friends were fighting in front, to advance and occupy the vacant space. When the Highlanders had taken their ground, his lordship cried out, "My brave Highlanders, now is your time!" The words were scarcely uttered, when they rushed forward, accompanied by the 33d, and the volunteers of Ireland. The charge was irresistible, and the centre of the enemy was completely overthrown. Meanwhile the right of the enemy, which was enveloped in the smoke of the fire, advanced unperceived, and gained the ground on which the Highlanders had been formerly posted as a reserve. Unaware of the fate of their companions, they gave three cheers for victory; but their joy was of short duration, for, the smoke immediately clearing up, they saw their mistake; and a party of Highlanders turning on them, the greater part threw down their arms, whilst the remainder flew in all directions. The loss of the British in this decisive action was 3 officers and 66 men killed, and 17 officers and 226 rank and file wounded. Lieutenant Archibald Campbell and 3 soldiers of the 71st were killed, and Captain Hugh Campbell, Lieutenant John Grant, 2 sergeants, and 30 privates wounded.[1]

Though the battle of the 16th of August

[1] In a letter communicated to General Stewart by Dr Chisholm of Bristol, an eye-witness, the writer says that there were many acts of individual prowess. One will suffice. "A tough stump of a Sutherland Highlander, of the name of Mackay, afterwards my own batman, entered the battle with his bayonet perfectly straight, and brought it out twisted like a cork-screw, and with his own hand had put to death seven of the enemy."

was decisive, yet as General Sumpter with a strong corps occupied positions on the Catawba river, which commanded the road to Charleston, it was necessary to dislodge him. For this purpose Colonel Tarleton was directed to proceed with the cavalry, and a corps of light infantry, under Captain Charles Campbell of the 71st. On the morning of the 18th they came in sight of Fishing Creek, and observing some smoke at a short distance on their right, the sergeant of the advanced guard halted his party, and went forward to reconnoitre. He observed an encampment with arms piled, and, with the exception of a few sentinels and some persons employed in cooking, the soldiers were reposing in groups apparently asleep. The sergeant reporting what he had seen to Captain Campbell, the latter, who commanded in front, fearing a discovery, formed such of the cavalry as had come up, and with 40 of the Highlander light infantry rushed quickly forward, secured the piled arms, and surprised the camp. The success was complete; a few men were killed, nearly 500 surrendered prisoners, and the rest fled in all directions. The loss was trifling, but the Highlanders had in an especial manner to regret the death of Captain Campbell, who was killed by a random shot.

The American general, Morgan, having entered South Carolina, in December 1780, with about 1100 men, Colonel Tarleton was detached with some infantry, of which the first battalion of the 71st formed a part, and a small body of cavalry. On the morning of the 17th of January 1781, intelligence was received that General Morgan was posted on a rising ground in front, which was thinly covered with pine trees. The front line was drawn up on the top of the rising ground, and the second, four hundred paces in rear of the first. Colonel Tarleton instantly formed in order of battle. In front he placed the 7th, or fusileers, the infantry of the British legion, and the light infantry; the Highlanders and cavalry formed the reserve. The line, exhausted by running at a rapid pace, received the fire of the enemy at the distance of thirty or forty yards, which did considerable execution. The fire was returned, but without spirit and with little effect; and it was kept up on both

sides for ten or twelve minutes, neither party advancing. The light infantry then made two attempts to charge, but were repulsed with loss. In this state of matters the Highlanders were ordered up, and advancing rapidly to the charge, the enemy's front line instantly gave way; and this retrograde motion being observed by the second line, which had not yet been engaged, it immediately faced to the right and inclined backwards, and by this skilful manoeuvre opened a space by which the front line retreated. Eager to pursue, the Highlanders followed the front line, when Colonel Howard, who commanded the enemy's reserve, threw in a destructive fire upon the 71st, when within forty yards of the hostile force. So disastrous was the effect of this fire, that nearly one half of the Highlanders fell; and the rest were so scattered over the ground, on which they pursued, that they could not be united to form a charge with the bayonet. Though checked, the Highlanders did not fall back, probably expecting that the first line and the cavalry would come up to their support; but they were mistaken: and after some irregular firing between them and Colonel Howard's reserve, the front line of the Americans rallied, returned to the field, and pushed forward to the right flank of the Highlanders. Alone, and unsupported, and almost overpowered by the increasing numbers of the enemy, the Highlanders "began to retire, and at length to run, the first instance (may it be the only one!) of a Highland regiment running *from* an enemy!!" A general rout ensued; few of the infantry escaped, but the cavalry saved themselves by the speed of their horses. The loss of the British, in this disastrous affair, exceeded 400 men. The Highland officers were perfectly satisfied with the conduct of their men, and imputing the disaster altogether to the bad dispositions of Colonel Tarleton, made a representation to Lord Cornwallis, not to be employed again under the same officer, a request with which his lordship complied.

The main body of the American army under General Green retreated northward after this action, and Lord Cornwallis made every exertion to follow them. Previous to the march the two battalions of the 71st, being greatly reduced, were consolidated into one, and formed in brigade with the Welsh fusileers and 33d regiment. General Green retreated to Guildford Court-house, where on the 16th of March he prepared for battle. He drew up his army in three lines: the first occupied the edge of a wood with a fence in front of Hogstie farm; the second a wood of stunted oaks at some distance in the rear; and the third line was drawn up in the more open parts of the woods and upon cleared ground. The front line of the British was formed of the German regiment of De Bos, the Highlanders and guards under the Honourable General Leslie on the right; and the Welsh fusileers, 33d regiment, and 2d battalion of guards under Brigadier-General Charles O'Hara, on the left. The cavalry were in the rear, supported by the light infantry of the guards and the German Jagers.

The order of battle being completed, the attack began at one o'clock. The Americans, covered by the fence in their front, reserved their fire till the British were within thirty or forty paces, at which distance they opened a most destructive fire, which annihilated nearly one-third of Colonel Webster's brigade. The fire was returned by the brigade, who rushed forward on the enemy. These abandoned their fence, and retreated on the second line. The contest was maintained with greater pertinacity on the more open ground, where the regiment of De Bos and the 33d retreated and advanced repeatedly before they succeeded in driving the enemy from the field. A party of the guards pressing forward without observing a body of cavalry placed in the right flank as a reserve, were charged in flank, had their line broken, and lost several men. The enemy, who had retreated, emboldened by the effect of this charge, halted, turned their face to the field, and recommenced firing. Whilst matters were in this state, and the Hessians warmly engaged, the Highlanders, who had rapidly pushed round the flank, appeared on a rising ground in rear of the enemy's left, and rushing forward with shouts, made such an impression on the Americans that they immediately fled, leaving their guns and ammunition behind. In this well-con

tested action every corps fought separately, each depending on its own firmness; and having to sustain the weight of so greatly superior numbers, the issue was for some time doubtful. The British had 7 officers and 102 non-commissioned officers and rank and file killed, among whom were Ensign Grant and 11 soldiers of the 71st; and 20 officers and 419 non-commissioned officers and rank and file wounded, including 4 sergeants and 46 soldiers of the same regiment.

No solid advantage was gained by this battle, as Lord Cornwallis found it necessary to retreat, and was even obliged to leave his wounded behind in a house in the neighbourhood. The British took the direction of Cross Creek, followed close in the rear by the Americans. The settlement of Cross Creek was possessed by emigrant Highlanders, who had evinced great loyalty during the war; and they now offered to bring 1500 men into the field, and to furnish every necessary except arms and ammunition, but stipulated that they should be commanded by officers from the line. This reasonable offer was declined; but it was proposed to form them into what was called a provincial corps of the line. This proposition was rejected by the emigrant Highlanders, who retired to their settlements, after a negotiation of twelve days. The army then marched for Wilmington, where it arrived on the 17th of April. Here Lord Cornwallis halted till the 26th, when he proceeded on the route to Petersborough. After traversing several hundred miles of a country chiefly hostile, he arrived at Petersborough on the 20th of May, where he formed a junction with Major-general Philips, who had recently arrived from New York with 3000 men. With the united forces, which amounted to 6000 men, Lord Cornwallis proceeded to Portsmouth, and whilst he was preparing to cross the river at St James's island, the Marquis de la Fayette, ignorant of the strength of the British army, gallantly attacked Colonel Thomas Dundas's brigade, with 2000 men. The Marquis was repulsed, but not without a warm contest.

Arriving at Portsmouth, Lord Cornwallis continued his march to Yorktown, and took up a position on the York river, on the 22d of

II.   3 o

August. The place selected was an elevated platform, on the banks of the river, nearly level. On the right of the position, extending from the river, was a ravine about forty feet in depth, and upwards of one hundred yards in breadth ; a line of entrenchments, with a hornwork, formed the centre. Beyond the ravine, on the right of the position, was an extensive redoubt, and two smaller ones on the left, also advanced beyond the entrenchments. These defences, which constituted the chief strength of the camp, were not completed when General Washington, who had been lately joined by the Count de Rochambeau, took up a position at the distance of two miles from the British lines. His force consisted of 7000 French and 12,000 Americans, being thrice as numerous as that of the British, which did not exceed 5950 men.

General Washington immediately proceeded to erect batteries, and to make his approaches. He first directed his fire against the redoubt on the right, which after four days' bombardment was reduced to a heap of sand. He did not, however, attempt an assault on this point of the position, but turned his whole force against the redoubts on the left, which he carried by storm, and turned the guns of the redoubts on the other parts of the entrenchments. Some soldiers of the 71st, who had manned one of these redoubts, conceiving that the honour of the regiment was compromised by their expulsion from the redoubt, sent a petition through the commanding officer to Lord Cornwallis, for permission to retake it ; but as his lordship did not think that the acquisition would be of much importance, under existing circumstances, be declined.

Finding his position quite untenable, and his situation becoming every hour more critical, the British commander determined to decamp at midnight with the *elite* of his army, to cross the river, and leave a small force in the works to capitulate for the sick and wounded, the former being very numerous. The plan would have succeeded had not the passage of the river been rendered dangerous, if not impracticable, by a squall of wind. The first division was embarked, and some of the boats had reached Gloucester Point on the

opposite shore, when the General countermanded the enterprise in consequence of a storm which arose. Judging farther resistance hopeless, Lord Cornwallis made proposals of capitulation, and the terms being adjusted, the British troops marched out with their arms and baggage on the 8th of October 1781, and were afterwards sent to different parts of the country. The garrison had 6 officers and 150 non-commissioned officers and rank and file killed, and 6 officers and 319 non-commissioned officers and rank and file wounded. Lieutenant Fraser and 9 soldiers of the 71st were killed, and 3 drummers and 19 soldiers wounded.

The military services of this army, which were now closed, had been most arduous. In less than twelve months they had marched and countermarched nearly 2000 miles, had been subjected to many severe hardships, and besides numerous skirmishes had fought two pitched battles, in all of which they had been victorious ; yet all their exertions were unavailing in the general contest.

With this misfortune also ended the military career of the Fraser Highlanders, who remained prisoners till the conclusion of the war. True to their allegiance, they resisted to a man the solicitations of the Americans to join their standard and settle among them, thus exhibiting a striking contrast to many soldiers of other corps, who, in violation of their oath, entered the American ranks. In other respects the conduct of the Highlanders was in perfect keeping with this high state of moral feeling and daring, not one instance of disgraceful conduct ever having occurred in the old 71st. The only case of military insubordination was that which happened at Leith in April 1779, of which an account has been given in the history of the 42d regiment ; but it is clear that no fault was attributable to the men of the detachment in question who merely insisted on the fulfilment of the engagement which had been entered into with them.[2]

The regiment returned to Scotland on the termination of hostilities, and was discharged at Perth in 1783.

KEITH'S AND CAMPBELL'S HIGH-LANDERS,

OR

THE OLD EIGHTY-SEVENTH AND EIGHTY-EIGHTH REGIMENTS.

1759—1763.

Keith's Highlanders — Germany — Campbell's High-landers — Germany — Zeirenberg — Fellinghausen — Continental Notions of Highlanders—Brucher Muhl —Reduction of regiments.

THE first of these regiments consisted of three companies of 105 men each. A relation of the celebrated Field-Marshal Keith, Major Robert Murray Keith, who had served in the Scotch Brigade in Holland, was appointed to the command. About the end of the year 1759 this regiment joined the allied army in Germany under Prince Frederick of Bruns-wick.

The Highlanders were not long in the allied camp when they were brought into action. On the 3d of January 1760 the Marquis de Vogue attacked and carried the town of Herborn, and made a small detachment of the allies who were posted there prisoners. At the same time the Marquis Dauvet made himself master of Dillenburg, the garrison of the allied troops retiring into the castle, where they were closely besieged. Prince Ferdinand no sooner understood their situation than he began to march with a strong detachment for their relief on the 7th of January, when he attacked and defeated the besiegers. On the same day "the High-landers under Major Keith, supported by the hussars of Luckner, who commanded the whole detachment, attacked the village of Eybach, where Beau Fremonte's regiment of dragoons was posted, and routed them with great slaughter. The greater part of the regiment was killed, and many prisoners were taken, together with two hundred horses and all their baggage. The Highlanders distinguished them-selves on this occasion by their intrepidity, which was the more remarkable, as they were no other than raw recruits, just arrived from their own country, and altogether unacquainted with discipline." The Highlanders had 4 men killed and 7 wounded.[3]

Prince Ferdinand was so well satisfied with

[3] Smollett.

the conduct of this body, that he recommended to the governor not only to increase it to 800 men, but to raise another regiment of equal strength, to be placed under his serene high-ness. This recommendation was instantly at-tended to, and, in a few weeks, the requisite number of men was raised in the counties of Argyle, Perth, Inverness, Ross, and Sutherland. The command of the new regiment was con-ferred on John Campbell of Dunoon; but power was reserved to the Earls of Suther-land and Breadalbane, the lairds of Macleod and Innes, and other gentlemen in the north, to appoint captains and subalterns to com-panies raised on their respective estates. Major Macnab, son of the laird of Macnab; Captain Archibald Campbell, brother of Achallader; John Campbell of Auch, and other officers, were recommended by Lord Breadalbane; and Macleod, who raised a com-pany in Skye, appointed his nephew, Captain Fothringham of Powrie to it. Sir James Innes, chief of that name, who succeeded to the estates and Dukedom of Roxburgh in the year 1810, was also appointed to a company.

Keith's regiment was embodied at Perth and Campbell's at Stirling, and being em-bodied at the same time, and ordered on the same service, an interchange of officers took place. Embarking for Germany they joined the allied army, under Prince Ferdinand, in 1760, and were distinguished by being placed in the grenadier brigade.

The allied army moved from Kalle on the 30th of July 1760, in consequence of the ad-vance of the French, who took up a position on the river Dymel. The hereditary prince of Brunswick, who had passed that river the pre-ceding day, was directed by Prince Ferdinand to turn the left of the enemy, who were posted between Warburg and Oehsendorff, whilst he himself advanced in front with the main body of the army. The French were attacked almost at the same moment both in flank and rear, and defeated with considerable loss. In an account of the battle written by Prince Ferdinand to George II., he says, "that the loss of the allies, which was moderate, fell chiefly upon Maxwell's brave battalion of English grenadiers and the two regiments of Scots Highlanders, which did wonders. Colonel

Beckwith, who commanded the whole brigade formed of English grenadiers and Scots Highlanders, distinguished himself greatly." None of the Highlanders were killed, but Lieutenant Walter Ogilvie, and two privates were wounded.

Another affair soon occurred in which the Highlanders also distinguished themselves. Prince Ferdinand, having determined to beat up the quarters of a large French detachment stationed at Zeirenberg, pitched upon five battalions, with a detachment of the Highlanders and eight regiments of dragoons, for this service. This body began their march on the night of the 5th of August, and when within two miles of the town the corps proceeded by three different roads—Maxwell's brigade of grenadiers, the regiment of Kingsby, and the Highlanders, keeping together. They marched in profound silence, and though their tramp was at last heard by the French, the surprise was too sudden for effectual resistance. "The Scots Highlanders mounted the breaches sword in hand, supported by the Chasseurs. The column of English grenadiers advanced in good order and with the greatest silence. In short, the service was complete, and the troops displayed equal courage, soldier-like conduct, and activity." [4] The loss of the Highlanders in this affair was 3 privates killed and 6 wounded

The hereditary prince being hard pressed by Marshal de Castries, was reinforced from the camp at Warburg. The Highlanders joined him on the 14th of October shortly after he had been attacked by the Marshal, who had compelled him to retire. The prince now attacked the French commander in his turn, but was unsuccessful, being obliged again to retire after a warm contest, which lasted from five till nine in the morning. The Highlanders, who "were in the first column of attack, were the last to retreat, and kept their ground in the face of every disadvantage, even after the troops on their right and left had retired. The Highlanders were so exasperated with the loss they sustained that it was with difficulty they could be withdrawn, when Colonel Campbell received orders from an aide-de-camp sent by the prince, desiring him to retreat as to persist in maintaining his position longer

[4] Military M....

would be a useless waste of human life." In this action Lieutenants William Ogilvie and Alexander Macleod of the Highlanders, 4 sergeants, and 37 rank and file were killed, and Captain Archibald Campbell of Achallader, Lieutenants Gordon Clunes, Archibald Stewart, Angus Mackintosh of Killachy, and Walter Barland, and 10 rank and file wounded.[5]

On the preceding night an attempt was made by Major Pollock, with 100 grenadiers and the same number of Keith's Highlanders, to surprise the convent of Closter Camp, where a detachment of the enemy was posted, and where, it was supposed, the French commander and some of his officers were to pass the night; but this attempt miscarried. On reaching the sentinel of the main-guard Major Pollock rushed upon him and ran him through the body with his sword. The wounded man, before falling, turned round upon his antagonist and shot him with a pistol, upon which they both fell dead.

The next affair in which the Highlanders were engaged was the battle of Fellinghausen, in July 1762. The commander in chief, in a general order, thus expressed his approbation of the conduct of the corps in this action: "His serene highness, Duke Ferdinand of Brunswick, has been graciously pleased to order Colonel Beckwith to signify to the brigade he has the honour to command his entire approbation of their conduct on the 15th and 16th of July. The soldier-like perseverance of the Highland regiments in resisting and repulsing the repeated attacks *of the chosen troops of France*, has deservedly gained them the highest honour. The ardour and activity with which the grenadiers pushed and pursued the enemy, and the trophies they have taken, justly entitle them *to the highest* encomiums. The intrepidity of the little band of Highlanders merits the greatest praise." Colonel Beckwith, in making his communication, added, that "the humanity and generosity with which the soldiers treated the great flock of prisoners they took, did them as much honour as their subduing the enemy." In this action Major Archibald Campbell of

[5] At this time the corps was joined by a reinforcement of 400 men from Johnstone's Highlanders, and ... aft rwar.. by 200 of Macl.. ...

Achallader, who had been promoted only a week before,[6] and Lieutenants William Ross and John Grant, and 31 rank and file, were killed; and Major Archibald Macnab, Captain James Fraser, Lieutenants Archibald Macarthur, Patrick Campbell, and John Mackintosh, brother of Killachy and father of Sir James Mackintosh, 2 sergeants, and 70 privates, were wounded.

No enterprise of any moment was attempted till the 28th of June 1762, when Prince Ferdinand attacked the French army at Graibenstein, and defeated them. The French lost upwards of 4000 men in killed, wounded, and prisoners, including 200 officers, whilst that sustained by the allies did not exceed 700 men. The British troops, who were under the command of the Marquis of Granby, "behaved with a bravery not to be paralleled, especially our grenadiers and Highlanders."

The Highlanders, from the distinction they had earned in these different encounters, now began to attract the especial notice of the Germans. At a time when an entire ignorance prevailed among the people of England respecting the Highlanders, it is not to be wondered at that the Germans should have formed the most extraordinary notions of these mountaineers. In common with the English they looked upon the Highlanders as savages; but their ignorance went farther, for the people of Germany actually believed that the Highlanders were still strangers to Christianity. "The Scotch Highlanders," says an article which appeared in the *Vienna Gazette* of 1762, "are a people totally different in their dress, manners, and temper from the other inhabitants of Britain. *They are caught in the mountains when young,* and still run with a surprising degree of swiftness. As they are strangers to fear, they make very good soldiers when disciplined. The men are of low stature, and the most of them old or very young. They discover an extraordinary submission and love for their officers, who are all young and handsome. From the goodness of their dispositions in every thing——

for the boors are much better treated by these savages than by the polished French and English; from the goodness of their disposition, which, by the by, shows the rectitude of human nature before it is vitiated by example or prejudice, it is to be hoped that their king's laudable, though late, endeavours to civilise and instruct them in the principles of Christianity will meet with success!" The article adds, that the "French held them at first in great contempt, but they have met with them so often of late, and seen them in the front of so many battles, that they firmly believe that there are twelve battalions of them in the army instead of two. Broglio himself has lately said that he once wished that he was a man of six feet high, but that now he is reconciled to his size since he has seen the wonders performed by the little mountaineers." An acquaintance with the Highlanders soon dissipated the illusions under which the Germans laboured.

The Highlanders were not engaged in the battle of Johannisberg, in which the allies were worsted; but on the 21st of September, in the subsequent action at Brucher Mühl, they took a part. The French occupied a mill on one side of the road, and the allies a redoubt on the other, and the great object of both parties was to obtain possession of a small post which defended the bridge at Brucher Mühl. At first a slight cannonade was opened from a few guns, but these were speedily augmented to twenty-five heavy pieces on each side. In the post occupied by the allies there was only at first 100, but during the action, which lasted without intermission for fifteen hours, no less than seventeen regiments were successively brought forward, replacing one another after they had spent their ammunition. Both sides remained in their respective positions, and although the contest was long and severe the allies lost only 600 in killed and wounded. The Highland corps had Major Alexander Maclean and 21 rank and file killed, and Captain Patrick Campbell and Lieutenant Walter Barland, 3 sergeants, and 58 rank and file wounded.

On the conclusion of hostilities in November 1762 the Highlanders were ordered home. In the three campaigns in which they had

---

[6] The cause of his promotion was his having, with a party of Highlanders, rescued General Griffin, afterwards Lord Howard of Walden, from a strong detachment of the enemy. Major Campbell was brother of Achallader, who, by his classical learning and acquirements, attracted the notice of Lord Lyttleton.

served they had established a well earned reputation for bravery, and so great was the estimation in which they were held by the Dutch,
that, on their march through Holland, they
were welcomed with acclamations, particularly
by the women, who presented them with laurel
leaves,—a feeling which, it is said, was in
some measure owing to the friendly intercourse
which had previously existed between the
inhabitants and the Scotch brigade.

After landing at Tilbury Fort, the regiments
marched for Scotland, and were received everywhere on their route with the most marked
attention, particularly at Derby, the inhabitants of which town presented the men with
gratuities in money. Among various reasons
assigned for the remarkable predilection shown
by the people of Derby, the most probable
is, a feeling of gratitude for the respect shown
by the Highlanders to the persons and pro-
perties of the inhabitants when visited by them
in the year 1745.

Keith's regiment was marched to Perth and
Campbell's to Linlithgow, and they were reduced in July 1763.

The total loss of these corps was 150 men
besides 7 officers killed, and 170 men, and 13
officers, wounded.

EIGHTY-NINTH HIGHLAND
REGIMENT

1759—1765

Raising of the Regiment—India—Reduction

THE war in which Great Britain was engaged
requiring at this time increased exertions on
the part of the government, it was resolved
to raise, in addition to Keith's Highlanders,
another regiment in those parts of the Highlands where the influence of the Gordon
family prevailed. At the solicitation of the
Dowager Duchess of Gordon, Major Staates
Long Morris, to whom she had been lately
married, was appointed to raise the regiment,
and to strengthen his interest amongst the
youth of the North, her eldest son by her
former husband, the late Duke of Gordon, then
a youth at college, was appointed a captain,
his brother, Lord William, a lieutenant, and

his younger brother, Lord George, an ensign.
The object of the duchess in obtaining these
appointments was to counteract the political
influence of the Duke of Argyle during the
minority of her son. Major Morris was so
successful that, in a few weeks, 760 men were
collected at Gordon Castle, who, in December
1759, were marched to Aberdeen.

The regiment embarked at Portsmouth for
the East Indies in December 1760, and arrived
at Bombay in November following. The
Duke of Gordon was desirous of accompanying
the regiment, but his mother, at the especial
request of George II, induced him to remain
at home to finish his education.

The 89th had no particular station assigned
it, but kept moving from place to place till
a strong detachment under Major Hector
Munro joined the army under the command of
Major Carnac, in the neighbourhood of Patna.
Major Munro then assumed the command, and
being well supported by his men, quelled a
formidable mutiny among the troops. After
the ringleaders had been executed, and discipline restored, Major Munro attacked the enemy
at Buxar, on the 23d of October 1764, and
though the force opposed to him was five times
as numerous as his own, he overthrew and
dispersed it. The enemy had 6000 men killed,
and left 130 pieces of cannon on the field,
whilst his majesty's troops had only 2 officers
and 4 rank and file killed. Major Munro
received a letter of thanks on the occasion from
the President and Council of Calcutta. "The
signal victory you gained," they say, "so as
at one blow utterly to defeat the designs of the
enemy against these provinces, is an event
which does so much honour to yourself, Sir,
in particular, and to all the officers and men
under your command, and which, at the same
time, is attended with such particular advantages to the Company, as call upon us to
return you our sincere thanks." For this
important service Major Munro was immediately promoted to the brevet rank of Lieutenant-
colonel.

The services of the regiment being no longer
required, it was ordered home, and was reduced
in the year 1765. It has been remarked, as a
singular circumstance attending their service,
that although five years embodied, four of

which were spent in India, or on the passage going and returning, none of the officers died, nor was there any promotion or other change among them, except the change of Lord William Gordon to the 76th regiment, and the promotion of his successor to his lieutenancy. The same good conduct which distinguished the other Highland corps was not less conspicuous in this,—not one man out of eight of the companies, numbering in all 780, having been brought to the halberts. Of the whole regiment only six men suffered corporal punishment.

- - - - - - - - -

JOHNSTONE'S HIGHLANDERS,
OR
ONE HUNDRED AND FIRST REGIMENT.
1760—1763.

THIS regiment, which consisted of five companies, of 5 sergeants and 105 rank and file each, was raised in the year 1760 by the following gentlemen, viz. Colin Graham of Drainie, James Cuthbert of Milncraigs, Peter Gordon of Knockespic, Ludovick Grant of the family of Rothiemurchus, and Robert Campbell, son of Ballivolin. These all received captain's commissions.

After the companies were completed they assembled at Perth, and thence were marched to Newcastle, where they remained till near the end of the year 1761, when they were sent to Germany, to reinforce Keith's and Campbell's Highlanders. Their officers did not accompany them, but were ordered back to the Highlands to raise six additional companies of the same strength as the other five. This service was soon performed, 600 men having assembled at Perth in a few months. Major, afterwards Sir James Johnstone of Westerhall was appointed to the command of the corps, with the rank of major-commandant. The major, Adjutant Macveah, and Sergeant-major Coxwell, were the only persons in the 101st regiment not Highlanders. Lieutenant-general Lord George Beauclerk reviewed the regiment at Perth in 1762, and declared that he had never seen a body of men in a more "efficient state, and better fitted to meet the enemy." They had, however, no opportunity of realizing the expectations formed of them, not having been called into active service. The regiment was reduced at Perth in August 1763.

LORD MACLEOD'S HIGHLANDERS,
FORMERLY SEVENTY-THIRD REGIMENT,
NOW SEVENTY-FIRST OR GLASGOW
HIGHLAND LIGHT INFANTRY.
1777—1818.
I.

Raising of the Regiment—First Battalion in India—Perambuecum—Porto-Novo—Cuddalore—Number of Regiment changed to 71st—War with Tippoo Saib—Bangalore—Seringapatam—Nundydroog—Savendroog—Seringapatam—Ceylon—Home—Cape of Good-Hope—Buenos Ayres—Home—Peninsula—Roleia—Vimiera—Corunna—Flushing—Sobral—Zibriera—Fuentes d'Onor—Albuera—Arroyo-del-Molinos—Ciudad-Rodrigo—Badajoz—Almaraz—Fort-Napoleon—Salamanca—Alba-de-Tormes—Vittoria—La Puebla—Maya—Lizasso—Eguaros—Doña Maria—Pyrenees—Altobispo—The Nive—St Pierre—Sauveterre—Orthes—Aire—Tarbes—Toulouse—Waterloo—Champs Elysées.

THIS regiment took its orignal name from Lord Macleod, eldest son of the Earl of Cromarty, both of whom were engaged in the rebellion of 1745. Having on account of his youth, received an unconditional pardon for his share in that transaction, Lord Macleod went abroad in quest of employment in foreign service. He sojourned some time at Berlin with Field Marshal Keith, through whose interest, it is believed, he obtained a commission in the Swedish army. At this time his means were so limited that he was unable to equip himself for the service, but the Chevalier de St George, on the recommendation of Lord George Murray, sent him a sum of money to defray the expenses of his outfit. He is described by Lord George as "a young man of real merit," who, he was hopeful, would gain the good opinion of those under whom he was to serve. This expectation was fully realized, and after serving the crown of Sweden twenty-seven years with distinguished efficiency, he obtained the rank of Lieutenant-general.

Though exiled so long from his native country, his attachment to the land of his birth was not in the least abated, and, desirous of revisiting it, he returned to England in the year 1777, and was presented to George III., who received him very graciously. At the suggestion of Colonel Duff of Muirtown, who had served in Keith's Highlanders, and encouraged by the favourable reception he met with in the North, he offered his services to raise a regiment. The offer was accepted, and although without property or political consequence, yet so great was the influence of his name, that 840 Highlanders were raised and marched to Elgin in a very short time. In addition to these, 236 Lowlanders were raised by Captains the Honourable John Lindsay, David Baird, James Fowlis, and other officers, besides 34 English and Irish, who were enlisted in Glasgow, making in all 1100 men. The corps was embodied at Elgin, and inspected there by General Skene in April 1778. About this time letters of service were issued for raising a second battalion of the same size as the first,—a service which was speedily performed. The men of both battalions, of whom nearly 1800 were from those parts of the Highlands where the interest of Lord Macleod's family had once predominated, were of a robust constitution and of exemplary behaviour.

FIRST BATTALION.

Colonel—John Lord Macleod.
Lieut.-Colonel—Duncan M'Pherson.

Majors.

John Elphinston.   James Mackenzie.

Captains.

George Mackenzie.   Hugh Lamont.
Alexander Gilchrist.   Hon. James Lindsay.
John Shaw.   David Baird.
Charles Dalrymple.

Captain Lieutenant and Captain, David Campbell.

Lieutenants.

A. Geddes Mackenzie.   Simon Mackenzie.
Hon. John Lindsay.   Philip Melvill.
Abraham Mackenzie, Adjt.   John Mackenzie.
Alexander Mackenzie.   John Borthwick.
James Robertson.   William Gunn.
John Hamilton.   William Charles Gorrie.
John Hamilton.   Hugh Sibbald.
Lewis Urquhart.   David Rainnie.
George Ogilvie.   Charles Munro.
Innis Munro.

Ensigns.

James Duncan.   George Sutherland.
Simon Mackenzie.   James Thrall.
Alexander Mackenzie.   Hugh Dalrymple.
John Sinclair.

Chaplain—Colin Mackenzie.
Adjutant—Abraham Mackenzie.
Quartermaster—John Lytrott.
Surgeon—Alexander MacDougall.

SECOND BATTALION.

Colonel—John Lord Macleod.
Lieut.-Colonel—The Hon. George Mackenzie

Majors.

Hamilton Maxwell.   Norman Macleod.

Captains.

Hon. Colin Lindsay.   Mackay Hugh Baillie.
John Mackintosh.   Stair Park Dalrymple.
James Foulis.   David Ross.
Robert Sinclair.   Adam Colt.

Lieutenants.

Norman Maclean.   Angus Mackintosh.
John Irving.   John Fraser.
Rod. Mackenzie, senior.   Robert Arbuthnot.
Charles Douglas.   David MacCulloch.
Rod. Mackenzie, junior.   Murdoch Mackenzie.
Phineas Mackintosh.   George Fraser.
John Mackenzie, senior.   John Mackenzie, junior.
Alexander Mackenzie.   Martin Eccles Lindsay.
Phippa Wharton.   John Dallas.
Laughlan MacLaughlan.   David Ross.
Kenneth Mackenzie.   William Erskine.

Ensigns.

John Fraser.   John Forbes.
John MacDougal.   Æneas Fraser.
Hugh Gray.   William Rose.
John Mackenzie.   Simon Fraser, Adjutant.

Chaplain—Æneas Macleod.
Adjutant—Simon Fraser.
Quartermaster—Charles Clark.
Surgeon—Andrew Cairncross.

The first battalion, under Lord Macleod, embarked for the East Indies in January 1779, and arrived in Madras Roads on the 20th of January 1780. The second battalion, under the command of the Honourable Lieut.-Colonel George Mackenzie, brother of Lord Macleod, was sent to Gibraltar, where it landed two days before the arrival of the first battalion at Madras.

The second battalion formed part of the garrison of Gibraltar during the siege, which lasted upwards of three years. In this, the only service in which it was engaged, the battalion had 30 privates killed and 7 sergeants, and 121 rank and file wounded. In May 1783 it returned to England, and was reduced at Stirling in October following. The officers who were regimentally senior in rank had liberty granted to join the first battalion in India.

The first battalion joined the army under Major-General Sir Hector Munro, and assembled at St Thomas's Mount, near Madras, in July 1780. This force amounted to 5209 men, and, with the exception of one battalion of the Company's European troops and the Grenadiers of another and 800 Highlanders, consisted of native troops.

This young and untried regiment had scarcely arrived in India, when Hyder Ali, forcing his way through the Ghauts, at the head of 100,000 men, burst like a mountain torrent into the Carnatic. He had interposed his vast army between that of the British, commanded by Sir Hector Monro, and a smaller force, under the command of Colonel Baillie, which were endeavouring to form a junction. The latter having, though victorious, sustained a serious loss in an engagement with Hyder Ali's troops, sent to the commander an account of his difficult position, stating that, from the loss he had sustained and his total want of provisions, he was equally unable to advance or remain in his then situation. With the advice of a council of war, Sir Hector judged the only course was to endeavour to aid Colonel Baillie, with such a reinforcement as would enable him to push forward in defiance of the enemy. The detachment selected for this enterprise consisted of about 1,000 men under Colonel Fletcher; and its main force was composed of the grenadier and infantry companies of Lord Macleod's regiment, commanded by Captain Baird. Hyder Ali having gained intelligence of this movement, sent a strong body to cut them off on their way, but, by adopting a long circuitous route, and marching by night, they at length safely effected a junction with Colonel Baillie. With the most consummate skill, however, Hyder, determining that they should never return, prepared an ambuscade, into which, early on the morning of the 10th of September, they unwarily advanced. The enemy, with admirable coolness and self-command, reserved their fire till the unhappy British were in the very midst of them. The army under the command of Colonels Baillie and Fletcher, and Captain Baird, marched in column. On a sudden, whilst in a narrow defile, a battery of twelve guns opened upon them, and, loaded with grape-shot, poured in upon their right flank. The British faced about; another battery opened immediately upon their rear. They had no choice therefore, but to advance; other batteries met them here likewise, and in less than half an hour fifty-seven pieces of cannon, brought to bear on them at all points, penetrated into every part of the

British line. By seven o'clock in the morning, the enemy poured down upon them in thousands: Captain Baird and his grenadiers fought with the greatest heroism. Surrounded and attacked on all sides, by 25,000 cavalry, by thirty regiments of Sepoy infantry, besides Hyder's European corps, and a numerous artillery playing upon them from all quarters, within grape shot distance, yet did this gallant column stand firm and undaunted, alternately facing their enemies on every side of attack. The French officers in Hyder's camp beheld with astonishment the British Grenadiers, under Captain Baird's command, performing their evolutions in the midst of all the tumult and extreme peril, with as much precision, coolness, and steadiness, as if upon a parade ground. The little army, so unexpectedly assailed, had only ten pieces of cannon, but these made such havoc amongst the enemy, that after a doubtful contest of three hours, from six in the morning till nine, victory began to declare for the British. The flower of the Mysore cavalry, after many bloody repulses, were at length entirely defeated, with great slaughter, and the right wing, composed of Hyder's best forces, was thrown into disorder. Hyder himself was about to give orders for retreat, and the French officer who directed the artillery began to draw it off, when an unforeseen and unavoidable disaster occurred, which totally changed the fortune of the day. By some unhappy accident the tumbrils which contained the ammunition suddenly blew up in the centre of the British lines. One whole face of their column was thus entirely laid open, and their artillery overturned and destroyed. The destruction of men was great, but the total loss of their ammunition was still more fatal to the survivors. Tippoo Saib, the son of Hyder, instantly seized the moment of advantage, and without waiting for orders, fell with the utmost rapidity, at the head of the Mogul and Carnatic horse, into the broken square, which had not had time to recover its form and order. This attack by the enemy's cavalry being immediately seconded by the French corps, and by the first line of infantry, determined at once the fate of our unfortunate army. After successive prodigies of valour, the brave Sepoys were almost to a man cut to pieces. Colonels

Baillie and Fletcher, assisted by Captain Baird, made one more desperate effort. They rallied the Europeans, and, under the fire of the whole immense artillery of the enemy, gained a little eminence, and formed themselves into a new square. In this form did this intrepid band, though totally without ammunition, the officers fighting only with their swords and the soldiers with their bayonets, resist and repulse the myriads of the enemy in thirteen different attacks; until at length, incapable of withstanding the successive torrents of fresh troops which

Sir David Baird, from a painting by Raeburn.

were continually pouring upon them, they were fairly borne down and trampled upon, many of them still continuing to fight under the very legs of the horses and elephants. To save the lives of the few brave men who survived, Colonel Baillie had displayed his handkerchief on his sword, as a flag of truce; quarter was promised, but no sooner had the troops laid down their arms than they were attacked with savage fury by the enemy. By

the humane interference, however, of the French officers in Hyder's service, many lives were saved. Colonel Fletcher was slain on the field. Colonel Baillie, severely wounded, and several other officers, with two hundred Europeans, were made prisoners. When brought into the presence of Hyder, he, with true Asiatic barbarism, received them with the most insolent triumph. The British officers, with a spirit worthy of their country, retorted with an indignant coolness and contempt. "Your son will inform you," said Colonel Baillie, "that you owe the victory to our disaster, rather than to our defeat." Hyder angrily ordered them from his presence, and commanded them instantly to prison. Captain Baird had received two sabre-wounds on his head, a ball in his thigh, and a pike-wound in his arm. He lay a long time on the field of battle, narrowly escaping death from some of the more ferocious of the Mysore cavalry, who traversed the field spearing the wounded, and at last being unable to reach the force under Munro, he was obliged to surrender to the enemy.

The result of this battle was the immediate retreat of the main army under Sir Hector Munro to Madras. Colonel Baillie, Captain Baird, and five other British officers were marched to one of Hyder's nearest forts, and afterwards removed to Seringapatam, where they were joined by others of their captive countrymen, and subjected to a most horrible and protracted imprisonment. It was commonly believed in Scotland that Captain Baird was chained by the leg to another man; and Sir Walter Scott, writing in May 1821 to his son, then a cornet of dragoons, with his regiment in Ireland, when Sir David was commander of the forces there, says, "I remember a story that when report came to Europe that Tippoo's prisoners (of whom Baird was one) were chained together two and two, his mother said, 'God pity the poor lad that's chained to our Davie!'" She knew him to be active, spirited and daring, and probably thought that he would make some desperate effort to escape. But it was not the case that he was chained to another. On the 10th of May all the prisoners had been put in irons except Captain Baird; this indignity he was not subjected to till the 10th of November following. "When they were about," says his biographer, "to put the irons on Captain Baird, who was completely disabled in his right leg, in which the wound was still open, and whence the ball had just then been extracted, his friend Captain Lucas, who spoke the language perfectly, sprang forward, and represented in very strong terms to the Myar the barbarity of fettering him while in such a dreadful state, and assured him that death would be the inevitable termination of Captain Baird's sufferings if the intention were persisted in. The Myar replied that the Circar had sent as many pairs of irons as there were prisoners, and they must be put on. Captain Lucas then offered to wear two sets himself, in order to save his friend. This noble act of generosity moved the compassion even of the Myar, who said he would send to the Kellidar, (commander of the fort,) to open the book of fate. He did so, and when the messenger returned, he said the book had been opened, and Captain Baird's fate was good; and the irons were in consequence not put on at that time. Could they really have looked into the volume of futurity, Baird would undoubtedly have been the last man to be spared."[1] Each pair of irons was nine pounds weight. Captain Lucas died in prison. Captain Baird lived to revenge the sufferings which he and his fellow-prisoners endured by the glorious conquest of Seringapatam on the 4th of May, 1799.

Some time after the battle of Conjeveram, Lord Macleod took ship for England, having, it is said, differed in opinion with General Munro on the subject of his movements, particularly those preceding Colonel Baillie's disaster. He was succeeded in the command of the 73d by Colonel James Crawford, who, with the regiment now reduced to 500 men, joined the army under Sir Eyre Coote on the morning

[1] *Life of Sir David Baird*, vol. i. p. 44.

of the 1st of July 1781, when about to attack the enemy at Porto Novo.

General Coote's army did not exceed 8000 men, of which the 73d was the only British regiment. The force under Hyder Ali consisted of 25 battalions of infantry, 400 Europeans, between 40,000 and 50,000 horse, and above 100,000 matchlock men, peons, and polygars, with 47 pieces of cannon. Notwithstanding this immense disparity of force, Sir Eyre Coote determined to attack Hyder, and, accordingly, drew up his army in two lines, the first commanded by Major-general Hector Munro, and the second by Major-general James Stewart. A plain divided the two armies, beyond which the enemy were drawn up on ground strengthened by front and flanking redoubts and batteries. General Coote advanced to the attack at nine o'clock, and, after a contest of eight hours, the enemy was forced from all his entrenchments, and compelled to retire.

The 73d was on the right of the first line, and led all the attacks, to the full approbation of General Coote, whose notice was particularly attracted by one of the pipers, who always blew up his most warlike sounds whenever the fire became hotter than ordinary. This so pleased the General that he cried aloud, "Well done, my brave fellow, you shall have a pair of silver pipes for this!" The promise was not forgotten, and a handsome pair of pipes was presented to the regiment, with an inscription in testimony of the General's esteem for its conduct and character.

After a variety of movements, both armies again met, August 27th, near Perambaucum, the spot so fatal to Colonel Baillie's detachment.

"Perhaps there come not within the wide range of human imagination scenes more affecting, or circumstances more touching, than many of our army had that day to witness and to bear. On the very spot where they stood lay strewed amongst their feet the relics of their dearest fellow soldiers and friends, who near twelve months before had been slain by the hands of those very inhuman monsters that now appeared a second time eager to complete the work of blood. One poor soldier, with the tear of affection glistening in his eye, picked up the decaying spatterdash of his valued brother, with the name yet entire upon it, which the tinge of blood and effects of weather had kindly spared. Another discovered the club or plaited hair of his bosom friend, which he himself had helped to form, and knew by the tie and still remaining colour. A third mournfully recognised the feather which had decorated the cap of his inseparable companion. The scattered clothes and wings of the flank companies of the 73d were everywhere perceptible, as also their helmets and skulls, both of which bore the marks of many furrowed cuts.

These horrid spectacles, too melancholy to dwell upon, while they melted the hardest hearts, inflamed our soldiers with an enthusiasm and thirst of revenge such as render men invincible; but their ardour was necessarily checked by the involved situation of the army."[2]

Hyder Ali, in anticipation of an attack, had taken up a strong position on ground intersected by deep water courses and ravines. The British commander formed his line of battle under a heavy fire, which the troops bore with firmness. An obstinate contest took place, which lasted from nine in the morning till sun-set. Hyder then abandoned his position, leaving General Coote master of the field of battle. The loss of the British was upwards of 400 killed and wounded, almost all native troops.

Colonel Crawford having become second in command, in consequence of the departure of General Munro for England, and the disabling of General Stewart in the last-mentioned action, Captain Shaw assumed the command of the 73d regiment. It continued attached to General Coote's army, and was present at the battles of Sholungar on the 27th of September 1781, and of Arnee on the 2d of June 1782.[3]

Having obtained reinforcements from England, General Stewart, who had recovered from his wounds, and succeeded to the command of the army on the death of General Coote, who died in April 1783, resolved to attack Cuddalore, the garrison of which had also obtained considerable additions from the Isle of France. General Stuart accordingly appeared before the place on the 6th of June 1783, and as M. Bussy, who commanded the garrison, was active in increasing his means of defence, he determined to make a speedy attack, and fixed the morning of the 13th for that purpose. The firing of three guns from a hill was to be the signal for a simultaneous assault at three different points; but in consequence of the noise of the cannonade which was immediately opened, the signals were not distinguished, and the attacks were not made at the same time. The enemy were thus enabled to direct their whole forces against each successive attack, and the result was, that one of the divisions was driven back. In the ardour of the pursuit, the besieged evacuated their redoubts, which were instantly taken possession of by Lieutenant-colonel Cathcart with the Grenadiers, and Lieutenant-colonel Stuart "with the precious remains of the 73d regiment." Though Colonel Stuart's party were forced to retire from the more advanced posts, yet as they retained possession of the principal redoubts, the advantage already was on the side of the British. In the belief that the French would retire from all their advanced posts during the night, General Stuart did not attempt to carry them. This expectation was realised. In this affair the 73d had Captains Alexander Mackenzie, and the Honourable James Lindsay, Lieutenants Simon Mackenzie and James Trail, 4 sergeants and 80 rank and file killed; and Captain John Hamilton, Lieutenants Charles Gorrie, David Rannie, John Sinclair, James Duncan, and George Sutherland, 5 sergeants, and 107 rank and file wounded. The casualties of the enemy exceeded 1000 men.

The following flattering compliment formed part of the general orders issued by the Commander-in-chief at the conclusion of the battle :—" I am also grateful to Captain Lamont and the officers under his command, who gallantly led the *precious remains* of the 73d regiment through the most perilous road to glory, until exactly one half of the officers and men of the battalion were either killed or wounded."

[2] Cannon's 71st, p. 16.

[3] In these encounters the regiment suffered little loss. Munro in his narrative mentions the following case : "I take this opportunity of commemorating the fall of John Doune Mackay, corporal in Macleod's Highlanders, son of Robert Doune, the bard whose singular talent for the beautiful and extemporaneous composition of Gaelic poetry, was held in such esteem. This son of the bard had frequently revived the spirits of his countrymen, when drooping in a long march, by singing the humorous and lively productions of his father. He was killed by a cannon-shot, and buried with military honours by his comrades the same evening."

With the aid of 2400 men from the fleet, under Admiral Suffrein, Bussy made a spirited sortie on the 25th of June, but was driven back with great loss. Hostilities terminated on the 1st of July in consequence of accounts of the signature of preliminaries of peace between Great Britain and France having been received. The army returned to St Thomas's Mount at the conclusion of the definitive treaty of peace, in March, 1784.

In consequence of the arrangements made when the second battalion was reduced, the Honourable Lieutenant-Colonel George Mackenzie, and some other officers of that corps, joined the regiment in 1785. Next year the number of the regiment was changed to the 71st, on which occasion it received new colours. The same year the corps sustained a heavy loss by the death of Colonel Mackenzie, when Captain (afterwards General Sir David) Baird was appointed Major. Lord Macleod died in 1789, and was succeeded in the Colonelcy by the Honourable Major-General William Gordon. The strength of the regiment was at this time about 800 men, having been kept up to that number by occasional detachments from Scotland.

The war between Tippoo Saib and the East India Company, which broke out in 1790, brought the regiment again into active service. In May of that year, the 71st and Seaforth's Highlanders (now the 72d), joined a large army assembled at Trichinopoly, the command of of which was assumed by Major-General Meadows. The right wing was commanded by Lieutenant-Colonel James Stuart, and the left by Lieutenant-Colonel Bridges, while the two Highland regiments formed the second brigade. In the campaign against Tippoo, the 71st followed all the movements of the army. The flank companies were employed in the attack on Dindegul, and the regiment was after the capture of that place, engaged in the siege of Palacatcherry.

Lord Cornwallis joined the army early in 1791 as Commander-in-chief, and, after various movements, encamped close to Bangalore on the 5th of March. He made an assault on the 21st, and carried the place with little loss. The attack was led by the flank companies, including those of the 71st, all under the com-

mand of the Honourable John Lindsay and Captain James Robertson, son of Principal Robertson the historian.

Having obtained a reinforcement of 10,000 well mounted native cavalry and some European troops from the Carnatic, Lord Cornwallis advanced upon Seringapatam, and on the 13th of May came within sight of the enemy, drawn up a few miles from the town, having the river on their right, and the heights of Carrighaut on their left. On the 15th the enemy were forced from a strong position, and driven across the river into the island on which the capital stands. In this affair the 71st had Lieutenant Roderick Mackenzie, and 7 rank and file killed, and Ensign (afterwards Lieutenant-Colonel of the 50th regiment[4]) Chas Stewart, and 74 rank and file wounded.

The advanced state of the season, and other unfavourable circumstances operating against a siege, Lord Cornwallis retired to Bangalore. From this place he detached Major Gowdie to attack Nundydroog, a strong fortified granite rock of great height. Except on one side this fortress was inaccessible, and care had been taken to strengthen that part by a double line of ramparts, and an outwork covered the gate by a flanking fire. Notwithstanding its great elevation, and very steep ascent, Nundydroog could still be approached, though it required immense labour to render the approaches available. After fourteen days' intense exertion, the besiegers succeeded in drawing up some guns, and erecting batteries on the face of a craggy precipice, from which they made two breaches, one on the re-entering angle of the outwork, and the other in the curtain of the outer wall.

Moving with his whole army towards Nundydroog, on the 18th of October, Lord Cornwallis made preparations for storming the place. An assault by night having been determined upon, Lieutenant Hugh Mackenzie, (afterwards paymaster of the 71st,) with twenty grenadiers of the 36th and 71st regiments, was to lead the attack on the right, and Lieutenant Moore, with twenty light infantry, and two flank companies of the same regiment, under the command of Lieutenants Duncan and Kenneth Mackenzie, was to lead the left. The whole was under the command of Captain (afterwards

He died in Spain, in the year 1810.

Lieutenant-General) James Robertson, supported by Captain (afterwards Major-General)
Burns, with the grenadiers, and Captain Hartly
with the light infantry of the 36th regiment.
Whilst waiting the signal to advance, one of
the soldiers whispered something about a *mine*.
General Meadows overhearing the observation,
took advantage of the circumstance, by intimat-
ing that there *was* a mine, but it was "a mine
of gold." This remark was not thrown away
upon the troops.

Apprehensive of an assault, the enemy had
provided themselves with huge masses of granite, to hurl down upon the besiegers when
they should attempt to ascend the rock. The
assault was made on the morning of the 19th
of October, in a clear moonlight, and in spite
of every obstacle the assailants effected a lodgement within one hundred yards of the breach.
Driven from the outward rocks, the enemy attempted to barricade the gate of the inner rampart; but it was soon forced, and the place
carried with the loss of 30 men amongst the
native troops killed and wounded, principally
from the stones which were rolled down the
rock.

Encouraged by this success, Lord Cornwallis
next laid siege to Savendroog, the strongest
rock in the Mysore, and hitherto deemed impregnable. This stronghold was considerably
higher than Nundydroog, and was separated
by a chasm into two parts at the top, on each
of which parts was a fort, but each independent
of the other. The arduous duty of reducing this
stronghold was intrusted to Lieutenant-Colonel
Stuart, who had already distinguished himself
in other enterprises. Some of the outworks
were battered, preparatory to an assault, which
was fixed for the 21st of December. Accordingly on the morning of that day, the flank
companies of the 52d, the two Highland regiments and the 76th, were assembled under the
command of Lieutenant-Colonel Nisbet of the
52d, and at eleven o'clock in the forenoon, the
party advanced to the assault to the air of
Britons Strike Home, performed by the band
of the 52d regiment. The assailants then ascended the rock, clambering up a precipice
which was so nearly perpendicular, that after
the capture of the place the men were afraid to
descend. The citadel on the eastern top was

soon carried, and eventually the whole of the
rock, the assailants losing only two men. This
success was soon followed by the capture of all
the other strongholds in the Mysore.

Bent upon the capture of the Sultan's capital, the possession of which would, it was supposed, finish the war, Lord Cornwallis, in the
month of January 1792, put his army in motion
for Seringapatam, of which place he came in
sight on the 4th of February. On the evening of the 6th he formed his army into three
columns; the right column consisting of the
36th and 76th regiments, being under the command of General Meadows; the centre one, consisting of the 52d, with the 71st and 74th Highland regiments, under Lord Cornwallis, with
Lieutenant-Colonels James Stuart and the
Honourable John Knox; and the left column,
being the 72d Highland regiment under Lieutenant-Colonel Maxwell. The native troops
were divided in proportion to each column.
General Meadows was to penetrate the enemy's
left, after which he was to attempt to open and
preserve the communication with Lord Cornwallis's division, by directing all his efforts towards the centre. Part of the centre division,
under Colonel Stewart, was to pierce through
the centre of the enemy's camp, and attack the
works on the island, while Colonel Maxwell,
with the left wing was directed to force the
works on Carrighaut Hill, and descending thence
to turn the right of the main division, and
unite with Colonel Stuart. The three columns
began to move at eight o'clock in the evening.
"The head of the centre column led by the flank
companies of the regiment, after twice crossing
the Lockary, which covered the right wing of
the enemy, came in contact with their first line,
which was instantly driven across the north
branch of the Cavery, at the foot of the glacis
of the fort of Seringapatam. Captain Lindsay,
with the grenadiers of the 71st, attempted to
push into the body of the place, but was
prevented by the raising of the drawbridge a
few minutes before he advanced. He was here
joined by some grenadiers and light infantry
of the 52d and 76th regiments. With this
united force he pushed down to the Loll
Bang, where he was fiercely attacked by a body
of the enemy, whom he quickly drove back
with the bayonet. His numbers were soon

afterwards increased by the grenadier company of the 74th, when he attempted to force his way into the Pettah (or town,) but was opposed by such overwhelming numbers that he did not succeed. He then took post in a small redoubt, where he maintained himself till morning, when he moved to the north bank of the river, and joined Lieutenant-Colonels Knox and Baird, with the troops who formed the left of the attack. During these operations the battalion companies of the 52d, 71st, and 72d regiments forced their way across the river to the island, overpowering all that opposed them. At this moment, Captain Archdeacon, commanding a battalion of Bengal seapoys, was killed. This threw the corps into some confusion, and caused it to fall back on the 71st, at the moment that Major Dalrymple was preparing to attack the Sultan's redoubt, and thus impeded his movements. However, the redoubt was attacked, and instantly carried. The command was given to Captain Sibbald, who had led the attack with his company of the 71st. The animating example and courage of this officer made the men equally irresistible in attack, and firm in the defence of the post they had gained. The enemy made several vain attempts to retake it. In one of these the brave Captain Sibbald was killed. Out of compliment to this officer, the Commander-in-chief changed the name from Sultan's to Sibbald's redoubt. In this obstinate defence the men had consumed their ammunition, when, by a fortunate circumstance, two loaded oxen of the enemy, frightened by the firing, broke loose from their drivers, and taking shelter in the ditch of this redoubt, afforded an ample and seasonable supply. The command of this post was assumed by Major Kelly of the 74th regiment, who had gone up with orders from the Commander-in-chief, and remained there after the death of Captain Sibbald. The Sultan seemed determined to recover this redoubt distinguished by his own name, and directed the French troops to attack it. But they met with no better success than the former, notwithstanding their superior discipline."[5]

The loss of the enemy in this affair was estimated at 4000 men and 80 pieces of cannon. That on the side of the assailants was 535 men

[5] Stewart' Sket'h.

killed and wounded. Of the 71st, Captain Sibbald and Lieutenant Baine, 2 sergeants, and 34 rank and file were killed; and Ensigns Duncan Mackenzie, and William Baillie, 3 sergeants, and 67 rank and file wounded.

On the 9th of February Major-General Robert Abercromby, with the army from Bombay, consisting of the 73d and 75th Highland, and 77th, besides some native regiments, joined the besieging army. Operations for the siege were begun the same day; but nothing particular occurred till the 18th, when Major Dalrymple, to cover the opening of the trenches, crossed the Cavery at nine o'clock at night, and surprised and routed a camp of Tippoo's horse. During the three following days traverses were finished; and on the 22d, the enemy, after a warm contest, were defeated by a part of the Bombay army under General Abercromby. This was the last effort of the Sultan, who sued for peace, and obtained it at the expense of nearly one-half of his dominions, which he ceded to the East India Company.

On the termination of the war, the 71st, now under the command of Lieutenant-colonel David Baird, was marched to the neighbourhood of Trichinopoly, where they remained till the breaking out of the war with France, in 1793. The flank companies were employed on the expedition against Ceylon, in the month of August that year, in which enterprise Captain Gerrie was severely wounded, and 11 men were killed and wounded.

On the 2d of January 1797, the regiment was inspected by Major-general Clarke, who issued the following general order :—

"Major-General Clarke has experienced infinite satisfaction, this morning, at the review of His Majesty's 71st regiment.

" He cannot say that on any occasion of field exercise he ever was present at a more perfect performance.

" When a corps is so striking in appearance, and so complete in every branch of its discipline, little can occur to the Commander in-chief to particularise. He cannot but notice, however, that the 71st regiment has excited his admiration for its expertness in those parts of its exercise which are most essential, and most difficult to execute. He alludes to its order and regularity when moving in line ; its extreme accuracy in preserving distances, and the neatness and promptitude that are so evident in all its formations. So much perfection in a corps, whose services in India will long be held in remembrance, does the greatest honour to Lieut.-Colonel Baird and all his officers, to whom and the corps at large, the Commander-in-chief desires to offer his best thanks."

In October 1797, in consequence of orders, all the soldiers fit for service, amounting to 560 men, were drafted into the 73d and 74th regiments; those unfit for service, along with the officers and non-commissioned officers, sailed from Madras for England on the 17th of October, and arrived in the Thames in August 1798. The regiment was then removed to Leith, and thence to Stirling, after an absence of nearly 18 years from Scotland [e]

As a mark of indulgence, a general leave of of 2 months was granted to the officers and men of the 71st, to enable them to visit their friends and families, after so long an absence from their native country.

The regiment remained in Scotland till June, 1800, when it was removed to Ireland, having previously received an accession of 600 volunteers from the Scottish fencible regiments. This augmented the corps to 800 men, of whom 600 were Highlanders. On the 24th of April, 1801, Lieutenant-Colonel Pack joined and assumed command of the regiment. In August 1803, Major-General Sir John Francis Cradock was appointed Colonel of the 71st, in succession to General the Honourable William Gordon. A second battalion was ordered to be embodied at Dumbarton, in the year 1804. From the success with which the recruiting for this battalion was carried on in Glasgow, and the favour shown to the men by the inhabitants, the corps acquired the name of the "Glasgow Highland Light Infantry."

The first battalion sailed from Cork on the 5th of August, 1805, on the expedition against the Cape of Good Hope, (of which an account will be found under the head of the Sutherland Regiment,) and reached its destination on the 4th of January, 1806. On this service the regiment had 6 rank and file killed, and Brevet-Lieutenant-Colonel Robert Campbell, 5 sergeants, and 67 rank and file wounded.

This enterprise was followed by that against Buenos Ayres, of which the 71st formed the chief force. The expedition reached the Rio de la Plata on the 8th of June, and passing Monte Video, anchored opposite to the city of Buenos Ayres, on the 24th. The troops and the marines of the fleet, amounting together to about 1400 men, landed the following evening without opposition. Next forenoon the troops moved forward to the village of Reduction in full view of the enemy, who were posted on the brow of an adjoining eminence. The enemy, after firing a few shots, retired into the city. On the 27th the passage of the Rio Chuelo was forced, and the result was that the city surrendered. The Spaniards, however, soon attempted to regain what they had lost, and in the beginning of August collected a force of 1500 men in the neighbourhood; but these were attacked and dispersed by General Beresford, with a detachment of the 71st, and the corps of St Helena. Notwithstanding their dispersion, however, these troops collected again, and on the 10th of August, surprised and cut off a sergeant's guard. Next day the town was abandoned by the British, who retired to the fort, and seeing no prospect of relief, capitulated the same evening. The 71st lost in this expedition Lieutenant Mitchell and Ensign Lucas, and 91 non-commissioned officers and privates were killed and wounded.

After the capitulation of General Whitelock's army, the regiment was restored to liberty, and embarked with the troops for England. The regiment landed in Ireland and marched to Middleton and afterwards to Cork, where it received a reinforcement of 200 men from the second battalion, by which the effective force was increased to 920 men. On the 21st of April, 1808, the regiment received new colours instead of those they had surrendered at Buenos Ayres. The colours were presented by General Floyd, a veteran officer, who had frequently witnessed the gallantry of the 71st in India. He made an eloquent speech on the occasion, the conclusion of which was as follows:—

[e] On the 23d of May 1821, His Majesty King George the Fourth was graciously pleased to authorise the 71st to bear on the regimental colour and appointments the word "HINDOOSTAN," in commemoration of its distinguished services in the several actions in which it had been engaged, while in India, between the years 1780 and 1797

"SEVENTY-FIRST,

"I am directed to perform the honourable duty of presenting your colours.

"Brave SEVENTY-FIRST! The world is well acquainted with your gallant conduct at the capture of *Buenos Ayres*, in South America, under one of His Majesty's bravest generals.

"It is well known that you defended your conquest with the utmost courage, good conduct, and discipline to the last extremity. When diminished to a handful, hopeless of succour, and destitute of provisions, you were overwhelmed by multitudes, and reduced by the fortune of war to lose your liberty, and your well-defended colours, but not your honour. Your honour, SEVENTY-FIRST regiment, remains unsullied. Your last act in the field covered you with glory. Your generous despair, calling upon your general to suffer you to die with arms in your hands proceeded from the genuine spirit of British soldiers. Your behaviour in prosperity,—your sufferings in captivity,—and your faithful discharge of your duty to your King and country, are appreciated by all.

"You who now stand on this parade, in defiance of the allurements held out to base desertion, are endeared to the army and to the country, and your conduct will ensure you the esteem of all true soldiers,—of all worthy men, —and fill every one of you with honest martial pride.

"It has been my good fortune to have witnessed, in a remote part of the world, the early glories and gallant conduct of the SEVENTY-FIRST regiment in the field; and it is with great satisfaction I meet you again, with replenished ranks, and with good arms in your hands, and with stout hearts in your bosoms.

"Look forward, officers and soldiers, to the achievement of new honours and the acquirement of fresh fame.

"Officers, be the friends and guardians of these brave fellows committed to your charge.

'Soldiers, give your confidence to your officers. They have shared with you the chances of war; they have bravely bled along with you; they will always do honour to themselves and you. Preserve your regiment's reputation for valour in the field and regularity in quarters.

"I have now the honour to present the ROYAL COLOUR.

This is the KING's COLOUR.

"I have now the honour to present your REGIMENTAL COLOUR.

"This is the colour of the SEVENTY-FIRST regiment.

"May victory for ever crown these colours."

The expectations which General Floyd had formed of the regiment were soon to be realised. In the month of June the first battalion of the regiment embarked at Cork for Portugal, in the expedition under Sir Arthur Wellesley, which sailed on the 13th of July. The fleet arrived in Mondego Bay on the 29th, and the forces, amounting to 10,000 men, landed early in August. In a few days a body of 5000 troops from Gibraltar joined the army. General Wellesley made a forward movement towards Lisbon on the 9th of August, and was joined on the 11th by 6000 Portuguese, but being destitute of provisions and military stores he could not proceed. The British army reached Caldas on the 14th—four companies of the 60th and Rifle corps pushing forward to the village of Brilos, then in possession of the enemy. An affair of advanced posts now took place, which ended in the occupation of the village by the British. This was the commencement of a series of battles and operations which raised the military fame of Great Britain to the highest pitch, overtopping all the glories of Marlborough's campaigns. Lieutenant Bunbury and a few privates of the Rifle corps were killed on this occasion.

The French under General Laborde, amounting to upwards of 5000 men, took up a position on the heights of Roleia, whither they were followed by the British on the 17th. These heights were steep and very difficult of access, with only a narrow path leading to the summit; but notwithstanding the almost insuperable obstacles which presented themselves, the position was carried by the British, after a gallant resistance by the French, who were forced to retreat at all points. The light company of the 71st was the only part of the regiment engaged, the remainder being employed in manœuvring on the right flank of the French. The company had only one man killed and one wounded.

II.

3 Q

The regiment acted a conspicuous part in the battle of Vimeira, which took place on the 21st of August 1808.

It was Sunday morning, and the men were engaged in washing their clothes, cleaning their fire-locks, and in other employments, when the French columns made their appearance on the opposite hills, about half-past eight. "To arms" was sounded, and everything being packed up as soon as possible, the 71st, along with the other brigaded regiments, left the camp ground, and moved across a valley to the heights on the east of Vimeira.

The grenadier company of the 71st greatly distinguished itself, in conjunction with a sub-division of the light company of the 36th regiment. Captain Alexander Forbes, who commanded the grenadier company, was ordered to the support of some British artillery, and, seizing a favourable opportunity, made a dash at a battery of the enemy's artillery immediately in his front. He succeeded in capturing five guns and a howitzer, with horses, caissons, and equipment complete. In this affair alone the grenadier company had Lieutenants John Pratt and Ralph Dudgeon and 13 rank and file wounded, together with 2 men killed.[7]

The French made a daring effort to retake their artillery, both with cavalry and infantry; but the gallant conduct of the grenadier company, and the advance of Major-General Ferguson's brigade, finally left the guns in the possession of those who had so gallantly captured them.

George Clark, one of the pipers of the regiment, and afterwards piper to the Highland Society of London, was wounded in this action, and being unable to accompany his corps in the advance against the enemy, put his pipes in order, and struck up a favourite regimental air, to the great delight of his comrades. This is the second instance in which the pipers of the 71st have behaved with particular gallantry, and evinced high feeling for the credit and honour of the corps.

[7] Lieut.-General Sir Harry Burrard landed during the action, but did not assume the command. Lieut.-General Sir Hew Dalrymple landed on the following day, and took command of the army. The force under Lieut.-General Sir John Moore was also disembarked during the negotiation, which subsequently took place, making the British army amount to 32,000 men.

During the advance of the battalion, several prisoners were taken, among whom was the French general, Brennier. Corporal John M'Kay, of the 71st, who took him, was afterwards promoted to an ensigncy in the Fourth West India Regiment.

The result of this battle was the total defeat of the enemy, who subsequently retreated on Lisbon, with the loss of twenty-one pieces of cannon, twenty-three ammunition waggons, with powder, shells, stores of all descriptions, and 20,000 rounds of musket ammunition, together with a great many officers and soldiers killed, wounded, and taken prisoners.

The conduct of the battalion, and of its commanding officer, Lieut.-Colonel Pack, was noticed in the public despatches, and the thanks of both Houses of Parliament were conferred on the troops.

The following officers of the 71st were wounded in the battle of Vimeira :—Captains Arthur Jones and Maxwell Mackenzie; Lieutenants John Pratt, William Hartley, Augustus M'Intyre, and Ralph Dudgeon; Ensign James Campbell, and Acting Adjutant R. M'Alpin.

The 71st subsequently received the royal authority to bear the word "Vimeira" on the regimental colour and appointments, in commemoration of this battle.

The "Convention of Cintra," signed on the 30th of August, was the result of this victory. By its provisions the French army evacuated Portugal, which thus became freed from its oppressors.

In September, Lieutenant-General Sir John Moore assumed the command and made dispositions for entering Spain. The 71st was brigaded with the 36th and 92d regiments under Brigadier-General Catlin Crawfurd, and placed in the division under the command of Lieutenant-General the Honourable John Hope, afterwards the Earl of Hopetoun. On the 27th October the division left Lisbon, and joined the forces under Moore at Salamanca. The regiment took part in the disastrous retreat under Sir John Moore to Corunna, and along with the rest of the army suffered dreadfully from the severity of the weather, want of food and clothing, and disease.

"At this period the situation of the British

army was dispiriting in the extreme. In the midst of winter, in a dreary and desolate country, the soldiers, chilled and drenched with the heavy rains, and wearied by long and rapid marches, were almost destitute of fuel to cook their victuals, and it was with extreme difficulty that they could procure shelter. Provisions were scarce, irregularly issued, and difficult of attainment. The waggons, in which were their magazines, baggage, and stores, were often deserted in the night by the Spanish drivers, who were terrified by the approach of the French. Thus baggage, ammunition, stores, and even money were destroyed to prevent them falling into the hands of the enemy; and the weak, the sick, and the wounded were necessarily left behind. The 71st suffered in proportion with the rest, and by weakness, sickness, and fatigue, lost about 93 men."[8]

In January 1809, Lieutenant-General Francis Dundas was appointed from the 94th regiment to be Colonel of the 71st, in succession to Sir John Francis Cradock, removed to the 43d.

On the 11th of January the army under Moore arrived at Corunna, where the furious battle was fought in which this famous leader got his death-wound. We have already, in our account of the 42d, given sufficient details of this engagement. While waiting for the transports some skirmishing took place with the French, in which four companies of the 71st were warmly engaged, and lost several men in killed and wounded. In the general battle on the 16th, the 71st, being placed on the extreme left of the British line, had little to do therein. In commemoration of this battle, and of the conduct of the regiment during the expedition, the 71st was authorised to bear the word *Corunna* on the regimental colours and appointments.

On the 17th of January the army embarked for England, and reached Plymouth about the end of the month, where the men were received by the people with the utmost enthusiasm, and were welcomed into every house as if they had been relations.[9] The battalion in which was the 71st was marched to Ashford barracks, where it remained for some time. In June the first battalion was increased by the addition of

several officers and 311 non-commissioned officers and men from the second battalion which continued to be stationed in Scotland, and by a number of volunteers from the militia.

In March 1809, the royal authority was granted for the 71st to be formed into a light infantry regiment, when it was directed that the clothing, arming, and discipline should be the same as those of other regiments of a similar kind. However, it cannot be said to have ceased to be a Highland regiment, for the men were permitted to retain such parts of the national dress as might not be inconsistent with their duties as a light corps. Lieutenant-Colonel Pack wrote to the Adjutant-General, in April 1810, on the subject, and received the following reply from headquarters:—

"HORSE GUARDS, 12th April 1810.

"SIR,—Having submitted to the Commander-in Chief your letter of the 4th instant, I am directed to state, that there is no objection to the 71st being denominated *Highland Light Infantry Regiment*, or to the retaining of their pipes, and the Highland garb for the pipers; and that they will, of course, be permitted to wear caps according to the pattern which was lately approved and sealed by authority.[1]

"I have, &c.

WILLIAM WYNYARD,

"Deputy-Adjutant-General.

"Lieut.-Colonel Pack,
"71st Regiment."

The 71st was next employed on the disastrous expedition to Walcheren, for which the most gigantic preparations had been made. The troops amounted to 40,000 men, commanded by Lieutenant-General the Earl of Chatham, while the naval portion consisted of 39 ships of the line, 36 frigates, and numerous gunboats and bomb-vessels, and other small craft, under Admiral Sir James Strachan.

---

[8] Cannon's *History of the 71st Regiment*, p. 73.
[9] *Journal of a Soldier of the 71st*.

[1] The bonnet *cocked* is the pattern cap to which allusion is made in the above letter. This was in accordance with Lieutenant-Colonel Pack's application; and with respect to retaining the pipes, and dressing the pipers in the Highland garb, he added, "It cannot be forgotten how these pipes were obtained, and how constantly the regiment has upheld its title to them. These are the honourable characteristics which must preserve to future times the precious remains of the old corps, and of which I feel confident His Majesty will never have reason to deprive the 71st regiment."

On the 16th of July, the first battalion of the 71st, consisting of 3 field-officers, 6 captains, 27 subalterns, 48 sergeants, and 974 drummers and rank and file, embarked at Portsmouth on board the *Belleisle* and *Imperieuse*. The expedition sailed from the Downs on the 28th of July, and in about thirty hours reached Roompot Channel, when the 71st was the first to disembark. It was brigaded with the 68th and 85th regiments, under the command of Brigadier-General the Baron de Rottenburg, in the division commanded by Lieutenant-General Alexander Mackenzie Fraser, and the corps of Lieutenant-General Sir Eyre Coote. The light brigade, consisting of the 71st, 68th, and 85th light infantry, were landed under cover of the fire of some small craft, and immediately on landing came in contact with the enemy's sharpshooters, who fell back skirmishing. Two of the companies of the 71st captured four guns and several prisoners. A battery and flagstaff on the coast were taken possession of by the 10th company of the 71st, and in place of a flag, a soldier's red jacket was hoisted on it. Further details of this expedition we take the liberty of copying from Cannon's history of this regiment.

"This advance having succeeded at all points, and the enemy having fallen back on *Flushing* and *Middelburg*, the army was disembarked. The advance then dividing, proceeded by different routes. The 71st moved by the sea dyke on a fort called *Ter Veer*, the situation and strength of which was not sufficiently known, an enemy's deserter having given but imperfect intelligence respecting it.

After nightfall the column continued to advance in perfect silence, with orders to attack with the bayonet, when, on a sudden, the advance-guard fell in with an enemy's party, who came out for the purpose of firing some houses which overlooked the works. The column following the advance-guard had entered an avenue or road leading to the fort, when the advance commenced the action with the enemy, who, retiring within the place, opened a tremendous fire from his works with artillery and musketry. Some guns pointing down the road by which the battalion advanced did great execution, and the 71st had Surgeon Charles Henry Quin killed, and about 18 men killed and wounded. The column, after some firing, retired, and the place was the next day regularly invested by sea and land. It took three days to reduce it, when it capitulated, with its stores, and a garrison of 800 men.

Flushing having been invested on the 1st of August, the 71st, after the surrender of Ter Veer, were ordered into the line of circumvallation, and placed on the extreme left, resting on the Scheldt. The preparations for the attack on the town having been completed, on the 13th a dreadful fire was opened from the batteries and bomb-vessels, and congreve rockets having been thrown into the town, it was on fire in many places. The ships having joined in the attack, the enemy's fire gradually slackened, and at length ceased. A summons being sent in, a delay was demanded, but being rejected, the firing recommenced.

On the 14th of August one of the outworks was carried at the point of the bayonet by a party of detachments and two companies of the 71st under Lieutenant-Colonel Pack.

In this affair Ensign Donald Sinclair, of the 71st, was killed ; Captain George Spottiswoode and a few men were wounded.

Flushing, with its garrison of 6000 men, capitulated on the 15th of August, and the right gate was occupied by a detachment of 300 men of the first or Royal Scots, and the left gate by a detachment of similar strength of the 71st under Major Arthur Jones. The naval arsenal, and some vessels of war which were on the stocks, fell into the hands of the British.

The 71st shortly after proceeded to Middelburg, where the battalion remained for a few days, when it was ordered to occupy *Ter Veer*, of which place Lieutenant-Colonel Pack was appointed commandant, and Lieutenant Henry Clements, of the 71st, town major. The battalion remained doing duty in the garrison until this island, after the works, &c., were destroyed, was finally evacuated on the 22d of December.

On the 23d of December, the battalion embarked in transports, and sailed for England, after a service of five months in a very unhealthy climate, which cost the battalion the loss of the following officers and men:—

	Officers.	Sergeants, Drummers, and Rank and File.
Died on service	1	57
Killed	2	19
Died after return home	2	9
Total	5	85

In passing Cadsand, that fort opened a fire on the transports, one of which, having part of the 71st on board, was struck by a round shot, which carried off Sergeant Steele's legs above the knees.

On the 25th of December, the first battalion of the 71st disembarked at Deal, and marched to Brabourne-Lees Barracks, in Kent, where it was again brigaded with the 68th and 85th light infantry, and was occupied in putting itself in an efficient state for active service." [2]

In May 1810, the battalion removed to Deal Barracks, and while here Lieutenant-Colonel Pack was removed from the regiment to become a brigadier in the Portuguese army. In the early part of September the battalion received orders to prepare six companies for foreign service, which was done by drafting into the 1st, 2d, 3d, 4th, 6th, and 10th companies the most effective officers and men belonging to the other companies. When completed, the companies altogether consisted of 30 officers, 42 sergeants, and 615 rank and file. These companies sailed on the 15th September from the Downs in two frigates, and disembarked at Lisbon on the 26th of the same month, when the men were quartered in two convents. "To my great joy," says the _Journal of a Soldier of the 71st,_ "we paraded in the grand square, on the seventh day after our arrival, and marched in sections, to the music of our bugles, to join the army: having got our camp equipments, consisting of a camp-kettle and bill-hook, to every six men; a blanket, a canteen, and haversack, to each man. Orders had been given that each soldier, on his march, should carry along with him three days' provision. Our mess of six cast lots who should be cook the first day, as we were to carry the kettle day about; the lot fell to me. My knapsack contained two shirts, two pairs of stockings, one pair of overalls, two shoe-brushes, a shaving box, one pair of spare shoes, and a few other articles; my great-coat and

[2] Cannon's _History of the 71st Regiment,_ pp. 77-79.

blanket above the knapsack; my canteen with water was slung over my shoulder, on one side; my haversack, with beef and bread, on the other; sixty round of ball-cartridge, and the camp-kettle above all." [3]

At Mafra, to which place the detachment marched on the 2nd of October, it was joined by Lieutenant-Colonel the Honourable Henry Cadogan, who assumed the command. The detachment joined the army under Wellington at Sobral on the 10th, and was brigaded with the 50th and 92d regiments, under Major-General Sir William Erskine, in the first division under Lieutenant-General Sir Brent Spencer. We cannot do better than quote from the simple but graphic journal already referred to :—

"We had not been three hours in the town, and were busy cooking, when the alarm sounded. There were nine British and three Portuguese regiments in the town. We were all drawn up and remained under arms, expecting every moment to receive the enemy, whose skirmishers covered Windmill Hill. In about an hour the light companies of all the regiments were ordered out, along with the 71st. Colonel Cadogan called to us, at the foot of the hill, 'My lads, this is the first affair I have ever been in with you; show me what you can do, now or never.' We gave a hurra, and advanced up the hill, driving their advanced skirmishers before us, until about half-way up, when we commenced a heavy fire, and were as hotly received. In the meantime the remaining regiments evacuated the town. The enemy pressed so hard upon us, we were forced to make the best of our way down the hill, and were closely followed by the French, through the town, up Gallows Hill. We got behind a mud wall, and kept our ground in spite of their utmost efforts. Here we lay upon our arms all night.

Next morning, by day-break, there was not a Frenchman to be seen. As soon as the sun was fairly up, we advanced into the town, and began a search for provisions, which had now become very scarce; and, to our great joy, we found a large store-house full of dry fish, flour, rice, and sugar, besides bales of cloth. All now became bustle and mirth; fires were

[3] _Memorials of the late War,_ p. 76.

kindled, and every man became a cook. Scones[4] were the order of the day. Neither flour nor sugar were wanting, and the water was plenty; so I fell to bake myself a flour scone. Mine was mixed and laid upon the fire, and I, hungry enough, watching it. Though neither neat nor comely, I was anticipating the moment when it would be eatable. Scarce was it warm ere the bugle sounded to arms. Then was the joy that reigned a moment before turned to execrations. I snatched my scone off the fire, raw as it was, put it into my haversack, and formed. We remained under arms until dark, and then took up our old quarters upon Gallows Hill, where I ate my raw scone, sweetly seasoned by hunger. In our advance to the town we were much entertained by some of our men who had got over a wall the day before, when the enemy were in the rear; and now were put to their shifts to get over again, and scarce could make it out.

Next morning the French advanced to a mud wall, about forty yards in front of the one we lay behind. It rained heavily this day, and there was very little firing. During the night we received orders to cover the bugle and tartans of our bonnets with black crape, which had been served out to us during the day, and to put on our great-coats. Next morning the French, seeing us thus, thought we had retired, and left Portuguese to guard the heights. With dreadful shouts they leaped over that wall before which they had stood, when guarded by British. We were scarce able to withstand their fury. To retreat was impossible; all behind being ploughed land, rendered deep by the rain. There was not a moment to hesitate. To it we fell, pell-mell, French and British mixed together. It was a trial of strength in single combat: every man had his opponent, many had two." In the first of these affairs the detachment had 8 men killed and 34 wounded. In Wellington's despatch concerning the affair of the 14th, the names of Lieutenant-Colonels Cadogan and Reynell were particularly mentioned. John Rea, a soldier of the 6th company of the 71st behaved on this occasion with so much gallantry, and so particularly distinguished himself, that he

[4] This flat cakes.

received a silver medal, inscribed "To John Rea, for his exemplary courage and good conduct as a soldier at Sobral, 14th October 1810."

On the 15th October the 71st retired between the lines at Tibreira, a continuation of those at Torres Vedras. Here the detachment remained along with the other regiments watching Marshal Massena, until the latter was compelled to retire from want of provisions in the nights between the 14th and 15th November. He was followed by the allied forces, and the 71st, along with the rest of its division, were quartered in and about Almoster from the 20th to the 26th. Massena took up a position in the vicinity of Santarem, and Wellington, after some manœuvring, placed himself in front of the enemy, having his headquarters at Cartano. The 71st was quartered in a convent at Alquintrinha, where the detachment remained until March 1811. In this month two companies of the 1st battalion arrived in the Peninsula to reinforce the regiment, other two coming out in July. On the night of the 5th of March, the French gave the British army the slip, deceiving the latter by placing wooden guns in their batteries, and stuffing old clothes with straw, which they put in place of their sentinels. It was two days before the trick was discovered. The British army immediately followed in pursuit, but did not come up with the enemy until they reached the Aguida on the 9th of April. The division, in which was the 71st, was posted at Abergaria, a small town on the frontiers of Spain, where it remained till the 30th April, when, on account of the movements of the enemy, the British army was moved out of its cantonments, and was formed in line on the high ground about two miles in rear of Fuentes d'Onor.

"On the 3rd of May, at day-break, all the cavalry and sixteen light companies occupied the town. We stood under arms until three o'clock, when a staff-officer rode up to our colonel, and gave orders for our advance. Colonel Cadogan put himself at our head, saying, 'My lads, you have had no provisions these two days; there is plenty in the hollow in front, let us down and divide.' We advanced as quick as we could run, and met the light companies retreating as fast as they could. We continued to advance at double-quick time, our firelocks at the trail, our bonnets in our hands. They called to us, 'Seventy-first, you will come back quicker than you advance.' We soon came full in front of the enemy. The colonel cried, 'Here is food, my lads; cut away.' Thrice we waved our bonnets, and thrice we cheered; brought our firelocks to the charge, and forced them back through the town.

How different the duty of the French officers from ours! They, stimulating the men by their example; the men vociferating, each chafing each until they appear in a fury, shouting, to the points of our bayonets. After the first huzza, the British officers, restraining their men, still as death—'Steady, lads, steady,' is all you hear, and that in an under tone.

During this day the loss of men was great. In our retreat back to the town, when we halted to check the enemy, who bore hard upon us, in their attempts to break our line, often was I obliged to stand with a foot upon each side of a wounded man, who wrung my soul with prayers I could not answer, and pierced my heart with his cries to be lifted out of the way of the cavalry. While my heart bled for them, I have shaken them rudely off.

We kept up our fire until long after dark. About one o'clock in the morning we got four ounces of bread served out to each man, which had been collected out of the haversacks of the Foot Guards. After the firing had ceased, we began to search through the town, and found plenty of flour, bacon, and sausages, on which we feasted heartily, and lay down in our blankets, wearied to death. Soon as it was light the firing commenced, and was kept up until about ten o'clock, when Lieutenant Stewart, of our regiment, was sent with a flag of truce, for leave to carry off our wounded from the enemy's lines, which was granted; and, at the same time, they carried off theirs from ours. We lay down, fully accoutred, as usual, and slept in our blankets. An hour before day we were ready to receive the enemy.

About half-past nine o'clock, a great gun from the French line, which was answered by one from ours, was the signal to engage. Down they came, shouting as usual. We kept them at bay, in spite of their cries and formidable looks. How different their appearance from ours! their hats set round with feathers, their beards long and black, gave them a fierce look. Their stature was superior to ours; most of us were young. We looked like boys; they like savages. But we had the true spirit in us. We foiled them in every attempt to take the town, until about eleven o'clock, when we were overpowered, and forced through the streets, contesting every inch.

During the preceding night we had been reinforced by the 79th regiment, Colonel Cameron commanding, who was killed about this time. Notwithstanding all our efforts, the enemy forced us out of the town, then halted, and formed close column betwixt us and it. While they stood thus the havoc amongst them was dreadful. Gap after gap was made by our cannon, and as quickly filled up. Our loss was not so severe, as we stood in open files. While we stood thus, firing at each other as quick as we could, the 88th regiment advanced from the lines, charged the enemy, and forced them to give way. As we passed over the ground where they had stood, it lay two and three deep of dead and wounded. While we drove them before us through the town, in turn, they were reinforced, which only served to increase the slaughter. We forced them out, and kept possession all day." [*]

The 71st took 10 officers and 100 men prisoners, but lost about half their number in killed and wounded. Those killed were Lieutenants John Consell, William Houston, and John Graham, and Ensign Donald John Kearns, together with 4 serjeants and 22 rank and file.

Captains Peter Adamson and James M'Intyre, Lieutenants William M'Craw, Humphrey Fox, and Robert Law (Adjutant), Ensigns Charles Cox, John Vandeleur, and Carique Lewin, 6 serjeants, 3 buglers, and 100 rank and file, were wounded. Two officers, with several men, were taken prisoners.

In commemoration of the gallantry displayed in this prolonged action, the 71st subsequently received the royal authority to bear the words

[*] *Memorials of the late War*, pp. 87–91.

Fuentes d'Onor" on the regimental colour and appointments

Viscount Wellington particularly mentioned the name of Lieut.-Colonel the Honourable Henry Cadogan in his despatch, and being highly gratified with the conduct of the 71st on this occasion, directed that a non-commissioned officer should be selected for a commission According to his Lordship's recommendation, Quartermaster-Serjeant William Gavin was shortly afterwards promoted to an ensigncy in the regiment [6]

The 71st, on the 11th of May, returned to Alborgaria, where it remained till the 26th, when it was marched to reinforce Marshal Beresford's army, then besieging Badajos After a variety of marchings, the battalion went into camp at Toro de Moro, where it remained a month, and was recruited by a detachment of 350 from the 2d battalion, stationed at Deal The battalion returned along with Wellington's army on the 20th of July to Borba, where it remained until the 1st of September, when it removed to Portalegre, and thence marched to Castello de Vido on October 4th

On the 22nd of October, we received information that General Gnard, with 4000 men, infantry and cavalry, was collecting contributions in Estremadura, and had cut off part of our baggage and supplies We immediately set off from Portalegre along with the brigade commanded by General Hill, and, after a most fatiguing march, the weather being very bad, we arrived at Malpartida. The French were only ten miles distant By a near cut, on the Merida road, through Aldea del Cano, we got close up to them, on the 27th, at Alcuesca, and were drawn up in columns, with great guns ready to receive them They had heard nothing of our approach We went into the town It was now nigh ten o'clock, the enemy were in Arroyo del Molino, only three miles distant We got half a pound of rice served out to each man, to be cooked immediately Hunger made little cooking necessary The officers had orders to keep their men silent We were placed in the houses, but our wet and heavy accoutrements were, on no account, to be taken off At twelve o'clock

we received our allowance of rum, and, shortly after, the serjeants tapped at the doors, calling not above their breath We turned out, and at slow time continued our march

The whole night was one continued pour of rain Weary, and wet to the skin, we trudged on, without exchanging a word, nothing breaking the silence of the night save the howling of the wolves The tread of the men was drowned by the pattering of the rain When day at length broke we were close upon the town The French posts had been withdrawn into it, but the embers still glowed in their fires During the whole march the 71st had been with the cavalry and horse-artillery, as an advanced guard

General Hill rode up to our colonel, and ordered him to make us clean out our pans (as the rain had wet all the priming), form square, and retire a short distance, lest the French cavalry had seen us, and should make an attack, however, the drift was so thick, they could not—it blew right in their faces when they looked our way The Colonel told us off in three divisions, and gave us orders to charge up three separate streets of the town, and force our way, without halting, to the other side We shouldered our arms The general, taking off his hat, said, 'God be with you—quick march' On reaching the gates, we gave three cheers, and in we went, the inhabitants calling, 'Live the English,' our piper playing 'Hey Johnny Cope,' the French swearing, fighting in confusion, running here and there, some in their shirts, some half accoutred The streets were crowded with baggage, and men ready to march, all now in one heap of confusion On we drove our orders were to take no prisoners, neither to turn to the right nor left, until we reached the other side of the town

As we advanced I saw the French general come out of a house, frantic with rage Never shall I forget the grotesque figure he made, as he threw his cocked hat upon the ground, and stamping upon it, gnashed his teeth When I got the first glance of him he had many medals on his breast In a minute his coat was as bare as a private's

We formed under cover of some old walls. A handful of French stood in view We got orders to fire : not ten pieces in a company went off, the powder was again so wet with the rain. A brigade of Portuguese artillery came up. We gave the enemy another volley, leaped the wall, formed column, and drove them over the hill ; down which they threw all their baggage, before they surrendered. In this affair we took about 3000 prisoners, 1600 horse, and 6 pieces of artillery, with a great quantity of baggage, &c.

We were again marched back to Portalegre, where the horses were sold and divided amongst the men according to their rank. I got 2s. 6d."[7]

The 71st remained in Portalegre till March 1812, having taken part, during the January of that year, in the expulsion of the French from Estremadura. After the capture of Badajos by Wellington on the 6th of April, the 71st, and the other troops under the command of Lieutenant-General Sir Rowland Hill, retired into Andalusia. Wellington, having armed the Tagus against Marshal Marmont, Sir Rowland Hill's force took post at Almendralejos for the purpose of watching Marshal Soult. Here the 71st remained from the 13th April to the 11th May, when it along with the rest of Sir R. Hill's corps marched to Almaraz to destroy the bridge of boats there. On the 18th of May it reached the height on which the castle of Mirabete stands, five miles from Almaraz.

"On the evening of the third day, General Hill ordered our left companies to move down to the valley, to cover his reconnaisance. When he returned, the officers were called. A scaling ladder was given to each section of a company of the left wing, with the exception of two companies. We moved down the hill in a dismal manner ; it was so dark we could not see three yards before us. The hill was very steep, and we were forced to wade through whins and scramble down rocks, still carrying the ladders. When day-light, on the morning of the 19th, at length showed us to each other, we were scattered all over the foot of the hill like strayed sheep, not more in one place than were held together by a ladder. We halted, formed, and collected the ladders, then moved on. We had a hollow to pass through to get at the battery. The French had cut a part of

the brae-face away, and had a gun that swept right through into the hollow. We made a rush past it, to get under the brae on the other side. The French were busy cooking, and preparing to support the other fort, thinking we would attack it first, as we had lain next it.

On our approach the French sentinel fired and retired. We halted, fixed bayonets, and moved on in double-quick time. We did not receive above four shots from the battery, until we were under the works, and had the ladders placed to the walls. Their entrenchment proved deeper than we expected, which caused us to splice our ladders under the wall ; during which time they annoyed us much, by throwing grenades, stones, and logs over it ; for we stood with our pieces cocked and presented. As soon as the ladders were spliced, we forced them from the works, and out of the town, at the point of the bayonet, down the hill and over the bridge. They were in such haste, they cut the bridge before all their men had got over, and numbers were either drowned or taken prisoners. One of our men had the honour to be the first to mount the works.

Fort Napoleon fired two or three shots into Fort Almaraz. We took the hint from this circumstance, and turned the guns of Almaraz on Fort Napoleon, and forced the enemy to leave it.

We moved forward to the village of Almaraz, and found plenty of provisions, which had been very scarce with us for some days."[8]

The whole of this brilliant affair was concluded in about 15 minutes, the regiment losing Captain Lewis Grant, 1 sergeant, and 7 rank and file, killed ; Lieutenants William Lockwood and Donald Ross, 3 sergeants, and 29 rank and file wounded. The names of 36 non-commissioned officers and soldiers were inserted in regimental orders for conspicuous bravery on this occasion, and "Almaraz" was henceforth inscribed upon the regimental colours. Both in the Brigade and General Orders, the 71st was particularly mentioned.

From this time to the 7th of November the 71st was occupied with many tedious marchings and countermarchings in accordance with the movements of the enemy. It occupied Alba de

[7] M . . . . W . , p. 94.   [8] M . . . . W . , p. 98.

II.   3 R

Tormes from the 7th till the 13th of November, and during that period sustained a loss, in action with the enemy, of 1 sergeant and 6 rank and file killed, and 1 bugler and 5 rank and file wounded. The army retired from this part and began to return on Portugal; and after various slight skirmishes with the enemy, reached Puerto de Baños in December, where it re-mained till April 1812, being then removed to Bejar, which it occupied till May 21st. In December the 1st battalion was joined by a draft of 150 men from the 2nd. On the 20th of June the battalion along with the rest of its division encamped at La Puebla, in the neighbourhood of Vitoria.

On the morning of the 21st, the two

Monument in Glasgow Cathedral to Colonel the Honourable Henry Cadogan.

armies being in position, the 71st was ordered to ascend the heights of La Puebla to support the Spanish forces under General Morillo. Forward they moved up the hill under a very heavy fire, in which fell mortally wounded their commander Colonel Cadogan, who, in falling, requested to be carried to a commanding height, from which he might take a last farewell of the regiment and the field.

"The French had possession of the top, but we soon forced them back, and drew up in column on the height, sending out four companies to our left to skirmish. The remainder

Scarce were we upon the height, when a heavy column, dressed in great-coats, with white covers on their hats, exactly resembling the Spanish, gave us a volley, which put us to the right about at double-quick time down the hill, the French close behind, through the whins. The four companies got the word, the French were on them. They likewise thought them Spaniards, until they got a volley that killed or wounded almost every one of them. We retired to the height, covered by the 50th, who gave the pursuing column a volley which checked their speed. We moved up the remains of our shattered regiment to the height. Being in great want of ammunition, we were again served with sixty rounds a man, and kept up our fire for some time, until the bugle sounded to cease firing.

We lay on the height for some time. Our drought was excessive; there was no water upon the height, save one small spring, which was rendered useless. At this time the major had the command, our second colonel being wounded. There were not 300 of us on the height able to do duty, out of above 1000 who drew rations in the morning. The cries of the wounded were most heart-rending.

The French, on the opposite height, were getting under arms: we could give no assistance, as the enemy appeared to be six to one of us. Our orders were to maintain the height while there was a man of us. The word was given to shoulder arms. The French at the same moment got under arms. The engagement began in the plains. The French were amazed, and soon put to the right about, through Vitoria. We followed, as quick as our weary limbs would carry us. Our legs were full of thorns, and our feet bruised upon the roots of the trees. Coming to a bean field at the bottom of the heights, the column was immediately broken, and every man filled his haversack. We continued to advance until it was dark, and then encamped on a height above Vitoria.

This was the dullest encampment I ever made. We had left 700 men behind. None spoke; each hung his head, mourning the loss of a friend and comrade. About twelve o'clock a man of each company was sent to receive half a pound of flour for each man at the rate

of our morning's strength, so that there was more than could be used by those who had escaped. I had fired 108 rounds this day."[9]

The loss of the regiment in the battle of Vitoria was dreadful. Colonel the Honourable Henry Cadogan, Captain Hall, Lieutenants Fox and Mackenzie, 6 serjeants, 1 bugler, and 78 rank and file were killed; Brevet Lieutenant-Colonel Cother; Captains Reed, Pidgeon, and Grant; Lieutenants Duff, Richards, M'Intyre, Cox, Torriano, Campbell, and Cummeline; 13 serjeants, 2 buglers, and 255 rank and file were wounded.

The enemy retired to Pampeluna, followed by the British, who afterwards marched towards the Pyrenees, the 71st reaching Maya upon the 8th of July. At Maya, on July 25th,——of which, as of other Peninsular battles, details will be found in the account of the 42nd,——the 71st behaved with marked bravery, maintaining their position to the last, and, when their ammunition was exhausted, hurling stones upon the enemy to impede their advance. The 71st had 3 sergeants and 54 rank and file killed, and 6 sergeants and 77 rank and file wounded.

The army under General Hill continued retiring until the 30th of July, when a strong position was taken up at Lizasso. Here they were attacked by the French, the 71st taking an active part in the engagement, and losing 1 sergeant, and 23 rank and file killed, and 2 sergeants and 34 rank and file wounded.

In the action in the pass of Doña Maria on the 31st, the 71st distinguished itself, and had 1 sergeant and 29 rank and file killed, and 2 sergeants and 45 rank and file wounded. For the part taken in these engagements the 71st was authorised to bear the word "Pyrenees" on its colours and appointments. Between the 14th of June and the 7th August, the regiment lost in killed and wounded, 33 officers, 6 buglers, and 553 rank and file.

For nearly three months after the last engagement the regiment was encamped on the heights of Roncesvalles, where the men were principally engaged in the construction of block-houses and batteries, and in the formation of roads for artillery, during which they suffered dreadfully from the inclemency of the weather. On the night of October 11th a strong party of the

French made an attack upon an advance of 15 men of the 71st under Sergeant James Ross, but the small band, favoured somewhat by their position and the darkness, maintained its ground, and forced the enemy to retire. At the request of Lieutenant-General Sir William Stewart, each of the 16 men was presented with a medal.

After the battle of Nivelle, in which the 71st did not take part, the regiment occupied part of the town of Cambo, and was there joined by a detachment of 16 men of the 2nd battalion (then in Glasgow), under the command of Lieutenant Charles Henderson. On the 9th of December the 71st crossed the Nive without loss, the regiment forming upon the top of the opposite height, and sending out two companies after the enemy, who, however, eluded pursuit. The enemy retired on Bayonne, and General Hill disposed his army with the right on the Adour, the left above the Nive, and the centre, in which was the 71st, at St Pierre, across the high road to St Jean Pied-de-Port.

"All the night of the 11th December we lay in camp upon the face of a height, near the Spaniards. In the afternoon of the 12th, we received orders to move round towards Bayonne, where we were quartered along the main road. There we remained until we received orders to march to our own right, to assist a Spanish force which was engaged with superior numbers. We set off by day-light on the morning of the 13th towards them, and were moving on, when General Hill sent an aide-de-camp after us, saying, 'That is not the direction,—follow me.' We put to right-about, to the main road towards Bayonne. We soon came to the scene of action, and were immediately engaged. We had continued firing, without intermission, for five hours, advancing and retreating, and lost a great number of men, but could not gain a bit of ground. Towards evening we were relieved by a brigade which belonged to another division. As many of us as could be collected were drawn up. General Hill gave us great praise for our behaviour this day, and ordered an extra allowance of liquor to each man. We were marched back to our old quarters along the road-side. We lay upon the road-side for two or three days, having two or three

leagues to the rear, carrying the wounded to the hospital. We were next cantoned three leagues above Bayonne, along the side of the river. We had strong picquets planted along the banks. The French were cantoned upon the other side. Never a night passed that we were not molested by boats passing up and down the river, with provisions and necessaries to the town. Our orders were to turn out and keep up a constant fire upon them while passing. We had two grasshopper guns planted upon the side of the river, by means of which we one night sunk a boat loaded with clothing for the army, setting it on fire with red-hot shot.

Next day we were encamped in the rear of the town, being relieved by a brigade of Portuguese. We remained in camp two or three days, expecting to be attacked, the enemy having crossed above us on the river. We posted picquets in the town, near our camp. At length, receiving orders to march, we moved on, until we came to a river on our right, which ran very swift. Part of the regiment having crossed, we got orders to come to the right-about, and were marched back to our old camp-ground. Next morning we received orders to take another road toward Salvatierra, where we encamped that night, and remained until the whole army assembled the following day.

About two o'clock in the afternoon we were under arms, and moved towards the river, covered by a brigade of artillery. We forded, and continued to skirmish along the heights until the town was taken. We lost only one man during the whole time. We encamped upon the other side of the town, and next morning followed the line of march, until we came before a town called Aris. We had severe fighting before we got into it. We were led on by an aide-de-camp. The contest lasted until after dark. We planted picquets in different streets of the town, the enemy did the same in others. Different patroles were sent out during the night, but the French were always found on the alert. They retired before day-light, and we marched into the town with our music at the head of the regiments. The town appeared then quite desolate, not worth twopence, but we were not three days in it, until the French that left it, coming back, opened their shops and houses, and it became a fine lively place "[1]

In the action of the 13th December the 71st lost Lieutenant-Colonel Mackenzie, Lieutenants Campbell and Henderson, 2 sergeants, and 24 men killed; Captains Barclay and Grant, Lieutenants M'Intyre and Torriano, and 37 men wounded For these services the regiment bears "*Nive*" on its colours On the 26th February 1814 the regiment was in action at Sauveterre, and on the 27th took part in the battle of Orthez, although it appears that in the latter it sustained little or no loss It bears "*Orthez*" on its colours

Two divisions of the French army having retired to Aire, after the action of the 27th of February, Lieutenant-General Sir Rowland Hill moved upon that town to dislodge them Upon the 2d of March the French were found strongly posted upon a ridge of hills, extending across the great road in front of the town, having their right on the Adour The second division attacked them along the road, seconded by a Portuguese brigade, and drove them from their position in gallant style Lieutenant James Anderson and 17 rank and file were killed; Lieutenant Henry Frederick Lockyer, 1 sergeant, and 19 rank and file, were wounded

A detachment from the second battalion, consisting of 1 captain, 4 subalterns, and 134 rank and file, under the command of Major Arthur Jones, joined at Aire

On the 25th of March part of the battalion was engaged in an affair at Tarbes, in which Lieutenant Robert Law was wounded, and upon the 10th of April was in position at Toulouse, where some of the companies were employed skirmishing, and sustained a loss of 1 sergeant and 3 rank and file killed; 6 rank and file were wounded [2]

On the 10th of April the regiment marched to Toulouse, in order to attack it It was drawn up in column behind a house, and sent out the flank companies to skirmish; the French, however, evacuated Toulouse on the night of the 11th, when the 71st and the other regiments entered the town The following interesting incident in connection with the attack on Toulouse, is narrated by a soldier of the 71st in his *Journal* —

"I shall ever remember an adventure that happened to me, towards the afternoon We were in extended order, firing and retiring I had just risen to run behind my file, when a spent shot struck me on the groin, and took the breath from me 'God receive my soul!' I said, and sat down resigned. The French were advancing fast. I laid my musket down and gasped for breath I was sick, and put my canteen to my head, but could not taste the water, however, I washed my mouth, and grew less faint I looked to my thigh, and seeing no blood, took resolution to put my hand to the part, to feel the wound My hand was unstained by blood, but the part was so painful that I could not touch it At this moment of helplessness the French came up One of them made a charge at me, as I sat pale as death In another moment I would have been transfixed, had not his next man forced the point past me 'Do not touch the good Scot,' said he; and then addressing himself to me, added, 'Do you remember me?' I had not recovered my breath sufficiently to speak distinctly I answered, 'No' 'I saw you at Sobral,' he replied Immediately I recognised him to be a soldier whose life I had saved from a Portuguese, who was going to kill him as he lay wounded 'Yes, I know you,' I replied 'God bless you!' cried he, and, giving me a pancake out of his hat, moved on with his fellows; the rear of whom took my knapsack, and left me lying I had fallen down for greater security I soon recovered so far as to walk, though with pain, and joined the regiment next advance "[3]

On the afternoon of April 12th word came that Napoleon had abdicated, and shortly after peace was proclaimed, and a treaty concluded between France and England

The 71st marched from Toulouse to Blaachfort, where it was encamped for about a fortnight, after which it proceeded to Bordeaux, where it embarked on the 15th of July, arriving in Cork on the 28th of that month Shortly afterwards the regiment proceeded to Limerick, where it lay for the rest of the year, and where Colonel

---

[1] *Memorials of the late War*, p. 123
[2] Cannon

Reynell assumed the command in December In January 1815 the first battalion of the 71st embarked at Cork, and proceeded to America but peace having been concluded with the United States, its destination was changed, in consequence of Napoleon having again broken loose, and resumed his former dignity of Emperor of the French Thus England was once more embroiled in war The 71st was in consequence transhipped in a small craft, and sent to Ostend, where it disembarked on April 22nd It was then marched to Leuze, where, quartered in the surrounding villages, it lay till June 16th, 1815, under the command of Colonel Reynell It was brigaded with the first battalion of the 52nd, and eight companies of the 95th regiment (Rifles), the brigade being commanded by Major General Frederick Adam, and the division by Lieutenant-General Sir Henry Clinton The first battalion had at this time 997 rank and file The regiment was drilled every day, and on the morning of June 16 was proceeding to its drill ground as usual, when it was ordered immediately to advance upon Nivelles, where it arrived late at night On the same day Blucher had been attacked at Ligny, and Wellington had successfully met Marshal Ney at Quatre Bras, in which action the 71st had no chance of taking part, although they had their own share of the fighting at Waterloo On the morning of the 17th the 71st took the road to Waterloo, and along with the other regiments of the brigade took up a position behind Hougoumont, where they lay under arms, amid pouring rain all night Two hours after daybreak, General Hill came down and took away the 10th company to cover his reconnaissance, and shortly after, the regiment set to cleaning their arms, and preparing for action All the opposite heights were covered by the enemy

The artillery had been tearing away since daybreak in different parts of the line About twelve o'clock we received orders to fall in for attack We then marched up to our position, where we lay on the face of a brae, covering a brigade of guns We were so overcome by the fatigue of the two days' march, that scarce had we lain down until many of us fell asleep We lay thus about an hour and a half, under a dreadful fire, which . . . .

while we had never fired a shot The balls were falling thick amongst us

About two o'clock a squadron of lancers came down, hurrahing, to charge the brigade of guns they knew not what was in the rear The general gave the word, ' Form square ' In a moment the whole brigade were on their feet, ready to receive the enemy The general said, ' Seventy-first, I have often heard of your bravery, I hope it will not be worse to-day than it has been ' Down they came upon our square We soon put them to the right-about

Shortly after we received orders to move to the heights Onwards we marched, and stood, for a short time, in square, receiving cavalry every now and then The noise and smoke were dreadful We then moved on in column for a considerable way, and formed line , gave three cheers, fired a few volleys, charged the enemy, and drove them back

At this moment a squadron of cavalry rode furiously down upon our line Scarce had we time to form The square was only complete in front when they were upon the points of our bayonets Many of our men were out of place There was a good deal of jostling for a minute or two, and a good deal of laughing Our quarter-master lost his bonnet in riding into the square , got it up, put it on, back foremost, and wore it thus all day Not a moment had we to regard our dress. A French general lay dead in the square , he had a number of ornaments upon his breast Our men fell to plucking them off, pushing each other as they passed, and snatching at them

We stood in square for some time, whilst the 13th dragoons and a squadron of French dragoons were engaged The 13th dragoons retiring to the rear of our column, we gave the French a volley, which put them to the right-about, then the 13th at them again They did this for some time , we cheering the 13th, and feeling every blow they received

The whole army retired to the heights in the rear, the French closely pursuing to our formation, where we stood, four deep, for a considerable time As we fell back, a shot cut the straps of the knapsack of one near me it fell, and was rolling away He snatched it up, saying ' in no' . . . . , . u are all I have in the world,' tied it on the best manner he could, and marched on.

Lord Wellington came riding up. We formed square, with him in our centre, to receive cavalry. Shortly the whole army received orders to advance. We moved forwards in two columns, four deep, the French retiring at the same time. We were charged several times in our advance. This was our last effort ; nothing could impede us. The whole of the enemy retired, leaving their guns and ammunition, and every other thing behind. We moved on towards a village, and charged right through, killing great numbers, the village was so crowded. We then formed on the other side of it, and lay down under the canopy of heaven, hungry and weary to death. We had been oppressed, all day, by the weight of our blankets and great-coats, which were drenched with rain, and lay upon our shoulders like logs of wood." [4]

The 71st had Brevet Major Edmund L'Estrange, aide-de-camp to Major-General Sir Denis Pack, and Ensign John Tod killed. The following officers were wounded : the Lieutenant-Colonel commanding the battalion, Colonel Thomas Reynell ; Brevet Lieutenant-Colonel Arthur Jones ; Captains Samuel Reed, Donald Campbell, William Alexander Grant, James Henderson, and Brevet Major Charles Johnstone ; Lieutenants Joseph Barrallier, Robert Lind, John Roberts, James Coates, Robert Law, Carique Lewin, and Lieutenant and Adjutant William Anderson.

The number of serjeants, buglers, and rank and file killed amounted to 29 ; 166 were wounded, and 36 died of their wounds." [5]

The 71st afterwards marched to Paris with the rest of the army, and was encamped in the Champs Elysées, continuing there till the beginning of November, when it proceeded to Versailles, and to Viarmes in December. On the 21st of December the second battalion was disbanded at Glasgow, the effective officers and men being transferred to the first battalion.

In January 1816 the regiment marched to the Pas de Calais, where it was cantoned in several villages. On the 21st of June the 71st was formed in hollow square upon the *bruyère*

[4] *Memorials of the late War*, p. 132.
[5] Cannon's *History of the 71st Regiment*, p. 110.

of Rombly for the purpose of receiving the medals which had been granted by the Prince Regent to the officers and men for their services at Waterloo, when Colonel Reynell addressed the regiment as follows :—

"SEVENTY-FIRST,—The deep interest which you will all give me credit for feeling in everything that affects the corps, cannot fail to be awakened upon an occasion such as the present, when holding in my hands, to transfer to yours, these honourable rewards bestowed by your sovereign for your share in the great and glorious exertions of the army of His Grace the Duke of Wellington upon the field of Waterloo, when the utmost efforts of the army of France, directed by Napoleon, reputed to be the first captain of the age, were not only paralysed at the moment, but blasted beyond the power of even a second struggle.

"To have participated in a contest crowned with victory so decisive, and productive of consequences that have diffused peace, security, and happiness throughout Europe, may be to each of you a source of honourable pride, as well as of gratitude to the Omnipotent Arbiter of all human contests, who preserved you in such peril, and without whose protecting hand the battle belongs not to the strong, nor the race to the swift.

"I acknowledge to feel an honest and, I trust, excusable exultation in having had the honour to command you on that day ; and in dispensing these medals, destined to record in your families the share you had in the ever memorable battle of Waterloo, it is a peculiar satisfaction to me that I can present them to those by whom they have been fairly and honourably earned, and that I can here solemnly declare that, in the course of that eventful day, I did not observe a soldier of this good regiment whose conduct was not only creditable to the English nation, but such as his dearest friends could desire.

"Under such agreeable reflections, I request you to accept these medals, and to wear them with becoming pride, as they are incontestable proofs of a faithful discharge of your duty to your king and your country. I trust that they will act as powerful talismans, to keep you, in your future lives, in the paths of honour, sobriety, and virtue."

The regiment received new colours on the 13th of January 1817; they were presented by Major-General Sir Denis Pack, a name intimately associated with some of our Highland

Major-General Sir Denis Pack, K.C.B. From a painting in possession of Mrs Reynell Pack.

regiments. On this occasion he addressed them as follows :—

"SEVENTY-FIRST REGIMENT,—Officers, non-commissioned officers, and soldiers, it affords me the greatest satisfaction, at the request of your commanding officer, Colonel Reynell, to have the honour of presenting these colours to you.

"There are many who could perform the office with a better grace, but there is no one, believe me, who is more sensible of the merit of the corps, or who is more anxious for its honour and welfare.

"I might justly pay to the valour and good conduct of those present the compliments usual on such occasions, but I had rather offer the expression of my regard and admiration of that excellent *esprit-de-corps* and real worth which a ten years' intimate knowledge of the regiment has taught me so highly to appreciate. I shall always look back with pleasure to that long period in which I had the good fortune to be your commanding officer, and during which time I received from the officers the most cordial and zealous assistance in support of discipline; from the non-commissioned officers proofs of the most disinterested regard for His

Majesty's service and the welfare of their regiment; and I witnessed on the part of the privates and the corps at large a fidelity to their colours in South America, as remarkable under such trying circumstances as their valour has at all times been conspicuous in the field. I am most happy to think that there is no drawback to the pleasure all should feel on this occasion. Your former colours were mislaid after a fête given in London to celebrate the Duke of Wellington's return after his glorious termination of the peninsular war, and your colonel, General Francis Dundas, has sent you three very handsome ones to replace them. On them are emblazoned some of His Grace's victories, in which the 71st bore a most distinguished part, and more might be enumerated which the corps may well be proud of. There are still in our ranks valuable officers who have witnessed the early glories of the regiment in the East, and its splendid career since is fresh in the memory of all. Never, indeed, did the character of the corps stand higher; never was the fame of the British arms, or the glory of the British empire more pre-eminent than at this moment, an enthusiastic recollection of which the sight of these colours must always inspire.

"While you have your present commanding officer to lead you, it is unnecessary for me to add anything to excite such a spirit; but were I called upon to do so, I should have only to hold up the example of those who have fallen in your ranks, and, above all, point to the memory of that hero who so gloriously fell at your head." [6]

After remaining in France until the end of October 1818, the 71st embarked for England, and arrived at Dover on the 29th of that month, proceeding to Chelmsford, where the establishment was reduced from 810 to 650 rank and file.

From 1818 to 1822 this regiment performed garrison duties at various places in England, a mere enumeration of which would not be interesting, and is needless here. While at Chatham in 1821, the strength of the regiment was reduced to 576 rank and file. In 1822 it sailed from Liverpool for Dublin, where it

[6] Colonel the Honourable Henry Cadogan, who was mortally wounded at Vitoria on the 21st of June 1813.

arrived on the 3rd of May, and remained there till the beginning of October, when it was marched to the south of Ireland Here it remained until May 1824, having its headquarters at Fermoy, with detachments stationed at various villages in order that disturbances might be suppressed and order maintained The nature of the duties which the regiment had to perform can be seen by reference to our account of the 42nd about this period In January 1824 Lieutenant-General Sir Gordon Drummond was removed from the colonelcy of the 88th to that of the 71st, vacant by the death of General Francis Dundas.

In May the regiment proceeded to Cork to re-embark for North America, but before doing so, Colonel Sir Thomas Arbuthnot, commanding the regiment, received very gratifying addresses from the magistrates and inhabitants of Fermoy, praising highly the conduct of the regiment, which had now the esteem of all classes The 71st embarked at Cork for North America on the 14th, 16th, 17th, and 18th of May 1824, and arrived at Quebec about a month thereafter, at which place the headquarters of the regiment was stationed The 71st remained in America performing garrison duty at various places till 1831 In May 1827 the headquarters was removed to Montreal, preparatory to the change, the service companies were inspected by Lieutenant-General the Earl of Dalhousie, who assured Lieutenant-Colonel Jones that he never had seen any regiment in more perfect order In May 1828 the regiment removed to Kingston, where it remained for a year, and where it suffered much from fever and ague From this place headquarters removed to Toronto in June 1829, and companies were sent out to occupy various posts, the 71st remained there for two years

In June 1825 the strength of the regiment had been increased to 710 rank and file, who were formed into 6 service and 4 depôt companies, the latter stationed in England, the movements of the former we have been narrating In August 1829 the depôt companies removed from Gravesend to Berwick-on-Tweed, and in June 1830 from the latter place to Edinburgh Castle In September 1829 Major General Sir Colin Halkett succeeded General Drummond as colonel of the 71st

In May 1831 the service companies returned to Quebec, where they stayed four months, sailing in October for Bermuda, where they were stationed till September 1834 While at Bermuda, in Febuary 1834, the tartan plaid scarf was restored to the 71st by authority of the King In September of that year the 6 service companies left Bermuda for Britain, arriving at Leith in October 19th The regiment was stationed at Edinburgh till May 1836, when it embarked for Ireland, and was stationed at Dublin till June 1837, when it proceeded to Kilkenny The regiment remained in Ireland till April 1838, on the 16th of which month the 6 service companies again sailed from Cork to Canada The four depôt companies remained in Ireland till June 1839, when they sailed from Cork to Scotland, and were stationed at Stirling While in Ireland, March 1838, Major-General Sir Samuel Ford Whittingham succeeded Sir Colin Halkett to the colonelcy of the regiment, and he again was succeeded in March 1841 by Lieutenant-General Sir Thomas Reynell, formerly so intimately associated with the regiment as its lieutenant-colonel The strength of the regiment was in August 1838 increased to 800

During 1840 the 6 service companies were stationed at St John's, Lower Canada

The service companies proceeded from St John's to Montreal, in two divisions, on the 27th and 28th of April 1842

In consequence of the augmentation which took place in the army at this period, the 71st regiment was ordered to be divided into two battalions, the 6 service companies being termed the first battalion, and the depôt, augmented by two new companies, being styled the reserve battalion The depôt was accordingly moved from Stirling to Chichester in 1842, and after receiving 180 volunteers from other corps, was there organised into a battalion for foreign service

The reserve battalion of the 71st, under the command of Lieutenant-Colonel James England, embarked at Portsmouth in Her Majesty's troop-ship "Resistance," which sailed for Canada on the 13th of August 1842, and landed at Montreal on the 23d of September, where the first battalion was likewise stationed, under the command of Major William

Denny, who, upon the arrival of Lieutenant-Colonel England, took charge of the reserve battalion

The reserve battalion marched from Montreal to Chambly on the 5th of May 1843, and arrived there on the same day

The first battalion, under the command of Lieutenant-Colonel England, embarked at Quebec for the West Indies in the ' Java" transport, on the 20th of October 1843 The headquarters disembarked at Grenada on the 15th of December following

The headquarters of the first battalion embarked on the 25th of December 1844, at Grenada, for Antigua,[7] where it remained till April 1846 It proceeded to Barbadoes, leaving that in December for England, arriving at Spithead, January 25th 1847 The first battalion, on landing, proceeded to Winchester, where it remained till July, when it was removed to Glasgow, and in December left the latter place for Edinburgh Here it remained till April 1848, when it was removed to Ireland

In February 1848, on the death of Sir Thos Reynell, Lieutenant General Sir Thos Arbuthnot succeeded to the colonelcy of the 71st, and on his death, in January 1849, it was conferred on Lieutenant-General Sir James Macdonell

In compliance with instructions received upon the occasion of Her Majesty's visit to Dublin, the headquarters of the first battalion, with the effectives of three companies, proceeded from Naas to that garrison on the 28th of July, and were encamped in the Phœnix Park The three detached companies also joined at the encampment on the same day On the 13th of August the head-quarters and three companies returned to Naas

The headquarters and two companies of the reserve battalion, under the command of Lieutenant-Colonel Sir Hew Dalrymple, Bart, proceeded from St John's to Montreal in aid of the civil power, on the 28th of April 1849 The headquarters and three companies quitted Montreal and encamped on the Island of St Helen's on the 30th of June, but returned to St John's on the 16th of July On the 17th of August 1849, the headquarters and two

[7] C . . . . 71 . . . .

companies proceeded from St John's to Montreal in aid of the civil power, and returned to St John's on the 6th of September.

In April 1850 the first battalion proceeded from Naas to Dublin

The headquarters and two companies of the reserve battalion quitted St John's and Chambly on the 21st of May 1850, and arrived at Toronto on the 23rd of that month, where the battalion was joined by the other companies, and it continued there during the remainder of the year

In May 1852 the reserve battalion proceeded from Toronto to Kingston On the 8th of June following, Lieutenant-Colonel Hew Dalrymple, Bart, retired from the service by the sale of his commission, and was succeeded by Lieutenant-Colonel Nathaniel Massey Stack [8]

On the 18th of February 1848, Lieutenant-General Sir Thomas Arbuthnot, K C B, from the 9th Foot, was appointed colonel of the regiment in room of Lieutenant-General Sir Thomas Reynell, Bart, who had died, and on the death of the new colonel, about a year after, Lieutenant General Sir James Macdonell, K C B, from the 79th Foot, was appointed to the colonelcy of the regiment

Instructions having been received for the battalion to embark at Glasgow for Ireland, three companies proceeded to Dublin on the 27th, and the headquarters, with the three remaining companies, embarked on board the "Viceroy" steamer on the 1st of May, and arrived at Dublin on the 2nd Companies were detached to various places, and the headquarters proceeded from Dublin to Naas on the 20th of May

On the 4th of July Lieutenant-Colonel William Denny, having arrived from Canada, assumed the command of the battalion, when Lieutenant-Colonel Sir Hew Dalrymple, Bart, proceeded to join the reserve battalion

H R H Major General Prince George of Cambridge, commanding the Dublin district, made the autumn half-yearly inspection of the regiment on the 13th of October, on which occasion H R H expressed personally to the regiment his satisfaction and approbation of their appearance and steadiness under arms,

[8] C m r H . . . . 71 . T . . . . pp 122, 123

and the marked improvement that had been effected.

In compliance with instructions received, on the occasion of the expected visit of Her Majesty to Dublin, the headquarters, with the effectives of three companies, moved from Naas to Dublin on the 28th of July, and encamped in the Phœnix Park. The three detached companies also joined the encampment on the same day.

The Queen having arrived on the 6th of August, the battalion had the honour of sharing in the grand review which took place in the park on the 9th, in presence of Her Majesty and Prince Albert, after which a highly complimentary general order was issued, expressing the high approval of Her Majesty and Prince Albert of the conduct of the troops present at the review.

On the 10th of August Her Majesty and Prince Albert and the Royal Family left Dublin, and the 71st furnished a guard of honour under Captain T. H. Colville, at the railway station; and on the 11th, the lieutenant-general commanding marked his very high appreciation of the services of the troops stationed in Dublin during the above auspicious occasion, by publishing another highly complimentary general order.

In addition to the remarks in the general order of Lieutenant-General Sir Edward Blackeney, which reflected so much credit on the 71st Highland Light Infantry, in common with the other regiments in garrison, Major-General H.R.H. Prince George of Cambridge was graciously pleased to express his approbation of the high state of efficiency and good conduct of the battalion; and as its stay in Dublin was intended to be during Her Majesty's visit, the headquarters and three companies returned to Naas on the 13th of August, detaching on the same day three companies to Maryborough, Carlow, and Newbridge.

During the months of March and April 1850, the various scattered companies of the 71st were removed to Dublin, where the whole battalion was stationed at the Richmond Barracks.

A draft of the reserve battalion, consisting of 2 subalterns, 2 sergeants, and 90 rank and file, embarked at Cork for Canada on the 4th of May of the same year.

The state of discipline in the regiment was reported to be good on its arrival in Dublin, and during its stay in that garrison it was most favourably reported upon. The accompanying extracts, which were conveyed to the commanding officer, by order, are creditable to the character of the regiment:—

"Asst. Adjt.-General's Office,
"Dublin, 21st July 1851.

"The Commander-in-Chief is glad to find that his Royal Highness considers the recruits lately joined to be of a superior description, and that he is enabled to speak with unqualified praise on the state of the discipline to which the regiment has arrived since it formed part of the garrison of Dublin.

"George Mylins,
"Asst. Adj.-Gen."

"Officer Commanding
"1st Bat. 71st Regt."

The following is an extract from a letter received from the Adjutant-General of the Forces, having reference to the confidential report of H.R.H. the Duke of Cambridge, of the 1st battalion of the 71st Highland Light Infantry, for the second period of 1850:—

"Asst. Adjt.-General's Office,
"Dublin, 28th January 1851.

"The progress made by this battalion during the half year is extremely satisfactory to the Commander-in-Chief, and in the highest degree creditable to Lieutenant-Colonel Denny and his officers, who may congratulate themselves on having brought the battalion into a state of efficiency of which it certainly could not boast when the lieutenant-colonel assumed the command.

"W. F. Forster, A. A.-G."

During 1851 and 1852 the regiment remained in Ireland, moving about in detachments from place to place, and performing efficiently a variety of duties, agreeable and disagreeable, in that disturbed country, and sending off now and then small parties to join the reserve battalion in Canada. In August the regiment removed to Kilkenny.

On the 1st of November 1852, a communication was received for the battalion to be held in readiness for embarkation for the Mediterranean, and in compliance therewith, the service and depôt companies were formed on the 1st of January 1853, and on the 3rd the battalion received new colours On the arrival of the battalion at Cork, the old colours were placed over a tablet erected at Kinsale, to the memory of the late Lieutenant General Sir Thomas Arbuthnot, a native of that place, who commanded the regiment for many years During February and March the regiment sailed in detachments for Corfu.

By a War Office letter of 20th of February 1854, the regiment was to be augmented, from the 1st of April, by one pipe-major and five pipers

The reserve battalion remained in Canada from 1849 to 1853, having been stationed successively at St John's, Toronto, Kingston, and Quebec, returning from Canada in 1854, and forming the depôt of the regiment at Canterbury in October

On the outbreak of the Crimean war all the effectives, with a proportion of officers, consisting of 1 major, 3 captains, 6 subalterns 20 serjeants, 6 buglers, and 391 rank and file—total, 417—were ordered to proceed to the Crimea, and embarked at Portsmouth, on board the "Royal Albert," November 24, and landed at Balaclava on the 20th of December The first battalion joined the reserve in February 1855

Major General A F Mackintosh, Commander of the Forces in the Ionian Islands, issued the following order prior to the embarkation of the first battalion from Corfu for the Crimea, in January 1855 —

"General Order

"DEPUTY QR -MASTER GENERAL'S OFFICE, "Corfu, 24th January 1855

" The Major-General commanding addresses a few words to the 71st Light Infantry on their departure for the seat of war

"The Major-General first saw the 71st a good many years ago, on a day when their commanding officer fell at their head, he has since often met the regiment in various parts of the world, and has always remarked among both the officers and men of the regiment that high military spirit and personal activity still conspicuous, which caused it to be selected and org nised a light corp

" They are now about to appear on a scene where their predecessors in the regiment have so often distinguished themselves—the field of battle,—and the Major-General wishes them a prosperous passage, followed by a glorious career

"R WALPOLE,
"Dep Qr -Mr General "

During the time the 71st was in the Crimea, it had no chance of distinguishing itself in any great action, as had the 42d, and the other two Highland regiments with which it was brigaded Nevertheless, the 71st had many fatiguing and critical duties to perform, which it did with efficiency, as will be seen, it was mainly occupied in expeditions to various parts of the Crimea.

The regiment embarked on the 3rd of May on board the "Furious" and the 'Gladiator" steam frigates, forming part of the first expedition to Kertch, returning to Balaclava on the 8th The regiment moved to the front on the 9th of May, and joined the third brigade of the fourth division in camp, before Sebastopol, performing satisfactorily the very trying duties in the trenches Here, however, it did not long remain, as on May 22nd it embarked at Balaclava, on board the steam frigates "Sidon" and "Valorous," and proceeded to Kertch with the expeditionary force of the allied army

Landing at Kamiesch Bouroun, about five miles from Kertch, on the 24th of May, under cover of the gun-boats, it bivouacked that night, and marched to Kertch the following morning, proceeding the same day to Yenikali, where it encamped

The regiment re-embarked at Yenikali on the 10th of June on board the steam frigates 'Sidon' and "Valorous," to return to the headquarters of the army, but was again disembarked—the headquarters and right wing at Yenikali on June the 12th, and the left wing at Cape St Paul on the 14th—to protect these points, in conjunction with a French and Turkish force One company moved into Kertch from Yenikali, August 4th, and the left wing from Cape St Paul to Kertch, September 22nd

Three companies, under Major Hunter, embarked at Kertch, September 24th, and proceeded with the French on a joint expedition to Taman Taman and Phanagoria were bombarded by the French and English gunboats, and taken possession of by the allied expeditionary force on the same day A large supply of hutting material and fuel was obtained for the use of the troops from these places, after which they were fired and abandoned The expedition returned to Kertch on the 3rd of October

A draft, consisting of 1 captain, 5 subalterns, 4 sergeants, and 121 rank and file from the reserve companies at Malta, landed at Balaclava in August, was moved to the front, and attached to the Highland division in camp before Sebastopol It was present at the fall of Sebastopol, under the command of Major Campbell, and joined the headquarters of the regiment at Yenikah on the 2nd of October

Until the 22nd of June 1856, the various companies were kept moving between Yenikali and Kertch On that date Kertch and Cape St Paul were handed over by the regiment to the Russian authorities, the whole of the French and Turkish forces having previously evacuated that part of the Crimea.

The headquarters and six companies embarked on board the steamship " Pacific," and two companies on board the " Gibraltar," on the 22nd of June, for passage to Malta

During the stay of the 71st in Malta, from July 1856 to January 1858, there is nothing of importance to record

The regiment received orders by telegram from England to proceed overland to India on the evening of the 2nd of January 1858, and on the morning of the 4th it embarked on board H M. ship " Princess Royal" and the steam frigate "Vulture" The headquarters and right wing arrived at Bombay on February 6th, and the left wing on the 8th, the right wing proceeding to Mhow by bullock train in detachments of about forty daily, the first of which left Bombay on the 26th of February, and the last arrived at Mhow, March 17th It marched from Mhow on the 30th March to join the Central India Field Force, and joined the second brigade at Mote on May 3rd It was present at the action in Rose's attack on the enemy at Koonch, May 7th, when eight men fell dead in the ranks, and upward of

twenty officers and men had to be carried from the field on account of the heat of the sun It was present also at the actions at Muttra and Deapoora, 16th and 17th May, at the latter places the principal attacks of the enemy were repulsed by this regiment Lieutenant-Colonel Campbell commanding the brigade, Major Rich commanding the regiment, and Battalion Major Lottus, were specially mentioned by the major-general The regiment was present at the battle of Gowlowlee, May 22nd, the occupation of Calpee, May 23rd, and it marched on Gwalior with the 1st Brigade Central India Field Force, at the action of Moorar on the 16th of June, in which the 71st took a prominent part It was while rushing on at the head of a company of this regiment that Lieutenant Wyndham Neave fell mortally wounded, and that Sergeant Hugh M'Gill, 1 corporal, and 2 privates were killed Lieutenant-Colonel Campbell, Major Rich, and Lieutenant Scott were specially mentioned, and Sergeant Ewing and Private George Rodgers were recommended for the Victoria Cross

On the evening of the 18th of June the regiment formed part of a column for the support of Brigadier Smith's brigade, and advanced on Gwalior with the whole force on the 19th and 20th

After the capture of Gwalior on the 20th of June, the headquarter's wing marched back to Moorar cantonments, where it was stationed till the 12th of August, when it returned to Gwalior, and was stationed at the Lushker and Phool Bagh, and returned again to Moorar on the 6th of June 1859

On the 11th of November 1858, a detachment from headquarters went on field-service to the Sind River, had two skirmishes with the rebels, and returned to Gwalior on the 9th of February 1859

On the 29th of November 1858, another detachment from headquarters went on field service, and had skirmishes with the rebels at Ranode and Namewass At the latter place three were killed This detachment returned to Gwalior on 27th of May 1859

The left wing marched from Bombay on the 11th of March 1858, and arrived at Mhow on 17th or April, and on the 9th of June a

company was detached from Mhow to Indore
The greater portion of the left wing proceeded
on field service, under Major General Michel,
C B, and on 2nd September 1858 was present
at the action at Rajghur In the action at
Mongrowlee, on September the 15th, the 71st
had one private killed In the action at
Sindwaho on October the 19th, and that at
Koorai on October the 25th, the 71st had
no casualties The left wing arrived at
Bhopal on the 17th of November 1858, and
marched to Goonah on the 17th of January
1859

On the 25th of November a party of 50
rank and file left Mhow on camels, with a
column under command of Major Sutherland,
92d Highlanders, and were engaged with the
rebels at Rajpore on the same day, after which
they returned to Mhow

On the 1st of January 1859, the company
stationed at Indore marched from that place
en route to join a column on service under
Brigadier-General Sir R Napier, K C B, and
was present at the attack of the Fort or Na-
harghur, 17th of January, where two privates
were wounded Captain Lambton was specially
mentioned for his daring attack

The headquarters of the regiment were
inspected by the Commander-in-Chief, Lord
Clyde, on the 2nd of December 1859 His Excellency expressed his satisfaction, both with
what he himself saw and the reports which
he had received regarding the state of the
regiment from other sources The report
made by Lord Clyde to H R H the General
Commanding-in-Chief, produced the following
letter from the Adjutant-General of the
Forces, highly complimentary to the commanding officer and all ranks of the regiment —

" HORSE GUARDS,
" 24th January 1860

" Sir,—His Royal Highness the General
Commanding-in-Chief is much gratified to
hear from General Lord Clyde, Commander-
in-Chief in India, that at his Lordship's last
visit to the station occupied by the regiment
under your command, he found it in the
highest order

" After the recent arduous and continuous
duties on which it has been employed and

credit is due to its commanding officer, Colonel
William Hope, and to every rank in the
corps, and H R H requests that his opinion
may be communicated to them accordingly —
I have the honour to be, &c

                        " G A WETHERAL,
                          "Adjutant General
" Officer Commanding
" 71st Highlanders "

In the month of January 1860, intimation
was received of the death of Lieutenant-
Colonel R D Campbell, C B, in London, on
the 4th of December 1859, and the command
of the 71st devolved on Lieutenant-Colonel
Hope, C B

On the 22nd of July cholera broke out in the
regiment It first appeared in the hospital in
cantonments, but the next day spread to the
barracks, and, two or three days later, reached
the fortress of Gwalior The companies in
cantonments, with the exception of one,
moved under canvas, two of those in the
fort moved down into quarters at the Phool
Bagh Notwithstanding these movements
the epidemic continued until the beginning
of September, and did not finally disappear
until the 16th of that month, having carried
off 1 colour-sergeant, 2 sergeants, 2 corporals,
1 piper, 1 bugler, and 62 men, 11 women and
11 children

On the 11th of November 1860 the order for
the relief was received, and on the 20th of the
next month the regiment marched for Sealkote, Punjab, having been relieved at Gwalior
by the 27th Inniskillings

The state of discipline of the regiment
while in the Gwalior district can be gathered from the following extract from a report
from the Political Agent Gwalior, to the
Government of India, dated 15th June
1860 —

" When it was determined in June last to
post a British force at the Lushker, the people
expected with dread and deprecation a violent
and dangerous, at least a rude and overbearing
soldiery, but Her Majesty's 71st Highlanders
soon dispelled their fears and created pleasant
feelings

" His Highness and the best informed
men of the Durbar have assured me that
those soldiers who for ten months in the

Phool Bagh have, by their manners, habits, dealings, and whole demeanour, so conciliated the respect and regards of all, that nothing would be more acceptable than the domestication of such a force in the capital.

"The Durbar considers further, that it would bring to Gwalior incalculable industrial advantages, through affording a constant supply of superintendents of public works and skilled labourers.

"I venture to express the hope, that his Excellency may consider the Durbar's view of the conduct of Her Majesty's 71st, commanded by Lieutenant-Colonel Campbell, C.B., a very high and true compliment, as worthy of express recognition as good conduct in the field. It is in my humble judgment a most fully deserved compliment.

"AD. A. CHARTERS MACPHERSON,
"*Political Agent.*"

"CAMP AGRA,
"*29th November* 1859.

"MY LORD,—As your Lordship is going to Gwalior, I trust you will not think that I exceed my office, if I venture to send you an extract from a report of June last, in which I attract the attention of the Government to the admirable conduct of Her Majesty's 71st Highlanders, and to its appreciation by Maharajah Scindia and his people.

"The importance of such conduct on the part of the first British troops stationed at the capital of Gwalior might scarcely be over stated.

"Having lived with the 71st at the Phool Bagh for about twelve months, my pride in them as soldiers and countrymen must be my excuse to your Lordship for venturing upon this irregular communication of my impressions. General Napier's views will, I trust, confirm them.

"AD. A. CHARTERS MACPHERSON,
"*Political Agent.*"

Various drafts joined the service companies in 1860. The regiment marched into Sealkote on Sunday, the 17th of February 1861.

The brigadier-general, commanding the Lahore division, made his first half-yearly inspection of the regiment on the 26th of April

1861, and published the following order on the conclusion of this duty:—

"*Extract from Station Orders, dated Sealkote,
27th April* 1871.

"Brigadier-General Ferryman, C.B., having completed the inspection of the 71st Highland Light Infantry, begs to express to Lieut.-Col. Rich and the regiment his great satisfaction with everything he has seen. The drill is excellent; it could not be better; and the officers are well instructed. He will, therefore, have much pleasure in making a very high report to the Commander-in-Chief of everything he has witnessed."

The regiment remained at Sealkote till the 1st of November 1862, when headquarters and seven companies marched *en route* to Nowshera, and arrived at that station on the 21st of the same month, having detached one company at Attock to garrison the fortress.

On the 14th of October 1863, headquarters, under Lieut.-Col. Hope, C.B., moved from Nowa-Killa in the Yuzufzai country, arriving on the 18th of October at Nowshera, where the sick were left. At Nowa-Killa was assembled the force about to be employed in the hill country to the eastward, and the command was assumed by Brigadier-General Sir Neville Chamberlain, K.C.B. The object of the expedition was to destroy Mulka, on the Mahabun Mountains, the stronghold of certain Hindostanee refugees, generally known as the Sitana Fanatics, who infested our frontier and preyed on the villages. Mulka is just beyond our frontier line, and in the territory of the Indoens.

The direct route to Mulka by the Chinglae Pass being reported to be stockaded, it was decided to take the more circuitous one by the Umbeylah Pass and the Chumla Valley. The brigadier-general decided on having a small native force at Nowa-Killa, and forming a depôt for the European troops at Roostum, which is near the entrance to the Umbeylah Pass, and directed the sick and the regimental band to remain there accordingly. 99 men of the 71st of all ranks were detached to remain at Roostum under Lieut. Boulderson.

The force marched in two divisions,—the first, all of native troops under command of

Lieut.-Col Wilde, C B, of the corps of Guides, on 19th October, and the second, which included all the European troops, on the 20th of October, under the brigadier-general

The pass was seized by Lieut Col Wilde without difficulty, but owing to the rugged nature of the ground, the so-called road being merely a path hardly practicable for loaded cattle, the troops were not concentrated at the crest of the pass until nearly 8 o'clock in the evening, and the baggage, of which much was lost or destroyed, was not all up for four days The heavy guns were shifted on to elephants at the bottom of the pass, and got up without much difficulty

On the 21st more ground to the front was taken, and the regiment marched down in the direction of Umbeylah about a quarter of a mile, and encamped on a small piece of level ground, and not far from a small stream of water On the 22nd a reconnaissance was made in the Chumla Valley under the orders of Lieut.-Col Taylor, C E, with a small body of native cavalry, supported by the 20th Native Infantry This party penetrated some distance into the valley without being molested, but on its return near sunset it was attacked near the village of Umbeylah, and sustained some loss Their assailants, who were chiefly of the Boneyir tribe, followed up the 20th Native Infantry in great numbers, and commenced a general attack upon the force, which was immediately turned out and placed in position with some difficulty owing to the darkness The attack was, however, repulsed with heavy loss to the enemy and slight loss on the British side, the 71st sustaining none. This attack by the Boneyir was not anticipated

There was no intention of entering the Boneyir Valley, the pass of which is close to the village of Umbeylah, but this had not been explained to them They were doubtless unwilling to allow a force to enter even the Chumla Valley, the inhabitants of which are closely connected with them, and the opportunity of attacking the invaders at a disadvantage, as they thought, was not to be lost by these warlike mountaineers

The unexpected hostility of this numerous and [...] [...] [...] [...] [...] [...]

regarding the baggage, and the delay now become necessary to bring up additional supplies, entirely changed the aspect of affairs, and it became apparent that the force must remain on its present ground for some days at least, orders were accordingly given to throw up breastworks along the front and flanks The front line, which was across the valley or pass, was chiefly occupied by the European troops, while the flanks, which were on the hills on each side, were entirely occupied by native troops, until the 26th

On the 25th, 100 men under command of Captain Aldridge, and 15 marksmen, were employed in meeting a slight attack made on the right flank, but no casualty occurred in the 71st On the 26th, the marksmen, 1 sergeant and 15 men, were with an equal number of the 101st Royal Bengal Fusiliers ordered up to the left flank, which was threatened Shortly afterwards, Major Parker with 150 men of the 71st proceeded as a further reinforcement Both these parties obtained great praise for steadiness and gallantry in this, the most serious attack that had yet occurred The marksmen occupied the post called the Eagle's Nest, which was several times attacked by the enemy in great numbers, and with great determination Many were shot down when close to the breastwork

Major Brownlow, 20th Native Infantry commanding the post, made a most favourable report of the conduct of this small party, and especially named privates William Clapperton and George Stewart as having exhibited great gallantry and coolness These men's names afterwards appeared in General Orders, and they were recommended for the "medal for service in the field"

The conduct of the party under Major Parker was also eulogised by Lieut.-Col Vaughan, who commanded the picquets on the left flank, and Major Parker's name was afterwards specially brought to the notice of the Commander-in-Chief On this day the casualties were, 1 killed and 5 wounded Major Parker's party remained on the heights during the 26th and 27th, and was relieved on the 28th by equal numbers of the 101st regiment

On the 28th the regiment assisted in repulsing a very spirited, but not well-sustained attack made by the enemy about dawn on the front line of the picquets in the valley, when 3 men were wounded.

On several days the regiment furnished a strong working party to make a new road, leading from the right flank to the village of Umbeylah. On the 6th of November an armed party, under Ensign C. B. Murray, was ordered out to cover the working party, and about a mile from the nearest post it soon became evident that the enemy intended to molest the party. Accordingly, about 11 A.M. a reinforcement of 50 men, under Captain Mounsey, proceeded to the threatened point. Captain Mounsey was placed by the commanding officer, Major Harding, at a point considerably higher than that occupied by Ensign Murray, and nearer to camp, where he materially assisted in protecting Ensign Murray's left flank, which was threatened. Soon after 1 o'clock the working party was withdrawn. Corresponding orders were, however, omitted to be sent to Ensign Murray's party, which consequently held its ground along with a party of the 20th Native Infantry; and Captain Mounsey having been ordered to take up a fresh position still higher up the hill, the party under Ensign Murray, no longer assisted by the flank fire of the other, could only hold its ground, and was nearly surrounded.

About 2 P.M. Ensign Murray was killed, and other casualties having occurred, Major Harding, who had joined soon after, decided on holding the ground till dark, when he hoped to be able to carry off the wounded, which could not be done under the enemy's fire. Major Harding finally retired without the wounded, but was killed in the retreat. Captain Mounsey having proceeded to the point to which he was directed, assisted by parties of the Guide corps and 1st Punjab Infantry, twice charged and drove the enemy off; and, without casualty to his own party, protected some wounded officers and men until they could be removed. For this service he was specially mentioned to the Commander-in-Chief, as was also Lieutenant Davidson of the Indian army, attached to, and doing duty with the 71st, for gallantry in assisting a wounded

officer. In addition to the above-named officers, sergeant J. B. Adams and 2 privates were killed, and 5 wounded.

On the 18th of November, at daylight, a change of position was effected, and the whole force was concentrated on the heights, which up to that time had been on the right flank. The movement was completed by 8 o'clock A.M., without molestation, and apparently without the knowledge of the enemy, who soon afterwards appeared in great force in the valley and occupied the abandoned position.

An attack on Captain Griffan's battery, which was supported by two companies of the 71st, was at first threatened, but the enemy soon turned his attention to the post occupied by the 14th Native Infantry, commanded by Major Ross, and which had now become our advanced post on the left. Repeated attacks were made on this post. Reinforcements being called for, Captain Smith's company, 2 officers and 34 bayonets, was pushed forward about 2 P.M. The enemy was in great force, and between 5 and 6 P.M. the picquets were obliged to retire to a second line of breastwork. During its occupation of the advance line and in the retreat, Captain Smith's company suffered severely. The captain himself had his leg broken by a matchlock ball, and was cut down. Lieutenant Gore Jones of the 79th, who was attached to the company, was shot in the head. The picquet reformed in the second line, and were joined by two companies of the 71st under Major Parker, who resumed command. They were furiously attacked, but after a severe hand-to-hand struggle repulsed the enemy at all points, and retained possession of the ground until after nightfall, when the whole were withdrawn by the brigadier-general, as the occupation of this point was not considered necessary or advisable. Major Parker was specially mentioned for this service.

There were killed on this occasion Captain C. F. Smith, Lieutenant Gore Jones, and 4 privates; the wounded were Sergeant John Hunter and 4 privates.

On the morning of the 19th Captain Aldridge was shot, when returning from visiting the advance sentries of the Lalloo picquet. Four companies of the regiment relieved an equal number of the 101st on the upper picquet, on which the enemy continued firing all day, when 2 privates were wounded.

The 101st took the picquets of the upper camp, and also held the advanced post known as the Craig picquet. About 3 P.M. the enemy made a sudden and furious attack in great force on the Craig picquet, and succeeded in obtaining possession of it. The 71st was at once ordered to re-take it. This post was situated on the apex of a very steep and rocky hill, of which the enemy had disputed possession on several occasions. Supported by a concentrated artillery fire and by two native corps, the 5th Ghoorkas and the 5th Punjab Infantry, the regiment, led by Colonel Hope, C.B., soon regained possession, and the combined force drove the enemy back over the nearest hill. A heavy flanking fire was maintained on the enemy by the water picquet, which also suffered some loss. The loss of the regiment was severe. The post was held that night by 270 of the 71st, under Major Parker, who also assumed command of the regiment. Brigadier-General Sir N. Chamberlain was wounded in the attack, and eventually had to resign command of the force to Major-General Garvock.

His Excellency the Commander-in-Chief, Sir Hugh Rose, signified his entire approval of the gallantry of the regiment and of all the troops employed on this occasion. Casualties on the 20th of November 1863,—killed, 6 privates; wounded, Colonel W. Hope, C.B., 2 sergeants, 3 corporals, and 20 privates.

After his repulse with very heavy loss on the 20th, the enemy refrained from attacking any of our posts until the 15th of December, during which interval Major-General Garvock took command, and the 7th Fusiliers and the 93rd Highlanders having arrived, the duty became less severe. Previous to the arrival of these regiments no soldier in camp could be said to be off duty day or night. An exchange of posts from the upper camp to the lower was the only relief, the upper camp being much more exposed.

On the 15th December, the regiment being on picquet duty, did not accompany the portion of the force which, under the major-general, with Brigadiers Turner and Wilde,

commanding brigades, advanced and drove the enemy from all its posts in front, and from the village of Lalloo, but assisted in repulsing a very determined counter attack made by a strong force on the Craig picquet and upper camp generally.

On the 16th the major-general advanced and again defeated the enemy at the village of Umbeylah, which with Lalloo was burned. On the following morning the enemy sent into the major-general's camp and tendered submission, which was accepted. A small force was detached with a strong party of Boneyirs co-operating, to destroy Mulka. This was done without actual opposition, but this force was very critically situated for a short time.

The regiment returned to Nowa-Killa, and reached Nowshera on the 30th, whence it marched on the 4th of January 1864, reaching Peshawur on the 5th.

On the 21st the regiment was inspected by His Excellency, Sir Hugh Rose, G.C.B., Commander-in-Chief, who expressed himself in the most complimentary manner with reference to the conduct of the regiment in the late campaign. He called the three men whose names had appeared in General Orders—privates Malcolm, Clapperton, and Stewart—to the front, and addressed some words of approval and encouragement to them.

On the 28th of April the regiment was inspected by Major-General Garvock, who also spoke in high terms of its conduct and discipline.

On the 23rd of October, pursuant to orders from England, the regiment marched to Calcutta for embarkation. It arrived at Rawul Pindee on the 30th; and on the 1st of November the half-yearly inspection was made by Sir John Garvock, G.C.B.

The regiment having been called on to furnish volunteers to regiments serving in the Bengal Presidency, 200 men volunteered, and were transferred to other regiments.

On the 9th of November the regiment resumed its march by Lahore, Umritsur, and Loodiana to Umballa, where it arrived on the 13th of December; and on the following day was present at a general parade of the troops in the station, where medals for gallant service in the field were presented by Major-General Lord George Paget to Sergeant Major John Blackwood, and privates Macdonald, Malcolm, Clapperton, and Stewart, for distinguished conduct in the field The Sergeant-Major was also granted a pension of £15 in addition to the medal

The regiment arrived at Delhi, on the 26th of December, and on the 4th of January 1865, one wing proceeded by rail to Allahabad, and was followed next day by the other wing

On the 21st and 23d the regiment proceeded by rail to Chinsurah, 25 miles from Calcutta, where it remained until it embarked—the right wing and head-quarters, under the command of Colonel Hope, on the 4th of February, in the steamship "Mauritius," and the left wing, commanded by Major Gore, in the "Albert Victor," on the 14th of February The right wing arrived and disembarked at Plymouth on the 29th of May, having touched at Madras, the Cape, and Fayal It remained at Plymouth until the 7th of June, when it was sent to Leith in H M's ship "Urgent," and arrived in Edinburgh on the 12th, where it occupied the Castle

The left wing arrived at Gravesend on the 19th of June, where it landed, and was afterwards taken round to Leith by the "Urgent," and joined the head-quarters in Edinburgh Castle on the 25th of June

The following General and Divisional Orders were published previous to the regiment quitting India —

Extract of Divisional Order by Major-General Sir John Garvock, K C.B , commanding Peshawur Division

"RAWUL PINDEE, 1st November 1864
"The 71st Highland Light Infantry being about to leave the Peshawur Division, en route to England, the Major-General commanding desires to offer them his best wishes on the occasion

"He has known the regiment for a number of years He was very intimately associated with it in the Mediterranean, and his interest in it is now naturally increased in no small degree by its having served under him in the field and done its part, and done it well, in obtaining for him those honours which Her Majesty has been pleased to confer

"The Major-General had not assumed the command of the Yuzufzai Field Force when the 71st re-captured the Craig Picquet, but he well knows that it was a most gallant exploit

"Sir John Garvock, K C B , begs Colonel Hope, C B , and the officers, non-commissioned officers, and soldiers of the 71st Highland Light Infantry, to believe that, although they will be soon no longer under his command, he will continue to take the liveliest interest in their career, and he now wishes them a speedy and prosperous voyage "

General Orders
By His Excellency the Commander-in-chief

"HEAD-QUARTERS, CALCUTTA,
27th January 1865

"The services of the 71st Highland Light Infantry in India entitle them, on their departure for England, to honourable mention in general orders

"A wing of the regiment on their arrival in India in 1858 joined the Central India Field Force, and His Excellency is therefore enabled to bear testimony to the good services which they performed, and the excellent spirit which they displayed during that campaign

"The regiment more recently distinguished itself under their commanding officer, Colonel Hope, C B , in the late operations on the frontier

"Sir Hugh Rose cannot, in justice to military merit, speak of the 71st in a General Order without reverting to an earlier period, when in two great campaigns in Europe they won a reputation which has earned them an honoured page in history

"Sir Hugh Rose's best wishes attend this distinguished regiment on their leaving his command for home

"By order of His Excellency the Commander-in-chief.

E HAYTHORN,
"Colonel, Adjutant General "

The depot companies, commanded by Brevet-Major Lambton, joined the regiment in Edinburgh, and the establishment of the regiment was fixed at 12 companies, with 54 sergeants, 31 buglers and pipers, and 700 rank and file

The autumn inspection was made by Major-General Walker, on the 4th of October 1865

"HORSE-GUARDS, 13th February 1866.

"SIR,

"Referring to your confidential report on the 71st regiment, dated the 4th of October last, in which you represent that a sword is worn by the officers which is not regulation, I am directed by the Field-Marshal Commander-in-chief, to acquaint you that H.R.H. having seen the sword in question, has no objection to the continuance of its use, the 71st being a Light Infantry Regiment.

"For levees, &c., the basket hilt should be worn, which, it is understood, can be made removable, and the cross-bar substituted at pleasure.

"I have, &c.,

"J. TROWBRIDGE, D.A.G.

"Major-General Walker, C.B.,
    Commanding North Britain."

In October 1865, during the stay of the regiment in Edinburgh Castle, it sustained the loss by death of Brevet Lieutenant-Colonel Parker, on which occasion the following Regimental Order was published by Colonel Hope :—

"The Commanding Officer regrets to have to announce to the regiment the demise of Brevet Lieutenant-Colonel Parker, which occurred this morning at 8 A.M. Colonel Hope feels certain that the announcement will be received with the deepest regret for the loss sustained, as well by the regiment, as by Her Majesty's service generally. Lieutenant-Colonel Parker has departed after a service of twenty-three years in the regiment, many of which he passed in distant countries and in active services against the enemies of his country. On more than one occasion, and as recently as 1863, his services in the field met with such approbation from general officers under whom he served, as to induce them to name him in public despatches.

"Colonel Hope can only express his opinion that no officer more faithfully and ably sustained the honour and reputation of the regiment than did Lieutenant-Colonel Parker, and that none better merited the honours done him."

In February 1866, the regiment removed to Aldershot, where the spring inspection was made on the 2nd of May 1866 ; and also the autumn inspection by Brigadier General Sir

Alfred Horsford, K.C.B., who was pleased to comment highly on the appearance and discipline of the regiment.

In December the regiment removed to Ireland, and was distributed in Fermoy, Cork, and Ballincollig ; head-quarters being at Fermoy.

On the 27th November 1867, Colonel Hope retired from the command of the regiment, which he had held for many years, and in which capacity he had gained alike the esteem and love both of officers and men. His retirement, which was forced upon him by his continued ill health, was felt to be an occasion upon which each individual member of the regiment lost a valued friend as well as a brave commander. On leaving he issued the following Order :—

"Colonel Hope has this day (18th of November 1867), relinquished the command of the regiment, which he has held for eight years, and handed it over to Major Macdonnell, who also will be his successor.

"Having served so many years—in fact, from his boyhood—in the regiment, and having commanded for the last eight years, he need hardly say that he quits the 71st with the greatest sorrow and regret.

"It has been his anxious wish at all times to maintain intact the reputation of the regiment as it was received by him ; and this wish has, he believes, been gratified. .

"Since the regiment was embodied, now 90 years ago, in all parts of the world,—in India, in the Cape of Good Hope, in South America, in Spain,—the 71st has been equally renowned for conduct and discipline—in the field before the enemy, during a long peace, and in quarters at home and abroad. It has also received the approbation of superior military authorities.

"Since the breaking out of the war with Russia, it has seen service in the Crimea, and the Indian Mutiny brought it once more to India, where its early laurels were won.

"In the Central Indian Campaign of 1858, the regiment served under Sir Hugh Rose, and received commendations from that distinguished officer (now Lord Strathnairn), as it did with other commanders, with whom that desultory campaign brought it into contact.

"1863 again saw the regiment in the Yuzufzai Hills, opposed to the warlike tribes of Central Asia. Colonel Hope can never forget the devotion of all officers and soldiers in the short but arduous campaign, nor the handsome terms in which Lord Strathnairn, then the Commander-in-Chief in India, acknowledged their services on its termination.

"Colonel Hope is well aware that this short recital of the regimental history is well known to all the older officers and soldiers, many of whom took part in the exploits of the 71st during the last twelve years, but he mentions them now that they may be known and remembered by the younger members, and with the confident hope that it will never be for-

Monument erected in Glasgow Cathedral.
WILLIAM BRODIE, R.S.A., Sculptor

gotten that the 71st has a reputation and a name in the British army, which must be maintained at all hazards.

"Colonel Hope now bids farewell to all his comrade officers and soldiers with every good wish for their prosperity and happiness."

The command of the regiment now devolved upon Major John Ignatius Macdonnell, who obtained his promotion to Lieutenant-Colonel by Colonel Hope's retirement. He took over the command with the good wishes and confidence of every one, having served in the regiment from the date of his first commission, on the 26th of April 1844, and been with it during the Crimea, Central Indian, and Yuzufzai campaigns

The detachment of the regiment at Tralee was inspected by Lord Strathnairn, Commander of the Forces in Ireland, October 28th, 1867, and favourably reported upon

During the stay of the 71st in the south of Ireland, parts of it were on several occasions called out in aid of the civil authorities during the Fenian disturbances, and it was held to be greatly to the credit of the regiment, that during this trying time with the inhabitants of the south of Ireland in open revolt against Her Majesty's authority, there were no complaints of quarrels or other disturbances between any civilians and soldiers of the 71st

The establishment of the regiment was increased from the 1st of April 1868 to the following standard —12 companies, 1 colonel, 1 lieutenant-colonel, 2 majors, 12 captains, 14 lieutenants, 10 ensigns, 1 paymaster, 1 adjutant, 1 quarter master, 1 surgeon, 1 assistant-surgeon, 57 sergeants, 31 buglers and pipers, and 800 rank and file

On the 22nd of July 1868, the regiment removed from Dublin to the Curragh, where it remained during summer, employed exclusively in practising field manœuvring, and in taking part in movements on a large scale with the rest of the division

General Lord Strathnairn inspected the regiment before leaving his command, and expressed his regret at losing it, while he still further complimented it on its steadiness and good behaviour

Two depot companies having been formed, they proceeded on the 9th of October for Aberdeen, to join the 15th depot battalion there

On the 17th of October the regiment left the Curragh, and embarked at Dublin on board H M S "Simoom" for Gibraltar, where it arrived on the 22d, disembarked on the 23d, and encamped under canvas on the North Front Camping Ground until the 29th, whence it marched into quarters and was distributed between Europa and Buena Vista Barracks

On the 13th of March 1870 the regiment sustained the l-- by l-r'b, of its C-l--l,

General the Hon Charles Grey, on which occasion the following Order was published by the commanding officer —

"It is with the deepest regret that the commanding officer has to announce to the regiment the death of General the Hon Charles Grey, Colonel of the 71st Highland Light Infantry This officer has peculiar claims on the sympathy of the regiment, from the deep interest he has always taken in its welfare, and his warm attachment to a corps in which he served for upwards of ten years On all occasions he had exerted his powerful interest to promote every measure required for the honour of the officers, non commissioned officers, and men, and never did he cease to watch with the kindliest feelings the varied and honourable career in distant lands of his old regiment, which he had been so proud of commanding in his early life

"The officers will wear regimental mourning for the period of one month'

The vacancy in the colonelcy was filled up by the appointment thereto of Lieutenant-General Robert Law, K H, which was notified to the regiment by the commanding officer in the following terms —

"The commanding officer has much pleasure in informing the regiment that Lieutenant-General Robert Law, K H, has been appointed colonel of the regiment, as successor to the late General the Honourable Charles Grey

The following account of General Law's services in the 71st will sufficiently inform the regiment how much he is entitled to their respect"

Lieutenant-General Law served with the 71st Light Infantry on Sir John Moore's retreat at the action of Lago and the battle of Corunna, the expedition to Walcheren, Liége, Ter Verre, and Flushing, subsequently in Portugal, Spain, and the south of France, from 1810 to 1814; the action of Sobraon, the entering of the lines of Torres Vedras, the pursuit of Massena through Portugal, the battle of Fuentes d'Onor, on the 3rd and 5th of May 1811 (where he was wounded in two places), the covering the two last sieges of Badajos, the surprise and defeat of Girard's corps at Arroyo del Molino, the storming and destruction of the enemy's tête du pont and other work at Almar--, the defence of the Alba-de-Tormes; the battles in the Pyrenees, in July 1813, where, on the 30th, the command of an important post devolved upon him; the attack on Sorauren; the capture at Elizondo of the convoy of supplies destined for the relief of Pamplona; the battles of the Nivelle and the Nive; the action at the Bridge of Cambo; the affair at Hellette, St Palais, Arrivarelle, and Garris; and the action at Aire. He was employed in command of an armed boat on night duties; in the affair with picquets on the river Adour; at the battle of St Pierre near Bayonne, on the 13th of December 1813; at the battle of Orthes; and the action at Tarbes, where he was wounded.

In the foregoing services he was long Adjutant of his regiment, and latterly acted as such to the light battalion of his brigade. He served also in the campaign of 1815, including the battle of Waterloo, where he was severely wounded by a cannon shot, which also killed his horse; he served also three years in the Army of Occupation in France, and received the war-medal with six clasps, and was made a K.H.

On the 1st of April the strength of the regiment was reduced to 10 companies (including 2 depot companies), consisting of 34 officers, 49 sergeants, 26 buglers and pipers, and 600 rank and file.

On the 5th of November 1869, the depot moved from Aberdeen to Fort-George; and on the 1st of April 1870, an order having been issued for the abolition of depot battalions, they proceeded to join the head-quarters of the 72d Highlanders at Buttevant, to which regiment they were attached and joined on the 7th of April 1870. On the 15th of August the establishment of the rank and file of the regiment was increased to 650, the other ranks remaining unaltered.

On the 24th of April 1873, the regiment embarked at Gibraltar for Malta. Previous to embarking, it was inspected by General Sir W. F. Williams, Bart., G.C.B., who, in his address, after his inspection, spoke of the appreciation in which the regiment was held by himself, and by the whole garrison and inhabitants of Gibraltar, for their soldier-like qualities, their smartness, and steadi-

ness on duty, and their general good conduct, and added, "I myself personally regret your approaching departure, and I am certain that feeling is shared by every one in the place, but I also feel convinced that you will equally keep up the same good character in your new quarters. I wish you all health and happiness, and a good passage to your destination."

Under the new system the 71st Highland Light Infantry has been linked with the 78th (Ross-shire) Highlanders, forming the 55th Brigade, head-quarters at Fort-George.

We have much pleasure in being able to present our readers with authentic steel portraits of two of the most eminent Colonels of the 71st Highland Light Infantry. That of the first Colonel, John Lord Macleod, is from the original painting in the possession of the Duchess of Sutherland, at Tarbat House, Ross-shire; and that of Sir Thomas Reynell, Bart., from a painting in the possession of Mrs Reynell Pack, at Avisford House, Arundel, Sussex.

ARGYLE HIGHLANDERS,
OR
OLD SEVENTY-FOURTH HIGHLAND REGIMENT.
1778—1783.

Raising of the Regiment—America—Penobscot—Return home—Disbanded.

THIS regiment was raised by Colonel John Campbell of Barbreck, who had served as captain and major of Fraser's Highlanders in the Seven Years' War. To him letters of service were granted in December 1777, and the regiment was completed in May 1778, when it was inspected at Glasgow by General Skene. The lower orders in Argyleshire, from their proximity to the sea, being more addicted to the naval than to the land service, did not embrace the military profession with the same alacrity as the other Highlanders; and the result was, that only 590 Highlanders entered this regiment. The remainder were Lowlanders recruited in Glasgow and the western districts of Scotland. With the exception of 4, all the officers were Highlanders, of whom 3 field-officers, 6 captains, and 14 subalterns, were of the name of Campbell.

The 74th embarked at Greenock in August 1778, for Halifax, in Nova Scotia, where they were garrisoned along with the Edinburgh Regiment (the 80th) and the Duke of Hamilton's (the 82d), all under the command of Brigadier-General Francis Maclean. In spring, 1779, the grenadier company, commanded by Captain Ludovick Colquhoun of Luss, and the light company by Captain Campbell of Balnabie, were sent to New York, and joined the army immediately before the siege of Charlestown.

The battalion companies, with a detachment of the 82d regiment, under the command of Brigadier-General Maclean, embarked at Halifax in June of the same year, and took possession of Penobscot. With the view of establishing himself there, the brigadier proceeded to erect defences; but before these were completed, a hostile fleet from Boston, with 2000 troops on board, under Brigadier-General Lovel, appeared in the bay, and on the 28th of July effected a landing on a peninsula, where the British were erecting a fort. The enemy immediately began to erect batteries for a siege; but their operations met with frequent interruption from parties that sallied from the fort. Meanwhile General Maclean proceeded with his works, and not only kept the enemy in complete check, but preserved the communication with the shipping, which they endeavoured to cut off. Both parties kept skirmishing till the 13th of August, on the morning of which day Commodore Sir George Collier entered the bay with a fleet to relieve the brigadier. The enemy immediately raised the siege, and retired to their ships, but a part only were able to escape. The remainder, along with the sailors of some of their ships which had grounded, formed themselves into a body, and attempted to penetrate through the woods; but running short of provisions, they afterwards quarrelled among themselves, and fired on each other till all their ammunition was spent. After upwards of 60 had been killed and wounded in this affray, the rest dispersed in the woods, where numbers perished. In this expedition, the 74th had 2 sergeants and 14 privates killed, and 17 rank and file wounded.

General Maclean returned to Halifax with the detachment of the 82d, leaving Lieutenant-Colonel Alexander Campbell of Monzie with the 74th at Penobscot, where they remained till the termination of hostilities, when they embarked for England. They landed at Portsmouth, whence they marched for Stirling, and, after being joined by the flank companies, were reduced in the autumn of 1783.

MACDONALD'S HIGHLANDERS,

OR

OLD SEVENTY-SIXTH HIGHLAND REGIMENT.

1777—1784.

Raising of the Regiment—Refusal to embark—America—Made prisoners—Return home—Disbanded.

LETTERS of service were granted in December 1777 to Lord Macdonald to raise a regiment in the Highlands and Isles, of which corps his lordship was offered the command; but he declined the commission, and at his recommendation, Major John Macdonell of Lochgarry was appointed lieutenant-colonel commandant of the regiment. Lord Macdonald, however, exerted his influence in the formation of the corps, and as a good selection of officers was made from the families of the Macdonalds of Glencoe, Morar, Boisdale, and others of his own clan, and likewise from those of other clans, as Mackinnon, Fraser of Culduthel, Cameron of Callart, &c., a body of 750 Highlanders was soon raised. Nearly 200 men were raised in the Lowlands by Captains Cunningham of Craigends, and Montgomery Cunningham, and Lieutenant Samuel Graham. These were kept together in two companies, and another body of men, principally raised in Ireland by Captain Bruce, formed a third company, all of which were kept perfectly distinct from the Highlanders. The regiment was inspected at Inverness in March 1778 by General Skene, and amounted to 1086 men, including non-commissioned officers and drummers.

The regiment was then quartered in Fort-George, where it remained twelve months under the command of Major Donaldson, who, from his long experience, was well calculated to train them properly.

Being removed to Perth in March 1779, the regiment was again reviewed by General Skene on the 10th, and, being reported complete, was ordered to march to Burntisland for the purpose of embarking for America. Shortly after their arrival at Burntisland, numbers of the Highlanders were observed in parties in earnest conversation together. The cause of this consultation was soon known. Each company, on the evening of the third day, gave in a written statement, complaining of non-performance of promises, of their bounty-money being withheld, &c., and accompanied by a declaration, that till their grievances were redressed, they would not embark. They demanded that Lord Macdonald should be sent for to see justice done to them. No satisfactory answer having been returned within the time expected, the Highlanders marched off in a body, and took possession of a hill above Burntisland. To show that these men had no other end in view but justice, they refused to allow some young soldiers, who had joined them in a frolic, to remain with them, telling them that as they had no ground for complaint, they ought not to disobey orders.

The Highlanders remained for several days on the hill without offering the least violence, and sent in parties regularly to the town for provisions, for which they paid punctually. During this interval, Major Donaldson, assisted by Lieutenant David Barclay the paymaster, investigated the claims of the men, and ascertained that they were well founded, and Lord Macdonald having arrived, his lordship and the major advanced the money, and paid off every demand at their own risk. On a subsequent investigation of the individual claims, when sent to the Isle of Skye, it was ascertained that all, without exception, were found to be just,[9] a circumstance as honourable to the claimants as it was disgraceful to those who had attempted to overreach them.

This disagreeable affair being fortunately settled, the regiment embarked on the 17th of March; but before their departure, all the men of Skye and Uist sent the money they had received home to their families and friends.[1]

Major Donaldson being unable to accompany the regiment on account of the delicate state of his health, and Lieutenant-Colonel Macdonell having been taken prisoner on his passage from America, where he had been serving with Fraser's Highlanders, the command of the regiment devolved on Major Lord Berridale.

The transports, with the 76th on board, touched at Portsmouth, and while lying at Spithead, the regiment was ordered to the relief of Jersey, which the enemy had attacked; but before reaching the island the French had been repulsed. They then proceeded on the voyage, and landed at New York in August. The flank companies were then attached to the battalion, composed of the flank companies of the other regiments, and the battalion companies were quartered between New York and Staten Island. In February 1781, these companies embarked for Virginia with a detachment of the army, commanded by Major-General Phillips. The light company, being in the second battalion of light infantry, also formed a part of the expedition.

Lord Berridale, who had, by the death of his father this year, become Earl of Caithness, having been severely wounded at the siege of Charlestown, returned to Scotland, and was succeeded in the command of the regiment by the Hon. Major Needham, afterwards Earl of Kilmorey, who had purchased Major Donaldson's commission.

General Phillips landed at Portsmouth, Virginia, in March, and having joined the detachment under General Arnold, the united detachments formed a junction with the army of Lord Cornwallis in May. The Macdonald Highlanders, on meeting with men who had braved the dangers of the field, considered themselves as an inferior race, and sighed for an opportunity of putting themselves on an equality with their companions in arms, and they did not wait long.

The celebrated Marquis de la Fayette, anxious to distinguish himself in the cause which he had espoused, determined to attack Lord Cornwallis's army, and in pursuance of this intention pushed forward a strong corps, which forced the British piequets. He then formed his line, and a warm contest immediately began, the

[9] Stewart. [1] Ibid.

weight of which, on the side of the British, was sustained by the brigade of Colonel Thomas Dundas, consisting of the 76th and 80th regiments. These corps, which were on the left, were drawn up on an open field, while the right of the line was covered by woods. Coming up in the rear of the 76th, Lord Cornwallis gave the word to charge, which being responded to by the Highlanders, they rushed forward with great impetuosity upon the enemy, who, unable to stand the shock, turned their backs and fled, leaving their cannon and 390 men, killed and wounded, behind them.[a]

After the surrender of Lord Cornwallis's army, the 76th was marched in detachments as prisoners to different parts of Virginia. During their confinement, many attempts were made by their emigrant countrymen, as well as by the Americans, to induce them to join the cause of American independence; but not one of them could be induced by any consideration to renounce his allegiance.

The regiment, on its return to Scotland, was disbanded in March 1784 at Stirling Castle.

ATHOLE HIGHLANDERS,
OR
OLD SEVENTY-SEVENTH HIGHLAND REGIMENT.
1778—1783.

Raising of the Regiment—Ireland—Mutiny—Disbanded.

On the application of the young Duke of Athole, government granted him authority to raise a regiment of 1000 men for the service of the State, with power to appoint officers. The command of this corps was given to Colonel James Murray, son of Lord George Murray.

The Athole Highlanders were embodied at Perth, and in June 1778 were marched to Port-Patrick, and embarked for Ireland, where they remained during the war. They were thus deprived of an opportunity of distinguishing themselves in the field; but their presence in Ireland was attended with this advantage, that they supplied the place of other troops, who would probably have been less exemplary in their conduct amongst a people whose passions were excited by misgovernment.

The terms on which the men had enlisted were to serve for three years, or during the war. On the conclusion of hostilities, they, of course, expected to be disbanded; but instead of this they were transported to England, and marched to Portsmouth for embarkation to the East Indies. On the march they were made acquainted with the intentions of Government; and so far from objecting to a continuance of their service, they showed no disinclination to embark, and when they first saw the fleet at Spithead, as they crossed Portsdown-hill, they pulled off their bonnets, and gave three cheers for a brush with Hyder Ali. They had scarcely, however, taken up their quarters at Portsmouth, when the face of matters changed. The minds of the men, it is said, were wrought upon by emissaries from London, who represented the unfaithfulness of Government in sending them abroad after the term of their service had expired. It was even insinuated that they had been sold to the East India Company at a certain sum per man, and that the officers were to divide the money amongst themselves. These base misrepresentations had their intended effect, and the result was that the soldiers resolved not to embark. The authority of the officers was despised; and after a scene of uproar and confusion, which lasted several days, during which the Highlanders attempted to obtain possession of the main-guard and garrison parade, the order to embark was countermanded by Government.

---

[a] "At the moment Lord Cornwallis was giving the orders to charge, a Highland soldier rushed forward and placed himself in front of his officer, Lieutenant Simon Macdonald of Morar, afterwards major of the 92d regiment. Lieutenant Macdonald having asked what brought him there, the soldier answered, 'You know that when I engaged to be a soldier, I promised to be faithful to the king and to you. The French are coming, and while I stand here, neither bullet nor bayonet shall touch you, except through my body!'

"Major Macdonald had no particular claim to the gener . . . . that which never failed to be binding on the true Highlander,—he was born on his officer's estate, where he and his forefathers had been treated with kindness,—he was descended of the same family (Clanranald),—and when he enlisted he promised to be a faithful soldier. He was of the branch of the Clanranald family, whose patronymic is Maceachen, or the sons of Hector; the same branch of which Marshal Macdonald, Duke of Tarentum, is descended."

S . . . .

One account of this affair, dated at Portsmouth, and published in February 1783, contains the following details:—"The Duke of Athole, his uncle, Major-General Murray, and Lord George Lennox, have been down here, but the Athole Highlanders are still determined not to go to the East Indies. . They have put up their arms and ammunition into one of the magazines, and placed a very strong guard over them, whilst the rest of the regiment sleep and refresh themselves. They come regularly and quietly to the grand parade, very cleanly dressed, twice a-day, their adjutant and other officers parading with them. One day it was proposed to turn the great guns of the rampart on the Highlanders; but this scheme was soon overruled. Another time it was suggested to send for some marching regiments quartered near the place, upon which the Highlanders drew up the draw-bridges, and placed sentinels at them."

"You may be assured," says another account, "I have had my perplexities since the mutiny commenced in the 77th regiment; but I must do the men the justice to confess, that excepting three or four drunken fellows, whose impudence to their officers could only be equalled by their brutality, the whole regiment have conducted themselves with a regularity that is surprising; for what might not have been expected from upwards of one thousand men let loose from all restraint? Matters would never have been carried to the point they have, but for the interference of some busy people, who love to be fishing in troubled waters. The men have opened a subscription for the relief of the widow of the poor invalid,* for whose death they express the greatest regret. On their being informed that two or three regiments were coming to force them to embark, they flew to their arms, and followed their comrade leaders through the town, with a fixed determination to give them battle; but on finding the report to be false, they returned in the same order to their quarters. The regiment is not to go to the East Indies contrary to their instructions, which has satisfied them, but will be attended with disagreeable consequences to the service; and since the debates in the House

of Commons on the subject, I should not wonder if every man intended for foreign service refused going, for the reasons then given, which you may depend on it they are now well acquainted with."

Mr Eden, afterwards Lord Auckland, secretary for Ireland, in the Parliamentary debates on the mutiny, bore honourable testimony to the exemplary conduct of the regiment in Ireland:—"He had happened," he said, "to have the 77th regiment immediately under his observation during sixteen months of their garrison duty in Dublin, and though it was not the most agreeable duty in the service, he must say that their conduct was most exemplary. Their officers were not only men of gentlemanly character, but peculiarly attentive to regimental discipline. He having once, upon the sudden alarm of invasion, sent an order for the immediate march of this regiment to Cork, they showed their alacrity by marching at an hour's notice, and completed their march with a despatch beyond any instance in modern times, and this too without leaving a single soldier behind."

This unfair and unworthy attempt on the part of Government created a just distrust of its integrity, and had a most pernicious effect on its subsequent endeavours to raise men in the Highlands. Alluding to this unfortunate affair, General Stewart observes, that "if Government had offered a small bounty when the Athole Highlanders were required to embark, there can be little doubt they would have obeyed their orders, and embarked as cheerfully as they marched into Portsmouth."

The fault resting entirely with Government, it wisely abstained from pushing matters further by bringing any of the men to trial. The regiment was immediately marched to Berwick, where it was disbanded in April 1783, in terms of the original agreement.

---

* He was killed when the Highlanders made the attempt to take possession of the main-guard and garrison parade.

SEAFORTH'S HIGHLANDERS,
FORMERLY
THE SEVENTY-EIGHTH,
NOW
THE SEVENTY-SECOND REGIMENT,
OR DUKE OF ALBANY'S OWN HIGHLANDERS.

I.

1778—1858.

Raising the Regiment—First Officers—Disaffection at Leith—"The affair of the Macraes"—Embarkation for India—Death of Lord Seaforth—Effects of scurvy—Joining Sir Eyre Coote's army—Joining Major-General James Stuart's army—Led by Colonel Fullarton against Tippoo Sahib—Palghatcherri—Number of the Regiment changed to 72nd—Recruiting—War with Tippoo Sahib—Stuart's dilemma—Palghatcheri—Ordered home—Fort Dindigal—Stuart takes Palghatcheri—Lord Cornwallis—Bangalore—Ootradroog—Forlorn hope of Sergeant Williams—Valour of the 72nd—Siege of Seringapatam—Storming of Savendroog—Ootradroog—Sailing for India—The Mauritius—Landing at the Cape of Good Hope—Arrival at Calcutta—Lands again at Cape Town—Captain Gethin's death—Return home—Permitted to assume the name of the Duke of Albany's Own Highlanders—The Cape of Good Hope again—Graham's Town—The Kaffir War in 1835—The Governor-General at the camp—The Kaffirs attack the Fingoes—End of the Kaffir War—Permitted to add "Cape of Good Hope" to the colours—At Graham's Town—At Cape Town—Home.

The late Duke of York's Cipher and Coronet.

HINDOOSTAN.
CAPE OF GOOD HOPE.
SEVASTOPOL.
CENTRAL INDIA.

KENNETH MACKENZIE, grandson of the Earl of Seaforth, whose estate and title were forfeited in consequence of his concern in the rebellion of 1715, having purchased the family property from the Crown, was created an Irish peer, by the title of Lord Viscount Fortrose. In the year 1771, Government restored to him the family title of Earl of Seaforth. To evince his gratitude for this magnanimous act, the Earl, in the year 1778, offered to raise a regiment on his estate for general service. This offer being accepted by his Majesty, a corps of 1130 men was speedily raised, principally by gentlemen of the name of Mackenzie, his lordship's clan.

Of these about 900 were Highlanders, 500 of whom were raised upon Lord Seaforth's own estate, and the remainder upon the estates of the Mackenzies of Scatwell, Kilcoy, Applecross, and Redcastle, all of whom had sons or brothers in the regiment. The remainder were raised in the Lowlands, of whom 43 were English and Irish.

The following is the first list of officers:—

Lieut.-Col.-Commandant—Kenneth, Earl of Seaforth.

Major—James Stuart (from Capt. 64th Regt.)

Captains.

T. F. M. Humberston.	George Mackenzie.
Robert Lumsdaine.	Hugh Frazer.
Peter Agnew.	Hon. Thos. Maitland.
Kenneth Mackenzie.[b]	Charles Halkett.[c]

Captain Lieutenant—Thomas Frazer.

Lieutenants.

Donald Moody.	George Mackenzie.
William Sutherland.	Charles Gladoning.
Colin Mackenzie.	William Sinclair.
Kenneth Mackenzie.	Charles Mackenzie.
Patrick Haggard.	John Campbell.
Thomas Mackenzie.	James Stewart.
George Innes.	Robert Marshall.
Charles M'Gregor.	Philip Anstruther.
David Melville.	Kenneth Macrae.
George Gordon.	John M'Innes.
James Gualie.	

Ensigns.

James Stewart.	Robert Gordon.
James Finney.	John Mitchell.
Aulay M'Aulay.	Ewen M'Lennan.
Malcolm M'Pherson.	George Gordon.

Staff.

Chaplain.—Wm. Mackenzie.
Surgeon.—John Walters.
Adjutant.—James Finney.
Quarter-master.—George Gunn.

The regiment was embodied at Elgin, in May 1778, and was inspected by General Skene, when it was found so effective that not one man was rejected. In the month of August the regiment marched to Leith for embarkation to the East Indies; but they had not been quartered long in that town when symptoms of disaffection began to appear among them. They complained of an infringement of their engagements, and that part of their pay and bounty was in arrear. Being wrought upon by some emissaries, the men refused to embark, and, marching out of Leith with pipes

---

[b] From the Dutch Service.
[c] From the Austrian service.

playing, and two plaids fixed on poles instead of colours, they took up a position in the immediate vicinity of Edinburgh on Arthur's Seat, on which they remained several days. During this time they were amply supplied with provisions and ammunition by the inhabitants of the capital, who had espoused their quarrel. The causes of complaint having been inquired into, after much negotiation, in which the Earls of Dunmore and Seaforth, Sir James Grant of Grant, and other gentlemen connected with the Highlands, took an active and prominent part, the grievances were removed, and the soldiers being satisfied, marched down the hill with pipes playing, with the Earls of Seaforth and Dunmore, and General Skene at their head, and returned to their quarters at Leith. From the great number of the clan Macrae that were in the regiment, the mutiny was called "The affair of the Macraes."

At Leith the regiment embarked with the greatest cheerfulness, accompanied by their colonel, the Earl of Seaforth. The intention of sending them to India being for the present abandoned, one half of the regiment was sent to Guernsey, and the other to Jersey. At the end of April 1781, however, both divisions assembled at Portsmouth, where, on the 12th of June, they embarked for the East Indies, being then 973 strong, rank and file. Though the men were all in excellent health, they suffered so severely from the effects of the voyage and the change of food, that before reaching Madras on the 2nd of April 1782, 247 of them had died of scurvy, and out of all that landed, only 369 were fit to carry arms. The death of Seaforth, their chief, who expired before the regiment reached St Helena, threw a damp over the spirits of the men, and it is said to have materially contributed to that prostration of mind which made them more readily the victims of disease.

As the service was pressing, such of the men as were able to march were immediately sent up the country under Major James Stuart; but many of them being still weak from the effects of scurvy, suffered greatly on the march. The men were sinewy and robust, and such as had escaped the scurvy were greatly injured by the violence of the sun's beams, the effects of which were not so injurious to men of more slender habits. They joined the army of Sir Eyre Coote at Chingleput in the beginning of May; but he found them so unfit for service that he ordered the corps into quarters, and put the few who remained healthy into the 73rd or Macleod's Highlanders, the only European corps then with the army.

The men gradually recovered, and in the month of October upwards of 600 were fit for duty. The colours of the regiment were again unfolded, and in April 1783 they joined the army destined to attack Cuddalore, under Major-General James Stuart (of the family of Torrance).

On the 25th of June, the enemy made a sally on the British lines, but were repulsed at every point, losing 150 men in killed and prisoners, including among the latter the Chevalier Dumas.

Notwithstanding the termination of hostilities with France in January 1783, the war with Tippoo Sahib was continued. Colonel Fullarton, who had marched on Cuddalore, finding he was no longer needed in that quarter, retraced his steps southward, reinforced by Seaforth's Highlanders and other troops, thus augmenting his force to upwards of 13,000 men. This army was employed several months in keeping down some turbulent chiefs; and in October Colonel Fullarton marched on Palghatcherri, after securing some intermediate forts. Lieutenant-Colonel Humberston Mackenzie, of the 100th regiment, who succeeded about this time to the command of the 78th, in consequence of the death of his cousin, the Earl of Seaforth, as well as to his title and estates, had intended to attack this place the preceding year, but he abandoned the attempt. After a fatiguing march through thick woods and a broken country, Colonel Fullarton reached the place early in November, and immediately laid siege to it. The garrison might have made a long and vigorous defence; but an event occurred which hastened the fall of Palghatcherri. The enemy having taken shelter from a shower of rain, the Hon. Captain Sir Thomas Maitland advanced unperceived with his flank corps, and drove the enemy through the first gateway, which he entered; but his progress was checked at the second, which was shut. Being immediately reinforced, he prepared to force an entrance; but the enemy, afraid of an assault, immediately surrendered.

On the 30th of April this year the regiment lost their new colonel, who died of wounds received on board the "Ranger" sloop of war on the 7th of April 1783, in an action with a Mahratta fleet while on his return from Bombay. He was succeeded in the command of the regiment by Major-General James Murray, from the half-pay of the 77th regiment.

In consequence of the peace, Seaforth's regiment having been raised on the condition of serving for three years, or during the war,—those of the men that adhered to this agreement were allowed to embark for England; while those that preferred staying in the country received the same bounty as other volunteers. The number of men who claimed their discharge on the 10th of August 1784 reduced the regiment to 425 rank and file; but so many men volunteered into the corps from the different regiments ordered home (among whom was a considerable number of Highlanders who had formerly enlisted into the 100th Regiment with Colonel Humberston Mackenzie), that the strength was at once augmented to 700 men. At the end of the next year the regiment received 423 men from various regiments.

On the 12th of September 1786 the number of the regiment was changed to the 72nd, in consequence of the reduction of senior regiments.

On the 25th of December 1787 the establishment was reduced to the following numbers:—1 captain, 1 lieutenant-colonel and captain, 1 major and captain, 7 captains, 22 lieutenants, 8 ensigns, 1 chaplain, 1 adjutant, 1 quartermaster, 1 surgeon, 2 mates, 30 sergeants, 40 corporals, 20 drummers, 2 fifers, 710 privates, including 40 contingent men.

It was soon found necessary, however, again to increase the strength of the regiment, and recruiting was carried on with success. A considerable detachment joined on the 18th of August 1789; so that in the following year, when war commenced with Tippoo, the 72nd was nearly 800 strong, while the men were healthy, seasoned to the climate, well-disciplined, and highly respectable in their moral conduct. In this highly efficient condition they

formed part of the army under Major-General Meadows on the 23rd of July 1790.

The first service of the 72nd was under Colonel Stuart, being ordered along with other troops to attack Palghatcheri, which on a former occasion had been the scene of success to a corps now destined to sustain a disappointment. The detachment being overtaken by the rains which fell in almost unprecedented abundance, Colonel Stuart got so beset with the mountain streams that, for a short time, he could neither proceed nor retire; and when the waters abated he returned to headquarters. In this enterprise the 78th had Captain George Mackenzie and 23 rank and file killed, and 3 sergeants and 44 rank and file wounded.

After a short rest, the same officer, with the same troops under his command, was detached against Dindigul, before which he arrived on the 16th of August 1790. This is one of those granite rocks so common in that part of India. The fort on the summit had lately been repaired, and mounted with 14 guns, the precipice allowing of only one point of ascent. The means of attack, both in guns and ammunition, were very deficient. A small breach, however, was made on the 20th; and Colonel Stuart resolved to assault, small as the breach was, judging that more loss would be sustained by delay than by an immediate attack, since, in addition to other difficulties, he was short of ammunition. Accordingly, on the evening of the 21st of August, the attack was made. The defences were unusually complete, and the resistance more determined than had been experienced on any former occasion. Every man that reached the summit of the breach was met and forced down by triple rows of spikes from the interior of the rampart. After a bold but fruitless effort, they were repulsed with loss. But the enemy was so intimidated, and dreaded so much the consequence of a second and perhaps successful attack, that he surrendered next morning, ignorant of their opponent's want of ammunition, the real cause of the premature attack.

Colonel Stuart again proceeded against Palghatcherri, and on the 21st of September opened two batteries within five hundred yards of the place; and though the fortification had been partly strengthened, and in a short time the place was taken by Colonel Fullarton, he succeeded the same day in making a practicable breach. Preparations were made for an assault the following morning; but before daylight the enemy offered to surrender on terms which were acceded to. Leaving a garrison in the place, Colonel Stuart joined the army in the neighbourhood of Coimbatore on the 15th of October, after which the regiment followed all the movements of the army till the 29th of January 1791, when Lord Cornwallis arrived and assumed the command.

The 72nd was engaged along with the 71st in the second attack on Bangalore, the first attack on Seringapatam, and the attack on Savendroog and Ootradroog. On the evening of March 7, 1791, the pettah of Bangalore was stormed, and the siege of the town was immediately commenced. During the night, the 72nd Highlanders were posted under the outer pettah wall, close to the gate. "The enemy kept up a sharp fire; their shots, which were many of them thirty-two pounders, came very close to the regiment, making a great rattling in the trees and bamboo hedge, near the line; but no casualties occurred."[7]

At four o'clock on the afternoon of the 20th of March, six companies of the regiment marched into the trenches; and on the evening of the following day the regiment was ordered to prepare to take part in storming the fortress. The grenadier company was to join the storming party appointed to advance by the left approach; the light company, that by the right approach; and the battalion companies were formed on the right of the parallel, to support the grenadiers. Three of the 72nd grenadiers joined the forlorn hope under Sergeant Williams of the 76th regiment. Lieutenant Campbell states in his Journal :— "The storming party primed and loaded, and sat down on their arms. Our batteries, both gun and mortar, kept firing frequently during the evening. At a quarter before eleven we got into motion; an opening was made in the centre of the second parallel; the signal for storming was given—three guns in quick succession—and out we rushed. The

covered way instantly appeared as a sheet of fire, seconded from the fort, but with no aim or effect; our batteries answered with blank cartridge; and we were in the covered way in a moment, and on the breach as quick as thought. I pushed on, carried forward by a powerful impulse, and found myself at the top of the breach with the front files. The grenadiers immediately turned off to the right with a huzza; their progress was suddenly stopped by an opening; the fort was hung with blue lights; a heavy fire was opened upon us, but with little effect; the difficulty was overcome, and our troops ascended the ladders with every possible expedition. The grandest and most striking sight I ever beheld was the rushing up of the troops to the top of the breach, and the ascent of the grenadiers in crowds by the scaling-ladders. We now heard the grenadiers' march beating in every quarter; our soldiers shouted with joy, and we swept round the ramparts, with scarce anything to oppose us. Every enemy that appeared had a bayonet in him instantly. The regiments that supported us came in by the gateway, and cleared the town below, where numbers were killed. In two hours we were in thorough possession of the fort, and Lieutenant Duncan, of the 71st regiment, pulled down the flag and put his own sash in its place. The Union flag was afterwards hoisted, and the troops gave three cheers."

On this occasion the regiment had 6 rank and file killed, and 1 sergeant and 23 rank and file wounded. In the orders issued on the following day by Lord Cornwallis, the following passage occurs :—

"The conduct of all the regiments which happened, in their turn, to be on duty that evening did credit in every respect to their spirit and discipline; but his Lordship desires to offer the tribute of his particular and warmest praise to the European grenadiers and light infantry of the army, and to the 36th, 72nd, and 76th regiments, who led the attack and carried the fortress, and who by their behaviour on that occasion furnished a conspicuous proof that discipline and valour in soldiers, when directed by zeal and capacity in officers, are irresistible.

"Lieut. Colonel Stuart (72nd Regiment)

---

[7] "Journal of Lieutenant Ronald Campbell, of the Grenadier Company, 72nd Regiment," 2 vols. folio. MS.

may be assured that Lord Cornwallis will ever retain the most grateful remembrance of the valuable and steady support which that officer afforded him, by his military experience and constant exertions to promote the public service."

The army advanced to the siege of Seringapatam on the 4th of May, and on the 15th as it approached the place, the Sultan's position was attacked by the 72nd, with other regiments. The enemy was driven from every post, and towards the close of the action the 72nd ascended an eminence and captured a round redoubt. The regiment had about 20 men killed and wounded, among the latter being Captain Braithwaite and Lieutenant Whitlie. The army, nearly all its provisions and other stores being exhausted, retreated to the vicinity of Bangalore.

On the morning of the 21st of December the 72nd took part in the storm of the strong fortress of Savendroog. The right attack was made by the light companies of the 71st and 72nd, supported by a battalion company of the 72nd; the left attack by the two flank companies of the 76th and grenadier company of the 52nd; the centre attack under Major Fraser of the 72nd, by the grenadiers and two battalion companies of the 72nd, two companies of the 52nd, the grenadiers of the 71st, and four companies of sepoys, supported by the sixth battalion of sepoys; the whole under Lieut.-Colonel Nisbitt, of the 52nd regiment. The storming-parties proceeded to their stations; the band of the 52nd took post near them, and suddenly striking up the tune *Britons, strike home*, the whole rushed forward with the most heroic ardour. The Mysoreans made a feeble defence, and in less than two hours the British were in possession of the fort, with the trifling loss of five men wounded. The troops were thanked in General Orders, for their very gallant conduct.

Two days afterwards the troops advanced against Ootradroog. On the 24th, two battalion companies of the 52nd and 72nd regiments, supported by the 26th sepoys, attacked the pettah by escalade, and were speedily in possession of the town. "Lieutenant M'Innes, senior officer of the two 72nd companies, applied to Captain Scott for liberty to follow the Pei-

tives up the rock, saying he should be in time to enter the first gateway with them. The captain thought the enterprise impracticable. The soldiers of M'Innes's company heard the request made, and not doubting of consent being given, had rushed towards the first wall, and were followed by M'Innes. The gate was shut: but Lieutenant M'Pherson arrived with the pioneers and ladders, which were instantly applied, and our people were within the wall as quick as thought, when the gate was unbolted, and the two companies entered. The enemy, astonished at so unexpected an attempt, retreated with precipitation. M'Innes advanced to the second wall, the men forced open the gate with their shoulders, and not a moment was lost in pushing forward for the third wall; but the road, leading between two rocks, was so narrow that only two could advance abreast; the pathway was, in consequence, soon choked up, and those who carried the ladders were unable to proceed. At the same time, the enemy commenced throwing huge stones in numbers upon the assailants, who commenced a sharp fire of musketry, and Lieut.-Colonel Stuart, who had observed from a distance this astonishing enterprise, sent orders for the grenadiers not to attempt anything further. Lieutenant M'Pherson forced his way through the crowd, causing the ladders to be handed over the soldiers' heads, from one to another, and before the colonel's orders could be delivered, the gallant Highlanders were crowding over the third gateway. The enemy fled on all hands; the foremost of our men pursued them closely, and gained the two last walls without opposition—there were five walls to escalade. The garrison escaped by the south-east side of the fort, over rocks and precipices of immense depth and ruggedness, where many must have lost their lives. By one o'clock, our two companies were in possession of every part of the fort, and M'Innes had planted the colours on the highest pinnacle, without the loss of a single man. The Kiledar and two of his people were taken alive. Colonel Stuart declared the business to be brilliant and successful, beyond his most sanguine hopes."[8] Thus was the important fortress of Outra-Durgum captured by two

Lieutenant Campbell's Journal.

companies of Highlanders (Major Petrie's, and Captain Hon. William M. Maitland's) of the 72nd regiment; the officers with the two companies were Lieutenants M'Innes, Robert Gordon, —— Getty, and Ensign Andrew Coghlan. Lieutenant M'Pherson conducted the pioneers. They all were thanked in General Orders by Earl Cornwallis, who expressed his admiration of the gallantry and steadiness of the officers and soldiers engaged in this service.

The rainy season being over, it was resolved to make a second attack on Seringapatam, to which place the army marched in the beginning of February 1792. The sultan had taken up a formidable position to cover his capital, and was attacked during the night of the 6th of February. The regiment formed part of the left division under Lieutenant-Colonel Maxwell, which advanced to the attack in the following order:—Grenadier Company, 72nd; Light Company, 72nd, with scaling ladders; pioneers; 23rd native infantry; 72nd regiment; 1st and 6th native infantry. The share taken by the 72nd in the attack on the place we shall give in the words of the journal of Lieutenant Campbell of the 72nd, quoted several times already:—

"We (the 72nd) moved from the left along the north side of the ridge of hills extending from the Carrighaut pagoda to the Cappalair rocks; by ten at night we found ourselves near the base of the hill, where the officers were directed to dismount. When we were about two hundred yards from the lower entrenchment, our grenadiers filed off from the right with trailed arms, a serjeant and twelve men forming the forlorn hope. When about fifty yards from the works, the sentinel challenged us, and instantly fired his piece, which was followed by a scattered fire from the rest of their party. We rushed among them, and those who did not save themselves by immediate flight were shot or bayoneted. The greatest number of them ran down to the Carriagat pagoda, where they made a stand, and kept up a smart fire until we were almost close to them; then retired under our fire to the foot of the hill, where they were joined by a strong body from the plain, and made a stand at a small choultry (or caravan-serai,

from which a flight of steps led to the bridge across the nulla. By this time the general attack on the enemy's lines had commenced, and there was an almost connected sheet of fire from right to left—musketry, guns, and rockets rending the air with their contending noise. We sat upon the brow of the hill a few minutes, while our men were recovering their breath, and had a commanding prospect of the whole attack, though nearly three miles in extent, as we contemplated the scene before us, the grandest, I suppose, that any person there had beheld. Being rested a little, Colonel Maxwell led us down the hill under a smart fire. We rushed forward and drove the enemy across the nulla in great haste, although they stood our approach wonderfully. We crossed the bridge under a constant fire, the enemy retreating as we advanced; we crossed the Lokany river, the opposite bank of which was well covered by a *bound-hedge*, and their fire did execution. A serjeant of grenadiers was killed, Captain Mackenzie mortally wounded, Major Fraser and Captain Maitland shot through their right arms, besides other casualties. After we had penetrated the *bound-hedge*, the enemy took post behind an extensive choultry; but nothing could stop the ardour of our men: we charged without loss of time, and soon dislodged the enemy, who retreated along the banks of the Cavery to a second choultry, where their numbers were reinforced. We had now got into their camp, upon the right flank of their lines; they retreated steadily before us, and our fire and bayonets did great execution among them, the road being strewed with their bodies. We charged and dislodged them from the second choultry; here Lieutenant M'Pherson of the grenadiers was wounded. We pursued the enemy to a large pagoda; they attempted to cross the river, but the place was so crowded with guns, tumbrils, bullocks, elephants, camels, followers, and Heaven knows what, that we were in the midst of them before they could escape, and for some minutes there was nothing but shooting and bayoneting. Colonel Maxwell came up with the 23rd native infantry; the sepoys of the 14th native battalions advanced; they took us for the enemy, and fired, but their officers suppressed the fire before much injury was done. The 71st regiment also joined us, and preparations were made to cross the river and force the lines on the opposite side. Colonel Baird requested me to lead with twenty men; I instantly rushed into the stream, followed by twenty grenadiers of the 72nd regiment; we pushed on through holes, over rocks and stones, falling and

71st and 72nd regiments advanced to the pettah, from which the inhabitants had fled, and we released a number of Europeans from prison. About seven o'clock the 72nd marched into the famous *Llal Baugh*, or, as I heard it translated, '*garden of pearls*,' and were posted in one of the walks during the day."

The loss of the regiment in this brilliant victory over Tippoo Sahib was Captain Thomas Mackenzie and 14 men killed; Major Hugh Fraser, Captain the Honourable William Maitland, Lieutenants M'Pherson and Ward, 1 serjeant, and 42 men wounded. This victory was the means of inducing the Sultan Tippoo to sue for peace, which he obtained on ceding half of his dominions, and paying £3,500,000, part of which was given as a gratuity to the troops, along with six months' batta or field allowance.

The 72nd returned to Wallahabad, where it remained till 1795, with a brief absence in August 1793, when it took part in an expedition against the French settlement of Pondicherry on the Coromandel coast.[9] The 72nd performed trench and other duty, and had only two men killed.

On the death of General Murray, the colonelcy of the regiment was conferred on Major-General Adam Williamson, March 19, 1794.

In 1795, the 72nd under their old commander-colonel, Major-General James Stuart, took part in the expedition against the Dutch

From a Painting by Sir Thomas Lawrence.
General James Stuart, who died in 1815, after 54 years' service.

stumbling at every step, the enemy's shot reducing our numbers; and myself, with about half a dozen grenadiers, arrived at a smooth part of the stream which proved beyond our depth; five of us, however, got over; but the regiments did not venture to follow and we returned with difficulty. An easy passage had been found out lower down; the 71st and 72nd regiments had got into the island; the flank companies of the 52nd, 71st, and 74th regiments forded higher up, and the enemy, seeing our troops on all sides of them, betook themselves to flight.

"About one o'clock in the morning the

[9] On the 12th of August, as the grenadiers and Captain Gordon's company of the 72nd were on duty in the trenches, exposed to a burning sun, and a severe cannonade from the fortress, Colonel Campbell, field officer of the trenches, sent his orderly to Lieutenant Campbell of the grenadiers requesting that the piper of the grenadiers might be directed to play some *pibrachs*. This was considered a strange request to be made at so unsuitable a time; it was, however, immediately complied with; "but we were a good deal surprised to perceive that the moment the piper began, the fire from the enemy slackened, and soon after almost entirely ceased. The French all got upon the works, and seemed more astonished at hearing the bagpipe, than we with Colonel Campbell's request."—*Lieutenant Campbell's Journal*.

settlements of Ceylon, where the regiment remained from August 1795 till March 1797, taking part in various operations with but little loss of men. At the siege of Trincomalee, the 72nd had Ensign Benson, 2 serjeants, and 7 rank and file wounded. Major Fraser, who was promoted to the lieutenant-colonelcy of the regiment in September 1793, was detached against the fort of Batticaloa, which surrendered to him on the 18th of that month.

The 72nd was removed to Pondicherry preparatory to embarking for England in March 1797, previous to which the men who were fit for service were drafted into corps remaining in India. The skeleton of the regiment embarked at Madras on the 10th of February 1798, and on arriving in England, it was ordered to Perth, which it reached in August that year. For its distinguished services in India, it was authorised to bear "Hindoostan" on its colours.

In October of the same year, Major-General James Stuart succeeded General Adam Williamson as colonel.[1] Lieutenant-Colonel Fraser died in May 1801; he was loved and respected by the regiment, with which he had been in many a hard-fought field. Some high ground near Seringapatam, the scene of his gallantry, was named "Fraser's Hill." He bequeathed £500 to the officers' mess, to be appropriated in such a manner as should best commemorate his attachment to the corps and his esteem for the officers.

In 1804, when a French invasion was feared, a second battalion was added to the regiment, formed of men raised in Aberdeen for limited service, under the "Limited Service Act." It was embodied at Peterhead, and remained in Scotland for some time.

In 1805 the 72nd, commanded by Lieutenant-Colonel Colquhoun Grant, embarked with the secret expedition under Major-General Sir David Baird, which sailed in August for the Cape of Good Hope, then possessed by the Dutch. The expedition anchored in Table Bay on the 4th of January 1806; and on the morning of the 6th, the Highland brigade, composed of the 71st, 72nd, and 93rd regiments, effected a landing, the light companies

of the two former regiments driving the Dutch sharpshooters from the contiguous heights.[2] After gaining a complete victory, and pursuing the enemy three miles under a burning sun, the Highlanders were ordered to halt, and the first brigade continued the pursuit.[3] In Sir David Baird's despatch, he spoke as follows of the Highland brigade and of the 72nd:—

"The Highland brigade advanced steadily under a heavy fire of round shot, grape, and musketry. Nothing could resist the determined bravery of the troops, headed by their gallant leader, Brigadier-General Ferguson; and the number of the enemy, who swarmed the plain, served only to augment their ardour and confirm their discipline. The enemy received our fire and maintained his position obstinately; but in the moment of charging, the valour of British troops bore down all opposition, and forced him to a precipitate retreat.

"Your lordship will perceive the name of Lieutenant-Colonel Grant among the wounded; but the heroic spirit of this officer was not subdued by his misfortune, and he continued to lead his men to glory, as long as an enemy was opposed to His Majesty's 72nd regiment."

The regiment lost 2 rank and file killed; Lieutenant-Colonel Grant, Lieutenant Alexander Chisholm, 2 sergeants, and 34 rank and file wounded.

On the 10th of January, the regiment marched to Wineberg barracks; and on the 11th, Lieutenant M'Arthur of the 72nd was detached with thirty men of the regiment, to take possession of Hout's Bay. "After Lieutenant M'Arthur's departure, it was ascertained that the enemy had a strong garrison at Hout's

[1] Stewart's Sketches, ii. pp. 187-9.

[2] An account of the part taken by the Highland brigade in further operations at the Cape will be found under the 93rd regiment.

[3] "The soldiers suffered excessively from the heat of the sun, which was as intense as I ever felt it in India; though our fatigue was extreme, yet, for the momentary halt we made, the grenadier company (72nd) requested the pipers might play them their regimental quick step, CABAR FEIDH, to which they danced a Highland reel, to the utter astonishment of the 59th regiment, which was close in our rear."— Journal of Captain Campbell, Grenadier Company, 72nd regiment.
Properly speaking, Cabar Feidh is not the regimental quickstep, but the warning for the regiment to get ready for parade. In "marching past" in quick time, the tune played by the band is "Highland ..." and in double time the pipers play Cabar F...

CABAR FEIDH;

OR,

GATHERING OF THE 72ND HIGHLANDERS.

ARRANGED FOR THE BAGPIPES.

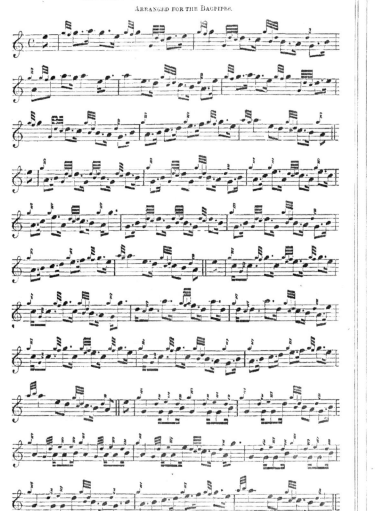

Bay, and Major Tucker of the 72nd was sent after him on horseback, to detain him until a reinforcement should arrive; but the lieutenant had reached the vicinity of the place with much expedition, and finding how matters stood, showed his men rank entire, and only partially, but to the most advantage. Having procured pen, ink, and paper, he summoned the garrison to unconditional surrender, otherwise he would blow the place about their ears, assault the works, and give no quarter. The Dutch immediately surrendered at discretion, and when the major arrived, he found Lieutenant M'Arthur in full possession of the works, consisting of a strong block-house and two batteries."[4]

The 72nd remained about the Cape till 1810, when it embarked 800 men to take part with troops from India in the capture of Mauritius.

Having on the 3rd of December arrived well to windward of the Isle of France, it was ascertained that the Indian army had landed the previous morning at Point Cannonnière, and was menacing the enemy's position. The transports carrying the Cape brigade were in consequence ordered to proceed to the mouth of Port Louis Harbour, where the 72nd was held in momentary readiness to land in the rear of the enemy's lines, should he have attempted to defend them. The French captain-general, who affected to despise the Indian Sepoys, against whom he had declared he would defend himself, was by this movement afforded the opportunity of seeing that the Cape brigade was absolutely present and threatening to land. This circumstance, to use his own words, "determined the immediate surrender of the Mauritius." Accordingly, on the 5th of December 1810, the regiment landed and remained on that island, taking its tour of the detachment and garrison duties during upwards of three years, during which period it obtained the respect and approbation of the inhabitants in a very eminent degree; and the universal regret expressed by the latter on the departure of the corps was in terms that would leave no doubt of its sincerity.

In 1809 King George III. approved of the regiment discontinuing to wear the Highland

4 " " p' in Campbell' Journal.

costume, which, however, was restored to it in 1823, with the exception of the kilt, for which the trews were substituted. In September 1811 the strength of the first battalion was augmented to 1000 rank and file, and was completed by drafts from the 2nd battalion, then in Ireland.

In April 1815, Lieutenant-General Rowland, Lord Hill, was appointed colonel of the 72nd in room of the deceased General Stuart; and Lord Hill was succeeded, in February 1817, by Major-General Sir George Murray.

The regiment remained at the Cape till June 1815, when it embarked for India, bearing on its colours "Cape of Good Hope" for its eminent services in South Africa. The destination of the regiment was India; but when it arrived there in September 1814, the war against the Rajah of Nepaul had terminated, and it was ordered back to the Cape, landing at Cape Town in March 1816. The war in Europe having terminated, the second battalion of the regiment was disbanded at Londonderry, the men either volunteering into incomplete regiments or receiving their discharge.

In June 1817 four companies of the regiment removed to Graham's Town to relieve the 21st Light Dragoons. These companies were distributed along the Great Fish River, to carry on a line of posts intended to defend the frontiers against the depredations of the warlike tribes of Kaffirs, that were continually committing acts of hostility and aggression. Notwithstanding the arduous and toilsome nature of their duties, and their frequent exposure to the inclement weather, the men of the 72nd remained remarkably healthy.

On the 3rd of February 1819, the regiment had to regret the loss of Captain Gethin, who, with one sergeant and a private, was killed near the post of De Bruin's Drift, on an excursion against the Kaffirs. It appears those savages had entered the colony and taken off some cattle belonging to a boor in the neighbourhood of Gethin's post. On the circumstance being reported, he instantly set out with a patrol in pursuit, and, coming upon their traces, pushed forward in advance with some of the men and boors, who were mounted, and came up with the cattle in a thick part of the bush. Depending on the support of the boors, who were well armed, in the event of an attack, he, with the few men that had accompanied him, fearlessly entered, and was proceeding to drive the cattle out, when they were attacked and surrounded by the Kaffirs; and though the cowardly boors were within hearing, and had among them the owner of the cattle, not one had the spirit to render the least assistance. Captain Gethin and his party behaved with the greatest bravery, fully determined to sell their lives as dearly as possible. He defended himself with the butt of his gun till he fell, overpowered by numbers and exertion : his body was found afterwards, pierced with thirty-two wounds. By this unfortunate affair was lost to the regiment a highly respected and valuable soldier, and to the service a brave and intelligent officer, whose gallant conduct in the Peninsula, particularly at the capture of San Sebastian, had been rewarded by promotion.

The regiment remained at the Cape, always having a detachment on the frontiers, till December 1821, when it embarked for England. At its departure, it received the approbation of the Governor-General, Lord Charles Somerset, for the exemplary and steady conduct of the men during their residence at the Cape.

On its arrival in England, in March 1822, the 72nd proceeded to Fort Cumberland; and, after moving about among various stations, it took up its quarters in Jersey and Guernsey in May 1823, in which year Sir George Murray removed to the 42nd, and was succeeded in the colonelcy of the 72nd by Lieutenant-General Sir John Hope. In this same year, the conduct of the regiment having on all occasions been so soldierly and exemplary, on the recommendation of the Commander-in-Chief, the Duke of York and Albany, George IV. was pleased to authorise that the 72nd should resume the Highland costume, with the exception of the kilt, trews being substituted. At the same time, as a special mark of royal favour, the regiment was authorised to assume the title of " The Duke of Albany's Own Highlanders;" and in June 1824 His Majesty approved of the 72nd using as a regimental badge the Duke of Albany's cipher and coronet, to be borne on the regimental colours.

The 72nd remained in the Channel Islands

till April 1824, and on leaving was presented with addresses by the authorities and principal inhabitants, expressing their high admiration of its discipline, and of the peaceful and orderly behaviour of the men. After staying a short time at Plymouth, the regiment proceeded to Scotland, landing on the 13th of September at Newhaven, from which it marched to Edinburgh Castle, headed by its colonel, Lieutenant-General Sir John Hope. Detachments were sent to Stirling, Fort-William, and Dumbarton.

While in Edinburgh, in August 1825, the regiment received new colours, which were presented to the colonel, Sir John Hope, by Lady Hope. In presenting them to the regiment, Sir John addressed it as follows :—

" In delivering to your charge these colours, which have been presented to the 72nd regiment by Lady Hope, I am fully aware that I am not addressing a newly-raised corps, whose name and character have yet to be acquired. As it has pleased His Majesty to confer so distinguished an honour on the regiment as to permit the 72nd to assume the name of the Duke of Albany's Own Highlanders, I cannot omit congratulating the corps on having received so flattering and honourable a mark of approbation, and expressing my conviction that this additional badge, which is now placed on these colours, will afford a new and powerful inducement for maintaining the high character which the 72nd regiment has so long and so deservedly possessed. I feel particularly gratified that the honour of delivering these colours has devolved on me, and that their presentation should also have taken place in the capital of the country where the regiment was first raised, and after its return from a long period of honourable and distinguished service. The country being now at peace, there is no opportunity for the 72nd to gain fresh honours by victories in the field; but the regiment may deserve and obtain almost equal honour and credit by setting an example of discipline and good conduct on home service, which becomes now particularly incumbent when so highly distinguished by being named after His Royal Highness the Commander-in-Chief, to whom the whole army is indebted for the present state of order and discipline to which it has attained. That the 72nd will ever continue to deserve the approbation of His Royal Highness I make no doubt: and I have now to offer my most sincere good wishes for the prosperity of the corps collectively, and of every individual officer, non-commissioned officer, and private soldier of the regiment."

The regiment left Edinburgh for Ireland during the same month, the Lord Provost and Magistrates of the city thanking the men for their exemplary conduct.

While in Ireland—where it was divided into detachments posted at various places—the regiment, in September 1827, was formed into six service and four depôt companies, the former proceeding to London, and taking duty at the Tower. In June 1828, it was inspected at Canterbury by Lord Hill, who complimented it by stating " that although it had been his lot to see and serve with most of the regiments in the service, he felt he should not be doing full justice to the 72nd Highlanders if he did not express his particular approbation of everything connected with them, and add, that he had never before seen a regiment their equal in movements, in appearance, and in steadiness under arms."

In the end of the same month the service companies of the regiment again embarked for the Cape of Good Hope, where its reputation had already been so well established, and reached it on the 11th October. On disembarking at the Cape of Good Hope, it was quartered in the main barracks at Cape Town until it was removed on the 1st of October 1832 to the Castle. During this period it furnished in its tour the detachments at Simon's Bay and Rotten Island. From the latter part of 1829 to the end of 1830 a company was employed in making a road through Hottentot Holland Kloof, since called " Sir Lowry's Pass." With this exception, nothing occurred to interrupt the usual routine of garrison duty, until the 31st of December 1834, when an express having arrived with the unexpected intelligence that a great part of the eastern frontier district was overrun and plundered by the Kaffirs, the Governor, Major-General D'Urban, immediately directed a wing of the regiment to be held in readiness for embarkation · and on the 2nd of January

1835 Nos. 3 and 5, with the Light Companies, under the command of Major Maclean, immediately sailed for Algoa Bay. On the 6th, the Grenadier Company marched to Simon's Bay, and embarked in His Majesty's 16-gun ship "Trinculo," in which the Governor took his passage to the frontier. Lieutenant-Colonel Peddie, K.H., with the remaining companies, proceeded, in four divisions, overland to Uitenhage, where the lieutenant-colonel with the first division arrived on the 16th, after a harassing journey of ten days, and was joined on the three succeeding days by the remaining divisions.

A detachment, consisting of Captain Sutherland, one subaltern, and forty rank and file, which rejoined the head-quarters at Grahamstown on the 12th of February, was left here for the protection of the town until a local force could be organised. Lieut.-Colonel Peddie, with the remainder, marched for Grahamstown on the 20th of January, arriving there on the 23rd, and finding at the Diedsty the three companies which had preceded them by sea, except the Light Company. With the latter and a small mounted force Captain Jervis had, on the 16th, been sent to re-occupy Fort Willshire. This, with all the military posts on the frontier, except Fort Beaufort and Hermann's Kraal, had been abandoned to the Kaffirs, and sacked by them.

At this time the Kaffirs had swept off nearly all the cattle in the colony, and were returning with their booty to the most distant and secure parts of their own country, while the Governor was at Grahamstown awaiting the arrival of armed boors and Hottentots, who hastened from the remote districts, and were collecting supplies for the prosecution of the war in Kaffirland. On the 27th of January, Major Cox, of the 75th regiment, had collected a force, of which Captain Jervis, with forty men of the Light Company, and the whole mounted force at Fort Willshire, formed part, for the purpose of bringing off the missionaries and traders, who were assembled at Burns Hill in Kaffirland : this service they successfully executed. During their absence, however, which had the effect of weakening the garrison of the fort, then under the orders of Lieutenant Bent, Royal Engineers, on the 29th of January the

Kaffirs, in overwhelming numbers, made a sudden attack on the cattle-guard. Although assistance was promptly afforded from the fort, which was not a thousand paces distant, and though the guard made a most gallant resistance, yet the Kaffirs succeeded in killing Corporal Davidson, and Privates Arnut, Webster, and Woods, of the Light Company, with two Hottentots of the new levies that composed it, and carried off all the cattle.

As it had been ascertained by Lieutenant-Colonel England, 75th regiment, that the Fish River Bush was occupied by the Kaffirs in great force, Captain Murray, with his company, marched, on the 31st of January, to Trompetter's Drift, to join a force collected there for the purpose of clearing the country; and Major Maclean, with 100 men of the 72nd, also marched thither on the 7th of February to reinforce this command, which was now under the direction of Lieutenant-Colonel Smith, C.B., and which returned to Grahamstown on the 17th of February. The next day, the Commander-in-Chief in General Orders, congratulated the troops—"all of whom behaved admirably"—"upon the complete success which has crowned their recent operations, and by which the necessary and important object has been gained of driving the hostile tribes from the woods and fastnesses of the Great Fish River. The enterprise was one of no ordinary difficulty. The enemy was numerous, and well armed with muskets, and was determined to hold his ground, which, from the rugged and well-wooded ravines, was singularly adapted to his peculiar mode of fighting. The enemy was routed everywhere, and driven from his strongholds and over the Keiskamma, with a great loss in killed and wounded, and all his possessions in cattle, of which 4000 head, with large quantities of sheep and goats, fell into our hands."

During these operations there were lost altogether eleven killed and eleven wounded, of whom three killed and four wounded belonged to the 72nd regiment.

For some time after this the Kaffirs continued inactive, and made no more incursions, while the Governor confined himself to organising the new levies, and providing for the security of the country during the absence of the army.

On the 6th of February 1835 a patrol from Fort Willshire, which had been reinforced by the Albany Burger Force and the Bathurst Yeomanry, discovered that a large body of the Kaffirs, estimated at 3000, had passed into the Fish River Bush, and next day Captain Jervis, with 120 men, proceeded to "Breakfast Key," and following the *spoor* (foot-marks), soon saw the Kaffirs, who kept up a well-sustained fire on the patrol as it approached the Bush. On being reinforced, however, by the George Burghers from the camp at Somerset Mount, and a three-pounder, the patrol succeeded in taking all the cattle that the enemy had brought up for his subsistence, thus inflicting on him a very severe blow.

The Kaffirs, however, retreated lower down the Fish River Bush, and near Trompetter's Drift fell in with a party of the Port Elizabeth Yeomanry, and killed eight of their number, with a loss on their part of only nine men—relatively speaking, a very small proportion. On the 8th, the Grenadier Company of the 75th regiment relieved Captain Jervis and the Light Company at Fort Willshire, which was marched that night to Breakfast Key, and next day formed part of the Force under Colonel Smith, which, on the following day, cleared the Bush of the Kaffirs, who retreated across the Keiskamma. The Government notice reports the loss of the Kaffirs as 150 killed, and our loss as 9 killed and 11 wounded. Sergeant Burt was the only man of the 72nd that suffered at this time: he had somehow unaccountably fallen a few paces in the rear of his company, and was immediately overpowered. Colonel Smith pursued the Kaffirs with his whole force, and a camp was formed at Macomo's Old Kraal, to which, on the 11th of March, the Light Company proceeded; and on the 18th it was joined by the rest of the regiment.

The Governor, having confided the protection of the colony to Lieut.-Colonel England, and the 75th regiment, with some local corps arrived on the 28th at the camp on the Brak River to which the troops at Macomo's Kraal had moved on the 25th. On the day after the Governor's arrival he issued an order distributing the army in four divisions, as follows :—

1st Division—Lieut.-Colonel Peddie near Fort Willshire; two guns Royal Artillery, the gunners of which, as well as the guns attached to the 3rd division, were selected from the 72nd regiment; the 72nd Highlanders; a detachment of the Cape Mounted Rifles, under Major Lowen; the 1st battalion Provisional Infantry; and the Swellend Burgher Force.

2nd Division—Lieut.-Colonel Somerset on the Clusie; two guns Royal Artillery; Cape Mounted Riflemen; Burgher Force; George Burgher Force; Uitenhage Force; and Albany Force.

3rd Division—Major Cox, 75th Regiment, Block Drift; two guns Royal Artillery; detachment of Cape Mounted Rifles; 2d Battalion Colonial Infantry; Beaufort Burgher Force; and the Kat River Legion.

4th Division—Field-Commandant Wyk, at Tambookie Vley, consisted of the Cradock and Somerset Burgher Forces.

On the 30th of March, the first division, with the headquarters of the Commander-in-Chief, broke up the camp at the Brak River, simultaneously with other divisions, at their various points, entered Kaffirland at Execution Drift, above Fort Willshire, and encamped that night on the Kebeca. The next day, April the 1st, this division encamped on the Debè Flats, and on the evening of the 2nd, Captain Jervis was despatched with the Light Company to the Upper Amatola, where he joined Major Cox, with the Kat River Legion, on the 3rd. These, with their combined force, succeeded in killing several Kaffirs, and taking 800 head of cattle, many horses, and immense flocks of goats, which were sent into the Debè Camp on the 4th, Major Cox following with his whole division. On the 3rd the first division left the Debè, penetrated to the fastnesses in rear of T'Slambie's Kop, and not meeting with the enemy in force, returned to the camp the same night, having succeeded in killing some stragglers, while the force sustained a loss of one man killed and one wounded. On the 6th the army left the Debè, and the third division entered the Keiskamma Hoek, while the baggage and supplies marched with the first division to the Buffalo.

The first division encamped on the left bank of the Buffalo, where Fort Beresford was afterwards built, and the second division encamped about three miles further down the river. Early on the morning of the 7th, Captain Murray, with 100 men of the regiment, and three companies of the First Provincial Battalion, was despatched to the principal ridge of Buffalo Mountain, with the view of intercepting any Kaffirs that might be retreating from the third division, which was advancing from the Keiskamma Hoek, and from the fourth, which was advancing from Klip Platts across the Bontebok to the rear of the mountains. About daybreak they came to a high, rugged cliff, called Murray's Krantz, and here found 600 chosen Kaffir warriors, under the guidance of Tyali, son of Dushanie, awaiting the attack, under the mistaken notion of the impregnability of their position.

On the 8th of April, Captain Murray, at the head of his company, gallantly climbed the cliff, although the Kaffirs, not content with the usual weapons, hurled down masses of rock on the attacking party. At length, however, the savage warriors fled, leaving a large number of killed on the ground, but not until Captain Murray and four of his men had been severely wounded by the assegais.[5] The result of this affair was the capture of 4000 head of cattle, the only loss on the British side being 1 sergeant of the Provincial Battalion, who was shot by a Hottentot deserter while driving the cattle out of the bush.

The patrol returned to the camp at night, and the Commander-in-Chief, in a General Order, thanked all the officers and troops employed in the affair. The conclusion of the General Order is in the following gratifying terms :—"The intrepid and determined perseverance of Captain Murray, who, though severely wounded, continued his exertions to the end of the day, with his company of the 72nd, was of the highest order, and deserves the especial thanks of the Commander-in-Chief."

On the evening of the 8th of April all the troops were assembled at their respective points of attack, and prepared for a concentrating movement on the mountains in which

.I v r , a du v j v hn u l , the Kaffirs.

3 Y

the Keiskamma, Kaboosie, and Buffalo take their rise. Sir Benjamin D'Urban, with the second division and the mounted part of the first, was at the Posts of the Buffalo; Major Cox and the third division, at the head of the Keiskamma Hoek; Van Wyk, with the fourth, was on the plains to the northward, while Colonel Peddie, leaving the camp at mid night with four companies of the regiment and the First Provincial Battalion, ascended the Iseli Berg; and having, early on the morning of the 9th, divided his forces into two columns, he penetrated the fastnesses of the Isidingi or Mount Kempt. The Kafirs, now perceiving that they were attacked at every point, fled in the utmost dismay, and several thousand head of cattle became the reward of this movement; while on our side we had only to lament the loss of 1 man killed and 4 wounded, among whom was Field Commander Van Wyk. This success is thus recorded in General Orders :—

" The hostile chiefs of the tribes of Tyali, Macomo, Bothma, Eno, and others, were at length compelled to assemble in the rocky woods near the sources of the Buffalo, with their followers, to the number of at least 7000 men, and had avowed their determination to defend themselves to the last. From these fastnesses, however, notwithstanding their impervious nature, they were immediately driven,—the troops penetrating them everywhere, each column in its ordered course; and they have scattered and dispersed in various directions, disheartened and dismayed, with a great loss of killed and wounded (among whom are some of the sons and relations of the chiefs), and in cattle to the number of ten thousand head. The Commander-in Chief desires to express his warmest approbation of the conduct of all the troops; their excellent marching, their patient endurance of fatigue, and the brilliant gallantry with which they drove the enemy before them wherever they were to be found, alike deserve his praise and the thanks which he offers to Lieut.-Col Peddie, commanding the first division, Lieut. Col Somerset, the second, Major Cox, the third, and Field Commandant Van Wyk, the fourth, as well as the officers and soldiers of their respective divisions."

On the 11th of April Sir Benjamin D'Ur-

ban, leaving the third and fourth divisions to harass and pursue the now discomfited Kaffirs, advanced to the river Kei in person with the two remaining divisions, the first taking the more direct road, the second moving in a parallel direction, but nearer the sea.

The first division crossed the Kei on the 16th, and now, upon entering the territories of Hintza, an order was issued forbidding any unprovoked hostility, and directing that all pillage or ill treatment of the inhabitants should be repressed with the utmost rigour.

The first division encamped at Butterworth on the 17th, and on the 19th were joined by the second division, which had captured 3000 head of cattle, which Colonel Somerset had sent to the rear.

The Governor, having been engaged in fruitless negotiations with Hintza for some days, at length had recourse to hostile measures; and war was accordingly formally proclaimed on the morning of the 21st, on which day Colonel Smith, with the mounted force of the first division, started in pursuit of Hintza, and the regiment, with the First Provisional Battalion, marching in the direction of the Izolo, where they encamped on the 25th. There they were joined by Colonel Smith, who had taken the 12,000 head of cattle, which were sent to be guarded by the second division, that still remained at Butterworth.

On the 26th, Colonel Smith, with a large patrol, of which Captain Murray and two companies of the regiment formed a part, marched to the T'Somo and returned to the camp on the 29th, when Colonel Smith reported the result of these two days' operations :—"Nearly 15,000 head of cattle have fallen into our hands, many of the enemy have been shot, whilst our loss has been trifling; and the savages have again been taught that neither woods, ravines, nor mountains can secure them from the pursuit of British troops. More difficult and fatiguing marches troops never encountered, and these happy results would not have been obtained without extraordinary exertions."

Meanwhile, these movements and their results had a dire effect on Hintza, and upon the Commander in-Chief's assurance of a safe-conduct for himself and also that of other persons who would be admitted to treat for him, he came into the camp on the 29th of April with his ordinary retinue of fifty followers, and had an immediate conference with the Commander in-Chief.

The next morning a treaty was formally agreed to, and hostilities suspended. Hintza, together with Krieh, his principal son, and their followers, continued in the camp at their own desire; and on the 2nd of May they accompanied the troops, when the latter took their departure from the Izolo, and commenced their retrograde movement.

At a deserted trading station, where the division halted during the middle of the day, and where Bokoo, Hintza's brother, and a chief joined the party, an express was received by Colonel Somerset that the Kaffirs were massacring the Fingoes, who had placed themselves under British protection, and were preparing to accompany the retreat of the troops. Sir Benjamin d'Urban thereupon summoned to his presence Hintza and his suite, who up to this period had been under no restraint, and informed them that, after sufficient time had elapsed for the Kaffirs to be made aware of the perilous situation of the sovereign, for each Fingo who should be murdered two Kaffirs should be hanged, and that the first selected should be Hintza and his brother Bokoo. On the division moving and encamping on the Debakazi, the whole of the now captive guests and followers were disarmed, and most of them dismissed the camp. The few whom the chief Hintza was allowed to retain, together with Bokoo, Krieh, and the Hemraden, were placed under a guard of 1 captain, 2 subalterns, and 90 men of the regiment, who had orders to use extraordinary measures of precaution, and to shoot any of their prisoners except Krieh, should there be an attempt at escape or rescue.

The Governor remained here some days, and on the 9th Colonel Somerset, having previously marched towards the colony with the Fingoes and captured cattle, moved on with the division, now augmented by the greater part of the Cape corps, and encamped on the left bank of the Kei at Lapstone Drift. Here, on the morning of the 10th, the Commander-in-Chief declared, under a royal salute, and in presence of Hintza, who was marched a prisoner into the square for the purpose, that the Kei was to be the future boundary of the colony, and that the chiefs Macomo, Tyali, Eno, Bethina, T'Slambie, Dushani, &c., and their tribes, were for ever expelled from the new territory, and would be treated as enemies if found therein. The territory was named the province of Queen Adelaide. The Commander-in-Chief gave as his reason for taking this step, " the absolute necessity of providing for the future security of the colony against unprovoked aggression, which could only be done by removing these treacherous and irreclaimable savages to a safer distance."

After this, Hintza was informed by the Governor that he would retain Krieh and Bokoo as the hostages required by the treaty entered into at the Izolo, and that he had a right to send him to Cape Town as a prisoner of war, but would refrain from doing so on his accompanying Colonel Smith through the country, and exerting his authority to collect the horses and cattle due. Upon Hintza engaging to do so, he was marched back to the guard, and his arms restored to him. He was shortly after handed over by the 72nd to a party of the corps of Guides, and proceeded with Colonel Smith accordingly. As soon as the party, with which was Captain Murray with two companies of the regiment, amounting in all to 500 men, had marched on the destined service, the Governor broke up his camp and marched to the Impotshane, where a Post named " Wardens" was immediately commenced.

On the morning of the 17th the party under Colonel Smith rejoined headquarters, having, in the words of the General Order, " marched 218 miles in seven days." They had crossed the Bashee, taken 3000 head of cattle, and succeeded in bringing off 1000 Fingoes, who from their remote situation had been unable before to join their countrymen, now under British protection. Major White, with a detachment of the Cape corps, was cut off whilst reconnoitring the country. This was the only loss on the British side. Hintza, however, met with his death while attempting to make his escape on the 14th, near the N'gabaxa. Although he had already received two severe wounds, he was shot by one of the corps of Guides, formerly a Kaffir trader, of the name of Southey. Even those who attempt to justify the deed characterise it as an untoward event.

On the following day, the 18th of May, Sir Benjamin d'Urban entered into a treaty with Kreli, now the principal chief, who took upon himself his father's engagements, and was permitted to receive the border tribes: Bokeo and Valanna being left as hostages, the young chief was escorted into his own country. During these transactions Major Cox had not been inactive, but had perpetually harassed the Kaffirs, now seeking individual safety, and was on the point of entering into negotiations with Macomo and Tyali, who on the 13th were prepared to come into his camp, when they received a message from Hintza that he was a prisoner, and advising them to take care of themselves. This advice they followed, although they did not retaliate by detaining Major Cox, who was in their power, without the means of resistance.

On the 20th of May, the work being finished, and a force of 2 subalterns and 80 rank and file of the regiment being left behind to garrison the place, the remainder marched to the Kemga, and halting there, constructed a Post, called Fort Wellington. Having left 1 subaltern and 25 rank and file of the regiment, and some provisional troops, to garrison it, the division marched to Brownlie's missionary station, on the Buffalo, which it reached on the 23rd. Here the Governor determined on fixing the future capital of the province, which was named King William's Town; a fort, named "Fort Hill," being completed and garrisoned, the plan of the town was laid out, and the troops commenced hutting themselves.

On the 10th of June the Governor left King William's Town, and, the division being broken up, gave over the command of the troops to Colonel Smith. On the 12th the Light Company marched to join Captain Jervis at the sources of the Buffalo, where a Post called Fort Beresford was constructed; and on the same day, Captain Lacy, with 30 men of his company and some provisional troops, marched to form a Post at Mount Coke, called Fort Murray. The exertions of the troops

continued unremitting, not only in completing the works of the different Posts, but also in patrolling the country. For their success in these duties they were repeatedly thanked in General Orders.

On the 9th of July a new Post, named Fort Cox, was established at Burn's Hill by Major Cox, and garrisoned by a detachment of the 75th Regiment. During the whole of this month patrolling was continued with unabated activity, but the Kaffirs, now become desperate, were successful in their efforts at Keiskamma. Lieutenant Baillie and a patrol of 30 men of the 1st Provisional Battalion were overpowered and killed to a man on the Committy flats, whilst retreating from the Keiskamma Hoek. Fifteen men of a foraging party from King William's Town were killed at the Kamka, or Yellow Wood Trees; and on the 20th, Gazela made a vigorous but unsuccessful attack upon Fort Wellington, when Private Storey of the 72nd was killed.

On the 8th of August the Kaffirs made a successful attack on the Fingoes in the Cedul Territory, carrying off all their cattle; and on intelligence being received at King William's Town, a large patrol of the regiment under Major Maclean was sent in pursuit. Their rations having, however, been expended, they were compelled to return without being able to retake the cattle or attack the Kaffirs with effect, although the latter hovered about with loud shouting and cheers during the march, and kept up a desultory fire on the detachment. In consequence of the report made by Major Maclean, and intelligence obtained that Macomo and Tyali were in great force on the Amatola and Izinuka mountains during the night of the 11th of July, Major Maclean and 40 men of the regiment, and 150 Provisionals from King William's Town, and 1 officer and 40 men of the 72nd, with 40 of the Provisionals from Fort Beresford, and the Kat River legion from Camp Adelaide, were assembled at Fort Cox. At no period since the commencement of hostilities did affairs wear a more unsatisfactory aspect. The Kaffirs, emboldened by success, watched from their fastness, the movements of the troops, and took advantage of every circumstance to harass them and cut off stragglers. They made frequent and incessant forays within the colony: the difficulty and expense of providing for the large force necessarily kept up increased every day: the Dutch Burgher force had been allowed to return to their homes; and among the now dispirited Hottentot levies, discontent and insubordination were making rapid progress. Under such circumstances Sir Benjamin D'Urban took the most effectual means to put a speedy end to the war. He again called out a large proportion of the Burgher force, whom he now ordered to receive a fixed rate of pay; and at the same time he despatched Brigade-Major Warden to Fort Cox to treat with the frontier Kaffirs, on condition of their becoming British subjects. An opportunity soon offered. Major Cox, having barely sufficient garrison in Fort Cox, divided the remainder and the reinforcement that were concentrated at his Post into three divisions, which, sallying from the fort, were everywhere successful, occasioning considerable loss to the enemy. They reassembled at the Gwali, where, a communication having been opened with the chiefs, Major Cox bivouacked.

The next day Major Warden having arrived from Fort Cox, he with Major Cox and an interpreter, all unarmed, proceeded about two miles from the camp to meet the chiefs, who had assembled with a body guard of 800 men, 300 of whom had firearms. Their conference came to a happy conclusion, Mácomo and Tyali each sending an assegai to the Governor in token of submission and readiness to pass under the English rule.

A suspension of hostilities was mutually agreed upon, and the camp was soon filled with unarmed Kaffirs, who expressed the greatest delight at the event. On the 21st of August a second conference was held below Fort Cox, and on this occasion the Kaffirs, to the number of 4000, of whom a great part were mounted, and upwards of 400 of them armed with guns, drew up with an evident attempt at display, and considerable pretension to military regularity. They received the overtures of Major Warden with but slight attention, and took little pains to conceal that

they were not indisposed to a renewal of the contest. This altered feeling was no doubt in a great measure produced by the circumstance that 2000 head of cattle had during the few preceding days fallen a prey to their marauding parties, which Macomo pretended had been sent out in ignorance of the truce. In consequence of this display, and in the event of the necessity of recommencing hostilities, Fort Cox was reinforced from King William's Town and Fort Beresford.

On the 2nd of September H.M.S. "Romney" had arrived in Algoa Bay with the 27th regiment and drafts for the 72nd and 75th. It is a curious circumstance, and shows how readily the Kaffirs obtain information, that the officers at Fort Cox knew of the arrival of troops in the bay from the Kaffir messenger Platjè, long before they received the intelligence through the usual channel of the post. To the exaggerated accounts which the Kaffirs had received of the additional force may with great probability be ascribed their changed demeanour on the 7th, when Macomo and Tyali accepted the terms offered by Colonel Smith, and, as a proof of their sincerity, returned with him to Fort Cox.

On the 8th of September Sir Benjamin D'Urban arrived at Fort Willshire for the purpose of negotiating with the chiefs, and shortly after a treaty of peace was concluded, and hostilities finally brought to a close.

During this contest, which had lasted nearly nine months, although the regiment had but little opportunity of distinguishing itself, it invariably maintained a high character for good conduct, not a single instance of crime of any description having occurred in the corps during the whole campaign. It repeatedly received the praise of Sir Benjamin D'Urban, and had the satisfaction of seeing the approbation of His Majesty William IV. recorded in the following words:—

"It affords His Majesty high gratification to observe that in this new form of warfare His Majesty's forces have exhibited their characteristic courage, discipline, and cheerful endurance of fatigue and privation."

During the month of October the detachments of the regiment at Forts Warden and Wellington were relieved by the 75th regiment, whose headquarters were now at Fort Cox; and upon the 18th, the headquarters having been relieved by the 75th regiment at King William's Town, marched for Grahamstown, where they arrived on the 26th, consisting of only two companies, the others being distributed in Forts Cox, Beresford, and Murray.

Government having at the end of 1836 given up the new province of Queen Adelaide, it was evacuated by the troops, when the regiment, having its headquarters at Grahamstown, furnished detachments to various forts.

On the 17th of March 1836 the regiment was permitted to bear on its colours and appointments the words "Cape of Good Hope," in commemoration (as the order from the Horse Guards expresses it) of the distinguished gallantry displayed by the 72nd regiment at the capture of the town and garrison of the Cape of Good Hope, on the 8th of January 1806, when it formed part of the second or Highland brigade employed on that occasion. On the 20th of January 1837, by an order from the Horse Guards, His Majesty was also graciously pleased to allow the regiment to bear on its colours and appointments the word "Hindoostan," in commemoration of the meritorious services of the regiment while in India from 1782 to 1798.

The regiment remained with the headquarters at Grahamstown, furnishing detachments to the different outposts until the month of October 1838, when orders were received for the corps to be held in readiness to proceed to Cape Town, on being relieved by the 27th regiment. The regiment, on its arrival at Cape Town, occupied quarters in the castle and main barracks, and furnished detachments to Simon's Town and Rotten Island. A detachment of troops having been ordered to proceed to Port Natal on the east coast of Africa, and take possession of it in the name of Her Majesty, the 72nd Highlanders furnished for this duty 1 captain, 2 subalterns, 1 assistant surgeon, 4 sergeants, 2 drummers, and the Light Company completed to 86 rank and file. This detachment, under the command of Major Charteris, military secretary to His Excellency Major-General Sir G. Napier, K.C.B., embarked on the

19th of November 1838, landing at Port Natal on the 3d of December, and were immediately employed in the erection of buildings for the protection of stores, and the construction of works for the defence of the Post.

The regiment remained during the year 1839 at Cape Town, and in that period received two drafts from the depot companies, consisting in all of 1 major, 1 captain, 3 subalterns, 3 sergeants, and about 170 rank and file. The detachment from Port Natal returned to Cape Town under Captain Jervis of the 72nd on the 2nd of January 1840, when His Excellency Major-General Sir George Napier, K.C.B., was pleased to express in General Orders his entire satisfaction with their conduct during absence from headquarters. The regiment had in September 1839 received orders to be held in readiness to embark for England, on being relieved from home by the 25th regiment, and the latter troops landed at the Cape in the month of March 1840. Previous to the regiment embarking for England the following address was presented to it, signed by all the principal inhabitants of Cape Town and its vicinity :—

"*To the officers, non-commissioned officers, and private soldiers of H.M. 72nd Highlanders.*

"We, the undersigned merchants and other inhabitants of the Cape of Good Hope, cannot permit the embarkation of the 72nd from the shores of this colony to take place without recording some expression of the sense we entertain of the general deportment and estimable conduct of the regiment during the twenty-five years it has been stationed in this garrison. The character of the 72nd Highlanders throughout that period has been uniformly and permanently marked towards the public by good order, sobriety, and discipline; while on every occasion on which its assistance has been sought, its services have been promptly, cheerfully, and effectively rendered. In parting with a regiment whose conduct has been so exemplary, and in which many of us have found personal friends, to whom we have been long and faithfully attached, we are anxious to express, however feebly, before you quit the colony, an acknowledgment of our regret at your departure, and to convey to you, how ever inadequately, our cordial wishes for your happiness wherever you may be stationed, and that you may long continue to enjoy that distinguished renown which the 72nd Highlanders have so honourably achieved in the service of their country."

On the embarkation of the 72nd, the following General Order was issued by Major-General Sir George Napier, commanding the forces at the Cape :—

"His Excellency the Commander-in-Chief cannot permit the 72nd Highlanders to embark for England, from the colony of the Cape of Good Hope, in which they have been stationed for the long period of twelve years, without his expressing his marked approbation of the conduct of this highly-disciplined and exemplary corps while under his immediate command ; and from the reports His Excellency has received from Colonel Smith, the Deputy-Quartermaster-General, under whose orders this regiment has been during the greater part of the above period, including a very arduous and active service in the field, His Excellency is enabled to record, which he does with great satisfaction, the very meritorious services of the 72nd Highlanders in whatever duty they have been engaged, whether in the field or in quarters.

"His Excellency begs to assure Major Hope, the officers, non-commissioned officers, and soldiers of the 72nd regiment, that he will ever feel a lively interest in their welfare."

On the 11th of April 1840 the regiment embarked in two divisions for England. The headquarters landed at Portsmouth on the 8th of the following June, and marched immediately to Fort Cumberland. The second division landed also at Portsmouth on the 18th of the same month, and proceeded to the same place.

On the 1st of July Colonel Arbuthnot joined and assumed the command ; and by a regimental order of the same date, the ten companies were consolidated, the depôt companies being stationed in Portsmouth at the period of the arrival of headquarters from the Cape. On the 6th of July the headquarters marched into Portsmouth, and occupied quarters in that garrison.

On the death of Sir John Hope, the colonelcy of the regiment was conferred upon Major-General Sir Colin Campbell (*not* Lord Clyde) in August 1836.

II.

1841—1873.

The Duke of Wellington presents new colours to the 72nd — Gibraltar — Barbadoes — Trinidad — Nova Scotia—Return to Europe—Embark for Malta—To the Crimea—Home—Channel Islands—Shorncliffe —Presentation of colours—Arrive in India in 1857 —Shorncliffe—New Colours—Old Colours destination —To Portsmouth — Bombay — Calaba — Guzerat— Tankaria—Baroda—Ahmedabad—Deesa — Nusseerabad—Mount Aboo—Death of Major Mackenzie of Glacket at Burra—The 72nd joins Major-General Roberts—Operations against Kotah—Strength of the Force—Major Thelluson—Sawah—Jehaspoor —Bhoondee—The Chumbul—The Rajah of Kotah— Major Burton and his Sons murdered—Kotah taken—Its immense strength—Lieutenant Cameron's gallantry—Lala—Fall of Kotah—Cavalry pursuit of the Rebels—Leave Kotah for Neemuch— Mokundurra Pass—Neemuch again—Colonel Parke commands this Station—Nusseerabad—Mutiny of the Army of Sindiah at Gwalior—The Bunnas— Kotarja — Brigadier-General Parke — Oodeypoor— Jhalra Patun —- Soosneer — Rajgurgh — Sironj— Sarungpoor—Indore—Bhopal—Beoar—Mungowlee —The Betwah—Borassa—Bhopal saved— Rao Sahib —Tantea Topee—The Nerbudda crossed by the Rebels — Hooshungabad — Churwah — Chicalda— Mhow—Indore—Chapeira—Angur—Palace of Chotah Oodeypoor—Pertabghur—Operations in the Jeysulmeer Districts on the Indus—Brigadier-General Parke's Operations north of Kotah—Tantea Topee captured and executed—Rao Sahib and Feroze Shah, Prince of Delhi — Major-General Michel's wonderful Marches—Lieutenant Vasey's March of 3000 Miles—The 72nd Medal for the Suppression of the Indian Mutiny—Victoria Cross conferred on Lieutenant Cameron—Mhow—Indore —Inspections — Leave Mhow—Nargaon — Leave Poonah—Return Home—Edinburgh—Prince Alfred opens the Museum of Arts and Sciences—The 72nd as a Guard of Honour—Inspection by General F. W. Hamilton, C.B.—Colonel Payn, C.B., commands—Aldershot—Inspection—Major Hunter in command — Manchester—Dublin—Limerick—Buttevant—Ordered to India—Proceed to Cork—Appointment of General Arbuthnot as Colonel of the 72nd—Arrive at Alexandria—Umballah—Lieutenant Thomson's Death—Reviewed by General Lord Napier of Magdâla—Inspected by Major-General Fraser Tytler, C.B., at Umballah—Kussowlee and Dugshai.

IN July 1841 the regiment, now joined by the depôt companies, proceeded from Portsmouth to Windsor, where, in January 1842, it was presented with new colours by Field-Marshal His Grace the Duke of Wellington, in the quadrangle of the castle, and in presence of Her Majesty the Queen, Prince Albert, and the King of Prussia. The Duke addressed the 72nd as follows : —

"Colonel Arbuthnot, and you, gentlemen officers, and you, non-commissioned officers and soldiers of the 72nd Highland Regiment, I have attended here this day, in compliance with the wish of your commanding officer, and by permission of Her Majesty, to present to you your new colours.

"These colours have been consecrated by one of the highest dignitaries of our Church, and are presented to you in the presence of Her Majesty, and of her illustrious and royal guest, the King of Prussia, of Prince Albert, and of a number of the most distinguished personages. They are composed of the colours of the three nations, and bear the cipher of Her Majesty; and I have no doubt, from your previous character and your present high state of discipline, that you will guard them under every circumstance to the utmost of your power.

"These colours you are henceforth to consider as your head-quarters, and in every circumstance, in all times of privation and distress, you will look to them as your rallying point; and I would again remind you that their presentation is witnessed by the monarch of one of the most powerful nations in Europe —a nation which boasts of an army which has heretofore been a pattern for all modern troops, and which has done so much towards contributing to the general pacification of Europe. And I am happy to be able to show His Majesty a regiment in such high order. I have long known the 72nd Highland Regiment. Half a century has now nearly elapsed since I had the pleasure of serving in the same army with them on the plains of Hindoostan, and then they were famous for their high order and discipline. Since that period they have been engaged in the conquest of some of the most valuable colonies of the British Crown, and latterly in performing most distinguished services at the Cape of Good Hope. Fourteen years out of the last sixteen they have spent in foreign service, and, with only eighteen months at home for their re-formation and their redisciplining, appear in their present high state of regularity and order. The best part of a long life has been spent by me in barracks, camps, and cantonments; and it has been my duty as well as my inclination always to study how best to promote the health and discipline of the troops; and I have always found it to be done only by paying the strictest regard to regularity and good order, with the greatest attention to the orders of their superiors. I address myself now particularly to the older soldiers, and wish them to understand that their strict attention to their discipline and respect to their officers will often have the best effect upon the younger soldiers; and it is, therefore, their duty to set a good example to their juniors by so doing. By these means alone can they expect to command the respect and regard of the community among whom they are employed. And I have made it my business to inquire particularly, and am rejoiced to find that the 72nd has always commanded that respect and regard, wherever it has been stationed, to which its high state of discipline and order so justly entitles it.

"You will, I am sure, always recollect the circumstances under which these colours are now committed to your charge, having been consecrated by one of the highest dignitaries of the Church, in the presence of Her Majesty, who now looks down upon you, and of her royal visitors. I give them into your charge, confident that at all times, under all circumstances, whether at home or abroad, and in all trials and privations, you will rally round them, and protect them to the utmost of your power."

To this address Colonel Arbuthnot made the following reply:—

"My Lord Duke, it would be highly presumptuous in me if I were to make any reply to the address which your Grace has delivered to us; but I cannot avoid stating that it is impossible for me, and indeed, I may add, out of the power of any one, to express how deeply I, my officers, non-commissioned officers, and men, feel the high honour which has been conferred on us by having had our colours presented to us by the greatest soldier the world has ever seen, and that in the presence of our Sovereign, His Majesty the King of Prussia, and Field-Marshal His Royal Highness Prince Albert."

In 1843 the regiment removed to Ireland, where it remained till November 1844, when it embarked from Cork for Gibraltar. The depôt companies remained in Ireland till September 1847, when they removed to Paisley in Scotland.

After the decease of Lieutenant-General Sir Colin Campbell, on the 13th of June 1847, Lieut.-General Sir Neil Douglas, K.C.B., K.C.H., was appointed Colonel of the regiment on the 12th of the following July.

During the whole of its service at Gibraltar, the regiment was constantly employed in furnishing working parties and artificers to assist in the construction of the new line of fortifications extending from the Light House at Europa Point to Little Bay, and from the New Mole to Chatham Counter-Guard. This magnificent work was proceeding with wonderful rapidity when the regiment left Gibraltar.

On the 14th of June 1847 it had been notified in garrison orders that the 72nd would re-embark, in the coming autumn, for the West Indies; and on the arrival of the reserve battalion of the 67th Regiment, the service companies embarked on the 15th of February 1848 on board the "Bombay," hired transport, and sailed on the 18th of February for Barbadoes. Previous to the embarkation, the following complimentary order was issued by his Excellency General Sir Robert Thomas Wilson, Governor and Commander-in-Chief of the Forces at Gibraltar:—

"GIBRALTAR, *February* 12, 1848.

"The eminently soldier-like qualities, the correct and zealous performance of all duties, and the general reputable conduct of the 72nd Highlanders during their service in Gibraltar, entitle them to the fullest encomiums of the General commanding. Wherever the regiment goes, the General commanding is confident that it will confer credit on the profession; and on quitting this station it leaves an impression of esteem on the garrison and the community that absence will neither impair nor efface."

After a favourable passage of twenty-three days, the regiment arrived in Carlisle Bay, Barbadoes, on the 12th of March 1848, landed on the 14th, and occupied quarters in the Brick Barracks, St Ann's. At this time the 66th regiment, which had arrived from Gibraltar about three weeks previously, occupied the Stone Barracks at St Ann's. These had been vacated in January by the 88th regiment, which encamped on the Savanna in consequence of its having been attacked with yellow fever, of which many died, during December and January, including the commanding officer, Lieut.-Colonel Phibbs. But the regiment was now healthy, and had proceeded to relieve the detachments of the 19th regiment in the islands, which corps had assembled at Barbadoes, and thence proceeded to Canada. In April, however, some men of the 66th were admitted into hospital with yellow fever, and several deaths occurred. This continued until August, when the cases became so numerous, that early in September the regiment was moved into camp in rear of the Brick Barracks. In October, the men of the Royal Artillery were also encamped; and in this month the 72nd, which had hitherto been remarkably healthy, was visited by this terrible disease. On the 13th of October, the assistant-surgeon, Dr Irwin, died of it, and it spread very rapidly among the men. On the 15th of November, the regiment moved out of the Brick Barracks into tents, erected about a mile distant, on the site of a former naval hospital, which had been destroyed by the hurricane of 1831. Nevertheless, the disease continued to spread until the end of December; and within the three months, 12 out of 14 officers, 26 non-commissioned officers, and 177 men, were attacked; and of these 4 officers, 17 non-commissioned officers, and 42 men, died. After this, however, only one other case occurred, that of Captain Maylan, who was taken ill on the 21st of January, and expired on the 25th.

By circular memorandum, dated Horse Guards, the 29th of January 1849, the regiment, being in the colonies, was ordered to be reduced to 770 rank and file.

In consequence of riots at St Lucia, a detachment of the 72nd, consisting of 1 captain, 3 subalterns, and 100 rank and file, was sent off at a few hours' notice, on the 12th of March. When it arrived, however, order had been restored; but the detachment remained at St Lucia, being quartered at Pigeon Island, until it was relieved by a company of the 66th, on the 16th of June.

In consequence of a riot at Trinidad, the flank companies were sent off to that island at a few hours' notice, on the 10th of October, and were afterwards detached to St Joseph's and San Fernando

On the 19th of December 1849, the head-quarters embarked at Barbadoes, on board the "Princess Royal" transport, for Trinidad, where they landed on the 24th of December, and occupied the barracks at St James's, thus relieving the head-quarters of the 88th Regiment The flank companies joined and formed the head-quarters of the regiment in the commencement of January, having been relieved by No 4 company

The distribution of the regiment at this period was as follows —

At Trinidad,	Grenadier, Light, and No 4 Companies
,, Demerara,	No 1 and No 2 Companies
,, Grenada,	No 3 Company
,, Tobago,	Detachment of 30 men

The regiment continued detached as above until the 12th of May 1851, when the head-quarters, having been relieved by the head-quarters of the 34th Regiment, embarked at Trinidad for Barbadoes, where they landed on the 23rd and again occupied the Brick Barracks, the several detachments above mentioned having previously been conveyed there under the command of Major Gaisford On the 8th of July, the regiment having been relieved by the 69th regiment from Malta, embarked on board H M S "Hercules" for Halifax, Nova Scotia, and on its arrival, on the 30th, marched into the South Barracks

On the 8th of September the 72nd commenced its march for New Brunswick to relieve the 97th, and on the 26th of the same month the head-quarters arrived at Fredericton, relieving the head-quarters of the 97th

On the 1st of March 1854, 132 men were transferred from the depôt to the 42nd and 79th Highlanders, which corps had been ordered to form part of the expedition sent to the East against Russia At the same time an order was given that the recruiting parties of the regiment should raise men for the corps sent on service, so that at this time the 72nd was about 330 rank and file under the establishment, and with little prospect of being recruiting to it.

On the 5th of May 1854, Lieut-Colonel Freeman Murray retired from the command of the regiment, having exchanged with Lieut-Colonel William Raikes Faber This officer, however never joined, but on the 23rd of June 1854 he exchanged with Lieut-Colonel James Fraser of the 35th Regiment

On the 7th of October 1854, the service companies stationed at Halifax, Nova Scotia, under command of Major R P Sharp, were ordered to hold themselves in readiness to embark for Europe on the shortest notice On the 12th of the same month they embarked on board the steamer "Alps" for conveyance to Dublin, and landed at Kingston on the 24th, proceeding at once by railway to Limerick, where they occupied the New Barracks, the depôt, under the command of Major J W Gaisford, having arrived there a few days previously

On the 1st of November 1854, Lieut-Colonel James Fraser assumed the command of the regiment, which was at once formed into twelve companies, while the depôt and service companies were amalgamated On the 23rd a letter was received from the Horse Guards desiring that the regiment should be held in readiness to embark for Malta

On the 1st of December 1854, Lieut-Colonel James Fraser retired from the command of the 72nd, by the sale of his commission, and was succeeded by Major R P Sharp, this being the first occasion on which the Lieutenant-Colonelcy had been given in this regiment for many years On this day also the regiment was again formed into eight service and four depôt companies, the latter being under the command of Major J W Gaisford On the 9th the service companies left Limerick by railway for Buttevant, and shortly afterwards proceeded to Cork, where they embarked on board H M S "Neptune," for Malta, where they arrived on the 4th of January 1855, occupying the Floriana Barracks

On the 22nd of May the regiment embarked, under the command of Lieut-Colonel R P Sharp, on board the "Alma" steamship, and sailed from Malta for service in the Crimea The full strength of the regiment was, on embarking—2 field officers, 8 captains, 10 lieu-

36 corporals, 17 drummers, and 514 privates. The regiment arrived at Balaklava on the 29th of May, and remained at anchor outside the harbour until the 31st, when it sailed to join the expedition at Kertch, under Lieutenant-General Sir George Brown. It reached Kertch on the following day, and remained on board ship until the 10th. While the regiment was at Kertch, cholera broke out in a most malignant form, and during the last six days it carried off 2 sergeants, 1 drummer, and 19 privates. It ceased, however, as soon as the ship left.

On the same day (the 10th of June) the 72nd arrived at Balaklava, disembarked on the 13th, encamped that night on the plain, and marched to the front of Sebastopol on the following day, where it was attached to a brigade composed of the 3rd and 31st Regiments, under the command of Colonel Van Straubenzee of the 3rd. On the 15th the 72nd commenced doing duty in the trenches of the right attack. On the 30th of this month it was appointed to the Highland brigade, composed of the 42nd, 79th, and 93rd Highlanders, under the command of Brigadier-General Cameron of the 42nd. This brigade was the 2nd of the 1st division; the other brigade was that of the Guards; the whole being under Major-General Sir Colin Campbell, who had the local rank of lieutenant-general. The 72nd continued doing duty in the trenches until the 26th of August, on which day the Highland brigade was moved to Kamara in support of the Sardinian outposts, an attack being expected in that direction, notwithstanding the repulse which the enemy had received from the French and Sardinian troops at the Traktir [6] Bridge, on the Tchernaya River, on the 16th of August 1855.

On the 18th of June the greater part of the regiment was in the trenches under the command of Major William Parke, while the remaining few were stationed under the command of Lieut.-Colonel Sharp, in rear of the 21-gun battery. In the beginning of July, however, Lieut.-Colonel Sharp, having obtained sick-leave of absence to England, handed over the command of the 72nd to Major Parke.

[6] TRAKTIR, a frequent name of villages and towns in the Crimea, simply means village. Krru is a farm.

It should be mentioned that, on the 22nd of June, a second lieutenant-colonel and 4 captains, with the proportionate number of subalterns, were added to the establishment of the regiment, which, by a War-Office circular of the 20th of August, was now fixed at 16 companies, consisting of 1 colonel, 2 lieutenant-colonels, 2 majors, 16 captains, 26 lieutenants, 14 ensigns, 7 staff-officers, 109 sergeants, 100 corporals, 47 drummers and pipers, and 1900 privates.

On the 16th of July, a draft, under the command of Captain Cecil Rice, composed of 3 subalterns, 1 staff-officer, 3 sergeants, 2 drummers, and 245 rank and file, joined from the depôt of the regiment, among whom was a large proportion of volunteers from other corps. After these had been in camp and done duty in the trenches for about a fortnight, cholera broke out again in the regiment, and carried off 35 men belonging, with only one exception, to the last draft. This terrible disease lasted about six weeks.

The brigade marched from the camp at Kamara, on the 8th of September, to the trenches, and occupied the 3rd parallel during the time the French stormed and took the Malakoff Tower and works, and during the unsuccessful attempt of the English to take the Redan. Between 4 and 5 o'clock that afternoon, the 72nd was ordered to the 5th parallel, holding the part of it situated in front of the Redan, and was to have led the storming party in another attack on the Redan at daylight on the 9th of September, had not the Russians evacuated the south side of Sevastopol during the night. How masterly their retreat was is well known.

The Commander-in-Chief, Lieutenant-General Simpson, soon afterwards resigned. He had been appointed to the supreme command on the death of Lord Raglan, in June 1855, and soon after the fall of Sevastopol was succeeded by Major-General Codrington.

Quarter-Master John Macdonald, of the 72nd, was wounded by a Minié bullet on the 8th, soon after the regiment entered the trenches, and died from the effects of the wound on the 16th of September. In him the regiment lost a most useful, active, and intelligent officer. The loss of the regiment on the 8th were slight—1 private killed, 1 sergeant, 2 corporals, and 16 privates wounded.

On the 15th of September, Lieut.-Colonel Gaisford arrived from England, and assumed command of the regiment from Major Parke. Lieut.-Colonel Gaisford returned to England, however, at the end of October, having retired from the service by the sale of his commission, and was succeeded by Lieut.-Colonel William Parke, who again assumed the command of the regiment. From this time the 72nd was constantly employed on fatigue duty, carrying up wooden huts from Balaklava, as it had been decided that the Highland brigade,—which had been joined by the 1st and 2nd battalions of the Royal Regiment, and the 92nd Highlanders from Gibraltar,—should now be made into the Highland division. The 2nd brigade consisted of the Royal Regiment, the 71st Highland Light Infantry (at Kertch), and the 72nd Highlanders, under Brigadier-General Home, C.B., of the 20th Regiment, and was quartered near Kamara during the winter.

On the 3d of October 1855, Sir Colin Campbell suddenly left for England, the command of the division devolving on Brigadier-General Cameron, C.B., of the 1st brigade, who obtained the local rank of major-general on being confirmed in the command. Temporarily, he was succeeded in the command of the 1st brigade by Colonel M. Atherley of the 92d Highlanders.

On the 11th of November 1855, Sir William Codrington, K.C.B., succeeded General Simpson in command of the army, with the local rank of lieutenant-general.

On the 12th of October the regiment had moved into huts in their new encampment for the winter, the situation being most favourable, well sheltered, with good water, and plenty of wood for fuel. This spot had been occupied by Turkish troops during the summer. The winter, during part of December, January, and February, was severe, with unusually rapid variations of temperature. The regiment, nevertheless, continued remarkably healthy, being well fed and admirably clothed, besides having received a field allowance of 6d. *per diem* of extra pay.

The first issue of silver medals for the Crimea took place on the 12th of December

1855. A large number of officers, non-commissioned officers, and private soldiers, received distinctions.

Sir Colin Campbell returned to the Crimea on the 15th of February 1856, and was appointed to the command of a corps d'armée, which, however, was never collected or embodied.

On the 1st of March, it appeared in general orders that an armistice had been signed, the conditions of which were : a suspension of arms ; that the river Tchernaya, from the ruins of the village of Tchernaya to Sevastopol, should be the boundary line, and that no one should be allowed to cross the river. On the 30th, a treaty of peace was signed in Paris ; and on the 2nd of April salutes were fired to announce and commemorate the peace of the allied armies in the Crimea. The communication with the interior of the country was soon opened, and the great majority of the officers of the British army took advantage of the permission.

On the 17th of April a review of the British army was held on the heights in front of Sevastopol in honour of General Lüders, the Russian Commander-in-Chief at that time. Marshal Pelissier, Le Duc de Malakoff, and the Sardinian Commander-in-Chief, were present. The British cavalry were all at Scutari, with the exception of the 11th Hussars, who had wintered there.

In the beginning of June the army began to embark from the Crimea ; and on the 15th the 72nd was ordered from the camp near the mountain gorge leading into the valley of Vernutka, which extends in the direction of Baidar into Kadikoi, the other regiments of the Highland division having embarked for England. On the 16th of June the 72nd marched into Kadikoi, and occupied huts, being attached to the brigade under Brigadier-General Warren. It was employed on fatigues, shipping stores, &c., from Balaklava, until it embarked and sailed for England in H.M.S. "Sanspareil." After a most favourable passage, the "Sanspareil" anchored off Spithead on the 29th of July.

The 72nd disembarked on the 31st of July, at Portsmouth, proceeding on the same day to the camp at Aldershot ; and on the 1st of

August, under the command of Lieutenant-Colonel Parke, it was inspected by Her Majesty the Queen. The regiment paraded in the grounds attached to the Royal Pavilion, and Her Majesty was graciously pleased to express her entire approbation of its appearance, and the steadiness of the men under arms.

On the 16th of August the 72nd Highlanders were inspected by H.R.H. the Duke of Cambridge, the General Commanding in Chief, who expressed himself as thoroughly satisfied with the appearance and soldierlike bearing of the men.

On the 27th of the same month, the head-quarters of this regiment, consisting of the flank companies, Nos. 3, 4, and 5, left Aldershot by railroad for Portsmouth, and embarked that afternoon for Guernsey, disembarking on the 28th. The men were dispersed in detachments over the whole island. The regiment was thus in a most unsatisfactory position, being divided into so many small detachments after a lengthened period of nearly twelve years' foreign service, during a great part of which they had been similarly dispersed. A new system, however, was adopted of consolidating the depôts of all regiments, whether at home or abroad, into battalions, under lieutenant-colonels or colonels. In accordance with this regulation, the four companies of the 72nd were ordered from Paisley to Fort George, to be formed into a battalion with those of the 71st and the 92nd Highlanders, under the command of Lieutenant-Colonel Taylor, late second lieutenant-colonel of the 79th Highlanders.

On the 22nd of April 1857, the head-quarters, with grenadier and light companies of the regiment, left Guernsey, and arrived at Portsmouth the following morning; thence proceeding direct to Shorncliffe Camp. The detachment from Alderney, under Major Mackenzie, had arrived on the 21st, and the remainder of the regiment arrived on the 27th, under Major Thellusson. Before leaving the island of Guernsey, however, the following address was presented to the regiment from the Bailiff, on behalf of the Royal Court of the island:——

"GUERNSEY, *April* 22, 1857.

"Sir,—I have the honour, on behalf of the Royal Court of the island, to express the regret that it feels at the departure of the 72nd Highlanders. The inhabitants of Guernsey rejoiced at receiving on their shores a corps which had borne its part in maintaining in the Crimea the glory of the British arms. The soldierlike bearing of the men, and the friendly dispositions that they have so generally evinced, will long be borne in mind by all classes of society. To the officers the acknowledgments of the Royal Court are more especially due, for their ready co-operation with the civil power, and their constant endeavour to promote a good understanding with the inhabitants. In giving expression to the feelings of consideration and esteem entertained by the Royal Court towards yourself and the corps under your command, I have the further gratification of adding that wherever the service of their country may call them, in peace or in war, the 72nd Highlanders may feel assured that the best wishes of the people of Guernsey will ever attend them.—I have the honour to be, Sir, your most obedient humble servant,

"PETER STAFFORD CAREY,
"*Bailiff of Guernsey.*

"To Lieutenant-Colonel Parke,
"Commanding 72nd Highlanders."

The 72nd regiment remained in camp at Shorncliffe during the summer of 1857. On the 5th of August an order of readiness was received for the immediate embarkation of the regiment for India, the establishment of the regiment to be augmented to 1200 rank and file. On the 24th the 72nd were inspected at Shorncliffe by H.R.H. the Duke of Cambridge, General Commanding in Chief, who was graciously pleased to present the regiment with new colours. The regiment received H.R.H. in line, with the usual royal salute. The new colours, placed in front of the centre of the line, were then consecrated by the chaplain of the brigade, the Rev. J. Parker, and were received from the hands of H.R.H. by Lieutenants Brownlow and Richardson, who then, accompanied by the grenadier company, under Captain Rice, trooped the new colours up and down the line, the old colours having been cased and carried off with the usual honours.[7] The regiment was then formed into three sides of a square, and addressed by H R H, who passed the highest encomiums upon its conduct, discipline, and appearance. The regiment then marched past in slow and quick time, and went through several manœuvres under the personal superintendence of H R H, who was again pleased to express to Lieut.-Colonel Parke, in command of the regiment, his entire and unqualified approbation.

On the 26th, the first detachment of the 72nd, consisting of 296 men and 14 officers, under the command of Major Thellusson, left Shorncliffe for Portsmouth, and the same day embarked in the "Matilda Atheling," for Bombay. On the 4th of September, the head-quarters of the regiment, consisting of the grenadier, No 4, and the light companies, under Lieut.-Colonel Parke, left Shorncliffe for Portsmouth, and embarked in the screw steamer "Scotia" for Bombay also, sailing on the 8th of the same month. The "Scotia" anchored in Bombay harbour on the 9th of December, head-quarters landing the next day, and occupying the barracks at Colaba.

On the 28th of December the steamer "Prince Albert," with a detachment of three companies of this regiment, under Major Mackenzie, and on the 5th of January 1858 the "Matilda Atheling" arrived. The whole regiment was now together in Colaba, four companies being encamped under the command of Lieut.-Colonel William Parke.

The strength of the regiment in January 1858 was—3 field officers, 10 captains, 19 subalterns, 8 staff-officers, 58 sergeants, 18 drummers and fifers, 41 corporals, and 766 privates, making a total of 923.

On the 31st of December the regiment was placed under orders for Goojerat, and on the 14th of January 1858 it embarked on board the East India Company's steamers "Auckland" and "Berenice" for the Bay of Cambay, and disembarked at Tankaria, Bunder, on the 17th. On the following day it left Tankaria for Baroda, which it reached on the 23rd, where 200 men were detained by the British resident at the court of the Guicowar of

Baroda and Goojerat, in case of force being required in the disarming of the people. Notwithstanding the constant exposure and severe marching to which these detachments were subjected, the men throughout the whole regiment continued very healthy.

The two companies of the regiment which had been left in Bombay soon joined the others at Baroda, although they were not kept together, but were moved by companies from village to village, collecting arms and carrying out executions. The remaining six companies of the regiment left Baroda on the 23rd of January, and reached Ahmedabad on the 31st, and Deesa on the 13th of February. The climate at this season is favourable to marching, the nights and early mornings being cold, so that the men suffered little from fatigue, and remained in excellent health, although recently landed after a long voyage. On the 15th of this month, the regiment left Deesa for Nusseerabad, and on the 18th a few delicate men of the regiment were left at Mount Aboo, the sanitarium station for European troops in this command, these were to rejoin as soon as the regiment should return into quarters.

On the 5th of March 1858, at a village called Beawr, the regiment sustained a great loss by the death, from small-pox, of Major Mackenzie, the senior major of the regiment, and an officer held in universal esteem. After this depressing incident, every precautionary measure was taken, and this dreadful disease did not spread. The regiment reached Nusseerabad on the 8th, where it joined the division under Major-General Roberts, of the East India Company's Service, destined for the field-service in Rajpootanah, but more especially for operations against the city of Kotah. The cantonment of Nusseerabad no longer remained, having been laid in ruins by the mutineers. The force here collected consisted of one troop of Horse Artillery (Bombay), two batteries Bombay Artillery, 18 heavy siege train guns of different calibres, one company R E, one company Bombay Sappers, four small mountain-train guns (mortars), 1st regiment of Bombay Lancers, a strong detachment of Sind irregular horse (Jacob's), a detachment of Gwalior irregular horse, H.M.'s 72nd Highlanders, the 83rd and 95th regiments, the 10th and 12th Native Infantry. This force was divided into one cavalry and two infantry brigades, the cavalry under Colonel Smith, 3rd Dragoon Guards, who had not joined. The first infantry brigade was under Colonel Macan of the Company's service, and consisted of H.M.'s 95th Regiment, a wing of H.M.'s 83rd, with the 10th and 12th Native Infantry. The second Infantry Brigade, under Lieut.-Colonel Parke of the 72nd Highlanders, consisted of Her Majesty's 72nd, a wing of the 83rd, and the 13th regiment native infantry, which latter regiment joined on the march to Kotah, having marched from Hyderabad in Sind. A second troop of Bombay Horse Artillery likewise joined the division from Sind after its departure from Nusseerabad. All the artillery of the force was under Lieut.-Colonel Price, R.A.

The cavalry was placed temporarily under the command of Lieut.-Colonel Owen, of the 1st Bombay Lancers. This force was soon increased by the arrival of Her Majesty's 8th Hussars and two squadrons of the 2nd Bombay Cavalry.

On the 11th of March, the 72nd, under the command of Major Thellusson, who had succeeded Lieut.-Colonel Parke, the first being one day in advance, left Nusseerabad with the second brigade, en route to Kotah, a distance of 112 miles. The principal places passed through were Sawoor, strongly fortified; Jhajpoor, a straggling, ill-defended town; and Bhoondee. This last was a very strong position, situated on the face of a ridge of mountains, approached on one side through a narrow winding gorge, capable of being defended with ease. This gorge or narrow valley runs below the city of Bhoondee, and opens out into a vast plain overlooked by the city and castle. Bhoondee is surrounded by substantially-built irregular walls, bastions and defences extending to the summit of the mountain, on whose side this curious, interesting, and beautiful city is built. Here the second brigade joined the first, only two days' march from Kotah.

On the 22nd of March, the division reached Kotah, and encamped on the left bank of the river Chumbul, opposite the city; but it was subsequently forced to shift its position more to the rear, to avoid the enemy's artillery, the round-shot from which reached the camp. The 72nd was on the extreme right of the line of the encampment, and the cavalry on the extreme left, the whole army being exactly opposite the city, and parallel with the river.

The immediate cause of these operations against Kotah was as follows:—The Rajah of Kotah had always professed himself an ally of the British Government, and for many years a British Resident had been attached to his court; but when the mutiny at Neemuch broke out among the Bengal troops, the British Resident, Major Burton, had left Kotah for a short time for some purpose. During his absence, however, the Rajah warned Major Burton against returning to Kotah, as the inhabitants had joined the rebellion, and considerable numbers of mutineers from Nusseerabad, Mundesoor, and Neemuch, had taken up their quarters in the city. Nevertheless, Major Burton returned to Kotah, and with his two sons was barbarously murdered. The Rajah refused to join his subjects against the British Government, shut himself up in his palace, which was situated in one of the strongly fortified quarters of the city, and was regularly besieged by his own subjects, now aided by their fellow rebels, from the neighbouring states of Rajpootanah. To avenge the murder of the British Resident, and to inquire into, and if necessary punish, the conduct of the Rajah, were the primary objects of the expedition, of which the 72nd regiment now formed a part.

On the 24th of March, two batteries were erected on the banks of the Chumbul, one on the right and the other on the left of the British position. On these the enemy opened a steady and well-directed fire. On the 26th, at the invitation of the Rajah, Major-General Roberts placed a body of troops in the entrenched quarter of the city, which was still in the Rajah's possession; while 200 men of Her Majesty's 83rd regiment and the rifle company of the 13th Native Infantry crossed over the river. On the 27th, 28th, and 29th, preparations were made for bringing over some of the heavy ordnance and mortars to be placed in position within the Rajah's quarters, as it had been decided by the Major-General to assault the enemy's portion of the city on the 30th, after a few hours' heavy fire from all the guns and mortars. Accordingly, at two o'clock A.M. of that day, three columns of 500 men each passed over in large, square, flat-bottomed boats into the Rajah's city; the reserve was under Colonel Macan. The leading column of the assault, under Lieutenant-Colonel Raimes, of the 95th, was composed of 260 men of the 72nd and 250 of the 13th Native Infantry; the second column, under Lieutenant-Colonel Holmes, of the 12th Native Infantry, of a similar number of Her Majesty's 95th regiment, with the 10th regiment of Native Infantry; the third column, of 200 of the 83rd, with the 12th Native Infantry.

The column to which the 72nd belonged took up its position in the rear of a wall which separated the Rajah's quarters from that part of the city held by the rebels, close to the Hunnyman Bastion. The design was to blow open a gap in the wall sufficiently large to admit of the 72nd making a rush through it upon the enemy; the engineers, however, found the wall too solid to admit of a successful result, and at eleven o'clock A.M., the regiment was ordered to the Kittenpole Gate, which had been strongly built up. This was instantly blown out by the engineers, and the column, headed by the 72nd under Major Thellusson, rushed through, and turned immediately to the right, under cover of a party placed on the walls of the fortifications of the Rajah's quarters. But little resistance was offered, and the advance of the column was rapid, the principal object of attack being a bastion called the Zooraivoor, on the outer walls of the city. On the approach of the column, a few shots were fired by matchlockmen, but Enfield rifles cleared the way; and on the 72nd reaching the bastion, most of the enemy had fled, while some, throwing themselves from the ramparts, were dashed to pieces at the bottom. The column then proceeded along the top of the outer wall of the city as far as the Soorjpole Gate, one of the principal entrances, through which a considerable body of the enemy was making a

precipitate retreat; the gateway was at once taken possession of, and the column rushed into the city itself. No sooner, however, had the regiment left the walls than the matchlock-men opened fire from a strongly-built stone house, facing the gateway, an entrance into which was attempted by Lieutenant Cameron of the 72nd with a small party of men. This officer in a very gallant manner dashed up a narrow passage and stair-case leading into the upper part of the building, when he was met by a determined band of rebels, headed by "The Lalla," the commander-in-chief of the rebels. Lieutenant Cameron was cut down and severely wounded, while one man of the Royal Engineers, and one of the 83rd, who happened to be with the party, were killed, and one of the 72nd was wounded. Lieutenant-Colonel Parke deemed it expedient not to risk more lives in the narrow, dark, and intricate passages of the building; and accordingly he ordered the company of Royal Engineers to lay powder-bags and effect an opening by that means; this was immediately done, and some of these determined fanatics were destroyed by the explosion, the remainder being slain by the troops. A few other instances of desperate resistance occurred, but anything like united, determined opposition was nowhere encountered.

The other two columns had been equally successful, and by the evening of the 30th of March 1858 the city of Kotah, one of the strongest positions in India, was in possession of the British. Upwards of 70 guns of various calibres, some very heavy, besides a vast amount of powder and war material, fell into the hands of the captors. The escape of the rebels was unfortunately not intercepted by the cavalry. On the 31st, the detachment of the 72nd was relieved by a party of the regiment which had remained in camp.

The casualties of the 72nd on the 30th were few, considering the importance of the victory. One officer, Lieutenant Cameron, was wounded, and one private killed and eight wounded. The victory was gained by a clever flank movement, which turned the enemy's position and rendered their defences useless. This point in tactics, the rebels never sufficiently attended to, and consequently repeatedly lost battles by allowing their flanks to be turned.

On the 18th of April the 72nd left Kotah, and on the 2nd of May the regiment reached Neemuch, having on the march from Kotah passed through the Mokundurra Pass, a long narrow valley between two ranges of hills, easily rendered formidable by a small number of men, and unfortunately known in Indian history for Colonel Monson's disastrous retreat thence. At Neemuch, new barracks were nearly completed for the men, but no accommodation of any kind for officers. Nothing but a mass of ruins remained of this once extensive cantonment, which had been completely destroyed by the mutineers of the Bengal Army, who had been quartered here.

The force at Neemuch now consisted of a wing of the 2nd Bombay Cavalry, six guns of Bombay field artillery, one company of Royal Engineers, one company of Royal Artillery without guns, the 72nd Highlanders, one company of Her Majesty's 95th regiment, and one wing of the Bombay Native Infantry. The remainder of the division was at Nusseerabad, with the exception of a column under Colonel Smith of the 3rd Dragoon Guards, consisting of a wing of the 8th Hussars, a wing of the 1st Bombay Lancers, one troop Bombay Horse Artillery (Lieutenant-Colonel Blake's), Her Majesty's 95th Regiment, and a Native Infantry Regiment, which had been detached to Goonah, to keep open the communications between Jhansee and Indoor in the rear of Sir Hugh Rose's division.

The 72nd was now once more in quarters. The conduct, discipline, and health of the men from the time of their landing in India was quite unexceptionable, the regiment remaining perfectly efficient in every sense, though considerably under the proper number of its establishment. The recruiting, however, at the dépôt quarters at Aberdeen proved most satisfactory.

The regiment continued under the command of Major Thellusson, Lieutenant-Colonel Parke having been appointed to command the station at Neemuch.

On the 6th of June, four companies of the regiment were suddenly ordered to Nusseerabad under Major Rock, in consequence of the mutiny of the main body of the army belonging to Sindhiah of Gwalior. On the 20th of June this detachment of the regiment reached Nusseerabad, and immediately took the field with a strong column under the command of Major-General Roberts. This force consisted of one troop Bombay Horse Artillery, a wing of Her Majesty's 8th Hussars, a wing of the 1st Bombay Cavalry, and some Belooch Horse, a detachment of Her Majesty's 72nd Highlanders, Her Majesty's 83rd regiment, a regiment of native infantry, four 9-pounder guns Bombay Artillery, and a small siege train.

Major-General Roberts proceeded with the column in the direction of Jeypoor to cover and protect that city, which was threatened by a large army of rebels under the Rao Sahib and Tantea Topee. These two noted leaders, after the capture of Gwalior in June by Sir Hugh Rose, crossed the river Chumbul at the northern extremity of Kerowlee District, at the head of ten or twelve thousand men, and entered the Jeypoor territory. On the advance, however, of Major-General Roberts, the enemy turned south, marched on the city of Tonk, pillaged the suburbs, capturing four field-pieces, and in good order, on the approach of the British troops, made a rapid retreat in a south-easterly direction to Bhoondee.

Major-General Roberts now detached a small force, composed of horse-artillery, cavalry, and the four companies of 72nd Highlanders, besides some native infantry, to take up the pursuit; but owing to excessive rains, this service was one of great difficulty, and the men were exposed to unusual hardships and privations. Such was the state of the weather that, for several days consecutively, not even the rebels could move.

On the 14th of August, Major-General Roberts, after a rapid succession of forced marches, came up with the enemy near the village of Kattara on the Bunas river, a few miles north of the city of Oodeypoor, where the rebels had taken up a good position. On the advance of the hussars and horse artillery, they abandoned their guns and fled; their loss, it was calculated, having exceeded 1000 men killed.

Simultaneously with these operations, a

column, including 350 rank and file of the regiment, under Lieutenant-Colonel Parke, recently appointed Brigadier of the 1st Class, moved out from Neemuch to co-operate with Major-General Roberts in the direction of Odeypoor, the head-quarters. On the 18th of this month, the column under Brigadier Parke received orders to pursue the scattered and fugitive rebel forces, and was reinforced by the head-quarters and a wing of the 13th Regiment Native Infantry, a wing of H.M. 8th Hussars, 250 Belooch horse, and a detachment of Goojerat irregular cavalry. Notwithstanding the utmost efforts on the part of the pursuing column, the enemy completely outstripped it by the extraordinary rapidity of their flight. They took a direct easterly course between the rivers Bunas and Bairas, retreating into the mountains and rocky fastnesses to the north of Chittoor, proceeding as far as the Chumbul river, which they crossed on the 23rd of August, without being intercepted by the pursuing column. This, probably, would not have happened had not the information supplied by the political authorities been incorrect. On the evening of the 23rd, Brigadier Parke reached the Chumbul; but he was unable to cross on account of the rapid swelling of the stream and the completely worn-out condition of the cavalry that had been detached from Major-General Roberts's column for the pursuit. The force accordingly returned, reaching Neemuch on the 28th, the infantry having marched upwards of 220 miles between the 11th and 23rd of August.

On the 5th of September, the Neemuch or 2nd Brigade of the Rajpootanah Field Force was again ordered to take the field, under the command of Brigadier Parke. This force consisted of 200 men of the 2nd Bombay Light Cavalry; one troop 8th Hussars; one company 11th Royal Engineers; 500 of the 72nd Highlanders, under Major Thellusson; four 9-pounder guns, Bombay Artillery; two mountain-train mortars; two siege-train mortars; and 450 of the 15th Regiment Bombay Native Infantry.

The object of this expedition was to attack the rebels, who were reported as being in position at Jhalra Patoon, having obtained possession of the Fort, containing upwards of 40 pieces of artillery, and a great amount of treasure. Here they had been joined by the Rajah's troops, who opened the gates of the city as well as those of the Fort, which is distant about 3 miles; the Rajah fled for protection to the nearest British force at Soosneer.

The rebels, now considerably augmented in numbers and completely re-equipped, hearing of the advance of the force from Neemuch, left Jhalra Patoon and moved south towards Soosneer, as if intending to attack a small body of British troops, detached from Mhow and encamped at Soosneer under the command of Lieutenant-Colonel Lockhart, of the 92nd Highlanders. The 2nd Brigade Rajpootanah Field Force accordingly marched to Sakoondai Ford, crossed the Chumbul river, and went direct to Soosneer. The rebels, however, did not attack Lieutenant-Colonel Lockhart, who was joined shortly afterwards by Major-General Michel, commanding the Malwah Division, together with reinforcements.

On the morning of the 15th of September, the 2nd Brigade Rajpootanah Field Force left Soosneer, heavy artillery firing having been heard to the eastward. The brigade accordingly marched in that direction to Mulkeera on the Sind river, a branch of the Kalli-Sind. It was ascertained that Major-General Michel had overtaken the rebels near Rajgurh, attacked, defeated, and captured all their guns, in number twenty-seven. The rebel forces, computed at 10,000 to 12,000 men, fled in hot haste and re-assembled at Sironj, a small state and large Mohammedan city in Rajpootanah.

Major-General Michel now directed the 2nd Brigade Rajpootanah Field Force to take up a position at Sarungpoor on the Bombay and Agra grand trunk road, the object being to cover Indore, the head-quarters of the Maharajah Holkar, and containing a numerous and most disaffected population. It was therefore a matter of paramount importance to frustrate any endeavour on the part of the rebels even to appear in that immediate neighbourhood. The Major-General, after the action at Rajgurh, likewise took a south easterly course in order to attack the rebels, covering at the same time the state and city of Bhopal.

A few days afterwards, the brigade was transferred, as a temporary arrangement, to the Malwah Division, and placed under the orders of Major-General Michel. At end of September, when it marched to Beawr on the grand trunk road. The 72nd, as part of the brigade, was now employed in keeping open the communications with the rear and covering the advance of the column under the Major-General through Sironj to the eastward towards the river Betwah.

The enemy having been again attacked by the Major-General, on the 9th of October, near a place called Mungowlee, sought refuge in the Chundairee jungles, and the 2nd Brigade Rajpootanah Field Force received orders to march by Sironj to these jungles. The rebels, however, crossed the Betwah and took a more easterly course, thus causing change in the intended movements of the brigade, which, after a few days' halt at Sironj, was ordered to Bhorasso on the Betwah river.

On the 25th of October information was received that the rebels had been again attacked by the Major-General and driven south, as if intending to make a descent on the city of Bhopal.

The 2nd brigade Rajpootanah Field Force accordingly left Bhorasso on the night of the 25th of October, marched direct on Bhopal, and bivouacked near that city on the evening of the 28th, thus having accomplished a distance of about 110 miles in 74 hours. The important and wealthy city of Bhopal was thus saved from falling into the hands of the Rao Sahib and Tantéa Topee; for there was no doubt whatever that the Begum's troops would have joined the rebels. For this service, the thanks of the Governor in Council (Bombay) and of Sir Henry Somerset, the Commander-in-Chief of the Presidency, were received.

Soon after the arrival of the brigade in Bhopal, the rebel forces crossed the river Nerbudda about 40 miles to the eastward of Hoosungabad, and proceeded due south through the Poochpoonah range of mountains to the banks of the Taptee river. Major-General Michel, C.B., with a column composed of cavalry and horse artillery, followed rapidly to Hoosungabad, and ordered the 2nd brigade Rajpootanah Field Force to do likewise. On the 9th of November the brigade reached Hoosungabad, crossed the Nerbudda on the 11th, and remained on the south side till the 14th. One wing of the regiment, under Major Norman, was now ordered to remain with a portion of the brigade at Hoosungabad, whence the headquarters of the regiment and the brigade marched *en route* to Charwah in a south-west direction. At Charwah another change was made in the disposing of this regiment. Brigadier Parke was ordered by the major-general to assume command of a column composed of light and irregular cavalry, with 100 men of the 72nd Highlanders mounted on riding camels, to pursue with the utmost speed the rebels, who had entirely changed their course, having turned north-west, making for the fords of the Nerbudda in the vicinity of Chicoolda. This last-named detachment of the regiment was composed of the light and No. 4 companies, under Lieutenant Vesey. The headquarters of the regiment and the wing under Major Thellusson were shortly afterwards ordered up to Mhow, which they reached on the 5th of December 1858, and on the 8th they were ordered to Indore, where they remained until the 5th of January 1859, on which day they returned to Mhow, and went into quarters. The detachment which had remained under Major Norman in November at Hoosungabad recrossed the Nerbudda, and was ordered north through Sehoor to Chapeira, and thence south again to Angoor.

The detachment under Lieutenant Vesey continued with the pursuing column under Brigadier Parke. The operations of this small force commenced on the 23rd of November 1858, and on the 1st of December, after having marched 250 miles in nine days, including the passage of the Nerbudda near Chicoolda, it came up with the enemy at daylight, and attacked him near the town and palace of Chhota Oodepoor, on the road to Baroda, the capital of Goojerat. The rebel forces were under the Rao Sahib and Tantéa Topee. These were completely dispersed, and suffered considerable loss; but it was impossible to obtain satisfactory accounts of the results, or to strike a heavy blow on these rebel hordes, who scattered themselves in all directions. In the course of ten days, however, the rebels again collected their forces, and marched through dense jungles due north by Banswarra to Sulumboor, a large and important city, strongly fortified, belonging to an independent but disaffected Rajah, who secretly gave all the aid in his power to the rebels, furnishing supplies in a country both barren and very thinly inhabited——the only inhabitants of these vast forest and mountainous districts being the aboriginal Bheels.

The rebels, however, being closely pressed by the pursuing column under Brigadier Parke, entered the open country again near Pertabgurh. Here they were met by a small force from Neemuch, under Major Rocke, 72nd Highlanders. This force consisted of 150 men of the 72nd, a small detachment of H.M.'s 95th Regiment, a few native infantry and cavalry, and two 9-pounder guns Royal Artillery. The rebels advanced late in the evening, but he was well and steadily received by Major Rocke's small detachment. For a considerable time a heavy fire was kept up; but the object of the rebels being to gain the open country, and rid themselves as rapidly as possible of the presence of the numerous small columns of British troops which had been stationed to watch the Banswarra and Sulumboor jungles, they availed themselves of the night, and effected their escape to the eastwards to Soosueer, crossing the Chumbul and the Kolli-Sind rivers. From the want of cavalry, Major Rocke's column could not take up the pursuit, and therefore shortly afterwards returned to Neemuch.

The detachment under Lieutenant Vesey, with the column of pursuit, now followed the course taken by the enemy, keeping to the westward, but nearly parallel to it, there being several other fresh columns in closer pursuit. Towards the middle of January, Brigadier Parke's column passed through the Mokundurrah Pass, and thence to the Gameotch Ford, near Kotah, to Jeypoor, by Bhoondee, the rebels with extraordinary rapidity having crossed the Chumbul near Indoorgurh, and again entered the Jeypoor territory. The y

were attacked by a column from Agra, under Brigadier Showers, and driven westward towards the borders of the Jeysoolmeer sandy districts bordering upon the deserts that extend to the Indus. Major-General Michel, with a strong column, entered Rajpootanah, and took a position on the highroad between Nusseerabad and Neemuch, ordering Colonel Somerset to watch the mountain passes south of Nusseerabad in the range of mountains separating Marwar and Jeypoor. Two other columns were also out from Nusseerabad, all trying to intercept the rebel forces. Brigadier Parke held the country between Samboor Lake and Jeypoor to the north, and extending south to Kishengurh, near Ajmeer. After several skirmishes with the British forces, the rebels marched due south, and, in the middle of February, crossed the Aravulli range of mountains at or near the Chutsebooj Pass, within a few "cess"[8] of Colonel Somerset, who, with a fine brigade of fresh cavalry and mounted infantry, took up the pursuit, but was unable to overtake his flying foe. The rebels had now recourse to stratagem, and feeling at last much distressed, they pretended to sue for truces. About 200 of the Ferozeshah's followers surrendered. The British columns were halted, and the rebel leaders availed themselves of the opportunity, to return eastward with their now (as rumour had it) disheartened followers greatly reduced in numbers, and sought refuge in the Sironj and Shahabad jungles.

In March 1859 the pursuing column under Brigadier Parke was ordered to Jhalra Patoon, there to halt and watch the country lying to the south as far as Booragoon, and north to the Kotah district.

In the beginning of April the rebel leader Tantéa Topee, who had separated from the main body of the rebels, was captured by means of treachery on the part of a surrendered rebel chief, Maun Singh, and executed at Sipree. The two remaining rebel leaders now were Rao Sahib and Ferozeshah, Prince of Delhi, son of the late king; the latter having managed to escape from Oude with

* Forty-one "cess" are equal to a degree, or 69 English miles. One cess (or kos) is thus nearly equal to one mile and seven-tenths. It varies, however, in different parts of the country.

about 2000 followers, joined the Rao Sahib in January 1859, before crossing the Chumbul into the Kerowlee and Jeypoor territories.

The rebel forces were now so much scattered, and such numbers had been slain, that it was deemed advisable to order as many European troops as possible into quarters. The detachment under Lieutenant Vesey accordingly left Jhalra Patoon, and regained headquarters at Mhow on the 21st of April. Brigadier Parke, with Captain Rice, of the 72nd (his orderly officer), and some irregular cavalry, remained in the field until 16th June 1859, on which day they returned into head-quarters at Mhow, and the regiment was again in cantonments.

To enter into the details of the extraordinary pursuit and campaign of the division under Major-General Michel, C.B., in Central India and Rajpootanah, would be out of place. Suffice it to say that the regiment under the command of Major Thellusson, from July 1858 to May 1859, was constantly in the field, engaged in perhaps the most arduous and trying service which has ever fallen to the lot of British soldiers in India. Disastrous marches, unsuccessful campaigns, attended by all the miseries of war, have occurred undoubtedly in India; but, for a constant unceasing series of forced marches, frequently without excitement, the campaign under Major-General Michel stands unsurpassed. The results were most satisfactory. The pacification and restoration of order and confidence in Central India were the completion of Sir Hugh Rose's brilliant campaign in 1858.

The thanks of both houses of Parliament were offered to Major-General Sir John Michel, K.C.B., and the troops under his command, being included in the general thanks to the whole army under Lord Clyde.

The conduct, discipline, and health of the regiment during all the operations in 1858-9 were excellent. The detachment of the regiment under Lieutenant Vesey, on its

arrival at headquarters at Mhow, had been under canvas in the field since January 1858, with the exception of five weeks at Neemuch, and had marched over 3000 miles. The headquarters of the regiment were in Neemuch during May, June, and July 1858; with the exception of this period, they likewise were in the field from January 1858 to January 1859.

In consequence of the services of the regiment, above enumerated, it became entitled to a medal, granted for the suppression of the Indian Mutiny of 1857-8.

Brigadier Parke returned from field service on the 16th of June, and took over the command of the regiment from Lieutenant-Colonel Thellusson.

Major-General William Parke, C.B.

From a Photograph by Mayall.

The following promotions and appointments were made in the regiment in 1858-9. Lieutenant-Colonel Parke was nominated a Companion of the Bath on March 22, 1859, and was appointed aide-de-camp to the Queen, with the rank of colonel in the army, on April 26, of the same year. Major Thellusson was promoted to the brevet rank of lieutenant-colonel in the army on July 20, 1858. Captain Norman was promoted to the rank of brevet-major on July 20, 1858. Sergeant-major James Thomson was promoted to the rank of ensign on October 15, and appointed adjutant to the regiment on December 31, 1858.

The Victoria Cross was conferred on Lieutenant A. S. Cameron of the 72nd, on November 11, 1859, for conspicuous bravery at Kotah on March 30, 1858.

The field force under Major Rocke returned to Mhow on January 5, 1860, having marched through India to the confines of the Bengal Presidency, a distance of 400 miles, and ensured the peace of the territories of Sindiah, Holkar, and other minor chiefs, and prevented the outbreak which had been expected to take place during the late cold season.

Brigadier Horner, C.B., concluded the half-yearly inspection of the regiment on May 3, and found the state of discipline so admirable, that he was pleased to remit the unexpired term of imprisonment of men under sentence of court-martial.

In December 1863, His Excellency Sir William Mansfield, K.C.B., Commander-in-Chief, Bombay Presidency, inspected the regiment, and addressed it in nearly the following words:—"Seventy-second, I have long wished to see you. Before I came to this Presidency, I had often heard from one who was a great friend of yours, as well as of my own, Sir Colin Campbell, now Lord Clyde, that of all the regiments he had known in the course of his long service, he had not met with one in which discipline and steadiness in the field, as well as the most minute matters of interior economy, all the qualities, in fact, which contribute to make a good regiment, were united in so eminent a degree as in the 72nd Highlanders, when serving in his division in the Crimea, under the command of Lieutenant-Colonel Parke. I have never met Colonel Parke, but I have heard of the reputation he made at your head. It will afford me very great satisfaction to report to His Royal Highness Commanding-in-Chief, and to write as I shall do to Lord Clyde, that from the reports of all the general officers you have served under in India, and now, from my own personal observation, the 72nd Highlanders have in no

way deteriorated during their service in India, but are now under my old friend and brother officer, Colonel Payn, in every respect, on the plains of Hindoostan, the same regiment that, when serving under Sir Colin Campbell on the shores of the Crimea, was considered by him a pattern to the British army." After the inspection, his Excellency requested Lieutenant-Colonel Payn, C.B., to express to Lieutenant and Adjutant J. Thomson, and Quarter-master D. Munro, his sense of the zeal and ability which they had displayed in assisting their commanding officer to carry out the institutions that were now in full working order in the regiment.

By a General Order, dated 3d September 1863, the Queen, in commemoration of the services of the 72nd Highlanders in Her Majesty's Indian dominions, was graciously pleased to command that the words "Central India" be worn on the colours, &c., of the regiment.

In October 1864 the regiment was inspected by Major-General Edward Green, C.B., when he forwarded a letter to Colonel Payn, from which we give the following extract:—

"The regiment under your command being about to leave this division, I desire to express to you my entire satisfaction with the manner in which duty has been performed by the officers and soldiers during eighteen months that I have been associated with them as commander of the division. The perfect steadiness under arms, the neat and clean appearance of the soldiers at all times, the small amount of any serious crimes, the order in which everything is conducted as regards the interior economy, makes the 72nd Highlanders quite a pattern corps, and a source of pride to a general officer to have such a regiment under his command. . . . .

" As senior regimental officer in this brigade, you have assisted and supported me with a readiness and goodwill most advantageous to the public service, and as, in all probability, I may never again have any official communication with the 72nd Regiment, I have to beg that you will accept my hearty acknowledgments. Read this letter at the head of the regiment at a convenient opportunity, and permit it to be placed among the records of the Duke of Albany's Own Highlanders."

The regiment being under orders to leave Central India, three companies marched from Mhow on the 26th of October for Sattarah, and two companies for Asseergurh. On the 11th of February 1865, the headquarters and five companies left Mhow for Poonah. The regiment had been stationed there since January 1859. On the 1st of March the regiment was distributed as under:—

Headquarters, with two companies, Nos 4 and 6, Poonah—Colonel Payn, C.B. Detachment of three companies, Nos. 5, 7, and 10, Sattarah—Lieutenant-Colonel Rocke. Detachment of three companies, Nos. 1, 3, and 9, Khandallah—Major Rice. Detachment of two companies, Nos. 2 and 8, Asseergurh—Captain Ffrench. Nothing requiring record occurred until the 15th of July, when the regiment was placed under orders to proceed to Great Britain.

The order to volunteer into other regiments serving in India (usually given to corps on departure from that country) was issued on the 6th of September. The volunteering commenced on the 14th, and continued till the 17th, during which time 272 men left the 72nd Highlanders to join various other regiments.

On the 13th of October, a detachment, consisting of 1 captain, 5 subalterns, 1 assistant surgeon, 5 sergeants, 6 corporals, 2 drummers, and 72 rank and file, went by railroad to Bombay, and embarked on the same day on board the freight ship "Talbot." After a prosperous though somewhat lengthened voyage of 108 days, this detachment landed at Portsmouth on the 31st of January 1866, and proceeded to Greenlaw, near Edinburgh, where it awaited the arrival of the headquarters of the regiment.

On the 6th of November Brigadier-General J. C. Heath, inspected the headquarters at Poonah, and expressed his satisfaction at the steady and soldier-like manner in which it moved upon parade, commending the good behaviour of the men, and the "particularly advanced system of interior economy existing in the regiment."

The detachments from Sattarah and Asseergurh, having joined headquarters, the regiment left Poonah, under command of Major Hunter (Major Crumbie being at Bombay on duty, and the other field-officers on leave), and proceeded by rail to Bombay, embarking on the 16th on board the freight ship, the "Tweed."

On afternoon of the 18th of November, the "Tweed" weighed anchor, and on the evening of February 10, having passed the Needles, she reached Spithead, and there, at her anchorage, rode through a terrible hurricane which lasted twenty-four hours, during which many vessels near her were lost, dismasted, or wrecked. Proceeding to Gravesend, the regiment disembarked there on February 15th, and proceeded by rail to Edinburgh Castle on the 21st, and released the 71st Highland Light Infantry. The strength of the regiment on arriving in Great Britain, including the depot companies at Stirling, was:—

Field Officers,	3
Captains,	12
Lieutenants,	14
Ensigns,	10
Staff,	5
Total Officers,	44
Sergeants,	42
Drummers and Pipers,	21
Corporals,	36
Privates,	578
Total Non-Commissioned Officers and Privates,	677
Grand Total,	721

The depot, under command of Captain Beresford, joined the headquarters shortly after their arrival at Edinburgh.

During the stay of the 72nd in Edinburgh no event of importance occurred, and the conduct of the men was highly satisfactory. At the various half-yearly inspections, Major-General F. W. Hamilton, commanding in North Britain, expressed himself as thoroughly satisfied with the discipline and appearance of the regiment, as well as with its interior economy, which, as will have been noticed, also elicited the commendation of the officers who inspected the regiment in India.

On May 9th, the regiment embarked on board H.M.S. "Tamar" at Granton, and landing on the 13th went by rail to Aldershott, where it was placed in camp under canvas.

On October 7th, Major-General Renny, commanding the 1st Brigade of Infantry at

Aldershott, inspected the regiment under Major Cecil Rice, and subsequently thus expressed himself to the latter officer :——" I could see at a glance the regiment was beautifully turned out, and, indeed, everything is as good as it is possible to be. Such a regiment is seldom seen, and I will send the most favourable report I am able to make to the Horse Guards."

Of the 72nd, as of other regiments during time of peace, and especially when stationed at home, there is but little that is eventful to record. The regiment was kept moving at intervals from one place to another, and wherever it was stationed, and whatever duties it was called upon to perform, it invariably received the commendation of the military officials who were appointed to inspect it, as well as the hearty good-will of the citizens among whom it was stationed. We shall conclude our account of the brave 72nd, which, as will have been seen, has all along done much to ward off the blows of Britain's enemies, and enable her to maintain her high position among the nations of the world, by noticing briefly its movements up to the present time.

On October 24th, the regiment, now commanded by Major Hunter, left Aldershott by rail for Manchester, taking with it every one belonging to the regiment on its effective strength. The regiment remained at Manchester till February 1st, 1868, when it proceeded, under the command of Major Cecil Rice, to Ireland, arriving at Kingston on the 5th, and marching to Richmond barracks, Dublin.

A detachment under command of Captain F. G. Sherlock, consisting of 1 captain, 2 subalterns, and 2 companies, proceeded on the 25th by rail to Sligo, in aid of the civil power, returning to Dublin on March 6th. Major C. Rice commended the good behaviour of the detachment while on duty at Sligo. "It is by such conduct," he said, "that the credit and good name of a regiment are upheld."

Colonel W. Payn, C.B., rejoined from leave of absence on the 12th of March, and resumed command of the regiment.

In April, their Royal Highnesses the Prince and the Princess of Wales visited Dublin; and on the 18th, the installation of His Roy [

Highness as a Knight of the Order of St Patrick took place at a special chapter of the order, held in St Patrick's Cathedral, His Excellency the Duke of Abercorn, Lord-Lieutenant of Ireland, presiding as Grand-Master. The regiment, under Colonel Payn, C.B., was on that day on duty in York Street.

On the 20th of April the whole of the troops in Dublin were paraded in the Phœnix Park, in review order, in presence of H.R.H. the Prince of Wales, the Princess of Wales, and H.R.H. the Duke of Cambridge, Field-Marshal, commanding-in-chief.

On September 16th the 72nd was ordered to Limerick, where it remained till the end of October 1869. On the 21st the headquarters and three companies, under the command of Major Beresford, proceeded by rail to Buttevant in county Cork. On the 22nd, five companies proceeded by rail to the Cove of Cork, viz, three companies under command of Captain Sherlock to Camhden Fort, and two companies under the command of Captain Tanner to Carlisle Fort. On the 25th, " F " (Captain Guinness's) company proceeded from Clare Castle to Tipperary to join "A" (Captain Fordyce's) company at the latter place.

On June 27th, 1870, orders were received for the embarkation of the regiment for India on or about February 19th, 1871. In the months of June and July 276 volunteers were received from various corps on the home establishment, and 191 recruits joined in June, July, and August. On October 4th, orders were received for the regiment to proceed to Cork.

On the transfer of General Sir John Aitchison, G.C.B., to the Colonelcy of the Scots Fusilier Guards, General Charles G. J. Arbuthnot, from the 91st Foot, was appointed colonel of the regiment, under date August 27, 1870. On the decease of General C. G. J. Arbuthnot in 1870, Lieutenant-General Charles Gascoyne was appointed colonel of the regiment, under date October 22, 1870.

On January 16th, 1871, the depot of the regiment was formed at Cork, and on the 21st the headquarters and the various companies, with the whole of the women, and children, and heavy baggage of the regiment, under the command of Captain Payn, sailed from Queenstown on board H.M. troop-ship "Crocodile" for India, where the 72nd had so recently won high and well-deserved honours. The regiment arrived at Alexandria on March 7th, and proceeded overland, to Suez, from which, on the 9th, it sailed in the "Jumna" for Bombay. The regiment arrived at Bombay on March 24th, embarked next morning, and proceede in three divisions by rail to Deoleea, where it remained till the 28th. On that and the two following days the regiment proceeded in detachments to Umballah, where it was to be stationed, and where it arrived in the beginning of April.

On May 3rd the regiment paraded for inspection by H.E. the Commander-in-Chief, Lord Napier of Magdala, but owing to the lamentable death of Lieutenant and Adjutant James Thomson—who, it will be remembered, was promoted from the rank of sergeant-major in 1858, for distinguished service in India—who was killed by a fall from his horse on parade, the regiment was dismissed to its quarters. On the evening of that date the remains of the late Lieutenant Thomson were interred in the cemetery, his Excellency the Commander-in-Chief and staff-officers of the garrison, and all the officers and men of the regiment off duty, attending the funeral.

The following regimental mourning order was published by Colonel Payn, C.B., on the occasion of this melancholy occurrence :—" A good and gallant soldier has passed from amongst us, and Colonel Payn is assured that there is no officer, non-commissioned officer, or soldier in the 72nd Highlanders, but feels that in the death of Lieutenant and Adjutant Thomson the regiment has suffered an irretrievable loss. He was endeared to every one from the highest to the lowest for his many estimable qualities, and nobody appreciated his worth and value more than Colonel Payn himself. He had served thirty years as soldier and officer in the 72nd, and was the oldest soldier in it; and the welfare of the regiment was invariably his first thought, his chief desire. He was just and impartial in

carrying out every duty connected with the regiment. His zeal and abilities as an officer were unequalled, and he was killed in the actual performance of his duties on parade, in front of the regiment that he dearly loved, and it will be long before he is forgotten by those whose interests were his chief study."

On December 20th and 21st, the regiment proceeded to the camp of exercise, Delhi, under command of Major Beresford. It was attached to the 1st Brigade 3rd Division, which was commanded by Colonel Payn, the division being under the orders of Major-General Sir Henry Tombs, K.C.B., V.C.

On January 17th, 1872, the regiment was suddenly recalled to Umballah, owing to an outbreak among the Kukah Sikhs. The regiment was highly complimented by the Commander-in-Chief, Lord Napier of Magdala, and Major-General Sir Henry Tombs, for the discipline and efficiency it displayed whilst serving at the camp. On February 9th, the regiment was inspected by Major-General Fraser-Tytler, C.B., at Umballah, when he expressed himself highly pleased with the general efficiency of the regiment.

Having received orders to move to Peshawur, the 72nd left Umballah on the 27th of October 1873, and marched the whole way, a distance of 476 miles, or 46 marches, although there is rail as far as Lahore.

We have much pleasure in being able to present our readers with authentic steel portraits of three of the gallant colonels of this famous regiment :—That of its first Colonel-Commandant, Kenneth, Earl of Seaforth, from a painting by Sir Joshua Reynolds; that of Sir George Murray, G.C.B., and G.C.H., who was for some time also Colonel of the 42nd Royal Highlanders, which is given on the plate of colonels of that regiment; and that of Sir Neil Douglas, K.C.B. and K.C.H., appointed from the 81st Regiment on the 12th of July 1847. This portrait is from a painting by Sir John Watson Gordon, late president of the Royal Scottish Academy.

SUCCESSION LISTS OF COLONELS, FIELD AND STAFF OFFICERS, &c, OF THE 72ND HIGHLANDERS

COLONELS

NAMES	Date of Appointment to Regiment.	Country	Remarks
Kenneth, Earl of Seaforth	29th Dec 1777	Scotland	Lieut -Col Commandant 29th Dec 1777 Died at sea Aug 1781
Thomas Frederick M Humberston	13th Feb 1782	England	Lieut Col 13th Feb 1782 Died 30th April 1783
James Murray	1st Nov 1789	Scotland	Laeut Col 1st Nov 1783, Col 1786, Lieut - Gen 1793 Died 19th March 1794
Sir Adam Williamson, K B,	1st March 1794	Scotland	Lieut General 1797 Died 21st Oct 1798
James Stuart	23d Oct 1798	Scotland	Lieut Col Commandant Feb 1782 Died in 1815
Rowland, Lord Hill, G C B	26th April 1815	England	Removed to 53d Foot 24th Feb 1817
Sir Geo Murray, G C B, G C H	24th Feb 1817	Scotland	Removed to 42d Regiment 6th Sept 1823
Sir John Hope G C H	6th Sept 1823	Scotland	Died at Rothesay, 1st Aug 1836
Sir Cohn Campbell, K C B	15th Aug 1836	Scotland	Died in London, 13th June 1847
Sir Neil Douglas, K C B	12th July 1847	Scotland	Removed to 78th Regiment, 29th Dec 1851
John Aitchison	29th Dec 1851	Scotland	Removed to Scots F Guards, 27th Aug 1870
General C G J Arbuthnot	27th Aug 1870	Scotland	From the 91st Foot, and died in Oct 1870
Charles Gascoyne	22d Oct 1870	England	

LIEUTENANT-COLONELS

H Monckton	18th Jan 1807	England	Appointed Major General
W N Leitch	29th Dec 1814	England	Placed on Half Pay on Reduction, 25th Dec 1818
Felix Calvert	9th Aug 1821	England	Exchanged to Half-Pay, 25th Sept 1826
C G J Arbuthnot	1st Oct 1825	Scotland	Appointed to 90th, 17th May 1831
Thomas Francis Wade	17th May 1831	Ireland	Retired upon Half Pay, 20th April 1832
John Peddie	28th Aug 1837	Scotland	Appointed to 90th, 23d Feb 1838
C G J Arbuthnot	23d Feb 1838	Scotland	Appointed Col in the Army, 28th June 1838
Lord Arthur Lennox	14th April 1843	Scotland	Exchanged to Half-Pay, 25th Feb 1845
Charles Gascoyne	25th Feb 1845	England	Exchanged to Half Pay, 11th Sept 1849
Freeman Murray	11th Sept 1849	Scotland	Exchanged to Half Pay, 5th May 1854
W R Faber	5th May 1854	England	Exchd to 35th, 23d June 1854 Never joined
James Fraser	23d June 1854	Scotland	Retired 1st Dec 1854
R P Sharp	1st Dec 1854	Ireland	Placed on Half Pay by Reduction, 10th Nov 1856
J W Gaisford	22d June 1855	England	Retired 23d Nov 1855
William Parke	23d Nov 1855	England	Exchanged to 53d, 14th Aug 1860
C H Somerset	25th Aug 1857	England	Retired 19th Aug 1862
William Payn	14th Aug 1860	England	Appointed Brigadier-General in India 14th June 1872
Richard Rocke	19th Aug 1862	England	Placed on Half Pay by Reduction, 15th Feb 1866
M De la Pour Beresford	14th June 1872	England	Still serving in 1873

MAJORS

Benjamin Graves	24th Sept 1812	England	Exchanged to 12th Regiment 5th May 1815
John Carter	11th Dec 1813	England	Exchanged to 7th Regiment 27th April 1823,
William Frith	5th May 1815	Ireland	Exchanged to 55th Regiment
John Rolt	29th Aug 1822	Ireland	Appointed Lieut Col unattached
T G Fitzgerald	27th April 1823	Ireland	Retired 26th Aug 1824
M H Drummond	24th July 1823	Scotland	Appointed Lieut Col unattached 16th June 1825 Died on passage to West Indies, 13th Jan 1826
Frederick Brownlow	26th Aug 1824	Ireland	Exchanged to Half Pay, 19th Nov 1825
W L Moberly	19th May 1825	England	Appointed Lieut Col 96th Regiment
Charles Middleton	16th June 1825	Scotland	Appointed Lieut Col unattached 19th Nov 1825

MAJORS—Continued.

NAMES.	Date of Appointment to Regiment.	Country.	Remarks.
George Hall	19th Nov. 1825	England	Exchanged to Half-Pay, 7th Aug. 1835.
C. M. Maclean	1st Feb. 1827	Scotland	Promoted Lieut.-Col. 3d W. I. Regiment.
Frederick Hope	7th Aug. 1835	Scotland	Exchanged to Half-Pay, 27th Sept. 1842.
Henry Jervis	27th Sept. 1842	England	Appointed Lieut.-Col. Provisional Battalion, Chatham.
Richard P. Sharp	8th March 1850	England	Promoted Lieut.-Col. 72nd, 1st Dec. 1854.
J. W. Gaisford	19th July 1850	England	Promoted Lieut.-Col. 72nd, 22d June 1855.
William Parke	1st Dec. 1854	England	Promoted Lieut.-Col. 72nd, 23d Nov. 1855.
James Mackenzie	22d June 1855	Scotland	Died in the East Indies, 5th March 1858.
A. D. Thellusson	23d Nov. 1855	England	Retired 14th Aug. 1860.
Richard Rocke	6th March 1858	England	Promoted Lieut.-Col. 72nd, 19th Aug. 1862.
C. J. W. Norman	14th Aug. 1860	England	Retired 5th March 1861.
Alexander Crombie	5th March 1861	Scotland	Retired 9th Nov. 1866.
T. C. H. Best	19th Aug. 1862	England	Retired 20th Feb. 1863.
Cecil Rice	20th Feb. 1863	England	Promoted Lieut.-Col. Half-Pay, 28th May 1870.
Charles F. Hunter	9th Nov. 1866	Scotland	Retired 14th July 1869.
M. De la Poer Beresford	14th July 1869	England	Promoted Lieut.-Col. 72nd, 14th June 1872.
Francis Brownlow	28th May 1870	Ireland	Still serving in 1873.
W. H. Clarke	14th June 1872	England	Still serving in 1873.

PAYMASTERS.

J. C. C. Irvine	27th Sept. 1810	Ireland	Exchanged to Half-Pay, 15th Oct. 1825.
William Graham	15th Oct. 1825	Scotland	Died in London, 30th Dec. 1848.
Rowland Webster	29th May 1849	England	Appointed to Coast Brigade Royal Artillery.
George Fowler	6th May 1862	England	Resigned.
C. M. Dawes	30th Aug. 1864	England	Exchanged to 30th Regiment.
J. Cassidy	22d Feb. 1871	Scotland	Still serving in 1873.

ADJUTANTS.

Richard Coventry	11th Jan. 1810	England	Appointed to Veteran Battalion 1819.
Henry Jervis	25th May 1819	England	Promoted Captain 19th Sept. 1826.
Michael Adair	19th Sept. 1826	Ireland	Promoted Captain Half-Pay 10th March 1837.
Charles Moylan	14th April 1837	Ireland	Resigned 26th June 1840.
J. T. Hope	26th June 1840	Scotland	Resigned 15th April 1842.
Henry Rice	16th April 1842	England	Promoted Captain 12th Nov. 1847.
Alexander Crombie	24th Dec. 1847	Scotland	Promoted Captain 6th June 1854.
C. C. W. Vesey	25th Aug. 1854	England	Resigned 1st May 1857.
Hon. S. R. H. Ward	1st May 1857	Ireland	Promoted Captain 17th Regt. 10th Sept. 1858
James Thomson	31st Dec. 1858	Scotland	Died 3d May 1871 at Umballa, East Indies: the cause was a fall from his horse, on parade.
T. A. A. Barstow	4th May 1871	Scotland	Still serving in 1873.

QUARTERMASTERS.

William Benton	1st Nov. 1804	Scotland	Retired on Half-Pay 25th July 1822.
George Mackenzie	25th July 1822	Scotland	Exchanged to Half-Pay 26th May 1825.
John Macpherson	9th Sept. 1823	Scotland	Retired on Half-Pay 2d March 1838.
Samuel Brodribb	2d March 1838	England	Appointed to 14th Dragoons.
William Hume	24th April 1838	Scotland	Retired on Half-Pay 23d July 1847.
John Lindsay	23d July 1847	Scotland	Died at Barbadoes, 21st Nov. 1848.
Michael Boden	20th April 1849	Ireland	Retired 30th April 1852.
John Macdonald	30th April 1852	Scotland	Died of wounds received in the trenches before Sevastopol 8th Sept. 1855.
Donald Munro	30th Nov. 1855	Scotland	Exchanged to 91st Highlanders.
Peter Murray	24th Jan. 1865	Scotland	Exchanged to 10th Regiment.
T. H. Smith	30th Sept. 1868	Scotland	Still serving in 1873.

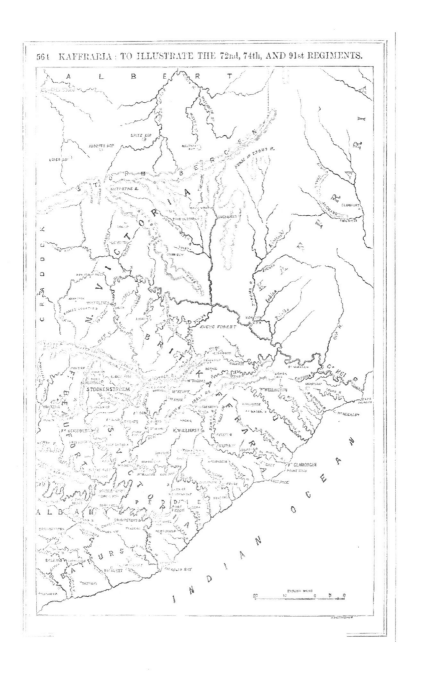

ABERDEENSHIRE HIGHLAND REGIMENT,

OR

OLD EIGHTY-FIRST.

1777—1783.

THIS regiment was raised by the Honourable Colonel William Gordon, brother of the Earl of Aberdeen, to whom letters of service were granted for that purpose in December 1777. Of 980 men composing the regiment, 650 were from the Highlands of Aberdeenshire. The clan Ross mustered strongly under Major Ross; when embodied it was found that there were nine men of the name of John Ross in the regiment.

The corps was marched to Stirling, whence it was removed to Ireland, where the regiment continued three years. In the end of 1782 it was removed to England, and in March of the following year embarked at Portsmouth for the East Indies immediately after the preliminaries of peace were signed, notwithstanding the terms of agreement, which were the same as those made with the Athole Highlanders. The men, however, seemed satisfied with their destination, and it was not until they became acquainted with the conduct of the Athole men, that they refused to proceed. Government yielded to their demand to be discharged, and they were accordingly marched to Scotland, and disbanded at Edinburgh in April 1783. Their conduct during their existence was as exemplary as that of the other Highland regiments.

ROYAL HIGHLAND EMIGRANT REGIMENT,

OR

OLD EIGHTY-FOURTH.

1775—1783.

Two Battalions—First Battalion—Quebec—Second Battalion—Settle in Canada and Nova Scotia.

THIS battalion was to be raised from the Highland emigrants in Canada, and the discharged men of the 42nd, of Fraser's and Montgomery's Highlanders, who had settled in North America after the peace of 1763. Lieutenant

Colonel Alan Maclean (son of Torloish), of the late 104th Highland Regiment, was appointed lieutenant-colonel commandant of the first battalion. Captain John Small, formerly of the 42nd, and then of the 21st Regiment, was appointed major-commandant of the second battalion, which was to be raised from emigrants and discharged Highland soldiers who had settled in Nova Scotia. Each battalion was to consist of 750 men, with officers in proportion. The commissions were dated the 14th of June 1775.

Great difficulty was experienced in conveying the recruits who had been raised in the back settlements to their respective destinations. A detachment from Carolina was obliged to relinquish an attempt to cross a bridge defended by cannon, in which Captain Macleod, its commander, and a number of the men were killed. Those who escaped reached their destination by different routes.

When assembled, the first battalion, consisting of 350 men, was detached up the River St Lawrence, but hearing that the American General Arnold intended to enter Canada with 3000 men, Colonel Maclean returned with his battalion by forced marches, and entered Quebec on the 13th of November 1776. The garrison of Quebec, previous to the arrival of Colonel Maclean, consisted of only 50 men of the Fusiliers and 700 militia and seamen. General Arnold, who had previously crossed the river, made a spirited attempt on the night of the 14th to get possession of the outworks of the city, but was repulsed with loss, and forced to retire to Point au Tremble.

Having obtained a reinforcement of troops under General Montgomery, Arnold resolved upon an assault. Accordingly, on the 31st of December he advanced towards the city, and attacked it in two places, but was completely repulsed at both points. In this affair General Montgomery, who led one of the points of attack, was killed, and Arnold wounded.

Foiled in this attempt, General Arnold took up a position on the heights of Abraham, and by intercepting all supplies, reduced the garrison to great straits. He next turned the blockade into a siege, and having erected batteries, made several attempts to get possession of the lower town; but Colonel Maclean, to whom the defence of the place had been entrusted by General Guy Carlton, the commander-in-chief, defeated him at every point[9] After these failures General Arnold raised the siege and evacuated Canada.

The battalion after this service was employed in various small enterprises during the war, in which they were generally successful They remained so faithful to their trust, that notwithstanding that every inducement was held out to them to join the revolutionary standard, not one native Highlander deserted Only one man was brought to the halberts during the time the regiment was embodied

Major Small, being extremely popular with the Highlanders, was very successful in Nova Scotia, and his corps contained a greater proportion of them than the first battalion Of ten companies which composed the second battalion, five remained in Nova Scotia and the neighbouring settlements during the war, and the other five, including the flank companies joined the armies of General Clinton and Lord Cornwallis The grenadier company was in the battalion, which at Eataw Springs " drove all before them," as stated in his despatches by Colonel Alexander Stuart of the 3d Regiment

In the year 1778 the regiment, which had hitherto been known only as the Royal Highland Emigrants, was numbered the 84th, and orders were issued to augment the battalions to 1000 men each Sir Henry Clinton was appointed colonel in chief The uniform was the full Highland garb, with purse of racoon's skin The officers wore the broad sword and dirk, and the men a half-basket sword At the peace the officers and men received grants of land, in the proportion of 5000 acres to a field officer, 3000 to a captain, 500 to a subaltern, 200 to a sergeant, and 100 to a private soldier The men of the first battalion settled in Canada, and those of the second in Nova Scotia, forming a settlement which they named Douglas Many of the officers, however, returned home

[9] Colonel Maclean, when a subaltern in the Scotch brigade in Holland, was particularly noticed by Count Lowendahl for his bravery at Bergen op-Zoom in 1774 See the notice of Loudon's Highlanders

FORTY-SECOND OR ROYAL HIGHLAND REGIMENT
SECOND BATTALION
NOW THE SEVENTY THIRD REGIMENT
1780—1809

Raising of the Regiment—First list of Officers—St Iago—India—Ponanee—Bednoor—Anantapoor—Mangalore — Jillycherry — Bombay — Dinapore—Cawnpore— Fort-William—Seringapatam—Pondicherry—Ceylon—Madras—Mysore—Home—Ceases to be a Highland Regiment

ABOUT 1780 the situation of Great Britain was extremely critical, as she had not only to sustain a war in Europe, but also to defend her vast possessions in North America and the East Indies In this emergency Government looked towards the north for aid, and although nearly 13,000 warriors had been drawn from the country north of the Tay, within the previous eighteen months, it determined again to draw upon the Highland population, by adding a second battalion to the 42nd regiment

The following officers were appointed to the battalion —

Colonel—Lord John Murray, died in 1787, the oldest General in the army

Lieutenant Colonel—Norman Macleod of Macleod, died in 1801, a Lieutenant General

Major—Patrick Græme, son of Inchbraco, died in 1781

Captains

Hay Macdowall, son of Garthland, a lieut -gen, who was lost on his passage from India in 1809	John Macgregor
	Cohn Campbell, son of Glenure
James Murray, died in 1781	Thomas Dalyell, killed at Mangalore in 1783
John Gregor	David Lindsay
James Drummond, afterwards Lord Perth, died in 1800	John Grant, son of Glenormiston, died in 1801

Lieutenants

John Grant	John Wemyss, died in 1781
Alexander Macgregor of Balhaldy, died Major of the 65th regiment in 1795	Alexander Dunbar, died in 1783
Dugald Campbell, retired in 1787	John Oswald [1]
	Æneas Fraser, died captain, 1784
James Spens, retired Lieutenant-Colonel of the 72d regiment in 1798	Alexander Maitland
	Alexander Ross, retired in 1784

Ensigns

Charles Sutherland	William White
John Murray Robertson	Charles Maclean
Alexander Macdonald	John Macpherson, killed at Mangalore
Robert Robertson	
John Macdonald	

[1] This officer, the son of a goldsmith in Edinburgh, was very eccentric in his habits He became a furious republican, and going to France on the breaking out of the revolution, was killed in 1793 in La Vendée at the head of a ... of ... he had obtained ...

Chaplain.—John Stewart, died in 1781.
Surgeon.—Thomas Farquharson.
Adjutant.—Robert Leslie.
Mate.—Duncan Campbell.
Quarter-master.—Kenneth Mackenzie, killed at
Mangalore.

The name of the 42nd Regiment was a sufficient inducement to the Highlanders to enter the service, and on the 21st of March 1780, only about three months after the appointment of the officers, the battalion was raised, and soon afterwards embodied at Perth.

In December the regiment embarked at Queensferry, to join an expedition then fitting out at Portsmouth, against the Cape of Good Hope, under the command of Major-General William Meadows and Commodore Johnstone. The expedition sailed on the 12th of March 1781, and falling in with the French squadron under Admiral Suffrein at St Iago, was there attacked by the enemy, who were repulsed. Suffrein, however, got the start of the expedition, and the commander, finding that he had reached the Cape before them, proceeded to India, having previously captured a valuable convoy of Dutch East Indiamen, which had taken shelter in Saldanha Bay. As the troops had not landed, their right to a share of the prize-money was disputed by the commodore, but after a lapse of many years the objection was overruled.

The expedition, with the exception of the "Myrtle" transport, which separated from the fleet in a gale of wind off the Cape, arrived at Bombay on the 5th of March 1782, after a twelve months' voyage, and on the 13th of April sailed for Madras. The regiment suffered considerably on the passage from the scurvy, and from a fever caught in the island of Joanna; and on reaching Calcutta, 5 officers, including Major Patrick Græme, and 116 non-commissioned officers and privates had died.

Some time after the arrival of the expedition, a part of the troops, with some native corps, were detached against Palghatcheri, under Lieutenant-Colonel Mackenzie Humberston of the 100th Regiment, in absence of Lieutenant-Colonel Macleod, who, being on board the Myrtle, had not yet arrived. The troops in this expedition, of which seven companies of the Highlanders formed a part, took the field on the 2nd of September 1782, and

after taking several small forts on their march, arrived before Palaghatcheri on the 19th of October. Finding the place much stronger than he expected, and ascertaining that Tippoo Sahib was advancing with a large force to its relief, Colonel Humberston retired towards Ponanee, closely pursued by the enemy, and blew up the forts of Mangaracotah and Ramgurh in the retreat.

At Ponanee the command was assumed by Lieutenant-Colonel Macleod. The effective force was reduced by sickness to 380 Europeans, and 2200 English and Travancore sepoys, and in this situation the British commander found himself surrounded by 10,000 cavalry and 14,000 infantry, including two corps of Europeans, under the French General Lally. Colonel Macleod attempted to improve by art the defences of a position strong by nature, but before his works were completed, General Lally made a spirited attack on the post on the morning of the 29th of November, at the head of the European troops: after a warm contest he was repulsed.

The conduct of the Highlanders, against whom Lally directed his chief attack, is thus noticed in the general orders issued on the occasion :—" The intrepidity with which Major Campbell and the Highlanders repeatedly charged the enemy, was most honourable to their character." In this affair the 42nd had 3 sergeants and 19 rank and file killed, and Major John Campbell, Captains Colin Campbell and Thomas Dalyell, Lieutenant Charles Sutherland, 2 sergeants, and 31 rank and file wounded.

After this service, Colonel Macleod with his battalion embarked for Bombay, and joined the army under Brigadier-General Matthews at Cundapoor, on the 9th of January 1793. On the 23rd General Matthews moved forward to attack Bednoor, from which the Sultan drew most of his supplies for his army. General Matthews was greatly harassed on his march by flying parties of the enemy, and in crossing the mountains was much impeded by the nature of the country, and by a succession of field-works erected on the face of these mountains. On the 26th of February, the 42nd, led by Colonel Macleod, and followed by a corps of sepoys, attacked these positions with the bayonet, and were in the breastwork before the enemy were aware of it. Four hundred of the enemy were bayonetted, and the rest were pursued to the walls of the fort. Seven forts were attacked and taken in this manner in succession. The principal redoubt, distinguished by the appellation of Hyder Gurh, situated on the summit of the highest ghaut or precipice, presented a more formidable appearance. It had a dry ditch in front, mounted with twenty pieces of cannon, and might have offered considerable resistance to the advance of the army, if well defended; but the loss of their seven batteries had so terrified the enemy, that they abandoned their last and strongest position in the course of the night, leaving behind them eight thousand stand of new arms, and a considerable quantity of powder, shot, and military stores. The army took possession of Bednoor the following day, but this triumph was of short duration, as the enemy soon recaptured the place, and took General Matthews and the greater part of his army prisoners.

Meanwhile the other companies were employed with a detachment under Major Campbell, in an enterprise against the fort of Anantapoor, which was attacked and carried on the 15th of February with little loss. Major Campbell returned his thanks to the troops for their spirited behaviour on this occasion, "and his particular acknowledgments to Captain Dalyell, and the officers and men of the flank companies of the 42nd regiment, who headed the storm." As the Highlanders on this occasion had trusted more to their fire than to the bayonet, the major strongly recommended to them in future never to fire a shot when the bayonet could be used.

The Highlanders remained at Anantapoor till the end of February, when they were sent under Major Campbell to occupy Carrical and Morebedery. They remained in these two small forts till the 12th of April, when they were marched first to Goorspoor and thence to Mangalore. Here the command of the troops, in consequence of the absence of Lieutenant-Colonels Macleod and Humberston devolved upon Major Campbell, now promoted to the brevet rank of lieutenant-colonel. General Matthews having been suspended, Colonel Macleod, now promoted to the rank of brigadier-general, was appointed to succeed him.

Encouraged by the recapture of Bednoor, Tippoo detached a considerable force towards Mangalore, but it was attacked and defeated by Colonel Campbell, on the 6th of May. Little loss was sustained on either side, but the enemy left all their guns. The Highlanders had 7 privates killed, and Captain William Stewart and 16 rank and file wounded.

Tippoo, having now no force in the field to oppose him, advanced upon Mangalore with his whole army, consisting of 90,000 men, besides a corps of European infantry from the Isle of France, a troop of dismounted French cavalry from the Mauritius, and Lally's corps of Europeans and natives. This immense force was supported by eighty pieces of cannon. The garrison of Mangalore was in a very sickly state, there being only 21 sergeants, 12 drummers, and 210 rank and file of king's troops, and 1500 natives fit for duty.

With the exception of a strong outpost about a mile from Mangalore, the place was completely invested by the Sultan's army about the middle of May. The defence of the outpost was intrusted to some sepoys, but they were obliged to abandon it on the 23rd. The siege was now prosecuted with vigour, and many attacks were made, but the garrison, though suffering the severest privations, repulsed every attempt. Having succeeded at length in making large breaches in the walls, and reducing some parts of them to a mass of ruins, the enemy repeatedly attempted to enter the breaches and storm the place; but they were uniformly forced to retire, sustaining a greater loss by every successive attack. On the 20th of July a cessation of hostilities was agreed to, but on the 23rd the enemy violated the truce by springing a mine. Hostilities were then resumed, and continued till the 29th, when a regular armistice was entered into. Brigadier-General Macleod anchored in the bay on the 17th of August, with a small convoy of provisions and a reinforcement of troops; but on learning the terms of the armistice, the general, from a feeling of honour, ordered the ships back to Tellicherry, to the great disappointment of the half-famished garrison. Two reinforcements which arrived off the coast successively on the 22nd of November, and the last day of December, also returned to the places whence they had come.

About this time, in consequence of the peace with France, Colonel Cossigny, the French commander, withdrew his troops, to the great displeasure of the Sultan, who encouraged the French soldiers to desert and join his standard. Some of them accordingly deserted, but Colonel Cossigny having recovered part of them, indicated his dissatisfaction with Tippoo's conduct, by ordering them to be shot in presence of two persons sent by the Sultan to intercede for their lives.

The misery of the garrison was now extreme. Nearly one-half of the troops had been carried off, and one-half of the survivors were in the hospital. The sepoys in particular were so exhausted that many of them dropped down in the act of shouldering their firelocks, whilst others became totally blind. Despairing of aid, and obliged to eat horses, frogs, dogs, crows, cat-fish, black grain, &c., the officers resolved, in a council of war, to surrender the place. The terms, which were highly honourable to the garrison, were acceded to by the Sultan, and the capitulation was signed on the 30th of January 1784, after a siege of nearly nine months. In the defence of Mangalore, the Highlanders had Captain Dalyell, Lieutenants Macpherson, Mackenzie, and Mackintyre, 1 piper and 18 soldiers killed; and Captains William Stewart, Robert John Napier, and Lieutenants Murray, Robertson, and Welsh, 3 sergeants, 1 piper, and 47 rank and file wounded. The corps also lost Mr Dennis the acting chaplain, who was shot in the forehead by a matchlock ball whilst standing behind a breastwork of sand-bags, and looking at the enemy through a small aperture.

Alluding to the siege of Mangalore, Colonel Fullarton says that the garrison, under its estimable commander, Colonel Campbell, "made a defence that has seldom been equalled, and never surpassed;" and Colonel Lindsay observes, in his Military Miscellany, that "the defence of Colberg in Pomerania, by Major Heiden and his small garrison, and that of Mangalore in the East Indies, by Colonel Campbell and the second battalion of the Royal Highlanders, now the 73rd regiment,

are as noble examples as any in history." The East India Company showed a due sense of the services of the garrison, by ordering a monument to be erected to the memory of Colonel Campbell,[2] Captains Stewart and Dalyell, and those who fell at the siege, and giving a handsome gratuity to the survivors.

The battalion embarked for Tellicherri on the 4th of February 1784, where it remained till April, when it departed for Bombay. It was afterwards stationed at Dinapoor in Bengal, when, on the 18th of April 1786, the battalion was formed into a separate corps, with green facings, under the denomination of the 73rd regiment, the command of which was given to Sir George Osborne. It was at first intended to reduce the junior officers of both battalions, instead of putting all the officers of the second on half-pay; but on representations being made by the officers of both battalions, the arrangement alluded to was made to save the necessity of putting any of the officers on half-pay.

In December 1787, the 73rd removed to Cawnpore, where it remained till March 1790, when it was sent to Fort William in Bengal. Next year the regiment joined the army in Malabar, under the command of Major-General Robert Abercromby. Major Macdowall being about this time promoted to the 57th, was succeeded by Captain James Spens.

With the view of attacking Seringapatam, Lord Cornwallis directed General Abercromby to join him with all his disposable force, consisting of the 73rd, 75th, and 77th British, and seven native regiments. He accordingly began his march on the 5th of December 1791, but owing to various causes he did not join the main army till the 16th of February following. The enemy having been repulsed before Seringapatam on the 22nd, entered into preliminaries of peace on the 24th, when the war ended.

[2] Colonel Campbell died at Bombay. His father, Lord Stonefield, a lord of session, had seven sons, and the colonel was the eldest. After the surrender of Mangalore the Sultan showed him great courtesy, and, after deservedly complimenting him upon his gallant defence, presented him with an Arabian charger and sabre. Tippoo had, however, little true generosity of disposition, and the cruelties which he inflicted on General M'Gowr and his army show that he was second to his father Hyder.

The 73rd was employed in the expedition against Pondicherry in 1793, when it formed part of Colonel David Baird's brigade The regiment, though much reduced by sickness, had received from time to time several detachments of recruits from Scotland, and at this period it was 800 strong In the enterprise against Pondicherry, Captain Galpine, Lieutenant Donald Macgregor, and Ensign Tod were killed

The 73rd formed part of the force sent against Ceylon in the year 1793, under Major General James Stuart It remained in the island till 1797, when it returned to Madras, and was quartered in various parts of that presidency till 1799, when it joined the army under General Harris

This army encamped at Mallavelly on the 27th of March, on which day a battle took place with the Sultan, Tippoo, whose army was totally routed, with the loss of 1000 men, whilst that of the British was only 69 men killed and wounded Advancing slowly, the British army arrived in the neighbourhood of the Mysore capital, Seringapatam, on the 5th of April, and took up a position preparatory to a siege, the third within the space of a few years The enemy's advanced troops and rocket-men gave some annoyance to the picquets the same evening, but they were driven back next morning by two columns under the Hon Colonel Arthur Wellesley and Colonel Shaw , an attempt made by the same officers the previous evening having miscarried, in consequence of the darkness of the night and some unexpected obstructions The Bombay army joined on the 30th, and took up a position in the line, the advanced posts being within a thousand yards of the garrison A party of the 73th, under Colonel Hart, having dislodged the enemy on the 17th, established themselves under cover within a thousand yards of the fort , whilst at the same time, Major Macdonald of the 73rd, with a detachment of his own and other regiments, took possession of a post at the same distance from the fort on the south On the evening of the 20th, another detachment, under Colonels Sherbrooke, St John, and Monypenny, drove 2000 of the enemy from an entrenched position within eight hundred

yards of the place, with the loss of only 5 killed and wounded, whilst that of the enemy was 250 men On the 22nd the enemy made a vigorous though unsuccessful sortie on all the advanced posts They renewed the attempt several times, but were as often repulsed with great loss Next day the batteries opened with such effect that all the guns opposed to them were silenced in the course of a few hours The siege was continued with unabated vigour till the morning of the 4th of May, when it was resolved to attempt an assault Major General Baird, who, twenty years before, had been kept a prisoner in chains in the city he was now to storm, was appointed to command the assailants, who were to advance in two columns under Colonels Dunlop and Sherbrooke , the Hon Colonel Arthur Wellesley commanding the reserve The whole force amounted to 4376 firelocks Everything being in readiness, at one o'clock in the afternoon the troops waited the signal, and on its being given they rushed impetuously forward, and in less than two hours Seringapatam was in possession of the British The Sultan and a number of his chief officers fell whilst defending the capital In this gallant assault, Lieutenant Lalor of the 73rd was killed, and Captain William Macleod, Lieutenant Thomas, and Ensigns Antill and Guthrie of the same regiment, were wounded

Nothing now remained to complete the subjugation of Mysore but to subdue a warlike chief who had taken up arms in support of the Sultan Colonel Wellesley was detached against him with the 73rd and some other troops, when his army was dispersed, and the chief himself killed in a charge of cavalry

In 1805 the regiment was ordered home, but such of the men as were inclined to remain in India were offered a bounty The result was that most of them volunteered, and the few that remained embarked at Madras for England, and arrived at Gravesend in July 1806 The remains of the regiment arrived at Perth in 1807, and in 1809 the ranks were filled up to 800 men, and a second battalion was added The uniform and designation of the corps was then changed, and it ceased to be a Highland regiment

74th HIGHLANDERS.

1787–1846.

I.

Raising of Four new Regiments—Original establishment of Officers of 74th—Goes to India—Mysore—Kistnagherry—Seringapatam—Incident at Pondicherry—Patriotic Liberality of the 74th—Seringapatam again—Storming of Ahmednuggur—Battle of Assaye—Battle of Argaum—Return home—Captain Cargill's recollections—Highland dress laid aside—The Peninsula—Busaco—Various skirmishes—Fuentes d'Onor—Badajoz—Cindad Rodrigo—Badajoz—Salamanca—Vitoria—Roncesvalles—Nivelle—Nive—Orthes—Toulouse—Home—Medals—Burning of the old colours—Nova Scotia—The Bermudas—Ireland—Barbadoes—West Indies—North America—England—Highland garb restored.

Assaye (with the elephant).	Salamanca.
Seringapatam.	Vitoria.
Busaco.	Pyrenees.
Fuentes d'Onor.	Nivelle.
Ciudad Rodrigo.	Orthes.
Badajoz.	Toulouse.
	Peninsula.

In the year 1787 four new regiments were ordered to be raised for the service of the state, to be numbered the 74th, 75th, 76th, and 77th. The first two were directed to be raised in the north of Scotland, and were to be Highland regiments. The regimental establishment of each was to consist of ten companies of 75 men each, with the customary number of commissioned and non-commissioned officers. Major-General Sir Archibald Campbell, K.B., from the half-pay of Fraser's Highlanders, was appointed colonel of the 74th regiment.[1]

The establishment of the regiment was fixed at ten companies, consisting of—

[1] Leader on the next page.

1 Colonel and Captain.	1 Adjutant.
1 Lieutenant-Colonel and Captain.	1 Quartermaster.
	1 Surgeon.
1 Major and Captain.	2 Surgeon's Mates.
7 Captains.	30 Sergeants.
1 Captain-Lieutenant.	40 Corporals.
21 Lieutenants.	20 Drummers.
8 Ensigns.	2 Fifers, and
1 Chaplain.	716 Privates.

A recruiting company was afterwards added, which consisted of—

1 Captain.	8 Corporals.
2 Lieutenants.	4 Drummers.
1 Ensign.	30 Privates.
8 Sergeants.	

Total of Officers and Men of all ranks, 902.

The regiment was styled "The 74th Highland Regiment of Foot." The uniform was the full Highland garb of kilt and feathered bonnet, the tartan being similar to that of the 42nd regiment, and the facings white; the use of the kilt was, however, discontinued in the East Indies, as being unsuited to the climate.

The following were the officers first appointed to the regiment:—

Colonel—Archibald Campbell, K.B.
Lieutenant-Colonel—Gordon Forbes.

Captains.

Dugald Campbell.	William Wallace.
Alexander Campbell.	Robert Wood.
Archibald Campbell.	

Captain-Lieutenant and Captain—Heneage Twysden.

Lieutenants.

James Clark.	John Alexander.
Charles Campbell.	Samuel Swinton.
John Campbell.	John Campbell.
Thomas Carnie.	Charles Campbell.
W. Coningsby Davies.	George Henry Vansittart.
Dugald Lamont.	Archibald Campbell.

Ensigns.

John Forbes.	John Wallace.
Alexander Stewart.	Hugh M'Pherson.
James Campbell.	

Chaplain—John Ferguson.
Adjutant—Samuel Swinton.
Quartermaster—James Clark.
Surgeon—William Henderson.

As the state of affairs in India required that reinforcements should be immediately despatched to that country, all the men who had been embodied previous to January 1788 were ordered for embarkation, without waiting for the full complement. In consequence of these orders, 400 men, about one-half Highlanders, embarked at Grangemouth, and sailed from Chatham for the East Indies, under the command of Captain William Wallace. The regiment having been completed in autumn, the recruit followed in February 1789, and arrived at Madras in June in perfect health. They joined the first detachment at the cantonments of Poonamallee, and thus united, the corps amounted to 750 men. These were now trained under Lieutenant-Colonel Maxwell, who had succeeded Lieutenant-Colonel Forbes in the command, and who had acquired some experience in the training of soldiers as captain in Fraser's Highlanders.

In connection with the main army under Lord Cornwallis, the Madras army under General Meadows, of which the 74th formed a part, began a series of movements in the spring

Major General Sir Archibald Campbell, Bart., K.C.B.
From a painting by J. C. Wood.

of 1790. The defence of the passes leading into the Carnatic from Mysore was intrusted to Colonel Kelly, who, besides his own corps, had under him the 74th; but he dying in September, Colonel Maxwell [2] succeeded to the command.

The 74th was put in brigade with the 71st and 72nd Highland regiments. The regiment

[2] This able officer was son of Sir William Maxwell of Monreith, and brother of the Duchess of Gordon. He died at Culloden in 1783.

suffered no loss in the different movements which took place till the storming of Bangalore, on the 21st of March 1791. The whole loss of the British, however, was only 5 men. After the defeat of Tippoo Sahib at Seringapatam, on the 15th of May 1791, the army, in consequence of bad weather and scarcity of provisions, retreated upon Bangalore, reaching that place in July.

The 74th was detached from the army at Nundeedroog on the 21st of October, with three Sepoy battalions and some field artillery, under Lieutenant-Colonel Maxwell, into the Baramahal country, which this column was ordered to clear of the enemy. They reached the south end of the valley by forced marches, and took the strong fort of Penagurh by escalade on the 31st of October, and after scouring the whole of the Baramahal to the southward, returned towards Caverypooram, and encamped within five miles of the strong fort of Kistnagherry, 50 miles S.E. of Bangalore, on the 7th of November. Lieutenant-Colonel Maxwell determined on attacking the lower fort and town immediately, and the column advanced from the camp to the attack in three divisions at ten o'clock on that night; two of these were sent to the right and left to attack the lower fort on the western and eastern sides, while the centre division advanced directly towards the front wall. The divisions approached close to the walls before they were discovered, succeeded in escalading them, and got possession of the gates. The enemy fled to the upper fort without making much resistance, and the original object of the attack was thus gained. But a most gallant attempt was made by Captain Wallace of the 74th, who commanded the right division, to carry the almost inaccessible upper fort also. His division rushed up in pursuit of the fugitives; and notwithstanding the length and steepness of the ascent, his advanced party followed the enemy so closely that they had barely time to shut the gates. Their standard was taken on the steps of the gateway; but as the ladders had not been brought forward in time, it was impossible to escalade before the enemy recovered from their panic.

During two hours, repeated trials were made to get the ladders up, but the enemy hurling down showers of rocks and stones into the road, broke the ladders, and crushed those who carried them. Unluckily, a clear moonlight discovered every movement, and at length, the ladders being all destroyed, and many officers and men disabled in carrying them, Lieutenant-Colonel Maxwell found it necessary to order a discontinuance of the assault.

The retreat of the men who had reached the gate, and of the rest of the troops, was conducted with such regularity, that a party which sallied from the fort in pursuit of them was immediately driven back. The pettah, or lower town, was set fire to, and the troops withdrawn to their camp before daylight on the 8th of November.

The following were the casualties in the regiment on this occasion:—Killed, 2 officers, 1 sergeant, 5 rank and file; wounded, 3 officers, 47 non-commissioned officers and men. The officers killed were Lieutenants Forbes and Lamont; those wounded, Captain Wallace, Lieutenants M'Kenzie and Aytone.

The column having also reduced several small forts in the district of Ossoor, rejoined the army on the 30th of November.

In the second attempt on Seringapatam, on the 6th of February 1792, the 74th, with the 52nd regiment and 71st Highlanders, formed the centre under the immediate orders of the Commander-in-Chief. Details of these operations, and others elsewhere in India, in which the 74th took part at this time, have already been given in our accounts of the 71st and 72nd regiments. The 74th on this occasion had 2 men killed, and Lieutenant Farquhar, Ensign Hamilton, and 17 men wounded.

On the termination of hostilities this regiment returned to the coast. In July 1793 the flank companies were embodied with those of the 71st in the expedition against Pondicherry. The following interesting episode, as related in Cannon's account of the regiment, occurred after the capture of Pondicherry:—

The 74th formed part of the garrison, and the French troops remained in the place as prisoners of war. Their officers were of the old *régime*, and were by birth and in manners gentlemen, to whom it was incumbent to show every kindness and hospitality. It was found, however, that both officers and men, and the French population generally, were strongly tinctured with the revolutionary mania, and some uneasiness was felt lest the same should be in any degree imbibed by the British soldiers. It happened that the officers of the 74th were in the theatre, when a French officer called for the revolutionary air, "*Ça Ira*;" this was opposed by some of the British, and there was every appearance of a serious disturbance, both parties being highly excited. The 74th, being in a body, had an opportunity to consult, and to act with effect. Having taken their resolution, two or three of them made their way to the orchestra, the rest taking post at the doors, and, having obtained silence, the senior officer addressed the house in a firm but conciliatory manner. He stated that the national tune called for by one of the company ought not to be objected to, and that, as an act of courtesy to the ladies and others who had seconded the request, he and his brother officers were determined to support it with every mark of respect, and called upon their countrymen to do the same. It was accordingly played with the most uproarious applause on the part of the French, the British officers standing up uncovered; but the moment it was finished, the house was called upon by the same party again to uncover to the British national air, "God save the King." They now appealed to the French, reminding them that each had their national attachments and recollections of home; that love of country was an honourable principle, and should be respected in each other; and that they felt assured their respected friends would not be behind in that courtesy which had just been shown by the British. Bravo! Bravo! resounded from every part of the house, and from that moment all rankling was at an end. They lived in perfect harmony till the French embarked, and each party retained their sentiments as a thing peculiar to their own country, but without the slightest offence on either side, or expectation that they should assimilate, more than if they related to the colour of their uniforms.

As a set-off to this, it is worth recording that in 1798, when voluntary contributions for the support of the war with France were being offered to Government from various parts of the British dominions, the privates of the 74th, of their own accord, handsomely and patriotically contributed eight days' pay to assist in carrying on the war,—"a war," they said, "unprovoked on our part, and justified by the noblest of motives, the preservation of our individual constitution." The sergeants and corporals, animated by similar sentiments, subscribed a fortnight's, and the officers a month's pay each.

of this campaign, and had its full share in the storming of Seringapatam on the 4th of May 1799.

The troops for the assault, commanded by Major-General Baird, were divided into two columns of attack.[9] The 74th, with the 73rd regiment, 4 European flank companies, 14 Sepoy flank companies, with 50 artillerymen, formed the right column, under Colonel Sherbroke. Each column was preceded by 1 sergeant and 12 men, volunteers, supported by an advanced party of 1 subaltern and 25 men. Lieutenant Hill, of the 74th, commanded the advanced party of the right column. After the successful storm and cap-

Plan of the
BATTLE OF ASSAYE,
SEPT. 23, 1803.

A, the ford from Peepulgaon to Warroor; B, the rising ground which protected the advance; C, four old mangoes; D, screen of prickly pear, covering Assaye; E E E E 50,000 of the enemy's cavalry.

Besides reinforcements of recruits from Scotland fully sufficient to compensate all casualties, the regiment received, on the occasion of the 71st being ordered home to Europe, upwards of 200 men from that regiment. By these additions the strength of the 74th was kept up, and the regiment, as well in the previous campaign as in the subsequent one under General Harris, was one of the most effective in the field.

The 74th was concerned in all the operations

ture of the fortress, the 74th was the first regiment that entered the palace.

The casualties of the regiment during the siege were:—Killed, 5 officers, and 45 non-commissioned officers and men. Wounded, 4 officers, and 111 non-commissioned officers and men. Officers killed, Lieutenants Irvine, Farquhar, Hill, Shaw, Prendergast. Officers

_____

[9] For further details see the history of the 73rd regiment page 570, vol. ii.

wounded, Lieutenants Fletcher, Aytone, Maxwell, Carrington.

The regiment received the royal authority to bear the word "Seringapatam" on its regimental colour and appointments in commemoration of its services at this siege.

The 74th had not another opportunity of distinguishing itself till the year 1803, when three occasions occurred. The first was on the 8th of August, when the fortress of Ahmednuggur, then in possession of Sindiah, the Mahratta chief, was attacked, and carried by assault by the army detached under the Hon. Major-General Sir Arthur Wellesley. In this affair the 74th, which formed a part of the brigade commanded by Colonel Wallace, bore a distinguished part, and gained the special thanks of the Major-General and the Governor-General.

The next was the battle of Assaye, fought on the 23rd of September. On that day Major-General the Hon. Arthur Wellesley attacked the whole combined Mahratta army of Sindiah and the Rajah of Berar, at ASSAYE, on the banks of the Kaitna river. The Mahratta force, of 40,000 men, was completely defeated by a force of 5000, of which not more than 2000 were Europeans, losing 98 pieces of cannon, 7 standards, and leaving 1200 killed, and about four times that number wounded on the field. The conduct of the 74th in this memorable battle was most gallant and distinguished; but from having been prematurely led against the village of Assaye on the left of the enemy's line, the regiment was exposed, unsupported, to a most terrible cannonade, and being afterwards charged by cavalry, sustained a tremendous loss.

In this action, the keenest ever fought in India, the 74th had Captains D. Aytone, Andrew Dyce, Roderick Macleod, John Maxwell; Lieutenants John Campbell, John Morshead Campbell, Lorn Campbell, James Grant, J. Morris, Robert Neilson, Volunteer Tew, 9 sergeants, and 127 rank and file killed; and Major Samuel Swinton, Captains Norman Moore, Matthew Shawe, John Alexander Main, Robert Macmurdo, J. Longland, Ensign Kearnon, 11 sergeants, 7 drummers, and 270 rank and file wounded. "Every officer present," says Cannon, "with the regiment

was either killed or wounded, except Quartermaster James Grant, who, when he saw so many of his friends fall in the battle, resolved to share their fate, and, though a non-combatant, joined the ranks and fought to the termination of the action." Besides expressing his indebtedness to the 74th in his despatch to the Governor-General, Major-General Wellesley added the following to his memorandum on the battle :—

"However, by one of those unlucky accidents which frequently happen, the officer commanding the piquets which were upon the right led immediately up to the village of Assaye. The 74th regiment, which was on the right of the second line, and was ordered to support the piquets, followed them. There was a large break in our line between these corps and those on our left. They were exposed to a most terrible cannonade from Assaye, and were charged by the cavalry belonging to the Campoos; consequently in the piquets and the 74th regiment we sustained the greatest part of our loss.

"Another bad consequence resulting from this mistake was the necessity of introducing the cavalry into the action at too early a period. I had ordered it to watch the motions of the enemy's cavalry hanging upon our right, and luckily it charged in time to save the remains of the 74th and the piquets."

The names especially of Lieutenants-Colonel Harness and Wallace were mentioned with high approbation both by Wellesley and the Governor-General. The Governor-General ordered that special honorary colours be presented to the 74th and 78th, who were the only European infantry employed "on that glorious occasion," with a device suited to commemorate the signal and splendid victory.

The device on the special colour awarded to the 74th appears at the head of this account. The 78th for some reason ceased to make use of its third colour after it left India, so that the 74th is now probably the only regiment in the British army that possesses such a colour, an honour of which it may well be proud.

Captain A. B. Campbell of the 74th, who had on a former occasion lost an arm, and had afterwards had the remaining one broken at the wrist by a fall in hunting, was seen in the thickest of the action with his bridle in his teeth, and a sword in his mutilated hand, dealing destruction around him. He came off unhurt, though one of the enemy in the charge very nearly transfixed him with a bayonet, which actually pierced his saddle.[4]

The third occasion in 1803 in which the 74th was engaged was the battle of Argaum, which was gained with little loss, and which fell chiefly on the 74th and 78th regiments, both of which were specially thanked by Wellesley. The 74th had 1 sergeant and 3 rank and file killed, and 1 officer, Lieutenant Langlands,[5] 5 sergeants, 1 drummer, and 41 rank and file wounded.

Further details of these three important affairs will be found in the history of the 78th regiment.

In September 1805, the regiment, having served for sixteen years in India, embarked for England, all the men fit for duty remaining in India.

The following Order in Council was issued on the occasion by the Governor, Lord William Bentinck :—

"*Fort St George, 5th Sept.* 1805.

" The Right Honourable the Governor in Council, on the intended embarkation of the remaining officers and men of His Majesty's 74th regiment, discharges a duty of the highest satisfaction to his Lordship in Council in bestowing on that distinguished corps a public testimony of his Lordship's warmest respect and approbation. During a long and eventful period of residence in India, the conduct of His Majesty's 74th regiment, whether in peace or war, has been equally exemplary and conspicuous, having been not less remark-

able for the general tenor of its discipline than for the most glorious achievements in the field.

" Impressed with these sentiments, his Lordship in Council is pleased to direct that His Majesty's 74th regiment be held forth as an object of imitation for the military establishment of this Presidency, as his Lordship will ever reflect with pride and gratification, that in the actions which have led to the present pre-eminence of the British Empire in India, the part so nobly sustained by that corps will add lustre to the military annals of the country, and crown the name of His Majesty's 74th regiment with immortal reputation.

" It having been ascertained, to the satisfaction of the Governor in Council, that the officers of His Majesty's 74th regiment were, during the late campaign in the Deccan, subjected to extraordinary expenses, which have been aggravated by the arrangements connected with their embarkation for Europe, his Lordship in Council has been pleased to resolve that those officers shall receive a gratuity equal to three months' batta, as a further testimony of his Lordship's approbation of their eminent services.

" By order of the Right Honourable the Governor in Council.

" J. H. WEBB,
"*Secretary to the Government.*"

Besides the important engagements in which the 74th took part during its long stay in India, there were many smaller conflicts and arduous services which devolved upon the regiment, but of which no record has been preserved. Some details illustrative of these services are contained in Cannon's history of the 74th, communicated by officers who served with it in India, and afterwards throughout the Peninsular War. Captain Cargill, who served in the regiment, writes as follows :—

"The 74th lives in my recollection under two aspects, and during two distinct epochs.

" The first is the history and character of the regiment, from its formation to its return as a skeleton from India ; and the second is that of the regiment as it now exists, from its being embarked for the Peninsula in January 1810.

" So far as field service is concerned, it has been the good fortune of the corps to serve

---

[4] Welsh's "Military Reminiscences," vol. i. p. 178.

[5] A powerful Arab threw a spear at him, and, drawing his sword, rushed forward to finish the lieutenant. But the spear having entered Langland's leg, cut its way out again, and stuck in the ground behind him. Langlands grasped it, and, turning the point, threw it with so true an aim, that it went right through his opponent's body, and transfixed him within three or four yards of his intended victim. All eyes were for an instant turned on these two combatants, when a Sepoy rushed out of the ranks, and patting the lieutenant on the back, exclaimed, " Atcha Sahib ! Chote atcha kecah !" " Well Sir! very well done." Such a ludicrous circumstance, even in a moment of such extreme peril, raised a very hearty laugh among the soldiers.—Welsh's "Military Reminiscences," vol. i. p. 194.

during both periods, on the more conspicuous occasions, under the great captain of the age; under him also, during the latter period, it received the impress of that character which attaches to most regiments that were placed in the same circumstances, which arose from the regulations introduced by His Royal Highness the Duke of York, and the practical application of them by a master mind in the great school of the Peninsular War. Uniformity was thus given; and the 74th, like every other corps that has had the same training, must acknowledge the hand under which its present character was mainly impressed. But it was not so with the 74th in India. At that time every regiment had its distinctive character and system broadly marked, and this was generally found to have arisen from the materials of which it had been originally composed, and the tact of the officer by whom it had been embodied and trained. The 74th, in these respects, had been fortunate, and the tone and discipline introduced by the late Sir Archibald Campbell, together with the chivalrous spirit and noble emulation imbibed by the corps in those earlier days of Eastern conquest, had impressed upon the officers the most correct perception of their duties, not only as regards internal economy and the gradation of military rank, but also as regards the Government under which they served. It was, perhaps, the most perfect that could well exist. It was participated in by the men, and certainly characterised the regiment in a strong degree.

"It was an established principle in the old 74th, that whatever was required of the soldier should be strikingly set before him by his officers, and hence the most minute point of ordinary duty was regarded by the latter as a matter in which his honour was implicated. The duty of the officer of the day was most rigidly attended to, the officer on duty remaining in full uniform, and without parting with his sword even in the hottest weather, and under all circumstances, and frequently going the rounds of the cantonments during the night. An exchange of duty was almost never heard of, and the same system was carried into every duty and department, with the most advantageous effect upon the spirit and habits of the men.

"Intemperance was an evil habit fostered by climate and the great facility of indulgence; but it was a point of honour among the men never to indulge when near an enemy, and I often heard it observed, that this rule was never known to be broken, even under the protracted operations of a siege. On such occasions the officers had no trouble with it, the principle being upheld by the men themselves.

"On one occasion, while the 74th was in garrison at Madras, and had received a route to march up the country, there was a mutiny among the Company's artillery at the Mount. The evening before the regiment set out it was reported that they had some kind of leaning towards the mutineers; the whole corps felt most indignant at the calumny, but no notice was taken of it by the commanding officer. In the morning, however, he marched early, and made direct for the Mount, where he unfurled the colours, and marched through the cantonments with fixed bayonets. By a forced march he reached his proper destination before midnight, and before dismissing the men, he read them a short but pithy despatch, which he sent off to the Government, stating the indignation of every man of the corps at the libellous rumour, and that he had taken the liberty of gratifying his men by showing to the mutineers those colours which were ever faithfully devoted to the service of the Government. The circumstance had also a happy effect upon the mutineers who had heard the report, but the stern aspect of the regiment dispelled the illusion, and they submitted to their officers."

The losses sustained by the regiment in officers and men, on many occasions, of which no account has been kept, were very great, particularly during the last six years of its Indian service.

That gallant veteran, Quarter-master Grant, who had been in the regiment from the time it was raised, fought at Assaye, and returned with it to England, used to say that he had seen nearly three different sets of officers during the period, the greater part of whom had fallen in battle or died of wounds, the regiment having been always very healthy.

Before the 74th left India, nearly all the men who were fit for duty volunteered into other regiments that remained on service in that country. One of these men, of the grenadier company, is said to have volunteered on nine forlorn hopes, including Seringapatam.

The regiment embarked at Madras in September 1805, a mere skeleton so far as numbers were concerned, landed at Portsmouth in February 1806, and proceeded to Scotland to recruit, having resumed the kilt, which had been laid aside in India. The regiment was stationed in Scotland (Dumbarton Castle, Glasgow, and Fort-George), till January 1809, but did not manage to recruit to within 400 men of its complement, which was ordered to be completed by volunteers from English and Irish, as well as Scotch regiments of militia. The regiment left Scotland for Ireland in January 1809, and in May of that year it was ordered that the Highland dress of the regiment should be discontinued, and its uniform assimilated to that of English regiments of the line; it however retained the designation *Highland* until the year 1816, and, as will be seen, in 1846 it was permitted to resume the national garb, and recruit only in Scotland. For these reasons we are justified in continuing its history to the present time.

It was while in Ireland, in September 1809, that Lieutenant-Colonel Le Poer Trench, whose name will ever be remembered in connection with the 74th, was appointed to the command of the regiment, from Inspecting Field-Officer in Canada, by exchange with Lieutenant-Colonel Malcolm Macpherson; the latter having succeeded that brave officer, Lieutenant-Colonel Swinton, in 1805.

In January 1810 the regiment sailed from Cork for the Peninsula, to take its share in the warlike operations going on there, landing at Lisbon on February 10. On the 27th the 74th set out to join the army under Wellington, and reached Vizeu on the 6th of March. While at Vizeu, Wellington inquired at Colonel Trench how many of the men who fought at Assaye still remained in the regiment, remarking that if the 74th would behave in the Peninsula as they had done in India, he ought to be proud to command such a regiment. In reply to this at Duke's estimate

to have had an exceedingly high estimate of this regiment, which he took occasion to show more than once. It is a curious fact that the 74th had never more than one battalion; and when, some time before the Duke's death, "Reserve Battalions" were formed to a few regiments. He decided "that the 74th should not have one, as they got through the Peninsula with one battalion, and their services were second to none in the army."

The regiment was placed in the 1st brigade of the 3rd division, under Major-General Picton, along with the 45th, the 88th, and part of the 60th Regiment. This division performed such a distinguished part in all the Peninsular operations, that it earned the appellation of the "Fighting Division." We of course cannot enter into the general details of the Peninsular war, as much of the history of which as is necessary for our purpose having been already given in our account of the 42nd regiment.

The first action in which the 74th had a chance of taking part was the battle of Busaco, September 27, 1810. The allied English and Portuguese army numbered 50,000, as opposed to Marshal Massena's 70,000 men. The two armies were drawn upon opposite ridges, the position of the 74th being across the road leading from St Antonio de Cantara to Coimbra. The first attack on the right was made at six o'clock in the morning by two columns of the French, under General Regnier, both of which were directed with the usual impetuous rush of French troops against the position held by the 3rd division, which was of comparatively easy ascent. One of these columns advanced by the road just alluded to, and was repulsed by the fire of the 74th, with the assistance of the 9th and 21st Portuguese regiments, before it reached the ridge. The advance of this column was preceded by a cloud of skirmishers, who came up close to the British position, and were picking off men, when the two right companies of the regiment were detached, with the rifle companies belonging to the brigade, and drove back the enemy's skirmishers with great vigour nearly to the foot of the sierra. The French, however, renewed the attack in greater force, and the Portuguese regiment on the left being thrown into confusion the 74th was placed in a most critical position, with its left flank exposed to the overwhelming force of the enemy. Fortunately, General Leith, stationed on another ridge, saw the danger of the 74th, and sent the 9th and 38th regiments to its support. These advanced along the rear of the 74th in double quick time, met the head of the French column as it crowned the ridge, and drove them irresistibly down the precipice. The 74th then advanced with the 9th, and kept up a fire upon the enemy as long as they could be reached. The enemy having relied greatly upon this attack, their repulse contributed considerably to their defeat. The 74th had Ensign Williams and 7 rank and file killed, Lieutenant Cargill and 19 rank and file wounded. The enemy lost 5000 killed and wounded.

The allies, however, retreated from their position at Busaco upon the lines of Torres Vedras, an admirable series of fortifications contrived for the defence of Lisbon, and extending from the Tagus to the sea. The 74th arrived there on the 8th of October, and remained till the middle of December, living comfortably, and having plenty of time for amusement. The French, however, having taken up a strong position at Santarem, an advanced movement was made by the allied army, the 74th marching to the village of Togarro about the middle of December, where it remained till the beginning of March 1811, suffering much discomfort and hardship from the heavy rains, want of provisions, and bad quarters. The French broke up their position at Santarem on the 5th of March, and retired towards Mondego, pursued by the allies. On the 12th, a division under Ney was found posted in front of the village of Redinha, its flank protected by wooded heights. The light division attacked the height on the right of the enemy, while the third division attacked those on the left, and after a sharp skirmish the enemy retired across the Redinha river. The 74th had 1 private killed, and Lieutenant Crabbie and 6 rank and file wounded. On the afternoon of the 15th of March the third and light divisions attacked the French posted a Fez de Arouce, and dispersed their left and centre, inflicting great loss. Captain Thomson and 11 rank and file of the 74th were wounded in

The third division was constantly in advance of the allied forces in pursuit of the enemy, and often suffered great privations from want of provisions, those intended for it being appropriated by some of the troops in the rear. During the siege of Almeida the 74th was continued at Nave de Aver, removing on the 2nd of May to the rear of the village of Fuentes d'Onor, and taking post on the right of the position occupied by the allied army, which extended for about five miles along the Dos Casas river. On the morning of the 3rd of May the first and third divisions were concentrated on a gentle rise, a cannon-shot in rear of Fuentes d'Onor. Various attacks and skirmishes occurred on the 3rd and 4th, and several attempts to occupy the village were made by the French, who renewed their attack with increased force on the morning of the 5th May. After a hard fight for the possession of the village, the defenders, hardly pressed, were nearly driven out by the superior numbers of the enemy, when the 74th were ordered up to assist. The left wing, which advanced first, on approaching the village, narrowly escaped being cut off by a heavy column of the enemy, which was concealed in a lane, and was observed only in time to allow the wing to take cover behind some walls, where it maintained itself till about noon. The right wing then joined the left, and with the 71st, 79th, and other regiments, charged through and drove the enemy from the village, which the latter never afterwards recovered. The 74th on this day lost Ensign Johnston, 1 sergeant, and 4 rank and file, killed; and Captains Shawe, M'Queen, and Adjutant White, and 64 rank and file, wounded.

The 74th was next sent to take part in the siege of Badajos, where it remained from May 28 till the middle of July, when it marched for Albergaria, where it remained till the middle of September, the blockade of Ciudad Rodrigo in the meantime being carried on by the allied army. On the 17th of September the 74th advanced to El Bodon on the Agueda, and on the 22nd to Pastores, within three miles of Ciudad Rodrigo, forming, with the three companies of the 60th, the advanced guard of the third division. On the 25th, advanced thirty squadrons of cavalry, fourteen battalions of infantry, and twelve guns, direct upon the main body of the third division at El Bodon, and caused it to retire, surrounded and continually threatened by overwhelming numbers of cavalry, over a plain of six miles, to Guinaldo.

The 74th, and the companies of the 60th, under Lieut.-Colonel Trench, at Pastores, were completely cut off from the rest of the division by the French advance, and were left without orders; but they succeeded in passing the Agueda by a ford, and making a very long detour through Robledo, where they captured a party of French cavalry, recrossed the Agueda, and joined the division in bivouac near Fuente Guinaldo, at about two o'clock on the morning of the 26th. It was believed at headquarters that this detachment had been all captured, although Major-General Picton, much pleased at their safe return, said he thought he must have heard more firing before the 74th could be taken. After a rest of an hour or two, the regiment was again under arms, and drawn up in position at Guinaldo before daybreak, with the remainder of the third and the fourth division. The French army, 60,000 strong, being united in their front, they retired at night about twelve miles to Alfayates. The regiment was again under arms at Alfayates throughout the 27th, during the skirmish in which the fourth division was engaged at Aldea de Ponte. On this occasion the men were so much exhausted by the continued exertions of the two preceding days, that 125 of them were unable to remain in the ranks, and were ordered to a village across the Coa, where 80 died of fatigue. This disaster reduced the effective strength of the regiment below that of 1200, required to form a second battalion, which had been ordered during the previous month, and the requisite strength was not again reached during the war.

The 74th was from the beginning of October mainly cantoned at Aldea de Ponte, which it left on the 4th of January 1812, to take part in the siege of Rodrigo. The third division reached Zamora on the 7th, five miles from Rodrigo, where it remained during the siege. The work of the siege was most laborious and trying, and the 74th had its own share of

trench-work. The assault was ordered for the 19th of January, when two breaches were reported practicable.

The assault of the great breach was confided to Major-General M'Kinnon's brigade, with a storming party of 500 volunteers under Major Manners of the 74th, with a forlorn hope under Lieutenant Mackie of the 88th regiment. There were two columns formed of the 5th and 94th regiments ordered to attack and clear the ditch and fausse-braie on the right of the great breach, and cover the advance of the main attack by General M'Kinnon's brigade. The light division was to storm the small breach on the left, and a false attack on the gate at the opposite side of the town was to be made by Major-General Pack's Portuguese brigade.

Immediately after dark, Major-General Picton formed the third division in the first parallel and approaches, and lined the parapet of the second parallel with the 83rd Regiment, in readiness to open the defences. At the appointed hour the attack commenced on the side of the place next the bridge, and immediately a heavy discharge of musketry was opened from the trenches, under cover of which 150 sappers, directed by two engineer officers, and Captain Thomson of the 74th Regiment, advanced from the second parallel to the crest of the glacis, carrying bags filled with hay, which they threw down the counterscarp into the ditch, and thus reduced its depth from 13½ to 8 feet. They then fixed the ladders, and General M'Kinnon's brigade, in conjunction with the 5th and 94th Regiments, which arrived at the same moment along the ditch from the right, pushed up the breach, and after a sharp struggle of some minutes with the bayonet, gained the summit. The defenders then concentrated behind the retrenchment, which they obstinately retained, and a second severe struggle commenced. Bags of hay were thrown into the ditch, and as the counterscarp did not exceed 11 feet in depth, the men readily jumped upon the bags, and without much difficulty carried the little breach. The division, on gaining the summit, immediately began to form with great regularity, in order to advance in a compact body and fall on the rear of the garrison, who were still nobly defending the retrenchment of the great breach. The contest was short but severe; officers and men fell in heaps, as Cannon puts it, killed and wounded, and many were thrown down the scarp into the main ditch, a depth of 30 feet; but by desperate efforts directed along the parapet on both flanks, the assailants succeeded in turning the retrenchments. The garrison then abandoned the rampart, having first exploded a mine in the ditch of the retrenchment, by which Major-General M'Kinnon and many of the bravest and most forward perished in the moment of victory. General Vandeleur's brigade of the light division had advanced at the same time to the attack of the lesser breach on the left, which, being without interior defence, was not so obstinately disputed, and the fortress was won.

In his subsequent despatch Wellington mentioned the regiment with particular commendation, especially naming Major Manners and Captain Thomson of the 74th, the former receiving the brevet of Lieutenant-Colonel for his services on this occasion.

During the siege the regiment lost 6 rank and file killed, and Captains Langlands and Collins, Lieutenants Tew and Ramadge, and Ensign Atkinson, 2 sergeants, and 24 rank and file, killed.

Preparations having been made for the siege of Badajos, the 74th was sent to that place, which it reached on the 16th of March (1812), taking its position along with the other regiments on the south-east side of the town. On the 19th the garrison made a sortie from behind the Picurina with 1500 infantry and a party of cavalry, penetrating as far as the engineers' park, cutting down some men, and carrying off several hundred entrenching tools. The 74th, however, which was the first regiment under arms, advanced under Major-General Kempt in double quick time, and, with the assistance of the guard of the trenches, drove back the enemy, who lost 300 officers and men. The work of preparing for the siege and assault went on under the continuance of very heavy rain, which rendered the work in the trenches extremely laborious, until the 25th of March, when the batteries opened fire against the hitherto impregnable fortress; and on that night Fort Picurina was assaulted and carried by 500 men of the third division, among

whom were 200 men of the 74th under Major Shawe. The fort was very strong, the front well covered by the glacis, the flanks deep, and the rampart, 14 feet perpendicular from the bottom of the ditch, was guarded with thick slanting palings above; and from thence to the top there were 16 feet of an earthen slope.[6] Seven guns were mounted on the works, the entrance to which by the rear was protected with three rows of thick paling. The garrison was about 300 strong, and every man had two muskets. The top of the rampart was garnished with loaded shells to push over, and a retrenched guardhouse formed a second internal defence. The detachment advanced about ten o'clock, and immediately alarms were sounded, and a fire opened from all the ramparts of the work. After a fierce conflict, in which the English lost many men and officers, and the enemy more than half of the garrison, the commandant, with 86 men, surrendered. The 74th lost Captain Collins and Lieutenant Ramadge killed, and Major Shawe dangerously wounded.

The operations of trench-cutting and opening batteries went on till the 6th of April, on the night of which the assault was ordered to take place. "The besiegers' guns being all turned against the curtain, the bad masonry crumbled rapidly away; in two hours a yawning breach appeared, and Wellington, in person, having again examined the points of attack, renewed the order for assault.

"Then the soldiers eagerly made themselves ready for a combat, so furiously fought, so terribly won, so dreadful in all its circumstances, that posterity can scarcely be expected to credit the tale, but many are still alive who know that it is true."[7]

It was ordered, that on the right the third division was to file out of the trenches, to cross the Rivillas rivulet, and to scale the castle walls, which were from 18 to 24 feet high, furnished with all means of destruction, and so narrow at the top, that the defenders could easily reach and overturn the ladders.

The assault was to commence at ten o'clock, and the third division was drawn up close to the Rivillas, ready to advance, when a lighted

'Nap.'s' Peninsular War. Ibid.

carcass, thrown from the castle close to where it was posted, discovered the array of the men, and obliged them to anticipate the signal by half an hour "A sudden blaze of light and the rattling of musketry indicated the commencement of a most vehement contest at the castle Then General Kempt,—for Picton, hurt by a fall in the camp, and expecting no change in the hour, was not present,—then General Kempt, I say, led the third division He had passed the Rivillas in single files by a narrow bridge, under a terrible musketry, and then reforming, and running up the rugged hill, had reached the foot of the castle, when he fell severely wounded, and being carried back to the trenches met Picton, who hastened forward to take the command Meanwhile his troops, spreading along the front, reared their heavy ladders, some against the lofty castle, some against the adjoining front on the left, and with incredible courage ascended amidst showers of heavy stones, logs of wood, and burning shells rolled off the parapet, while from the flanks the enemy plied his musketry with a fearful rapidity, and in front with pikes and bayonets stabbed the leading assailants, or pushed the ladders from the walls, and all this attended with deafening shouts, and the crash of breaking ladders, and the shrieks of crushed soldiers, answering to the sullen stroke of the falling weights "⁵

The British, somewhat baffled, were compelled to fall back a few paces, and take shelter under the rugged edges of the hill But by the perseverance of Picton and the officers of the division, fresh men were brought, the division reformed, and the assault renewed amid dreadful carnage, until at last an entrance was forced by one ladder, when the resistance slackened, and the remaining ladders were quickly reared, by which the men ascended, and established themselves on the ramparts

Lieutenant Alexander Grant of the 74th led the advance at the escalade, and went with a few men through the gate of the castle into the town, but was driven back by superior numbers On his return he was fired at by a French soldier lurking in the gateway, and mortally wounded in the back of the head

He was able, however, to descend the ladder, and was carried to the bivouac, and trepanned, but died two days afterwards, and was buried in the heights looking towards the castle Among the foremost in the escalade was John M'Lauchlan, the regimental piper, who, the instant he mounted the castle wall, began playing on his pipes the regimental quick step, "The Campbells are comin'," as coolly as if on a common parade, until his music was stopped by a shot through the bag, he was afterwards seen by an officer of the regiment seated on a gun-carriage, quietly repairing the damage, while the shot was flying about him After he had repaired his bag, he recommenced his stirring tune

After capturing the castle, the third division kept possession of it all night, repelling the attempts of the enemy to force an entrance About midnight Wellington sent orders to Picton to blow down the gates, but to remain quiet till morning, when he should sally out with 1000 men to renew the general assault This, however, was unnecessary, as the capture of the castle, and the slaughtering escalade of the Bastion St Vincente by the fifth division, having turned the retrenchments, there was no further resistance, and the fourth and light divisions marched into the town by the breaches In the morning the gate was opened, and permission given to enter the town

Napier says, "5000 men and officers fell during the siege, and of these, including 700 Portuguese, 3500 had been stricken in the assault, 60 officers and more than 700 men being slain on the spot The five generals, Kempt, Harvey, Bowes, Colville, and Picton were wounded, the first three severely" At the escalade of the castle alone 600 officers and men fell "When the extent of the night's havoc was made known to Lord Wellington, the firmness of his nature gave way for a moment, and the pride of conquest yielded to a passionate burst of grief for the loss of the gallant soldiers" Wellington in his despatch noticed particularly the distinguished conduct of the third division, and especially that of Lieutenant-Colonels Le Poer Trench and Manners of the 74th

The casualties in the regiment during

Collins, Lieutenants Ramadge and Grant, 1 sergeant, and 22 rank and file. Wounded, 10 officers, Lieut.-Colonel the Hon. R. Le Poer Trench, Captain Langlands, Brevet-Major Shawe, Captains Thomson and Wingate, Lieutenants.Lister, Pattison, King, and Ironside, Ensign Atkinson, 7 sergeants, and 91 rank and file.

The 74th left Badajoz on the 11th of April, and marched to Pinedono, on the frontiers of Beira, where it was encamped till the beginning of June, when it proceeded to Salamanca. Along with a large portion of the allied army, the 74th was drawn up in order of battle on the heights of San Christoval, in front of Salamanca, from the 20th to the 28th of June, to meet Marshal Marmont, who advanced with 40,000 men to relieve the forts, which, however, were captured on the 27th. Brevet-Major Thomson of the 74th was wounded at the siege of the forts, during which he had been employed as acting engineer.

On the 27th Picton having left on leave of absence, the command of the third division was entrusted to Major-General the Hon. Edward Pakenham.

After the surrender of Salamanca the army advanced in pursuit of Marmont, who retired across the Douro.[1] Marmont, having been reinforced, recrossed the Douro, and the allies returned to their former ground on the heights of San Christoval in front of Salamanca, which they reached on the 21st of July. In the evening the third division and some Portuguese cavalry bivouacked on the right bank of the Tormes, over which the rest of the army had crossed, and was placed in position covering Salamanca, with the right upon one of the two rocky hills called the Arapiles, and the left on

the Tormes, which position, however, was afterwards changed to one at right angles with it. On the morning of the 22nd the third division crossed the Tormes, and was placed in advance of the extreme right of the last-mentioned position of the allied army. About five o'clock the third division, led by Pakenham, advanced in four columns, supported by cavalry, to turn the French left, which had been much extended by the advance of the division of General Thomières, to cut off the right of the allies from the Ciudad Rodrigo road. Thomières was confounded when first he saw the third division. for he expected to see the allies in full retreat towards the Ciudad Rodrigo road. The British columns

Lieut.-Colonel the Hon. Sir Robert Le Poer Trench.
From a bust in possession of his daughter, Mrs Burrowes.

formed line as they marched, and the French gunners sent showers of grape into the advancing masses, while a crowd of light troops poured in a fire of musketry.

"But bearing on through the skirmishers with the might of a giant, Pakenham broke the half-formed line into fragments, and sent

---

[1] The two opposing armies were encamped for some time on the opposite side of the Douro, and parties of the officers and men of both armies used to meet daily, bathing in the river, and became so familiar and friendly that the practice was forbidden in a general order.

the whole in confusion upon the advancing supports."[1] Some squadrons of light cavalry fell upon the right of the third division, but the 5th Regiment repulsed them. Pakenham continued his "tempestuous course" for upwards of three miles, until the French were "pierced, broken, and discomfited." The advance in line of the 74th attracted particular notice, and was much applauded by Major-General Pakenham, who frequently exclaimed, "Beautifully done, 74th; beautiful, 74th!"

Lord Londonderry says, in his Story of the Peninsular War :—

"The attack of the third division was not only the most spirited, but the most perfect thing of the kind that modern times have witnessed.

"Regardless alike of a charge of cavalry and of the murderous fire which the enemy's batteries opened, on went these fearless warriors, horse and foot, without check or pause, until they won the ridge, and then the infantry giving their volley, and the cavalry falling on, sword in hand, the French were pierced, broken, and discomfited. So close indeed was the struggle, that in several instances the British colours were seen waving over the heads of the enemy's battalions."

Of the division of Thomières, originally 7000 strong, 2000 had been taken prisoners, with two eagles and eleven pieces of cannon. The French right resisted till dark, when they were finally driven from the field, and having sustained a heavy loss, retreated through the woods across the Tormes.

The casualties in the regiment at the battle of Salamanca were :—Killed, 3 rank and file. Wounded, 2 officers, Brevet-Major Thomson and Lieutenant Ewing, both severely; 2 sergeants, and 42 rank and file.

After this the 74th, with the other allied regiments, proceeded to Madrid, where it remained till October 20, the men passing their time most agreeably. But, although there was plenty of gaiety, Madrid exhibited a sad combination of luxury and desolation ; there was no money, the people were starving, and even noble families secretly sought charity.

In the end of September, when the distress was very great, Lieutenant-Colonel Trench

and the officers of the 74th and 45th Regiments, having witnessed the distress, and feeling the utmost compassion for numbers of miserable objects, commenced giving a daily dinner to about 200 of them, among whom were some persons of high distinction, who without this resource must have perished. Napier says on this subject, that "the Madrileños discovered a deep and unaffected gratitude for kindness received at the hands of the British officers, who contributed, not much, for they had it not, but enough of money to form soup charities, by which hundreds were succoured. Surely this is not the least of the many honourable distinctions those brave men have earned."

During the latter part of October and the month of November, the 74th, which had joined Lieutenant-General Hill, in order to check the movement of Soult and King Joseph, performed many fatiguing marches and counter marches, enduring many great hardships and privations, marching over impassable roads and marshy plains, under a continued deluge of rain, provisions deficient, and no shelter procurable. On the 14th of November the allied army commenced its retreat from Alba de Tormes towards Ciudad Rodrigo, and the following extract from the graphic journal of Major Alves of the 74th will give the reader some idea of the hardships which these poor soldiers had to undergo at this time :—"From the time we left the Arapeiles, on the 15th, until our arrival at Ciudad Rodrigo, a distance of only about 15 leagues, we were under arms every morning an hour before daylight, and never got to our barrack until about sunset, the roads being almost unpassable, particularly for artillery, and with us generally ankle deep. It scarcely ceased to rain during the retreat. Our first endeavour after our arrival at our watery bivouack, was to make it as comfortable as circumstances would admit ; and as exertion was our best assistance, we immediately set to and cut down as many trees as would make a good fire, and then as many as would keep us from the wet underneath. If we succeeded in making a good enough fire to keep the feet warm, I generally managed to have a tolerably good sleep, although during the period I had scarcely ever a dry shirt. To add to our misery, during the retreat we were deficient in provisions, and had rum only on two days. The loss of men by death from the wet and cold during this period was very great. Our regiment alone was deficient about thirty out of thirty-four who had only joined us from England on the 14th, the evening before we retreated from the Arapiles."

The 74th went into winter quarters, and was cantoned at Sarzedas, in the province of Beira, from December 6, 1812, till May 15, 1813.

During this time many preparations were made, and the comfort and convenience of the soldiers maintained, preparatory to Wellington's great attempt to expel the French from the Peninsula.

The army crossed the Douro in separate divisions, and reunited at Toro, the 74th proceeding with the left column. Lieutenant-General Picton had rejoined from England on the 20th May.

On the 4th of June the allies advanced, following the French army under King Joseph, who entered upon the position at Vittoria on the 19th of June by the narrow mountain defile of Puebla, through which the river Zadorra, after passing the city of Vittoria, runs through the valley towards the Ebro with many windings, and divides the basin unequally. To give an idea of the part taken by the 74th in the important battle of Vittoria, we cannot do better than quote from a letter of Sir Thomas Picton dated July 1, 1813.

"On the 16th of May the division was put in movement; on the 18th we crossed the Douro, on the 15th of June the Ebro, and on the 21st fought the battle of Vittoria. The third division had, as usual, a very distinguished share in this decisive action. The enemy's left rested on an elevated chain of craggy mountains, and their right on a rapid river, with commanding heights in the centre, and a succession of undulating grounds, which afforded excellent situations for artillery, and several good positions in front of Vittoria, where King Joseph had his headquarters. The battle began early in the morning, between our right and the enemy's left, on the high craggy heights, and continued with various success for several hours. About twelve o'clock the third division was ordered to force

the passage of the river and carry the heights in the centre, which service was executed with so much rapidity, that we got possession of the commanding ground before the enemy were aware of our intention. The enemy attempted to dislodge us with great superiority of force, and with forty or fifty pieces of cannon. At that period the troops on our right had not made sufficient progress to cover our right flank, in consequence of which we suffered a momentary check, and were driven out of a village whence we had dislodged the enemy, but it was quickly recovered; and on Sir Rowland Hill's (the second) division, with a Portuguese and Spanish division, forcing the enemy to abandon the heights, and advancing to protect our flanks, we pushed the enemy rapidly from all his positions, forced him to abandon his cannon, and drove his cavalry and infantry in confusion beyond the city of Vittoria. We took 152 pieces of cannon, the military chest, ammunition and baggage, besides an immense treasure, the property of the French generals amassed in Spain.

"The third division was the most severely and permanently engaged of any part of the army; and we in consequence sustained a loss of nearly 1800 killed and wounded, which is more than a third of the total loss of the whole army."

The 74th received particular praise from both Lieutenant-General Picton and Major-General Brisbane, commanding the division and brigade, for its alacrity in advancing and charging through the village of Arinez.

The attack on and advance from Arinez seems to have been a very brilliant episode indeed, and the one in which the 74th was most particularly engaged. The right wing, under Captain M'Queen, went off at double quick and drove the enemy outside the village, where they again formed in line opposite their pursuers. The French, however, soon after fled, leaving behind them a battery of seven guns.

Captain M'Queen's own account of the battle is exceedingly graphic. "At Vittoria," he says, "I had the command of three companies for the purpose of driving the French out of the village of Arinez, where they were strongly posted; we charged through the village and the enemy retired in great confusion. Lieutenants Alves and Ewing commanded the companies which accompanied me. I received three wounds that day, but remained with the regiment during the whole action; and next day I was sent to the rear with the other wounded. Davis (Lieutenant) carried the colours that day, and it was one of the finest things you can conceive to see the 74th advancing in line, with the enemy in front, on very broken ground full of ravines, as regularly, and in as good line as if on parade. This is in a great measure to be attributed to Davis, whose coolness and gallantry were conspicuous; whenever we got into broken ground, he with the colours was first on the bank, and stood there until the regiment formed on his right and left."

Captain M'Queen, who became Major of the 74th in 1830, and who died only a year or two ago, was rather a remarkable man; we shall refer to him again. Adjutant Alves tells us in his journal, that in this advance upon the village of Arinez, he came upon Captain M'Queen lying, as he thought, mortally wounded. Alves ordered two of the grenadiers to lift M'Queen and lay him behind a bank out of reach of the firing, and there leave him. About an hour afterwards, however, Alves was very much astonished to see the indomitable Captain at the head of his company; the shot that had struck him in the breast having probably been a spent one, which did not do him much injury.

Major White (then Adjutant) thus narrates an occurrence which took place during the contest at Arinez:—"At the battle of Vittoria, after we had forced the enemy's centre, and taken the strong heights, we found ourselves in front of a village (I think Arinez) whence the French had been driven in a confused mass, too numerous for our line to advance against; and whilst we were halted for reinforcements, the 88th Regiment on our left advanced with their usual impetuosity against the superior numbers I have spoken of, and met with a repulse. The left of our regiment, seeing this, ran from the ranks to the assistance of the 88th; and I, seeing them fall uselessly, rode from some houses which sheltered us to rally them and bring them back. The piper

(M'Laughlan, mentioned before) seeing that I could not collect them, came to my horse's side and played the 'Assembly,' on which most of them that were not shot collected round me. I was so pleased with this act of the piper in coming into danger to save the lives of his comrades, and with the good effect of the pipes in the moment of danger, that I told M'Laughlan that I would not fail to mention his gallant and useful conduct. But at the same time, as I turned my horse to the right to conduct the men towards our regiment, a musket ball entered the point of my left shoulder, to near my back bone, which stopped my career in the field. The piper ceased to play, and I was told he was shot through the breast; at all events he was killed, and his timely assistance and the utility of the pipes deserves to be recorded." It was indeed too true about poor brave M'Laughlan, whose pipes were more potent than the Adjutant's command; a nine-pound shot went right through his breast, when, according to the journal of Major Alves, he was playing "The Campbell's are comin'" in rear of the column. It is a curious circumstance, however, that the piper's body lay on the field for several days after the battle without being stripped of anything but the shoes. This was very unusual, as men were generally stripped of everything as soon as they were dead.

When the village was captured and the great road gained, the French troops on the extreme left were thereby turned, and being hardly pressed by Sir Rowland Hill's attack on their front, retreated in confusion before the advancing lines towards Vittoria.

The road to Bayonne being completely blocked up by thousands of carriages and animals, and a confused mass of men, women, and children, thereby rendered impassable for artillery, the French retreated by the road to Salvatierra and Pamplona, the British infantry following in pursuit. But this road being also choked up with carriages and fugitives, all became confusion and disorder. The French were compelled to abandon everything, officers and men taking with them only the clothes they wore, and most of them being barefooted. Their loss in men did not, however, exceed 6000, and that of the allies was nearly as great. That of the British, however, was more than twice as great as that of the Spanish and Portuguese together, and yet both are said to have fought well, but as Napier says, "British troops are the soldiers of battle."

The French regiments which effected their escape arrived at Pamplona and took shelter in the defile beyond it, in a state of complete disorganisation. Darkness, and the nature of the ground unfavourable for the action of cavalry, alone permitted their escape, at the distance of two leagues from Vittoria the pursuit was given up.

The following Brigade Order was issued the day after the battle —

"Major-General Brisbane has reason to be highly pleased with the conduct of the brigade in the action of yesterday, but he is at a loss to express his admiration of the conduct of the Honourable Colonel Le Poer Trench and the 74th Regiment, which he considers contributed much to the success of the day."

The casualties in the 74th at the battle of Vittoria were — Killed, 7 rank and file, wounded, 5 officers, Captains M'Queen and Ovens, Adjutant White, and Ensigns Hamilton and Shore, 4 sergeants, 1 drummer, and 31 rank and file

The army followed the retreating French into the Pyrenees by the valley of Roncesvalles

Of the various actions that took place among these mountains we have already given somewhat detailed accounts when speaking of the 42nd. The 74th was engaged in the blockade of Pamplona. And while thus employed, on the 15th of July, its pickets drove in a reconnoitring party of the garrison, the regiment sustaining a loss of 3 rank and file killed and 1 sergeant and 6 rank and file wounded. On the 17th the blockade of Pamplona was entrusted to the Spaniards, and the third, fourth, and second divisions covered the blockade, as well as the siege of San Sebastian, then going on under Lieutenant-General Sir Thomas Graham

Marshal Soult, with 60,000 men, advanced on the 25th to force the pass of Roncesvalles, and compelled the fourth division, which had been moved up to support the front line of the allies, to retire, on the 26th it was joined by the third division in advance at Zubiri. Both divisions, under Sir Thomas Picton, took up a position on the morning of the 27th July, in front of Pamplona, across the mouth of the Zubiri and Lanz valleys. At daylight on the 30th, in accordance with Wellington's orders, the third division, with two squadrons of cavalry and a battery of artillery, advanced rapidly up the valley of the Zubiri skirmishing on the flank of the French who were retiring under General Foy. About eleven o'clock, the 74th being in the valley, and the enemy moving in retreat parallel with the allies along the mountain ridge to the left of the British, Lieut.-Colonel Trench obtained permission from Sir Thomas Picton to advance with the 74th and cut off their retreat. The regiment then ascended the ridge in view of the remainder of the division, which continued its advance up the valley. On approaching the summit, two companies, which were extended as skirmishers, were overpowered in passing through a wood, and driven back upon the main body. Though the regiment was exposed to a most destructive fire, it continued its advance, without returning a shot, until it reached the upper skirt of the wood, close upon the flank of the enemy, and then at once opened its whole fire upon them

A column of 1500 or 1600 men was separated from the main body, driven down the other side of the ridge, and a number taken prisoners, most of those who escaped were intercepted by the sixth division, which was further in advance on another line. After the 74th had gained the ridge, another regiment from the third division was sent to support it, and pursued the remainder of the column until it had surrendered to the sixth division. Sir Frederick Stoven, Adjutant-General of the third division, who, along with some of the staff came up at this moment, said he never saw a regiment behave in such a gallant manner

The regiment was highly complimented by the staff of the division for its conspicuous gallantry on this occasion, which was noticed as follows by Lord Wellington, who said in his despatch,—

"I cannot sufficiently applaud the conduct of all the general officers, officers, and troops, throughout the whole of the

" The movement made by Sir Thomas Picton merited my highest commendation; the latter officer co-operated in the attack of the mountain by detaching troops to his left, in which Lieutenant-Colonel the Hon Robert Trench was wounded, but I hope not seriously "

The regiment on this occasion sustained a loss of 1 officer, Captain Whitting, 1 sergeant, and 4 rank and file killed, and 5 officers, Lieut.-Colonel the Hon Robert Le Poer Trench, Captain (Brevet-Major) Moore, and Lieutenants Pattison, Duncomb, and Jew, 4 sergeants, and 36 rank and file wounded

The French were finally driven across the Bidasoa into France in the beginning of August

At the successful assault of the fortress of San Sebastian by the force under Sir Thomas Graham, and which was witnessed by the 74th from the summit of one of the neighbouring mountains, Brevet Major Thomson of the 74th, was employed as an acting engineer, and received the brevet rank of Lieutenant-Colonel for his services

After various movements the third division advanced up the pass of Zagaramurdi, and on the 6th October encamped on the summit of a mountain in front of the pass of Echalar; and in the middle of that month, Sir Thomas Picton having gone to England, the command of the third division devolved upon Major-General Sir Charles Colville The 74th remained encamped on the summit of this bare mountain till the 9th of November, suffering greatly from the exposure to cold and wet weather, want of shelter, and scarcity of provisions, as well as from the harassing piquet and night duties which the men had to perform Major Alves[2] says in his journal that the French picquets opposite to the position of the 74th were very kind and generous in getting the soldiers' canteens filled with brandy,— for payment of course

Pamplona having capitulated on the 31st of October, an attack was made upon the French position at the Nivelle on the 10th of November, a detailed description of which has

[2] This officer was present with the 74th during the whole of its service in the Peninsula, and kept an accurate daily journal of all the events in which he was concerned He was afterwards Major of the depôt battalion in the Isle of Wight.

been given in the history of the 42nd. The third, along with the fourth and seventh divisions, under the command of Marshal Beresford, were dispersed about Zagaramurdi, the Puerto de Echellar, and the lower parts of these slopes of the greater Rhune, which descended upon the Sarre On the morning of the 10th, the third division, under General Colville, descending from Zagaramurdi, moved against the unfinished redoubts and entrenchments covering the approaches to the bridge of Amotz on the left bank of the Nivelle, and formed in conjunction with the sixth division the narrow end of a wedge The French made a vigorous resistance, but were driven from the bridge, by the third division, which established itself on the heights between that structure and the unfinished redoubts of Louis XIV The third division then attacked the left flank of the French centre, while the fourth and seventh divisions assailed them in front The attacks on other parts of the French position having been successful, their centre was driven across the river in great confusion, pursued by the skirmishers of the third division, which crossed by the bridge of Amotz The allied troops then took possession of the heights on the right bank of the Nivelle, and the French were compelled to abandon all the works which for the previous three months they had been constructing for the defence of the other parts of the position

The 74th was authorised to bear the word "Nivelle" on its regimental colour, in commemoration of its services in this battle; indeed it will be seen that it bears on its colours the names of nearly every engagement that took place during the Peninsular War The French had lost 51 pieces of artillery, and about 4300 men and officers killed, wounded, and prisoners, during the battle of the Nivelle; the loss of the allies was about 2700 men and officers.

On the 9th of December the passage of the Nive at Cambo having been forced by Sir Rowland Hill, the third division remained in possession of the bridge at Ustariz On the 13th the French having attacked the right between the Nive and the Adour at St Pierre, were repulsed by Sir Rowland Hill after a very severe battle; and the fourth, sixth, and two brigades of the third division were moved across the Nive in support of the right.

The 74th, after this, remained cantoned in farm-houses between the Nive and the Adour until the middle of February 1814.

Lieutenant-General Sir Thomas Picton having rejoined the army, resumed the command of the third division in the end of December 1813. Many acts of outrage and plunder had been committed by the troops, on first entering France, and Sir Thomas Picton took an opportunity of publicly reprimanding some of the regiments of his division for such offences, when he thus addressed the 74th:—"As for you, 74th, I have nothing to say against you, your conduct is gallant in the field and orderly in quarters.' And, addressing Colonel Trench in front of the regiment, he told him that he would write to the colonel at home (General Sir Alexander Hope) his report of their good conduct. As Lieutenant-General Picton was not habitually lavish of complimentary language, this public expression of the good opinion of so competent a judge was much valued by the regiment.

The next engagement in which the 74th took part was that of Orthes, February 27, 1814. On the 24th the French had concentrated at Orthes, with their front to the river Gave de Pau, while the third division was at the broken bridge of Bereaux, five miles lower down the river, on the 25th, crossing to the other side next day. On the 27th, when the sixth and light divisions crossed, the third, and Lord Edward Somerset's cavalry, were already established in columns of march, with skirmishers pushed forward close upon the left centre of the French position. During the whole morning of the 27th a slight skirmish, with now and then a cannon shot, had been going on with the third division, but at nine o'clock Wellington commenced the real attack. The third and sixth divisions took without difficulty the lower part of the ridges opposed to them, and endeavoured to extend their left along the French front with a sharp fire of musketry. But after three hours' hard fighting, during which the victory seemed to be going with the French, Wellington changed his plan of attack, and ordered the third and sixth divisions to be thrown *en masse* on the left centre of the French position, which they

carried, and established a battery of guns upon a knoll, from whence their shot ploughed through the French masses from one flank to another.[9] Meantime Hill had crossed the river above Orthes, and nearly cut off the French line of retreat, after which the French began to retire, step by step, without confusion. The allies advanced, firing incessantly, yet losing many men, especially of the third division, whose advance was most strongly opposed. The retreat of the French, however, shortly became a rout, the men flying in every direction in scattered bands, pursued by the British cavalry, who cut down many of the fugitives.

During the first advance Lieutenant-General Sir Thomas Picton particularly remarked to Major-General Brisbane the steady movement of his brigade; and the latter reported to him the notice he had taken of the gallantry of Sergeant-Major Macpherson, of the 74th, upon which Sir Thomas Picton expressed to the sergeant-major his pleasure to hear such a good report of him, and on the following day, during a short halt on the march, desired Lieutenant-Colonel Manners, who commanded the regiment in the absence of Lieutenant-Colonel Trench, to write his recommendation, which he did on a drum-head; the sergeant-major was consequently promoted to a commission on the 31st of March following, and was afterwards a captain in the regiment.

The casualties in the regiment at the battle of Orthes were—1 sergeant and 7 rank and file killed; and 5 officers, Captain Lyster, Lieutenant Ewing (mortally—dying shortly afterwards), Lieutenant Ironside, Ensigns Shore and Luttrell, 1 sergeant, 1 drummer, and 17 rank and file wounded.

The 74th, along with the other regiments of the third division, was kept moving about until the 7th of March, when it was cantoned at Aire, on the left bank of the Adour. On the 18th the whole allied army advanced up both sides of the Adour, the French falling back before them. The third division was in the centre column, which on the 19th came up with a division of the French, strongly posted amongst some vineyards, two miles in front of the village of Vic-en-Bigorre. The third divi-

Napier.

sion attacked the French and drove them before it, and encamped in the evening about three miles beyond the town of Vic-en-Bigorre

The Marquis of Wellington stated in his despatch —" On the following day (the 19th) the enemy held a strong rear guard in the vineyards in front of the town of Vic en-Bigorre, Lieutenant General Picton, with the third division and Major-General Rock's brigade, made a very handsome movement upon this rear-guard, and drove them through the vineyards and town"

Two officers of the regiment, Lieutenant Atkinson and Ensign Flood, were wounded in this affair

On the 20th, after some sharp fighting, in which the 74th lost a few men, the right column of the allies crossed the Adour at Tubes, and was encamped with the rest of the army upon the Larret and Arros rivers The French retreated towards Toulouse, and on the 26th the allied army came in sight of the enemy posted behind the Touch river, and covering that city Details having already been given, in our account of the 42nd Regiment, concerning this last move of Soult, we need only mention here that the third, fourth, and sixth divisions passed over the Garonne by a pontoon bridge fifteen miles below Toulouse on the 3d of April On the 10th about six o'clock in the morning, the various divisions of the British army advanced according to Wellington's previously arranged plan The part taken in the battle of Toulouse by the 74th is thus narrated by Major Alves in his journal —

" Shortly after daylight the division was put in motion, with orders to drive all the enemy's outposts before us, and although acting as adjutant, I was permitted by Colonel Trench to accompany the skirmishers With but feeble opposition we drove them before us, until they reached the tête-de-pont on the canal leading into Toulouse, on the right bank of the Garonne, on arriving there I mentioned to Captain Andrews of the 74th, that I thought we had gone far enough, and reconnoitered very attentively the manner in which it was defended by strong palisades, &c I then returned to where the regiment was halted, and ment, where I saw Lieut. Colonel Trench

and that nothing further could possibly be done without artillery to break down the palisades He immediately brought me to General Brisbane, to whom I also related my observations as above, who directed me to ride to the left and find out Sir Thomas Picton, who was with the other brigade, and to tell him my observations After riding about two miles to the left I found Sir Thomas, and told him as above stated, who immediately said, in presence of all his staff, ' Go back, sir, and tell them to move on' This I did with a very heavy heart, as I dreaded what the result must be, but I had no alternative About a quarter of an hour afterwards the regiment moved from where it was halted We experienced a loss of 30 killed and 100 wounded, out of 350, in the attempt to get possession of the tête-de-pont, and were obliged to retire without gaining any advantage The attack was the more to be regretted, as Lord Wellington's orders were that it was only to be a diversion, and not a real attack"

The casualties in the regiment at the battle of Toulouse were 4 officers, Captains Thomas Andrews and William Tew, Lieutenant Hamilton, and Ensign John Parkinson, 1 sergeant, and 32 rank and file killed, and 5 officers, Brevet-Major Miller, Captain Donald M'Queen,[1] and Lieutenants Jason Hassard, William Gra-

---

[1] This brave officer, who died only quite recently, and who had been made a Military Knight of Windsor only a few months before his death, was severely wounded through the lungs He had been in almost every battle fought during the Peninsular War, and seldom came out without a wound, yet he became Major of his regiment only in 1830, though for his conduct in the Peninsula he received the silver war medal with nine clasps For some years he was barrack master at Dundee and Perth In 1835, as a recognition of his meritorious services in the Peninsula, he was made a Knight of the Royal Hanoverian Guelphic Order The following incident in which he was concerned at Toulouse is worth narrating — When left for dead on the field, and his regiment had moved on, a soldier, his foster brother, named John Gillanders, whom he had taken with him from his native parish as a recruit, missed his captain, and hurried back through a heavy fire, searched for and found him, and carried him to the rear There were few places for shelter, and the faithful soldier, loaded with his almost insensible burden, pushed his way into a house which was filled with officers, and called out for a bed In the room there was a bed, and on it lay a wounded officer He heard the entreaty of the soldier, and saw the desperate condition of the officer he carried, and at once exclaimed, " That poor fellow needs the bed more than I do," and rose and gave it up That officer was the gallant Sir Thomas

ham, and E. J. Crabbe, 4 sergeants, and 94 rank and file wounded.

The French abandoned the city during the night of the 11th of April, and the allies entered it in triumph on the 12th, on the forenoon of which day intelligence arrived of the abdication of Napoleon and the termination of the war. The officers charged with the intelligence had been detained near Blois "by the officiousness of the police, and the blood of 8000 men had overflowed the Mount Rhune in consequence."[2]

After remaining in France for some time the 74th embarked in the beginning of July, and arrived at Cork on the 25th of that month.

The record of the services of the 74th during these eventful years will be sufficient to prove how well the corps maintained the high character it had at first acquired in the East Indies, and how well it earned the distinction for gallantry in the field and good conduct in quarters.

In consideration of the meritorious conduct of the non-commissioned officers and men of the regiment during the war, Colonel Trench applied to the Commander-in-Chief to authorise those most distinguished among them to wear silver medals in commemoration of their services. The sanction of the Commander-in-Chief was conveyed to Colonel Trench in a letter from the Adjutant-General, bearing date "Horse Guards, 30th June 1814."

Facsimile of the Medal.
From the collection of Surgeon-Major Fleming, late of the 4th Dragoon Guards.

Medals were accordingly granted to the deserving survivors of the campaign, who were divided into three classes: first class, men who had served in eight or nine general actions; second class, in six or seven general actions; third class, in four or five general actions.

The regiment remained in Ireland till May 1818, not having had a chance of distinguishing itself at the crowning victory of Waterloo, although it was on its way to embark for Belgium when news of that decisive battle arrived. While at Fermoy, on the 6th of April 1818, the regiment was presented with new colours. The colours which had waved over the regiment in many a hard-fought field, and which had been received in 1802, were burned, and the ashes deposited in the lid of a gold sarcophagus snuff-box, inlaid with part of the wood of the colour-staves, on which the following inscription was engraved:—"This box, composed of the old standards of the Seventy-fourth regiment, was formed as a tribute of respect to the memory of those who fell, and of esteem for those who survived the many glorious and arduous services on which they were always victoriously carried, during a period of sixteen years, in India, the Peninsula, and France. They were presented to the regiment at Wallajahbad in 1802, and the shattered remains were burned at Fermoy on the 6th of April 1818."

The 74th embarked at Cork for Halifax, Nova Scotia, on the 13th of May, leaving one depôt company, which was sent to the Isle of Wight. The companies were divided between St John's, Newfoundland, St John's, New Brunswick, and Frederickton, where were head-quarters and five companies. The regiment remained in North America till 1828, in August of which year proceeding to Bermudas, which it left at the end of the next year for Ireland, where it arrived in the beginning of 1830. In 1818 the regiment had been reduced to ten companies of 65 rank and file each, and in 1821 it was further reduced to eight companies of 72 rank and file. In 1825, however, the strength was augmented to ten companies—six service companies of 86 rank and file, and four depôt companies of 56 rank and file each.

The regiment remained in Ireland till 1834, during part of which time it was actively employed in suppressing the outrages consequent on the disturbed state of the country. In the

divided

into four depot and six service companies; three of the latter were sent to Barbadoes, while the headquarter division, consisting of the three remaining companies, was sent to the island of Grenada. In November 1835 the two service divisions were sent to Antigua, where they remained till February 1837. From thence the headquarter division proceeded to St Lucia, and the other three companies to Demerara, both divisions being sent to St Vincent in June of the same year. The regiment was kept moving about among these western islands till May 1841, when it proceeded to Canada, arriving at Quebec at the end of the month. While the regiment was stationed at Trinidad it was attacked by fever and dysentery, which caused great mortality; and fever continued to prevail among the men until the regiment removed to Trinidad. With this exception the 74th remained remarkably healthy during the whole of its residence in the West Indies.

The 74th remained in the North American colonies till 1845, being removed from Canada to Nova Scotia in May 1844, and embarking at Halifax for England in March 1845. On arriving in England in the end of that month, the service companies joined the depot at Canterbury.

While the regiment was stationed in Canterbury, Lieutenant-Colonel Crabbe, commanding the regiment, submitted to the Commander-in-Chief, through the colonel (Lieutenant-General Sir Phineas Ryall), the earnest desire of the officers and men to be permitted to resume the national garb and designation of a Highland regiment, under which the 74th had been originally embodied.

The lieutenant-colonel having himself first joined the regiment as a Highland corps in the year 1807, and having served with it continuously during the intervening period, knew by his own experience, and was able to certify to the Commander-in-Chief, how powerfully and favourably its character had been influenced by its original organisation; and also that throughout the varied services and changes of so many years, a strong national feeling, and a connection with Scotland by recruiting, had been constantly maintained. Various considerations, however, induced an application for permission

to modify the original dress of kilt and feathered bonnet, and with the resumed designation of a Highland corps, to adopt the trews and bonnet as established for the 71st regiment.

His Grace the Duke of Wellington was pleased to return a favourable answer to the application, in such terms as to render his consent doubly acceptable to the corps, causing it to be intimated to the colonel, by a letter from the adjutant-general, bearing date 'Horse Guards, 13th August 1845,' that he would recommend to Her Majesty that the 74th Regiment should be permitted to resume the appellation of a Highland regiment, and to be clothed "accordingly in compliment to the services of that regiment so well known to his Grace in India and in Europe."

In the "Gazette" of the 14th November 1845 the following announcement was published:—

"War Office, 8th November 1845.

"Memorandum,—Her Majesty has been graciously pleased to approve of the 74th foot resuming the appellation of the 74th (Highland) Regiment of foot, and of its being clothed accordingly; that is, to wear the tartan trews instead of the Oxford mixture; plaid cap instead of the black chaco; and the plaid scarf as worn by the 71st Regiment. The alteration of the dress is to take place on the next issue of clothing, on the 1st of April 1846."

The national designation of the regiment was of course immediately resumed, and the recruiting has been since carried on solely in Scotland with uniform success.

It was directed by the Adjutant-General that the tartan now to be worn by the 74th should not be of the old regimental pattern, that being already in use by two other regiments (the 42nd and 93rd), but that it should be distinguished by the introduction of a white stripe. The alteration of the regimental dress took place as ordered, on the 1st of April 1846.

In May 1846, Lieutenant-Colonel Crabbe, who had been connected with the regiment for forty years, retired on full pay, and took leave of the regiment in a feeling order. Major Crawley was promoted to the lieutenant-colonelcy in his place.

II.

1846–1853.

AFTER being stationed a short time at Canterbury and Gosport, the 74th removed to Scotland in detachments in the months of August and September 1846, two companies being sent to Dundee, three to Paisley, one to Perth, headquarters and three companies to Aberdeen, and detachments to Stirling and Dunfermline. In November of the same year, all the companies united at Glasgow, and in July 1847 the regiment proceeded to Ireland. While stationed at Dublin, the 74th, in consequence of the disturbed state of Tipperary, was sent to that county on July 29th, to be employed as part of a movable column under Major-General Macdonald. The regiment, along with the 75th and 85th, a half battery of Artillery, a detachment of Sappers, and three companies of the 60th Rifles, the whole forming a movable column, was kept moving about in the neighbourhood of Thurles and Ballingarry during the month of August. Happily, however, the column had none of the stern duties of war to perform, and returned to Dublin in the beginning of September, after having suffered much discomfort from the almost incessant rain which prevailed during the time the men were under canvas.

The 74th remained in Ireland till March 1851, on the 16th of which month it sailed in the "Vulcan" from Queenstown, having been ordered to South Africa to take part in the sanguinary Kaffir War of that period, in which, as will be seen, the regiment maintained its well-won reputation for valour in the faithful performance of its duty. The 74th arrived in Simon's Bay, Cape of Good Hope, on the 11th of May, when it was ordered to proceed to Algoa Bay to join the first division at Fort Hare, under Major-General Somerset, who was engaged in active operations against

the Kaffirs and Hottentots. Having arrived at Algoa Bay on the 16th, the regiment disembarked at Port Elizabeth, where, owing to the want of transport for the camp equipage, it remained for a few days before proceeding to Grahamstown, which, from want of grass and the consequent weak condition of the oxen, it did not reach till the 27th of May.[1]

While the 74th was at Grahamstown, a sudden outbreak of the Hottentots at the mission station of Theopolis occurred. Four companies of the regiment, under the command of Lieutenant-Colonel Fordyce, together with a few native levies, proceeded to the scene of disturbance, and succeeded in destroying the rebel camp, and capturing about 600 head of cattle: the Hottentots, however, made their escape.

The regiment having resumed its march for Fort Hare, arrived at that place on June 12th, and encamped near the fort. Though but a few days in the country, Colonel Fordyce saw that the ordinary equipment of the British soldier was in no way suited to African campaigning, and while at Fort Hare he made a complete change in the appearance of the regiment. The dress bonnets, scarlet tunics, black pouches, and pipe-clayed cross belts, were put away in the quartermaster's stores. Common brown leather pouches and belts were issued, while an admirable substitute for the tunic was found in the stout canvas frocks of which a couple are served out to each soldier proceeding on a long sea voyage. These had been carefully preserved when the regiment landed, and now, with the aid of copperas and the bark of the mimosa bush, were dyed a deep olive brown colour, which corresponded admirably with that of the bush, and was the least conspicuous dress of any regiment in the field, not excepting the Rifle Brigade and 60th, both of which corps had a battalion engaged. The cuffs and shoulders were strapped with leather, and this rough-looking but most serviceable tunic was worn by both officers and men as long as they were actively employed in the field. The forage cap, with a leather peak, completed the costume.

[1] On its arrival in South Africa, the 74th, with the exception of about 80, mainly Irishmen, consisted of men raised in the northern counties of Scotland.

On the 18th of June Major-General Somerset ordered the following troops, divided into brigades, to form a camp in advance for field operations:—

First Brigade—Lieutenant-Colonel Fordyce, 74th Highlanders: the 74th Highlanders; the 91st Regiment; the 1st European Levy; and the Alice European Levy.

Second Brigade—Lieutenant-Colonel Sutton, Cape Mounted Riflemen: the George Levy, the Graaff Reynett Levy, the Kat River Levy, and the Fingo Levies.

Cavalry Brigade—Major Somerset, Cape Mounted Riflemen: the Royal Artillery, the Cape Mounted Riflemen, the George Mounted Levy, and Blakeway's Horse; and besides, a detachment of Royal Sappers and Miners, under the orders of Lieutenant Jesse, R.E., Deputy Quartermaster-General.

These troops marched from Fort Hare on the 24th for the Quesana River, near the base of the Amatola Mountains, where a standing camp was formed.

The division moved before daylight on the 26th of June, and ascended in two columns the western range of the Amatola heights, halting on the ridge while Major-General Somerset reconnoitered the position of the enemy. While doing so, his escort was attacked, but on the arrival of a reinforcement the enemy was driven from his position, and forced into the valley below. While these operations were in progress, the 74th Highlanders, Cape Mounted Rifles, European and Kat River Levies, with the Alice and Port Elizabeth Fingoes, were moved into the Amatola basin. A formidable body of the enemy, chiefly Hottentots, were now seen strongly posted on the extreme point of the ridge of the northern range of the Amatolas, partly concealed and well covered by large stones and detached masses of rock; these the 74th, flanked by the Alice and Port Elizabeth Fingoes, under Lieutenant-Colonel Ferdyce, was ordered to dislodge. The enemy opened a galling fire upon the advancing troops, but the 74th deployed into extended line, and having opened fire, drove the Hottentots from their position and gained the summit. After moving along the ridge, which was intersected by a narrow strip of forest bush, the troops were again attacked, and three men of the 74th

killed. Having halted for a short time to refresh themselves, the 74th, flanked by the Fort Beaufort Fingoes, was again moved on the enemy's position, when some sharp firing took place, and the enemy was compelled to abandon his position altogether, retiring into the forest and mountains. The division descended into the Amatola basin, and at 5 P.M. bivouacked for the night. It was reported that some Gaika chiefs and a considerable number of the enemy were killed on this occasion; while the casualties in the 74th were one corporal and two privates killed, and one officer, Lieutenant W. W. Bruce, and nine men wounded. Nothing of importance occurred during the next two days, and on the 29th the division marched to the camp on the Quesana.

The conduct of the 74th in the above services was highly spoken of in various orders, but we need only quote from a general order by Lieutenant-General Sir Harry Smith, Bart., dated "Headquarters, King William's Town, 3rd of July, 1851:—

"Lieutenant-Colonel Fordyce and the 74th Highlanders seized every opportunity of assailing them and driving them before them, and the Major-General reports in the strongest terms of admiration the gallantry and the discipline of the corps."

On the 2nd of July the division again ascended the Amatolas, and its operations were thus detailed by Major-General Somerset in the following letter to the Deputy Quartermaster-General:—

"CAMP ON THE KAMKA OR YELLOW WOODS,
"3d July 1851.

"SIR,—I have the honour to acquaint you, for the information of his Excellency the Commander-in-Chief, that I proceeded with my division yesterday morning, and ascended the Amatola, with the view of clearing the eastern range of the Victoria Heights, and also of again attacking the enemy's fastnesses in the forest, at the southern point of Hogg's Back Ridge. This latter point was thoroughly cleared by the European Levy and a company of the 91st, under Lieutenant Mainwaring. The enemy abandoned the forest when their huts were destroyed, and took refuge in the extreme and highest points of the Chumie Mountains. I then directed my attention to the southern point of the Victoria Heights, placing a gun under Lieutenant Field ; the 74th Highlanders, under Lieutenant-Colonel Fordyce ; and the Cape Mounted Rifles, under Major Somerset, in position on the middle ridge. I detached the Graaff Reynett Levy, under Captain Heathcote, senior, the Fort Beaufort Fingoes, under Captain Verity, and destroyed all the kraals east of the Victoria range. While this movement was going on, I detached Captains Cumbers and Ayliff with their levies, and Captain Hobbs with the Kat River Levy, down the valley of the Amatola, destroying all the kraals at the base of the middle ridge, and nearly succeeded in capturing the Kaffir chief Oba or Waba, Tyali's son, whom I saw lately with the Commander-in-Chief at Fort Cox, as it was his kraal that was surprised by the Kat River Levy under Captain Hobbs, and his wives and family, with all their household property, were captured, including the chief's crane feathers for his tribe, his smart forage cap and jacket, given to him by his Excellency, and much other property ; and distinctly saw the chief ride off from his kraal just before the patrol got there. The enemy was completely routed, and made off in every direction. In my attack on the Amatola position on the 26th instant, the chiefs Beta and Pitoi, the son of Vongya (brother of the late Tyali), were killed, and many others of less note. This information I have received from the Kaffir Dakana, residing at the Quilli station."

In a despatch from the Governor, Lieutenant-General Sir Harry Smith, Bart., to Earl Grey, the regiment is mentioned as follows:—

"Major-General Somerset speaks in the highest terms of Lieutenant-Colonel Fordyce and the 74th Regiment, recently arrived from England, upon whom the brunt of these operations fell in the first division."

During the next month the standing camp of the division was moved about from place to place, and patrolling parties were constantly sent out to check the depredations of the enemy. About the middle of August, when the standing camp was fixed at Riet Fontein, Major-General Somerset proceeded to Lower Albany with a large portion of the division, leaving Lieutenant Colonel Fordyce, of the 74th High-

landers, in command of the troops remaining in camp.

Lieutenant-Colonel Sutton, Cape Mounted Rifles, commanding at Fort Beaufort, communicated with Lieutenant-Colonel Fordyce, about the beginning of September, regarding many bold and frequently successful attempts at the robbery of cattle made by the hordes of Kaffirs in the neighbourhood of that post, which it became necessary, if possible, to check. A force, consisting of 11 officers and 245 men of the 74th Highlanders, 3 officers and 36 men of the Cape Mounted Rifles, and 22 officers and 372 men of the various levies in camp and at Fort Beaufort, were assembled at Gilbert's farm, on the Klu Klu, on the night of the 7th of September, and marched about 2 o'clock A.M. on the 8th, under Lieutenant-Colonel Fordyce, to the lower edge of the Kroome, where they arrived at dawn, but found none of the enemy in that locality. The force ascended the Kroome heights by the steep and difficult ridge called the Wolf's Head. It being well known that the enemy, under the Gaika chief Macomo, were in great force in the adjacent valleys of the Waterkloof, Fuller's Hoek, and Blinkwater, it was determined to halt in a hollow, where there was good water, until future operations were determined upon. Strong picquets were posted on the surrounding ridges, and the usual precautions taken to guard against surprise. Some large bodies of the enemy were seen collecting at various points, and about 3 P.M. the alarm was given that the Kaffirs were approaching in great force. They ran almost with the speed of greyhounds, but the troops, many of whom had to toss away their half-cooked dinners, got under arms with the utmost promptitude, and were soon posted in extended order on the ridges surrounding the bivouac, reinforcing the picquets. The enemy approached in swarms from all quarters of the contiguous bush, and as soon as they were within range, opened fire, which they kept up without intermission for about half an hour. Their force, at the lowest computation, was about 2000 men, and was led by Macomo in person, who was seen riding about on a white charger, well out of range. The troops being posted behind a ridge, were enabled to keep up a sharp fire without much danger to themselves, and the enemy were soon compelled to withdraw to the bush. Nearly half of the ammunition being now expended, the troops were ordered to retire; and Lieutenant-Colonel Sutton, with a few mounted men, was directed to occupy the pass leading from Kroome heights to Niland's farm. Between two and three hundred mounted Kaffirs were now seen endeavouring to turn the left flank, but they were kept in check, and all the troops were enabled to gain the pass—a narrow defile, in many parts of which not more than four or five men could walk abreast. The retreat was going on with perfect regularity, when a strong force of the enemy opened fire from the bush, and a detachment of the Fort Beaufort Fingoes became panic-stricken, rushing among the regular troops in great disorder, and thereby preventing them from using their arms with effect against the enemy. This no doubt encouraged the Kaffirs, who, seizing the advantage, rushed from the bush and stabbed many of the men with their assegais. The enemy continued their fire until the troops cleared the bush, but they scarcely showed themselves beyond it. The ammunition being nearly expended, the retreat was continued until the force arrived at Gilbert's farm, which they did shortly after dark, and bivouacked there for the night, sending an express to Riet Fontein for waggons to convey the wounded to camp. The casualties in the regiment on this occasion were 8 privates killed, and 1 officer, Lieutenant John Joseph Corrigan, 1 corporal, and 8 privates wounded. Hans Hartung, who had for many years been bandmaster of the regiment, and was much respected by all ranks, lost his life on this occasion; he had accompanied the force as a volunteer.

The troops returned to Riet Fontein and Fort Beaufort, on the following day.

An officer,[2] who was with the regiment during the whole of this war, states that this was the only instance in which the 74th really met the Kaffirs face to face, and the latter even then had the advantage of possessing a thorough knowledge of the intricacies of the

[2] Captain Thackeray, who is intimately acquainted with the history of his old regiment, and to whom we are greatly indebted for having carefully revised this history of the 74th Highlanders, and otherwise lent us valuable assistance and advice.

bush, and were in overwhelming numbers. There were numerous hand-to-hand conflicts, and several of the enemy were killed with the bayonet.

Major-General Somerset having arrived at Riet Fontein in September, the division marched on the 3rd of October to Fort Beaufort and encamped there, awaiting the arrival of reinforcements from the second division, under Lieutenant-Colonel Michel, of the 6th Regiment, intended to act with the first division in a combined attack on the Waterkloof, Kroome Heights, and Fuller's Hoek.

The necessary preparations having been made, Lieutenant-Colonel Fordyce marched on the 13th of October with the Reserve Battalion 12th Regiment, Beaufort West Levy, Graaf Reynett Mounted Levy, and Fort Beaufort Mounted Troop. The Major-General had previously proceeded with the Cape Mounted Riflemen and Fort Beaufort Fingo Levy to meet Lieutenant-Colonel Michel on his march from King William's Town.

The force under Lieutenant-Colonel Fordyce arrived at the Gola River on the afternoon of the 13th, and on the southern point of the Kroome Heights about sunrise next morning. The Waterkloof and Kroome Heights were that morning enveloped in a dense fog, which for a time prevented Lieutenant-Colonel Fordyce from acting in concert with the Major-General, according to previous arrangement; but about noon the fog cleared away, and the Major-General was then seen to be engaged with the enemy at the head of the Waterkloof. Lieutenant-Colonel Fordyce joined him with his brigade, and the enemy having been dispersed, they all marched to Mandell's farm, where they remained until the morning of the 16th.

The force was now divided. Lieutenant-Colonel Fordyce's brigade, reinforced by the Reserve Battalion 91st Regiment, marching by the Bush Nek to the entrance of the Waterkloof; while the remainder of the division, under the personal command of the Major-General, proceeded to the head of the Waterkloof. Lieutenant-Colonel Fordyce, on his arrival at the entrance of the Waterkloof, extended a line of skirmishers across the valley, seeing but few of the enemy, and meeting with no opposition until they emerged from the bush at the head of the Waterkloof, when a brisk fire was opened upon them; fresh skirmishers were thrown out, and the enemy dispersed. The force then joined the Major-General near Mount Misery, and the division marched to Eastland's Farm and bivouacked. The casualties in the regiment on this occasion were 2 privates killed, and 1 lance-corporal and 1 private wounded.

In another skirmish at the head of the Waterkloof, on the 23rd, 2 privates were killed and 2 wounded.

Various operations were carried on at the head of the Waterkloof and Kroome heights until the 28th, when Lieut.-Colonel Fordyce's brigade was ordered to the Blinkwater, where it arrived the same day, having been in the field exposed to heavy rains, and frequently with only one blanket per man, and since the 13th without tents.

The Commander-in-Chief, Sir Harry Smith, spoke, in his general order of October 31, in deservedly high terms of the conduct of the officers and men in these most trying duties; for this kind of desultory warfare, entailing constant marches from place to place without shelter, amid almost constant frost, snow, wind, and rain, and frequently with short supplies of food, and even of ammunition, against an immense number of savages, with whom it is impossible to come to close quarters, is far more trying to the temper and endurance of soldiers than a series of pitched battles with a powerful, well-disciplined, and well-equipped enemy.

This particular post of the enemy, at the head of the Waterkloof, was one which seemed almost impregnable, although it was held by only a few hundred Hottentots. The rebels had taken up a position near the summit of the Kloof, which they had fortified with a breastwall of detached rocks, from behind which they long bade defiance to all efforts to eject them. Occasionally, when the British soldiers were receding from the bush, the enemy would appear on the open ground, firing at the former with fatal precision, and seeming as if to invite them to open combat. Our brave soldiers accepting the challenge, and returning towards the Hottentots, or "Totties," as they

were facetiously called, the latter would precipitately retreat to their stronghold, reappearing when their opponents' backs were turned, sending death to many a poor fellow, whose brave comrades could never get a chance to avenge him. Such a mode of warfare is harassing in the highest degree. It was at the deathful Waterkloof that the 74th sustained the loss of one of its bravest and best-beloved officers.

The troops belonging to the second division having marched to King William's Town, and the Major-General having assembled at the Blinkwater all the available force of the first division, he ascended the Blinkwater Hill on the 4th of November, and bivouacked at Eastland's Farm, leaving the tents and baggage at the Blinkwater under a guard.

On the morning of the 6th of November the infantry under Lieutenant-Colonel Fordyce marched about two hours before daylight, the cavalry under the Major-General following at dawn, to the head of the Waterkloof, where, as we have said, a considerable party of the enemy was seen posted in strong positions. The infantry, under Lieutenant-Colonel Fordyce, were ordered to attack the position. The Colonel led his men in column into the Waterkloof, when suddenly his march was arrested by a rocky precipice which flanked him in the form of a semicircle, where he found the enemy in considerable force, and these knew too well the rules of military tactics to let so favourable an opportunity escape for inflicting a penalty. Though the bayonets of our brave soldiers seemed powerless in such a position—for they had to contend against an enemy concealed among inaccessible rocks—yet Colonel Fordyce placed his men in position for an assault, and it was while calmly surveying them to see that all was ready for the desperate work, that he was struck in the side by a ball, which proved fatal to him in a quarter of an hour. His last words, it is said, were, "What will become of my poor regiment?" He was indeed the father of his regiment, looking with parental solicitude after the comforts of men, women, and children, and by all he was lamented with unfeigned sorrow.[a] His men, notwithstanding their irre-

[a] We regret very much that after making all possible

parable loss, stood firm against the enemy, and the Major-General having arrived and assumed the command, the enemy was driven from his position, and the troops bivouacked for the night on Mount Misery, near the scene of the day's operations.

The casualties in the regiment on this occasion were 2 officers (Lieutenant-Colonel Fordyce and Lieutenant Carey), 2 sergeants, and 2 privates killed; and 1 officer, Lieutenant Gordon (who died shortly afterwards), and 8 men wounded. The greater number of the casualties on this occasion occurred in No.

2 company, under the command of Lieutenant Carey, until he was mortally wounded, and then of Lieutenant Philpot. They were opposed to a strong body of the enemy posted behind rocks, but being assisted by the light company, they succeeded in dislodging it.

The bodies of the dead were next day carried in a mule waggon for burial at Post Retief—15 miles across the table-land. "The funeral will never be forgotten by those who were present. The thunder, mingled with the booming artillery, rolled grandly and solemnly among the mountains. As the rough deal coffins were borne

Death of Lieutenant-Colonel Fordyce.
From "Campaigning in Kaffirland," by Captain Wm. Ross King, 74th Highlanders (now Lieut.-Colonel Unattached).

out, the 'firing party,' dripping wet, and covered with mud, presented arms, the officers uncovered, and we marched in slow time out of the gate and down the road—the pipers playing the mournful and touching 'Highland Lament'—to where the graves had been dug, a few hundred yards from the Post."

The following division order by Major-General Somerset by no means exaggerates the soldierly merits of Colonel Fordyce:—

"CAMP BLINKWATER,
"Nov. 9th, 1851.

"It is with the deepest regret that Major-General Somerset announces to the division inquiries, we have been unable to obtain a portrait of this distinguished officer; indeed, his brother, General Fordyce, informs us that no good portrait of the Colonel exists.

the death of Lieutenant-Colonel Fordyce, commanding the 74th Highlanders. He fell, mortally wounded, in action with the enemy, on the morning of the 6th, and died on the field.

"From the period of the 74th Highlanders having joined the first division, their high state of discipline and efficiency at once showed to the Major-General the value of Lieutenant-Colonel Fordyce as a commanding officer; the subsequent period, during which the Major-General had been in daily intercourse with Lieutenant-Colonel Fordyce, so constantly engaged against the enemy in the field, had tended to increase in the highest degree the opinion which the Major-General had formed of Lieutenant-Colonel Fordyce as a commander of the highest order, and one of Her Majesty's ablest officers, and whom he now so deeply laments (while he truly sympathises with the 74th Highlanders in their irreparable loss), as an esteemed brother soldier."

Small parties of the enemy having again taken up positions near the head of Fuller's Hoek, they were attacked and dislodged on the 7th; and on the following day the division marched to its camp at the Blinkwater.

The 74th was engaged in no enterprise of importance for the next two months, head-quarters having meantime been removed to Fort Beaufort. In January 1852 preparations were made under Major-General Somerset, by the first and second divisions, for a combined movement to destroy the enemy's crops in the Chumie Hoek, Amatolas, and on the left bank of the Keiskamma River. The Major-General marched from Fort Beaufort on the 26th of January 1852 for that purpose, with a force which included upwards of 250 of all ranks of the 74th. Detachments of the regiment were left at Post Retief, Blinkwater, Riet Fontein, and Fort Beaufort.

The Major-General, with the force under his command, arrived at the Amatolas on the 27th, and on the 28th commenced the destruction of the enemy's crops, which was carried on at the Amatolas, Chumie Hoek, and near the Gwali Mission Station, up to the 24th of February, with little interruption from the enemy and no loss to the regiment.

The destruction of that part of the crops allotted to the first division having been com-pleted, the Major-General marched on the 25th en route for Haddon on the Koonap River, where he arrived on the 29th, and formed a standing camp.

At about two o'clock on the morning of the 4th of March, a patrol under Lieutenant-Colonel Yarborough, 91st Regiment, consist-ing of all the available men of that corps and of the 74th Highlanders, together with a troop of the Cape Mounted Riflemen, marched to the Waterkloof to destroy a number of kraals belonging to a party of the enemy who had located themselves on the sides of the moun-tain near Browne's Farm. This force arrived at the scene of operations about sunrise, and immediately attacked the kraals, which they completely destroyed, and captured a number

of horses and cattle which were concealed in a dense bush in an adjacent kloof. These kraals were well defended by the enemy, and the time necessarily occupied in securing the horses and cattle allowed the enemy to collect in large numbers from every part of the Water-kloof. They kept up an incessant fire upon the troops until their arrival at Nel's Farm, where a position was taken up by the 74th and 91st Regiments, which kept the enemy in check until the horses and cattle were driven beyond their reach, after which the enemy dispersed, and the troops returned to camp. The casualties in the regiment on this occa-sion were 1 private killed and 4 wounded.

On the 7th of March the Commander-in-Chief arrived at the Blinkwater with all the available force of the 2nd division, for the purpose of carrying out, in connection with the 1st division, a combined movement against the Fuller's Hoek, the Waterkloof, and Kroome Heights, which were still occupied by Macomo and his best warriors. These opera-tions were carried on between the 10th and the 16th of the month, and the regiment was engaged with the enemy on several occasions during that time, but happily without sustain-ing any loss. 410 women, among whom was Macomo's great wife, many children, 130 horses, 1000 head of cattle, and a number of goats were captured, together with some arms and ammunition, and all the property in Macomo's Den.

The Commander-in-Chief, in referring to these six days' operations in a general order, spoke of them as a success which may well be expected to lead to a permanent and lasting peace. "The Kaffir tribes," he said, "have never been previously thus punished, and the expulsion over the Kei being effected, tran-quillity on a permanent basis may be hoped for. No soldiers ever endured greater fatigues, or ever encountered them with more constant cheerfulness and devotion to their sovereign and country."

On the 16th of March the 1st division re-turned to its standing camp, which had been removed on the 13th to the Gola River, near the entrance of the Waterkloof; and the troops belonging to the 2nd division returned to their stations.

The Waterkloof, Fuller's Hoek, and Blinkwater being now considered cleared of the enemy, the Commander-in-Chief ordered a combined movement to take place against large bodies of the enemy that had established themselves between the Kaboosie Mountains and the Kei River. To effect this, the 1st division marched on the morning of the 18th of March; and having been joined on the 26th at the Thorn River by a burgher force, which was to co-operate with the troops, reached the Thomas River on the 29th, where a standing camp was formed. The 2nd division, at the same time, sent patrols to the Kaboosie Nek, Keiskamma Hoek, and the banks of the Kei River, and a large number of burghers was in the field co-operating with the troops.

On the 5th of April a patrol, under Lieutenant-Colonel Napier, Cape Mounted Riflemen, consisting of 162 men, from the headquarters of the 74th, along with detachments of the various other corps, marched for the junction of the Thomas and the Kei Rivers, where it was supposed large numbers of the enemy's cattle were concealed.

This force arrived at and bivouacked on the Quantine, a branch of the Thomas River, on the evening of the 5th, and on the following morning resumed their march in three separate columns. Large herds of cattle were seen about ten o'clock in the morning near the junction of the Thomas and the Kei Rivers, and signal fires were lighted up by the enemy in various directions. After a successful contest of several hours' duration, in which 100 of the enemy were supposed to have been killed, this force captured, with little loss, large numbers of cattle, horses, and goats, with which they returned to the standing camp on the Thomas River. The Commander-in-Chief, Lieutenant-General Sir Harry Smith, Bart., in a general order, spoke in the highest terms of these services, as being of such a character that a speedy termination of the war might be looked for, which must lead to the establishment of permanent peace to the country.

The standing camp was moved on the 10th of April to the Windvogel, a branch of the Kei River. Lieutenant-General the Hon. George Cathcart, appointed Governor and Commander-in-Chief of the Cape of Good Hope in succession to Sir Harry Smith, who was recalled, having assumed the command and arrived at King William's Town, Major-General Somerset proceeded to that town to receive instructions regarding future operations.

Lieutenant-General Sir Harry George Wakelyn Smith, G.C.B., Bart., on resigning the command, bade farewell to the army which he had so efficiently commanded in a general order, in which he said:—

"I have served my Queen and country many years; and, attached as I have ever been to gallant soldiers, none were ever more endeared to me than those serving in the arduous campaign of 1851 and 1852 in South Africa. The unceasing labours of night marches, the burning sun, the torrents of rain, have been encountered with a cheerfulness as conspicuous as the intrepidity with which you have met the enemy in so many enterprising fights and skirmishes in his own mountain fastnesses and strongholds, and from which you have always driven him victoriously."[4]

During the next few months the 74th was kept incessantly moving about in detachments from one post to another, the bare recital of which movements would only fatigue the reader. The regiment was constantly employed either on patrol, in waylaying parties, or on escort duties, the work involved in such movements being, as we have already said, far more trying and fatiguing to the soldier

[4] There is no doubt that the energetic Sir Harry Smith was made the scape-goat of the shortcomings of the Government at home. Among other things, he had been accused "of using the language of hyperbole in describing the numerous rencontres which have occurred, and of giving praise to the gallant officers and troops as well as burghers." Possessing, however, some experience in war, he says, in his spirited despatch to Earl Grey, dated Camp, Blinkwater, March 17, 1852, "I must maintain that such is not the case. Troops acting in the open field expect not the stimulus of praise; the soldier sees his foe, and his British courage rises at each step; but he who, after perhaps a night-march of great length, has to ascend mountains, or penetrate dense bush and ravines, filled probably with a daring and intrepid enemy, as resolute as athletic, ready to murder any one who may fall into his hands, and when warfare is of the most stealthy and enterprising kind, appreciates the praise of his commander, because, when his acts are conspicuously daring, he is conscious he deserves it. He does his duty; but human nature renders even the soldier's intrepid heart sensible of the approbation of his superior; which he is proud to know may reach the eye of his parents and friends."

than a regular series of field operations against a large and thoroughly disciplined army. The high value of these irritating duties could only be fully appreciated by the superior officers who were watching the progress of the operations from day to day, and by the terrified colonists, whose lives and property the brave soldiers were doing their best, under great hardship, to protect. That the 74th, as well as the other regiments, really were the protectors of the colonists in South Africa, and performed their duties as such with honour and credit to themselves, all who were in a position to form an opinion concur in admitting. We have only heard of one instance in which an attempt was made to sully the honour and honesty of the 74th; that was by the Rev. Henry Renton, a Scotch missionary, who at a public meeting in Glasgow made some remarks reflecting on the conduct of the 74th Highlanders. We cannot believe that a Scotchman would maliciously attempt to sully the honour of a Highland regiment; and, of course, a Christian minister never so far should forget himself as to give utterance to a statement which he does not believe has a foundation in truth, especially when that statement, as in the present case, involves the reputation of so many of his fellow-countrymen, and, it is to be presumed, fellow-Christians. That the Rev. Henry Renton, whose honesty of intention, then, we cannot doubt, was under a misapprehension when he rashly—perhaps in a gush of "holy rapture," as Burns puts it—made this statement at the public meeting in Glasgow, is clear from the following letter written on the subject by Major-General Somerset:—

"GRAHAMSTOWN, *August* 18, 1852.

"SIR,—Having observed in several of the public journals that, at a recent public meeting, Mr Renton, a Scotch minister, took occasion to attack the character of the 74th Highlanders for their conduct when encamped at the Gwali Station on the Chumie River, in the month of February last, stating that the men of that corps had plundered and destroyed the garden of the widow Chalmers while the savage enemies had always spared her property; I desire to state, in justice to the 74th Highlanders under your command, that the statement is a false and gratuitous attack on your gallant regiment, whose unvaried discipline and excellent conduct have ever met my fullest approbation.

"Shortly after the troops arrived in camp at Gwali, a guard was detached to afford Mrs Chalmers protection, and if any produce was taken out of her garden, it must have been in total ignorance that any person was residing on the property—the Kaffirs who had been residing on the grounds having all fled into the bush.

"I consider the attack of Mr Renton, whose character is so well known on the frontier, to be an attempt to enhance the value of his statements in favour of those barbarians whose atrocities he has attempted to palliate, and whose cause he so earnestly patronises.

"You will be good enough to make this expression of my sentiments known to the 74th Highlanders under your command.

"I have the honour to be, &c,

"H. SOMERSET,
"Major-General.

"To Major Patton,
"Commanding 74th Highlanders."

Major-General Somerset having been appointed to the Staff in India, Colonel Buller, C.B., Rifle Brigade, assumed the command of the 1st division on the 27th of August 1852.

Lieutenant-Colonel John Macduff, from the St Helena Regiment, having been appointed to the 74th Highlanders, joined at Fort Beaufort on the 17th of October 1852, and assumed the command of the regiment.

The Commander-in-Chief having determined upon sending an expedition into the Abasutus country against Moshesh, to enforce the payment of a fine of cattle and horses imposed upon that chief, the detachments from Fort Browne, Koonap Port, Riet Fontein, Post Retief, joined headquarters at Fort Beaufort in the beginning of November, and on the 10th of that month the headquarters, under Lieutenant-Colonel Macduff—strength, 2 captains, 5 subalterns, 3 staff, 12 sergeants, 5 buglers, and 244 rank and file—marched for Burghersdorp, where the forces intended for the expedition were to assemble under the

II.   4 o

personal command of His Excellency the Commander-in-Chief. A detachment was left at Fort Beaufort under Major Patton, consisting of 2 captains, 1 subaltern, 2 staff, 11 sergeants, 4 buglers, and 141 rank and file.

On the 11th of November, the force was joined by a detachment of artillery and 2 guns under Captain Robinson, and a detachment of the Cape Mounted Rifles, under Major Somerset, the whole being under the command of Lieutenant-Colonel Macduff. Proceeding by stages towards its destination, the force was joined on the 16th by Captain Brydon's company from Whittlesea, consisting of about 150 men, increasing the strength to 1 lieutenant-colonel, 3 captains, 6 subalterns, 3 staff, 17 sergeants, 7 buglers, and 404 rank and file; on the 17th to the Honey Klip River; on the 18th to Klaas Smidts River; on the 19th to the Vleys on the Stormberg Mountains; on the 20th to the Stormberg River, on the 22nd it reached Burghersdorp, and joined the troops under Lieutenant-Colonel Eyre of the 73rd regiment, who had arrived at Burghersdorp on the previous day.

On the 23rd, the headquarters of the Cape Mounted Rifles joined the force, and on the 28th, His Excellency the Commander-in-Chief arrived, and the troops were divided into brigades, the 74th Highlanders, the 2nd (Queen's Regiment), and one Rocket Battery, forming the first brigade of infantry, under Lieutenant-Colonel Macduff, 74th Highlanders.

On the 28th of November, the march was recommenced by brigades, and the village of Plaatberg was reached on the 13th.

Moshesh's sons, Nehemiah and David, arrived in camp the same evening, and on the 15th, that chief himself appeared and had an interview with the governor, who informed him that if his fine of horses and cattle was not paid within three days, he would be obliged to go and take them.

On the 18th, Nehemiah arrived with 3450 head of cattle; but the remainder not having been sent within the stipulated time, the cavalry and 2nd brigade advanced on the 19th to the Drift on the Caledon River, leaving the camp and cattle at Plaatberg in charge of the 1st brigade. This force moved against Moshesh on the morning of the 20th,

and after a sanguinary contest on the Berea Mountain, which lasted during the day, captured 4500 head of cattle, and some horses and goats. During that night Moshesh sent a letter to the Governor, saying that he had been severely punished, and suing for peace, which the Governor granted on the 21st, and the troops returned to camp on the 22nd.

One company of the 2nd, or Queen's, and one of the 74th, under Captain Bruce, marched for Plaatberg on the afternoon of the 19th, and reinforced the troops engaged. The cattle were sent for distribution to Bloem Fontein, and the troops commenced their march on their return to the colony on the 24th of December. On their arrival at the Orange River, it was found so swollen from recent rains that the troops, waggons, and baggage had to be conveyed across on two pontoons, which operation occupied six days.

The troops marched on their return to the colony by nearly the same route by which they had advanced, a detachment of the regiment, under Captain Bruce, of 2 sergeants, 1 bugler, and 40 rank and file, being left at Whittlesea.

The Governor and Commander-in-Chief took his leave of the troops in a general order dated "Camp Boole Poort, 26th December 1852," in which he spoke in the highest terms of their conduct during the expedition.

Lieutenant-Colonel Eyre also, on resigning command of the division, published a division order, in which he spoke of the general character of all non-commissioned officers and soldiers as having been most exemplary. "To the officers generally he feels that his thanks are especially due; their example and exertions have rendered his task of commanding very easy." Among the officers particularly named by Lieutenant-Colonel Eyre were,—Lieutenant-Colonel Macduff of the 74th Highlanders, commanding the 1st brigade, from whose judgment and experience he derived great assistance; Captain Hancock, 74th Highlanders; Lieutenant and Adjutant Falconer, 74th Highlanders, acting Brigade-Major, and Dr Fraser, 74th Highlanders, &c.

The first brigade, under Lieutenant-Colonel Macduff, arrived at Bryce's Farm, on the Kat River, on the 19th of January, 1853. On the following day the regiments composing the brigade returned to their stations; the 74th proceeding to Fort Beaufort, where it arrived on the 21st, and where, on the 20th, a small detachment from the regimental depôt had joined.

In the beginning of February orders were received for the regiment to proceed to King William's Town to reinforce the 2nd division. It accordingly marched from Fort Beaufort on the 3rd, under Lieutenant-Colonel Macduff, leaving a small detachment at Fort Beaufort. The regiment arrived at King William's Town on the 7th, and was ordered to proceed to the Duhne or Itembi Mission Station, accompanied by detachments from the 12th Royal Lancers, the Royal Artillery, and the Cape Mounted Riflemen; the whole under the command of Lieutenant-Colonel Macduff, of the 74th Highlanders, the intention being to form a connecting link in a chain of posts surrounding the Amatolas. Numerous patrols were sent out to keep up a communication with the post at Kaboosie Nek, and to examine the country near the sources of the Kaboosie and the Buffalo rivers, and the valley between the Iseli range and Murray's Krantz.

Peace, however, having been established in March, the regiment marched from the Duhne Station to Fort Beaufort, arriving there on the 26th.

On the termination of the war, His Excellency published a general order, which we shall give at length, as serving to convey the idea formed by a competent judge of the urgent nature of the duties which the soldiers engaged in the Kaffir War had to perform, and also showing the important results of the operations in which the 74th bore so conspicuous a part.

"HEADQUARTERS, GRAHAMSTOWN,
"March 14, 1853.

"The Commander of the Forces congratulates the army under his command on the termination of the war of rebellion which has troubled the eastern frontier of Her Majesty's South African Dominions for more than two years, and which at one time assuming the character of a war of races, had it not been arrested by their gallantry, perseverance, and unparalleled exertions, must have overwhelmed the inhabitants of the eastern district of the colony. And indeed it is impossible to calculate the extent to which it might have reached.

"In conveying his thanks to the army for their meritorious services, His Excellency desires to include those of the Colonial service, Europeans, Fingoes, and Loyal Hottentots, who, under gallant leaders, nobly emulated the brilliant examples set them by Her Majesty's troops.

"The field of glory opened to them in a Kaffir war and Hottentot rebellion is possibly not so favourable and exciting as that which regular warfare with an open enemy in the field affords; yet the unremitting exertions called for in hunting well-armed yet skulking savages through the bush, and driving them from their innumerable strongholds, are perhaps more arduous than those required in regular warfare, and call more constantly for individual exertions and intelligence.

"The British soldier, always cheerfully obedient to the call, well knows that when he has done his duty, he is sure to obtain the thanks and good opinion of his gracious Queen.

"It is His Excellency's duty, and one which he has had the greatest pleasure in performing, to call Her Majesty's attention, not only on particular occasions, but generally, to the noble conduct of all officers, non-commissioned officers, and soldiers of this army, throughout the arduous contest in which they have been engaged; and they may rest assured it will not pass unheeded.

"It cannot fail to be an additional gratification to them to reflect that the result of their exertions has been the total and final clearance of the Waterkloof, Fish River, and all the other strongholds of the enemy within the colony. The surrender of the rebel chiefs, Sandilli, Macomo, and the Gaika people, who have been expelled from all their former territories, including the Amatolas, which now remain in possession of Her Majesty's troops, and the removal of that hitherto troublesome race to the banks of the Kei; the complete submission of the Bassutus, the Sambookies, and the Anna-Galiekas, and the extinction of the Hottentot rebellion; and

that thus, thanks to their noble exertions, where all was war and rebellion two years ago, general and profound peace reigns in South Africa."
    "A. J. CLOETE,
        "Quartermaster-General."

Colonel Buller, C.B., Rifle Brigade, commanding 1st Division, made his inspection of the regiment on the 5th of May, when he expressed to Lieutenant-Colonel Macduff his entire satisfaction with the regiment in every respect.

Before concluding our account of the doings of the 74th Highlanders during the Kaffir War, we must tell the story of an action which sheds more glory upon those who took part in it than a hundred well-fought battles, or the taking of many cities; an action in which discipline and self-denial triumphed gloriously over the love of dear life itself.

On the 7th of January 1852, the iron paddle troopship "Birkenhead," of 1400 tons and 556 horse-power, commanded by Master Commanding Robert Salmond, sailed from the Cove of Cork, bound for the Cape of Good Hope, with detachments from the depôts of ten regiments, all under the command of Lieutenant-Colonel Seton of the 74th Highlanders. Altogether there were on board about 631 persons, including a crew of 132, the rest being soldiers with their wives and children. Of the soldiers, besides Colonel Seton and Ensign Alexander Cumming Russell, 66 men belonged to the 74th.

The "Birkenhead" made a fair voyage out, and reached Simon's Bay, Cape of Good Hope, on the 23rd of February, when Captain Salmond was ordered to proceed eastward immediately, and land the troops at Algoa Bay and Buffalo River. The "Birkenhead" accordingly sailed again about six o'clock on the evening of the 25th; the night being almost perfectly calm, the sea smooth, and the stars out in the sky. Men, as usual, were told off to keep a look-out, and a leadsman was stationed on the paddle-box next the land, which was at a distance of about 3 miles on the port side. Shortly before two o'clock on the morning of the 26th, when all who were not on duty were sleeping peacefully below, the leadsman got soundings in 12 or 13 fathoms: ere he had time to get another cast of the lead, the "Birkenhead" wa

suddenly and rudely arrested in her course; she had struck on a sunken rock, surrounded by deep water, and was firmly fixed upon its jagged points. The water immediately rushed into the fore part of the ship, and drowned many soldiers who were sleeping on the lower troop deck.

It is easy to imagine the consternation and wild commotion with which the hundreds of men, women, and children would be seized on realising their dangerous situation. Captain Salmond, who had been in his cabin since ten o'clock of the previous night, at once appeared on deck with the other naval and military officers; the captain ordered the engine to be stopped, the small bower anchor to be let go, the paddle-box boats to be got out, and the quarter boats to be lowered, and to lie alongside the ship.

It might have been with the "Birkenhead" as with many other passenger-laden ships which have gone to the bottom, had there not been one on board with a clear head, perfect self-possession, a noble and chivalrous spirit, and a power of command over others which few men have the fortune to possess; this born "leader of men" was Lieutenant-Colonel Seton of the 74th Highlanders. On coming on deck he at once comprehended the situation, and without hesitation made up his mind what it was the duty of brave men and British soldiers to do under the circumstances. He impressed upon the other officers the necessity of preserving silence and discipline among the men. Colonel Seton then ordered the soldiers to draw up on both sides of the quarter-deck; the men obeyed as if on parade or about to undergo inspection. A party was told off to work the pumps, another to assist the sailors in lowering the boats, and a third to throw the poor horses overboard. "Every one did as he was directed," says Captain Wright of the 91st, who, with a number of men of that regiment, was on board. "All received their orders, and had them carried out, as if the men were embarking instead of going to the bottom; there was only this difference, that I never saw any embarkation conducted with so little noise and confusion."

Meanwhile Captain Salmond, thinking no doubt to get the ship safely afloat again and t t an her nearer to the shore, ordered the engineer to give the paddles a few backward turns. This only hastened the destruction of the ship, which bumped again upon the rock, so that a great hole was torn in the bottom, letting the water rush in volumes into the engine-room, putting out the fires.

The situation was now more critical than ever; but the soldiers remained quietly in their places, while Colonel Seton stood in the gangway with his sword drawn, seeing the women and children safely passed down into the second cutter, which the captain had provided for them. This duty was speedily effected, and the cutter was ordered to lie off about 150 yards from the rapidly sinking ship. In about ten minutes after she first struck, she broke in two at the foremast—this mast and the funnel falling over to the starboard side, crushing many, and throwing into the water those who were endeavouring to clear the paddle-box boat. But the men kept their places, though many of them were mere lads, who had been in the service only a few months. An eye-witness, speaking of the captain and Colonel Seton at this time, has said—"Side by side they stood at the helm, providing for the safety of all that could be saved. They never tried to save themselves."

Besides the cutter into which the women and children had been put, only two small boats were got off, all the others having been stove in by the falling timbers or otherwise rendered useless. When the bows had broken off, the ship began rapidly to sink forward, and those who remained on board clustered on to the poop at the stern, all, however, without the least disorder. At last, Captain Salmond, seeing that nothing more could be done, advised all who could swim to jump overboard and make for the boats. But Colonel Seton told the men that if they did so, they would be sure to swamp the boats, and send the women and children to the bottom; he therefore asked them to keep their places, and they obeyed. The "Birkenhead" was now rapidly sinking; the officers shook hands and bade each other farewell; immediately after which the ship again broke in two abaft the mainmast, when the hundreds who had bravely stuck to their posts were plunged with the sinking wreck into the sea. "Until the vessel totally disappeared," says an eye-witness, "there was not a cry or murmur from soldiers or sailors." Those who could swim struck out for the shore, but few ever reached it; most of them either sank through exhaustion or were devoured by the sharks, or were dashed to death on the rugged shore near Point Danger, or entangled in the death-grip of the long arms of sea-weed that floated thickly near the coast. About twenty minutes after the "Birkenhead" first struck on the rock, all that remained visible were a few fragments of timber, and the main-topmast standing above the water. Of the 631 souls on board, 438 were drowned, only 193 being saved: not a single woman or child was lost. Those who did manage to land, exhausted as they were, had to make their way over a rugged and barren coast for fifteen miles, before they reached the residence of Captain Small, by whom they were treated with the greatest kindness until taken away by H.M. steamer "Rhadamanthus."

The three boats which were lying off near the ship when she went down picked up as many men as they safely could, and made for the shore, but found it impossible to land; they were therefore pulled away in the direction of Simon's Town. After a time they were descried by the coasting schooner "Lioness," the master of which, Thomas E. Ramsden, took the wretched survivors on board, his wife doing all in her power to comfort them, distributing what spare clothes were on board among the many men, who were almost naked. The "Lioness" made for the scene of the wreck, which she reached about half-past two in the afternoon, and picked up about forty-five men, who had managed to cling to the still standing mast of the "Birkenhead." The "Lioness," as well as the "Rhadamanthus," took the rescued remnant to Simon's Bay.

Of those who were drowned, 357, including 9 officers, belonged to the army; the remaining 81 formed part of the ship's company, including 7 naval officers. Besides the chivalrous Colonel Seton and Ensign Russell, 48 of the 66 men belonging to the 74th perished.

Any comment on this deathless deed of heroic self-denial, of this victory of moral power over the strongest impulse, would be impertinent; no one needs to be told what to think of the simple story. The 74th and the other regiments who were represented on board of the "Birkenhead," as well as the whole British army, must feel prouder of this victory over the last enemy, than of all the great battles whose names adorn their regimental standards.

The only tangible memorial of the deed that exists is a monument erected by Her Majesty Queen Victoria in the colonnade of Chelsea Hospital; it bears the following inscription :—

"This monument is erected by command of Her Majesty Queen Victoria, to record the heroic constancy and unbroken discipline shown by Lieutenant-Colonel Seton, 74th Highlanders, and the troops embarked under his command, on board the "Birkenhead," when that vessel was wrecked off the Cape of Good Hope, on the 26th of February 1852, and to preserve the memory of the officers, non-commissioned officers, and men who perished on that occasion. Their names were as follows :—

"Lieutenant-Colonel ALEXANDER SETON, 74th Highlanders, commanding the troops; Cornet Rolt, Sergeant Straw, and 3 privates, 12th Lancers; Ensign Boylan, Corporal M'Manus, and 34 privates, 2nd Queen's Regiment; Ensign Metford and 47 privates, 6th Royals; 55 privates, 12th Regiment; Sergeant Hicks, Corporals Harrison and Cousins, and 26 privates, 43rd Light Infantry; 3 privates 45th Regiment; Corporal Curtis and 29 privates, 60th Rifles; Lieutenants Robinson and Booth, and 54 privates, 73rd Regiment; Ensign Russell, Corporals Mathison and William Laird, and 46 privates, 74th Highlanders; Sergeant Butler, Corporals Webber and Smith, and 41 privates, 91st Regiment; Staff-Surgeon Laing; Staff Assistant-Surgeon Robinson. In all, 357 officers and men. The names of the privates will be found inscribed on brass plates adjoining."

Lieutenant-Colonel Seton, whose high-mindedness, self-possession, and calm determination inspired all on board, was son and heir of the late Alexander Seton, Esq. of Mounie, Aberdeenshire, and represented the Mounie branch of the old and eminent Scottish house of Pitmedden. His death was

undoubtedly a great loss to the British army, as all who knew him agree in stating that he was a man of high ability and varied attainments; he was distinguished both as a mathematician and a linguist. Lord Aberdare (formerly the Right Honourable H. A. Bruce) speaks of Colonel Seton, from personal knowledge, as "one of the most gifted and accomplished men in the British army."[5]

III.

1853—1874.

Embarkation for India—Ten years in India—Malabar—Canara—New stand of Colours—Mrs Anson—A desperate duel — Lieut.-General Shawe becomes Colonel of the 74th——Indian Rebellion——The Kaffir War Medals—Storm of Sholapoor—Kopal—Nargoond—Leave to be discharged in 1858—The 74th embarks for England in 1864—Captain Thackeray in command of the 74th—Edinburgh—Aldershot—Receives the special commendation of H.R.H. Commanding-in-Chief.

ORDERS having been received that the 74th should hold itself in readiness to proceed to India, all the outlying detachments joined headquarters at Fort Beaufort. The regiment set out on November 10, 1853, to march for Port Elizabeth, where it arrived on the 18th, and from which, on the 20th, the headquarters and right wing were conveyed to Cape Town, where they embarked on board the freight-ship "Queen."

The "Queen" sailed from Table Bay on the 25th of November, and arrived at Madras on the 12th of January 1854. The 74th was destined to remain in India for the next ten years, during which time the movements of its various detachments were exceedingly complicated, and are difficult to follow even with the aid of a good map. Indeed, few regiments, we are sure, have been more broken up into small detachments than was the 74th, during its services at the Cape, and for the greater part of the time that it remained in India; for eight years from 1850, when the regiment was at Fermoy, in Ireland, it was broken up into small detachments, and it was only on the repeated petition of the commanding-officer to the War Office authorities that, in 1858, all the companies once more found themselves together : this was at Bellary, in the Madras Presidency, where headquarters had been stationed for some time.

After the arrival of headquarters and the right wing at Madras, the regiment was joined by a detachment from England, under Captain Jago. After headquarters had been about a week at Madras, it, along with four companies, re-embarked, on January 19, for Negapatam, about 180 miles further south, where it arrived next day, and remained till the 24th, when it set out to march for Trichinopoly, which it reached on the 2nd of February.

On the 7th of February a detachment, under Captain Brydon, consisting of 4 officers and 205 men, proceeded to Jackatalla (now Wellington, about ten miles south of Ootakemund, in the Neelgherri Hills), there to be stationed for the purpose of assisting in the building of barracks at that place.

Captain Jago, with the two companies which had been left at Madras, joined headquarters on the 13th, and a small detachment from England, under Lieutenant Davies, landed at Madras on the 13th, and arrived at Trichinopoly on the 27th of February.

The left wing of the service companies, which had left Cape Town some time after the rest of regiment, landed at Madras on the 19th of February, and embarked for Tranquebar. This detachment, on its march from Tranquebar to Trichinopoly, was unfortunately attacked by cholera, and lost 3 sergeants, 2 corporals, and 15 privates.

The headquarters marched for Jackatalla on the 15th of March, and arrived there on the 30th, having left a detachment at Trichinopoly, consisting of 2 captains, 5 subalterns, 1 assistant-surgeon, 10 sergeants, 4 drummers, and 220 rank and file, under command of Major Hancock, who was relieved of the command by Lieutenant-Colonel Monkland on the 3rd of April.

It would be tedious to follow the movements of the various detachments of the regiment in the performance of the ordinary routine duties which devolve on the British soldier when stationed in India. The headquarters remained at Jackatalla—where it was gradually joined by the various detachments which remained at Trichinopoly—till 1857. At fre-

quent intervals during this time, and while the regiment remained in India, it was joined by detachments of recruits from the depôt companies at home, and by volunteers from other regiments in India—it being a common custom, when a regiment was ordered home, to allow those of the men who wished to remain in India to volunteer into other regiments. If we may judge from the large detachments which the 74th received in this way, it must have had a very high reputation among the other regiments of Her Majesty stationed in India. Among the other additions which the 74th received while at Jackatalla was one which was made by Her Majesty's gracious pleasure, much, no doubt, to the gratification of the regiment, and one which to a Highland regiment is of no mean importance. The addition we refer to consisted of 1 pipe-major and 5 pipers, who joined in May 1854, and whose strains, no doubt, served often to remind the many Highlanders in the regiment of their homes far away in dear old Scotland. This accession was in addition to a pipe-major and a piper for each company, which have always been maintained in the regiment, and dressed at the expense of the officers.

In November of the same year that the regiment received the above important addition, it was inspected by Major-General J. Wheeler Cleveland, commanding the Southern Division, who, in a division order afterwards issued, expressed himself in complimentary and justly merited terms towards this distinguished regiment.

Colonel Macduff, having been appointed a brigadier of the 2nd class, and ordered to assume the command of the provinces of Malabar and Canara, handed over command of the regiment to Captain Brydon on the 7th of February 1855,—Lieutenant-Colonel Monkland, the next senior officer, having proceeded to Bangalore on sick-leave. But Captain and Brevet-Major Robert Bruce having joined, from leave of absence, on the 28th of February, assumed command of the regiment, and was relieved on the 9th of April by Lieutenant-Colonel Monkland.

A wing of the regiment having been ordered to relieve the 25th (King's Own Borderers) Regiment—132 volunteers from which joined the 74th—at Cannanoor, a detail of 8 officers, 1 surgeon, 13 sergeants, 16 corporals, 6 drummers, 3 pipers, and 304 privates, under command of Captain Jago, marched from headquarters on the 14th of February, and arrived at Cannanoor on the 1st of March, having *en route* detached No. 5 Company, under Captain Augustus Davies, to Malliapooram. The wing thus stationed at Cannanoor, on the Malabar coast, had to furnish so many strong detachments to the provinces of Malabar and Canara that it was necessary frequently to reinforce it from headquarters, as well as from England, so that very soon the number of companies at headquarters was reduced to four, the other six being with the left wing.

The 24th of May, being the anniversary of the birth of Her Most Gracious Majesty, was selected by the Hon. Mrs George Anson for presenting a stand of new colours to the regiment. His Excellency Lieutenant-General the Honourable George Anson, Commander-in-Chief of the Madras Army, and the staff of the Most Noble the Governor-General of India, the Marquis of Dalhousie, and a large concourse of spectators, were to be present, but the Governor-General was unfortunately prevented by illness from attending.

The new colours having been consecrated by the Rev. John Ruthven Macfarlane, the chaplain of the regiment, were handed to Lieutenants R. H. D. Lowe and H. R. Wolrige (the two senior subalterns present) by the Honourable Mrs Anson, who, in doing so, mentioned the various services of the regiment in a most complimentary manner; and His Excellency the Commander-in-Chief, after the review, was pleased to express himself in the most flattering terms with regard to the gallantry, efficiency, soldier-like bearing, and good conduct of the regiment.

In the month of September, the detachment stationed at Malliapooram, under the command of Captain Augustus Davies, was employed against some insurgent Moplahs in the neighbourhood, who had murdered Mr Conelly, Collector of Malabar, and in an affair on the 17th of that month 1 private was killed and 1 wounded.

During the performance of this duty a very remarkable incident occurred which is well worth putting on record. Captain Davies' company having been sent in quest of the Moplahs, came upon them, after a hot midday march of about eight or ten miles, at the house of a high caste Nair, which they had taken possession of after murdering the servant who had been left in charge. The house was no sooner surrounded by the soldiers than the Moplahs rushed forth, fired what arms they possessed at the 74th, killing a private; they then attacked the men with the Moplah war-knives. All the Moplahs were speedily despatched, not, however, before one of them had attacked Private Joseph Park, who transfixed the Moplah through the chest with his bayonet. The Moplah thereupon, although mortally wounded, seized the muzzle of Park's firelock—for the 74th was still armed with the old Brown Bess—and with a fierce blow of his war-knife, whilst still transfixed with the bayonet, cut Park's throat almost from ear to ear. Staggered with the blow, the firelock dropped from Park's hands, and the Moplah fell dead at his feet. After hovering between life and death for some weeks, Park ultimately recovered.

Colonel Macduff, having been relieved from the provinces of Malabar and Canara by the return of Brigadier Brown, rejoined headquarters, and assumed command of the regiment on the 31st of January 1856, and Lieutenant-Colonel Monkland proceeded to Cannanoor for the purpose of assuming command of the left wing. On the 14th of November, however, Colonel Macduff, as senior officer in the Presidency, having been ordered to proceed to Bellary as acting Brigadier in place of Colonel Brown of the 43d Foot, who had died, the command of the headquarters devolved upon Lieutenant-Colonel Monkland, who, however, retained it only a few weeks, as Colonel Macduff, having been relieved from the command of the Bellary Brigade by Colonel Pole, 12th Lancers, his senior, returned to headquarters at Jackatalla, and reassumed the command of the regiment on the 6th of February.

On the 16th of February 1857 notification of the appointment of Lieutenant-General Shawe to the colonelcy of the regiment, in place of Lieutenant-General Thomson, was received by the regiment.

During all this time, of course, the regular half-yearly inspection was made by Major-General Cleveland, who on every occasion was able to express himself perfectly satisfied with the state of the regiment.

On the 12th of April 1857, Enfield rifles were first issued to a portion of the regiment in accordance with the instructions from home directing their partial introduction into the army as an experiment.

On the 22d of July, in accordance with instructions received, the right wing and head-quarter companies proceeded en route to Bangalore by Mysore ; but on arriving at the latter place, their destination having been changed to Bellary (with the exception of 150 men, who, under command of Captain Falconer, followed by marches in charge of the families and baggage), the regiment was pushed on by transit to that station, Government being apprehensive of a rising among the Rajah's zemindars in the Mahratta country. As the sequel shows, the services of the regiment were soon called into requisition. A movable column having been formed under the command of Brigadier Whitlock, the grenadier company, made up to 100 men immediately on its arrival, proceeded on the 12th of August to join the force by way of Kurnool; and as soon as the arrival of the detachment under Captain Falconer, above referred to, rejoined headquarters on the 30th, the light company, also made up to 100 men, proceeded to join the column. These companies were all armed with the Enfield rifle —the right wing, on passing through Bangalore, having been furnished with this weapon. These two companies being on field service, and a wing of six companies being at Cannanoor, the headquarters of the regiment at Bellary was reduced to a skeleton of two weak companies.

On the 16th of September, Colonel Macduff being appointed Brigadier of the 2nd class on the permanent establishment of the Presidency, the command of the corps again devolved upon Colonel Monkland, at this time in command of the left wing at Cannanoor, but who now assumed the command at headquarters. On the following day a letter, considerably augmenting the establishment of the regiment, was received ; and on the 29th the headquarters, consisting of the two attenuated companies above referred to, was inspected by Major-General Donald Macleod,[6] commanding the ceded districts, who on the occasion expressed himself satisfied with everything that came under his notice.

Instructions having been received for the left wing at Cannanoor to join headquarters at Bellary, on the arrival of the 66th Foot at that station from England, the various detachments rejoined the wing, and the whole six companies marched, under the command of Captain Jago, on the 12th of January 1858, having all been furnished with the new Enfield rifle. The wing arrived at Bellary in daily batches by the 20th of February.

The regiment having been scattered in detachments, the medals which it had so honourably won in the Kaffir war of 1851-53 had not been presented to many of the men ; therefore, upon the six companies joining headquarters, Lieutenant-Colonel Monkland took an early opportunity of distributing to the meritorious those rewards for their distinguished conduct during that trying campaign.

Intimation having been received that the Rajah of Sholapoor was in arms against the Government, the two companies of the regiment, with Brigadier Whitlock, previously referred to, were detached to Sholapoor, at the storm and capture of which, on the 8th and 9th of February, they were present and took a prominent part.

On the 2nd, 3rd, and 4th of March, the regiment being, by good fortune, all together for a brief period, with the exception of two companies, Nos. 1 and 10, on field service, Major-General Donald Macleod again inspected it, and was pleased, as previously, to express himself much gratified with the discipline and interior economy of the regiment, as well as with its appearance on parade.

The day following the inspection, the 15th of March 1858, a detachment, under Captain Falconer, consisting of 2 captains, 4 subalterns, 1 staff-officer, 12 sergeants, 12 corporals, 3 pipers, and 280 privates, proceeded on field-

[6] This officer met his death by a sad mischance in 1873, at one of the London Metropolitan Railway Stations.

4 II

service to the southern Mahratta country, being placed at the disposal of the Bombay Government, and being ultimately stationed at Darwar.

On the 28th of May, a petty rajah or zemindar having taken possession of the Fort of Kopál, a field force from Bellary was immediately put in motion—No. 9 Company, under Captain Menzies, composing the European infantry with the force. Major Hughes, deeming it politic to nip in the bud this outbreak before it spread further in the Madras Presidency, pushed on the force as quickly as possible by forced marches, and arrived before Kopál on the 31st. The fort was stormed and recaptured on the 1st of June by No. 9 Company, which formed the storming party on the occasion, having 1 sergeant and 6 privates wounded, one of the latter dying on the 5th.

The same day on which the storm and capture of Kopál took place, Companies 2 and 6, under Captain Davies, having been, by direction of the Bombay Government, detached from the contingent stationed at Darwar, proceeded to Noorgoond, and stormed and captured the fort of that name, on which occasion only 1 private was wounded.

Government being apprehensive that the rebel leader, Tantéa Topee, was endeavouring to enter the Deccan and incite the Mahrattas, a field force under the command of Brigadier Spottiswood of the 1st Dragoon Guards, who had temporarily succeeded Brigadier Macduff in command of the Bellary Brigade, marched from Bellary on the 9th of November. The force consisted of the 74th Highlanders, 47th Regiment Native Infantry, one battery of Royal Artillery, 5th Light Cavalry, and one regiment of Mysore Horse. It proceeded by way of Kurnool to Hyderabad, arriving there on the 3rd of December. This force remained fully equipped and ready to move on any point until the 21st of January 1859, when it was broken up and taken on the strength of the Hyderabad subsidiary force. The 74th left Hyderabad on February 3rd, and reached Bellary on the 22nd of the same month.

Shortly before this, Major-General Macleod left his district, and it must be exceedingly gratifying to the 74th that an officer of his penetration, knowledge, and honesty of speech,

felt himself able to issue an order so highly complimentary as the following, dated "Headquarters, Ceded Districts, October 8th, 1858:"—

"The Major-General thanks Colonel Monkland for the excellent state of discipline and good behaviour of the men of the 74th Highlanders while the regiment remained at Bellary. The conduct of the men has been strikingly correct. A single case of irregularity in any soldier's conduct out of quarters has never been observed. . . . As the Major-General thinks it probable that during his period of command he will not again have the troops composing the column under his orders, he deems it right to express his high opinion of those composing it, and feels confident that opportunity is only wanting to prove that the Bellary column is second to none on field-service."

It was at this time that, at the repeated request of the commanding officer, the whole regiment was reunited at Bellary, where the strength of the regiment was found to be as follows:—1 colonel, 2 lieutenant-colonels, 2 majors, 10 captains, 14 lieutenants, 2 ensigns, 6 staff, 55 sergeants, 44 corporals, 20 drummers, 6 pipers, 942 rank and file, being a total of 1067; and on the 14th of June a draft of 16 recruits joined headquarters from England.

The period of service, under the "Limited Service Act" (of June 1847), of many of the men having long expired, and the country being considered quiet, authority for the discharge of such as desired it having been received, the regiment lost a large number of its best soldiers, and by the end of 1859 was considerably reduced in numbers.

Colonel Macduff—the division under Major-General Whitlock, including the 2nd Infantry brigade which he commanded, having been broken up—returned to Bellary, and assumed the command of the brigade at that station, having been repeatedly, during his absence on field-service, successfully engaged against the rebels.

There is but little to record out of the even tenor of the regiment's way from this time until it embarked for England in 1864. The 74th was of course regularly inspected every half-year by the superior officer whose duty it was to do so; and invariably a good report was given, not only of the discipline and bearing of the men, their knowledge of their business, and their smart and soldierly appearance, but also of their personal cleanliness, and the excellent interior economy of the regiment, and of the unanimity and good feeling that existed among all its ranks. Indeed, the terms in which Major-General Coffin, whose duty it was at this time frequently to inspect the regiment, spoke of the character and efficiency of the 74th, were such that Colonel Villiers seems to have been afraid that the men would be spoiled by so much praise, and in a regimental order of November 1860 sincerely hopes the high encomiums passed by the Major-General may not lead either officers or men to rest satisfied with the present state of the efficiency of their corps, but act as an additional incentive to renewed exertion on the part of every one concerned to render perfect what is now in their estimation considered good.

In a letter dated Horse Guards, 27th of March 1860, it is intimated that "the small amount of crime has been specially remarked by the Duke of Cambridge."

During this period some important changes took place among the superior officers of the regiment. Lieutenant-Colonel Menkland, who had been with the regiment since first he entered the army, exchanged in November 1859 to half-pay, with Lieutenant-Colonel James Villiers, who joined regimental headquarters from England in February 1860. This latter officer, however, was not destined to be long connected with the regiment, as he had the misfortune to be cut off by brain fever at Ramdroog on May 10, 1862.

The senior Lieutenant-Colonel of the regiment, Major-General (local rank) John Macduff, C.B., commanding the Oudh division of the Bengal Presidency, had been placed on half-pay on the 24th of January of this year, the date of his appointment to the Bengal staff, and the supernumerary Lieutenant-Colonelcy was thereby absorbed.

On the death of Lieutenant-Colonel Villiers, Major William Kelty Macleod, who had been in temporary command since that officer's departure on leave of absence on the 23rd of March, succeeded to the command, Colonel

Patton being absent in command of a brigade at Thagetmyo in Burmah.

The depôt of the regiment was during this period stationed at Aberdeen, and sent out frequent detachments of recruits to supply the deficiencies created in the service companies by men who left on the expiry of their term, and by the numerous batches of invalids whom it was found necessary to send home for the sake of their health.

A pattern dress bonnet had been supplied to the companies at Aberdeen in 1861 on trial, but not having been found durable, a new pattern was designed by Captain Palmer, commanding the depôt, and submitted by him to the clothing department for the approval of His Royal Highness the General Commanding-in-Chief, who was pleased to direct a letter to be sent to Captain Palmer, thanking him for his suggestion, and directing the pattern to be sealed and adopted by the regiment as its future head-dress.

The Indian mutiny medals having been received for the officers and men of the regiment who were engaged at the capture of the forts of Shorapoor, Noorgoond, and Kopál in 1858, they were presented at Bellary, in presence of the division, on the 23rd of September (being the sixtieth anniversary of the victory of Assaye), by Major-General Armstrong, commanding the ceded districts. He addressed the regiment in the following terms :—

"Major Macleod, officers, and men of the 74th Highlanders,—This is the anniversary of a memorable day in the annals of your regiment, and consequently I have selected it to perform a duty most agreeable to myself ; that is, to present in the presence of the assembled division the medals to so many officers and men of your distinguished regiment with which Her Most Gracious Majesty, our beloved Queen, has been pleased to reward the good and gallant services and conduct of her troops during the recent disturbances in Bengal and other parts of India. But before fulfilling this duty, I feel called upon to say a few words to you."

Major-General Armstrong then glanced rapidly at all the brilliant services performed by the 74th Highlanders, from Assaye to the Indian Mutiny, concluding as follows:—

" Bravery is the characteristic of the British

soldier, but the 74th Highlanders possesses also another claim to distinction, such as in all my long service I have never seen surpassed, and which has justly obtained for the regiment a high reputation—I mean that very best criterion of the good soldier, steady good conduct, obedience to orders, and the most perfect discipline at all times, whether in camp or quarters. You have now served in this division under my command for a year and a half, and it is particularly gratifying to me to be the medium of presenting so many of you with medals, honourable tokens of your service to your country, and the approbation of your Queen."

The medals were then fastened on the left breast of the officers and men by the General, assisted by several ladies, after which General Armstrong spoke again as follows:—

"I am quite sure there is not a man now wearing the decoration just fixed upon your breasts that will hereafter willingly be guilty of any act to tarnish this token of your Sovereign's favour. Long may you live, one and all, to wear the honours you have won! I greatly regret to think that the time is rapidly approaching when I shall lose the 74th Regiment from my command on its return to England. Many of you, no doubt, will volunteer for other regiments in India, and you may be assured that every well-conducted man will find a good recommendation to his new corps in his having served in a regiment possessing the high reputation of the 74th Highlanders. But others will be returning with the regiment to your native land, whither, if my life is spared, I may follow you at no distant period, when I hope to beat up the quarters of the regiment, and if so, I trust to see many of the medals I have this day presented to you still decorating the ranks of the corps. It will always be to me a proudly gratifying recollection that a regiment so gallant, so well behaved, and in every way distinguished, has served under my command.

"Major Macleod, and officers of the 74th, you may well feel a pride in your Highlanders. I trust that you, Major Macleod, will long be permitted to retain the command of them—a command which you have so ably and efficiently exercised for the advantage of the service, and the happiness and well being of all

ranks during the whole period the regiment has been under my orders."

On the 1st of January 1864, 261 men who had volunteered to other corps in the Madras Presidency were struck off the strength of the regiment; and on the 4th of the same month the regiment marched from Bellary en route to Madras, where it arrived on the 13th of February, and was ordered to encamp till the vessels were ready to convey it to England.

While in camp cholera broke out, and several deaths having occurred, the camp was at once removed to Palaveram, where, happily, the disease disappeared.

On the 7th of March the regiment proceeded to Madras and embarked for England—the headquarters and right wing under Major Jago (Major Macleod having been permitted to proceed to England by the overland route), and the left wing under Captain Thackeray.

On the 19th of June, the headquarters reached Spithead, where orders were received for the vessel to proceed to Gravesend, on arrival at which place the wing was transhipped, without landing, to the "Princess Royal" steamer, and proceeded to Leith, disembarking at Granton Pier on the 24th of June, and marching to Edinburgh Castle, there to be stationed. The left wing did not reach Edinburgh till the 29th of July, having been delayed at St Helena by the illness of the commander of the "Hornet."

Brevet-Colonel Patton, who had gone home from India on sick leave some weeks previously, joined headquarters on the 25th of June, and assumed the command; but on the 9th of September he retired upon half-pay, and Major Macleod was promoted to the lieutenant-colonelcy of the regiment.

The movements of the regiment, from its arrival in Edinburgh up to the present time, may be very briefly recorded, as there is but little to tell except its movements from one quarter to another. Its stay in Edinburgh was very brief, for in less than a year after its arrival, on May 1, 1865, it re-embarked at Granton for Portsmouth en route for Aldershot, where it arrived on the evening of the 4th. The 74th left behind its old colours, which were deposited in the armoury of Edinburgh Castle.

After a stay at Aldershot of a few months, the regiment got short notice to proceed to Dover, which it did on February 20, 1866, the admirable manner in which it turned out eliciting the special commendation of His Royal Highness the Commander-in-Chief. On its arrival at home, the strength of the regiment was of course considerably reduced, and in April 1866 it was still further reduced by two companies, the new establishment consisting of only 640 privates, with a proportionate number of officers and non-commissioned officers.

After a stay of six months at Dover, the 74th was ordered to Ireland, arriving at Cork, whence it proceeded to Limerick, where it stayed till September 26, 1867, on which day it went by rail to Dublin, where it occupied Richmond barracks. While at Limerick, detachments had been told off to do duty at Clare Castle and Nenagh. In consequence of Fenian riots, flying columns were sent out on several occasions, of which various companies of the 74th formed a part.

In November 1867, orders had been received for the regiment to hold itself in readiness to proceed to New Brunswick; its destination was, however, changed about a month later, when it received orders to make ready to proceed to Gibraltar; the depôt companies, consisting of 92 men, under Captain Thackeray and 3 subalterns, having, on January 27, 1868, sailed for Greenock in order to proceed to Fort-George, where it was to be stationed. The regiment sailed from Kingstown on February 2nd, on board H.M. ship "Himalaya," for Gibraltar, where it arrived on February 7th, disembarked on the 8th, and encamped on the North Front until the 13th, when it was removed to the South Barracks.

The 74th remained at Gibraltar till February 1872, on the 17th of which month headquarters and four companies under Colonel Macleod sailed for Malta, where it arrived on the 22nd. The left wing, under Major Jago, followed on the 7th of March, arriving at Malta on the 12th.

SUCCESSION LISTS OF COLONELS AND FIELD OFFICERS OF THE 74TH HIGHLANDERS.

COLONELS.

Sir Archibald Campbell, K.C.B.,   Oct. 12, 1787.

He was a Major-General, and the first Colonel of the 74th, which he raised. He died on the 31st of March 1791, and a monument was erected to his memory in Westminster Abbey.

Charles O'Hara, ... April 1, 1791.
From the 22nd Regiment in . . 1791.
Appointed Lieut.-General in . . 1793.
Governor of Gibraltar in 1798, and promoted to the rank of General. He died at Gibraltar, Feb. 21, 1802.

John, Lord Hutchinson, K.B.,   March 21, 1802.
M.P. for Cork in . . . . 1777.
Lieut.-Colonel of the Athole Highlanders in   1783.
Colonel of the 94th in . . . 1794.
Major-General in . . . . 1796.
Second in command in Egypt.
Chief in Egypt on the death of Abercromby,   1801.
Baron Hutchinson, . . . Dec. 5, 1801.
Governor of Stirling Castle in . . 1803.
Lieut.-General in . . . . 1803.
Colonel of the 57th in . . . 1806.
Colonel of the 18th Royal Irish in . 1811.
General in . . . . . 1813.
In 1825 became Earl of Donoughmore; and died June 29, 1832.

Sir John Stuart, K.B., Count of Maida, Sept 8, 1806.
Ensign 3d Foot Guards, . . . 1779.
Lieut.-Colonel, ... 1798.
Colonel in . . . . . 1796.
Brigadier-General in . . . 1800.
Major-General in . . . . 1802.
Gained the victory over the French at Maida, July 4, 1806; received the freedom of the city of London, and was appointed Colonel of the 74th, Sept. 8, 1806; Lieut.-General, April 25, 1808; Colonel of the 20th Dec. 29, 1808; Commander of the Western District of Great Britain, June 10, 1813; and died in 1815.

The Hon. Sir Alexander Hope, G.C.B., Dec. 29, 1809.
Ensign in the 63d Regiment. . March 6, 1786.
Lieut.-Colonel of the 14th, . . Aug. 27, 1794.
Governor of Tynemouth and Glifford's Fort, 1797.
Lieut.-Governor of Edinburgh Castle,   1798.
Deputy Adjutant-General, . . 1799.
Colonel in the Army, . . . Jan. 1, 1800.
Colonel of 5th West India Regiment, Oct., 30, 1806.
Major-General, ... 1808.
Colonel of the 74th, . . . Dec. 29, 1809.
Colonel of the 47th, . . . April 1812.
Lieut.-General, ... June 1813.
General, ... July 22, 1830.
Colonel of the 14th, . . . 1835.
G.C.B. and Lieut. Governor of Chelsea Hospital. He died on the 19th of May 1837.

James Montgomerie, . . . April 26, 1813.
  Ensign in the 51st, . . Sept. 13, 1773.
  Exchanged into the 13th Foot, . . 1775.
  Lieutenant, ... 1779.
  Promoted to the late 93rd, . . . 1780.
  To the 10th Foot, . . . 1786.
  Brigade-Major, ... 1794.
  Brevet-Major and Lieut.-Colonel of 6th West
    India Regiment, . . . 1795.
  Volunteered with Sir Ralph Abercromby, 1796.
  Commander of the troops at St Kitt's till 1798,
    when he exchanged into the 45th Regiment.
  Brevet-Colonel, . . . April 29, 1802.
  Lieut.-Colonel of the 64th, . . 1804.
  Brigadier-General in the West Indies, 1804.
  Governor of these Colonies till . . 1808.
  Major-General, . . . Oct. 25, 1809.
  Colonel of the 74th, . . April 26, 1813.
  Lieut.-General, . . . June 4, 1814.
  Colonel of the 80th Regiment, . June 13, 1823.
  Which he retained till his death in 1829.

The Hon. Sir Charles Colville, G.C.B.,
    G.C.H., ... June 13, 1823.
  Ensign in the 28th, . . Dec. 26, 1781.
  Lieutenant, ... 1787.
  Major in the 13th, . . . 1795.
  Lieut.-Colonel, . . . Aug. 26, 1796.
  Brevet-Colonel, . . . Jan. 1, 1805.
  Brigadier-General, . . . Dec. 25, 1805.
  Major-General, . . . July 25, 1810.
  Col. of the 5th Garrison Battalion, April 29, 1815.
  Lieut.-General, . . . Aug. 12, 1819.
  Colonel of the 74th, . . June 13, 1823.
  Governor of the Mauritius, . Jan. 1828.
  Removed to the 14th Regiment of Foot, 1834.
  Col. of the 5th Regiment of Foot, March 25, 1835.
  General, . . . Jan. 10, 1837.
  Died March 27, 1843.

Sir James Campbell, K.C.B., K.C.H. Dec. 12, 1834.
  Ensign 1st Royal Regiment of Foot, March 30, 1791.
  Lieutenant, . . . March 20, 1794.
  Half-pay, . . . Jan. 1796.
  42nd Highland Regiment, . Dec. 1797.
  Major in the Argyll Fencibles, . June 1799.
  Removed to the 94th, . . April 7, 1802.
  Lieutenant in the 94th, . Sept. 27, 1804.
  Brevet-Colonel, . . . June 4, 1813.
  Major-General, . . . Aug. 12, 1819.
  K.C.B., . . . Dec. 8, 1822.
  Colonel of the 94th, . . April 13, 1831.
  Removed to the 74th Regiment, Dec. 12, 1834.
  Died in Paris, May 6, 1835.

Sir Phineas Riall, K.C.H. . May 20, 1835.
  Ensign, ... Jan. 31, 1792.
  Lieutenant, . . . Feb. 28, 1794.
  Captain, . . . May 31, 1794.
  Major, ... Dec. 8, 1794.
  Lieut.-Colonel, . . . Jan. 1, 1800.
  Colonel, ... July 25, 1810.
  Major-General, . . . June 4, 1818.
  Lieut.-General, . . . May 27, 1825.
  Colonel of the 74th Regiment, May 20, 1835.
  General, ... Nov. 23, 1841.

  Sir Phineas Riall received a medal and one clasp for
Martinique and Guadaloupe; served in America in
1813, and was severely wounded at the battle of
Chippawa.

Sir Alexander Cameron, K.C.H., April 24, 1846.
  Ensign, ... Oct. 22, 1799.
  Lieutenant, . . . Sept. 6, 1800.
  Captain, ... May 6, 1805.
  Major, ... May 30, 1811.
  Lieut.-Colonel, . . . April 27, 1812.
  Colonel, ... July 22, 1830.
  Major-General, . . . June 28, 1838.
  Died at Inverailort, Fort-William, July 26, 1850.
  Served in Holland, 1799; expedition to Ferrol,
1800; Egypt, 1801 (severely wounded at the battle of
Alexandria); expedition to Germany, 1805; Copen-
hagen and battle of Kiöge, 1807; Portugal in 1808;
battles of Vimeiro and Corunna; Peninsula in 1809;
present at Busaco, Torres Vedras, Coa, Almeida,,
Fuentes d'Onor, &c., till severely wounded at Vit-
toria and obliged to return to England; served in the
campaign of 1814 and 1815, including Quatre Bras and
Waterloo (severely wounded).

Alexander Thomson, C.B., . Aug. 15, 1850.
  Ensign,. . . . Sept. 23, 1803.
  Lieutenant, . . . Feb. 29, 1804.
  Captain, ... May 14, 1807.
  Major, ... April 9, 1812.
  Lieut.-Colonel, . . . Sept. 21, 1812.
  Colonel,. . . . July 22, 1830.
  Major-General, . . . Nov. 23, 1841.
  Lieut.-General, . . . Nov. 11, 1851.
  Colonel 74th Regiment, . Aug. 15, 1850.
          Died 1856.
  Lieut.-General Thomson accompanied the 74th to
the Peninsula, landing at Lisbon in Jan. 1810, and was
present at the battle of Busaco, retreat to the lines of
Torres Vedras, advance of the army on Massena's
retreat therefrom, action at Foz d'Arouce (wounded),
battle of Fuentes d'Onor, siege and capture of Ciudad
Rodrigo, where he served as assistant engineer, and
for his services was promoted to the rank of Brevet-
Major; siege and capture of Badajoz, where he served
as assistant engineer, and was slightly wounded when
leading about 360 men of the party that stormed and
took the raveline of St Roque to reinforce the 3rd
division of the army which had taken the castle; siege
and capture of the forts of Salamanca, where he served
as assistant engineer, and was slightly wounded;
battle of Salamanca (severely wounded); siege of Burgos
and retreat therefrom; served as assistant engineer,
and had the blowing-up of the bridge of Villa Muriel
and the bridge at Cabezon entrusted to him; battle of
Vittoria, as second in command of the 74th; siege of
St Sebastian, where he served as assistant engineer,
and for his conduct was promoted to the brevet rank
of Lieut.-Colonel; battles of the Nivelle and the Nive,
passage of the Bidassoa, and battle of Orthes, besides
several skirmishes with his regiment at Alfayates, Villa
de Pastores Albidos, and other places. He received
the gold medal for St Sebastian, and the silver war
medal with nine clasps for the other battles and sieges.

Charles Augustus Shawe, . Nov. 24, 1856.
  Ensign, . . . May 26, 1808.
  Lieutenant and Captain, . April 23, 1812.
  Captain and Lieut.-Colonel, April 28, 1825.
  Major and Colonel, . . Aug. 8, 1837.
  Major-General, . . . Nov. 9, 1846.
  Lieut.-General, . . . June 20, 1854.
  General, ... March 6, 1863.
  Colonel 74th Foot, . . Nov 24, 1856.
  General Shawe served in the campaigns of 1810 and
1811, and part of 1812, in the Peninsula, including
the battle of Busaco. Served also in Holland and
Belgium from Nov. 1813 to 1814, and was severely
wounded at Bergen-op-Zoom. He received the war
medal, with three clasps, for Busaco, Fuentes d'Onor,
and Ciudad Rodrigo.

LIEUTENANT-COLONELS.

NAMES.	Date of Appointment to Regiment.	Date of Removal.	Remarks.
George Forbes	Oct. 12, 1787	Dec. 14, 1788	Died.
Hamilton Maxwell	Dec. 15, 1788	June 8, 1794	Died.
Marlborough Parsons Sterling	June 9, 1794	Dec. 4, 1795	Died.
Alexander Ross	Dec. 5, 1795	Dec. 3, 1796	Died.
Robert Shaw	Sept. 1, 1795	Dec. 24, 1798	Exchanged to 12th Foot.
Alexander Campbell	Dec. 4, 1796	July 25, 1810	Promoted Major-General.
William Harness	Dec. 24, 1798	June 7, 1800	Returned to 18th Foot, 7th June 1800.
Robert Shawe	June 7, 1800	Dec. 1, 1803	Resumed his situation in the Regiment 7th June 1800. Retired 1st Dec. 1803.
Samuel Swinton	Dec. 1, 1803	May 13, 1805	Promoted in 75th Regiment.
Malcolm M'Pherson	May 14, 1807	Sept. 21, 1809	Exchanged to Inspecting Field Officer, Canada.
Hon. Sir Robt. Le Poer Trench	Sept. 21, 1809	Mar. 14, 1823	Died.[1]
John Alexander Mein	Mar. 20, 1823	Nov. 5, 1841	Died.
Eyre John Crabbe	Nov. 6, 1841	May 1, 1846	Retired on Full-pay.
William White Crawley	May 1, 1846	July 10, 1846	Retired.
John Fordyce	July 10, 1846	Nov. 6, 1851	Killed in action, 6th of Nov. 1851, at Waterkloof, Cape of Good Hope.
Alexander Seton	Nov. 7, 1851	Feb. 26, 1852	Drowned in the wreck of the Birkenhead.
G. W. Fordyce	Feb. 27, 1852	July 30, 1852	Retired.
John MacDuff	July 30, 1852	Jan. 24, 1862	Promoted Major-General; since dead.
George Monkland	July 29, 1853	Nov. 4, 1859	Exchanged to Half-pay.
James Villiers	Nov. 4, 1859	May 10, 1862	Died.
W. D. P. Patton	May 11, 1862	Sept. 9, 1864	Retired on Half-pay.
William Kelty M'Leod	Sept. 9, 1864		Now (1874) commanding.

MAJORS.

NAMES.	Date of Appointment to Regiment.	Date of Removal.	Remarks.
Francis Skelly	Nov. 5, 1788	Nov. 30, 1793	Died.
Robert Shawe	Dec. 1, 1793	Mar. 28, 1795	Exchanged to 76th Foot.
Alexander Ross	Mar. 28, 1795	Dec. 4, 1795	Promoted Lieut.-Colonel.
Alexander Campbell	Dec. 25, 1795	Dec. 4, 1796	Promoted Lieut.-Colonel.
William Wallace	Sept. 2, 1795	Nov. 22, 1803	Promoted in the 19th Dragoons.
William Douglas	Dec. 4, 1796	May 17, 1799	Promoted in 85th Foot.
Samuel Swinton	May 17, 1799	Dec. 1, 1803	Promoted Lieut.-Colonel.
James Robertson	Nov. 22, 1803	Nov. 14, 1804	Retired.
Francis R. West	Dec. 1, 1803	Nov. 15, 1804	Retired.
Malcolm M'Pherson	Nov. 14, 1804	May 13, 1807	Promoted Lieut.-Colonel.
Hon. M'Donnell Murray	Nov. 15, 1804	Mar. 10, 1808	Died.
Edward Broughton	May 14, 1807	April 14, 1810	Retired.
Russell Manners[2]	May 11, 1808	April 18, 1822	Retired
Allan William Campbell[3]	April 5, 1810	Nov. 10, 1813	Died of wounds.
John Alexander Mein	Nov. 11, 1813	Mar. 20, 1823	Promoted Lieut.-Colonel.
David Stewart	April 18, 1822	Dec. 4, 1828	Exchanged to 65th Foot.
William Moore[4]	Mar. 20, 1823	Jan. 31, 1828	Retired.
Eyre John Crabbe	Jan. 31, 1828	Nov. 6, 1841	Promoted Lieut.-Colonel.
John William Hutchinson	Dec. 4, 1828	Oct. 22, 1830	Died.
Donald John M'Queen	Oct. 23, 1830	Oct. 3, 1834	Retired.
Thomas Mannin	Oct. 3, 1834	Oct 12, 1839	Died at sea.
William White Crawley	Oct. 13, 1839	May 1, 1846	Promoted Lieut.-Colonel.
John Casamir Harold	Nov. 6, 1841	Oct. 22, 1844	Exchanged to 11th Foot.
John Fordyce	Oct. 22, 1844	July 10, 1846	Promoted Lieut.-Colonel.
Augustus Francis Ansell	May 1, 1846	May 24, 1850	Retired on Half-pay.
Hon. Thomas O'Grady	July 10, 1846	Mar. 14, 1851	Retired.
Alexander Seton	May 24, 1850	Nov. 7, 1851	Promoted Lieut.-Colonel.
G. W. Fordyce	Mar. 14, 1851	Feb. 27, 1852	Promoted Lieut.-Colonel.
G. Monkland	Nov. 7, 1851	July 29, 1853	Promoted Lieut.-Colonel.
W. D. P. Patton	Feb. 27, 1852	May 11, 1862	Promoted Lieut.-Colonel.
E. W. L. Hancock	July 29, 1853	Jan. 26, 1858	Died.
William Kelty M'Leod	Jan. 27, 1858	Sept. 9, 1864	Promoted Lieut.-Colonel.
John Jago[5]	May 11, 1862	...	...
H. W. Palmer	Sept. 9, 1864	Oct. 4, 1864	Exchanged to 90th.
L. H. L. Irby	Oct. 4, 1864	Feb. 4, 1871	Exchanged to Half-pay.
Robert F. Martin	Feb. 4, 1871	...	

---

[1] His bust is on page 583, vol. ii.   [2] Brevet Lieut.-Colonel.   [3] Brevet Lieut.-Colonel, 30th June 1813 brevet Lieut.-Colonel, 9th Dec. 1874.
[4] Brevet Major, 21st June 1817.

SEVENTY-FIFTH REGIMENT

1787-1809

Raising of the Regiment—India—Home—Ceases to be a Highland Regiment

WHILE Major-General Sir Archibald Campbell was appointed Colonel of the 74th, the colonelcy of its coeval regiment, the 75th, was conferred on Colonel Robert Abercromby of Tullibody He had commanded a light infantry brigade during six campaigns in the American war , and as several companies of this brigade had been composed of the light infantry of the Highland regiments then in America, the colonel was well known to the Highlanders, and had acquired an influence among them rarely enjoyed by officers born south of the Grampians   There are instances, no doubt, such as those of the Marquis of Montrose and Viscount Dundee, and others of modern date, "where Highland corps have formed attachments to officers not natives of their country, and not less ardent than to the chiefs of old,"[8] and if the instances have been few, it must be attributed entirely to want of tact in officers themselves, who, from ignorance of the Highland character, or from some other cause, have failed to gain the attachment of the Highland soldiers

From personal respect to Colonel Abercromby, many of the Highlanders, who had served under him in America, and had been discharged at the peace of 1783, enlisted anew, and with about 300 men who were recruited at Perth, and in the northern counties, constituted the Highland part of the regiment According to a practice which then prevailed, of fixing the head quarters of a regiment about to be raised in the neighbourhood of the colonel's residence, if a man of family, the town of Stirling was appointed for the embodying of the 75th, it was accordingly regimented here in June 1788, and being immediately ordered to England, embarked for India, where it arrived about the end of that year

For eighteen months after its arrival in India,

[8] Jackson's *Characteristics*

the regiment was subjected to extreme severity of discipline by one of the captains, who appears to have adopted the old Prussian model for his rule   A more unfortunate plan for destroying the morale of a Highland regiment could not have been devised, and the result was, that during the existence of this discipline, there were more punishments in the 75th than in any other corps of the same description But as soon as the system was modified by the appointment of an officer who knew the dispositions and feelings of the Highlanders, the conduct of the men improved

The regiment took the field in 1790, under the command of Colonel Hartley, and in the two subsequent years formed part of the force under Major-General Robert Abercromby, on his two marches to Seringapatam.   The regiment was also employed in the assault on that capital in 1799, the flank companies having led the left columns [9] From that period down to 1804, the regiment was employed in the provinces of Malabar, Goa, Goojerat, and elsewhere, and in 1805 was with General Lake's army in the disastrous attacks on Bhurtpoor

The regiment was ordered home in 1806 , but such of the men as were desirous of remaining in India were left behind In 1809 there were not one hundred men in the regiment who had been born north of the Tay , on which account, it is believed, the designation of the regiment was at that time changed

The regiment, however, still retains its old number, and is known as the "Stirlingshire Regiment"   It has had a distinguished career, having been present in many of the engagements which we have had to notice in connection with the existing Highland regiments. As will be seen in our account of the 78th Highlanders, the 75th formed part of the force with which Sir Colin Campbell marched to the relief of Lucknow in November 1857, it having been left to guard the Alum Bagh while Sir Colin, with the rest of the force, made his way to the besieged garrison on the 14th of that month

[9] See histories of the 71st, 72nd, 73rd, and 74th regiments in this volume

MACKENZIE OF SEAFORTH LIEUT COLONEL.
Col. of 74th Highlrs 5th March 1793 — May 1793.
First Colonel.

SIR PATRICK GRANT, G.C.B. G.C.M.G.
Col of 72nd Decr 1854 to 1861.

THE 78th HIGHLANDERS, OR ROSS-SHIRE BUFFS.[1]

I.

1793 to 1796.

The Clan Mackenzie—The various Battalions of the 78th—Offers from F. H. Mackenzie, Esq. of Seaforth, to raise a Regiment for Government—Letter of service granted to F. H. Mackenzie, Esq., to raise a Regiment of Highlanders, to be numbered the 78th—The 1st Battalion—List of officers—Inspected and passed by Sir Hector Munro—Under Lord Moira in Guernsey—The Campaign of 1794–95 in Holland—The Regiment joins the Duke of York on the Waal — Nimeguen — Disastrous retreat on Deventer — The Regiment returns home — The Loyalist war in La Vendée—The Quiberon Expedition—Occupation of L'Ile Dieu—The Regiment returns home—Colonel F. H. Mackenzie's proposals to raise a 2nd Battalion for the 78th—Letter of Service granted to him for that purpose—List of Officers—Inspected and passed by Sir Hector Munro—Granted the title of the Ross-shire Buffs—Ordered to England—Difficulties prior to embarkation at Portsmouth—The Regiment sails on secret service—Capture of the Cape of Good Hope—The Regiment goes into quarters at Capetown, until the arrival of the 1st Battalion.

ASSAYE.
MAIDA.
JAVA.

PERSIA.
KOOSHAB.
LUCKNOW.

THE clan Mackenzie was, next to the Campbells, the most considerable in the Western Highlands, having built its greatness upon the fallen fortunes of the Macdonalds. Its military strength was estimated in 1704, at 1200 men; by Marshal Wade in 1715, at 3000 men; and by Lord President Forbes in 1745, at 2500 men; but probably all these conjectures were below the mark.[2]

[1] For this history of the 78th Highlanders up to the beginning of the Persian War, we are entirely indebted to Captain Colin Mackenzie, formerly an officer of the regiment, who is himself preparing a detailed history of the 78th.
[2] See page 23a, vol. ii.

II.

The clan Mackenzie furnished large contingents to the present 71st and 72nd Regiments when they were first raised.

In 1793, Francis Humberstone Mackenzie, heir-male of the family, and afterwards Lord Seaforth, raised the present 78th Highlanders, and a second battalion in the following year, when nearly all the men enlisted were from his own or his clansmen's estates in Ross-shire and the Lewis. Another second battalion was subsequently raised in 1804, when, Lord Seaforth being absent as Governor of Demerara, his personal influence was not of so much avail. However, again the greater part of the men were recruited on the estates of the clan by his brother-in-law, Colonel Alexander Mackenzie of Belmaduthy (who afterwards adopted the additional surname of Fraser, on succeeding to the Castle Fraser estates in right of his mother) and Colonel J. R. Mackenzie of Suddie. Several Fencible, Militia, and local Volunteer regiments were also raised among the Mackenzies at the end of the last and beginning of the present century.

As the early history of the 78th is a little complicated, owing to its having been twice augmented with a 2nd battalion, it is as well to remember the following chronology:—

1st Battalion—Letter of Service dated 7th March 1793.
2nd Battalion—Letter of Service dated 10th February 1794.
   Both Battalions amalgamated, June 1796.
2nd Battalion—Letter of Service, dated 17th April 1804.
   Both Battalions amalgamated, July 1817.

The regiment has ever since remained as a single battalion.

As early as the autumn of 1787 (when the 74th, 75th, 76th, and 77th Regiments were ordered to be raised for service in India), Francis Humberstone Mackenzie of Seaforth, lineal descendant and representative of the old earls of Seaforth, had made an offer to the King for the raising of a Highland corps on his estates in Ross-shire and the Isles, to be commanded by himself. As the Government, however, merely accepted his services in the matter of procuring recruits for the regiments of Sir Archibald Campbell and Colonel Abercromby (the 74th and 75th), he did not come prominently forward. On the 19th of May 1790, he again renewed his offer, but was informed that Government did not contemplate raising fresh corps, the establishment of the army having been finally fixed at 77 regiments.

Undismayed, however, by the manner in which his offers had been hitherto shelved, he was the first to step forward, on the declaration of war, and place his great influence in the Highlands at the disposal of the Crown. Accordingly, a Letter of Service, dated 7th March, 1793, was granted to him, empowering him, as Lieut.-Colonel Commandant, to raise a Highland battalion, which, as the first to be embodied during the war, was to be numbered the 78th. The strength of the battalion was to be 1 company of grenadiers, 1 of light

SEAFORTH'S
HIGHLANDERS

To be forthwith raifed for the DEFENCE of His Glorious Majefty KING GEORGE the Third, and the Prefervation of our Happy Conftitution in Church and State.

All LADS of *TRUE HIGHLAND BLOOD*, willing to fhew their Loyalty and Spirit, may repair to *SEAFORTH*, or the Major, *ALEXANDER MACKENZIE* of *Belmaduthy*; Or, the other Commanding Officers at Head Quarters, at where they will receive HIGH BOUNTIES, and *SOLDIER-LIKE ENTERTAINMENT*.

The LADS of this Regiment will LIVE and DIE together :— as they cannot be DRAUGHTED into other Regiments, and must be reduced in a BODY in their OWN COUNTRY.

Now for a Stroke at the Monfieurs my Boys ! KING George for ever !

HUZZA!

Notice posted throughout the Counties of Ross and Cromarty and the Island of Lewis.
Engraved from a photograph of the original poster.

infantry, and 8 battalion companies. Seaforth immediately appointed as his major his brother-in-law, Alexander Mackenzie of Belmaduthy, son of Mackenzie of Kilcoy, a captain in the 73rd Regiment, and a man in every way fitted for the post. A notice was then posted through the counties of Ross and Cromarty, and the island of Lewis.

Applications for commissions now poured in upon Seaforth ; and, besides his own personal friends, many who were but slightly known to him folicited favours for their relatives. The following is a list of those whose names were approved by the King :—

FIRST LIST OF OFFICERS.

Lieut.-Colonel Commandant.—F. H. Mackenzie, afterwards Lord Seaforth, Lieut.-Gen. 1808. Died 1815. [His portrait is on the Plate of the Colonels of the 78th and 79th Regiments.]

Lieut.-Colonel.—Alexander Mackenzie of Belmaduthy, afterwards of Castle Fraser, when he assumed the name of Fraser. Lieut.-General 1808. Died 1809.

Majors.
George, Earl of Errol, died 1799.
Alexander Mackenzie of Fairburn, Lieut. General 1809.

Captains.
Alexander Malcolm, died 1798.
Thomas Fraser of Leadclune.
John Mackenzie (Gairloch).
Gabriel Murray, Brevet-Major, killed at Tuil, 1794.

Alexander Grant, died 1807.
J. R. Mackenzie of Suddie, Major-General, killed at Talavera 1809.
Alexander Adams, Major-General 1814.
Hon. Geo. Cochrane, son of the Earl of Dundonald.
Captain-Lieutenant—Duncan Munro of Culcairn.

Lieutenants.

Colin Mackenzie.
James Fraser, retired 1795.
Charles Rose.
Hugh Munro, Captain of Invalids.
Charles Adamson.
William Douglas, son of Brigton, Lieut.-Colonel 91st Regiment.
George Bayley, promoted to 44th.
Thomas, Lord Cochrane, Captain Royal Navy.

Ensigns.

Duncan Macrae.
John Macleod, Colonel 1813.
J. Mackenzie Scott, Captain 57th, killed at Albuera, 1811.
Charles Mackenzie (Kilcoy).
John Reid.
David Forbes, Lieut.-Colonel, H.P.
Alexander Rose, Major of Veterans.
John Fraser.

Chaplain—The Rev. Alexander Downie, D.D.
Adjutant—James Fraser.
Quarter-Master—Archibald Macdougall.
Surgeon—Thomas Baillie. He died in India.

The martial spirit of the nation was now so thoroughly roused, and recruits poured in so rapidly, that, on the 10th of July, 1793, only four months after the granting of the Letter of Service, the regiment was inspected at Fort George, and passed by Lieut.-General Sir Hector Munro. Orders were then issued to augment the corps to 1000 rank and file, and 5 companies, including the flank ones, under the command of Major Alexander Mackenzie, were embarked for Guernsey. In October of the same year the remaining 5 companies were ordered to join their comrades.

"This was an excellent body of men, healthy, vigorous, and efficient; attached and obedient to their officers, temperate and regular; in short, possessing those principles of integrity and moral conduct which constitute a valuable soldier. The duty of officers was easy with such men, who only required to be told what duty was expected of them. A young officer, endowed with sufficient judgment to direct them in the field, possessing energy and spirit to ensure the respect and confidence of soldiers, and prepared on every occasion *to show them the eye of the enemy*, need not desire a command that would sooner and more permanently establish his professional character, if employed on an active campaign,

than that of 1000 such men as composed this regiment.

"Colonel Mackenzie knew his men, and the value which they attached to a good name, by tarnishing which they would bring shame on their country and kindred. In case of any misconduct, he had only to remonstrate, or threaten to transmit to their parents a report of their misbehaviour. This was, indeed, to them a grievous punishment, acting like the curse of Kehama, as a perpetual banishment from a country to which they could not return with a bad character."[a]

After being stationed a short time in Guernsey and the Isle of Wight, the 78th, in September 1794, embarked with the 80th to join Lord Mulgrave's force in Walcheren. While detained by contrary winds in the Downs, fever broke out on board the transports, which had recently brought back prisoners of war from the West Indies, and had not been properly purified; thus several men fell victims to the disease.

The British troops had landed in Holland, on the 5th of March, 1793, and since then the war had been progressing with varying success. Without, therefore, giving details of their operations during the first year and a half, we shall merely sketch the position they occupied when the 78th landed at Flushing.

On the 1st of July, 1794, the allies having decided to abandon the line of the Scheldt, the Duke of York retired behind the Dyle, and was there joined by Lord Moira and 8000 men. On the 22nd the Duke, having separated from the Austrians, established himself at Rosendaal, and there remained inactive in his camp the whole of August and the early part of September; but, on the 15th of September, Boxtel having fallen into the hands of General Pichegru, he was constrained to break camp and retire across the Meuse, and finally across the Waal, establishing his head-quarters at Nimeguen.

At this juncture the 78th and 80th reached Flushing, and found that Lord Mulgrave was ordered home. They therefore embarked with the 79th, 84th, and 85th, to join the Duke's army. Early in October the 78th landed at

[a] Stewart's *Sketches*.

Tuil, and proceeded to occupy the village of Rossem in the Bommeler-Waart, oi Island of Bommel, where they first saw the enemy, scarcely one hundred yards distant, on the opposite side of the river Here, through the negligence of a Dutch Emigrant Officer, a sad accident occured This person hearing voices on the bank of the river, and dreading a surprise, ordered his gunners to fire an iron 12-pounder, loaded with case shot, by which discharge the officer of the day, Lieut Archibald Christie, 78th, and a sergeant, were seriously wounded while visiting a sentry. They both recovered, but were unable to serve again, strange to say, the sentry escaped untouched While quartered here, by a tacit understanding, the sentries exchanged no shots, but it was observed that the French frequently fired howitzers with effect when the troops were under arms, and that, before the fire commenced, the sails of a certain windmill were invariably put in motion The owner was arrested, found guilty as a spy, and condemned to death, but was reprieved through the lenity of Lieut Colonel Mackenzie, the commandant, with the full understanding that, on a repetition of the offence, the last penalty would be enforced

About the end of October the 78th proceeded to Arnheim, the Duke of York's headquarters, and thence, by a night march, to Nimeguen, against which place the French were erecting batteries. On the 4th of November a sortie was made, when the 78th was for the first time under fire, and did such execution with the bayonet, as to call forth the highest encomiums from experienced and veteran officers The loss of the regiment in this engagement was Lieutenant Martin Cameron (died of his wounds) and seven men killed, wounded, Major Malcolm, Captain Hugh Munro, Captain Colin Mackenzie, Lieutenant Bayley, 4 sergeants, and 56 rank and file

On the 6th the regiment marched from Nimeguen to Arnheim, and finally to Dodewaart on the Waal, where they were brigaded with the 12th, the 33rd, under Lieut.-Colonel Arthur Wellesley (afterwards Duke of Wellington), and the 42nd under Major Dickson The General going home on leave, the command

devolved on Colonel Alexander Mackenzie of the 78th, who, however, still remained with his regiment

On the 2nd of December the Duke of York quitted Arnheim for England, and handed over his command to Lieut -General Harcourt.

On the 29th of December General Daendels, having crossed the Waal on the ice and driven back the Dutch, Major-General Sir David Dundas was ordered to dislodge him He, therefore, marched towards Thiel by Buren and Geldermalsen, and came up with the enemy at Tuil, which village he carried at the point of the bayonet with comparatively little loss, though Brevet Major Murray and three men of the light company, 78th, were killed by the bursting of a shell thrown from a distant battery After the action the troops lay on their arms in the snow until the evening of the 31st, and the French recrossed the Waal

On the 3rd of January 1795 the French repossessed themselves of Tuil, and on the 5th they drove in the British outposts at Meteren, capturing two three-pounders, which were, however, recovered later in the day They then attacked Geldermalsen The 78th were in advance, supported by the 42nd, when they were charged by a Republican cavalry corps, dressed in the same uniform as the French Emigrant Regiment of Choiseul They advanced towards the Highlanders with loud cries of " Choiseul ! Choiseul !" and the 78th, believing them to be that regiment, forbore to fire upon them until they were quite close, when, discovering the mistake, they gave them a warm reception, and those of the enemy who had penetrated beyond their line were destroyed by the 42nd The infantry then came up, the officers shouting "Avancez, Carmagnoles !" but the 78th, reserving their fire till the foe had almost closed with them, poured in such a withering volley, that they were completely demoralised and retreated in great confusion It was remarked that in this action the French were all half drunk, and one officer, who was wounded and taken, was completely tipsy The loss of the 78th was four men killed, and Captain Duncan Munro and seven men wounded It was on this occasion that a company of the 78th, commanded by Lieutenant Forbes, showed an example of steadiness that would have done honour to the oldest soldiers, presenting and recovering arms without firing a shot upon the cavalry as they were coming down. The whole behaved with great coolness, and fired nearly 60 rounds per man.

On the night of the 5th the troops retired to Buren. On the 6th the British and Hanoverians retired across the Leck, with the exception of the 6th Brigade, Lord Cathcart's, which remained at Kuilenburg. On the 8th both parties assumed the offensive, but the British advance was countermanded on account of the severity of the weather. It happened, however, luckily for the picquet of the 4th Brigade, which was at Burenmalsen, opposite to Geldermalsen, that the order did not reach Lord Cathcart until he had arrived at Buren, as being driven in, it must otherwise have been taken. Here a long action took place, which ended in the repulse of the French. The 4th and a Hessian Brigade went into Buren, and the British into the castle.

The day the troops remained here, a man in the town was discovered selling gin to the soldiers at such a low price as must have caused him an obvious loss, and several of the men being already drunk, the liquor was seized, and ordered by General Dundas to be divided among the different corps, to be issued at the discretion of commanding officers. Thus what the French intended to be a means of destruction, turned out to be of the greatest comfort and assistance to the men during their fearful marches through ice and snow. During the afternoon a man was apprehended at the outposts, who had been sent to ascertain whether the trick had taken effect, and whether the troops were sufficiently drunk to be attacked with success.

Abercromby and Hammerstein having been unable to reach Thiel, were, with Wurmb's Hessians, united to Dundas at Buren. On the 10th the French crossed the Waal, and General Regnier crossing the Oeg, drove the British from Ophensden, back upon Wageningen and Arnheim, with a loss of fifty killed and wounded. Abercromby, therefore, withdrew, and the British retired across the Rhine at Rhenen. This sealed the fate of Holland, and on the 20th General Pichegru entered Amsterdam.

The inclemency of the season increased, and the rivers, estuaries, and inundations froze as they had never been known to do before, so that the whole country, land and water, was one unbroken sheet of ice.

The Rhine was thus crossed on the ice on the night of the 9th of February, and for two more nights the 78th lay upon their arms in the snow, and then marched for Wyk. On the 14th Rhenen was attacked by the French, who were repulsed by the Guards, with a loss of 20 men; however, the same night it was determined to abandon the Rhine, and thus Rhenen, the Grand Hospital of the army, fell into the hands of the French, who, nevertheless, treated the sick and wounded with consideration. After resting two hours in the snow during the night, the 78th resumed their march, passed through Amersfoort, and about 11 A.M. on the 15th lay down in some tobacco barns, having marched nearly 40 miles. It had been decided to occupy the line of the Yssel, and Deventer therefore became the destination. On the 16th at daybreak the regiment commenced its march across the horrible waste called the Veluwe. Food was not to be obtained, the inhabitants were inhospitable; with the enemy in their rear, the snow knee deep, and blown in swirls by the wind into their faces, until they were partially or entirely blinded, their plight was most pitiable.

They had now a new enemy to encounter. Not only was the weather still most severe, and the Republicans supposed to be in pursuit, but the British had, in consequence of French emissaries, a concealed enemy in every Dutch town and village through which they had to pass. Notwithstanding the severity of the climate,—the cold being so intense that brandy froze in bottles—the 78th, 79th (both young soldiers), and the recruits of the 42nd, wore their kilts, and yet the loss was incomparably less than that sustained by the other corps.

After halting at Loo to allow the officers and men to take off their accoutrements, which they had worn day and night since the 26th December, they on the 18th marched to Hattem on the Yssel. Finally, on the 28th of March the 78th entered Bremen, and the army being embarked, the fleet sailed on the 12th of April.

On the 9th of May, 1795, the shores of Old England brought tears into the eyes of the war-worn soldiers, and the first battalion of the Ross-shire Buffs landed at Harwich, and proceeded to Chelmsford, where they took over the barracks After making up the returns, and striking off the names of all men supposed to be dead or prisoners, the regiment, which had embarked on the previous September 950 strong, and in excellent health, was found to be reduced to 600 men, which number included the disabled and sick who had not been yet invalided The 78th remained three weeks at Chelmsford, and marched to Harwich, where it was brigaded with the 19th, under command of General Sir Ralph Abercromby. It then proceeded to Nutshalling (now Nursling) Common, where a force was assembling under the Earl of Moira, with a view to making a descent on the French coast

On the 18th of August the 78th, in company with the 12th, 80th, and 90th Regiments, and some artillery, embarked under the command of Major-General W Ellis Doyle, and sailed for Quiberon Bay, the design was to assist the French Royalists They bore down on Noirmoutier, but finding the island strongly reinforced, and a landing impracticable, they made for L'Île Dieu, where they landed without opposition Here they remained for some time, enduring the hardships entailed by continued wet weather and a want of proper accommodation, coupled with an almost total failure of the commissariat, but were unable to assist Charette or his royalist companions in any way Finally, the expedition embarked in the middle of December, joined the grand fleet in Quiberon Bay, and proceeded with it to Spithead

On the 13th of October 1793, Seaforth made an offer to Government to raise a second battalion for the 78th Highlanders, and on the 30th Lord Amherst signed the king's approval of his raising 500 additional men on his then existing letter of service However, this was not what he wanted, and on the 28th of December he submitted three proposals for a second battalion to Government

On the 7th of February 1794, the Government agreed to one battalion being raised, with eight battalion and two flank companies, each

company to consist of "one hundred private men,"[4] with the usual complement of officers and non-commissioned officers But Seaforth's services were ill requited by Government, for while he contemplated raising a second battalion to his regiment, Lord Amherst had issued orders that it was to be considered as a separate corps The following is a copy of the letter addressed to Mr Secretary Dundas by Lieut-Colonel Commandant F H Mackenzie[5] —

"St Alban's Street,
'8th Feb 1794

" Sir,—I had sincerely hoped I should not be obliged to trouble you again, but on my going to-day to the War Office about my letter of service (having yesterday, as I thought, finally agreed with Lord Amherst), I was, to my amazement, told that Lord Amherst had ordered that the 1000 men I am to raise were not to be a second battalion of the 78th, but a separate corps It will, I am sure, occur to you that should I undertake such a thing, it would destroy my influence among the people of my country entirely, and instead of appearing as a loyal honest chieftain calling out his friends to support their king and country, I should be gibbeted as a jobber of the attachment my neighbours bear to me Recollecting what passed between you and me, I barely state this circumstance, and I am, with great respect and attachment, Sir, your most obliged and obedient servant,

"F H Mackenzie"

This argument had its weight, Lord Amherst's order was rescinded, and on the 10th February 1794, a letter of service was granted to Seaforth, empowering him, as Lieut.-Colonel Commandant, to add a second battalion to the 78th Highlanders, of which the strength was to be "one company of grenadiers, one of light infantry, and eight battalion companies."[6]

Stewart states that of this number 560 men were of the same country and character as the first, and 190 from different parts of Scotland, but he alludes to the first six companies, as the regiment was almost entirely composed of Highlanders

---

[4] The corporals were included in this number, which should therefore have appeared as "rank and file" instead of "private men"—C M
[5] Private papers of the late Lord Seaforth
[6] Extract from letter of service

The following is a list of the officers appointed to the regiment :—

Lieutenant-Colonel Commandant.
F. H. Mackenzie of Seaforth.

Lieutenant-Colonel.
Alexander Mackenzie of Fairburn, from first battalion.

Majors.
J. R. Mackenzie of Suddie, from first battalion.
Michael Monypenny, promoted to 73d, dead.

Captains.
J. H. Brown, killed in a duel in India.
Simon Mackenzie.
William Campbell, Major, killed in Java, 1811.
John Mackenzie, Major-General, 1813.
Patrick M'Leod (Geanies), killed at El Hamet, 1807.
[His portrait will be found on page 650.]
Hercules Scott of Benholm, Lieut.-Colonel 103d Regiment, 1814, killed in Canada.
John Scott.
John Macleod, Colonel, 1813, from first battalion.

Lieutenants.
James Hanson.
Alexander Macneil.
Æneas Sutherland.
Murdoch Mackenzie.
Archd. C. B. Crawford.
Norman Macleod, Lieut.-Colonel Royal Scots.
Thomas Leslie.
Alexander Sutherland, sen.
Alexander Sutherland, jun.
P. Macintosh.
John Douglas.
George Macgregor.
B. G. Mackay.
Donald Cameron.
James Hay.
Thomas Davidson.
William Gordon.
Robert Johnstone.
Hon. W. D. Halyburton, Colonel, half-pay.
John Macneil.
John Dunbar.

Ensigns.
George Macgregor, Lieut.-Colonel 59th Regiment.
Donald Cameron.
John Macneil.
William Polson.
Alexander Wishart.

Chaplain.—The Rev. Charles Proby.
Adjutant.—James Hanson.
Quarter-Master.—Alexander Wishart.

The records of this battalion having been lost many years since, the only knowledge we can derive of its movements is to be obtained from the Seaforth papers. The regiment was inspected and passed at Fort-George by Sir Hector Munro in June 1794. In July his Majesty authorised the regiment to adopt the name of "The Ross-shire Buffs" as a distinctive title. In August six companies embarked for England, and proceeded to Netley Camp, where they were brigaded with the 90th, 97th, and 98th. The troops suffered much from fever, ague, and rheumatism, the situation being very unfavourable; but here again the 78th was found to be more healthy than their neigh-bours. The young battalion was chafing at this enforced idleness, and longed to go on active service. On the 5th of November, the regiment marched from Netley, four companies proceeding to Poole, one to Wimborne, and one to Wareham, Corff Castle, &c.

In the end of February 1795, the second battalion of the 78th Highlanders, Lieut.-Colonel Alexander Mackenzie of Fairburn in command, embarked, under Major-General Craig, with a secret expedition. Major J. R. Mackenzie of Suddie, writing to Seaforth under date "Portsmouth, 4th March 1795," narrates the following unpleasant circumstance which happened on the day previous to embarkation :—

"The orders for marching from Poole were so sudden that there was no time then for settling the men's arrears. They were perfectly satisfied then, and expressed the utmost confidence in their officers, which continued until they marched into this infernal place. Here the publicans and some of the invalids persuaded the men that they were to be embarked without their officers, and that they would be sold, as well as lose their arrears. This operated so far on men who had never behaved ill before in a single instance, that they desired to have their accounts settled before they embarked. Several publicans and other villains in this place were guilty of the most atrocious conduct even on the parade, urging on the men to demand their rights, as they called it. Fairburn having some intimation of what was passing, and unwilling that it should come to any height, addressed the men, told them it was impossible to settle their accounts in the short time previous to embarkation, but that he had ordered a sum to be paid to each man nearly equal to the amount of their credit. This was all the publicans wanted, among whom the greatest part of the money rested. Next morning the men embarked in the best and quietest manner possible, and I believe they were most thoroughly ashamed of their conduct. I passed a most miserable time from receiving Fairburn's letter in London till I came down here, when it had all ended so well; for well as I knew the inclinations of the men to have been, it was impossible to say how far they might have been mi led.

"There is little doubt of the expedition being intended for the East. It is said the fleet is to run down the coast of Guinea, proceed to the Cape, which they hope to take by negotiation; but if unsuccessful, to go on to the other Dutch possessions."

The fleet sailed on the morning of Sunday the 1st of March. 1 major, 1 ensign, 4 sergeants, 1 drummer, and 124 privates were left behind; and the most of them, with others, were incorporated with the first battalion, on its amalgamation with the second battalion.

Holland having entirely submitted to France, as detailed in the record of the first battalion, and Britain being fully aware that submission to France became equivalent to a compulsory declaration of war against her, it behoved her to turn her attention to the Dutch colonies, which, from their proximity to India, would prove of immense importance to an enemy.

In June 1795 a British fleet under Sir G. Elphinstone arrived off the Cape, having Major-General Craig and the 78th Highlanders (second battalion) on board; and the commanders immediately entered into negotiations with Governor Slugsken for the cession of the colony to Great Britain in trust for the Stadtholder. A determination to resist the force having been openly expressed, the commanders determined to disembark their troops and occupy a position. Accordingly, the 78th and the Marines were landed at Simon's Bay on the 14th, and proceeded to take possession of Simon's Town without opposition. The Dutch were strongly posted in their fortified camp at Muysenberg, six miles on this side of Capetown; and accordingly a force of 800 seamen having been sent to co-operate with the troops on shore, the whole body moved to its attack; while the ships of the fleet, covering them from the sea, opened such a terrific fire upon the colonists that they fled precipitately. Muysenberg was taken on the 7th of August, and on the 9th a detachment arrived from St Helena with some field-pieces; but it was not till the 3rd of September, when Sir A. Clarke, at the head of three regiments, put into the bay, that an advance became practicable. Accordingly, the Dutch position at Wineberg was forced on the 14th, and on

the 15th Capetown capitulated, the garrison marching out with the honours of war. Thus, after a two months' campaign, during which they suffered severely from the unhealthiness of their situation, the scarcity of provisions, and the frequent night attacks of the enemy, this young battalion, whose conduct throughout had been exemplary in the highest degree, saw the object of the expedition accomplished, and the colony taken possession of in the name of his Britannic Majesty.

Under date "Cape of Good Hope, 19th September 1795," Lieut.-Colonel Alexander Mackenzie of Fairburn, commanding the second battalion of the 78th Highlanders, sends a long account of the transactions at the Cape to Lieut.-Colonel F. H. Mackenzie of Seaforth. We are sorry that our space permits us to give only the following extracts:—

"I think if you will not be inclined to allow that the hardships have been so great, you will at all events grant that the comforts have been few, when I assure you that I have not had my clothes off for nearly nine weeks, nor my boots, except when I could get a dry pair to put on.

". . . If the regiment is put on the East India establishment, which is supposed will be the case, it will be equally the same for you as if they were in India. I must observe it is fortunate for us that we are in a warm climate, as we are actually without a coat to put on; we are so naked that we can do no duty in town. . . .

"I cannot tell you how much I am puzzled about clothing. The other corps have all two years' clothing not made up, and I should not be surprised if this alone was to turn the scale with regard to their going to India. General Clarke advises me to buy cloth, but I fear putting you to expense; however, if the clothing does not come out in the first ship I shall be obliged to do something, but what, I am sure I don't know. I hope your first battalion may come out, as there cannot be a more desirable quarter for the colonel or the regiment. We are getting into excellent barracks, and the regiment will soon get well of the dysentry and other complaints. They are now immensely rich, and I shall endeavour to lay out their money properly for them. I shall bid you adieu by saying that I do not care how soon a good peace may be brought about. I think we have at last turned up a good trump card for you, and I daresay the Ministry will play the negotiating game well."

In Capetown the regiment remained quartered until the arrival of the first battalion in June 1796.

II.

1796–1817.

1st and 2d Battalions amalgamated——The Regiment sails for the Cape—The consolidation completed—Capture of a Dutch fleet—Ordered to India—Lucknow—Cession of Allahabad—Various changes of Quarters—Colonels Alexander Mackenzie and J. R. Mackenzie quit the Regiment—Ordered to Bombay—Join General Wellesley's Army—The Mahrattas—The Treaty of Bassein—Lake and Wellesley take the field—War between the British and the Mahrattas—Ahmednuggur taken—Battle of Assaye—Colours granted to the 74th and 78th—Wellesley's pursuit of the Enemy—Battle of Argaum—Gawilghur taken—The Regiment goes to Goojerat—From Bombay to Goa—Excellent conduct—Ordered to Madras and thence to Java—Landing near Batavia, which is invested—The Cantonment of Waltevreeden forced—The Fortification of Cornelis captured, when General Janssens flies—Colonel Gillespie defeats Janssens—The French army surrender and evacuate the Island—Rebellion of the Sultan of Djokjokarta—His Capital is taken, and he is deposed—Colonel Fraser and Captain Macpherson murdered by Banditti at Probolingo—Major Forbes defeats the Insurgents—Thanks of Government to the Regiment—Expeditions against the Islands of Bali and Celebes—The Regiment sails for Calcutta—Six Companies wrecked on the Island of Preparis—General Orders by the Indian Government—The Regiment lands at Portsmouth and proceeds to Aberdeen—Unfounded charge against the Highland Regiments.

On the 28th of November, 1795, the Duke of York had issued orders for the consolidation of both battalions, and accordingly, on the arrival of the 1st battalion from L'Ile Dieu, the work was commenced by the attachment to it of that part of the 2nd battalion which had been left behind. On the 26th of February, 1796, only seven weeks after its return from abroad, the battalion proceeded from Poole to Portsmouth, where it embarked for the Cape in two divisions under the command of Lieut.-Colonel Alexander Mackenzie of Belmaduthy, and sailed on the 6th of March. On the 30th of May the 78th arrived in Simon's Bay, and on the 1st of June landed and commenced its march to

Capetown. Here the work of consolidation was completed, and the supernumerary officers and men ordered home. The regiment now presented the appearance of a splendid body of men, and mustered 970 Highlanders, 129 Lowlanders, and 14 English and Irish, the last chiefly bandsmen. The Batavian Republic had formally declared war against England in May; and, accordingly, on the 3rd of August, apparently with the view of attempting the recapture of the Cape, a Dutch fleet under Admiral Lucas anchored in Saldanha Bay. General Craig, the commander of the troops, marched up a force, which included the grenadier and light battalions of the 78th. As the Dutch fleet, however, surrendered, the troops marched back to a place called Groenekloof, about half-way to Capetown, where they remained encamped for three or four weeks, when the 78th marched to Capetown, and occupied the hill near the Castle until the transports were ready to convoy them to India.

On the 4th of November the regiment embarked, and sailed on the 10th; it had a long passage, during which scurvy made its appearance, but to no formidable extent. On the 10th of February 1797 the transports reached Calcutta, and the following day the regiment marched into Fort-William. Ten days later it embarked in boats on the Hoogly, and proceeded to Burhampoor, the voyage occupying fourteen days. About the 1st of August, on the embarkation of the 33rd Regiment with the expedition intended against Manilla, the 78th proceeded to Fort William. In the beginning of October six companies were again embarked in boats, and proceeded to Chunar. From Chunar, about the end of November, the division, having drawn camp equipment from the magazine, was ordered to drop down to Benares, there to land, and form part of a large escort to the Governor-General (Sir John Shore), and the Commander-in-Chief (Sir A. Clarke), about to proceed to Lucknow. The division accordingly landed at Benares on the 6th of December and marched to Sheopoor, six miles on the road, where it halted to complete its field equipment. In the beginning of November, the 33rd having returned to Fort William, the second division of the 78th embarked and proceeded to Chunar, where it was landed and encamped until the following March

On the 9th of December the first division was joined by a part of the 3rd Native Infantry, some artillery with field-pieces, and two russallahs or squadrons of Irregular Hindoostani Cavalry, formerly the body-guard of General De Boigne, a Savoyard in Sindiah's service, and marched forward, forming the escort above mentioned. The march was continued without halting for fifteen days, which brought the force to the race-course of Lucknow, where it was joined by the remainder of the 3rd Native Infantry. It is unnecessary to enter here into the complications of native Indian politics. It is enough to say that on the death, in 1797, of the troublesome Asoph-ud-Dowla, the Nawaub Vizir of Oudh, he was succeeded by his equally troublesome and weak-minded son, Mirza Ali.

The young prince had barely ascended the throne, however, ere reports were brought to the Governor-General of his incapacity, faithless character, and prodigality. It was on receiving these reports, therefore, that Sir John Shore determined to proceed to Lucknow in person, and, by actual observation, satisfy himself of the merits of the case. The narrative is resumed from the regimental records of the 78th.

"On the frontier of the Nawaub Vizir's dominions, we had been met by the new Nawaub Vizir, Ali, a young lad of known faithless principles, with a large force, and his intentions being considered very suspicious, each battalion furnished a captain's outlying picquet, for the security of the camp at night, which was continued until after his deposition and the elevation of his successor, Saadut Ali, on the 22nd January 1798."

By skilful management Vizir Ali was secured without violence, and his uncle, Saadut Ali, placed in his stead.

On the 23rd of February, the 78th, the 1st Battalion Native Infantry, and a company of Artillery, under the command of Colonel Mackenzie of the 78th, marched for the Fort of Allahabad, which had lately been ceded to the British by Saadut Ali.

After various movements, the 78th found itself in garrison at Fort William in December

1800. In the October of that year Lieut.-Colonel Alexander Mackenzie had left for England, handing over his command to Lieut.-Colonel J. Randoll Mackenzie of Suddie.[7] And in the latter part of November Lieut.-Colonel Mackenzie also went to England, and was succeeded in the command of the regiment by Lieut.-Colonel Adams. The regiment remained in quarters at Fort William during the whole of 1801 and 1802.

In the middle of January, 1803, the 78th received orders to prepare for embarkation for Bombay, where head quarters arrived on the 26th of March, and immediately received orders to prepare for field service. The regiment re-embarked on the 4th of April, and proceeded to Bassein, where it landed on the 7th, and marched at once to join the camp of Colonel Murray's detachment at Sachpara, 7 miles from the town, being formed as an escort to His Highness the Peshwah, who had been driven from his dominions by Holkar during the previous October.

The detachment set out on the 18th of April, and marched by Panwell and the Bhore Ghât. In the beginning of June the 78th joined at Poonah the army under General Wellesley, destined to act against Sindiah and the Mahrattas. The regiment was posted to the brigade commanded by Lieut.-Colonel Harness,

[7] "During six years' residence in different cantonments in Bengal no material event occurred. The corps sustained throughout a character every way exemplary. The commanding officer's system of discipline, and his substitution of censure for punishment, attracted much attention. The temperate habits of the soldiers, and Colonel Mackenzie's mode of punishment, by a threat to inform his parents of the misconduct of a delinquent, or to send a bad character of him to his native country, attracted the notice of all India. Their sobriety was such that it was necessary to restrict them from selling or giving away the usual allowance of liquor to other soldiers.

"There were in this battalion nearly 300 men from Lord Seaforth's estate in the Lewis. Several years elapsed before any of these men were charged with a crime deserving severe punishment. In 1799 a man was tried and punished. This so shocked his comrades that he was put out of their society as a degraded man, who brought shame on his kindred. The unfortunate outcast felt his own degradation so much that he became unhappy and desperate, and Colonel Mackenzie, to save him from destruction, applied and got him sent to England, where his disgrace would be unknown and unnoticed. It happened as Colonel Mackenzie had expected, for he quite recovered his character. By the humane consideration of his commander, a man was thus saved from that ruin which a repetition of severity would have rendered inevitable."—Stewart.

80th Regiment, which was called the 4th brigade, with reference to the Grand Madras Army, from which General Wellesley was detached, but which formed the right of the General's force. Its post in line was the right of the centre, which was occupied by the park, and on the left of the park was the 74th Highlanders, in the brigade commanded by Colonel Wallace, 74th, and called the 5th Brigade. Besides these two brigades of infantry there was one of cavalry, commanded by Lieut.-Colonel Maxwell, 19th Light Dragoons; each brigade consisted of 1 European and 3 native regiments. The train consisted of four iron and four brass 12-pounders, besides two 5½-inch howitzers, and some spare field-pieces.

A very few days after the army moved forward the rainy season commenced, but was by no means a severe one; the great want of forage, however, at the commencement of this campaign, destroyed much cattle, and the 78th Highlanders, who were by no means so well equipped as the other corps, were a good deal distressed at first. The movements of the army were slow, making long halts, and not keeping in a straight direction till the beginning of August, when it encamped about 8 miles south of Ahmednuggur, in which position it was when negotiations were broken off and war declared with Dowlut Rao Sindiah and the Rajah of Berar, Ragojee Bhoonslah.

On the 8th of August the advanced guard was reinforced by the flank companies of the 74th and 78th Highlanders, and the city of Ahmednuggur was attacked and carried by storm in three columns, of which the advanced guard formed one, the other two being led by battalion companies of the same regiments. "The fort of Ahmednuggur is one of the strongest in India, built of stone and a strong Indian cement called *chunam*. It is surrounded by a deep ditch, with large circular bastions at short intervals, and was armed with guns in casemated embrasures, and with loopholes for musketry. The escarp was unusually lofty, but the casemates were too confined to admit of their being effectively employed, and the glacis was so abrupt that it offered good shelter to an enemy who could once succeed in getting close to the walls. The Pettah was a large and regular Indian town, surrounded by a wall of stone and mud 18 feet high, with small bastions at every hundred yards, but with no rampart broad enough for a man to stand upon. Here, both in the Pettah and the fort, the walls were perceived to be lined by men, whose appointments glittered in the sun. The Pettah was separated from the fort by a wide space, in which Sindiah had a palace and many valuables, surrounded with immense gardens, where the remains of aqueducts and many interesting ruins of Moorish architecture show the once flourishing condition of the Nizam's capital in the 16the century."[8] Having determined on taking the Pettah by escalade, General Wellesley ordered forward the stormers, who were led by the advanced guard. Unfortunately, on account of the height and narrowness of the walls, and the difficulty of obtaining footing, the men, having reached the top of the scaling ladders, were, one after the other as they came up, either killed or thrown down. At length, Captain Vesey, of the 1/3rd Native Infantry, having secured a bastion, a party of his men leaped down within the walls, and, opening a gate, admitted the remainder of the force; some skirmishing took place in the streets, but the enemy was speedily overcome, and though the fort continued to fire round-shot, it was with but little precision, and occasioned no damage.[9] The army lost 140 men, the casualties of the 78th being Captains F. Mackenzie Humberstone and Duncan Grant (a volunteer on this occasion), Lieut. Anderson of the Grenadier Company, and 12 men killed; and Lieut. Larkin of the Light Company, and 5 men wounded.

After the action the army encamped a long shot's distance from the fort, which was reconnoitred on the 9th, and a ravine having been discovered, not 300 yards from the wall, it was occupied, and a battery erected, which opened with four iron 12-pounders on the morning of the 10th. During that night the battery was enlarged, and two howitzers added to its arma-

[8] Cust's *Wars*.
[9] "A Mahratta chief, residing in the British camp, gave the following account of the action in a letter to his friends at Poonah:—'The English are a strange people, and their General a wonderful man. They came here in the morning, looked at the Pettah wall, walked over it, killed all the garrison, and then turned in to breakfast. Who can resist such men as these!'"
Cust's *War*.

ment, and the fire re opened on the 11th, on the evening of which day the Killedar capitulated, and next morning the garrison, to the number of 1400 men having marched out, the grenadiers of the 78th and a battalion of Sepoys took possession The victorious troops proceeded to the plunder of Sindiah's palace Its treasures can have been surpassed only by those of the Summer Palace at Pekin "There were found in it, besides many objects of European manufacture and luxury, the richest stuffs of India—gold and silver cloths, splendid armour, silks, satins, velvets, furs, shawls, plate, cash, &c "[1] Here, as afterwards, General Wellesley set his face against all such demoralising practices, but it was only after hanging a couple of Sepoys in the gateway, as a warning to the rest, that order could be restored and the native troops restrained

Along with the fort and city of Ahmednuggur, a province of the same name became subject to British authority This fortress, long regarded as the key of the Deccan, besides covering his communications with Poonah, afforded General Wellesley an invaluable depôt from which to draw supplies, and from its position overawed the surrounding population, and formed a bulwark of defence to the western territories of the Nizam [2]

The army remained for some days in the neighbourhood of Ahmednuggur, and then marching down the Nimderrah Ghât, directed its route to Toka, on the Godavery On the 24th it crossed the river in boats On the 17th of September the army encamped at Goonjee, the junction of the Godavery and Galatty, and thence moved to Golah Pangree on the Doodna, which it reached on the 20th

[1] Cust's *Wars*
[2] "It may not be known to the public, and perhaps not to the 78th Regiment itself, that the handsome black granite slab inserted in the Pettah wall of Ahmednuggur, bearing an inscription that on this spot fell, at the storming of the fort, Captain Thomas Mackenzie-Humberstone (son of Colonel Mackenzie Humberstone, who was killed at the close of the Mahratta War, 1783), also to the memory of Captain Grant, Lieutenant Anderson, the non-commissioned officers, and privates of that Regiment who fell on that occasion, was placed here as a memorial by the Honourable Mrs Stewart-Mackenzie (then Lady Hood), eldest daughter of Lord Seaforth (brother of Colonel Humberstone), when she visited this spot on her way from Poonah to Hyderabad, in March 1813 "—*Memorandum found among the papers of the late Colonel C. Mackenzie Fraser of Castle Fraser*

On the 24th of August the united armies of Sindiah and the Rajah of Berar had entered the territories of the Nizam by the Adjunteh Ghât, and were known to be occupying the country between that pass and Jalnah General Wellesley's plan of operations now was, if possible, to bring the enemy to a general action, but, if he failed in that object, at least to drive them out of the Nizam's country and secure the passes On the 19th of September he wrote to Colonel Stevenson, directing that officer to march upon the Adjunteh Ghât, he himself moving by Jafferabad upon those of Bhaudoola and Laukenwarra On the 21st, having obtained intelligence that the enemy lay at Bokerdun, he, after a personal interview with Colonel Stevenson at Budnapoor, arranged that their forces should separate, marching on the 22nd, and traversing two parallel roads about 12 miles apart. On the 22nd both officers broke camp, the General proceeding by the eastern route, round the hills between Budnapoor and Jalnah, and Colonel Stevenson moving to the westward On the 23rd General Wellesley arrived at Naulniah, and found that, instead of being 12 or 14 miles distant from the enemy's camp, as he had calculated, he was within 6 miles of it. General Wellesley found himself unable to make a reconnaissance without employing his whole force, and to retire in the face of the enemy's numerous cavalry would have been a dangerous experiment, but the hircarrahs having reported that the cavalry had already moved off, and that the infantry were about to follow, the General determined to attack at once, without waiting for Colonel Stevenson He, however, apprised Stevenson of his intention, and desired him to move up without delay On coming in sight of the enemy he was rudely undeceived as to his intelligence, for, instead of the infantry alone, the whole force of the allied Rajahs was drawn up on the further bank of the river Kaitna, ready to receive him

" The sight was enough to appal the stoutest heart thirty thousand horse, in one magnificent mass, crowded the right, a dense array of infantry, powerfully supported by artillery, formed the centre and left, the gunners were beside their pieces, and a hundred pieces of cannon, in front of the line, stood ready to vomit forth death upon the assailants. Wellington paused for a moment, impressed but not daunted by the sight. His whole force, as Colonel Stevenson had not come up, did not exceed 8000 men, of whom 1600 were cavalry; the effective native British were not above 1500, and he had only 17 pieces of cannon. But feeling at once that retreat in presence of so prodigious a force of cavalry was impossible, and that the most audacious course was, in such circumstances, the most prudent, he ordered an immediate attack."[3]

Before receiving intelligence of the enemy, the ground had been marked out for an encampment, and the cavalry had dismounted: General Wellesley ordered them to remount, and proceeded with them to the front. Of the infantry, the 1/2nd Native Infantry was ordered to cover the baggage on the marked ground, and to be reinforced by the rearguard as it came up. The 2/12th Native Infantry was ordered to join the left, in order to equalise the two brigades, which were to follow by the right, and the four brass light 12-pounders of the park were sent to the head of the line.

These dispositions did not cause above ten minutes' halt to the column of infantry, but the cavalry, moving on with the General, came first in sight of the enemy's position from a rising ground to the left of the road. This was within cannon-shot of the right of their encampment, which lay along the further bank of the river Kaitna, a stream of no magnitude, but with steep banks and a very deep channel, so as not to be passable except at particular places, chiefly near the villages. Sindiah's irregular cavalry formed the right; the troops of the Rajah of Berar, also irregulars, the centre; and Sindiah's regular infantry, the left. The latter was composed of 17 battalions, amounting to about 10,500 men, formed into 3 brigades, to each of which a body of regular cavalry and a corps of marksmen, called Allygoots, were attached. 102 pieces of their artillery were afterwards accounted for, but they probably had a few more.[4] The infantry were dressed, armed, and accoutred like British Sepoys; they were very fine bodies of men,

and though the English officers had quitted them, they were in an admirable state of discipline, and many French and other European officers held command among them. Their guns were served by Gollundaze, exactly like those of the Bengal service, which had been disbanded some little time previously, and were probably the same men. It was soon found that they were extremely well trained, and their fire was both as quick and as well-directed as could be produced by the British artillery. What the total number of the enemy was cannot be ascertained, or even guessed at, with any degree of accuracy; but it is certainly calculated very low at 30,000 men, including the light troops who were out on a plundering excursion, but returned towards the close of the action. The two Rajahs were in the field in person, attended by their principal ministers, and, it being the day of the Dusserah feast, the Hindoos, of which the army was chiefly composed, had religious prejudices to make them fight with spirit and hope for victory.

The force of General Wellesley's army in action was nearly 4700 men, of whom about 1500 were Europeans (including artillery), with 26 field-pieces, of which only four 12 and eight 6-pounders were fired during the action; the rest, being the guns of the cavalry and the battalions of the second line, could not be used.

On General Wellesley's approaching the enemy for the purpose of reconnoitring, they commenced a cannonade, the first gun of which was fired at twenty minutes past one o'clock P.M., and killed one of his escort. The General, although he found himself in front of their right, determined to attack their left, in order to turn it, judging that the defeat of their infantry was most likely to prove effectual, and accordingly ordered his own infantry column to move in that direction. Meanwhile some of the staff looked out for a ford to enable the troops to pass the Kaitna and execute this movement, and found one, which the enemy had fortunately left undefended, scarcely half a mile beyond their left flank, near the old fort of Peepulgaon, where the ground, narrowing at the confluence of the Kaitna and Juah, would prevent them from attacking with overwhelming numbers. The whole of this march was performed considerably within range of

[3] Alison's *History of Europe.*
[4] "It is now said that they had in their camp 128 guns."—*General Wellesley to Major Shaw, 28th September 1803.*

their cannon, and the fire increased so fast that by the time the head of the column had reached Peepulgaon, it was tremendously heavy, and had already destroyed numbers.

For some time the enemy did not discover Major-General Wellesley's design; but as soon as they became aware of it, they threw their left up to Assaye, a village on the Juah, near the left of their second line, which did not change its position. Their first line was now formed across the ground between the Kaitna and the Juah, the right resting upon the Kaitna, where the left had been, and the left occupying the village of Assaye, which was garrisoned with infantry and surrounded with cannon. They also brought up many guns from their reserve and second line to their first.

The British being obliged to cross the ford in one column by sections, were long exposed to the cannonade. After passing the river, their first line was formed nearly parallel to that of the enemy, at about 500 yards distance, having marched down the alignment to its ground. The second line rather out-flanked the first to the right, as did the third (composed of the cavalry) the second. The left of the first line was opposite the right of the enemy during the formation, and their artillery fired round-shot with great precision and rapidity, the same shot often striking all three lines. It was answered with great spirit by the first British line, but the number of gun-bullocks killed soon hindered the advance of the artillery, with the exception of a few guns which were dragged by the men themselves. The British lines were formed from right to left as follows:—

First Line.

The picquets, four 12-pounders, the 1/9th and 1/10th Native Infantry, and the 78th Highlanders.

Second Line.

The 74th Highlanders and the 2/12th and 1/4th Native Infantry.

Third Line.

The 4th Native Cavalry, the 19th Light Dragoons, and the 5th and 7th Native Cavalry.

Orders were now given for each battalion to attach a company to the guns, to assist and protect them during the advance. These orders, though immediately afterwards counter-manded, reached the 78th, and, consequently, the 5th battalion company, under Lieutenant Cameron, was attached to the guns.

Major-General Wellesley then named the picquets as the battalion of direction, and ordered that the line should advance as quickly as possible consistent with order, and charge with the bayonet without firing a shot. At a quarter to three the word was given for the line to advance, and was received by Europeans and Natives with a cheer. Almost immediately, however, it was discovered that the picquets were not moving forward as directed, and the first line received the word to halt. This was a critical moment, for the troops had got to the ridge of a small swell in the ground that had somewhat sheltered them, particularly on the left; and the enemy, supposing them to be staggered by the fire, redoubled their efforts, discharging chain-shot and missiles of every kind. General Wellesley, dreading the consequences of this check in damping the ardour of the troops, rode up to one of the native corps of the first line, and, taking off his hat, cheered them on in their own language, and repeated the word "March!" Again the troops received the order with loud cheers, and the three battalions of the first line, followed by the 1/4th, advanced in quick time upon the enemy with the greatest coolness, order, and determination.

The 78th, on coming within 150 yards of the enemy's line, withdrew its advanced centre sergeant, and the men were cautioned to be ready to charge. Soon after the battalion opposed to them fired a volley, and about the same time some European officers in the enemy's service were observed to mount their horses and ride off. The 78th instantly ported arms, cheered, and redoubled its pace, and the enemy's infantry, deserted by its officers, broke and ran. The 78th pushed on and fired, and coming to the charge, overtook and bayonetted a few individuals. The gunners, however, held firm to their guns, many being killed in the acts of loading, priming, or pointing; and none quitted their posts until the bayonets were at their breasts. Almost at the same moment the 1/10th Native Infantry closed with the enemy in the most gallant style; but the smoke and dust (which, aided by a high wind, was very great) prevented the troops from moving further to the right.

The 78th now halted for an instant to complete their files and restore exact order, and then moved forward on the enemy's second line, making a complete wheel to the right, the pivot being the right of the army, near the village of Assaye. The picquets having failed to advance, the 74th pushed up, in doing which they were very much cut up by grape, and were charged by the Mahratta cavalry, led by Sindiah in person. They suffered dreadfully, as did also the picquets and 2/12th; and they were only saved by a brilliant charge, headed by Lieut.-Colonel Maxwell. This part of the British line, though it broke the enemy's first line, did not gain much ground; and the enemy still continued in possession of several guns about the village of Assaye, from which they flanked the British line when it arrived opposite their second line.

Several of the enemy also coming up from

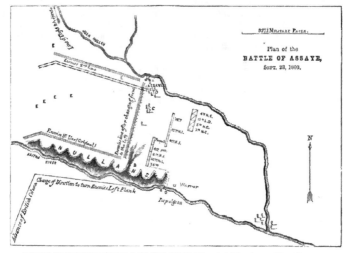

A, the ford from Peepulgaon to Waroor; B, the rising ground which protected the advance; C, four old mangoes; D, screen of prickly pear, covering Assaye; E E E E, 50,000 of the enemy's cavalry.

the bed of the river and other ways, attacked and killed a good many of the British artillerymen. A considerable number also who, after the fashion of Eastern warfare, had thrown themselves on the ground as dead, regained possession of the guns of their first line, which had been taken and passed, and from them opened a fire of grape upon the British rear. The guns of the 78th, with the escort under Lieutenant Cameron, escaped, and joined the regiment as it halted opposite to the enemy's second line.

The British infantry was now in one line, the 78th on the left of the whole; and as it had the longest sweep to make in the wheel, it came up last. When the dust cleared a body of the enemy's best cavalry was seen a little in advance of the left flank, purposing to turn it, on which the left wing of the 78th was thrown back at a small angle, and preparations were made for opening the two guns, which at that moment came up. It is impossible to say too much for the behaviour of the infantry at this awful crisis. Deprived of the assistance of their own artillery, having the enemy's second line, untouched and perfectly fresh, firing steadily upon them, flanked by round-shot from the right, grape pouring upon their rear, and cavalry threatening their left, not a word was heard or a shot fired; all waited the orders of the General with the composure of a field-day amidst a scene of slaughter scarcely ever equalled. This, however, was not of long duration; for the British cavalry came up and drove off the body of horse which threatened the left, and which did not wait to be charged, and General Wellesley ordered the principal part of the line to attack the enemy in front, while the 78th and 7th Native Cavalry moved to the rear and charged the guns which were firing thence. The enemy's second line immediately retired, one brigade in perfect order—so much so, that it repulsed an attack of the 19th Light Dragoons, at the head of which Colonel Maxwell was killed.

The 78th had great difficulty in clearing the field towards the rear and recovering the guns. The enemy strongly resisted, and three times forced them to change their front and attack each party separately, as none would give way until they were so attacked. Meanwhile, as the regiment marched against the one, the remainder kept up a galling fire of grape, till they were all driven off the field. The enemy's light troops, who had been out plundering, now appeared upon the ground, and the Mysore horse were ordered to attack them; however, they did not wait for this, but made off as fast as possible. About half-past four the firing entirely ceased, and the enemy set fire to his tumbrils, which blew up in succession, many of them some time later. The corps which retired at first in such good order soon lost it, and threw its guns into the river, four of which were afterwards found, exclusive of ninety-eight taken on the field of battle. Seven stand of colours were taken from the enemy. After plundering their dead, their camp, and bazaar, they retreated along the Juah for about ten miles and made a halt, but on moving again the flight became general. Then casting away their material of every kind, they descended the Adjunteh Ghât into Candeish, and made for the city of Burhanpoor, when they were described as having no artillery, nor any body of men that looked like a battalion, while the roads were strewed with their wounded and their dying.

The loss of the British was most severe. No part of the Mysore or Mahratta allies was actually engaged. Their infantry was with the baggage, and their cavalry not being in

uniform, the General was apprehensive of mistakes should any part of them come into action. Between one-half and one-third of the British actually in the field were either killed or wounded. The 78th was fortunate in having but a small proportion of the loss to bear. Lieutenant Douglas and 27 men were killed, and 4 officers, 4 sergeants, and 73 men were wounded. The officers wounded were Captain Alexander Mackenzie, Lieutenant Kinloch, Lieutenant Larkin, and Ensign Bethune (Acting Adjutant). Besides those mentioned, Colonel Adams received a contusion of the collar-bone which knocked him off his horse; Lieutenant J. Fraser a contusion of the leg; and all the other officers were more or less touched in their persons or their clothes. The sergeant-major was very badly wounded, and died a few days afterwards.

General Wellesley had two horses killed under him; and nearly all the mounted officers lost horses, some as many as three.

The loss of the enemy must have been terrible. The bodies of 1200 were found on the field, and it was said that 3000 were wounded. Owing to the part they played in the action, the cavalry were unable to pursue, and the enemy suffered much less in their retreat than they should otherwise have done. This fact, too, enabled many of their wounded to creep into the jungle, whence very few returned; but it is impossible to conjecture the total loss, and all computations probably fall short of the actual amount. Jadoon Rao, Sindiah's first minister, and the chief instigator of the war, was severely wounded, and died a few days afterwards; and Colonel Dorsan, the principal French officer, was also killed.

Such was the battle of Assaye, one of the most decisive as well as the most desperate ever fought in India.

Major-General Wellesley and the troops under his command received the thanks of the Governor-general in Council for their important services. His Majesty was pleased to order that the corps engaged should bear upon their colours and appointments an elephant, superscribed "Assaye," in commemoration of the victory; and honorary colours were granted to the 19th Light Dragoons, and the 74th and 78th Highlanders, by the government of India in a general order.[5] For some unknown reason the 78th ceased to use these special colours after leaving India, the 74th being the only one of the three regiments still possessing them.

After various independent movements, Colonel Stevenson, on the 29th of November, formed a junction with General Wellesley at Parterly, on which day the whole of the enemy's force was discovered drawn up on the plains of Argaum about six miles distant. Their line extended five miles, having in its rear the gardens and enclosures of Argaum, while in its front was the uncultivated plain, which was much cut up by watercourses. The Berar cavalry occupied the left, and the artillery and infantry the left centre. Sindiah's force, which occupied the right, consisted of one very heavy body of cavalry, with a number of pindarries or light troops on its right again.

The enemy, though nearly as numerous as at Assaye, were neither so well disciplined nor so well appointed, and they had besides only thirty-eight pieces of cannon. The British army, on the other hand, was more numerous than in the late engagement, having been reinforced by Colonel Stevenson's division. The British moved foward in one column to the edge of the plain. A small village lay between the head of the British columns and the line. The cavalry formed in close column behind this village; and the right brigade formed line in its front, the other corps following and forming in succession. The moment the leading picquet passed the village, the enemy, who was about 1200 yards distant, discharged 21 pieces of cannon in one volley. The native picquets and two battalions, alarmed by this noisy demonstration, which was attended with no injurious consequences, recoiled and took refuge behind the village, leaving the picquets of the 78th and the artillery alone in the field. By the exertions of the officers these battalions were again brought up into line,—not, however, till the 78th had joined and formed into line with the picquets and artillery.

The army was drawn up in one line of fifteen battalions, with the 78th on the right, having

the 74th on its immediate left, and the 94th on the left of the line, supported by the Mysore horse. The cavalry formed a reserve or second line. In the advance, the 78th directed its march against a battery of nine guns, which supported the enemy's left. In the approach, a body of 800 infantry darted from behind the battery, and rushed forward with the apparent intention of passing through the interval between the 74th and 78th. To close the interval, and prevent the intended movement, the regiments obliqued their march, and with ported arms moved forward to meet the enemy; but they were prevented by a deep muddy ditch from coming into collision with the bayonet. The enemy, however, drew up alongside the ditch, and kept up the fire until his last man fell. Next morning upwards of 500 dead bodies were found lying by the ditch. Religious fanaticism had impelled these men to fight.

With the exception of an attack made by Sindiah's cavalry on the left of Colonel Stevenson's division, in which they were repulsed by the 6th Native Infantry, no other attempt of any moment was made by the enemy. After this attack the whole of the enemy's line instantly gave way, leaving all their artillery on the field. They were pursued by the cavalry by moonlight till nine o'clock.

The loss of the British was trifling; no European officer was killed, and only nine wounded, one of whom had his thigh broken. The number of killed and wounded was small, and fell principally upon the 78th, which had eight men killed and about forty wounded; but no officer among the number. In the orders thanking the army for its exertions on this day, General Wellesley particularised the 74th and 78th :—"The 74th and 78th regiments had a particular opportunity of distinguishing themselves, and have deserved and received my thanks." Colonel Harness being extremely ill, Lieut.-Colonel Adams of the 78th commanded the right brigade in the action; and Major Hercules Scott being in command of the picquets as field-officer of the day, the command of the 78th fell to Captain Fraser. In this action, as at the battle of Assaye, a scarcity of officers caused the colours of the 78th to be carried by sergeants; and it

[5] See History of the 74th, vol. ii. p. 573.

II.

4 L

is noticeable that not a shot penetrated the colours in either action, probably owing to the high wind which prevailed and caused them to be carried wrapped closely round the poles. The names of the sergeants who carried the colours at Assaye were Sergeant Leavoch, paymaster's clerk, afterwards quarter-master; and Sergeant John Mackenzie, senior sergeant of the regiment, and immediately afterwards quarter-master's sergeant. At Argaum, Sergeant Leavoch, and Sergeant Grant, regimental clerk, afterwards an ensign, and now (1815, says the Record), a lieutenant in the regiment.

"At the battle of Assaye," General Stewart tells us, "the musicians were ordered to attend to the wounded, and carry them to the surgeons in the rear. One of the pipers, believing himself included in this order, laid aside his instrument and assisted the wounded. For this he was afterwards reproached by his comrades. Flutes and hautboys they thought could be well spared; but for the piper, who should always be in the heat of the battle, to go to the rear with the *whistlers* was a thing altogether unheard of. The unfortunate piper was quite humbled. However, he soon had an opportunity of playing off this stigma; for in the advance at Argaum, he played up with such animation, and influenced the men to such a degree, that they could hardly be restrained from rushing on to the charge too soon, and breaking the line. Colonel Adams was indeed obliged to silence the musician, who now in some manner regained his lost fame."

The next, and, as it turned out, the last exploit of General Wellesley's army, was against the strong fort of Gawilghur, which was taken by assault on the 13th of December. It, however, continued in the field, marching and counter-marching, till the 20th of July, 1804, when the 78th reached Bombay.

The regiment remained in quarters at Bombay till May, 1805, when five companies were ordered to Baroda in the Goojerat. The strength of the regiment was kept up by recruits, chiefly from the Scotch militia, and latterly by reinforcements from the second battalion, 800 strong, added to the regiment in 1804. In July, 1805, a detachment of 100 recruits arrived from Scotland. The regi-

ment removed to Goa in 1807, whence it embarked for Madras in March, 1811.

"The numerical strength of this fine body of men was less to be estimated than their character, personal appearance, efficiency, and health. Upwards of 336 were volunteers from the Perthshire and other Scotch militia regiments, and 400 were drafts from the second battalion, which had been seasoned by a service of three years in the Mediterranean. Such was the stature of many of the men that, after the grenadier company was completed from the tallest men, the hundred next in height were found too tall and beyond the usual size of the light infantry. The harmony which so frequently subsisted between Highland corps and the inhabitants of the countries where they have been stationed, has been frequently observed. In Goa it appears to have been the same as elsewhere. The Condè de Surzecla, Viceroy of Portuguese India, on the departure of the regiment from under his command, embraced that opportunity 'to express his sentiments of praise and admiration of the regular, orderly, and honourable conduct of His Britannic Majesty's 78th Highland regiment during the four years they have been under his authority, equally and highly creditable to the exemplary discipline of the corps, and to the skill of the excellent commander; and his Excellency can never forget the inviolable harmony and friendship which has always subsisted between the subjects of the regent of Portugal and all classes of this honourable corps.'" [6]

On the 14th of March, 1811, the regiment embarked, and sailed in three transports for Madras. Very few men were left behind sick. The strength embarked was 1027, of whom 835 were Highlanders, 184 Lowlanders, and 8 English and Irish.

The transports arrived at Madras on the 10th of April, but the regiment was not landed, and sailed on the 30th with the last division of troops detailed for the expedition under the command of Lieut.-General Sir Samuel Auchmuty, destined for the capture of Java.

On the 5th of June the last division of the

[6] Stewart's *Sketches.*

troops arrived at Malacca, when the army was formed into four brigades as follows:—The first or advanced brigade, under Colonel Gillespie, was composed of the flank battalions (formed by the rifle and light companies of the army), a wing of the 89th, a battalion of marines, of Bengal Light Infantry, and of volunteers, three squadrons of the 22nd Dragoons, and some Madras Horse Artillery. The left flank battalion was formed by the rifle and light companies of the 78th, the light company of the 69th, and a grenadier company of Bengal Native Infantry, and was commanded by Major Fraser of the 78th. The second brigade, commanded by Colonel Gibbs of the 59th, consisted of the 14th and 59th, and a battalion of Bengal Native Infantry. The third brigade, commanded by Colonel Adams of the 78th, was composed of the 69th and 78th, and a battalion of Bengal Native Infantry. The 78th was commanded by Brevet Lieut.-Colonel Campbell, and the light battalion by Major Forbes of the 78th. At Goa, a company of marksmen had been formed in the 78th, under the command of Captain T. Cameron, and at Madras they had received a rifle equipment and clothing. The reserve, under Colonel Wood, was composed entirely of Native Infantry. Attached to the army were detachments of Bengal and Madras Artillery and Engineers; and the whole force amounted to about 12,000 men, of whom about half were Europeans.

Early in June the fleet sailed from Malacca, and on the 4th of August came to anchor off the village of Chillingching, about twelve miles to the eastward of Batavia, and the troops landed without opposition. On the 7th the advance took up a position within two miles of Batavia, and on the 8th the magistrates surrendered the city at discretion.

It was understood that General Jumelle, with 3000 men, held the cantonment of Weltevreeden, about three miles from the city; and that about the same distance further on lay the strongly entrenched camp of Cornelis, where the greater portion of the French force, about 10,000 men, were posted under command of General Janson, the governor.

Before daybreak, on the morning of the 10th, the advance marched against Weltevreeden, and the enemy was discovered strongly posted in the woods and villages. His right was defended by the canal called the Slokan; his left was exposed, but the approach in front and flank was defended by a marsh and pepper plantations, and the road rendered impassable by a strong abbatis of felled trees. The enemy's infantry, enforced by four field-pieces served with grape, was drawn up behind this barrier, and commenced a destructive fire upon the head of the column as it advanced. Captain Cameron, who was in advance with his rifle company, was severely wounded, and a number of his men killed or disabled while entangled in the abbatis. Captain Forbes, with the aid of the light company, was then ordered to charge the obstacle; but he met with such resistance, that, after losing 15 out of 37 men, Colonel Gillespie directed him to retire and cross the ditch to the enemy's left. Lieutenant Munro was killed here while in command of a party detailed to cover the British guns. An order was now given to turn the enemy's left, which after a little delay succeeded,—"the grenadier company of the 78th, as in every Eastern field of fame, heading the attack." [7] The grenadiers, in company with a detachment of the 89th, under Major Butler, carried the enemy's guns after a most obstinate resistance, the gunners being cut down or bayoneted almost to a man. The general wrote—"The flank companies of the 78th (commanded by Captains David Forbes and Thomas Cameron) the detachment of the 89th, particularly distinguished themselves." The main body of the force shortly after came up, and the villages having been fired, the camp was occupied, and its war material, consisting of 300 guns, and a vast quantity of stores, taken possession of. The enemy's loss was said to be very heavy, and the Brigadier-General Alberti was dangerously wounded. The British loss fell principally upon the 78th and 89th, the former having 33 men killed and wounded, besides the officers mentioned. By the occupation of Weltevreeden, the army obtained a good communication with Batavia and the

Alison's H[ist] of Eur[ope].

fleet, a healthy situation, the command of the country and supplies, and a base of operations against the main position of Cornelis.

On the night of the 21st, when in company with the 69th, the 78th relieved Colonel Gillespie's brigade in the advance. Early on the morning of the 22nd, three English batteries being nearly completed, the enemy made a sortie from Cornelis, and obtained possession of two of them, whence they were driven by a party of the 78th, which happened, fortunately, to be in the trenches at the time, under Major Lindsay and Captain Macleod. The battery on the right was energetically defended by Lieutenant Hart and a company of the 78th, who repulsed the enemy's attack with considerable loss.

The camp of Cornelis was an oblong of 1600 by 900 yards. It was strongly entrenched: the river Jacatra or Liwong flowed along its west side, and the canal, called the Slokan, washed the east. Neither was fordable, and the banks of the river were steep and covered with jungle, while on the canal and beyond it powerful batteries were raised. The north and south faces were defended by deep ditches, which could be inundated at pleasure, and were strengthened with palisades, fraises, and chevaux de frise. These faces between the river and canal were further protected by seven formidable redoubts, constructed by General Daendels, and numerous batteries and entrenchments. A strong work also covered and protected the only bridge which communicated with the position, and which was thrown across the Slokan. The entire circumference of the works was about five miles; they were mounted with 280 pieces of cannon, and were garrisoned by over 10,000 men, of whom about 5000 were Europeans, and the remainder disciplined native regiments, commanded by French and Dutch officers.

Sir Samuel Auchmuty had broken ground on the 20th, at 600 yards distance from the works; and on the 24th, though no practicable breach had been made, the general being apprehensive of the danger of delay, determined upon an assault. The command of the principal attack was entrusted to Colonel Gillespie. The advance guard was formed by the rifle company of the 14th, while the grenadiers of the 78th led the column, to which the light and rifle companies also belonged. Immediately after midnight of the 25th Colonel Gillespie marched, but his advance was impeded by the darkness of the night and the intricacy of the country, which was parcelled out into pepper and betel gardens, and intersected with ravines, so that the troops were frequently obliged to move in single file. Towards daylight it was found that the rear division, under Colonel Gibbs, had strayed, but as it was impossible to remain long concealed, and to retreat would have been to abandon the enterprise, it was determined to assault without them. With the earliest streak of dawn the column was challenged, but the men, advancing with fixed bayonets at the double, speedily annihilated the enemy's picquets, and obtained possession of the protecting redoubt No. 3. At the same time the grenadiers of the 78th rushed up on the bamboo bridge over the Slokan, mingling with the fugitives, and thus prevented its destruction by them. Owing to the darkness still prevailing, many of the men fell over the bridge into the canal, and were with difficulty rescued; while everywhere the carnage was terrific, the road being enfiladed by numerous pieces of artillery. The left of the attack now stormed and carried a large redoubt, No. 4, to the left of the bridge, which was strongly palisaded, and mounted upwards of twenty 18-pounders, besides several 24 and 32-pounders. Colonel Gibbs also came up at this moment, and his force was joined by a portion of the 78th, under Captain Macleod and Lieut. Brodie, who carried the redoubt No. 1 to the right; but scarcely had his advance entered when it blew up with a tremendous explosion, by which many of both parties were killed. It was said that a train had been fired by some of the enemy's officers, but this has never been proved. Lieut.-Colonel Macleod's (69th) attack against redoubt No. 2 was also completely successful, though the army had to deplore the loss of that gallant officer in the moment of victory. "Major Yule's attack was equally spirited, but after routing the enemy's force at Campong Maylayo, and killing many of them, he found the bridge on fire, and was unable to penetrate further." [8] He therefore had to con-

[8] Sir Samuel Auchmuty's Despatch.

tent himself with firing across the river. The two attacks now joined, and, under Colonel Gillespie, advanced to attack a body of the enemy inforced by a regiment of cavalry, which was stationed on a rising ground above the fort, and protected their park of artillery. The fire was very heavy, and though the British actually reached the mouths of the enemy's guns, they were twice driven back, but rallying each time, they made a final charge and dislodged the enemy. Here Lieutenants Hart and Pennycuik of the 78th were wounded, the former having his thigh broken in two places by a grape-shot. The commander-in-chief now ordered a general attack upon the north face, which was led by Colonel Adams' brigade, and "the heroic 78th, which, though long opposed, now burst in with loud shouts in the front of the line, and successively carried the works on either hand." [9] The regiment, under Lieut.-Colonel Campbell, advanced along the high road, crossed the ditch and palisade under a very heavy fire of grape and musketry, and carried the enemy's work in that direction. Two companies, under Colonel Macpherson, proceeded along the bank of the Slokan and took possession of the dam-dyke, which kept back the water from the ditch, thus preventing the enemy from cutting it, and leaving the ditch dry for the main body of the regiment to cross. In this service "Captain Macpherson was wounded in a personal rencontre with a French officer." [1] The loss of the 78th in this part of the action was very heavy. Lieutenant-Colonel Campbell had both his thighs shattered by a grape-shot, and died two days afterwards, and Captain William Mackenzie and Lieutenant Matheson were also wounded. The regiment was necessarily much broken up in crossing the ditch and palisades, but soon re-formed, and completed the rout of the enemy.

In the space of three hours from the commencement of the action, all the enemy's works were in the possession of the British.

The loss of the enemy in killed, during the attack and pursuit, was nearly 2000. The wounded were estimated at about 3000, while between 5000 and 6000 prisoners were taken,

[9] Alison's *History of Europe*.
[1] Stewart's *Sketches*.

mostly Europeans, including a regiment of Voltigeurs lately arrived from France.

The main body of the 78th lost 1 field officer (Lieut.-Colonel Campbell) and 18 rank and file killed, and 3 sergeants and 62 rank and file wounded; its total of killed and wounded, including the three companies with Colonel Gillespie's attack, being 164.

A force, which had been sent by sea to Cheribon to intercept General Jansen's retreat into the eastern portion of the island, having arrived two days after he had passed, Sir Samuel Auchmuty determined to undertake the pursuit. Accordingly, on the 5th of September, he embarked at Batavia with the 14th and 78th Regiments, the grenadiers of the 3rd Volunteer Regiment, and some artillery and pioneers, less than 1000 men in all, with six field-pieces. The headquarters, grenadier, rifle, and one battalion company of the 78th sailed in the "Mysore," under Major Fraser, and the remaining seven companies, under Major Lindsay, in the "Lowjee Family." On the 12th the troops commanded by Major Lindsay landed at Samarang, and occupied the town without opposition, and learnt that a considerable body of the enemy, principally cavalry, was strongly posted upon the hills of Serondole, about 5 or 6 miles distant. On the 16th the whole force, under the command of Colonel Gibbs, advanced against Serondole at an early hour. Although the position of the enemy was most formidable, his troops gave way on all hands.

On the morning of the 18th a flag of truce arrived from General Jansen, accepting unconditionally any terms Sir Samuel Auchmuty might suggest. These were that the governor should surrender himself and his army prisoners of war, resign the sovereignty of Java and all the Dutch and French possessions in the East Indies into the hands of Great Britain, who should be left free with regard to the future administration of the island, the guarantee of the public debt, and the liquidation of paper money.

Thus the fertile island of Java and its rich dependencies, the last colonial possession of France, was wrested from her by British prowess.

The regiment remained in Java till September 1816, when it embarked for Calcutta. The only other enterprise we need mention in which the 78th was engaged while in Java was an expedition against the rebellious Sultan of Djokjokarta, when a great amount of treasure was captured, including two solid silver soup-tureens of antique design and exquisite finish, which the regiment still possesses. We must also mention the melancholy death, at Probolingo, on the 18th of May, 1813, of Lieut.-Colonel Fraser and Captain Macpherson at the hands of some fierce banditti, these officers being on a visit to a friend at Probolingo, when the banditti approached the place. Next day a detachment, consisting of 100 of the most active of the grenadier, rifle, and light companies, under Major Forbes of the 78th, marched against the banditti. After marching 64 miles in 18 hours the detachment came up with the main body of the banditti, and the commanding officers thought it advisable to make a halt, in order that the men might obtain some water before proceeding to the attack. The enemy seeing this, and mistaking the motive, advanced boldly and rapidly, headed by their chiefs. When within about 100 yards they halted for a moment, and again advanced to the charge at a run, in a close compact body, at the same time setting up a most dreadful yell. The men on this occasion showed a steadiness which could not be surpassed, not a shot being fired until the enemy was within a spear's length of their line, when they gave their fire with such effect that it immediately checked the advance, and forced the enemy to retreat with terrible loss. Upwards of 150 lay dead on the spot; one of their chiefs was killed, and two more, who were taken alive that afternoon, suffered the merited punishment of their rebellion. Only a few of the 78th were wounded. The detachment now moved on to Probolingo House, which it was supposed the insurgents would defend, but having lost their principal leaders they dispersed without making any further stand. Their force was estimated to have amounted to upwards of 2500 men. The same evening the bodies of Colonel Fraser and Captain Macpherson were brought in and interred in the square of Probolingo.

During the period of its residence in Java

the men of the regiment had suffered extremely from the climate. Of that splendid body of men, which in 1811 had left Madras 1027 strong, about 400 only now remained, and strange to say, it had been observed that the stoutest and largest men fell the first victims to disease.

The headquarters, in the "Guildford," sailed from Batavia roads on the 18th of September, and arrived safely at Calcutta on the 29th of October.

The "Frances Charlotte," with the remaining six companies, under Major Macpherson, had a fine passage up the Bay of Bengal, until the night of the 5th of November, when the vessel struck upon a rock about 12 miles distance off the island of Preparis. Fortunately the weather was moderate, but the ship carrying full sail at the time, struck with such violence that she remained fast, and in fifteen minutes filled to her main-deck.

"Now was displayed one of those examples of firmness and self-command which are so necessary in the character of a soldier. Although the ship was in the last extremity, and momentarily expected to sink, there was no tumult, no clamorous eagerness to get into the boats: every man waited orders, and obeyed them when received. The ship rapidly filling, and appearing to be lodged in the water, and to be only prevented from sinking by the rock, all hope of saving her was given up. Except the provisions which had been brought up the preceding evening for the following day's consumption, nothing was saved. A few bags of rice and a few pieces of pork were thrown into the boats, along with the women, children, and sick, and sent to the island, which was so rocky, and the surf so heavy, that they had great difficulty in landing; and it was not until the following morning that the boats returned to the ship. In the meantime, a small part of the rock on which the ship lay was found dry at low water, and covered with little more than a foot of water at full tide. As many as this rock could admit of (140 men) were removed on a small raft, with ropes to fix themselves to the points of the rock, in order to prevent their being washed into the sea by the waves at high water. The highest part of the rock was about 150 yards from the ship. It was not till the fourth day that the boats were able to carry all in the ship to the island, while those on the rock remained without sleep, and with very little food or water, till the third day, when water being discovered on the island, a supply was brought to them.

"During all this time the most perfect order and resignation prevailed, both on the island and on the rock. Providentially the weather continued favourable, or those on the rock must have been swept into the sea. In the evening of the fourth day the "Prince Blucher," Captain Weatherall, and the "Po," Captain Knox, appeared in sight, and immediately bore down to the wreck. They had scarcely taken the men from the rock, and begun to steer for the island, when it came on to blow a furious gale. This forced them out to sea. Being short of provisions, and the gale continuing with great violence, the commanders were afraid that they could not get back to the island in sufficient time to take the people on board[2] and reach a port before the stock was expended, and therefore bore away for Calcutta, where they arrived on the 23rd of November. Two fast-sailing vessels were instantly despatched with provisions and clothes, and, on the 6th of December, made the Island of Preparis. The people there were by that time nearly reduced to the last extremity. The allowance of provisions (a glass-full of rice and two ounces of beef for two days to each person) was expended, and they had now only to trust to the shell-fish which they picked up at low water. These soon became scarce, and they had neither lines to catch fish nor firearms to kill the birds and monkeys, the only inhabitants of the island, which is small and rocky, covered with low trees and brushwood. In this deplorable state the men continued as obedient, and the officers had the same authority, as on parade. Every privation was borne in common. Every man that picked

2 "On the 10th, the 'Prince Blucher,' Captain Weatherall, came in sight, and took on board Major Macpherson. Lieutenants Mackenzie and M'Crummin, with a considerable number of men and *all the women and children*. He would have taken the whole, but was driven off during the night by a severe gale, and obliged to proceed to Calcutta, leaving Captain M'Queen, Lieutenants M'Rae, Macleod, Brodie, Macqueen, and Smith, and 109 non-commissioned officers and privates on the island, which is barren and uninhabited."—*Record of Fr...*

up a live shell-fish carried it to the general stock, which was safe from the attempts of the half-famished sufferers. Nor was any guard required. However, to prevent any temptation, sentinels were placed over the small store. But the precaution was unnecessary. No attempt was made to break the regulations established, and no symptoms of dissatisfaction were shown, except when they saw several ships passing them without notice, and without paying any regard to their signals. These signals were large fires, which might have attracted notice when seen on an uninhabited island. Captain Weatherall required no signal. He met with some boards and other symptoms of a wreck, which had floated to sea out of sight of the island; and suspecting what had happened, immediately steered towards it. To his humanity the safety of the people on the rock may, under Providence, be ascribed; for, as the violence of the gale was such as to dash the ship to pieces, leaving no part visible in a few hours, the men must have been swept off the rock at its commencement.

"Five men died from weakness; several were drowned in falling off the kind of raft made to convey them from the ship to the rock; and some were drowned by the surf in going on shore; in all, fourteen soldiers and two Lascars were lost. Unfortunately, the gale that destroyed the ship blew off the island, so that no part of the wreck floated on shore. Had it been otherwise, some things might have been carried back to the island."[3]

Many men died subsequently, in consequence of their sufferings on this occasion. The officers and men lost the whole of their baggage, and upwards of £2000 of the funds of the regiment went down in the transport.

On the 9th the surviving officers and men were relieved; and, after a quick run to Calcutta, landed on the 12th of December. All were now assembled in Fort William, with the exception of one company in Java; and, having received orders to make preparations to embark for Europe, the following General Order was issued by his Excellency the Governor-General in Council:—

3 Stewart's Sketches.

"FORT WILLIAM,
"SATURDAY, 22nd February 1817.

"The embarkation of the 78th Regiment for Europe calls upon the Governor-General in Council to bear testimony to the conduct of that distinguished corps during its service in every part of India. It is most gratifying to this Government to pay to the regiment a tribute of unqualified applause; the zeal and gallantry so conspicuously manifested by the corps at Assaye, and so uniformly maintained throughout all its subsequent exertions in the field, not having been more exemplary than its admirable regularity and discipline on every other occasion. Such behaviour, while it must be reflected on by themselves with conscious pride, cannot fail to procure for the officers, non-commissioned officers, and soldiers of the 78th Regiment, the high reward of their sovereign's approbation."

An equally complimentary order was issued by the Commander-in-Chief.

The regiment embarked for England on board the "Prince Blucher" transport, Captain Weatherall, to whom in a measure they owed their lives, and sailed from the Sandheads on the 1st of March 1817. On the 5th of July the regiment arrived at Portsmouth, and re-embarked in the "Abeona" transport for Aberdeen. A few weeks later the 78th was was ordered to Ireland.

In rebutting an unfounded report as to the disaffection of the three Highland regiments, the 42nd, 78th, and 92nd, General Stewart says:—"The honour of Highland soldiers has hitherto been well supported, and Ross-shire has to boast that the 78th has all along maintained the honourable character of their predecessors. All those who value the character of a brave and virtuous race may look with confidence to this corps, as one of the representatives of the military and moral character of the peasantry of the mountains. In this regiment, twenty-three have been promoted to the rank of officers during the war. Merit thus rewarded will undoubtedly have its due influence on those who succeed them in the ranks."[4]

[4] Stewart's Sketches.
[5] Records of 2nd Battalion.

III.

1804—1856.

ON the 17th of April 1804, a letter of service was granted to Major-General Alexander Mackenzie-Fraser, Colonel of the 78th Highlanders, in which his Majesty was pleased to approve of a second battalion being added to that regiment, with a strength of 1000 men.

General Mackenzie-Fraser had been connected with the regiment ever since it was first raised in 1793, his brother-in-law, now Lord Seaforth, having appointed him its first Major; and it was chiefly owing to his unremitting zeal and attention at headquarters, in personally superintending and teaching the recruits, that its energy and discipline in the field became so early conspicuous. He therefore, when called upon to organise a young battalion, threw his whole soul into the task, and his vigorous mind rested not until he had collected around him a body of men in every way worthy of their predecessors.

"No officer could boast of circumstances more favourable to such an undertaking. Beloved by every one that had the good fortune of his acquaintance, he found no difficulty in selecting gentlemen possessed of various local interests in furtherance of his plan.

"The quality of the men, their youth and vigour, in short, we may say with confidence, the raw material was unexampled."[5]

LIST OF OFFICERS.

Colonel.

Major-General Alexander Mackenzie-Fraser of Castle Fraser, Colonel of 1st battalion.

Lieutenant-Colonel.

Patrick M'Leod, younger of Geanies, from 1st Battalion.

Majors.

David Stewart of Garth (author of the Sketches), Colonel, half-pay.
James Macdonell of Glengarry, Colonel and Major, Coldstream Guards.

Captains.

Alexander Wishart, from first battalion.
Duncan Macpherson.
James Macvean.
Charles William Maclean, from 42nd.
Duncan Macgregor, Major, half-pay.
William Anderson.
Robert Henry Dick, from 42nd, and afterwards Lieut.-Colonel 42nd.[6]
Colin Campbell Mackay of Bighouse, Major, half-pay.
George Mackay.

Lieutenants.

William Balvaird, Major, Rifle Brigade.
Patrick Strachan.
James Macpherson, killed in Java, 1814.
William Mackenzie Dick, killed at El Hamet, 1807.
John Matheson, Captain, half-pay.
Cornwallis Bowen.
William Mackenzie, Captain, half-pay.
Malcolm Macgregor.
James Mackay, Captain, half-pay.
Thomas Hamilton.
Robert Nicholson.
Charles Grant, Captain, half-pay.
Horace St Paul, Lieut.-Colonel, half-pay.
George William Bowes.
William Matheson.
William Cameron, Captain, half-pay.

Ensigns.

John Mackenzie Stewart.
John Munro, killed in Java, 1811.
Christopher Macrae, killed at El Hamet, 1807.
Roderick Macqueen.
Neil Campbell, Captain, half-pay.
John L. Strachan.
Alexander Cameron.
Alexander Gallie.
Robert Burnet, Captain, 14th.

Paymaster.—James Ferguson.
Adjutant.—William Mackenzie, Captain.
Quarter-Master.—John Macpherson.
Surgeon.—Thomas Draper, D.I.

Assistant-Surgeon.

William Munro, Surgeon, half-pay.

On the 25th of February 1805 the regiment embarked at Fort George, and landed at Dover on the 9th of March, whence it marched into quarters at Hythe, then under the command of Major-General Sir John Moore.[7]

[6] His portrait will be found on page 396, vol. ii.
[7] Before launching out into its history, it may be as well to state that the uniform of this battalion was formed on the exact model of the original dress of the first battalion, viz., a Highland jacket, neck and cuffs

On the 19th of the same month they were inspected by their Colonel, Major-General Mackenzie-Fraser, who published an order expressive of his high approval of the condition in which he found the regiment.

On the 23rd of the same month they were inspected by Major-General Sir John Moore, who conveyed in an order his approval of their appearance.

" As one of the objects I have in view is to point out such characteristic traits of disposition, principle, and habits as may be in any way interesting, I shall notice the following circumstance which occurred while this regiment lay at Hythe. In the month of June orders were issued for one field-officer and four subalterns to join the first battalion in India. The day before the field-officer fixed on for this purpose left the regiment, the soldiers held conferences with each other in the barracks, and in the evening several deputations were sent to him, entreating him, in the most earnest manner, to make application either to be allowed to remain with them or obtain permission for them to accompany him. He returned his acknowledgments for their attachment and for their spirited offer; but as duty required his presence in India, while their services were at present confined to this country, they must therefore separate for some time. The next evening, when he went from the barracks to the town of Hythe, to take his seat in the coach for London, two-thirds of the soldiers, and officers in the same proportion, accompanied him, all of them complaining of being left behind. They so crowded round the coach as to impede its progress for a considerable length of time, till at last the guard was obliged to desire the coachman to force his way through them. Upon this the soldiers, who hung by the wheels, horses, harness, and coach-doors, gave way, and allowed a passage. There was not a dry eye amongst the younger part of them. Such a scene as this, happening to more than 600 men, and in the streets

of light buff, edging and frogs trimmed with a narrow stripe of green, the button bearing the number of the regiment beneath a crown, the breastplate engraved with a G. R. circumscribed with the regimental motto, " Cuidich 'n Righ" ("Aids of the King"); and in all other respects the full Highland uniform as established by his Majesty's regulations.

of a town, could not pass unnoticed, and was quickly reported to General Moore, whose mind was always alive to the advantages of mutual confidence and esteem between officers and soldiers. The circumstance was quite suited to his chivalrous mind. He laid the case before the Commander-in-Chief; and his Royal Highness, with that high feeling which he has always shown when a case has been properly represented, ordered that at present there should be no separation, and that the

Major-General Alexander Mackenzie Fraser.
From Painting in possession of C. J. Mackenzie, Esq. of Portmore.

field-officer should return to the battalion in which he had so many friends ready to follow him to the cannon's mouth, and when brought in front of an enemy, either to compel them to fly or perish in the field."[8]

Having been ordered for foreign service, the regiment embarked at Portsmouth on the 28th of September 1805; but, hearing that the combined French and Spanish fleets had put to sea from Cadiz, the transports ran into the

[8] Stewart's *Sketches*. In relating the above interesting anecdote, it is generally understood that Stewart alludes to an incident in his own career.

Tagus, where they remained until intelligence arrived of the total destruction of the enemies' flotilla at Trafalgar. They then proceeded to Gibraltar, where they disembarked the first battalion of the 42nd and the second battalion of the 78th.

On the 2nd of May, 1806, the regiment embarked for Sicily, and landed at Messina on the 25th. There it was inspected by Major-General Sir John Stuart,[9] who, at the earnest solicitation of the spirited Queen of Naples, had determined on an expedition to Calabria against the French, Napoleon having annexed to his empire the kingdom of Naples. On the 16th of June, the 78th marched and encamped in the vicinity of Milazzo, under command of Brigadier-General Auckland.

On the 27th of June the regiment embarked at Milazzo, and, on the 1st of July, landed in the Bay of St Euphemia in Calabria without opposition. The force at first numbered 4200, but, being further augmented by the arrival of the 20th Regiment, the total was 4790 men, as opposed to 7000 of the enemy, with the addition of 300 cavalry. General Stuart, who expected a large accession of Calabrian volunteers to his standard, remained at St Euphemia till the 3rd, with the mortification of finding nothing but apathetic indifference among the people, where he had been led to expect a chivalrous loyalty and effectual support. On the evening of that day news was brought to him that General Regnier lay near the village of Maida, about ten miles distant, with a force of 4000 infantry and 300 cavalry, and that he was merely waiting for a reinforcement of 3000 men to attack the British and drive them back upon the sea. Stuart, who had no further assistance to expect, immediately made up his

[9] It is said that Sir John Stuart was greatly disappointed to find the second battalion of the 78th a "corps of boys," he having expected the 42nd to be sent to his command, and calculated on their assistance in his projected descent on Calabria. However, this disappointment was of but short duration, as his order of the 6th of July, after the battle of Maida, will testify.

mind to attack the French before the arrival of their fresh troops, which course would at least equalise numbers in the first instance, and give him the chance of beating them in detail. Accordingly, he marched the same night and halted within a short distance of the French camp; and, renewing the march at daylight, he crossed the River Amato, which covered the front of the enemy's position, near its mouth, and sent forward his skirmishers to the attack. However, as he advanced further into the plain, the truth suddenly broke upon him. Like Wellesley at Assaye, he had expected to encounter merely one-half of his adversary's force; like him, he found himself deceived. The whole French army was before him.

Stuart was a man of action; his decision once formed, he proceeded to act upon it. He would advance. To retreat would be certain ruin to the expedition, as he should be forced to re-embark even if he escaped defeat; the morale of his troops would be destroyed; and Calabria would be left hopelessly in the hands of the French. He knew that he had the veterans of Napoleon before him in a proportion of nearly two to one; but he preferred to trust to a cool head, British pluck, and British steel. The following was the disposition of his force :—

The light brigade, Lieut.-Colonel James Kempt, was composed of the light infantry companies of the 20th, 27th, 35th, 58th, and 81st Regiments, of two companies of Corsican Rangers under Lieut.-Colonel Hudson Lowe, and of 150 chosen men of the 35th Regiment under Major George Robertson. The first brigade, Brigadier-General Auckland, consisted of the 78th and 81st Regiments. The second, Brigadier-General Lowrie Cole, was formed of the grenadier companies of the 20th, 27th, 35th, 58th, and 81st, under the Hon. Lieutenant-Colonel O'Calloghan, and the 27th Regiment. The reserve, Colonel John Oswald, consisted of the 58th and Watteville Regiment.

Stewart, in his admirable *Sketches*, gives a most spirited and circumstantial account of the battle; and as he himself fought on the occasion, it has been thought better to give his narrative entire rather than to collate from other sources, especially as the regimental records are very destitute of information :—

"The army was drawn up, having in its rear the head of the bay, and in its front a broad and extensive valley, level in the centre, and bounded on both sides by high, and in some places precipitous, hills, with woods covering their sides in many parts, and in others with corn-fields up to a considerable height. This valley, which is of unequal breadth, being in some places four miles and in others not more than two, runs across the Calabrian peninsula, from St Euphemia to Cortona on the Adriatic, intersected at intervals to nearly one-half its breadth by high ridges, which run out at right angles from the mountains, forming the lateral boundaries of the plain. . . On the summit of one of these ridges, at somewhat more than four miles distant, the army of General Regnier was seen drawn up in columns, apparently ready either to descend to the plains or to wait the attack of the British. General Stuart had now to come to an instant decision. Disappointed of the support of the Calabrese, of whom not more than 1000 had joined, and these badly armed and worse disciplined, and therefore of no use in the attack, and being also informed that a reinforcement of 3000 men was expected by the enemy on the following day, he had no alternative but an immediate advance or a retreat, either to the ships or to some strong position.

" To retreat was little congenial to the spirit of the commander; and accordingly, actuated by the same confidence in his little army which had encouraged him to engage in the enterprise, he resolved upon advancing, little aware that the expected addition to the enemy's force had already taken place. While General Stuart's ignorance of this fact confirmed his resolution to attempt the strong position of the enemy, the consciousness of superior numbers gave additional confidence to General Regnier, who, looking down upon his enemy from his elevated position, could now count every file below; and who, as it is said, called out to his troops to mark his confidence in their invincible courage, and his contempt for the English, whose presumption in landing with so small a force he was determined to punish by driving them into the sea. Accordingly, giving orders to march, he descended the hill in three lines, through narrow paths in the woods, and formed on the plain below. His army consisted of more than 7000 men, with 300 cavalry, and a considerable train of field artillery. He drew up his troops in two parallel lines of equal numbers, with artillery and cavalry on both flanks, and with field-pieces placed in different parts of the line. To oppose this force, General Stuart placed in the front line the light brigade of Lieut.-Colonel Kempt on the right, the Highland regiment in the centre, and the 81st on the left.

"At eight o'clock in the morning, the corps composing the first line advanced, the enemy commencing his forward march (presenting a parallel front) nearly at the same moment. The distance between the armies was at the time nearly three miles, and the ground perfectly level, intersected only by drains, to carry off the water in the rainy season, but not so large as to intercept the advance of the field-pieces. When the first brigade moved forward, the second halted for a short time, and then proceeded, followed by the reserve. The forward movement of the opposing lines lessened the intervening distance in double ratio. The first brigade passed over several corn-fields with parties of reapers, who eagerly pointed out the advance of the enemy, then at a distance of less than a mile. On a nearer approach they opened their field-pieces; and, contrary to the usual practice of French artillery, with little effect, the greater part of the shot passing over the first line and not reaching the second.

"This was an interesting spectacle. Two armies in parallel lines, in march towards each other, on a smooth and clear plain, and in dead silence, only interrupted by the report of the enemy's guns; it was more like a chosen field fixed upon by a general officer for exercise, or to exhibit a sham fight, than, as it proved, an accidental encounter and a real battle. No two rival commanders could ever wish for a finer field for a trial of the courage and firmness of their respective combatants; and as there were some present who recollected the contempt with which General Regnier, in his account of the Egyptian expedition, had chosen to treat the British, there was a much

feeling, mixed up with the usual excitements, as, perhaps, in any modern engagement, excepting that most important of all modern battles, where Buonaparte for the first, and perhaps the last time, met a British army in the field.

"To the young Highlanders, of whom nearly 600 were under age, the officers, with very few exceptions, being equally young and inexperienced, it was a critical moment. If we consider a formidable line, which, from numbers, greatly outflanked our first line, supported by an equally strong second line, the glancing of whose bayonets was seen over the heads of the first, the advance of so preponderating a force on the three regiments of the first brigade (the second being considerably in the rear was sufficiently trying, particularly for the young Highlanders. . . . I have already noticed that the enemy's guns were not well served, and pointed too high; not so the British. When our artillery opened, under the direction of Major Lemoine and Captain Dougal Campbell, no practice could be more perfect. Every shot told, and carried off a file of the enemy's line. When the shot struck the line, two or three files on the right and left of the men thrown down gave way, leaving a momentary opening before they recovered and closed up the vacancy. The inexperienced young Highlanders, believing that all the vacant spaces had been carried off, shouted with exultation at the evident superiority. It is not often that in this manner two hostile lines, in a reciprocally forward movement, at a slow but firm pace, can make their observations while advancing, with a seeming determination to conquer or perish on the spot. These criticisms were, however, to be soon checked by the mutual forward movement on which they were founded. The lines were fast closing, but with perfect regularity and firmness. They were now within 300 yards' distance, and a fire having commenced between the sharp-shooters on the right, it was time to prepare for an immediate shock. The enemy seemed to hesitate, halted, and fired a volley. Our line also halted and returned the salute; and when the men had reloaded, a second volley was thrown in. The precision with which these two volleys were fired, and their effect, were quite remarkable. When the clearing-off of the smoke—there was hardly a breath of wind to dispel it—enabled us to see the French line, the breaks and vacancies caused by the men who had fallen by the fire appeared like a paling of which parts had been thrown down or broken. On our side it was so different, that, glancing along the rear of my regiment, I counted only 14 who had fallen by the enemy's fire. The smoke having cleared off so that the enemy could be seen, the line advanced at full charge. The enemy, with seeming resolution to stand the shock, kept perfectly steady, till, apparently intimidated by the advance, equally rapid and firm, of an enemy, too, who they were taught to believe would fly before them, their hearts failed, and they faced to the right-about, and fled with speed, but not in confusion. When they approached within a short distance of their second line, they halted, fronted, and opened a fire of musketry on our line, which did not follow up the charge to any distance, but halted to allow the men to draw breath, and to close up any small breaks in the line. They were soon ready, however, to advance again. A constant running fire was now kept up on the march, the enemy continuing the same, but retiring slowly as they fired, until they threw their first line on their second. They then seemed determined to make a resolute stand, thus giving our line the advantage of sooner closing upon them ; but they would not stand the shock ; they gave way in greater confusion than in the first instance. They had now lost a considerable number of men.

"At this period the enemy's cavalry attempted to charge, but either from the horses not being properly broke, or rather from the sharp running fire kept up in their faces, the dragoons could not, with all their exertions, bring them to the charge. At last, finding their efforts unavailing, they galloped round the flanks of their line to the rear, turned their horses loose, and fought on foot.

"Both lines of the enemy were now completely intermixed, and Regnier, who was seen riding about, and from his violent gesticulations seemingly in great agitation, seeing himself completely foiled in his attack on the front, and being driven back more than a mile, made an attempt to turn the left flank. For this purpose he brought some battalions by an oblique movement to the British left, and gained so much on that flank that the second line (the grenadier battalions and the 27th Regiment, which now came up under General Cole) could not form the line in continuation. Throwing back their left, they therefore formed an angle of about 60 degrees to the front line, and in this position opened a most admirably directed and destructive fire, which quickly drove back the enemy with great loss. While in this angular formation, the fire was incessantly and admirably sustained, till a circumstance occurred in the centre which gave the enemy a momentary advantage, but from which they afterwards suffered severely.

"On the side of the French there was a Swiss Regiment, commanded by an officer of the family of Watteville, a family which had also a regiment in our service, and in the field that day. The Watteville Regiment in the French service was dressed in a kind of light claret-coloured uniform, something like scarlet when much worn, and with hats so much resembling those of the band of our Watteville's, that when this corps was seen advancing from their second line, the Highlanders, in their inexperience, believed they were our own, who had in some manner got to the front ; and a word passed quickly to cease firing. The fire had accordingly slackened, before the voice of the mounted officers, whose elevated position enabled them to distinguish more clearly, could be heard, and the enemy, believing this relaxation to proceed from a different cause, advanced with additional boldness. This brought them so close that when the men were undeceived and recommenced firing, it was with such effect that, in ten minutes, the front was cleared, and the enemy driven back with great precipitation. Indeed, the precision with which the men took their aim during the whole action was admirable, and clearly established the perfect self-possession and coolness of their minds.

"Unwilling to break the continuity of the narrative of the proceedings on the centre and the left, where the action was now nearly finished, I have delayed noticing the movements of Lieut.-Colonel Kempt's light brigade. This corps had for some time been exercised in a uniform manner, under the training of that officer, and they now even exceeded the high expectations formed of them and their spirited commander. The party of the Corsican Rangers attached to the light infantry were on the right. When the line advanced within reach of musketry, they were sent out on the flank and in front to skirmish, but on the first fire from the enemy's sharp-shooters, they retreated in great haste. This, in some cases, would have been an inauspicious, if not a fatal commencement to a battle, when so much was to be done, and so much superior a force to be opposed. But here this repulse did not extend beyond those who gave way to the panic, and the light company of the 20th Regiment, who had the right of the line, rushed forward, and in an instant drove off the party which had advanced on the Corsicans, but with the loss of Captain Maclean, the only officer killed on that day. In a few minutes after this the two hostile lines came within charge distance; and the left of the enemy pushing forward, both lines had nearly met, when at this momentous crisis the enemy became appalled, broke, and endeavoured to fly, but it was too late;—they were overtaken with most dreadful slaughter.

"I now return to the centre and left, which continued hotly engaged, always vigorously pushing the enemy, who still endeavoured to gain upon the flank. But in this he was frustrated by the continued advance of the British, who preserved the same angular formation, the first line moving directly on its original front, and the second in an oblique direction, with its right touching the left of the first.

"The fire now slackened, the enemy having lost much ground, being repulsed in every attempt, and having sustained an unusual, and, indeed, altogether an extraordinary loss of men. But General Regnier, despairing of success against Colonel Kempt's light corps on the right, and still pushed by the troops in the centre and left, prepared to make a desperate push in order to take our line in flank on the left. At this moment the 20th Regiment marched up, and formed on the left, nearly at right angles to General Cole's bri-

gade. This regiment had that morning disembarked in the bay from Sicily (the scarcity of transports preventing their earlier arrival), and Lieut.-Colonel Ross having landed with great promptitude the moment he heard the firing, moved forward with such celerity, that he reached the left of the line as the enemy were pushing round to turn the flank. Colonel Ross formed his regiment with his right supported by the left of the 27th, and opposed a full front to the enemy. This reinforcement seemed to destroy all further hopes of the enemy. So feeble was this last attempt, that when Colonel Ross ordered out 80 men to act as sharpshooters in his front, they could not face even the small detachment.

"The battle was now over. The confidence which had animated the enemy during the greater part of the action appeared to have at last totally forsaken them; they gave way at all points in the greatest confusion, numbers, to assist their speed, throwing away their arms, accoutrements, and every encumbrance. . . .

"The disadvantage so frequently experienced in the transmarine expeditions of England, occasioned by the want of ships for the conveyance of a sufficient number of troops, was now severely felt; for though the field was most favourable for the operations of cavalry, that arm was, on the present occasion, totally wanting. As soon as the ships had landed the infantry at St. Euphemia, they were ordered back for the cavalry, who arrived the day after the battle. Few victories, however, have been more complete, and as under equal advantages of ground, of discipline in the troops, and ability in the commanders, a hard fought battle is the most honourable, if gained with little loss to the victors, and with great destruction to the vanquished, so that engagement must be particularly so, in which a greatly superior force is totally routed with a loss in killed of more than 30 to 1: that is, on the present occasion with a loss of 1300 killed of the French to 41 killed of the British.

"The disparity of numbers being so great, the proofs of courage and other military qualities, on the part of the victors, are conclusive. Equally decisive were the advantages on the side of the victors in regard to the subsequent operations of the campaign ; for while the English army was, on the following morning, but little diminished, and quite prepared to meet a fresh opponent, if such could have been brought against it, the enemy were so dispirited that on no after occasion did they attempt to make a stand, which indeed their reduced numbers rendered impossible. Their loss was 1300 killed and 1100 wounded, left on the field, besides the slightly wounded who retired to the rear. Upwards of 200 of the latter were taken afterwards in the hospital at Cotrone, on the opposite coast of the Adriatic.

"The loss of the Highlanders was 7 rank and file killed; Lieut.-Colonel Patrick M'Leod, Major David Stewart, Captains Duncan Macpherson and Duncan Macgregor, Lieutenant James Mackay, Ensigns Colin Mackenzie and Peter Macgregor, 4 sergeants, 1 drummer, and 69 rank and file wounded."

The British minister at the Sicilian court thus alluded to the battle in his despatch :— "There is not to be found in the annals of military transactions an enterprise prepared with more deliberate reflection or executed with greater decision, promptitude, and success, than the late invasion of Calabria by Sir John Stuart. I trust, therefore, you will not think me presumptuous for venturing to add my testimony of the high sense entertained by this court of the merits of the British General and of his gallant army, who, on the fertile plains of Maida, have added new trophies to those which the same troops had formerly earned, from the same enemy, on the sandy regions of Egypt."

The King of the Two Sicilies created Sir John Stuart, Count of Maida. In England he received the thanks of Parliament, a pension of £1000 per annum, the Order of the Bath, a sword of honour, and the freedom of the city of London.

In commemoration of this victory a gold medal was struck, and conferred upon all the superior officers who were present.

The troops were re-embarked on the 2nd of August, and on the night of the 9th the regiment made Messina harbour, and having been disembarked, was ordered to take over quarters in the town of Taormina, where it became subjected to the consequences of its fatigues and privations during the late campaign, frequently suffering from ill-health to the extent of from twenty to thirty men per month. On the 13th of October, however, it was ordered round to Syracuse, where it arrived on the 17th, and remained during the rest of its stay in Sicily, until it was ordered to embark and join the Egyptian expedition.

Early in 1807 an armament was fitted out in Sicily for the purpose of occupying Alexandria, Rosetta, and the adjoining coast of Egypt. The force on this occasion consisted of a detachment of artillery, the 20th Light Dragoons, the 31st, 35th, 78th, and De Rolle's regiment, and the corps of Chasseurs Britanniques, all under the command of Major-General Mackenzie-Fraser. The expedition sailed on the 6th of March, but, encountering bad weather, the "Apollo" frigate and nineteen transports were separated from the fleet. The remainder, with the commodore, anchored on the 16th off the Arab's Tower to the west of Alexandria. General Fraser, in consequence of the absence of so large a proportion of his force, hesitated about landing; but, being pressed by Major Misset, the British resident, who informed him that the inhabitants were favourably disposed, and that there were not more than 500 men in garrison, he disembarked his troops on the 17th and 18th. On the morning of the 19th took up a position on the same ground that the British army occupied in March 1801. The town, on being summoned, surrendered the next day, and in the evening the other transports anchored in Aboukir bay. Vice-Admiral Duckworth, with a fleet from the Dardanelles, arrived in the bay on the 22nd.

On the 27th of March a detachment, under Major-General Wauchope and Brigadier-General Meade, took possession, without opposition, of the forts and heights of Abûmandûr, a little above Rosetta. The capture of this place was the next object. General Wauchope, unconscious of danger, marched into the town at the head of the 31st Regiment. Not a human being was to be seen in the streets, nor was a sound to be heard. The troops wended their way through the narrow and deserted streets towards an open space or market-place in the centre of the town; but they had not proceeded more than half-way when the portentous silence was broken by showers of musketry from every house, from the first floor to the roof. Cooped up in these narrow lanes, the troops were unable to return the fire with any effect, nor, amidst the smoke in which they were enveloped, could they see their assailants, and could only guess their position from the flashes of their guns. They had, therefore, no alternative but to retire as speedily as possible; but, before they had extricated themselves, General Wauchope was killed, and nearly 300 officers and soldiers were killed and wounded. General Meade was among the wounded.

After this repulse the troops returned to Alexandria; but General Fraser, resolved upon the capture of Rosetta, sent back a second detachment, consisting of the 35th, 78th, and De Rolle's regiment, under the command of Brigadier-General the Hon. William Stewart and Colonel Oswald. This detachment, after some skirmishing, took possession of Abûmandûr on the 7th of April, and on the following day Rosetta was summoned to surrender, but without effect. Batteries were therefore speedily erected, and a position was taken up between the Nile and the gate of Alexandria; but, from the paucity of the troops, it was found impossible to invest the town on all sides, or prevent a free communication across the Nile to the Delta. The batteries opened their fire; but with no other effect than damaging some of the houses.

The enemy having erected some batteries on the Delta for the purpose of taking the British batteries in flank, Major James Macdonell of the 78th, with 250 men, under Lieutenant John Robertson, and 40 seamen from the Tigre, were detached on the 16th across the river, opposite to Abûmandûr, to destroy these batteries. To conceal his movements, Major Macdonell made a considerable circuit, and coming upon the rear of the batteries at sunrise, attacked the enemy, and driving him from the batteries, turned the guns upon the town. But as the enemy soon collected in considerable force, he destroyed the batteries, and embarking the guns, recrossed the river with only four men wounded.

General Stewart had been daily looking for a reinforcement of Mamelukes from Upper Egypt, but he was disappointed in this expectation. While a detachment of De Rolle's, under Major Vogelsang of that regiment, occupied El Hamet, another detachment, consisting of five companies of the Highlanders, two of the 35th Regiment, and a few cavalry and artillery under Lieut.-Colonel Macleod, was sent on the 20th to occupy a broad dyke or embankment, which, with a dry canal, runs between the Nile and the Lake Etko, a distance of about two miles. On reaching his destination, Colonel Macleod stationed his men, amounting to 720, in three divisions, with an equal number of dragoons and artillery between each. One of these he disposed on the banks of the Nile, another in the centre, and the third upon the dry canal.

Meanwhile the enemy was meditating an attack on the position, and on the morning of the 21st, while numerous detached bodies of their cavalry began to assemble round the British posts, a flotilla of about 70 djerms or large boats full of troops was observed slowly descending the Nile. With the intention of concentrating his force, and of retreating if necessary to the camp at Rosetta, Colonel Macleod proceeded to the post on the right, occupied by a company of the 35th and the Highland grenadiers. He had not, however, sufficient time to accomplish this object, as the enemy left their boats with great rapidity, and while they advanced on the left and centre posts, their cavalry, with a body of Albanian infantry, surrounded the right of the position, and attacked it furiously at all points. Colonel Macleod formed his men into a square, which, for a long time, resisted every effort of the enemy. Had this handful of men been attacked in one or two points only, they might have charged the enemy; but they were so completely surrounded that they could not venture to charge to any front of the square, as they would have been assailed in the rear the moment they faced round. At every successive charge made by the cavalry, who attempted, at the point of the bayonets, to cut down the troops, the square was lessened, the soldiers closing in upon the vacancies as their comrades fell. These attacks, though irregular, were bold, and the dexterity with which the assailants handled their swords proved fatal to the British.

This unequal contest continued till Colonel Macleod and all the officers and men were killed, with the exception of Captain Colin Mackay of the 78th and eleven Highlanders, and as many more of the 35th.[1] With this small band, Captain Mackay, who was severely wounded, determined to make a desperate push to join the centre, and several succeeded in the attempt; but the rest were either killed or wounded. Captain Mackay received two wounds, and was about reaching the post when an Arab horseman cut at his neck with such force that his head would have been severed from his body, had not the blow been in some measure neutralised by the cape of his coat and a stuffed neckcloth. The sabre, however, cut to the bone, and the captain fell flat on the ground, when he was taken up by Sergeant (afterwards Lieutenant) Waters, who alone escaped unhurt, and carried by him to the post.

During their contest with the right, the enemy made little exertions against the other posts; but when, by the destruction of the first, they had gained an accession of disposable force, they made a warm onset on the centre. An attempt was at first made to oppose them;

but the commanding officer soon saw that resistance was hopeless, and desirous of saving the lives of his men, he hung out a white handkerchief as a signal of surrender. The firing accordingly ceased, and the left, following the example of the centre, also surrendered. A general scramble of a most extraordinary kind now ensued amongst the Turks for prisoners, who, according to their custom, became the private property of the captors. In this *melée* the British soldiers were pulled about with little ceremony, till the more active amongst the Turkish soldiery had secured their prey, after which they were marched a little distance up the river, where the captors were paid seven dollars for every prisoner they had taken. Some of the horsemen, less intent upon prize-money than their companions, amused themselves by galloping about, each with the head of a British soldier stuck upon the point of his lance.

When General Stewart was informed of the critical situation of Colonel Macleod's detachment, he marched towards Etko, expecting that it would retreat in that direction; but not falling in with it he proceeded to El Hamet, where, on his arrival, he learned its unfortunate fall. With a force so much reduced by the recent disaster, and in the face of an enemy emboldened by success and daily increasing in numbers, it was vain to think of reducing Rosetta, and therefore General Stewart determined to return to Alexandria. He accordingly commenced his retreat, followed by the enemy, who sallied out from Rosetta; but although the sandy plain over which he marched was peculiarly favourable to their cavalry, they were kept in effectual check by the 35th and the 78th. No further hostile operations were attempted; and the prisoners, who had been sent to Cairo, having been released by capitulation, the whole army embarked for Sicily on the 22nd of September.

The loss of the 78th at El Hamet was 159 men, with Lieut.-Colonel Patrick Macleod, younger of Geanies, Lieutenants William Mackenzie Dick, Christopher Macrae, and Archibald Christie, killed. The officers taken prisoners were Captain Colin Campbell Mackay (severely wounded), Lieutenants John Matheson, Malcolm Macgregor, Alexander Gallie, P. Ryrie

---

[1] "Sergeant John Macrae, a young man, about twenty-two years of age, but of good size and strength of arm, showed that the broadsword, in a firm hand, is as good a weapon in close fighting as the bayonet. If the first push of the bayonet misses its aim, or happens to be parried, it is not easy to recover the weapon and repeat the thrust, when the enemy is bold enough to stand firm; but it is not so with the sword, which may be readily withdrawn from its blow, wielded with celerity, and directed to any part of the body, particularly to the head and arms, whilst its motions defend the person using it. Macrae killed six men, cutting them down with his broadsword (of the kind usually worn by sergeants of Highland corps), when at last he made a dash out of the ranks on a Turk, whom he cut down; but as he was returning to the square he was killed by a blow from behind, his head being nearly split in two by the stroke of a sabre. Lieutenant Christopher Macrae, whom I have already mentioned as having brought eighteen men of his own name to the regiment as part of his quota of recruits, for an ensigncy, was killed in this affair, with six of his followers and namesakes, besides the sergeant. On the passage to Lisbon in October 1805, the same sergeant came to me one evening crying like a child, and complaining that the ship's cook had called him English names, which he did not understand, and thrown some fat in his face. Thus a lad who, in 1805, was so soft and so childish, displayed in 1807 a courage and vigour worthy a hero of Ossian."—Stewart's *Sketch*.

II.

and Joseph Gregory (wounded), with Assistant-Surgeon Alexander Leslie.

"The death of Lieut.-Colonel Macleod was sincerely regretted by the battalion which he had hitherto commanded since its formation, and confirmed by his own example. He ever laboured to render the relative duties of officers and men merely habitual; his chief object was to establish a high character to his corps, and those common interests by which he found means to unite every individual.

Colonel Patrick Macleod of Geanies.
From the original Painting by Raeburn, in possession of
Colin Mackenzie, Esq. of Portmore.

The regiment still embraces his memory, which, combined with every pleasing retrospect to our little history, shall long be cherished amongst us with feelings of fraternal attachment and sincere respect."[2]

After returning to Sicily, the 78th joined an expedition under Sir John Moore, intended for Lisbon; but the regiment was withdrawn, and ordered to England, where it landed, and was marched to Canterbury in the spring of 1808.

[2] Records, 2d Battalion. He was succeeded in the command by Lieut.-Colonel John Macleod.

About this time several changes took place amongst the field-officers of the regiment. Lieutenant-Colonel Hercules Scott of the 1st battalion was removed to the 103d Regiment, and was succeeded by Major John Macleod from the 56th. Major David Stewart was promoted to the lieutenant-colonelcy of the Royal West India Rangers, and was succeeded by Major Robert Hamilton from the 79th Highlanders.

Shortly after the return of the regiment to England, it obtained a considerable accession of recruits raised from several Scotch militia regiments, chiefly from that of Perthshire, by Major David Stewart, who, in consequence of a wound received at Maida, had been obliged to return to Scotland. A detachment of 400 men, including 350 of the newly-raised men (of whom 280 were six feet in height and upwards, and of a proportionate strength of limb and person), was drafted to reinforce the second battalion in India. The remainder of the second battalion was then removed from Little Hampton, in Sussex, where they had been for a short time quartered, to the Isle of Wight, where they remained till August 1809, when a detachment of 370 men, with officers and non-commissioned officers, was sent on the unfortunate expedition to Walcheren, being incorporated with a battalion commanded by the Honourable Lieutenant-Colonel Cochrane. The men suffered greatly from fever and ague, which affected the rest of the troops, and were so emaciated that they did not recover their usual strength till the following year. Another draft of all the men fit for service in India was made in 1810, and joined the first battalion at Goa on the eve of the departure of the expedition against Batavia in 1811.

Lieut.-General Mackenzie-Fraser had had the command of a division in the Walcheren expedition, but the fever spared neither rank nor age, and the gallant and veteran colonel of the Ross-shire Buffs was struck down, and expired, to the inexpressible grief of the regiment, with which he had been connected since it was first raised. "'Twas now that we were doomed to sustain a loss, which was keenly felt by every rank, in the death of Lieut.-General Mackenzie-Fraser, adored in our first battalion, to whom his virtues were more particularly known; the same manifest qualities could not fail to have endeared him to every member of the second, and to draw from it a genuine tribute of heart-felt regret, whilst it mingles with the public voice its filial homage to the memory of such uncommon worth. Individually we lament the departure of a father and a friend—as a regiment we would weep over the ashes of the most beloved of colonels! Although the undeviating advocate of discipline and good order, never did the star of rank impose a humiliating deference upon those whose affection and esteem he never failed to secure by his boundless benevolence and gentle manners. To indulge in this heart-felt eulogy is not peculiarly our province—his country has already weighed his value—and in its acknowledgments he has amply received what was ever the proudest meed of his soul."[3]

Lieut.-General Sir James Craig succeeded to the command of the regiment on the 15th of September 1809, and on his death, about eighteen months afterwards, the colonelcy was conferred on Sir Samuel Auchmuty.

On the 10th of January, the same day that it landed, the 78th marched to Oudenbosch, the head-quarters of Sir Thomas Graham,[4] and his force of 8000 men, and the following day proceeded to Rosendaal, and thence to Calmp-thout. General Bülow had established his headquarters at Breda, and the object of the allied commanders was the investiture and reduction of Antwerp, and the destruction of the docks and shipping. On the 12th Colonel Macleod was ordered to march, so as to come up with the division of Major-General Kenneth Mackenzie, then moving upon Capelle, and arrived just before dark, when, notwithstanding a most fatiguing day's march, it was found that only three men had fallen out. On the 13th the division was under arms an

hour before daylight, and on the arrival of Sir Thomas Graham, Colonel John Macleod was appointed to the command of a brigade, consisting of the 25th (2nd battalion), 33rd, 56th, and 78th, when the command of the latter regiment devolved on Lieut.-Colonel Lindsay. The divisions of Majors-General Kenneth Mackenzie and Cooke, with their guns, were put in motion about 8 o'clock, on the road to Eeckeren, with the intention of feeling the environs of Antwerp, and reconnoitring the position of the enemy's fleet, in conjunction with the advance of General Bülow's corps. It was deemed necessary for this purpose to dispossess the enemy of the village of Merxem, within a few hundred yards of the outworks, and this service was confided by Major-General Mackenzie to Colonel Macleod.

The 78th, previously the left centre battalion of the brigade, was now brought to the front, by the special order of Sir Thomas Graham; and its light company, together with that of the 95th (rifle regiment), commenced skirmishing with the enemy among the hedges and thick underwood in advance, and to the left of the road. The regiment then moved forward in oblique échelon through the fields on the right, and formed line on the leading division. In advancing it became exposed to the fire of the enemy's sharp-shooters, who were firing from behind the hedges in front, the light companies of the 78th and 95th, having uncovered to the left when the line moved forward. It, however, wisely reserved its fire, as it would have had but little effect from the formation of the ground, which was completely intersected with hedges and frozen ditches; but a full view of the enemy was shortly after obtained in a small field close to the village. They appeared to be numerous, but retired before the fire of the 78th, which now opened and appeared to gall them very much. Colonel Macleod, seeing the necessity of an immediate assault, ordered up the Highlanders, who, without a moment's hesitation, rushed forward at the charge, and falling upon the enemy, drove them through and beyond the village. The light company had crossed the Breda Chaussée (which intersected the advance of the battalion, and forms the principle street of the village), and making a detour round that part of the village beyond

[3] Records, 2d Battalion.
[4] The victor of Barossa, afterwards Lord Lynedoch.

it swept everything before it, and came up on the flank of the battalion, which had arrived on the Antwerp side "Every appearance at the time, and subsequent accounts from sources likely to be correct, give reason to believe that there were upwards of 3000 men (the French themselves admit of 4 battalions), put to the most shameful flight by the 78th, not quite 300 men, and about 40 riflemen, and it may be assumed that the panic struck that day into the garrison of Antwerp prevented any subsequent sortie from the garrison till the day it was given up"

In their determined and steady onslaught, the 78th was exposed on both flanks to the fire of the enemy who were posted in houses commanding the entrance to the village, and had the regiment hesitated in its movements, their loss must have been very severe, but the rapidity with which they carried out their orders ensured success with a comparatively small loss The enemy left a large number of killed and wounded in the street, and the regiment took 25 prisoners Among the dead was found the body of the French Général de-division, Avy, said to have been an excellent officer The loss of the regiment in killed was Ensign James Ormsby, who carried the regimental colour, with nine rank and file left on the field, Lieutenant William Mackenzie, who was mortally wounded through the body, and died next morning upon the waggons, going to Calmpthout Colonel Macleod was very severely wounded in the arm, and Captain Sime and Lieutenants Bath and Chisholm were also severely wounded Lieutenant Mackenzie was extremely regretted by his brother officers, as he was a young man of a clear and strong mind, and a most promising officer

His Excellency Sir Thomas Graham, in a general order of January 13th, spoke of the conduct of the 78th and other regiments engaged in the highest terms "No veteran troops,' he said, "ever behaved better than these men, who met the enemy the first time, and whose discipline and gallantry reflect great credit on themselves and their officers"

This was the only enterprise in which the Highlanders were engaged in the Netherlands Their duties, until the return of the battalion

to Scotland in 1816, were confined to the ordinary details of garrison duty at Brussels, Nieuwpoort, and other places

In the month of March 1815, when in daily expectation of returning to England, accounts were received of the change of affairs in France Napoleon had returned from Elba, the Bourbons had fled, and the hundred days had commenced Orders were therefore issued immediately for the army to be in readiness to take the field

Nieuwpoort, a garrison town, nine miles from Ostend, and regarded as a frontier fortress, had been suffered to fall into a state of dilapidation when in the hands of the French, and since it had come into the possession of the government of the Netherlands, they had done nothing towards placing it in an efficient state for defence A company of German artillery, with some guns and stores, was sent there on the 19th of March, and the 2nd battalion of the 78th, mustering about 250 effective men, followed on the 22nd, when the garrison was placed under the command of Colonel Macleod Little respite from duty or labour was to be expected until the place was put out of all danger of being taken by a coup-de main On the 24th the garrison was augmented by a Hanoverian battalion, of between 500 and 600 men, and the works progressed so quickly, that they were completed and inspected by His Grace the Duke of Wellington on the 17th of April At this time the battalion was the least effective British regiment in the Netherlands in point of numbers, and when the army commenced its operations, it was so much further reduced by the unhealthiness of its station, as to have 70, 80, and finally 100 men totally disabled by ague It was therefore, unhappily, condemned to the daily routine of garrison duty and labour, and did not share in that glorious campaign which culminated in the victory of Waterloo

After repeated representations to the authorities of the extreme unhealthiness of their quarters, and the alarming increase of the numbers on the sick list, the matter happened to come to the ears of the commander of the forces, when His Grace ordered the immediate removal of the 78th to Brussels Here it remained for more than three months. During its former stay it had greatly ingratiated itself with the inhabitants, and on the present occasion, as soon as the rumour of its departure was circulated among them, they did all they could to have the order rescinded. Failing this, the Mayor of the city was called upon to make, in their name, the following declaration:—

"As Mayor of Brussels, I have pleasure in declaring that the Scotch Highlanders, who were garrisoned in the city during the years 1814 and 1815, called forth the attachment and esteem of all by the mildness and suavity of their manners and excellent conduct, insomuch that a representation was made to me by the inhabitants, requesting me to endeavour to detain the 78th regiment of Scotchmen in the town, and to prevent their being replaced by other troops."

Brussels was the last quarters of the battalion before its return home, but the same spirit as that breathed in the above testimony had been apparent in every part of the country. In no town was the regiment stationed where the inhabitants did not hail its advent with pleasure, and witness its departure with regret.

"This battalion was no more employed except on garrison duties, in the course of which the men conducted themselves so as to secure the esteem of the people of Flanders, as their countrymen of the Black Watch had done seventy years before. It is interesting to observe, at such distant periods, the similarity of character on the one hand, and of feelings of respect on the other. In examining the notices of what passed in 1744 and 1745, we find that an inhabitant of Flanders was happy to have a Highlander quartered in his house, as he was not only kind and peaceable in his own demeanour, but protected his host from the depredations and rudeness of others. We find also that in Germany, in 1761 and 1762, in regard to Keith's Highlanders, much was said of "the kindness of their dispositions in everything, for the boors were much better treated by those *savages*, than by the polished French and English." When such accounts are read and compared with those of what passed in 1814 and 1815, in which it is stated that "they were kind as well as brave"— "enfans de la famille" — "Lions in the

field, and lambs in the house;" — when these accounts of remote and recent periods are compared, they display a steadiness of principle not proceeding from accidental occurrences, but the result of natural dispositions originally humane and honourable.

"It is only justice to mention, that it was the conduct of this battalion, for eighteen months previous to June 1815, that laid the foundation of that favourable impression in the Netherlands, which was confirmed by the 42nd, and the other Highland regiments who had arrived only just previous to the battle of Waterloo, so that little could have been known to the Flemish of what their conduct in quarters might prove. Enough was known, however, to cause a competition among the inhabitants who should receive them into their houses."[5]

On the 24th of December, orders had been received to reduce the regiment by four companies, and the supernumerary officers had proceeded home.

The six remaining companies marched from Brussels, on the 5th of February, 1816, to Ostend, where they embarked for England, three companies sailing on the 10th, and three on the 11th. The right wing landed at Ramsgate on the 12th, and was ordered to march immediately to Deal Barracks. The left wing arrived at Ramsgate on the 16th, and was forwarded to Canterbury, where it was joined by the right wing next day.

Major-General Sir George Cooke, K.C.B., having been ordered to inspect the regiment, and report upon the number of men fit for service in India, and those to be discharged or placed in veteran battalions, found 20 sergeants, 9 drummers, and 253 rank and file fit for Indian service; and this being reported to the Horse Guards, the men were ordered to be held in readiness for embarkation, to join the 1st battalion.

An order for reducing the 2nd battalion was received from the Horse Guards, and carried into effect on the 29th of February 1816, the effective non-commissioned officers and men being transferred to the 1st battalion.

The colours of the regiment were presented to Colonel Macleod by Sir Samuel Auchmuty,

5 Stewart's *Sk. Char.*

the colonel of the regiment, to be by him preserved as "a pledge of the mutual attachment which subsisted between himself and the battalion."

To the records of the 2nd battalion Colonel Macleod appended the following remarks:—

"Colonel Macleod, in reading over the history of the 2nd battalion of the 78th Regiment, and considering its progress and termination under such happy circumstances, would do violence to his own feelings did he not subjoin his testimony to the interesting narrative in which he bore his share for nine years of the period. Were he capable of doing justice to his sentiments on a review of the proceedings of that period of his services in the battalion, those results from the grateful and best feelings of his heart must render the expression of them impracticable.

"To record the merits of all the officers that served under him would be unavailing, but he will sum up with an assertion, that no commanding officer in His Majesty's service has the pride to boast of never having for nine years found it necessary to place an officer under arrest; that no regulation for the discipline of the army had ever been violated, and that in every instance the rules of good breeding regulated the discharge of the duties of the officer and the gentleman; he never witnessed a dispute at the mess-table, nor ever heard of a quarrel from it: with what pleasure must he ever meet those who contributed so much to his personal comforts as a friend, and pride as an officer.

"To the conduct of the non-commissioned officers and men his exultation is equally due in their degree; their order and discipline on every occasion attracted the notice and approbation of general officers and inhabitants in quarters, and their marked admiration in the field. For their individual and collective attachment to him, he must ever consider them the dutiful children of a fond parent. . .

"As a lasting testimony of his approbation, and thanks to Lieut.-Colonel Lindsay, Major Macpherson, Major Colin Mackay, Lieut. and Adjutant Smith, Lieut. Chisholm, Quartermaster Gunn, and Surgeon Munro, the field officers and staff who so ably assisted him in the more immediate discharge of his duties at the

concluding services of the battalion, he desires that their names, as well as that of every officer composing the battalion, may be inserted in this conclusion of the narrative. He will retain a copy of it to remind him of those who have been his faithful friends, his valuable associates, and sharers in his everlasting esteem."

The reduction having been carried into effect, and the claims of the men to be discharged settled, the dépôt proceeded to Aberdeen, where it remained quartered till July 1817, when it was joined by the 1st battalion newly returned from India, and the two battalions of the 78th were once more consolidated.

On the 13th of July 1817, the 1st battalion landed at Aberdeen, and marched into barracks occupied by the dépôt of the 2nd battalion, with which it was immediately amalgamated, and the regiment has since remained as a single battalion. The regiment, now consisting of 638 rank and file, maintained its headquarters at Aberdeen, with detachments at Perth, and Forts George, William, and Augustus.[6]

Having received a route for Ireland, the headquarters marched from Aberdeen on the 31st of October, embarked at Port Patrick on the 22nd of November, and a few hours later landed at Donaghadee. Thence the regiment proceeded to Belfast, and having there received orders for Mullingar, it marched thither, and arrived at its destination on the 3rd of December; headquarters and four companies remained at Mullingar, and the remaining five (the 5th company being still in India), under Lieut.-Colonel Lindsay, proceeded to Tullamore, two small detachments being sent to Bally-mahon and Longford.

We need not follow the movements of the 78th during its stay in Ireland for nearly nine years, during which time it was broken up into numerous detachments, stationed at various small towns throughout the country, for the purpose of keeping in check the many disturbers of the peace with whom the country was at this period infested. Wherever the regiment was stationed while in Ireland at

---

[6] At these stations the regiment was inspected, and most favourably reported upon, by Major-General Hope.

this time, it invariably won the good-will and respect of the magistrates and people. When about to leave Mullingar, in June 1819, an extremely flattering series of resolutions was sent to Colonel Macleod by a meeting of magistrates and gentlemen held at Trim."

In October 1818 the Highland Society of London presented to the regiment twenty-five copies of the Poems of Ossian in Gaelic, " to be disposed of by the commanding officer of the regiment in such manner as he may judge most expedient, and as best calculated to promote the views of the Society." At the same time the secretary of the Highland Society conveyed the high respect which the Society entertained "for that national and distinguished corps and the wish on their part that it may long continue to cherish, as it now does, the noble sentiments of the patriotic Ossian." We need scarcely say that these sentiments were warmly reciprocated by Colonel Macleod, who then commanded the 78th. About a year after this, in September 1819, Colonel Macleod was promoted to the rank of major-general, and was succeeded in the command of the regiment by Lieutenant-Colonel Lindsay, who, on the reduction of the establishment of the regiment in September 1818, had been placed on half-pay.

The regiment was reviewed by the Right Honourable Sir David Baird, Commander of the Forces,[7] on the 24th of July, when its appearance and steadiness called forth his highest approbation.

On the 11th of August 1822, Lieutenant-General Sir Samuel Auchmuty, G.C.B., colonel of the regiment, died in Dublin, having been, a short time previously, appointed to the command of the forces in Ireland. He was succeeded in the regiment by Major-General Sir Edward Barnes, K.C.B.

When the regiment left Kilkenny for Dublin, in August 1824, a letter was received from the grand jury of the county Kilkenny, expressive of their high sense of the good conduct of the regiment during its stay of two years and a half in that county, and of their satisfaction at the unanimity which had at all times prevailed between them and the inhabi-

tants. The regiment would have changed its station the preceding year, but was allowed to remain at the particular request of the gentlemen of the county. Lieut.-Colonel Lindsay was appointed a magistrate of the counties of Kilkenny and Carlow, and Captain Lardy a magistrate of Carlow.

On the 13th of January 1826, the regiment moved from Fermoy to Cork. Orders were received on the 26th of January for the regiment to hold itself in readiness to embark for Ceylon, in consequence of which four service companies and six dépôt companies were immediately formed. On the 7th of March new arms were issued to the six service companies, and a selection of the old ones made for the dépôt. The old arms had been in possession more than nine years, but not having been originally good, were considered unfit to be taken to a foreign station. Some of the arms issued as new had been previously for a short time in the possession of the 42nd Highlanders.

The service companies of the regiment embarked at the Cove of Cork on board three ships, which sailed together on the morning of the 23rd of April, and arrived at Colombo on the 9th, the 17th, and the 28th of August respectively, after a favourable passage.

The regiment remained in garrison at Colombo, from its disembarkation until the 2nd of October 1828, when the first division marched for Kandy.

"It was a great satisfaction to the officers of the regiment, to receive from the officers of the civil service their testimony to the good conduct of the men, that during nearly three years' residence in Kandy no complaint had ever been made of ill treatment or injustice by them to any of the natives."

On the 2nd of August 1831, the regiment received routes for four companies to Trincomalee, and to Galle. The companies for Trincomalee, with the headquarters, disembarked at their destination on the 22nd of August.

A year after its arrival the station was attacked by cholera in its most malignant form, and the regiment suffered severely.

The crisis of the disease, both in the fort and in the hulk, was from the night of the 22nd to that of the 24th; in these 48 hours

---

[7] His portrait will be found on page 482, vol. ii.

25 men died. The cases after that became gradually fewer and less virulent, and, by the 2nd of November, the disease may be said to have entirely left the fort, though it continued to rage among the natives outside for a month or six weeks longer. Altogether, in the 78th, there were attacked 132 men, 10 women, and 3 children, and of these there died 56 men, 2 women, and 1 child.

The regiment, after this lamentable visitation, became tolerably healthy, and continued so during the remainder of its stay at Trincomalee; it returned to Colombo in October and November 1834, and remained there until September 1835, when it was ordered to Kandy.

Colonel Lindsay having embarked on leave of absence to England on the 11th of April 1836, the command of the regiment devolved on Major Douglas, who eventually succeeded to the lieutenant-colonelcy, on Colonel Lindsay selling out in April 1837.

The regiment remained in Kandy, detaching a company to Nuwera Ellia, until the orders were received for its return to England on the 28th of March 1837; and on the 1st and 3rd of August it marched in two divisions to Colombo. At the different inspections, Sir John Wilson, the Major-General commanding, expressed his satisfaction with the general appearance and conduct of the regiment, and previous to the embarkation on its return to England, he issued an order conveying the high opinion he had formed of officers and men during their service in Ceylon.

Two companies had embarked on board the "Numa" transport on the 15th of May, and on the 2nd of September following the headquarters embarked on board the "Barossa" transport, and sailed next day.

The deaths which took place during the service of the regiment in Ceylon were—Captains Macleod and Lardy, Paymaster Chisholm, and Assistant-Surgeon Duncan, with 295 men. Detachments had been received at various periods, but of the original number embarked from England, 1 field officer, 2 captains, 1 subaltern, 2 regimental staff, 3 sergeants, 4 drummers, and 208 rank and file returned. The total strength of the regiment on embarkation for England was—1 lieutenant-colonel, 5 captains, 9 subalterns, 3 regimental staff,

30 sergeants, 10 drummers, and 363 rank and file.

The headquarters landed at Limerick on the 9th of February 1838. The division in the "Numa" transport had previously landed at the same place in November 1837, both vessels having been driven into the Shannon by stress of weather and shortness of provisions. In the headquarters' ship, owing to its being later in the season, the officers and men suffered more severely from the intense cold and wet.

The detachment in the "Numa" transport, after landing, had joined the dépôt at Cork, and the headquarters, after remaining three weeks in Limerick to recover from the general debility occasioned by their late sufferings, marched to Buttevant, where the service and dépôt companies were reunited.

The regiment brought home a young elephant (an elephant being the regimental badge), which had been presented to the officers in Kandy by Major Firebrace of the 58th, and which had been trained to march at the head of the band.

Orders having been given to permit volunteers to be transferred to the 71st, 85th, and 93rd Regiments, to complete these corps previous to their embarking for America, 23 men volunteered to the 71st, and 38 to the 85th; 28 men were discharged as unfit for further service, thus leaving the regiment 183 below its establishment.

The regiment having been ordered to Glasgow, embarked in steamers at Cork, and landed in two divisions on the 8th of June 1838. In Glasgow it remained until August 1839, when it was ordered to Edinburgh. The establishment had been completed in June, and in August the order for augmenting regiments to 800 rank and file was promulgated, when the regiment recommenced recruiting, and finally completed its number in January 1840.

On the 17th of July the regiment embarked at Glasgow for Liverpool, where it arrived on the 22nd. Headquarters were at Burnley, and detachments were sent out to various places.

The regiment remained thus detached, in consequence of disturbances which had taken place in the manufacturing towns of Lancashire, until the 23rd of June 1841, when it was moved to Manchester. This was the first time the regiment had been together since its return from Ceylon. It left Manchester for Dublin on the 19th of November, and on the 1st of April 1842, it re-embarked for Liverpool, and proceeded by train to Canterbury, where it arrived on the 8th, having been ordered to hold itself in readiness for India. Volunteers were received from the 72nd, 79th, 92nd, and 93rd Highlanders, and from the 55th Regiment. The embarkation, on board six ships, was very hurried, owing to the disastrous news received from India.

The elephant, which had been brought from Ceylon, was presented to the Zoological Society of Edinburgh, previous to the regiment leaving Dublin.

The 78th sailed from Gravesend about the end of May, in various ships, and had arrived in Bombay by the 30th of July, with the exception of the "Lord Lynedoch," which did not arrive until a month after. The regiment landed at Panwel, *en route* for Poonah, marching by the same road that it took in 1803, when proceeding to reinstate the Peishwah on his musnud.

The regiment was quartered in Poonah until the 7th of April 1843, when it was ordered to Sindh. The right wing marched on the 7th. Lieutenant-Colonel Douglas being ordered on special duty to Sindh, the command of the regiment was taken over by Major Forbes. After several contradictory orders, a final order was received at Khandallah, to leave the families and heavy baggage, and embark immediately at Panwel for Kurráchee. There the headquarters and five companies landed on the 20th of May. The left wing having joined from Bombay after the rains, the regiment marched for Sukhur in two divisions. There was no beaten track, and native guides were procured to lead the column, but even these frequently went astray. The march was sometimes through dreary wastes of heavy sand, dotted with the cactus and other bushes, and at other times through the dry bed of a river. Frequently, when the regiment halted, there was no sign of water to be seen, but by digging a few feet down, in certain spots, the water would suddenly well up, and in a

short time form a little pond. The water would subside again after some hours, but men, camp followers, and cattle, received their supply, and the skins and other vessels would meanwhile be filled. The regiment marched into Sukhur apparently in excellent health, but disease must have been contracted on the way up, when passing through swampy tracts where the heat of the sun had engendered malaria.

"The excitement of the march kept the scourge from showing itself, but no sooner had the men settled in their barracks than a most virulent fever broke out, which continued, without cessation, throughout the stay of the regiment. Some lingered for weeks, some for days. It was not unfrequent to hear of the death of a man to whom one had spoken but half an hour previously. The hospital, a large one, was of course filled at once; some of the barrack-rooms were converted into wards, and at one time there were upwards of 800 men under treatment. Some hundreds of the less dangerously affected were marched about, a few paces, morning and evening, in hopes that by their being called 'convalescent,' the mind might act beneficially on the body, but as death called them away the group became less and less.

"Day after day we attended at the hospital for, in fact, funeral parade; for four or five, and then eight or nine, men died daily; you did not ask who had died, but how many. Firing parties were discontinued, not only that the sad volleys might not disturb the dying, but because there were no men for the duty. In the graveyard at Sukhur lie the bodies of hundreds of the regiment—officers, men, women, and children. Major-General Simpson, Sir Charles Napier's lieutenant (who afterwards commanded our armies in the Crimea), was at Sukhur at the time, and on his return to Hyderabad, caused to be erected there at his own expense a monument to the memory of all those who died, which feeling and tender act filled our hearts with the warmest gratitude. It was the spontaneous effusion of a truly noble mind. The remains of the regiment also erected a monument in St Giles' Cathedral, Edinburgh, to the memory of their comrades who died in Sindh.

II.

"The regiment lost, between the 1st of September 1844 and 30th of April 1845, 3 officers, 532 men, 68 women, 134 children —total, 737 souls

"The medical men attributed the sickness in a great degree to the improper time at which the regiment was moved, and the malaria engendered by the heat of the sun on the swampy plains which had been overflowed by the Indus The deaths continued very frequent all the time we remained, and at last, on the 21st and 25th of December 1844, we embarked, or rather the men crawled, on board common country boats, which conveyed us to Hydera-bad These boats were very imperfectly chuppered, i e, straw, reed, or matting roofed The sun struck through the thatching by day and the very heavy dews penetrated it by night, when it was extremely cold When we moored in the evening we used to bury our dead, and I sewed up many of the poor fellows in their blankets and rugs, the only substitutes for a coffin we had We dug the graves deep, and with the bodies buried the boxes and everything else that had belonged to them We put layers of thorns inside, round, and on the top of the graves, in hopes of preserving the remains of our poor comrades from the attacks of the troops of jackals swarming in the neighbourhood There were no stones to be had, so thorns and bushes well beaten down were all the protection we could give We were much pleased on learning afterwards that in many cases our efforts had been successful, and that the wild people who live near the river had respected the graves of the white men The two divisions of the regiment buried between Sukhur and Hydera-bad, nearly 100 men, besides women and children After its arrival the mortality still continued very great, and it was not until the warm weather set in that the sickness began to abate The miserable remains of as fine a regiment as ever was seen, left Hydera-bad in two parties, on the 24th of February and 4th of March 1845, respectively, for the mouth of the river, whence they went by steamer to Bombay Some of the officers of the regiment, myself among the number, were detained in Sindh on court-martial duty, when relieved some went to Bombay or Kurrachee,

and at the latter place heard reports to the effect that the mortality in the regiment was to be attributed to intemperance Indignation at this cruel and false charge, which was reported to Major Twopeny, caused him to write to Sir Charles Napier's military secretary Had not some of the officers of the regiment passed through Kurrachee, these reports might have been believed, for every exertion was made at the time to persuade the public that climate had nothing to do with the disease There was not a murmur heard in the regiment all the time of the plague, but the sur-vivors were determined to relieve the memory of their dead from such a charge, and prove that the will of God, and not alcohol, had caused the mortality. The canteen returns showed how little liquor had been consumed, and the officers, who daily visited the hospital and the barracks, not only in the common course of duty, but to tend, comfort, and read to the men, could not fail to have observed any irregularity, had any existed The poor dying men were not thinking of intoxicating liquors, but met death with the utmost firm-ness and resignation It was an accursed charge, and cannot be too highly censured When relieved from duty, the officers who had been detained joined the wreck of the regiment at Fort George, Bombay Invalid-ing committees sat, and most of the survivors were sent home, so that but a very small rem-nant of that once splendid corps slowly took its way to Poonah, which, two years before, it had left full of health, strength, and hope There the regiment got 100 volunteers from the 2nd Queen's, then going home, and between recruiting and volun-teering, by December 1845, 700 had joined These were afterwards always known as 'The 700'"[8]

At Bombay 105 non-commissioned officers and men were invalided, and the regiment in one division, amounting in number to 313 (being reduced by sickness to less than one-third its strength), proceeded to Poonah on the 4th of April 1845, but did not arrive there until the 18th, being unable to march more than six or seven miles a day

[8] Journal of Captain Keogh, late 78th Highlanders

"FORT-WILLIAM, 15th August 1845
" To the Secretary to Government,
     " Military Department, Bombay

"Sir,—I am directed to acknowledge the receipt of your letter, No 3167, of the 14th ultimo, and in reply, to express to you, for the information of the Government of Bombay, the satisfaction with which the Governor-General in Council has perused the correspondence to which it gave cover, so clearly proving, as it does, to be utterly unfounded, the report that intemperance had occasioned the sickness by which Her Majesty's 78th Highlanders was prostrated in Sinde, and which, unhappily, proved so fatal to that fine corps —I am, Sir, your most obedient servant,

(Signed)   " J STUART, Lieut -Col
              " Secretary to Government of India,
                  " Military Department "

The 78th left Goraporee lines, Poonah, on the 18th of December 1845, for Khirkee, six miles distant   The regiment returned to Poonah on the 14th of February 1846, and marched for Belgaum, under command of Lieutenant - Colonel Douglas, who died of fever at Hyderabad on the 1st of October 1849, while on staff employ, and was succeeded by Major Walter Hamilton

After being stationed at Khirkee and Belgaum for some time, the regiment left Belgaum for Bombay and Aden, on the 6th and 7th of November 1849   The left wing, under the command of Lieutenant Colonel W Hamilton, arrived at Aden on the 25th, and the right wing, under the command of Major H Stisted, proceeded to Colabba, Bombay, where it arrived on the 16th of the same month   An exchange of wings took place in October 1850, the headquarters still remaining at Aden

During the year 1851 the Arab tribes round Aden committed several outrages, in one of which, near Lahaj, in the month of March, Lieutenant Macpherson of the 78th was very dangerously wounded, having been stabbed in no fewer than seven places.   About a fortnight after this affair, as Lieutenant Delisser of the regiment was riding to Steamer Point (about five miles distant from the barracks), at eight o'clock A M, he was attacked by an Arab, armed with a crease or dagger, and wounded severely in the arm and slightly in the stomach   Lieutenant Delisser got off his horse, and, seizing the Arab, wrested the crease from his hand, and with one blow nearly severed his head from his body   The corpse was afterwards hung in chains at the entrance to the fortifications from the interior

The regiment being ordered to Poonah, the left wing, consisting of the light and Nos 5, 6, and 7 companies, under command of Major Colin Campbell M'Intyre, left Bombay for that station on the 10th of February 1853, and arrived on the 18th of the same month.   The right wing left Aden for Poonah in three detachments in January and February, and thus, after a separation of upwards of three years, the regiment was once more united at Poonah on the 5th of March 1853.

In the month of May 1854 new accoutrements and colours were furnished to the regiment by the estate of the late General Paul Anderson   The alteration in the new accoutrements consisted in a waist and cross-belt, instead of double cross-belts

The clothing of the whole army having been altered in the year 1856, the regiment was supplied with the Highland jacket.

IV

1857

War declared with Persia—Expedition despatched—Gen Stalker takes Resheer and Busheer—A second division despatched, of which the 78th forms part, and the whole placed under command of Sir James Outram—Expedition to Boorasjoon and destruction of the enemy's stores — Night attack and battle of KOOSHAB—General Havelock joins the second division—Naval and military expedition up the Euphrates—Mohammrah bombarded and taken—Flight of the Shah zada, Prince Khander Meerza, and his army—The Persian camps occupied—Expedition to Ahwaz, on the Karoon—The Shah-zada and his troops fly from 300 men to Shuster—Total destruction of the Persian dépôts of provisions at Ahwaz —Return of the expedition — Peace signed—Havelock's opinion of the 78th—The 78th sail from Persia, and arrive safely at Calcutta

THE Governor-General of India having declared war against Persia on the 1st of November 1856, an expedition was despatched the same month from Bombay to the Persian Gulf   The force consisted of one division only, comprising two infantry brigades, with cavalry, artillery, and engineers, the whole under the command of Major-General Stalker. Its strength was 5670 fighting men, of whom 2270 were Europeans, with 3750 followers, 1150 horses, and 430 bullocks, and its equipment and embarkation were completed in an incredibly short space of time, chiefly owing to the manly exertions of Lord Elphinstone, the Governor of Bombay. On the 6th of December a sufficiently large portion of the fleet arrived off Busheer to commence operations, and on the 7th a landing was effected at Ras Hallila, about twelve or thirteen miles below Busheer. On the 9th the expedition advanced against Resheer, which, after some resistance, was taken. Next day General Stalker formed his line of attack against Busheer, but after a bombardment of four hours, the Governor surrendered, and the garrison, to the number of about 2000 men, laid down their arms, and being conducted into the country, were set at liberty. Sixty-five pieces of artillery were found in the town, which now became the head-quarters of the army, an entrenched camp being formed, with a ditch 3 feet deep and 6 feet wide, and a parapet, about a mile beyond the walls.

This expedition was subsequently reinforced by a second division, of which the 78th Highlanders formed part. Early on the morning of the 7th of January 1857 the left wing, consisting of 12 officers and 388 men, commenced its march under the command of Major M'Intyre, and the head-quarters, consisting of 16 officers and 421 men, under the command of Colonel Stisted, started on the morning of the 8th. A depôt, consisting of 1 officer and 89 men, was left at Poonah in charge of Lieutenant Gilmore. After staying a short time at Khandallah, the regiment arrived at Bombay on the 19th, and embarked in three ships, which sailed the same day. Headquarters arrived off Busheer on July 1st, and disembarked immediately in light marching order, with no baggage except bedding, consisting of a settzingee, or cotton padded rug, and a pair of blankets. The left wing having arrived on the previous day, had already landed in the same order, and marched into the entrenched camp, where the whole regiment was assembled, occupying an outwork near the lines of the 64th Regiment, in which tents had been pitched for officers and men. Owing, however, to the insufficient

supply of these, 30 men, or 2 officers and their servants, had to find accommodation in a zowtee tent, 10 feet by 8. Both officers and men were received in camp with great hospitality, the men of the different companies of the 64th and 2d Bombay Europeans sending their rations of spirits and porter to the corresponding companies of the 78th.

It had come to the notice of Sir James Outram that the Persian Government were making vast preparations for the recovery of Busheer, and that Sooja-ool-Moolk, the Persian commander, and reputed to be the best general in the Persian army, had assembled a formidable force at the town of Boorasjoon, 46 miles from Busheer, where he had formed an entrenched camp. This force consisted of a total of 8450 cavalry and infantry.

The Persian force was well supplied with food and ammunition, and it had been intended that it should form the nucleus of a very large army assembling for the recovery of Busheer.

At six o'clock in the evening of the 3d of February the following force was drawn up, in two lines of contiguous columns at quarter-distance, outside the entrenched camp :—

Cavalry—3d Bombay Light Cavalry, 243 ; Poona Horse, 176. Infantry (Europeans)—H.M. 64th regiment, 780 ; H.M. 78th Highlanders, 739 ; 2d Bombay European Light Infantry, 693. Infantry, &c. (Natives)—Sappers, 118 ; 4th Bombay Rifle Regiment, 523 ; 20th Regiment Bombay N.I., 442 ; 26th Regiment Bombay N.I., 479 ; Beloochee Battalion, 460. Guns—3d Troop Horse Artillery, 6 ; 3d Light Field Battery, 6 ; 5th Light Field Battery, 6. Total sabres, 419 ; Europeans, 2212 ; Natives, 2022. Total men, 4653 ; guns, 18.

The force was not provided with tents or extra clothing of any kind ; but every man carried his great coat, blanket, and two days' cooked provisions.

After a march of 46 miles in forty-one hours, during which the troops were exposed to the worst of weather—cold winds, deluging storms of rain and thunder, and clouds of driving sand, the greater part of the march lying through a reedy swamp—the force reached the enemy's entrenched position near the town of Boorasjoon, on the morning of the 5th, but was

only in time to find the enemy abandoning it.
A smart brush, however, took place between
their rearguard and the British cavalry, in
which an officer and two or three troopers
received some slight wounds. By two o'clock
the force was in possession of the enemy's
entrenched camp, and great quantities of ammunition of all kinds, together with grain and
camp equipage, were captured, the enemy having gone off in a most hurried and disorderly
manner

"The 6th and 7th of February were passed
in the enemy's position, destroying stores and
searching for buried guns, which were afterwards ascertained to have been thrown down
wells; their carriages and wheels, being found
by us, were burned. Some treasure was also
discovered, and many horses and carriage cattle
secured. During this time no annoyance was
experienced from the enemy, though an alarm
on the night of the 6th caused the whole of
the troops to stand to arms. From information
received afterwards, and their own despatch,
this alarm was not altogether a groundless one,
as they fell up to our outposts; but finding the
troops under arms, and it being a bright moonlight night, they attempted nothing. Many
jokes were, however, current in camp next day
on the events of the night, the picket of one
regiment having taken a *door* prisoner, which
was leaning against a bush in a most suspicious
manner; and those of two other gallant corps
skirmished up to, and were very nearly having
a battle of their own with a patrol of the Poonah
Horse. However, all passed off without accident.

"Many spies were doubtless in our camp
during the entire period of our stay, and the
enemy were well informed of every movement; regardless of which, however, intercourse between the villagers and camp was
encouraged, and such strict precautions enforced that they should not be pillaged or ill-
treated, that they were civil if not friendly,
and at any rate gave no trouble."[9]

The troops had been somewhat exhausted
by their march of 46 miles through rain, mud,
morass, and sand in forty-one hours; but being
now recruited by their two days' rest, and Sir

James Outram having heard that the enemy
had succeeded in getting his guns through
the difficult pass of Maak, considered it
better to rest content with the moral effect
produced by the capture and destruction of
their stores, and accordingly ordered a return
to Busheer.

"At eight o'clock on the evening of the 7th,"
Captain Hunt says, "the return march to
Busheer was commenced, the column taking
with it as much of the captured stores as carriage was procurable for, and the military
Governor of Boorasjoon as a prisoner—this personage proving a double traitor. The General's
intention that the return march should be a
leisurely one had been so widely made known
through the force, that the stirring events then
so shortly to occur were little indeed expected
by any one. . . . Shortly after midnight a
sharp rattle of musketry in the rear, and the
opening of two horse artillery guns, put every
one on the *qui vive*, and that an attack in
force upon the rearguard was taking place became apparent to all. The column at once
halted, and then moved back to extricate the
baggage and protecting troops. These, however, were so ably handled by Colonel Honnor
(who was in command) as to need little assistance, save for the increasing numbers of the
assailants.

"In about half an hour after the first shot
was fired, not the rearguard only, but the
entire force, was enveloped in a skirmishing
fire. Horsemen galloped round on all sides,
yelling and screaming like fiends, and with
trumpets and bugles making as much noise as
possible. One of their buglers had the auda-
city to go close to a skirmishing company of
the Highlanders, and sound first the 'Cease
fire,' and afterwards, 'Incline to the left,'
escaping in the dark. Several English officers
having, but a few years since, been employed
in organising the Persian troops, accounted for
the knowledge of our bugle-calls, now artfully
used to create confusion. The silence and
steadiness of the men were most admirable,
and the manœuvring of regiments that followed, in taking up position for the remaining
hours of darkness, was as steady as an ordinary
parade, and this during a midnight attack,
with an enemy's fire flashing in every direc-

---

[9] Captain Hunt's (78th Highlanders) *Persian Campaign*.

tion, and cavalry surrounding, ready to take advantage of the slightest momentary confusion Pride may well be felt in the steadiness of any troops under such circumstances, and how much more so when, as on the present occasion, two-thirds had never before been under an enemy's fire The horsemen of the enemy were at first very bold, dashing close up to the line, and on one occasion especially to the front of the 78th Highlanders, but finding that they could occasion no disorder, and having been in one or two instances roughly handled by the cavalry and horse artillery, this desultory system of attack gradually ceased, and the arrangement of the troops for the remainder of the night was effected under nothing more serious than a distant skirmishing fire The formation adopted was an oblong, a brigade protecting each flank, and a demi-brigade the front and rear, field battery guns at intervals, and a thick line of skirmishers connecting and covering all, the horse artillery and cavalry on the flank of the face fronting the original line of march, the front and flanks of the oblong facing outwards, the baggage and followers being in the centre When thus formed the troops lay down, waiting for daylight in perfect silence, and showing no fire or light of any kind

"Scarcely was the formation completed when the enemy opened five heavy guns, and round shot were momentarily plunging through and over our position, the range of which they had obtained very accurately Our batteries replied, and this cannonade continued, with occasional intervals, until near daylight, causing but few casualties, considering the duration of the fire"

It appears that, in abandoning their position at Boorasjoon, Sooja-ool-Moolk (reputed to be the best officer in the Persian army), with his force, had taken the direct road to Shiraz by the Maak Pass, and the Elkanee, with his horse, had retired to the one leading to the Haft Moola, and that they had planned a night attack on the British camp on the night that the troops marched The explosion of the magazine at Boorasjoon gave the Persians the first intimation of the departure of the British force, when they hastened after it, in the expectation of being able to attack it on the line

of march, and possibly create confusion and panic in the dark

At daybreak on the 8th of February the Persian force, amounting to over 6000 infantry and 2000 horse, besides several guns, was discovered on the left rear of the British (north-east of the line of march) in order of battle The Persians were drawn up in line, their right resting on the walled village of KOOSHAB and a date grove, and their left on a hamlet with a round fortalice tower Two rising mounds were in front of their centre, which served as redoubts, behind which they placed their guns, and they had deep nullahs on their right front and flank, thickly lined with skirmishers Their cavalry, in considerable bodies, were on both flanks, commanded by the hereditary chief of the tribes in person The whole army was commanded by Sooja ool-Moolk

The British artillery and cavalry at once moved rapidly to the attack, supported by two lines of infantry, a third line protecting the baggage The first line was composed of the 78th Highlanders under Major M'Intyre, a party of Sappers on the right, the 26th Regiment Native Infantry, the 2nd European Light Infantry, and the 4th Regiment Bombay Rifles on the left of all" The second line had H M's 64th Regiment on its right, then the 20th Regiment Native Infantry, and the Belooch Battalion on its left. The light companies of battalions faced the enemy's skirmishers in the nullahs, and covered both flanks and rear of their own army A detachment of the 3d Cavalry assisted in this duty, and as the enemy showed some bodies of horse, threatening a dash on the baggage or wounded men, these were of considerable service. They had also in their charge the Governor of Boorasjoon, who, endeavouring to attract attention by placing his black Persian cap on a stick, and waving it as a signal to his countrymen, was immediately, and very properly, knocked off his horse, and forced to remain on his knees until the fortune of the day was decided

"The lines advanced directly the regiments had deployed, and so rapidly and steadily did the leading one move over the crest of a rising ground (for which the enemy's guns were laid) that it suffered but little, the Highlanders not having a single casualty, and the 26th Native

Infantry, their companion regiment in brigade, losing only one man killed, and having but four or five wounded. The 1st Brigade, 1st Division, fared worse, as the shot, passing over the regiments then in their front, struck the ranks, and occasioned the greatest loss of the day. The 2nd Brigade, 1st Division, suffered equally, but had more killed among their casualties especially in the 2nd European Light Infantry.

"During this time the cannonade had been continuous; but as the Persian fire in some degree slackened, our artillery advanced to closer action, making most beautiful practice, and almost silencing the opposing batteries. Some bodies of horse soon presented an opportunity for a charge, and the squadrons of the 3rd Cavalry and Tapp's Irregulars, who had hitherto been on the right front, dashed at them, accompanied by Blake's Horse Artillery, and made a most sweeping and brilliant charge, sabring gunners, and fairly driving the enemy's horse off the field. The infantry lines were still advancing rapidly, and in beautifully steady order, to sustain this attack, and were just getting into close action when the enemy lost heart, and his entire line at once broke and fled precipitately.

"More than 700 of their dead were left upon the field, with many horses; how many were slain in the pursuit, or died of their wounds, it was of course impossible to ascertain. No great number of prisoners (said to be about 100) fell into our hands; their own cowardly treachery in many instances, after having received quarter, enraged the men, and occasioned a free use of the bayonet. One or two men of consequence were, however, among those taken. These brilliant results were secured on our part with a loss of only 1 officer and 18 men killed, and 4 officers and 60 men wounded. Among the unfortunate camp-followers, however, crowded together during the preceding night attack, several were killed and wounded, and many not accounted for."[1]

The troops bivouacked for the day in the battlefield, and at night accomplished a march of twenty miles (by another route) over a country rendered almost impassable by the heavy rains which fell incessantly. Through sticky mud, half clay and sand, the column marched the whole night after the action. The guide misled the force, and at four o'clock in the morning of the 9th a halt was called to wait for daylight. In the midst of pelting rain, sunk knee-deep in mud, and exposed to a biting north-easterly wind, two hours were passed, without a tree even in sight, and the swamp around looking in the hazy light like a vast lake. Yet men and officers alike stretched themselves in the mire, endeavouring to snatch some sort of rest after their exhausting labours. The foot of Chah Gudack was at length reached by ten in the morning, whence, after a rest of six hours, the march was continued through deep swamps to Busheer, which was reached before midnight; the force having thus performed another most arduous march of forty-four miles, under incessant rain, besides fighting and defeating the enemy during its progress, within the short space of fifty hours. Though the men were tired and fagged, they were in excellent spirits.

In Sir James Outram's despatch to General Sir H. Somerset the name of Brigadier Stisted (78th) was particularly mentioned.

This wet march from Boorasjoon having completely destroyed the shoes of the men, Sir James Outram generously took upon himself to order that each man of the force should be supplied with a new pair free of expense, the cost of which was subsequently defrayed by Government. The marching hose of the 78th were all spoiled and rendered useless, and in many cases could only be taken off by being cut to pieces. A long gray stocking, procurable from the Government stores, was substituted, and continued to be worn until the adoption of the white spats in the following year.

On the return of the expedition it was the intention of General Outram immediately to proceed against the Fort of Mohammrah, situated at the junction of the Shut-el-Arab (the Euphrates) and the Karoon, but owing to the non-arrival of the requisite reinforcements from India, occasioned by tempestuous weather in the Gulf of Persia, and other causes, Sir James was unable to leave Busheer until the 18th of March. In the meantime the troops were

[1] Captain Hunt'. *P . . . . 'gn.*

busily employed in erecting five formidable redoubts, four in front and one in rear of the entrenched camp. While lying before Busheer the light company of the 78th was supplied with Enfield rifles.

Brigadier-General Havelock[2] having arrived in February, took command of the Indian division, and Brigadier Walker Hamilton, of the 78th Highlanders, arriving from Kurráchee, where he had been for some months

Major-General Sir Henry Havelock, K.C.B.

commanding the brigade, assumed command of the 1st Brigade, 2nd Division, which had hitherto been commanded by Colonel Stisted of the 78th; the latter officer now resumed the command of the regiment.

In the beginning of March the embarkation of the troops destined for the bombardment of Mohammrah commenced, and continued at intervals as the weather permitted, until the departure of General Outram on the 18th.

[2] This portrait is copied, by the permission of John Clark Marshman, Esq., and the Messrs Longman, from that in Marshman's *Memoirs of Major-General Sir Henry H..l..., K.C.B.*

The place of rendezvous for the expedition was about sixteen miles from the mouth of the Euphrates, opposite the village of Mohammrah. On the 16th of March the "Kingston" sailed from Busheer with 6 officers and 159 non-commissioned officers and rank and file, being No. 8 and the light company of the 78th, under Captain Hunt. These were followed on the 12th by headquarters, consisting of 9 officers and 228 men, under command of Colonel Stisted, accompanied by Brigadier-General Havelock; also by 6 officers and 231 men under Major M'Intyre. A few days previous to the attack on Mohammrah, Nos. 1, 2, and 3 companies, under Major Haliburton, joined the rest of the regiment.

All the ships comprising the expedition were assembled at the appointed rendezvous by the 21st of March, and the next two days were occupied in the arrangement of details for the attack.

For some months past the Persians had been strengthening their position at Mohammrah; batteries of great strength had been erected, consisting of solid earth, 20 feet thick and 18 feet high, with casemated embrasures on the northern and southern points of the banks of the Karoon and Shut-el-Arab, at the junction of the two rivers. These, with other earthworks, armed with heavy ordnance, completely commanded the passage of the latter river, and were so judiciously placed and so skilfully formed as to sweep the whole stream to the extent of the range of the guns down the river and across to the opposite shore. Indeed, everything that science could suggest and labour accomplish in the time appeared to have been done by the enemy, to prevent any vessel from passing up the river above their position. The banks, for many miles, were overgrown with dense date groves, affording a perfect cover for riflemen; and the opposite shore, being neutral (Turkish) territory, was not available for the erection of counter batteries.

The plan of action resolved upon was to attack the enemy's batteries with the armed steamers and sloops of war, and when the fire was nearly silenced, to pass up rapidly with the troops in small steamers towing boats, land the force above the northern forts, and immediately advance upon and attack the entrenched camp

The Persian army, numbering 13,000 men of all arms, with 30 guns, was commanded by the Shah zada, Prince Khanler Meerza, in person The strength of the British force was 4886 of all arms, together with five steamers of the Indian navy, and two sloops of war, the entire command of the expedition being committed to Commodore Young of that service, the 78th Highlanders numbered 830

On the morning of the 24th of March the fleet of ships of war and transports got under weigh, and made up the river to within three miles of the southern battery, opposite the village of Harteh, where they anchored

By nine o'clock on the morning of the 26th the fire of the heavy batteries was so reduced by the fire from a mortar raft, followed up by that from the vessels of war, that the rendezvous flag was hoisted by the "Feroze" as a signal for the advance of the troops in the small steamers and boats This was accomplished in admirable order, although at the time the fire from the batteries was far from being silenced The leading steamer was the "Berenice" carrying on her deck the whole of the 78th Highlanders and about 200 Sappers

Passing under the shelter of the ships of war, the troopships were brought to the banks above the forts, the water being sufficiently deep for them to lie close alongside the bank and skirmishers were at once thrown out to cover the disembarkation of the force In the meantime, the artillery fire from the Persian forts gradually ceased, and musketry was opened from them and from breastworks in their vicinity, and maintained with spirit for some time, when storming parties were landed, that drove out the defenders and took possession of their works and guns

By half-past one o'clock the troops were landed and formed, and advanced without delay in contiguous columns at quarter-distance, through the date groves and across the plain, upon the entrenched camp of the enemy,

who, without waiting for the approach of the British, fled precipitately after exploding their largest magazine, leaving behind them tents and baggage and stores, with several magazines of ammunition and 16 guns Their loss was estimated at about 200 killed

For the next few days, while the tents and the baggage were being disembarked, the army bivouacked under the date trees on the river-bank by day, and removed to the sandy plain by night, to avoid the unhealthy miasma.

It having been ascertained that the enemy had retreated to the town of Ahwaz, about 100 miles distant up the river Karoon, where they had large magazines and supplies, Sir James Outram determined to despatch an armed flotilla to that place to effect a reconnaisance

The expedition was placed under the command of Captain Rennie of the Indian navy, and consisted of three small armed steamers, towing three gunboats and three cutters, and carrying on board No 5 and the light company of the 78th, with Captain M'Andrew, Lieutenants Cassidy, Finlay, and Barker, and the grenadiers of the 64th Regiment, in all 300 men, under command of Captain Hunt of the 78th This force came in sight of Ahwaz on the morning of the 1st of April The whole Persian army was here observed posted in a strong position on the right bank of the Karoon It having been ascertained from some Arabs that the town itself, on the left bank, was nearly deserted, it was determined to land the party, advance upon Ahwaz, and, if possible, destroy the dépôt of guns and ammunition

At eleven in the morning the little band of 300 landed and advanced at once in three columns, covered by skirmishers, the whole party being extended in such a way that it appeared like a large body of men The left column consisted of the light company of the 78th, with its skirmishers and supports, both in one rank, the remainder of the company marching in columns of threes in single ranks with three paces distance between each man The grenadier company of the 64th and No 5 company of the 78th formed the right and centre columns in the same order The gun-boats were sent off in advance up the river, and taking up a position within shell-range of the enemy's ridges, opened fire upon them

The troops thus marched in a mimic brigade, advanced under cover of the gunboats' fire, and within an hour and a half Ahwaz was in their possession, and the Persian army, consisting of 6000 infantry, 5 guns, and a cloud of Bukhtyari horsemen, numbering upwards of 2000, was in full retreat upon Dizful, leaving behind it 1 gun, 154 stand of new arms, a great number of mules and sheep, and an enormous quantity of grain

Having remained at Ahwaz for two days, the plucky little force returned to Mohammrah, which it reached on the 5th of April, and where it received the hearty thanks of the General for the signal service which it had rendered [3]

On the very same day news was received that peace with Persia had been concluded at Paris on the 4th of March, but the British forces were to remain encamped at Mohammrah until the ratification of the treaty

On the 15th of April the regiment was inspected by Brigadier-General Havelock, C B, who expressed his extreme satisfaction at the highly efficient state in every respect in which he found it [4]

[3] Captain Hunt, 78th Highlanders, "Persian Campaign" We may remark that Captain Hunt's conduct of the Ahwaz force was very highly praised Sir James Outram says in his despatch to Sir Henry Somerset, "Great praise is also due to Captain Hunt, 78th Highlanders, who so successfully carried out the military operations," and Sir Henry acknowledges this by alluding to Captain Hunt, "whose excellent disposition of his small force I have remarked with much satisfaction" Captain Hunt also received the thanks of the Governor-General in Council This very promising officer unfortunately fell a victim to cholera during the Mutiny, and thus, at an early age, terminated a career which must have done honour to himself and reflected credit upon his regiment — O M

[4] "Of the 78th Highlanders Havelock had formed a very high estimate, and in his confidential report of that corps, made before leaving Persia, a copy of which was found among his papers, he had said — "There is a fine spirit in the ranks of this regiment I am given to understand that it behaved remarkably well in the affair at Kooshab, near Busheer, which took place before I reached the army, and during the naval action on the Euphrates, and its landing here, its steadiness, zeal, and activity, under my own observation, were conspicuous The men have been subjected in this service to a good deal of exposure, to extremes of climate, and have had heavy work to execute with their entrenching tools, in constructing

At length, on the 9th of May, a field force order was issued, directing the Indian division to be broken up, and the several regiments composing it to be sent to their respective destinations In this order Sir James Outram bade the troops farewell, and expressed in the very highest terms his admiration of their conduct in every respect

Thus ended the Persian campaign, during which the 78th had the good fortune to mature its campaigning qualities under the auspices of Outram and Havelock, names which were shortly destined to render its own illustrious

A medal was sanctioned to be worn by the troops engaged in the Persian campaign

In the regiment, Colonel Stisted, who for a time acted as brigadier, and afterwards commanded the regiment, was made a Companion of the Bath, and Captains Drummond, Hay, and Bouverie, who acted as majors of brigade at Busheer and Mohammrah, respectively, received brevet majorities The regiment received orders to place the words "Persia" and "Kooshab" upon its colours and appointments

On the 10th of May 1857, the 78th sailed from Mohammrah en route for Bombay Touching only at the port of Muscat, the vessels all arrived safe in Bombay harbour on the 22nd and 23rd, and there received the astounding intelligence that the entire Bengal army had mutinied, seized Delhi, and in many cases massacred all the Europeans The 78th was ordered to proceed immediately to Calcutta, along with the 64th, its old comrades, who had also just arrived from Persia Colonel Walter Hamilton, having arrived from Persia, took command of the regiment, which, numbering 28 officers and 828 men, was transferred to four ships, which arrived at Calcutta on the 9th and 10th of June

redoubts and making roads They have been, while I have had the opportunity of watching them, most cheerful, and have never seemed to regret or complain of anything but that they had no further chance of meeting the enemy I am convinced the regiment would be second to none in the service if its high military qualities were drawn forth It is proud of its colours, its tartan, and its former achievements" —Marshman's Memoirs of Havelock

V.

1857—1859.

ON the 10th of June 1857 the 78th High-landers proceeded to Chinsurah, where arrange-ments were made for their immediate transit to Benares. The grenadiers and No. 1 com-pany started on the 11th and 12th. On the night of the 13th, at 11 P.M., an order was received by express from Calcutta for the 78th to march immediately to Barrackpoor, and if possible reach that place by daybreak. The regiment marched to Barrackpoor, and after assisting in disarming the native troops, it returned to Chinsurah on the 16th, and the daily departure of detachments to Benares was resumed.

After a short halt at Benares the detach-ments proceeded to Allahabad, at which place a moveable column was being formed under Brigadier-General Havelock to advance against the mutineers. On arrival at that place it was

found that the whole of the country between it and Delhi was in the hands of the insur-gents; that Cawnpoor and Lucknow were in a state of siege; and a rumour, which eventually proved to be too true, stated that the British garrison of the former place had been induced to surrender, and had been basely massacred.[5]

On the 7th of July General Havelock ad-vanced from Allahabad with a small force of about 1000 British and a few Sikhs, with six guns, to endeavour to retake Cawnpoor and rescue Lucknow. His force consisted of a light field battery, a portion of the 1st Madras Fusi-liers, the 64th Regiment, and 78th Highlanders; of the latter were the grenadiers, Nos. 3, 6, and the light companies, numbering 305 men, be-sides 13 officers, under Colonel Walter Hamil-ton. The heat was intense, and the monsoon having just set in, the rain fell in torrents, rendering the entire country one large morass.

Major Renaud had been sent on with a small force as an advanced guard, and on the 10th General Havelock set out after him, coming up with him at moonlight, after a hard and long march. The united forces continued their march to Khaga, five miles from Futtehpoor, where Havelock commenced to encamp. His force now amounted to about 1400 Europeans and 400 natives, with 8 guns. While the camp was being pitched, the enemy, numbering about 3500, with 12 guns, was observed in the

[6] The garrison at Cawnpoor, under the command of Sir Hugh Wheeler, was induced to surrender, after a most heroic defence of three weeks, on promise of a safe conduct to Allahabad, and on condition that the force should march out under arms, with 60 rounds of ammunition to every man; that carriages should be provided for the conveyance of the wounded, the women, and the children; and that boats, victualled with a sufficiency of flour, should be in readiness, at the Suttee Chowra Ghât, or landing-place (on the Ganges), which lay about a mile from the British en-trenchment. On the morning of the 27th of June 1857 the garrison, numbering, with women and chil-dren, nearly 800, was marched down to the landing-place; but before the embarkation was completed, a fire of grape and musketry was opened upon the boats, and a fearful massacre took place. Only 125 women and children were spared from that day's massacre, and reserved for the more awful butchery of the 15th of July. Upwards of a hundred persons got away in a boat, but only four made good their escape, as within three days the boat was captured by the mutineers and taken back to Cawnpoor, where the sixty male occupants were shot, the women and children being put into custody with the 125 already mentioned. Our illustration is from a photograph, and shows the Fisherman's Temple. For full details of the Cawnpoor massacres, we may refer our readers to volume entitled *Cawnpore*, by G. O. Trevelyan.

distance bearing down upon a reconnoitering party which had been sent to the front under Colonel Tytler.

Futtehpoor constituted a strong position, and the enemy had already occupied the many advantageous positions, both natural and artificial. Among the rebel force was the 56th Bengal Native Infantry, the regiment which Havelock led on at Maharajpoor.

After the General had disposed his troops the action was soon decided. Captain Maude, pushing on his guns to point-blank range, electrified the enemy with his fire. The Madras Fusiliers gained possession of a hillock on the right, and struggled on through the inundation; the 78th, in extension, wading knee-deep in mud and water, kept up communication with the centre; the 64th gave strength to the centre and left; while on the left the 84th and Sikhs of Ferozepoor pressed back the enemy's right.

As the British force pressed forward, the rebel guns continued to fall into its hands; the rebels were driven by the skirmishers and

The Suttee Chowra Ghât, or Landing-Place.   Scene of the Second Massacre, 27th June 1857.

columns from every point, one after the other, of which they held possession, into, through, and beyond the town, and were very soon put to a final flight. General Havelock then taking up his position in triumph, halted his weary men to breakfast, having marched 24 miles, and beaten the enemy so completely that all their ammunition, baggage, and guns (11 in number) fell into his hands. The loss on the British side was merely nominal; but the moral effect on the mutineers of this their first reverse was immense.

During the action the heat was excessive, and 12 men died from exposure to the sun and fatigue. Next day General Havelock issued a Field-force Order, highly and justly complimenting the force for its conduct, which he attributed to the fire of British artillery, to English rifles in British hands, to British pluck, "and to the blessing of Almighty God on a most righteous cause."

On the 14th the moveable column recommenced its march, and after dislodging the rebels from a strong position at Aong, pushed on for Pandoo Nuddee, at the bridge of which place the enemy had prepared another strong position. Here, also, by the promptitude and admirable tactics of General Havelock, the rebels were completely routed; both on this occasion and at Aong they left behind them a number of heavy guns and a quantity of ammunition. It was on hearing the intelligence of the defeat of his troops at the Pandoo Nuddee that Nana Sahib put the finishing stroke to the atrocious conduct which has rendered his name an abhorrence to the whole civilized world, and which turned this warfare on the part of the English into "a most righteous cause" indeed. On the 15th of July this diabolical wretch filled up the measure of his iniquities; for it was on hearing that the bridge over the Pandoo Nuddee had been forced and his army driven back, that he ordered the immediate massacre of all the English women and children still in his possession.

Between four in the afternoon of the 15th, and nine in the morning of the 16th of July, 206 persons, mostly women and children of gentle birth, comprising the survivors of the massacre of 27th June and the captured fugitives from Futteghur,—who had been confined for a fortnight in a small building which has since been known in India as the Beebeegur, or House of the Ladies, in England as the House of the Massacre, —were butchered with the most barbarous atrocity, and their bodies thrown into a dry well, situated behind some trees which grew hard by. Our illustration, taken from a photograph, shows the Mausoleum erected over the well, and part of the garden which covers the site of the House of Massacre. Just within the doorway, at top of the flight of steps, may be seen the carved pediment which closes the mouth of the well. Around this pediment are carved the words —

Sacred to the perpetual memory of a great Company of Christian people, chiefly women and children. XVI Day of July MDCCCLVII

On the pediment has been erected, since our view was taken, an emblematical figure of an angel in front of a tall cross, carved in marble by Baron Marochetti.

At daybreak, on the 16th, Havelock's column

again moved on, the troops being strongly in hope of being able to save the wives and children of the murdered garrison of Cawnpoor, being ignorant of their brutal massacre. After a march of 16 miles the army halted in a mango grove at the village of Maharajpoor, to take refreshment and a slight rest in the shade from the powerful sun, before engaging the Nana, who was strongly posted about two miles off.

The camp and baggage being left here under proper escort, the column again moved at 2 o'clock P.M. The Fusiliers led, followed by two

Action near Cawnpoor, on the Afternoon of the 16th of July 1857

guns, then came the 78th Highlanders, in rear of whom was the central battery under Captain Maude, the 64th and 84th had two guns more in the rear, and the regiment of Ferozepoor closed the column.

Nana Sahib had taken up a strong position at the village of Aherwa, where the grand trunk road joined that which led to Cawnpoor. His entrenchments had cut and rendered impassable both roads, and his heavy guns, seven in number, were disposed along his position, which consisted of a series of villages. Behind these the infantry, consisting of mutinous troops and his own armed followers, numbering in all about 5000, was disposed for defence.

General Havelock resolved to take the position by a flank movement. Accordingly, after a short advance along the road, the column moved off to the right, and circled round the enemy's left. As soon as the Nana perceived Havelock's intention, he pushed forward on his left a large body of horse, and opened upon the British column a fire of shot and shell from all his guns.

Havelock's troops continued their progress until the enemy's left was entirely turned, and then forming line, the British guns opened fire upon the rebels' batteries, while the infantry advanced in direct échelon of regiments from the right, covered by a wing of the Fusiliers as skirmishers. "The opportunity had now arrived," wrote General Havelock in his despatch, "for which I have long anxiously waited, of developing the prowess of the 78th Highlanders. Three guns of the enemy were strongly posted behind a lofty hamlet, well entrenched. I directed this regiment to advance, and never have I witnessed conduct more admirable. They were led by Colonel Hamilton, and followed him with surpassing steadiness and gallantry under a heavy fire. As they approached the village they cheered and charged with the bayonet, the pipers sounding the pibroch. Need I add, that the enemy fled, the village was taken, and the guns captured." Until within a few hundred yards of the guns the line advanced in perfect order and quietness, with sloped arms. Here for a few moments they lay down to allow the fierce iron storm to pass over. At the word from the General, "Rise up, advance," they sprang to their feet, and with a cheer rushed upon the battery. General Havelock followed close in behind, and when the regiment was halted in rear of the village, exclaimed, "Well done, 78th, you shall be my own regiment! Another charge like that will win the day."

Having halted here for a few minutes to take breath, the regiment pushed on at the double march to a hamlet about 500 yards distant still held by the enemy, who were quickly dislodged from it. Meanwhile, the 64th and 84th regiments advanced on the left, and captured two guns strongly posted on the enemy's original right.

Nana Sahib having withdrawn his forces in the direction of Cawnpoor, and taken up a new position in rear of his first, the British infantry now changed line to the front and rear, while the guns were brought up. This was a work of great difficulty, the ground being very heavy and the bullocks worn out with fatigue. About this time the Nana sent some of his numerous cavalry to the British flanks and rear, which did some execution before they were repulsed. The rebel infantry appeared to be in full retreat when a reserve 24-pounder was opened on the Cawnpoor road which caused considerable loss to the British force; and under cover of its fire, at the same time two large bodies of cavalry riding insolently over the plain, and the rebel infantry once more rallied. "The beating of their drums and numerous mounted officers in front announced the definitive struggle of the Nana for his usurped dominion."

But the final crisis approached. The artillery cattle being tired out could not bring up the guns to the assistance of the British; and the Madras Fusiliers, 64th, 78th, and 84th formed in line were exposed to a heavy fire from the 24-pounder on the road, and from the musketry of the rebel skirmishers. Colonel Hamilton about this time had his horse shot under him by a musket ball. The General now called upon the infantry, who were lying down in line, to rise and make another steady advance. "It was irresistible," he wrote, "the enemy sent round shot into our ranks until we were within 300 yards, and then poured in grape with great precision." The gun was more immediately in front of the 64th, which regiment suffered severely by its fire; but the line advancing steadily upon the gun, at length charged with a cheer and captured it.

The enemy now lost all heart, and after a hurried fire of musketry gave way in total rout. Four of the British guns coming up by the road completed the discomfiture by a heavy cannonade; and as it grew dark the roofless artillery barracks were dimly descried in advance, and it was evident that Cawnpoor was once more in possession of the British.

The entire loss from the action of the day was about 100 killed and wounded—that of the 78th being 3 killed and 16 wounded. Many men also died from the effects of the sun and extreme fatigue, the 78th alone losing 5 men from this cause.

An incident occurred about this time which is worth recording. By some mistake a bugler sounded the " officers' call " in rear of the 78th. The officers of the regiment immediately assembled near the general—who was standing close by—imagining that he wished to see them. On finding out the mistake, General Havelock addressed them as follows:—"Gentlemen, I am glad of having this opportunity of saying a few words to you which you may repeat to your men. I am now upwards of sixty years old; I have been forty years in the service: I have been engaged in action about seven-and-twenty times; but in the whole of my career I have never seen any

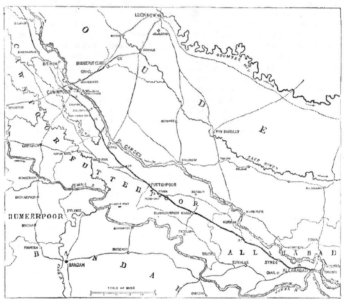

Sketch-Map to illustrate Brigadier-General Havelock's Military Operations during July and August 1857.
The numbers on the route are miles.

regiment behave better, nay more, I have never seen any one behave so well, as the 78th Highlanders this day. I am proud of you, and if ever I have the good luck to be made a major-general, the first thing I shall do, will be to go to the Duke of Cambridge and request that when my turn arrives for the colonelcy of a regiment, I may have the 78th Highlanders. And this, gentlemen, you hear from a man who is not in the habit of saying more than he means. I am not a Highlander, but I wish I was one."

The wounded were now gathered together and cared for, and the tired troops lay down for the night, when a crash that shook the earth woke them; Nana Sahib had blown up the great Cawnpoor magazine and abandoned the place.

The next morning a few troops were sent into the town, which was found to be entirely evacuated. The sight presented by the house of murder, and the well into which were thrown the mangled bodies of upwards of 200 women and children as yet scarcely cold, can never be effaced from the memories of those who witnessed it, and who, though fresh from the horrors of the battle-field, shuddered and wept at the revolting scene.

On the morning of the 17th, the force was joined by the camp and baggage, and encamped on the Cawnpoor parade-ground (where the 78th was last encamped in the year 1799), and on the 18th moved round to the western side of Cawnpoor, where General Havelock issued a stirring general order, his words burning with horror and righteous indignation at what had

taken place at Cawnpoor. "Your comrades at Lucknow are in peril," the order said, "Agra is besieged, Delhi still the focus of mutiny and rebellion. . . . Highlanders! it was my earnest desire to afford you the opportunity of showing how your predecessors conquered at Maida. You have not degenerated. Assaye was not won by a more silent, compact, and resolute charge than was the village near Jansenvoor on the 16th instant."

On the 20th of July, Brigadier General Neill arrived from Allahabad with 270 men.

Mausoleum over the Well at Cawnpoor.

Thus reinforced, Havelock began to cross the Ganges; and on the 25th, with his band of 1500, commenced his first march to relieve Lucknow, leaving General Neill to command at Cawnpoor. Though the season was that of the monsoon, and the country in a deluge, the troops took the field without tentage of any kind, getting such shelter as could be afforded by the deserted and ruined hamlets.

The strength of the 78th was 16 officers and 293 men, being the grenadiers, Nos 3, 6, and light companies.

On the 26th, the force moved forward a few miles and took up its quarter at the

village of Mungulwar, about six miles from Cawnpoor. On the morning of the 29th, it advanced to meet the rebels, who were stationed in great strength at the town of Oonao, and a small village close in front of it. The houses were surrounded by walled enclosures, every wall being loopholed, and a deep swamp protected the enemy's right.

The 78th and the 1st Madras Fusiliers, with two guns, began the attack. They drove the enemy from the gardens; but when they approached the village, where every house was loopholed, a destructive fire was opened upon them. From one house in particular the

line suffered a heavy musketry fire; Lieutenant Bogle with part of No 3 company was
ordered to attack it. He gallantly led on
the men through a narrow and strongly
defended doorway (the only means of ingress),
into a court filled with armed fanatics, but immediately on entering he fell severely wounded,
together with nearly all who had entered with
him. The defenders were ultimately overcome
by shells thrown into the house by the artillery. After an obstinate resistance, the mutineers were driven beyond the town, where they
rallied, but were soon put to flight, and their
guns taken.

After a halt of three hours the column
moved on, and in the afternoon came in sight of
Buseerutgunge, where the rebels again made
a stand. This town was walled, surrounded
by deep ditches, and had been strengthened
by earthworks. The gate in front was defended
by a round tower, mounting four heavy guns.
Behind the town was a wide nullah full of
water, crossed by a narrow causeway and
bridge.

The troops immediately deployed, the 64th
being ordered to turn the town on the left,
and penetrate between the bridge and the
enemy. The 78th and the Fusiliers advancing
on the front face, carried the earthworks and
drove out the enemy, capturing their guns. It
was now 6 P.M., and too dark, without cavalry,
to pursue the enemy through the swamps
beyond the causeway, over which the rebels
succeeded in escaping.

These two actions had cost the little force
12 killed and 76 wounded, and cholera had,
moreover, broken out. To send the sick and
wounded, numbering nearly 300, back to
Cawnpoor would have required an escort which
could not be spared, and Lucknow was still 36
miles away. Without reinforcements General
Havelock found the relief impossible, he therefore fell back to Mungulwar, which he reached
on the morning of the 31st. Here he remained
entrenched awaiting reinforcements from Cawnpoor, whither all the sick and wounded were
sent.

Brigadier-General Neill having thrown up
a strong entrenchment at Cawnpoor, sent over
all the men whom he could spare to Havelock,
who, with his force thus again increased to

about 1400 men, commenced on the 4th of
August his second march to relieve Lucknow.
The enemy were found on the following day
occupying their old position at Buseerutgunge.
They were driven from the town in confusion
and with severe loss, by Maude's battery, the
78th, and the Sikhs, and also from a position
which they had taken up across the nullah.
Their loss was supposed to be about 300,
that of the British being 2 killed and 23
wounded; Colonel Hamilton's charger was
killed under him.

The British force being again diminished by
sickness and the sword, General Havelock
was compelled to retire upon his old position
at Mungulwar. It was the only course he
could pursue, as to advance to Lucknow with
the small force at his command was to court
annihilation, and as a consequence the certain
destruction of the British garrison at Lucknow. Preparations were therefore made to
recross the river to Cawnpoor, which was now
threatened on all sides by the Dinapoor mutineers, the Gwalior contingent, and Nana Sahib
at Bithoor. Perceiving Havelock's intention
a large force of the enemy assembled at
Oonao, with the design of attacking the
British position at Mungulwar, or of annoying the force during its passage of the Ganges.
To obviate this the general moved out to
meet the mutineers in the morning of the
11th of August, after sending his force, now
reduced to about 1000 men, and all his baggage
and stores across the river. On Havelock's force
reaching Oonao, the enemy's advanced posts
fell back, and it bivouacked during the night
near the town.

On advancing the next day (July 29th) the
enemy were descried drawn up at the village of
Boorbeek Chowkey, about a mile from Buseerutgunge. Their centre rested on the village, and
their guns were conveniently placed behind a
series of high mounds, forming strong natural
defences, which they had scarped and otherwise
artificially improved. The British troops deployed, and, covered by artillery fire and
skirmishers, advanced in direct échelon of
battalions from the right, receiving, as they
came within range of the enemy's batteries,
a deadly fire of shell, grape, and round shot,
which was aimed with greater precision than

had hitherto been manifested by their artillery-men anywhere. The British guns on the right having sufficiently advanced to get a flanking fire on the enemy's line, the 78th charged a battery of three guns on the enemy's left, captured two of the guns, and turning them on the retreating hosts, pounded them with their own shell and grape, putting them completely to rout. At the same time the Madras Fusiliers repulsed a strong demonstration made by the enemy's cavalry on the right. The loss of the British in the action was 140 killed and wounded.

Having rested for two hours on the field, the column slowly retired to Mungulwar, and on the following morning, August 13th, re-crossed the Ganges to Cawnpoor, having been in the field, in an Indian monsoon, without tents, for twenty-three days, during which it had four times met and defeated the enemy.

In these four engagements the 78th lost 6 men killed and 2 officers, Lieutenant and Adjutant Macpherson and Lieutenant Bogle, and 6 men wounded. To Lieutenant Crowe of the 78th the Victoria Cross was subsequently awarded, as having been the first man to enter the battery at Boorbeck Chowkey, where the two guns were captured.

The regiment was joined at Cawnpoor by Colonel Stisted, Captain Archer, and No. 4 Company.

Early on the morning of the 16th of August the movable column marched against Bithoor, the residence of Nana Sahib, about 14 miles from Cawnpoor. About noon the column came in sight of the enemy, numbering in all, infantry and cavalry, about 4000, strongly posted. General Havelock called it "one of the strongest positions in India." The plain in front of the enemy's position was covered with thick sugar-cane plantations, which reached high above the heads of the men, and their batteries were defended by thick ramparts flanked by entrenched quadrangles. The whole position was again flanked by other villages and comprehended the town of Bithoor.

The enemy having opened upon the advancing British force a continued shower of shot and shell, and as the British guns made no impression upon them, it was resolved to have recourse to the bayonet, and a simultaneous advance of the line was ordered. While the Fusiliers moved upon the flanking villages, the 78th advanced upon the batteries, alternately lying down and moving on, as the volleys of grape issued from the enemy's guns. The rebels awaited the approach of the advancing men until the foremost entered the works, when they fled in confusion. The British troops pursued the enemy into and through the town, but being completely knocked up by exposure to the fierce sun, and by the great fatigue they had undergone, could follow the retreating rebels no further, and bivouacked on the ground they had won.

The 78th had in this affair only Captain Mackenzie and 10 men wounded, though several men died of cholera, which had again broken out.

The next morning the force returned to Cawnpoor, and took up a position on the plain of Subada, where General Havelock issued a commendatory and stirring note, in which he told the small force that it "would be acknow-ledged to have been the prop and stay of British India in the time of her severest trial."

During the next month the force rested at Cawnpoor, while reinforcements gradually arrived. Immediately on crossing the Ganges cholera broke out, and carried off a great number of the little band. The headquarters of the 78th lost from this cause alone 1 officer, Captain Campbell, and 43 men. The strength of the regiment was still further reduced by the departure of 1 officer and 56 men, sick and wounded, to Allahabad. At the end of the month, however, the five companies that had been left behind, and the detachment that came from Chinsurah by the steamer route, joined headquarters from Allahabad

In the middle of September the regiment was supplied with Enfield rifles, but there was little time left for giving the men any instruction in the use of that weapon.

The force despatched from England to assist in the Chinese war (the 23rd, 82nd, 90th, and 93rd Regiments) had been stopped at Singapore and brought to Calcutta. The 37th Regiment also arrived from Ceylon, and the 5th from Mauritius. Of these regiments, the 5th and 90th were immediately on arrival sent up the country, and reached Cawnpoor in the beginning of September. Sir James Outram also arrived at this time, having been appointed to the military command of the Cawnpoor and Dinapoor divisions.

A bridge of boats was thrown across the Ganges, and every preparation made for another attempt to relieve Lucknow, the garrison of which was still successfully and heroically holding out. On the 16th of September, Sir James Outram issued a division order, in which he generously resigned to Major-General Havelock the honour of leading on the force intended to make a second attempt to relieve Lucknow. This Sir James did "in gratitude for, and in admiration of the brilliant deeds in arms achieved by General Havelock and his gallant troops." Sir James was to accompany the force as a volunteer, and on the relief of Lucknow would resume his position at the head of the forces.

The army of relief was divided into two brigades of infantry and one of artillery, as follows :—First brigade of infantry, under Brigadier-General Neill, consisted of the 5th Fusiliers, 84th Regiment, 1st Madras Fusiliers, and 100 men of the 64th Regiment. Second brigade of infantry, under Colonel Walter Hamilton of the 78th, consisted of the 78th Highlanders under Colonel Stisted, 90th light infantry, and the Sikh regiment of Ferozepoor. The Artillery brigade, under Major Cooper, R.A., consisted of the batteries of Captain Maude, Captain Olphert, and Brevet-Major Eyre. The volunteer cavalry, a few irregulars, under Captain Barrow, and a small body of Engineers, accompanied the forces. The entire force was under the command of Brigadier-General Havelock, accompanied, as we have stated, by Major-General Outram as a volunteer.

The entrenchment at Cawnpoor having been completed was garrisoned by the 64th regiment under Colonel Wilson.

On the 18th of September an advance party, consisting of No. 8 and the Light Company of the 78th, the Sikh regiment, and four guns under Major M'Intyre of the 78th, was pushed across the river to form a *tête-de-pont* to enable the bridge to be completed on the enemy's side of the river. The men were exposed during the day to a skirmishing fire from the enemy, who also opened a few guns upon them from a distance, but with little effect. During the day these companies were relieved by Nos. 6 and 7 of the 78th, and Major Haliburton took command of the advanced party. Before daybreak on the 19th, this party, which was stationed all night on a dry sandbank in the middle of the Ganges, pushed quietly across the intervening islands to the mainland, in order to cover the advance of the force, which crossed with little opposition, the rebel army, after a slight show of resistance, retiring on their entrenched position about three miles off, towards Mungulwar.

The strength of the force amounted to about 3000, that of the 78th being 26 officers and 523 men ; Colonel Walter Hamilton being Brigadier, Colonel Stisted commanded the regiment.

On the morning of September 21st, the advance on Lucknow commenced, and the enemy's position was soon reached near Mungulwar, which for some weeks they had been busily employed in fortifying. The position, however, was soon carried, the enemy rapidly pursued, and many of them cut up by the British cavalry ; four guns and a colour were captured. The British loss was merely nominal.

Rain now commenced to pour in monsoon torrents, and hardly ceased for three days. Through it the force pushed in column of route over the well-known scenes of their former struggles, by Busseerutgunge and the village of Bunnee, when, about 2 o'clock in the afternoon of the 23rd, the enemy were descried in a strong position in the neighbourhood of Lucknow. The head of the column at first suffered from the fire of the enemy's guns as it was compelled to pass along the trunk road between morasses ; but these passed, the force quickly deployed into line, and the 2nd brigade advancing through a sheet of water drove back the right of the mutinous army, while the 1st Brigade attacked it in front. Victory soon declared for the British force, which captured five guns. The enemy's cavalry, however, 1500 strong, creeping through lofty cultivation, made a sudden irruption on the baggage in the rear of the relieving force, inflicting some loss on the detachment of the 90th that was guarding it. In this engagement the 78th lost 1 man killed and 6 wounded.

The British passed the night of the 23rd on the ground they had won, exposed, however, to a cannonade from the enemy's guns. On the morning of the 24th, their fire inflicted such loss on the British force, especially the 78th, which had 4 men killed and 11 wounded by it, that the General, having determined to halt this day to obtain rest previous to the attack on the city, found it necessary to retire the left brigade out of reach of the guns.

The 24th was spent in removing all the baggage and tents, camp-followers, sick and wounded, into the Alum Bagh, which, on the advance being made next day, was left in charge of Major M'Intyre of the 78th, with a detachment of 280 Europeans, some Sikhs, and 4 guns. Of these, Major M'Intyre, Lieutenant Walsh, and 71 non-commissioned officers and men, besides 34 sick and wounded, belonged to the 78th.

A short description of the desperate position of those whom Havelock hoped to rescue may not be out of place here.

In the month of June (1857), most of the native regiments at Lucknow, as elsewhere, having broken out into open mutiny, the Residency and a strong fort in the city called Muchee Bhorwan, were put in a state of defence for the protection of the Europeans. On the 30th of June, the garrison, consisting of 300 of H.M.'s 32nd Regiment, and a few Native infantry, cavalry, and artillery, marched out to Chinhut to meet a rebel army which was marching upon Lucknow; but the native gunners proved traitors, overturned the guns, cut the traces, and then deserted to the enemy. The remainder of the force thus exposed to a vastly superior fire, and completely outflanked, was compelled to make a disastrous retreat, with the loss of 3 guns and a great number killed and wounded.

The force being thus diminished the Muchee Bhorwan had to be evacuated. On the night of the 1st of July it was blown up, and the troops marched into the Residency, the investment of which the enemy now completed; and for three months the brave garrison had to undergo a siege regarding which the Governor-General of India justly writes, "There dou

not stand in the annals of war an achievement more truly heroic than the defence of the Residency of Lucknow."

This brave handful had heard through spies of the frightful tragedy of Cawnpoor; the dangers multiplied; the provisions were failing; more than 300 of the men had been killed, and many more had succumbed to disease, when the joyful sound of the British guns at the Alum Bagh, on the 23d of September, announced to them that relief was at hand.

And now came the rescue. On the morning of the 25th of September, General Havelock's force advanced from the Alum Bagh.

The enemy had taken up an exceedingly strong position at the village of Char Bagh, on the city side of the canal, the bridge over which was defended by several guns in position; they also occupied in force numerous gardens and walled enclosures on one side of the canal, from which they poured a most destructive musketry fire on the advancing troops.

The 1st brigade led, accompanied by Captain Maude's battery, and after a desperate resistance, in which one-third of the British artillerymen fell, they succeeded in storming the bridge of Char Bagh and capturing the guns, supported by the 2nd brigade, which now moved to the front, and occupying the houses on both sides of the street, bayoneted the defenders, throwing the slain in heaps on the roadside.

From this point the direct road to the Residency through the city was something less than two miles; but it was known to have been cut by trenches and crossed by barricades at short intervals, all the houses, moreover, being loopholed. Progress in this direction was impossible; so, the 78th Highlanders being left to hold the position until the entire force, with ammunition, stores, &c., had passed, the united column pushed on, detouring to the right along a narrow road which skirted the left bank of the canal. The advance was not seriously impeded until the force came opposite the Kaiser Bagh, or King's Palace, where two guns and a body of mercenary troops were entrenched, who opened a heavy fire of grape and musketry. The artillery with the column had to pass a bridge exposed to this fire, but

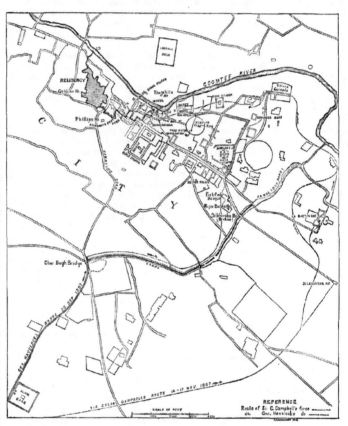

Plan illustrative of the Operations for the Relief of Lucknow in September and November 1857.

they were then shrouded by the buildings adjacent to the palace of the Furrah Buksh.

In the meantime the 78th was engaged in a hot conflict. As soon as the enemy perceived the deviation made by the main body, and that only a small force was left at the bridge of the Char Bagh, they returned in countless numbers to annoy the Highlanders. Two companies, Nos. 7 and 8, under Captains Hay and Hastings, were sent to occupy the more advanced buildings of the village; four companies were sent out as skirmishers in the surrounding gardens; and the remainder, in reserve, were posted in the buildings near the bridge.

The lane out of which the force had marched was very narrow and much cut up by the passage of the heavy guns, so that it was a work of great difficulty to convey the line of commissariat carts and cattle along it, and in a few hours the 78th was separated from the main body by a distance of some miles. The enemy now brought down two guns to within 500 yards of the position of the 78th, and opened a very destructive fire of shot and shell upon the advanced companies, while the whole regiment was exposed to a heavy musketry fire. This becoming insupportable, it was determined to capture the guns at the point of the bayonet. The two advanced companies, under Captains Hay and Hastings, and Lieutenants Webster and Swanson, formed upon the road, and by a gallant charge up the street captured the first gun, which, being sent to the rear was hurled into the canal. In the meantime the skirmishing companies had been called in, and they, together with the reserve, advanced to the support of Nos. 7 and 8. The united regiment now pushed on towards the second gun, which was still annoying it from a more retired position. A second charge resulted in its capture, but as there was some difficulty in bringing it away, and it being necessary to retire immediately on the bridge to keep open the communications, which were being threatened by the hosts who surrounded the regiment, the gun was spiked, and the 78th fell back upon the bridge, carrying with them numbers of wounded, and leaving many dead on the road. In the charge Lieutenant Swanson was severely wounded.

The entire line of carts, &c., having now passed, the regiment evacuated the position and bridge of the Char Bagh, and forming the rear-guard of the force, proceeded along the narrow lane taken by the column on the left bank of the canal. The rebels immediately seized the bridge, crossed it, and lined the right bank of the canal, where they were protected by a wall, from behind which they poured a galling musketry fire, and placing a gun upon the bridge, enfiladed the road along which the route of the 78th lay; thus the regiment was almost completely surrounded, and had to stand and protect its rear at every step. Captain Hastings was severely wounded, while making a brave stand with No. 8 company against the advancing mass of rebels; Captain Lockhart and a large number of men were also wounded here.

A report having been sent to the general that the 78th was hard pressed, the volunteer cavalry and a company of the 90th Regiment were sent back to its assistance; the lane, however, was too narrow for cavalry to work in, and they suffered severely. At length a point was reached, near Major Banks's house, where four roads meet; the 78th had no guide, the main body was far out of sight, and all that could be ascertained regarding the locality was that the turning to the left, which evidently led into the city, was the direct road to the Residency. The force therefore followed that route, which led through a street of fine houses loopholed and occupied by the rebels, to the gate of the Kaiser Bagh, or King's Palace, where it came in reverse upon the battery which was firing upon the main body near the Motee Mahul. After spiking the guns, the force pushed on under the walls of the Kaiser Bagh, and after being exposed to another shower of musketry from its entire length, the little column, consisting of the 78th and cavalry, about four o'clock in the afternoon, joined the main body near the entrance to the Furrah Buksh, where for a short time it obtained rest.

From this point the Residency was about half a mile distant, and as darkness was coming on, it was deemed most important to reach the Residency that night.

The 78th Highlanders and the regiment of Ferozepore were now directed to advance. "This column," wrote General Havelock in his despatch, " pushed on with a desperate gallantry, led by Sir James Outram and myself and staff, through streets of flat-roofed, loopholed houses, from which a perpetual fire was kept up, and overcoming every obstacle, established itself within the enclosure of the Residency. The joy of the garrison may be more easily conceived than described. But it was not till the next evening that the whole of my troops, guns, tumbrils, and sick and wounded, continually exposed to the attacks of the enemy, could be brought step by step within the *enceinte* and the adjacent palace of the Furrah Buksh. To form an adequate idea of the obstacles overcome, reference must be made to the events that are known to have occurred at Buenos Ayres and Saragossa."

Lieutenant Kirby was mortally wounded in this advance, while gallantly waving the Queen's colour which he had carried throughout the action. On his fall, Sergeant Reid of the grenadier company seized the colour and carried it for some distance, when assistant-surgeon M°Master took it from him, and carried it up to near the Residency gate, where he handed it over to Colour-sergeant Christie, by whom it was brought into the Residency. The regimental colour was carried throughout the day by Ensign Tweedie, 4th Bengal Native Infantry, who was attached to the regiment. Lieutenant Webster was killed within 200 yards of the gate; Lieutenant Crowe and Lieutenant and Adjutant Macpherson were wounded, and 2 officers attached to the regiment—Lieutenant Joly of the 32nd Regiment, and Lieutenant Grant of the Bengal army—were also wounded, the former mortally.

Early the next morning a party was sent out under Captain R. Bogle, of the 78th, to assist in bringing in the wounded, who had been left with the 90th Regiment and heavy guns in the Motee Mahul. While performing this duty Captain Bogle received a severe wound, of which he died two months afterwards.

A request for reinforcements having been sent by Major Haliburton of the 78th, who now commanded the troops at the Motee Mahul (his two seniors having fallen), the 5th regiment and part of the Sikhs were sent to assist him. In the forenoon another party was sent, consisting of 50 men of the 78th, under Captain Lockhart and Lieutenant Barker, who occupied the house called "Martin's House," on the bank of the Goomtee, which secured the communication between the palaces and the Motee Mahul. Here they were exposed during the whole day to a hot cannonade, until towards evening the house was a complete ruin.

In the meantime the wounded men were conveyed from the Motee Mahul under charge of their medical officers, Surgeons Jee of the 78th, and Home of the 90th, who had gallantly remained with them under the heavy fire to which they had been exposed for many hours. Some of them, with the former officer, reached the Residency in safety, but those under charge

of Surgeon Home were misled by a civilian, who had kindly volunteered to show the way. The enemy surrounded them; the doolie bearers fled, and the small escort, with a few wounded officers and men, took refuge in a neighbouring house, where during the whole day and night they were closely besieged by a large body of rebels, numbering from 500 to 1000, against whom the escort defended themselves and their wounded comrades in a most heroic manner. Those of the wounded, however, who were unable to leave their doolie, fell into the hands of the enemy, and were put to death with horrible tortures, some of them being burned alive. Lieutenant Swanson was one of the wounded of the 78th who were saved, but not until he had received two fresh wounds, one of which proved mortal. Privates James Halliwell, Richard Baker, and William Peddington of the 78th, were among those few gallant men who fought against such unequal odds. The first-named was rewarded with the Victoria Cross, as were also Surgeon Home of the 90th and two men of other regiments. The party was most fortunately saved from this perilous situation on the following morning, as will appear in the sequel.

After the wounded and commissariat stores had left the Motee Mahul by the river bank, it was found impossible to take the heavy guns by that way, and the only practicable route for them being the high road which ran through the enemy's position to the Furrah Buksh palace, it was resolved to attempt to bring them in by that route under cover of the night. The remainder of the 78th, under Colonel Stisted, was sent out from the Residency about sunset on the 26th to assist in this operation, together with two guns under Captain Olpherts, and some irregular cavalry. The 5th, and part of the Sikh Regiment had already been sent there in the early part of the day.

At three o'clock on the morning of the 27th the column was formed in perfect silence, the 78th leading, and the remainder following, with heavy guns and ammunition in the centre; the Sikhs covered each flank. Thus formed, the whole force proceeded undiscovered up to the enemy's posts. The leading division had nearly reached the palace when the alarm was given by the enemy's sentries, bugles sounded the "assembly," and confusion reigned in the rebel camp. The British soldiers now raised a cheer, and rushed on the opposing force into their own line of works, losing only 1 officer and 2 men killed, and 1 officer and 9 men wounded—2 of the latter belonging to the 78th.

The route of this little force fortunately lay through the square where, as above mentioned, a few men were heroically defending their wounded comrades in a most critical situation, and they were thus saved at a most opportune moment.

The relief of the Lucknow garrison having been thus gloriously accomplished, Sir James Outram resumed his position as the commander of the troops, and in an Order (dated the 26th of September 1857) he bears just and high testimony to the bravery and heroism of the troops and their leader, who thus accomplished a feat unsurpassed in history. Among the regiments specially mentioned in the Order is "the 78th Highlanders, who led the advance on the Residency, headed by their brave commander, Colonel Stisted."

In effecting the relief the army lost 535 in killed, wounded, and missing. The loss fell heaviest on the 78th, which throughout the day was exposed to more fighting than the rest of the force. This regiment alone lost 122 killed and wounded; 2 officers and 39 men being killed, and 8 officers and 73 men wounded, out of 18 officers and 428 men who left the Alum Bagh on the 25th. Besides the officers already named, Lieutenant Crowe was wounded.

The Victoria Cross was subsequently awarded to Lieutenant and Adjutant Macpherson, for "distinguished conduct in setting an example of heroic gallantry to the men of the regiment at the period of the action in which they captured two brass 9-pounders at the point of the bayonet."

The Victoria Cross was also conferred upon the regiment as a body, which was required to nominate one individual to wear it as its representative. On a vote being taken, it was almost unanimously agreed that it should be given to Assistant-Surgeon M'Master, upon whom accordingly it was conferred, "for the intrepidity with which he exposed himself to the fire of the enemy in bringing in and attend-

ing to the wounded on the 25th of September at Lucknow."

In addition to these, a Victoria Cross was conferred upon Colour-sergeant Stewart Macpherson and Private Henry Ward of the light company.

On the 26th the enemy were cleared away from the rear of the position, and on the 27th the palace, extending along the line of the river from the Residency to near the Kaiser Bagh, was also cleared and taken possession of for the accommodation of the troops.

At daylight on the 29th three columns, aggregating 700 men, attacked the enemy's works at three different points, destroyed the guns, and blew up the houses which afforded positions to the enemy for musketry fire. One of the columns was composed of 20 men of the 32nd Regiment, 140 men of the 78th (under Captains Lockhart and Hay, and Lieutenants Cassidy and Barker), and the 1st Madras Fusiliers.

The column fell in and filed out of the breach in the Sikh Square at daybreak, the advance consisting of the 32nd and the 78th, the Madras Fusiliers being in reserve. They formed silently under cover of some broken ground, and made a sudden dash upon the first gun, which was taken by the 32nd with a cheer, and burst by an artilleryman. The 78th, led by Captain Lockhart, who was slightly wounded, then charged a gun up a street leading to the right; the covering party of the first gun and a considerable body of the enemy rallied round this gun, which was twice fired as the regiment advanced up the lane. Sergeant James Young, of the 78th, the first man at the gun, bayoneted one of the enemy's gunners while reloading for the third discharge, and was severely wounded by a sword-cut. The rest of the gunners were shot or cut down, and some who had taken refuge in an adjoining house were destroyed by means of hand-grenades thrown in by the windows. Proceeding further, the regiment captured a small gun and some wall-pieces, which were brought in, the large gun being blown up. The position was retained while the engineers made preparations for blowing up the houses which it was deemed advisable to destroy; these being ready, the columns retired into the entrenchment, and the explosions took place. The loss of the 78th on this day was 1 man killed, and 1 officer and 8 men wounded.

Brigadier-General Neill having been killed on the 25th of September 1857, Colonel Stisted was appointed brigadier of the 1st brigade, and Major Haliburton assumed command of the regiment.

After the heavy loss sustained by the relieving force in pushing its way through the enemy, it was clearly impossible to carry off the sick, wounded, women, and children (amounting to not fewer than 1500) through five miles of disputed suburb; the want of carriage alone rendering it an impossibility. It was therefore necessary for the now considerably increased garrison to maintain itself in its present position on reduced rations until reinforcements should advance to its relief. Brigadier Inglis retained command of the old Lucknow garrison, reinforced by the volunteer cavalry, Madras Fusiliers, and a detachment of the 78th; while General Havelock commanded the field force that occupied the palaces and outposts.

One of the enemy's batteries, known as Phillip's Battery, still remained in a strong position close to the Residency, and continued to annoy the garrison by its fire; its capture, therefore, became necessary, and a force, consisting in all of 568 men, of which the 78th formed a part, was placed at the disposal of Colonel Napier, of the Bengal Engineers, on the 1st of October. On the afternoon of that day the column formed on the road leading to the Pyne Bagh, and advancing to some houses near the Jail, drove the enemy away from them and from a barricade, under a sharp musketry fire. The column having to work its way through strongly barricaded houses, it was late before a point was reached from which the enemy's position could be commanded. This having been obtained, and it being found, on reconnoitring, that the battery was in a high position, scarped, and quite inaccessible without ladders, it was determined to defer the assault till daylight. The position gained having been duly secured and loopholed, the men occupied the buildings for the night, and were subjected to a heavy fire from the battery.

On the morning of the 2nd the troops advanced, covered by a fire of artillery from the Residency entrenchment. A severe fire was opened from a barricade which flanked the battery on the right; but this being turned, the troops advanced and drove the enemy from the battery, capturing the guns, which had been withdrawn to some distance, and driving off the enemy, who defended them with musketry and grape. The guns having been destroyed, and Phillip's house blown up, the troops withdrew to their position of the previous night, the 78th having lost 1 man killed and 3 wounded.

The command of this sallying party now fell to Major Haliburton of the 78th, who, under instructions from the general, commenced on the 3rd of October to work from house to house with crowbar and pickaxe, with a view to the possibility of adapting the Cawnpoor road as the line of communication with the Alum Bagh. On the 4th, Major Haliburton was mortally wounded and his successor disabled. On the 6th the proceedings were relinquished, and the troops gradually withdrew to the post at the junction of the Cawnpoor road and Main Street, which was occupied by the 78th Highlanders, and retained by that regiment as a permanent outpost during the two months' blockade which ensued.

The regiment being greatly reduced, both in officers and men, the ten companies were told off into four divisions, each under the command of an officer—Captain Hay, Lieutenants Cassidy, Finlay, and Barker. The position was divided into three different posts, each defended by one of these divisions, the fourth being in reserve. By this arrangement, each man was on guard for three days and nights out of four, and on the fourth day was generally employed on a working party in erecting the defences.

Everything was now done by the garrison to strengthen its position; barricades were erected at all available points, the defences of the Residency were improved, and all the palaces and buildings occupied by the field force were put into a state of defence. One of the greatest dangers that the besieged had to apprehend was from the enemy's mines, which threatened the position of the British from every possible quarter, thus requiring the garrison to be continually on the alert, and to be constantly employed in countermining. In this the garrison was very successful, the underground attempts of the besiegers being outwitted on almost every hand, and many of their mines frequently destroyed. The outpost of the 78th, under Captain Lockhart (who on the death of Major Haliburton took command of the regiment, and held it during the rest of the siege), was vigorously assailed by these means by the enemy; but they were completely outwitted by some of the soldiers of the 78th (who volunteered for this work, for which they received extra pay at the rate of 10s. per diem), directed by Lieutenant Hutchinson, of the Bengal Engineers, and Lieutenant Tulloch, Acting Engineer.

The enemy kept so persistently sinking shafts and driving galleries towards the position occupied by the 78th, that in order to countermine them five shafts were sunk at several angles of the position, from each of which numerous galleries were driven, of a total length of 600 feet. Indeed, in regard to the mining operations in connection with the siege of Lucknow, Sir James Outram wrote, " I am aware of no parallel to our series of mines in modern war; 21 shafts, aggregating 200 feet in depth, and 3291 feet of gallery, have been erected. The enemy advanced 20 mines against the palace and outposts."

The post of the 78th was all this time exposed by day and night to a ceaseless fire of shot, shell, and musketry, and scarcely a day passed in which some casualty did not occur. The outer walls of the houses forming the post were reduced to ruins by round shot, and sharpshooters occupied the houses around to within 50 yards, watching for their prey. All the other regiments were similarly situated during the two months' blockade.

The rations had now for some time been reduced to one-half, and the troops, having left everything behind them at the Alum Bagh, had nothing to wear but the clothes they wore on entering. At length, however, tidings of relief arrived.

Sir Colin Campbell arrived at the Alum Bagh on the 12th of November with about 700 cavalry, 2700 infantry, and some artillery (being chiefly troops which had been engaged in the siege of Delhi), after having a smart skirmish

at Buntera, where Captain Mackenzie of the 78th was a second time wounded; that officer, with Lieutenant-Colonel Hamilton, Captain Archer, and several men of the 78th, having accompanied the relieving force. Changing the garrison of the Alum Bagh, where the 75th Regiment was left, Sir Colin Campbell formed a battalion of detachments of the 7th Fusiliers, the 64th and 78th Regiments, numbering in all about 400 men, of whom 118 belonged to the 78th, with Lieutenant-Colonel M'Intyre, Captain Archer, and Lieutenant Walsh, the battalion being commanded by Lieut.-Colonel Henry Hamilton of the 78th.

The commander-in-chief being further joined by a reinforcement of about 700 men (of the 23rd Fusiliers and 82nd Regiment), advanced from the Alum Bagh in the direction of Dilkhoosha Park, and after a running fight of about two hours, the enemy were driven through the park of the Martinière beyond the canal. The Dilkhoosha and Martinière were both occupied, and all baggage being left at the former place in charge of the regiment, the advance on Secundur Bagh commenced early on the 16th. This place, as well as the Shah Nujeef, was taken in the most gallant manner, the 93rd Highlanders forming part of the attacking force.

In the meantime Havelock's force had been employed in digging trenches and erecting batteries in a large garden held by the 90th Regiment; these were concealed by a lofty wall, under which several mines were driven for the purpose of blowing it down when the moment for action should arrive. It was determined by the general, that as soon as the commander-in-chief should reach Secundur Bagh, this wall should be blown in by the miners, and that the batteries should open on the insurgent defences in front, when the troops were to storm the three buildings known as the Hera Khanah, or Deer House, the Steam Engine House, and the King's Stables.

On the morning of the 16th, all the troops that could be spared from the defences were formed in the square of the Chuttur Munzil; at 11 A.M. the mines under the wall were sprung, and the batteries opened an overwhelming fire, which lasted for three hours, on the buildings beyond. When the breaches were declared practicable, the troops were brought up to the front through the trenches, and lay down before the batteries until the firing should cease, and the signal be given to advance. The storming parties were five in number, with nearly 800 men in all, each accompanied by an engineer officer and a working party. A reserve of 200 men, part of whom belonged to the 78th, under Major Hay of that regiment, remained in the palace square. The 78th storming party, 150 strong, was commanded by Captain Lockhart, and the working party by Lieutenant Barker, accompanied by an engineer officer.

The guns having ceased firing at half-past three in the afternoon, the bugle sounded the advance. "It is impossible," wrote General Havelock, "to describe the enthusiasm with which the signal was received by the troops. Pent up, inactive, for upwards of six weeks, and subjected to constant attacks, they felt that the hour of retribution and glorious exertion had returned. Their cheers echoed through the courts of the palace, responsive to the bugle sound, and on they rushed to assured victory. The enemy could nowhere withstand them. In a few minutes the whole of their buildings were in our possession."

Guns were mounted on the newly occupied post, and the force retired to its quarters. On the following day the newly-erected batteries opened fire upon the Tara Kotee (or Observatory) and the Mess House, while Sir Colin Campbell's artillery battered them from the opposite direction. In the afternoon these and the intermediate buildings were occupied by the relieving force, and the relief of the besieged garrison was accomplished.

All arrangements having been made for the silent and orderly evacuation of the Residency and palaces hitherto occupied by General Havelock's troops, the retreat commenced at midnight on the 22nd, and was carried out most successfully in perfect silence, the 78th Highlanders forming the rear-guard. When the 78th reached the last palace square, Sir James Outram, who was riding with it, halted the regiment for a few moments, and in a low but clear voice addressed to them a few words, saying that he had selected the 78th for the honour of covering the retire-

ment of the force, as they had had the post of honour, in advance, on entering to relieve the garrison, and none were more worthy of the post of honour in leaving it. The evacuation was so successfully accomplished, and the enemy were so completely deceived by the movements of the British force, that they did not attempt to follow, but, on the contrary, kept firing on the old position many hours after its evacuation.

The entire force reached the Dilkhoosha Park at four o'clock on the morning of the 23rd. Here the army sustained a great loss by the death of the brave and noble-minded Sir Henry Havelock, K C B, who died of dysentery brought on by the severe privations of the campaign.

Lieutenant-Colonel Hamilton's battalion of detachments was broken up, and that part of it belonging to the 78th joined the headquarters of the regiment, that officer assuming the command. For their services in Sir Colin Campbell's force, Lieutenants-Colonel H Hamilton and M'Intyre received the thanks of the Governor-General, and were afterwards created Companions of the Bath.

Between the 26th of September and the 22nd of November, the 78th lost in the defence of Lucknow 9 men killed, and 5 officers and 42 men wounded, the names of the officers were, Major Haliburton, Captain Bogle, Assistant-Surgeon M'Master, Captain Lockhart, Lieutenant Swanson, and Lieutenant Barker. The two first mentioned and Lieutenant Swanson, besides 27 men, died of their wounds during these two months.

As might be expected, Sir James Outram in his despatches spoke in the very highest terms of the conduct of the troops during this trying period, and the Governor-General in Council offered his hearty thanks to Brigadiers Hamilton and Stisted, and Captains Bouverie and Lockhart of the 78th, for their efficient co-operation. General Havelock's force was rewarded by a donation of twelve months' batta, which reward was also conferred on the original garrison of Lucknow. Colonel Walter Hamilton and Surgeon Jee of the 78th were made C B's, the former receiving the distinguished service pension of L 100 per annum, and the latter the Victoria

Cross; Captain Lockhart was made a Brevet-Major.

Mention should be made of the occupation and defence of the post at the Alum Bagh under Lieutenant-Colonel M'Intyre of the 78th, from the 25th of September until the arrival of Sir Colin Campbell's force. That officer, it may be remembered, was appointed to the command of the Alum Bagh, with detachments of regiments of about 200 Europeans, with some Sikhs, and foreigners. In it were placed the sick and wounded of the force, amounting to 128 (of whom 64 were wounded), the baggage, commissariat and ordnance stores. The native followers left them amounted to nearly 5000, and there was an enormous number of cattle of various descriptions. Though closely besieged by the enemy, and suffering greatly at first from scarcity of provisions, the small force held gallantly out until relieved, with a loss of only one European killed and two wounded during the 49 days' siege. For this service Lieutenant-Colonel M'Intyre received the special thanks of the Government.

On the afternoon of the 25th of November the whole force under Sir Colin Campbell encamped in the plain to the south of the Alum Bagh. On the 27th, the commander-in-chief moved off with General Grant's division in the direction of Cawnpoor, which was threatened by the Gwalior contingent, leaving Sir James Outram's division, now numbering 4000 men of all arms, to retain a defensive position at the Alum Bagh, with a view of keeping in check the masses of Lucknow rebels. Sir James took up a strong position, fortifications being erected at every possible point, and the force at his command being disposed in the most advantageous manner. The circuit of the entire position was nearly ten miles, and here the force remained for the next three months (December, January, and February), while Sir Colin Campbell, after retaking Cawnpoor, was engaged in recovering the Doab, and making preparations for a final assault upon the city of Lucknow. The numbers of the enemy daily increased in front of Sir James Outram's position, until they amounted to little less than 100,000. The unceasing activity of the enemy kept Outram's force continually on the alert.

Towards the end of December, Sir James learned that the enemy contemplated surrounding his position and cutting off supplies, and with that object had despatched to Guilee a force which took up a position between that village and Budroop, which places are about a mile distant from each other, and were about three miles to the right front of the British position. This force, on the evening of December 21st, amounted to about 4000 infantry, 400 cavalry, and 4 field guns.

Sir James moved out at 5 o'clock on the morning of the 22nd, with a force composed of 6 guns, 190 cavalry, 1227 infantry under Colonel Stisted of the 78th, including 156 of the 78th under Captain Lockhart. Notwithstanding the very unequal odds, the enemy were completely and brilliantly repulsed on all hands, 4 guns, and 12 waggons filled with ammunition being captured. In his Division Order of the next day Sir James Outram said, "The right column, under command of Lieutenant-Colonel Purnell, 90th Regiment, consisting of detachments of the 78th and 90th Regiments and Sikhs, excited his admiration by the gallant way in which, with a cheer, they dashed at a strong position held by the enemy, and from which they were met by a heavy fire, regardless of the overwhelming numbers, and 6 guns reported to be posted there. The suddenness of the attack, and the spirited way in which it was executed, resulted in the immediate flight of the enemy, with hardly a casualty on our side." In the same order, Sir James thanked Lieutenant-Colonel H. Hamilton for the manner in which he commanded the reserve, and Brigadiers Hamilton (78th) and Eyre, who had charge of the camp, for the way in which they kept the enemy in check.

After this successful repulse the enemy did not again attempt to surround the position, but continued day after day to make attacks upon it from their position in front. Want of space forbids us to give details of these attacks, every one of which, notwithstanding the overwhelming numbers of the rebels, was most brilliantly repulsed with but little loss to the British.

"Thus was this position before Lucknow held for three months by Sir James Outram's division, his troops being continually called on to repel threatened attacks, and frequently employed in defending the numerous picquets and outposts, all of which were exposed to the fire of the enemy's batteries."

The casualties of the 78th during this defence were only 8 men wounded.

On the 26th of January 1858, the 2nd brigade was paraded to witness the presentation of six good-conduct medals to men of the 78th Highlanders, on which occasion Sir James Outram addressed the regiment in terms in which, probably, no other regiment in the British army was ever addressed. Indeed, the ROSS-SHIRE BUFFS may well be proud of the high opinion formed of them by Generals Havelock and Outram, neither of whom were given to speaking anything but the severe truth. So extremely complimentary were the terms in which Sir James Outram addressed the 78th, that he thought it advisable to record the substance of his address in writing, lest the 78th should attribute anything to the excitement of the moment. In a letter addressed to Brigadier Hamilton he wrote,—— "What I did say is what *I really feel*, and what I am sure must be the sentiment of every Englishman who knows what the 78th have done during the past year, and I had fully weighed what I should say before I went to parade." We must give a few extracts from the address as Sir James wrote it:—

"Your exemplary conduct, 78th, in every respect, throughout the past eventful year, I can truly say, and *I do most emphatically declare*, has never been surpassed by any troops of any nation, in any age, whether for indomitable valour in the field or steady discipline in the camp, under an amount of fighting, hardship, and privation such as British troops have seldom, if ever, heretofore been exposed to. The cheerfulness with which you have gone through all this has excited my admiration as much as the undaunted pluck with which you always close with the enemy whenever you can get at him, no matter what his odds against you, or what the advantage of his position. . . . I am sure that you, 78th, who will have borne the brunt of the war so gloriously from first to last, when you return to old England, will be hailed and

rewarded by your grateful and admiring countrymen as the band of heroes, as which you so well deserve to be regarded."

In the meantime Sir Colin Campbell having relieved Cawnpoor and retaken the Doab, and having received large reinforcements from England, had assembled a large army for the capture of the city of Lucknow. This army was composed of an artillery division, an engineer brigade, a cavalry division, and four infantry divisions. The 78th Highlanders, consisting of 18 officers and 501 men, under Colonel Stisted, formed with the 90th Light Infantry, and the regiment of Ferozepore, the 2nd Brigade, under Brigadier Wanklin of the 84th Regiment, of the 1st Division under Major-General Sir James Outram, G.C.B. In the 2nd Division were the 42nd and 93rd Highlanders, and in the 3rd Division, the 79th Highlanders. The whole army amounted to 1937 artillery, 2002 engineers, 4156 cavalry, and 17,549 infantry, or a grand total of 25,664 effective men, to which was added during the course of the siege the Ghoorka army, under the Maharajah Jung Bahadoor, numbering about 9000 men and 24 guns.

We need not enter into the details of the siege of Lucknow, especially as the 78th was not engaged in the aggressive operations, particulars of which will be found in our histories of the 42nd, 79th, and 93rd. After nineteen days' incessant fighting, the city was taken complete possession of by the British, and the enemy put to utter route. During the siege operations the 78th was in position at the Alum Bagh, where the regiment sustained little more than the usual annoyance from the enemy, until the 16th, when the front and left of the position were threatened by large forces of the enemy's infantry and cavalry. Brigadier Wanklin had hardly time to dispose his troops in the best positions for supporting the outposts, when a determined advance of the enemy's line took place, their cavalry in myriads making a most brilliant charge on the front left picquets. A heavy fire from these, however, aided by that of the field artillery, who were detached to the left, caused them to turn and flee precipitately.

The 78th being thus not actively engaged during the siege, sustained a loss of only

1 officer, Captain Macpherson, and 2 men wounded.

The officers of the regiment honourably mentioned in the despatches were Colonel Stisted, C.B., Brevet Lieutenant-Colonel H. Hamilton, C.B., Brevet-Major Bouverie, on whom the brevet rank of Lieutenant-Colonel was conferred, Captain Macpherson, on whom the brevet rank of Major was conferred, and Lieutenant Barker. The brevet rank of Major was also conferred on Captain Mackenzie.

On the 29th of March 1858 the divisions of the army were broken up, and three new forces of all arms combined were formed as follows: —the Azimgurh Field Force under General Lugard, the Lucknow Field Force under General Sir Hope Grant, and the Rohilcund Field Force under Brigadier-General Walpole.

After going to Cawnpoor the 78th joined, on the 26th of April, the Rohilcund Field Force, among the regiments composing which were the 42nd, 79th, and 93rd Highlanders. On the same day Sir Colin Campbell arrived and took the command, moving on the following day to Bareilly, the enemy everywhere retiring before the advancing forces. Early on the morning of the 5th of May a movement was made upon Bareilly from Furreedpoor; but into the details of the hot work that took place here we need not enter : they will be found elsewhere. On the forenoon of the 7th, the 78th was sent to protect the heavy guns which were detached to the front for the purpose of shelling some large buildings intervening between the British force and the town, and which were supposed to be undermined.

On the morning of the 7th the town of Bareilly was finally reduced, and the Mussulman portion of it, where there were still detached parties of Ghazees remaining with the intention of selling their lives as dearly as possible, was cleared. In these affairs the 78th lost only 1 man killed and 1 officer, Lieutenant Walsh, and 1 man wounded.

The 42nd, 78th, and 93rd Highlanders were now left to garrison Bareilly, where the 78th remained till February 20th, 1859, having in the meantime received orders to prepare for embarkation to England; previous to which 176 of the men volunteered to join other corps remaining in India. Before leaving Bareilly, an order highly complimentary to the corps was issued by Brigadier-General (now Sir Robert) Walpole, K.C.B. We regret that space does not permit us to reproduce the order here, and for a similar reason we must pass over with as great brevity as possible the remaining history of the regiment; we have devoted considerable space to its periods of active service.

The regiment left Bareilly on the 20th of February, and on the 4th of March reached Agra, where a farewell order was received from the commander-in-chief to the regiment leaving India, in which he, as was to be expected, spoke in high terms of the 78th. The whole of the regiment was collected at Mhow on the 30th of March 1859, and here a banquet was given by the inhabitants of the station to the officers of the 64th and 78th, to welcome back to the Presidency of Bombay these two regiments which had been so distinguished in the late struggle.

On the 26th of March another complimentary order was received from Sir Henry Somerset, commander-in-chief of the Bombay army.

Finally, on the 28th of April, the whole regiment, which had been travelling in detachments, assembled at Bombay, and in honour of its arrival Commodore Wellesley, commander-in-chief of the Indian navy, ordered all H.M.'s ships to be dressed "rainbow-fashion."

On the evening of this day a grand entertainment was given to the 78th by the European inhabitants of Bombay, in the form of a banquet, to which were invited the non-commissioned officers, privates, women, and children of the regiment. A magnificent suite of tents was pitched on the glacis of the fort, and many days had been spent in preparing illuminations, transparencies, and other decorations, to add lustre to the scene. At half-past 7 o'clock P.M. the regiment entered the triumphal arch which led to the tents, where the men were received with the utmost enthusiasm by their hosts, who from the highest in rank to the lowest had assembled to do them honour. After a magnificent and tasteful banquet, speeches followed, in which the men of the ROSS-SHIRE BUFFS were addressed in a style sufficient to turn the heads of men of less solid calibre.

The entertainment was described in a local paper as "one of the most successful demonstrations ever witnessed in Western India."

The depôt had a few days previous to this arrived from Poonah, and joined the regiment after a separation of two years and four months.

Finally, the regiment embarked on the morning of the 18th in two ships, under the distinguished honour of a royal salute from the battery. The two ships arrived at Gravesend about the middle of September, and the regiment having been transhipped, proceeded to Fort-George, where it once more rested from its hard labours, after an absence of seventeen years from home. The strength of the regiment on leaving India was 21 officers, 44 sergeants, 30 corporals, 11 drummers, 424 privates, 30 women, and 67 children; 59 men only being left of those who came out with the regiment in 1842.

We may mention here, that during this year an alteration was made in the clothing of the pipers, the colour of whose uniform was changed from buff to a dark green.

VI.

1859—1874.

Reception of the regiment in the Northern Counties—Banquet at Brahan Castle—Regiment fêted at Nairn and Inverness—Medals for Persia—Removed to Edinburgh—Officers and men fêted at Edinburgh and Hamilton—Abolition of Grenadiers and Light Companies—Medals for the Indian Mutiny—Removed to Aldershot — thence to Shorncliffe—thence to Dover—The Duke of Cambridge's opinion of the 78th—Additional year's service granted to Indian men—Inauguration of the Monument on the Castle Hill, Edinburgh—Presentation of Plate and Pipe-major's Flag by the Countess of Ross and Cromarty—Lucknow Prize-money—Gibraltar—Retirement of Colonel M'Intyre—Retirement of Colonel Lockhart—His farewell Address—Canada—Presentation of Colours—Nova Scotia—Internal changes—Lieutenant-General Sir C. H. Doyle's opinion of the 78th—Home—Belfast—Aids the civil power—Fort-George—Aldershot.

As we have devoted so much space to a narrative of the active service of this distinguished regiment, we shall be compelled to recount with brevity its remaining history; this, however, is the less to be regretted, as, like most regiments during a time of peace, the history of the Ross-shire Buffs since the Indian mutiny is comparatively uneventful.

On the 1st of June 1859 Colonel Walter Hamilton was appointed to be Inspecting Field Officer of a recruiting district, by which the command of the regiment fell to Colonel Stisted, who, on the 30th of the following September, exchanged to the 93rd Highlanders with Colonel J. A. Ewart, C.B., aide-de-camp to the Queen.

The regiment being once more assembled on the borders of Ross-shire (the county from which it received its name), after an absence of twenty years, was received on all sides with a most hearty and spontaneous and certainly thoroughly well-deserved welcome. The northern counties vied with each other in showing civility to the regiment by giving banquets to the men and balls to the officers. Into the details of these fêtes we cannot of course enter. One of the most characteristic of these entertainments was a banquet given at Brahan Castle, by the Honourable Mrs Stewart Mackenzie, daughter of the Earl of Seaforth who raised the regiment, when a large family gathering of the Mackenzies of Seaforth assembled to do honour to the corps raised by their ancestors, on its return from the Indian wars. The regiment as a body was fêted by the inhabitants of the town and county of Nairn, and by the noblemen and gentlemen of the northern countries and burgh of Inverness at the latter town. The freedom of the burgh of Nairn was also conferred on Lieutenant-Colonel M'Intyre, and in both cases addresses were presented to the regiment, showing a high and well-deserved appreciation of the noble work done by the "Saviours of India." On entering Inverness, Colonel M'Intyre halted the regiment in front of the house of General John Mackenzie, the oldest officer then in the British army, and who originally raised the light company of the 78th Highlanders. The men gave three cheers for the gallant veteran before proceeding along the streets appointed for the procession to the banqueting hall.

In the month of November a large meeting was held at Dingwall, for the purpose of considering the propriety of presenting some lasting testimonial from all classes in the county of Ross to the Ross-shire Buffs. The result of the meeting will appear in the sequel.

Shortly after this, Nos 11 and 12 companies were formed into a dépôt, numbering 4 officers and 96 men, who, under Captain M'Andrew, proceeded to Aberdeen to join the 23rd dépôt battalion at that place

The medals for the Persian campaign were received in February 1860, and on the 18th of that month were issued to the regiment Out of the 36 officers and 866 men who served in Persia in the early part of the year 1857, only 15 officers and 445 men at this time remained on the strength of the regiment

The 78th left Fort-George in two detachments, on the 21st and 24th of February, for Edinburgh, where its reception was most enthusiastic. The streets were rendered almost impassable by the people that thronged in thousands to witness the arrival of the famous 78th In Edinburgh, as when at Fort-George, the people showed their appreciation of the services of the regiment by fêting officers and men On the 23rd of March the officers were entertained at banquet given by the Royal Company of Archers, Queen's Body-Guard for Scotland, and on the 21st of April a grand banquet was given to the officers and men by the citizens of Edinburgh, in the Corn Exchange

The 78th remained in Edinburgh till April 1861, furnishing detachments to Greenlaw and Hamilton The detachment stationed at the latter place was duly banqueted, and the free dom of the borough conferred upon Lieutenant-Colonel M'Intyre, C B

While in Edinburgh, in accordance with a circular from the Horse-Guards, dated May 30th, 1860, directing that all distinction between flank and battalion companies be abolished, the grenadiers and light companies ceased to exist, as such , the green heckles, grenades, and bugles being done away with, together with all distinction as to the size of the men, &c. This step, though no doubt conducive to the greater efficiency of the service, was not a little grievous to old officers, who as a rule took considerable pride in the stalwart men of the grenadier companies

On the 2nd of June, General Sir William Chalmers, K.C B, died at Dundee, and was succeeded in the coloneley of the regiment by Lieutenant-General Roderick M'Neil, formerly an officer of the 78th Highlanders

On the 9th of August the medals granted for the suppression of the Indian mutiny were presented to the regiment by Lady Havelock (widow of the late Sir Henry Havelock), who happened to be in Edinburgh at the time Out of about 900 of all ranks, who commenced the Indian campaign with the 78th in May 1857, only 350 remained at this time in the strength of the service companies, a few also being at the depôt at Aberdeen

The 78th left Edinburgh for Aldershot in detachments between April 27th and May 8th, 1861, remaining in huts till the end of August, when it removed into the permanent barracks After staying a year at Aldershot it was removed on the 15th of May 1862 to Shorncliffe, where it spent about another year, removing to Dover on the 26th of May 1863 Here it was quartered on the Western Heights, furnishing detachments regularly to the Castle Hill Fort, to be employed as engineer working parties. After staying in Dover until August 1864, the 78th embarked on the 5th of that month, under command of Colonel J A Ewart, C B, for Ireland, disembarking at Kingstown on the 8th, and proceeding to Dublin Here the regiment remained for another year, when it received the route for Gibraltar During this period there is little to record in connection with the peaceful career of the 78th

Since the return of the regiment from India, it had, of course, been regularly inspected, the inspecting officers, as was naturally to be expected, having nothing but praise to bestow upon its appearance, discipline, and interior economy Shortly after the arrival of the 78th at Aldershot, it was inspected by H.R H the Duke of Cambridge, who spoke of it in terms of the highest praise , "it was a noble regiment and admirably drilled," the Duke said

On the 19th of November 1861, an authority was received for an additional year's service to be granted to those officers and soldiers of the 78th Highlanders who formed part of the column that entered Lucknow under Sir Henry Havelock , and on the 6th of March, in the same year, a similar reward was granted to those who were left by Sir Henry Havelock in defence of the Alum Bagh post on the 25th of September 1857

Monument on the Castle-Hill, Edinburgh.

SACRED TO THE MEMORY OF THE OFFICERS, NON-COMMISSIONED OFFICERS, AND PRIVATE SOLDIERS OF THE LXXVIII REGIMENT WHO FELL IN THE SUPPRESSION OF THE MUTINY OF THE NATIVE ARMY OF INDIA IN THE YEARS MDCCCLVII AND MDCCCLVIII, THIS MEMORIAL IS ERECTED AS A TRIBUTE OF RESPECT BY THEIR SURVIVING BROTHER OFFICERS AND COMRADES, AND BY MANY OFFICERS WHO FORMERLY BELONGED TO THE REGIMENT.—ANNO DOMINI MDCCCLXI.

On the 15th of April 1862, a monument to the memory of the officers, non-commissioned officers, and privates of the 78th Highlanders, who fell in India during the suppression of the mutiny in 1857–58, and which had been erected on the Castle Esplanade at Edinburgh by the officers and men of the regiment, and others who had formerly served in the Ross-shire Buffs, was publicly inaugurated by Major-General Walker, C.B., commanding the troops in Scotland, in presence of the Scots Greys, the 26th Cameronians, and the Royal Artillery. The monument is in the form of a handsome and tasteful large Runic cross, an illustration of which we are glad to be able to give on the preceding page.

We mentioned above that a meeting had been held at Dingwall, to consider the propriety of presenting some testimonial to the Ross-shire Buffs from the county which gives the regiment its distinctive name. The outcome of the meeting was that, while the regiment was at Shorncliffe, on the 26th of June 1862, two magnificent pieces of plate, subscribed for by the inhabitants of the counties of Ross and Cromarty, were presented to the 78th by a deputation consisting of Keith Stewart Mackenzie (a descendant of Kenneth, Earl of Seaforth, who raised and equipped the regiment), Macleod of Cadbol, Major F. Fraser, and Lord Ashburton. The plate consists of a Centre Piece for the officers' mess, and a cup for the sergeants' mess, and bears the following inscription :—

Presented by the Counties of Ross and Cromarty to the 78th Highlanders or Ross-shire Buffs, in admiration of the gallantry of the regiment and of its uniform devotion to the service of the country. —1859.

A very handsome flag for the pipe-major was also presented by Keith Stewart Mackenzie of Seaforth to the regiment, which has six pipers.

While at Dover, on the 17th of October 1863, the first issue of the Lucknow prize-money was made, a private's share amounting to £1, 14s.; that of the various other ranks, from a corporal upwards, increasing in regular proportion, up to the Lieutenant-Colonel, who received 17 shares, amounting to £28, 18s.

On the 22nd of this month died the colonel of the 78th, General Roderick Macneil (of Barra), to whom succeeded Lieutenant-General Sir Patrick Grant, G.C.B.[1] In October of the following year, Lieutenant-Colonel Ewart, who had had command of the regiment for five years, retired on half-pay, and was succeeded by Major and Brevet-Colonel Colin Campbell M'Intyre, C.B.

It may be interesting to note here, that in compliance with a circular memorandum, dated Horse-Guards, 10th June 1865, the companies of the regiment, from July 17th, were designated by letters from A to M (excluding J), for all purposes of interior economy, instead of by numbers as hitherto.

The 78th had been at home for nearly six years, when on the 2nd of August 1865, it embarked at Kingstown for Gibraltar, the whole strength of the regiment at the time being 33 officers, 713 men, 74 women, and 95 children. Asiatic cholera was prevalent at Gibraltar at the time of the regiment's arrival, and it therefore encamped on Windmill Hill until the 18th of October. The loss of the regiment from cholera was only 5 men, 1 woman, and 1 child.

During the two years that the 78th remained at Gibraltar, in performance of the tedious routine duties incident to that station, the only event worthy of record here is the retirement on full pay, in October 1866, of Colonel M'Intyre, who had been so long connected with the regiment, and who, as we have seen, performed such distinguished service in India. He was succeeded by Lieutenant-Colonel Lockhart, C.B., who, in assuming the command of the regiment, paid, in a regimental order, a high and just compliment to his predecessor.

On the 6th of July 1867 the 78th embarked at Gibraltar for Canada. Previous to embarkation the regiment paraded on the Alameda, where his Excellency Lieutenant-General Sir Richard Airey, G.C.B., Governor of Gibraltar, bade the 78th "good-bye" in a short address highly complimentary to the regiment, and especially to Colonel Lockhart, who also, before his old regiment sailed, had to say farewell to it. Colonel Lockhart, after being connected

[1] See portrait on the steel plate of the Colonels of the 78th and 79th Regiments.

with the 78th for thirty years, was about to retire on full pay, and therefore on the morning of the 8th, before the vessel quitted the bay, he handed over the command of the regiment to Major Mackenzie; and on the evening of that day his farewell regimental order was issued, in which he exhibited the deepest feeling at having to bid farewell to his dear old regiment, as well as intense anxiety for the highest welfare of the men. The address is, indeed, very impressive, and we are sorry that space does not permit us to quote it here. "If any 78th man meets me in Scotland," the colonel said, "where, by God's permission, I hope to spend many

Centre Piece of Plate for the Officers' Mess.

happy days, I shall expect he will not pass me by; I shall not him."

After being transhipped at Quebec on board a river steamer, the regiment landed at Montreal on the 23rd of July. The regular routine of garrison duty at Montreal was relieved by a course of musketry instruction at Chambly, and by a sojourn in camp at Point Levis, on the fortification of which place the regiment was for some time engaged.

The only notable incident that happened during the stay of the regiment in Canada was the presentation to it of new colours, the old ones being sadly tattered and riddled, and stained with the life-blood of many a gallant officer. The new colours were presented to the regiment by Lady Windham, in the Champ de Mars, on the 30th of May 1868, amid a concourse of nearly ten thousand spectators. After the usual ceremony with regard to the old colours, and a prayer for God's blessing on the new by the Rev. Joshua Fraser, Lady Windham, in a few neat, brief, and forcible words, presented the new colours to Ensigns Waugh and Fordyce. Lieutenant-General C. A. Windham, the commander-in-chief, also addressed the regiment in highly complimentary terms. "Though he had not a drop of Scotch blood in his veins," he said, " he had exceedingly strong Scottish sympathies. It was under Scotchmen that he got his first military start in life, and under succeeding Scotchmen he had made his earlier way in the service. . . . . The 78th Highlanders had always conducted themselves bravely and with unsullied loyalty." At the déjeuner which followed, General Windham said that in the whole course of his service he had never seen a regiment which pulled together so well as the 78th, and among whom there were so few differences. All the toasts were, of course, drunk with Highland honours, and all went off most harmoniously down to the toast of the "Ladies," to which Lieutenant Colin Mackenzie had the honour to reply, advising his young brothers in arms to lose no time in coming under the sway of the "dashing white sergeant."

The old colours of the Ross-shire Buffs were sent to Dingwall, in Ross-shire, there to be deposited in the County Buildings or the Parish Church.

On the 8th of May 1869 the regiment left Montreal; and, after being transhipped at Quebec, proceeded to Halifax, Nova Scotia, where it arrived on the 14th of May. Previous to the regiment's leaving Montreal, a very warm and affectionate address was presented to it by the St Andrew's Society.

The regiment remained in Nova Scotia till November 1871, furnishing detachments regularly to St John's, New Brunswick. On several occasions since its return from India, the strength of the regiment had been reduced; and while at Halifax, on the 21st of April 1870, a general order was received, notifying a further reduction, and the division of the regiment into two depôts and eight service companies,

consisting in all of 34 officers, 49 sergeants, 21 drummers, 6 pipers, and 600 rank and file. This involved a redistribution of the men of some of the companies; and, moreover, depôt battalions having been broken up on the 1st of April, the depôt companies of the 78th Highlanders were attached to the 93rd Highlanders.

Lieutenant-General Sir Charles Hastings Doyle, K.C.M.G., commanding the forces in British North America, inspected the regiment on the 11th of October 1870, a day or two after which the following very gratifying letter was received by Lieutenant-Colonel Mackenzie, C.B., from Brigade-Major Wilsome Black :—" The general desires me to say that he is not in the habit of making flourishing speeches at half-yearly inspections of Queen's troops (although he does so to militia and volunteers), because her Majesty expects that all corps shall be in perfect order. When they are not, they are sure to hear from him, and a report made accordingly to the Horse Guards; but when nothing is said, a commanding officer will naturally take for granted that his regiment is in good order. The general, however, cannot refrain from saying to you, and begs you will communicate to the officers and men of the regiment under your command, that he was perfectly satisfied with everything that came under his observation at his inspection of your regiment on Tuesday last."

In compliance with orders received, the 78th, under the command of Lieutenant-Colonel Alexander Mackenzie, C.B., embarked on board H.M.'s troop-ship "Orontes," on the 25th of November 1871, and arrived at Queenstown, Ireland, on the 17th of December, where the regiment was transhipped and conveyed to Belfast, arriving in Belfast Lough on the 20th, and disembarking next day.

The strength of the regiment on its arrival in the United Kingdom was 32 officers and 472 non-commissioned officers and men, which on the 22nd of December was augmented by the arrival of the depôt battalion from Edinburgh, consisting of 2 officers and 45 non-commissioned officers and men. Shortly afterwards the strength of the regiment was augmented to 33 officers and 592 non-commissioned officers and privates; and in accordance with the Royal Warrant, dated October 30th, 1871, all the ensigns of the regiment were raised to the rank of lieutenant, the rank of ensign having been abolished in the army.

During its stay at Belfast the 78th regularly furnished detachments to Londonderry ; and on several occasions it had the very unpleasant and delicate duty to perform of aiding the civil power in the suppression of riots caused by the rancour existing between Orangemen and Roman Catholics in the North of Ireland. This trying duty the regiment performed on both occasions to the entire satisfaction of the Irish authorities as well as of the War Office authorities, receiving from both quarters high and well-deserved praise for its prudent conduct, which was the means of preventing greatly the destruction of life and property.

Under the new system of localisation of regiments, it was notified in a Horse Guards General Order, that the 71st Highland Light Infantry and the 78th Highlanders would form the line portion of the 55th infantry sub-district, and be associated for the purposes of enlistment and service. The counties included n this sub-district are Orkney and Shetland, Sutherland, Caithness, Ross and Cromarty, Inverness, Nairn, and Elgin, and the station assigned to the brigade depôt is Fort George. In accordance with this scheme, Major Feilden, with a small detachment, proceeded to Fort-George on the 9th of April, to form part of the brigade depôt.

The 78th embarked at Belfast on the 3rd of May 1873, under command of Colonel Mackenzie, C.B. The streets were densely crowded, and the people gave vent to their good feeling by cheering repeatedly as the regiment marched from the barracks to the quay. The regiment was transferred to the "Himalaya," which sailed on the 4th round the west and north coast of· Scotland, and anchored in Cromarty Bay on the evening of the 7th, headquarters and six companies disembarking opposite Fort George next day. Two companies remained on board and proceeded to Aberdeen, there to be stationed. A detachment of the companies at Aberdeen proceeded to Ballater on the 15th of May, as

a guard of honour to her Majesty the Queen, and again on the 14th of August.

The regiment was inspected by Major-General Sir John Douglas, K.C.B., on the 19th of May the report of the inspection being considered by H.R.H. the Field-Marshal Commanding-in-Chief as most satisfactory.

The 78th remained at Fort George for only one year, embarking on the 11th of May 1874, under command of Colonel Mackenzie, C.B., for conveyance to Portsmouth, en route to Aldershot. The regiment disembarked at Portsmouth on the 15th of May, and proceeded by special train to Farnborough, marching thence to Aldershot. A period of exactly twelve years had elapsed since the 78th was last at this camp.

On the 19th of May the 78th was brigaded with the 42nd, 79th, and 93rd Highlanders, at a review which took place in the presence of the Czar of Russia ; and it is worthy of note that these four kilted regiments are those that represented Scotland at the siege and fall of Lucknow. It is also a curious coincidence that Colonels Macleod, Mackenzie, M'Bean, and Miller all served with the regiments they led on this occasion before the Czar.

Major-General William Parke, C.B., commanding the 1st brigade, inspected the regiment on the 21st of May, and expressed himself highly pleased with the appearance and drill of the Ross-shire Buffs.

At the time we write, the establishment of this most distinguished regiment consists of 27 officers, 64 non-commissioned officers, drummers, and pipers, 40 corporals, and 480 privates, —the total of all ranks thus being 611.

We have the gratification of being able to present our readers with two authentic portraits on steel of two of the most eminent colonels of the Ross-shire Buffs. That of the first colonel, Francis Humberstone Mackenzie, Lord Seaforth, is from the original painting in the possession of Colonel Mackenzie Fraser, of Castle-Fraser ; and that of Sir Patrick Grant, G.C.B., G.C.M.G., is from a photograph by Bassano, kindly sent to us by Sir Patrick himself.

SUCCESSION LIST OF COLONELS AND FIELD OFFICERS OF THE 78th HIGHLANDERS.

COLONELS.

NAMES.	Date of Appointment.	Remarks.
Francis Humberstone Mackenzie, afterwards Lord Seaforth	March 7, 1793	Resigned command of the regiment, retaining his rank. Died, 11th January 1815.
Alex. Mackenzie of Belmaduthy, took the name of Fraser of Castle Fraser	May 3, 1796	Died a Lieutenant-General, September 1809, from fever contracted in the Walcheren expedition.
Sir James Henry Craig, K.C.B.	September 15, 1809	Died, 1812.
Sir Samuel Auchmuty, G.C.B.	January 13, 1812	Died, 1822.
Sir Edward Barnes, G.C.B.	August 25, 1822	Appointed to 31st Foot, 16th October 1834.
Sir L. Smith, Bart., K.C.B., G.C.H.	October 10, 1834	Appointed to the 40th Foot, 9th February 1837.
Paul Anderson, C.B., K.C.	February 9, 1837	Died, 28th December 1851.
Sir Neil Douglas, K.C.B., K.C.H.	December 28, 1851	From Colonel 72nd. Died, 30th Sept. 1853.
Sir W. Chalmers, C.B., K.C.H.	September 30, 1853	Died, 2d June 1860.
Roderick Macneil	June 3, 1860	Died, 22d October 1863.
Sir Patrick Grant, G.C.B., G.C.M.G.	October 23, 1863	Governor of Chelsea Hospital (1874).

LIEUTENANT-COLONELS.

Alex. Mackenzie of Belmaduthy	July 24, 1793	Promoted Colonel-Commandant 27th Feb. 1796.
Alex. Mackenzie of Fairburn	February 10, 1794	2nd Battalion of 1794. To 36th Regiment, 1797.
John Randoll Mackenzie of Suddie	February 27, 1796	A Col. in the army in 1794 ; he became a Major-General, and was killed at Talavera, 1809.
Alexander Malcolm	1795	Died, 1798.
John Mackenzie, Gairloch	1795	Placed on Half-pay, 1799.[9]
John Mackenzie, junior	1795	Placed on Half-pay, 1795.
Hay Macdowall	May 22, 1797	Col. in the army in 1795, Major-General in 1798, and was promoted to 40th Regiment, 1802. Lost on passage from India, 1809.
Alexander Adams	April 7, 1802	Promoted Major-General, 1814.
Patrick Macleod, Geanies	April 17, 1804	2nd Bat. 1804 ; Killed at El-Hamet, 21st Ap. 1807.
Hercules Scott, Benholm	July 23, 1807	To 103rd, 1808. Killed in Canada, 1814.
John Macleod, C.B.	May 12, 1808	2nd Battalion of 1804. Major-General, 1819.
James Macdonell, Glengarry	September 7, 1809	Exchanged to Coldstream Guards, 1810.
Sir Edward Michael Ryan, Kt.	February 21, 1811	Died in 1812.
James Fraser	May 1, 1812	Killed at Probolingo in Java, 1813.
Martin Lindsay, C.B.	November 25, 1813	Succeeded Colonel John Macleod in command, 12th Aug. 1819, and retired 27th April 1837.
David Forbes	July 28, 1814	Reduced on Half-pay, 1816.
Henry N. Douglas	April 28, 1837	Died, 1st October 1849.
Martin G. T. Lindsay	April 8, 1842	Exchanged, 15th April 1842.
Roderick Macneil	April 15, 1842	Colonel in the army June 17, 1828, and was promoted Major-General, 9th November 1846.
Jonathan Forbes	November 9, 1846	Retired, 10th December 1847.
E. Twopeny	December 10, 1847	Exchanged to 10th Foot.
Walter Hamilton, C.B.	October 2, 1849	Appointed Inspecting Field Officer, 1st June 1859.
Henry W. Stisted, C.B.	April 19, 1850	Exchanged to 93d Highlanders, 30th Sept. 1859.
John Alexander Ewart, C.B.	September 30, 1859	Retired on Half-pay, 28th October 1864.
Colin Campbell M'Intyre, C.B.	October 28, 1864	Retired on Full-pay, 2d October 1866.
Græme A. Lockhart, C.B.	October 2, 1866	Retired on Full-pay, 13th July 1867.
Alexander Mackenzie, C.B.	July 13, 1867	

MAJORS.

Alex. Mackenzie, Belmaduthy	March 8, 1793	Promoted Colonel-Commandant, 27th Feb. 1796.
George, Earl of Errol	July 24, 1793	To 1st Regiment Foot Guards, 1794. Died, 1799.
Alex. Mackenzie of Fairburn	July 24, 1793	To command of 2nd Battalion, 10th Feb. 1794.
John Randoll Mackenzie of Suddie	February 10, 1794	Promoted, 1794.
Michael Monypenny	October 23, 1794	Promoted to 72nd Regiment, 1798. Died, 1808.
Alexander Malcolm	May 2, 1794	Promoted, 1795.
John Mackenzie, Gairloch	May 3, 1794	Promoted, 1795.
John Mackenzie, junior	1794	Promoted, 1795.
Alexander Grant	1795	Retired, 1798. Died, 1807.
William Montgomery	1795	Promoted to 64th Regiment. Died 1800.
Alexander Adams	August 30, 1798	Promoted, 1802.

[9] "A General, and, at the time of his death, the oldest officer in the British army. He served with high distinction and without cessation from 1779 to 1814. He became a General (*full*) in 1837. So marked was his daring and personal valour, that he was known among his companions in arms as 'Fighting Jack.' General Mackenzie married Lilias, youngest daughter of Alexander Chisholm of Chisholm, and died 14th June 1860, aged 96."—Burke's *Peerage and Baronetage*. When the 78th Highlanders were received in Inverness with the utmost enthusiasm, on their return from the Indian Mutiny, General Mackenzie, verging on 100 years appeared on his balcony to bid them welcome . . . . by the su . . . . of those he had so often led to victory.—M.

MAJORS—continued.

NAMES.	Date of Appointment.	Remarks.
Hercules Scott, Benholm	May 9, 1800	Promoted, 1807.
Patrick Macleod, Geanies	November 18, 1802	To command of 2nd Battalion, 17th April 1804.
David Stewart, Garth	April 17, 1804	Promoted to Royal West Indian Rangers, 1808. Author of the *Sketches*.
James Macdonell, Glengarry	April 17, 1804	Promoted, 1809.
William Campbell	December 13, 1804	Killed at taking Fort Cornelis, in Java, 1810.
James Fraser	July 23, 1807	Promoted, 1813.
Robert Hamilton	April 21, 1808	Retired, 1810.
Martin Lindsay	January 4, 1810	Promoted, 1813.
David Forbes	August 29, 1811	Promoted, 1814.
Duncan Macpherson	November 7, 1811	Major of the regiment in 1820.
James Machean	December 14, 1811	Major of the regiment in 1820.
Duncan Macgregor	November 25, 1813	Reduced on Half-pay in 1816.
Colin Campbell Mackay, Bighouse	August 11, 1814	Reduced on Half-pay in 1816.
Joseph Bethune	June 14, 1821	
C. G. Falconer	June 26, 1823	
Henry N. Douglas	October 22, 1825	Promoted, 28th April 1837.
James Mill	April 8, 1826	
Benjamin Adams	May 7, 1829	Retired, 17th May 1838.
Martin G. T. Lindsay	April 28, 1837	Promoted, 8th April 1842.
Jonathan Forbes	May 18, 1838	Promoted, 9th November 1846.
E. Twopeny	April 8, 1842	Promoted, 10th December 1847.
R. J. P. Vassall	November 9, 1846	Exchanged to Half-pay.
Walter Hamilton	December 10, 1847	Promoted, 2d October 1849.
J. Burns	May 23, 1848	Exchanged to 2nd Foot.
Henry W. Stisted	May 26, 1848	Promoted, 19th April 1850.
T. J. Taylor	October 2, 1849	Died, 18th June 1850.
Henry Hamilton, C.B.	April 19, 1850	Appointed to the Staff, 1st July 1862.
Colin Campbell M'Intyre, C.B.	June 19, 1850	Promoted, 28th October 1864.
Graeme A. Lockhart, C.B.	July 1, 1862	Promoted, 2d October 1860.
Alexander Mackenzie	October 28, 1864	Promoted, 13th July 1867.
Oswald B. Feilden	October 2, 1866	
Augustus E. Warren	July 13, 1867	

ADJUTANTS.

James Fraser	March 8, 1793	Retired, 1794.
James Hanson	February 10, 1794	2nd Battalion of 1794. Became Adjutant of the consolidated Battalion in 1796. Retired.
Donald Fraser	October 1, 1794	
Alexander Wishart	October 20, 1797	Promoted.
John Hay	December 30, 1800	Died in India, 1803.
Joseph Bethune	June 25, 1803	Promoted.
William Mackenzie	April 17, 1804	2nd Battalion of 1804. Promoted.
Thomas Hamilton	September 26, 1805	Deceased.
John Cooper	October 15, 1807	Adjutant of the regiment till succeeded by Bull.
James Fraser	June 15, 1810	
William Smith	June 24, 1813	Adjutant of the 2nd Battalion when reduced.
J. E. N. Bull	May 4, 1826	Promoted, 19th October 1838.
S. M. Edington	October 19, 1838	Resigned, 31st August 1838.
C. Pattison	August 31, 1839	Promoted in Newfoundland Companies.
Hamilton Douglas Gordon	June 16, 1848	Promoted, 10th October 1850.
Laurence Pleydell Bouverie	October 10, 1850	Promoted, 22nd December 1854.
Herbert T. Macpherson, V.C.	December 22, 1854	Promoted, 6th October 1857.
Andrew C. Bogle, V.C.	October 6, 1857	Promoted, 5th November 1858.
G. D. Barker	November 5, 1858	Promoted, 2nd April 1861.
Thomas Mackenzie	April 2, 1861	Resigned, 16th May 1862.
Richard P. Butler	May 16, 1862	Retired, 21st November 1865.
George E. Lecky	November 21, 1865	Resigned, 27th February 1867.
Robert Lockhart Dalglish	February 27, 1867	Retired, 20th July 1867.
E. P. Stewart	July 20, 1867	Promoted, 7th July 1869.
C. E. Croker-King	July 7, 1869	Promoted, 17th July 1872.
Arthur Dingwall Fordyce	August 21, 1872	

PAYMASTERS.

Alexander bannerman	February 25, 1804	
James Ferguson	March 21, 1805	2nd Battalion of 1804. Deceased.
John Chisholm	December 11, 1817	Retired. Succeeded by Paymaster Taylor.
M. G. Taylor	August 26, 1836	Exchanged to 45th Foot.
E. Evans	July 7, 1846	Retired, 22nd April 1853.
Joseph Webster	April 22, 1853	Retired, 1st April 1864.
Charles Skrine	April 1, 1864	

QUARTER-MASTERS.

NAMES.	Date of Appointment.	Remarks.
Archibald Macdougal	March 8, 1793	Retired.
Alexander Wishart	February 10, 1794	2nd Battalion of 1794. Establishment reduced.
Duncan Macrae	January 23, 1801	To 76th Foot as Ensign.
John Leavoch	February 11, 1804	Promoted from Paymaster's Clerk. He carried the Queen's colour at Assaye and Argaum.
John Macpherson	April 17, 1804	2nd Battalion of 1804. Retired.
Alexander Waters	June 30, 1808	
William Smith	April 19, 1810	
William Gunn	August 6, 1812	Paymaster in Cape Mounted Rifles, May 31, 1839.
Joseph Webster	May 31, 1839	Promoted Paymaster, 22nd April 1853.
Patrick Carroll	April 22, 1853	Retired on Full-pay, 12th September 1856.
Charles Skrine	September 12, 1856	Promoted Paymaster, 1st April 1864.
Alexander Weir	April 26, 1864	

SURGEONS.

Thomas Baillie	March 8, 1793	Died in India, 1802.
William Kennedy	1794	2nd Battalion of 1794.
John Macandie	November 17, 1802	
Thomas Draper	April 17, 1804	2nd Battalion of 1804. Promoted Deputy Inspector-General.
Neil Currie	September 1, 1808	
William Munro	June 3, 1813	To Half-pay.
John M'Roberts, M.D.	November 13, 1817	
Robert Henry Bolton, M.D.	October 30, 1823	
Duncan Henderson	March 23, 1826	Exchanged to 14th Foot.
John M'Andrew	February 15, 1933	Appointed to 40th Foot.
James Burt	July 29, 1836	Appointed to 16th Dragoons.
Archibald Alexander	October 3, 1845	Exchanged to 56th Foot.
Arthur C. Webster	March 23, 1849	Transferred to 10th Hussars.
Joseph Jee, V.C. & C.B.	June 23, 1854	Exchanged to 1st Dragoons, 20th Sept. 1864.
L. C. Stewart	September 20, 1864	Promoted, 17th March 1867.
J. Meane	March 8, 1867	Appointed to the Staff, 6th March 1869.
V. M. M'Master, V.C.	March 6, 1869	Died, 22nd January 1872.
A. W. Beveridge, M.D.	February 17, 1872	

ASSISTANT-SURGEONS.—John Macandie (1795), Alex. Young (1795), John Bowen (1803), Wm. Munro (1805), Alex. Leslie (1805), Walter Irwin (1810), John Hughes (1811), Wm. Macleod (1814), George Maclean (1814), Duncan Henderson, M.D. (1817), Alex Duncan (1826), James Thomson (1826), Arthur Wood, M.D. (1826), James Young (1826), Wm. Robertson (1832), W. H. Allman (1842), John James (1842), G. Archer, M.D. (1839), J. Mitchell, M.D. (1843), D. R. M'Kinnon (1844), W. Bowie, M.D. (1844), J. Leitch, M.D. (1846), J. M'Nab, M.D. (1847), A. S. Willocks (1852), E. K. O'Neill (1854), V. M. M'Master (1855), S. S. Skipton, M.D. (1857), A. W. Beveridge, M.D. (1857), P. Kilgour (1866), N. Wade (1867), W. Johnston, M.D. (1872).

DRESS OF THE 78TH HIGHLANDERS—THE FULL HIGHLAND COSTUME.

Officers.—Kilt and belted plaid of Mackenzie tartan; scarlet Highland doublet, trimmed with gold lace according to rank, buff facings (patrol jacket and trews for fatigue dress); bonnet of black ostrich plumes, with white vulture hackle; Menzies tartan hose, red garter knots, and white spatterdashes (shoes and gold buckles, and Mackenzie tartan hose and green garter knots for ball dress); sporran of white goat's hair, with eight gold tassels (two long black tassels undress); buff leather shoulder-belt, with gilt breast plate; red morocco dirk belt, embroidered with gold thistles; dirk and skean-dhu, mounted in cairngorm and silver gilt; the claymore, with steel scabbard; round silver-gilt shoulder brooch, surmounted by a crown. The field officers wear trews, shoulder plaid, and waist belt. The Cabar Feidh on all appointments, with the Elephant, superscribed "Assaye."

Mess Dress.—Scarlet shell jacket, with buff rolling collar and facings, and gold shoulder-knots; Mackenzie tartan vest, with cairngorm buttons.

Sergeants.—Same as privates, with the exception of finer cloth and tartan. Staff sergeants wear the buff cross-belt and claymore, and shoulder plaid with brooch.

Privates.—Kilt and fly of Mackenzie tartan; scarlet Highland doublet, buff facings (buff jacket and trews for fatigue dress); bonnet of black ostrich plumes, with white hackle; sporran of white goat's hair, with two long black tassels; Menzies tartan hose, red garter knots, and white spatterdashes; the Cabar Feidh and the Elephant on the appointments.

Band.—Same as privates, with the exception of red hackles, grey sporrans, buff waist-belts and dirks, and shoulder plaids and brooch.

Pipers.—Same as privates, with the exception of green doublets, green hackles, Mackenzie tartan hose, green garter knots, grey sporrans, black shoulder and dirk belts, claymore, dirk, and skean-dhu, and shoulder plaids with round brooch.

Colonel Mackenzie, C.B., Major Forbes, and the company officers of the 78th presented their pipers, on the 21st of May 1875, with a beautiful set of pipe banners of the value of £100. The mottoes, devices, and honours of the corps are emblazoned on them, and they are considered the most costly flags that have ever been presented to the pipers of any regiment.

THE 79TH QUEEN'S OWN CAMERON HIGHLANDERS.

I.

1793—1853.

The Clan Cameron—Raising of the Regiment—Flanders—West Indies—Holland—Ferrol and Cadiz—Egypt—Ireland—A 2nd battalion—Proposed abolition of the kilt—Denmark—Sweden—Portugal—Corunna—Spain—The Peninsular War—Busaco—Foz d'Arouce—Fuentes d'Onor—Death of Colonel Philip Cameron—Lord Wellington's opinion of the 79th—Salamanca—Siege of Burgos—Vittoria—Pyrenees—Nivelle—Nive—Orthes—Toulouse—Home—Quatre Bras—Waterloo—France—Home—Chichester—Portsmouth—Jersey—Ireland—Canada—New Colours—Scotland—England—Gibraltar—"Bailie Nicol Jarvie"—Canada—Scotland—Chobham—Portsmouth.

EGMONT-OP-ZEE.   NIVE.
EGYPT (WITH SPHINX).   TOULOUSE.
FUENTES D'ONOR.   PENINSULA.
SALAMANCA.   WATERLOO.
PYRENEES.   ALMA.
NIVELLE.   SEBASTOPOL.
LUCKNOW.

THE Camerons are well known as one of the bravest and most chivalrous of the Highland clans. They held out to the very last as steadfast adherents to the cause of the Stuarts, and the names of Ewen Cameron, Donald the "gentle Lochiel," and the unfortunate Dr Cameron, must be associated in the minds of all Scotchmen with everything that is brave, and chivalrous, and generous, and unyieldingly loyal.

II.

The clan itself was at one time one of the most powerful in the Highlands; and the regiment which is now known by the clan name has most faithfully upheld the credit of the clan for bravery and loyalty; it has proved a practical comment on the old song, "A Cameron never can yield."

This regiment was raised by Alan Cameron of Erracht, to whom letters of service were granted on the 17th of August 1793. No bounty was allowed by Government, as was the case with other regiments raised in this manner, the men being recruited solely at the expense of the officers. The regiment was inspected at Stirling in January 1794, and at the end of the same month its strength was raised to 1000 men, Alan Cameron being appointed Lieutenant-Colonel Commandant.[1] The 79th was at first designated the "Cameronian Volunteers," but this designation was subsequently changed to "Cameron Highlanders."

The following is the original list of the officers of the 79th:—

Major-Commandant—Alan Cameron.
Major—George Rowley.
Captains.

Neil Campbell	Donald Cameron.
Patrick M'Dowall.	George Carnegie.

Captain-Lieutenant and Captain—Archibald Maclean.
Lieutenants.

Archibald Maclean.	Colin Maclean.
Alexander Macdonell.	Joseph Dewer.
Duncan Stewart.	Charles MacVicar.
John Urquhart.	

Ensigns.

Neil Campbell.	Donald Maclean.
Gordon Cameron.	Archibald Cameron.
Archibald Macdonell.	Alexander Grant.
Archibald Campbell.	William Graham.

Chaplain—Thomas Thompson.
Adjutant—Archibald Maclean.
Quartermaster—Duncan Stewart.
Surgeon—John Maclean.

After spending a short time in Ireland and the south of England, the 79th embarked in August 1794 for Flanders. During the following few months it shared in all the disasters of the unfortunate campaign in that country, losing 200 men from privation and the severity of the climate.[2]

Shortly afterwards the regiment returned to

[1] No portrait of this indomitable Colonel exists, or it should have been given as a steel engraving.
[2] Captain Robert Jameson's *Historical Record of the 79th.* To this record, as well as to the original manuscript record of the regiment, we are indebted for many of the following details.

England, and landed in the Isle of Wight, in April 1795. Its strength was ordered to be completed to 1000 men, preparatory to its embarkation for India. While Colonel Cameron was making every exertion to fulfil this order, he received an intimation that directions had been given to draft the Cameron Highlanders into four other regiments. This impolitic order naturally roused the indignation of the colonel, who in an interview[3] with the commander-in-chief deprecated in the strongest terms any such unfeeling and unwise proceeding. His representations were successful, and the destination of the regiment was changed to the West Indies, for which it embarked in the summer of 1795. The 79th remained in Martinique till July 1797, but suffered so much from the climate that an offer was made to such of the men as were fit for duty to volunteer into other corps, the consequence being that upwards of 200 entered the 42nd, while about a dozen joined four other regiments. The officers, with the remainder of the regiment, returned home, landing at Gravesend in August, and taking up their quarters in Chatham barracks. Orders were issued to fill up the ranks of the 79th, and by the exertions of Colonel Cameron and his officers a fresh body of 780 men was raised, who assembled at Stirling in June 1798. In the following year it was ordered to form part of the expedition to the Helder, landing at Helder Point, in North Holland, in August, when it was brigaded with the 2nd battalion Royals, the 25th, 49th, and 92nd Regiments, under the command of Major-General Moore. After various movements, the fourth division, under the command of Sir Ralph Abercromby, came up, on the 2nd of October, with the enemy, strongly posted near the village of Egmont-op-Zee. Notwithstanding the unfavourable nature of the ground, consisting of loose sand-hills, General Moore's brigade made such a vigorous attack with the bayonet, that the enemy were quickly driven from their position, and pursued over the sand-hills till night prevented further operations. In this enterprise, Captain James Campbell, Lieutenant Stair Rose, and 13 rank and file, were killed; and Colonel Cameron, Lieutenants Colin Macdonald, Donald Macniel, 4 sergeants, and 54 rank and file wounded. The regiment was specially complimented for its conduct both by the commander-in-chief and by General Moore; the former declaring that nothing could do the regiment more credit than its conduct that day. It embarked in the end of October, and landed in England on on the 1st of November.

In August 1800 the 79th embarked at Southampton as part of the expedition fitted out to destroy the Spanish shipping in the harbours of Ferrol and Cadiz. It arrived before Ferrol on the 25th, and shortly afterwards the brigade of which the regiment formed part, forced the enemy from their position and took possession of the heights of Brion and Balon, which completely commanded the town and harbour of Ferrol. Lieutenant-General Sir James Pulteney, however, did not see meet to follow out the advantage thus gained, and abandoned the enterprise. In this "insignificant service," as Captain Jameson calls it, the 79th had only Captain Fraser, 2 sergeants, and 2 rank and file wounded.

On the 6th of October the expedition landed before Cadiz, but on account of the very unfavourable state of the weather, the enterprise was abandoned.

In 1801 the Cameron Highlanders took part in the famous operations in Egypt, under Sir Ralph Abercromby; but as minute details of this campaign are given in the histories of the 42nd and 92nd Regiments, it will be unnecessary to repeat the story here. The 79th was brigaded with the 2nd and 50th Regiments, and took an active part in the action of March 13th, in which it had 5 rank and file killed, and Lieutenant-Colonel Patrick M'Dowall, Lieutenants George Sutherland and John Stewart, Volunteer Alexander Cameron, 2 sergeants, and 56 rank and file wounded.

In the general engagement of March 21st, in which the brave Abercromby got his death-wound, the light companies of the 79th and the other regiments of its brigade kept the

[3] "At this interview, Colonel Cameron plainly told the Duke, 'to draft the 79th is more than you or your Royal father dare do.' The Duke then said, 'The King my father will certainly send the regiment to the West Indies.' Colonel Cameron, losing temper, replied, 'You may tell the King your father from me, that he may send us to h——l if he likes, and I'll go at the head of them, but *he daurna draft us,*' —a line of argument which, it is unnecessary to add, proved to the Royal Duke perfectly irresistible."—Jameson' *H. . . . . . 11.*

enemy's riflemen in check in front, while the fight was raging hotly on the right. The regiment lost one sergeant killed, and Lieutenant Patrick Ross, 2 sergeants, and 18 rank and file wounded.

While proceeding towards Cairo with Major-General Craddock's brigade (to which the Cameron Highlanders had been transferred) and a division of Turks, they had a brush on the 9th of May with a French force, in which the 79th had Captain M'Dowall and one private wounded. At Cairo the regiment had the honour of being selected to take possession of the advanced gate, the "Gate of the Pyramids," surrendered to the British in terms of a convention with the French.

For its distinguished services during the Egyptian campaign, the Cameron Highlanders, besides receiving the thanks of the king and parliament, was one of the regiments which received the honour of bearing the figure of a Sphinx, with the word "Egypt," on its colours and appointments.

After staying a short time at Minorca, the regiment returned to Scotland in August 1802, whence, after filling up its thinned ranks, it was removed to Ireland in the beginning of 1803. In 1804 a second battalion was raised, but was never employed on active service, being used only to fill up vacancies as they occurred in the first battalion, until 1815, when it was reduced at Dundee.

In 1804 the question of abolishing the kilt seems to have been under the consideration of the military authorities, and a correspondence on the subject took place between the Horse-Guards and Colonel Cameron, which deserves to be reproduced for the sake of the Highland Colonel's intensely characteristic reply. In a letter dated "Horse Guards, 13th October 1804," Colonel Cameron was requested to state his "*private* opinion as to the expediency of abolishing the kilt in Highland regiments, and substituting in lieu thereof the tartan trews." To this Colonel Cameron replied in four sentences as follows :—

"GLASGOW, *27th October* 1804.

"SIR,—On my return hither some days ago from Stirling, I received your letter of the 13th inst. (by General Calvert's orders) respecting the propriety of an alteration in the mode of clothing Highland regiments, in reply to which I beg to state, freely and fully, my sentiments upon *that* subject, without a particle of prejudice in either way, but merely founded upon *facts* as applicable to these corps—at least as far as I am *capable*, from thirty years' experience, twenty years of which I have been upon *actual* service in all *climates*, with the description of men in question, which, independent of being myself a Highlander, and well knowing all the convenience and inconvenience of our native garb in the field and otherwise, and perhaps, also, aware of the probable source and clashing motives from which the suggestion now under consideration originally *arose*. I have to observe progressively, that in the course of the late war several gentlemen proposed to raise Highland regiments, some for general service, but chiefly for home defence ; but most of these corps were called from all quarters, and thereby adulterated with every description of men, that rendered them anything but real Highlanders, or even Scotchmen (which is not strictly synonymous), and the colonels themselves being generally unacquainted with the language and habits of Highlanders, while prejudiced in favour of, and accustomed to wear breeches, consequently *averse* to that free congenial circulation of pure wholesome air (as an exhilarating native bracer) which has hitherto so peculiarly befitted the Highlander for *activity*, and all the other necessary qualities of a soldier, whether for hardship upon scanty fare, *readiness in accoutring*, or making *forced marches, &c.,* besides the exclusive advantage, when halted, of drenching his kilt, &c., in the *next brook*, as well as washing his limbs, and drying *both*, as it were, by constant *fanning*, without injury to either, but, on the contrary, feeling clean and comfortable, while the buffoon tartan pantaloon, &c., with all its fringed frippery (as some mongrel Highlanders would have it) sticking wet and dirty to the skin, is not very easily pulled off, and *less so* to get on again in case of alarm or any other hurry, and all this time absorbing both wet and dirt, followed up by rheumatism and fevers, which ultimately make great havoc in hot and cold climates ; while it consists with knowledge, that the Highlander in his native garb always appeared more cleanly, and maintained better health in both climates than those who wore even the thick cloth pantaloon. Independent of these circumstances, I feel no hesitation in saying, that the proposed alteration must have proceeded from a whimsical idea, more than from the real comfort of the Highland soldier, and a wish to lay aside that national martial garb, the very sight of which has, upon many occasions, struck the enemy with terror and confusion,—and now metamorphose the Highlander from his real characteristic appearance and comfort in an odious incompatible dress, to which it will, in my opinion, be difficult to reconcile him, as a poignant grievance to, and a galling reflection upon, Highland corps, &c., as levelling that martial distinction by which they have been hitherto *noticed and respected*,—and from my own experience I feel well founded in saying, that if anything was wanted to aid the rack-renting Highland landlords in destroying that source, which has hitherto proved so fruitful for keeping up Highland corps, it will be that of abolishing their native garb, which His Royal Highness the Commander-in-chief and the Adjutant-General may rest assured will prove a complete death-warrant to the recruiting service in that respect. But I sincerely hope His Royal Highness will never acquiesce in so painful and degrading an idea (come from whatever quarter it may) as to strip us of our native garb (admitted hitherto our regimental uniform) and *stuff* us into a harlequin tartan pantaloon, which, composed of the usual quality that continues, as at present worn, useful and becoming for twelve months, will not endure six weeks' fair wear as a pantaloon, and when patched makes a horrible appearance—besides that the necessary quantity to serve decently throughout the year would become extremely expensive, but, above all, take away completely the appearance and conceit of a Highland soldier, in which case I would rather see him *staffed* in breeches, and abolish the distinction at once.—I have the honour to be, &c.

(Signed) "ALAN CAMERON,
"*Colonel 79th or Cameron Highlanders.*"
"To Henry Thorpe, Esq."

The regiment remained in Ireland till November 1805, when it was removed to England, where it did duty at various places till July 1807. In that month the 79th formed part of the expedition against Denmark, where it remained till the following November, the only casualties being four men wounded, during the bombardment of Copenhagen.

After a fruitless expedition to Sweden in May 1808, under Lt.-General Sir John Moore, the regiment was ordered, with other reinforcements, to proceed to Portugal, where it landed August 26th, 1808, and immediately joined the army encamped near Lisbon. After the convention of Cintra, the 79th, as part of Major-General Fane's brigade, joined the army under Sir John Moore, whose object was to drive the French out of Spain. Moore, being joined by the division under Sir David Baird, at Mayorga, had proceeded as far as Sahagun, when he deemed it advisable to commence the ever memorable retreat to Corunna, details of which have already been given. At Corunna, on the 16th of January 1809, the 79th had no chance of distinguishing itself in action, its duty being, as part of Lt.-General Fraser's division, to hold the heights immediately in front of the gates of Corunna; but "they also serve who only stand and wait." The embarkation was effected in safety, and on the army arriving in England in February, the 79th marched to Weeley Barracks, in Essex, about 10 miles from Chelmsford, where many of the men were shortly afterwards attacked with fever, though not a man died.[4]

[4] "In 1809, the 79th accomplished what no other regiment did. In January of that year they were in Spain at the Battle of Corunna, and returned to England in February, when 700 men and several officers suffered from a dangerous typhus fever, yet not a man died. In July they embarked 1002 bayonets for Walcheren, were engaged during the whole siege of Flushing in the trenches, yet had not a man wounded, and, whilst there, lost only one individual in fever—Paymaster Baldock, the least expected of any one. During the three months after their return

While in Portugal, Colonel Cameron, who had been appointed commandant of Lisbon with the rank of Brigadier-General, retired from the personal command of the regiment, after leading it in every engagement and sharing all its privations for fifteen years; "his almost paternal anxiety," as Captain Jameson says, "for his native Highlanders had never permitted him to be absent from their head." He was succeeded in the command of the regiment by his eldest son, Lt.-Colonel Philip Cameron.

After taking part in the siege of Flushing, in August 1809, the regiment returned to England, and again took up its quarters in Weeley Barracks, where it was attacked with fever, which carried off a number of men, and prostrated many more, upwards of 40 having to be left behind when the regiment embarked for Portugal in January 1810, to join the army acting under Sir Arthur Wellesley.

Meanwhile a number of men of the 79th, who had been left behind in Portugal on the retreat to Corunna, had, along with several officers and men belonging to other regiments, been formed into a corps designated the 1st battalion of detachments. The detachment of the 79th consisted of 5 officers, 4 sergeants, and 45 rank and file; and out of this small number who were engaged at Talavera de la Reyna on July 27th and 28th, 1809, 14 rank and file were killed, and one sergeant and 27 rank and file wounded.

Shortly after landing at Lisbon, the regiment was ordered to proceed to Spain to assist in the defence of Cadiz, where it remained till the middle of August 1810, having had Lts. Patrick M'Crummen, Donald Cameron, and 25 rank and file wounded in performing a small service against the enemy. After its return to Lisbon, the 79th was equipped for the field, and joined the army under Lord Wellington at Busaco on the 25th of September. The 79th was here brigaded with the 7th and 61st Regiments, under the command of Major-General Alan Cameron.

The regiment had not long to wait before taking part in the active operations carried on

to England, only ten men died, and in December of that same year again, embarked for the peninsula, 1002 strong."—Note by Dr A. Anderson, Regimental surgeon, p. 44 of H. S. Smith's *List of the Officers of the 79th.*

against the French by England's great general. Wellington had taken up a strong position along the Sierra de Busaco, to prevent the further advance of Marshal Massena; and the division of which the 79th formed part was posted at the extreme right of the British line. At daybreak on the 27th of Sept. the French columns, preceded by a swarm of skirmishers, who had nearly surrounded and cut off the picket of the 79th, advanced against the British right, when Captain Neil Douglas gallantly volunteered his company to its support, and opening fire from a favourable position, checked the enemy's advance, and enabled the picket to retire in good order. As the enemy's attack was changed to the centre and left, the 79th had no other opportunity that day of distinguishing itself in action. It, however, lost Captain Alexander Cameron[5] and 7 rank and file killed, Captain Neil Douglas, and 41 rank and file wounded.

After this battle, Wellington deemed it prudent to retire within the strong lines of Torres Vedras, whither he was followed by Massena, who remained there till the 14th of November, when he suddenly broke up his camp and retired upon Santarem, followed by Wellington. The French again commenced their retreat in the beginning of March 1811, closely pursued by the British army. During the pursuit several small skirmishes took place, and in a sharp contest at Foz d'Arouce, the light company of the 79th had 2 men killed, and 7 wounded. In this affair, Lt. Kenneth Cameron of the 79th captured the Lieutenant-Colonel of the 39th French infantry.

On the 2nd of May, Massena, desirous of relieving Almeida, which Wellington had invested, took up a position in front of Dos Casas and Fuentes d'Onor. "The English position," says Jameson, "was a line whose left extended beyond the brook of Onoro, resting on a hill supported by Fort Conception; the right, which was more accessible, was at Nave d'Aver, and the centre at Villa Formosa."

On the 3rd of May, Massena commenced

[5] "This gallant officer commanded the picket of the 79th, and could not be induced to withdraw. He was last seen by Captain (afterwards the late Lieut.-General Sir Neil) Douglas, fighting hand to hand with several French soldiers, to whom he refused to deliver up his sword. His body was found pierced with seven bayonet wounds."—Jameson's *Record*, p. 24.

his attack upon the English position, his strongest efforts being directed against the village of Fuentes d'Onor, which he seemed determined to get possession of. The defence of the position was entrusted to the 79th, along with the 71st Highlanders, with the 24th regiment and several light companies in support, the whole commanded by Lieutenant-Colonel Philip Cameron of the 79th. During the whole of the day the enemy in superior numbers made several desperate attempts to take the village, and indeed did manage to get temporary possession of several parts, "but after a succession of most bloody hand to hand encounters, he was completely driven from it at nightfall, when darkness put an end to the conflict."[6]

Early on the morning of the 5th of May, Massena, who in the meantime had been making dispositions for a renewal of the contest, again directed his strongest efforts against the position held by the 79th and its comrades. By the force of overwhelming numbers the French did succeed in carrying the lower portion of the village, at the same time surrounding and taking prisoners two companies of the 79th, which had got separated from the main body. Meantime, in the upper portion of the village a fierce and deadly contest was being waged between the French Grenadiers and the Highlanders, the latter, according to Captain Jameson, in numerous instances using their muskets as clubs instead of acting with the bayonet, so close and deadly was the strife maintained. "About this period of the action, a French soldier was observed to slip aside into a doorway and take deliberate aim at Colonel Cameron, who fell from his horse mortally wounded. A cry of grief, intermingled with shouts for revenge, arose from the rearmost Highlanders, who witnessed the fall of their commanding officer, and was rapidly communicated to those in front. As Colonel Cameron was being conveyed to the rear by his sorrowing clansmen, the 88th regiment, detached to reinforce the troops at this point, arrived in double-quick time; the men were now at the highest pitch of excitement, and a charge being ordered by Brigadier-General

[6] Jameson's *Record*.

Mackinnon, the enemy was driven out of the village with great slaughter. The post was maintained until the evening, when the battle terminated, and the Highlanders being withdrawn, were replaced by a brigade of the light division." [7]

In these fierce contests, besides Lt.-Colonel Cameron, who died of his wound, the 79th had Captain William Imlach, one sergeant, and 30 rank and file killed; Captains Malcolm Fraser and Sinclair Davidson, Lts. James Sinclair, John Calder, Archibald Fraser, Alexander Cameron, John Webb, and Fulton Robertson, Ensigns Charles Brown and Duncan Cameron, 6 sergeants, and 138 rank and file wounded, besides about 100 missing, many of whom were afterwards reported as killed.

The grief for the loss of Colonel Cameron, son of Major-General Alan Cameron, former and first colonel of the 79th, was deep and wide-spread. Wellington, with all his staff and a large number of general officers, notwithstanding the critical state of matters, attended his funeral, which was conducted with military honours. Sir Walter Scott, in his "Vision of Don Roderick," thus alludes to Colonel Cameron's death :—

" And what avails thee that, for Cameron slain,
   Wild from his plaided ranks the yell was given ?
 Vengeance and grief gave mountain-rage the rein,
 And, at the bloody spear-point headlong driven,
 The despot's giant guards fled like the rack of
   heaven." [8]

Wellington,—and many other officers of high rank,— sent a special letter of condolence to the colonel's father, Major-General Cameron, in which he speaks of his son in terms of the highest praise. "I cannot conceive," he says, "a string of circumstances more honourable and glorious than these in which he lost his life in the cause of his country."

[7] Jameson's *Record*, p. 27.
[8] In a note to this poem, Scott says that the 71st and 79th, on seeing Cameron fall, raised a dreadful shriek of grief and rage; "they charged with irresistible fury the finest body of French grenadiers ever seen, being a part of Bonaparte's selected guard. The officer who led the French, a man remarkable for stature and symmetry, was killed on the spot. The Frenchman who stepped out of the ranks to take aim at Colonel Cameron was also bayoneted, pierced with a thousand wounds, and almost torn to pieces by the furious Highlanders, who, under the command of Colonel Cadogan, bore the enemy out of the contested ground at the point of the bayonet."

Cameron was succeeded in the command of the regiment by Major Alexander Petrie, who, besides receiving a gold medal, had the brevet rank of Lt.-Colonel conferred on him; and the senior captain, Andrew Brown, was promoted to the brevet rank of Major.

How highly Lord Wellington esteemed the services performed by the 79th on these two bloody days, will be seen from the following letter:—

" VILLA FORMOSA, 8th May, 1811.

"SIR,—I am directed by Lord Wellington to acquaint you that he will have great pleasure in submitting to the Commander-in-Chief for a commission the name of any non-commissioned officer of the 79th regiment whom you may recommend, as his lordship is anxious to mark the sense of the conduct of the 79th during the late engagement with the enemy.
" I have the honour to be, &c.,
          (Signed)   " FITZROY SOMERSET.
"Major Petrie, Commanding
  " 79th Highlanders," &c.

Sergeant Donald M'Intosh was selected for this distinguished honour, and, on the 4th of June 1811, was appointed ensign in the 88th Regiment.

The 79th did not take part in any other engagement till the 22nd of July 1812, when it was present as part of the reserve division under Major-General Campbell at the great victory of Salamanca. Its services, however, were not brought into requisition till the close of the day, and its casualties were only two men wounded. Still it was deemed worthy of having the honour of bearing the word " Salamanca " on its colours and appointments, and a gold medal was conferred upon the commanding officer, Lt.-Colonel Robert Fulton, who had joined the regiment at Vellajes in September 1811, with a draft of 5 sergeants, and 231 rank and file from the 2nd battalion.

In the interval between Fuentes d'Onor and Salamanca the 79th was moved about to various places, and twice was severely attacked with epidemic sickness.

After the battle of Salamanca, the 79th, along with the rest of the allied army, entered Madrid about the middle of August, where it remained till the end of that month.

On the 1st of September the 79th, along with the rest of the army, left Madrid under Lord Wellington, to lay siege to Burgos, before which it arrived on the 18th : and on the morning of the 19th, the light battalion, formed by the several light companies of the 24th, 42nd, 58th, 60th, and 79th regiments, commanded by Major the Hon. E. C. Cocks of the 79th, was selected for the purpose of driving the enemy from their defences on the heights of St Michael's, consisting of a horn-work and flèches commanding the approach to the castle on the right.

"The attack was made by a simultaneous movement on the two advanced flèches, which were carried in the most gallant manner by the light companies of the 42nd and 79th; but a small post, close to and on the left of the horn-work, was still occupied by the enemy, from which he opened a fire upon the attacking party. Lieut. Hugh Grant, with a detachment of the 79th light company, was sent forward to dislodge him, but finding himself opposed to continually increasing numbers, he found it impossible to advance; but being equally resolved not to retire, he drew up his small party under cover of an embankment, and, possessing himself of the musket of a wounded soldier, he fired together with his men and gallantly maintained himself. The remainder of the company now coming up, the enemy was driven within the works; but this brave young officer was unfortunately mortally wounded, and died a few days afterwards, sincerely and deeply regretted.

The two light companies maintained the position until nightfall, when the light battalion was assembled at this point, and orders were issued to storm the horn-work at 11 P.M. A detachment of the 42nd and a Portuguese regiment were directed to enter the ditch on the left of the work, and to attempt the escalade of both demi-bastions, the fire from which was to be kept in check by a direct attack in front by the remainder of the 42nd. The light battalion was to advance along the slope of the hill, parallel to the left flank of the work, which it was to endeavour to enter by its gorge. The attack by the 42nd was to be the signal for the advance of the light battalion, the command of the whole being entrusted to Major-General Sir Denis Pack.[9]

In execution these arrangements, the troops at the appointed hour proceeded to the assault. The light companies, on arriving at the gorge of the work, were received with a brisk fire of musketry through the opening in the palisades, causing severe loss; they, however, continued to advance, and, without waiting for the application of the felling-axes and ladders, with which they were provided, the foremost in the attack were actually lifted over the palisades on each other's shoulders. In this manner, the first man who entered the work was Sergeant John Mackenzie of the 79th; Major Cocks, the brave leader of the storming party, next followed, and several others in succession.

In this manner, and by means of the scaling-ladders, the light battalion was, in a few minutes, formed within the work; and a guard, consisting of Sergeant Donald Mackenzie and twelve men of the 79th, having been placed at the gate leading to the castle, a charge was made on the garrison, which, numbering between 400 and 500 men, having by this time formed itself into a solid mass, defied every attempt to compel a surrender; in this manner the French troops rushed towards the gate, where, meeting with the small guard of the 79th, they were enabled, from their overwhelming numbers to overcome every opposition, and to effect their escape to the castle.

Sergeant Mackenzie, who was severely wounded in this affair,[1] and his small party behaved with the greatest bravery in their endeavours to prevent the escape of the French garrison; and bugler Charles Bogle of the 79th, a man of colour, was afterwards found dead at the gate, near a French soldier, the sword of the former and bayonet of the latter through each other's bodies.

The front attack had in the meantime completely failed, and a severe loss was sustained."[2]

The enemy having opened a destructive fire from the castle on the horn-work, the light battalion was withdrawn to the ditch of the curtain; and strong parties were employed during the night in forming a parapet in the gorge.

Afterwards a series of assaults was made against the castle, with but little success. In one of these Major Andrew Lawrie of the 79th was killed while entering a ditch, and encouraging on the party he led by escalade; and the Hon. Major Cocks met with a similar fate while rallying his picket during a night sortie of the French. The death of this officer was very much regretted by Wellington, who in his despatch of October 11, 1812, said he considered "his loss as one of the greatest importance to this army and to His Majesty's service." The army continued before Burgos till Oct. 21, when, being threatened by the advance of strong reinforcements of the enemy, it was deemed advisable to retreat towards the frontiers of Portugal.

At the siege of Burgos, besides the two officers just mentioned, the 79th had one sergeant and 27 rank and file killed; Captain William Marshall, Lt. Hugh Grant, Kewan J. Leslie, and Angus Macdonald, 5 sergeants, 1 drummer, and 79 rank and file wounded.

The regiment, with the rest of the army, remained in cantonments till the middle of May 1813; and in February of that year Lt.-Colonel Fulton retired from the command of the regiment, which was assumed by Lt.-Colonel Neil Douglas,[3] from the 2nd battalion.

Breaking up from winter-quarters about

---

[9] His portrait is on p. 504, vol. ii.

[1] "Sergeant Mackenzie had previously applied to Major Cocks for the use of his dress sabre, which the major readily granted, and used to relate with great satisfaction that the sergeant returned it to him in a state which indicated that he had used it with effect."

[2] Captain Jameson's Record.

[3] His portrait will be found on the steel-plate of Colonels of the 71st and 72nd Regiments.

the middle of May, the army advanced against the enemy, who occupied various strong positions on the north of the Douro, which, however, were precipitately evacuated during the advance of the British army. The enemy retired towards the north-east, in the direction of Burgos, which the British found had been completely destroyed by the French. In the action at Vittoria, in which the enemy was completely routed on the 21st of June, the 79th had not a chance of distinguishing itself in action, as it formed part of Major-General Pakenham's division, whose duty it was to cover the march of the magazines and stores at Medina de Pomar.

At the battle of the "Pyrenees," on the 28th of July, the 6th division, to which the 79th belonged, was assigned a position across the valley of the Lanz, which it had scarcely assumed when it was attacked by a superior French force, which it gallantly repulsed with severe loss; a similar result occurred at all points, nearly every regiment charging with the bayonet. The loss of the 79th was 1 sergeant and 16 rank and file killed; Lieutenant J. Kynock, 2 sergeants, and 38 rank and file wounded. Lt.-Colonel Neil Douglas had a horse shot under him, and in consequence of his services he was awarded a gold medal; and Major Andrew Brown was promoted to the brevet rank of Lt.-Colonel for his gallantry.

Along with the rest of the army, the 79th followed the enemy towards the French frontier, the next action in which it took part being that of Nivelle, November 19, 1813, fully described elsewhere. Here the steadiness of its line in advancing up a hill to meet the enemy excited the admiration of Sir Rowland Hill, and although its casualties were few, the part it took in the action gained for the regiment the distinction of inscribing "Nivelle" on its colours and appointments. Its loss was 1 man killed, and Ensign John Thomson and 5 men wounded.

Continuing to advance with its division, the 79th shared, on the 10th of December, in the successful attack on the enemy's entrenchments on the banks of the Nive, when it had 5 men killed, and Lt. Alexander Robertson, 2 sergeants, and 24 rank and file wounded.[4]

The enemy having retired to the Gave d'Oléron, and the severity of the weather preventing further operations, the 79th went into quarters at St Pierre d'Yurbe, and while here, in Feb. 1814, it marched over to the seaport town of St Jean de Luz to get a new supply of clothing, of which it stood very much in need.

In the battle of Orthes, on February 25th, the 79th had no opportunity of taking part, but took an active share, and suffered severely, in the final engagement at Toulouse.

Early on the morning of the 10th, the 6th division, of which the 79th, under the command of Sir Henry Clinton, formed part, along with the 42nd and 91st regiments, constituting the Highland Brigade of Sir Denis Pack, crossed the Garonne and the Ers at Croix d'Orade, following the 4th division, and halted near the northern extremity of the height (between and running parallel with the canal of Languedoc, and the river Ers) on which the enemy was posted, strongly fortified by entrenchments and redoubts. Arrangements were here made for a combined attack, the 6th division, continuing its march along the left bank of the Ers, filed by threes in double-quick time, close under the enemy's guns, from which a heavy cannonade of round and grape-shot was opened, occasioning considerable loss. "The Highland Brigade of Sir Denis Pack," Captain Jameson says, "halted about midway to the position, formed line to the right, and proceeded to ascend the hill. The light companies were now ordered out, and directed to conform to the movements of the brigade, General Pack having mingled with the former, and cheering them on. The grenadier company of the 79th was brought up as a reinforcement to the light troops; and after a vigorous resistance, the enemy was driven to a considerable distance down the opposite slope of the ridge. The pursuit was then discontinued, and a slackened and desultory fire of advanced posts succeeded.

The brigade had, in the meantime, formed on the Balma road across the height, the light companies were recalled, and final arrangements completed for an attack on the two centre redoubts of the enemy's position, designated respectively La Colombette and Le

---

[4] As the part taken by the 79th in the Peninsular battles has been described at some length in connection with the 42nd and other regiments, it is unnecessary to repeat the details here.

Tour des Augustins. The attack of the former or most advanced redoubt was assigned to the 42nd, and the latter to the 79th, the 91st and 12th Portuguese being in reserve. Both these redoubts were carried at a run, in the most gallant style, in the face of a terrific fire of round shot, grape, and musketry, by which a very severe loss was sustained. About 100 men of the 79th, headed by several officers, now left the captured work to encounter the enemy on the ridge of the plateau; but, suddenly perceiving a discharge of musketry in the redoubt captured by the 42nd in their rear, and also seeing it again in possession of the enemy, they immediately fell back on the Redoubt des Augustins. The Colombette had been suddenly attacked and entered by a fresh and numerous column of the enemy, when the 42nd was compelled to give way, and, continuing to retire by a narrow and deep road leading through the redoubt occupied by the 79th (closely pursued by an overwhelming force of the enemy), the alarm communicated itself from one regiment to the other, and both, for a moment, quitted the works.[5]

At this critical juncture, Lt.-Colonel Douglas having succeeded in rallying the 79th, the regiment again advanced, and in a few minutes succeeded in retaking, not only its own former position, but also the redoubt from which the 42nd had been driven. For this service, Lt.-Colonel Douglas received on the field the thanks of Generals Clinton and Pack, commanding the division and brigade; and the regiments in reserve having by this time come up, the brigade was moved to the right, for the purpose of carrying, in conjunction with the Spaniards, the two remaining redoubts on the left of the position. While, however, the necessary preparations were making for this attack, the enemy was observed to be in the act of abandoning them, thus leaving the British army in complete possession of the plateau and its works. The 79th occupied the Redoubt Colombette during the night of the 10th of April 1814.[6]

The importance of the positions captured by the 42nd and the 79th was so great, and the behaviour of these regiments so intrepid and gallant, that they won special commendation from Wellington, being two of the four regiments particularly mentioned in his despatch of the 12th of April 1814.

The 79th lost Captains Patrick Purves and John Cameron, Lt. Duncan Cameron; and 16 rank and file killed; the wounded were Captains Thomas Mylne, Peter Innes, James Campbell, and William Marshall; Lts. William M'Barnet, Donald Cameron, James Fraser, Ewen Cameron (1st), John Kynock, Ewen Cameron (2nd), Duncan Macpherson, Charles M'Arthur, and Allan Macdonald; Ensign Allan Maclean, Adjutant and Lt. Kenneth Cameron, 12 sergeants, 2 drummers, and 182 rank and file. Of those wounded, Lts. M'Barnet, Ewen Cameron (2nd), and 23 men died of their wounds. Of the 494 officers and men of the 79th who went into action at Toulouse, only 263 came out unwounded.

Lt.-Colonel Neil Douglas received the decoration of a gold cross for this action, in substitution of all his former distinctions; Major Duncan Cameron received the brevet rank of Lt.-Colonel in the army; and the 79th was permitted by royal authority to bear on its colours and appointments the word TOULOUSE, in addition to its other inscriptions. As a proof, likewise, of the distinction earned by it during the successive campaigns in the Peninsula, it was subsequently authorised to have the word PENINSULA inscribed on its colours and appointments.

Napoleon Buonaparte's abdication having put an end to further hostilities, the regiment, after remaining a few weeks in the south of France, embarked in July 1814, arriving at Cork on the 26th, and taking up its quarters in the barracks there. While here, in December, its ranks were filled up by a large draft from the 2nd battalion, and in the beginning of Feb. 1815, it set sail, along with several other regiments, for North America, but was driven back by contrary winds; the same happened to the expedition when attempting to sail again on the 1st of March. On the 3rd, the expedition was countermanded; and on the 17th the 79th sailed for the north of Ireland, to take up its quarters at Belfast, where it

---

[5] Whilst the enemy thus gained a temporary possession of the redoubts, Lieutenant Ford and seven men of the 79th, who were in a detached portion of the work, separated from its front face by a deep road, had their retreat cut off by a whole French regiment advancing along this road in their rear, when one of the men, with great presence of mind, called out "sit down," which hint was immediately acted on, with the effect of saving the party from being made prisoners, as the enemy supposed them to be wounded, *and a French officer shrugged his shoulders in token of inability to render them any assistance!*"

II.

[6] Jameson's *Historical Record*, p. 43.

4 U

706 HISTORY OF THE HIGHLAND REGIMENTS.

remained till May, when, with all the other available forces of Britain, it was called upon to take part in that final and fierce struggle with the great disturber of the peace of Europe, and assist in putting an end to his bloody machinations against the peace of civilised nations. The 79th, having joined Wellington's army at Brussels, was brigaded with the 28th, 32nd, and 95th Regiments, under the command of Major-General Sir James Kempt, the three regiments forming the first brigade of the fifth, or Sir Thomas Picton's division, the Royal Scots, 42nd, 44th, and 92nd regiments forming the other brigade under Major-General Pack.

The events from the night of the 15th to the 18th of June 1815 are so well known, and so many details are given in connection with the 42nd and 92nd Regiments, that it will be sufficient here to indicate the part taken in them by the 79th. The alarm having been rapidly spread of the approach of the French on the night of the 15th—the night of the famous ball well known to all readers of Byron,—preparations were immediately made for marching out, and by four o'clock on the morning of the 16th, the regiment, with its division, provisioned for three days, was on the road to Charleroi. In the passage of *Childe Harold* where Byron's famous description of the episode preceding Quatre Bras occurs, the poet thus refers to the Cameron Highlanders :—

" And wild and high the ' Cameron's Gathering ' rose,
  The war-note of Lochiel, which Albyn's hills
  Have heard, and heard, too, have her Saxon foes :—
  How in the noon of night that pibroch thrills
  Savage and shrill ! But with the breath which fills
  Their mountain-pipe, so fill the mountaineers
  With the fierce native daring which instils
  The stirring memory of a thousand years,
  And Evan's, Donald's fame rings in each clansman's
       ears !"

The division halted near the village of Waterloo to cook its provisions ; but before this could be accomplished it was ordered forward towards Quatre Bras, where it halted on the road, at the distance of about half a mile from the enemy, from whom the column was separated by a rising ground. After the two brigade companies had halted for a very short time on this road the division broke off to the left, lining the Namur Road, the banks

---

of which were from ten to fifteen feet high on each side. The Cameron Highlanders formed the extreme left of the British army, and the 92nd the right of the division, being posted immediately in front of Quatre Bras.

Scarcely had this position been taken up, when the enemy advanced in great force, sending out " a cloud of sharpshooters," who were met by the light companies of the first brigade, along with the 8th company and marksmen of the 79th. These maintained their ground bravely, despite the fearful execution done upon them by the overwhelming numbers of the enemy's sharpshooters, who picked out the officers especially, and the artillerymen serving the only two guns yet brought into action. At about four o'clock in the afternoon, the Cameron Highlanders had the honour of being ordered forward to cover the guns and drive the enemy from his advanced position, and gallantly did the regiment perform the service.

" The regiment," says Captain Jameson,[8] " cleared the bank in its front, fired a volley, and, charging with the bayonet, drove the French advanced troops with great precipitation and in disorder to a hedge about a hundred yards in their rear, where they attempted to re-form, but were followed up with such alacrity that they again gave way, pursued to another hedge about the same distance, from which they were a second time driven in confusion upon their main column, which was formed in great strength upon the opposite rising ground. The regiment, now joined by its detached companies, commenced firing volleys upon the enemy from behind the last-mentioned hedge, and in the course of fifteen minutes expended nearly all its ammunition. Whilst in this exposed situation, it was ordered to retire, which it accomplished without confusion, although it had a broad ditch to leap, and the first hedge to repass, when it formed line about fifty yards in front of its original position. Being here much exposed to the fire of the enemy's guns, it was ordered to lie down, and it continued thus for nearly an hour, when it was again directed to resume its first position on the road, and

---

[7] " Evan " and " Donald " are Sir Evan or Ewen Cameron, and Donald, the "Gentle Lochiel." Their portraits are on pages 296 and 519, vol. i.

[8] *Historical Record*, p. 51.

form in column as circumstances might require. Being afterwards repeatedly threatened by cavalry, it formed and moved forward in square, but without being attacked."

Meantime all the other regiments of the division were engaged; indeed, each battalion of the British army had to sustain, in several instances separately and independently, the whole weight of the superior French masses which bore down upon it. The enemy, however, notwithstanding the many advantages he had, seems to have failed in almost every attack, and the contest for that day ended about dusk decidedly in favour of the British.

The loss of the 79th was Captain John Sinclair, Lt. and Adjutant John Kynock, and 28 rank and file killed; Lt.-Colonel Neil Douglas, Brevet Lt.-Colonels Andrew Brown and Duncan Cameron; Captains Thomas Mylne, Neil Campbell, William Marshall, Malcolm Fraser, William Bruce, and Robert Mackay; Lieuts. Thomas Brown, William Maddock, William Leaper, James Fraser, Donald MacPhee, and William A. Riach; Ensign James Robertson, Volunteer Alexander Cameron, 10 sergeants, and 248 rank and file wounded. All the field officers, according to Captain Jameson, in addition to severe wounds, had their horses shot under them.

At dusk on the 17th the division took up its position among some corn-fields near the farm La Haye Sainte, under cover of a rising ground, the ridge opposite to which was lined by the enemy's columns. The 28th and 79th formed the centre of Picton's division, the left of the division extending towards Ohain, its right resting on the Brussels road.

About half-past ten on the morning of the 18th of June, the French began to move forward to the attack, under cover of a tremendous cannonade, spiritedly answered by the British artillery, posted in advance of a road which ran along the crest of the rising ground in front of the division, and on each side of which was a hedge. Kempt's brigade, deploying into line, advanced to this road, the light companies and the rifles descending into the valley, and maintaining a severe contest against overwhelming numbers. Meantime a heavy column of the enemy's infantry, advancing towards the right of the division, was warmly received by the 28th; and the 32nd and 79th, following up the advantage, each attacking the column opposed to it, a close and obstinate engagement followed, "shedding lasting honour on Kempt's brigade," till at length the enemy gave way in the greatest confusion.

It was during this contest that General Picton was killed and General Kempt severely wounded; but although unable, from the severity of the wound, to sit on horseback, the latter would not allow himself to be carried off the field. The column of the enemy thus routed was shortly afterwards surrounded and taken captive by Ponsonby's brigade of cavalry.

Shortly after this the first brigade, being threatened by a body of the enemy's cavalry, formed into squares, and soon afterwards returned to its former position on the road,[9] lining the hedge nearest the enemy, where it was exposed to a galling and destructive fire, both from the guns and sharpshooters, against whom the light companies of Kempt's brigade and the division rifles were several times sent.

After falling back for a supply of ammunition, the first brigade again moved forward, and a general charge having been made along the whole line about seven o'clock, the enemy gave way in all directions, pursued by the Prussians and the English cavalry. The fifth division rested for the night near the farm of *La Belle Alliance.*

The loss of the 79th was Captain John Cameron, Lts. Duncan Macpherson, Donald Cameron, and Ewen Kennedy, 2 sergeants, and 27 rank and file killed; Captains James Campbell, senior, Neil Campbell; Lts. Alexander Cameron, Ewen Cameron, Alexander Forbes, Charles Macarthur, and John Powling; Ensigns A. J. Crawford and J. Nash, 7 sergeants, 4 drummers, and 121 rank and file wounded. Captain Neil Campbell, Lts. Donald Cameron, John Powling, and 48 men died soon afterwards. The total number of officers and men who entered the engagement on the 16th was 776, and out of that only 297 came out on the 18th unwounded; the loss of the 79th exceeded by one that of any other regiment in the army, except the 3rd battalion of the 1st Foot Guards, which was almost annihilated.

Wellington, in his despatch of the 19th, mentions the regiment in terms of high praise; and, as in the case of Toulouse, it was one of the only four British regiments—the 28th, 42nd, 79th, and 92nd—specially mentioned in the despatch. The distinction of a Companionship of the Bath was conferred upon Lt.-Colonel Neil Douglas, and upon Brevet Lt.-Colonels Andrew Brown and Duncan Cameron; Capt. Thomas Mylne was promoted by brevet to be

[9] "During the formation, Piper Kenneth Mackay of the 79th, a brave Highlander, stepped outside of the bayonets and continued to play round the outside of the square, the popular air of '*Cogaidh na Sith*' with much inspiriting effect."—Jameson's *Historical Record.*

major in the army; and Lt. Alexander Cameron, upon whom, from the great loss sustained in superior officers, the command of the regiment ultimately devolved, was promoted to the brevet rank of major for his distinguished conduct. Each surviving officer and soldier received the decoration of the "Waterloo" silver medal, and was allowed to reckon two additional years' service.

The regiment, along with the rest of the army, proceeded on the 19th in pursuit of the enemy, arriving on July 8th at Paris, near which it was encamped till the beginning of December. While here, on the 17th of August, at the special request of the Emperor of Russia, Sergeant Thomas Campbell of the grenadiers, a man of gigantic stature, with Private John Fraser and Piper Kenneth Mackay, all of the 79th, accompanied by a like number of each rank from the 42nd and 92nd Highlanders, proceeded to the Palais Elysée in Paris, to gratify the Emperor's desire of examining the dress and equipments of the Highland regiments. Sergeant Campbell especially was most minutely inspected by the Emperor, who, says Campbell, "examined my hose, gaiters, legs, and pinched my skin, thinking I wore something under my kilt, and had the curiosity to lift my kilt to my navel, so that he might not be deceived." After asking Campbell many questions, the Emperor "requested Lord Cathcart to order me to put John Fraser through the 'manual and platoon' exercise, at which performance he was highly pleased. He then requested the pipers to play up, and Lord Cathcart desired them to play the Highland tune 'Cògaidh nà Sìth' (' war or peace'), which he explained to the Emperor, who seemed highly delighted with the music. After the Emperor had done with me, the veteran Count Platoff came up to me, and, taking me by the hand, told me in broken English that I was a good and brave soldier, and all my countrymen were. He then pressed my hand to his breast, and gave me his to press to mine."

In the beginning of December 1815, the 79th, as part of the Army of Occupation, went into cantonments in Pas de Calais, where it remained till the end of October 1818, when it embarked for England, taking up its quarters at Colchester on the 8th of November.

After moving from Chichester to Portsmouth, and Portsmouth to Jersey, the regiment, in May 1820, embarked at Plymouth for Ireland, where it took part in the critical and not very agreeable duty necessitated by the disturbed state of the country, details of which will be found in our account of the 42nd Royal Highlanders, who were in Ireland at the same time.

On quitting Jersey, the "States of the Island" transmitted to the commanding officer of the 79th an address, praising the regiment in the highest terms for its exemplary conduct while stationed in the island.

The 79th remained in Ireland till August 1825, being quartered successively at Fermoy, Limerick, Templemore, Naas, Dublin, and Kilkenny, furnishing detachments at each of these places to the district and towns in the neighbourhood. The regiment seems to have discharged its unpleasant duties as delicately and satisfactorily as did the 42nd Highlanders, and to have merited the esteem and respect of the people among whom it was stationed. On leaving Limerick, where it was quartered for nearly two years, the magistrates and council presented an address to the commanding officer, Lt.-Colonel Douglas, in which they say,—

"The mild manners and military deportment of the officers, as well as the excellent discipline and moral order of the brave men whom you so well command, are happily evinced in the general order which their uniform good conduct has excited in this city; and we beg of you to convey to them the expression of our highest approbation."

In April 1825, the regiment was augmented from eight to ten companies, of 740 rank and file, and in August, the six service companies embarked at Cork for Canada, under the command of Colonel Sir Neil Douglas, arriving at Quebec in the month of October, where they remained till June 1828. During this time, with the exception of a few months in Glasgow, the dépôt companies were stationed at various places in Ireland.

On the 24th of March 1828, Lt.-General Sir R. C. Ferguson, G.C.B.,[1] was appointed colonel of the regiment, in succession to Lt.-General Sir Alan Cameron, K.C.B., who had died at Fulham, Middlesex, on the 9th, after

[1] See his portrait on the steel-plate of Colonels of the 79th, 79th Highlanders.

being connected with the regiment for about thirty-five years.

On the 18th of June 1828, the anniversary of Waterloo, the 79th, which in that month had removed to Montreal, was presented with new colours, the gift of its new Colonel, Lt.-General Ferguson. The presentation, which was performed by Lady Douglas, took place on the Champs de Mars, in presence of a very numerous assemblage of the élite of the inhabitants of Montreal.

The regiment returned to Quebec in 1833, where it remained till its embarkation for England in 1836. In the October of that year, the service companies were joined at Glasgow by the dépôt companies, which had in the meantime been moving about from place to place in Ireland, England, and Scotland, being stationed for most of the time at various towns in the last mentioned country.

In September 1833, by the retirement of Sir Neil Douglas on half-pay, Brevet Lt.-Colonel Duncan Macdougal succeeded to the command of the regiment; and on the latter's retirement in March 1835, he was succeeded by Major Robert Ferguson.

The regiment remained in Glasgow till June 1837, removing thence to Edinburgh, where it was stationed till the following June, when it proceeded to Dublin. On account of the disturbed state of the manufacturing districts in the north of England in 1839, the regiment was ordered to proceed thither, being quartered at various places. Here it remained till about the end of 1840, when it was again ordered on foreign service, embarking at Deptford for Gibraltar, where it arrived in January 1841, and where it remained performing garrison duty till June 1848.

In April 1841, on the death of Sir R. C. Ferguson, Major-General the Honourable John Ramsay was appointed Colonel of the 79th, and was succeeded, on his death in July 1842, by Lt.-General Sir James Macdonell, G.C.B., whose portrait will be found on the plate of Colonels of the 78th and 79th Regiments. Meantime, on the retirement, in June 1841, of Lt.-Colonel Robert Ferguson, Major Andrew Brown succeeded to the command of the regiment, but exchanged in October following with Colonel John Carter. K.H., from the 1st Royals,

who retired in June 1842, and was succeeded by Major the Hon. Lauderdale Maule.

" The monotony of a regiment's life at Gibraltar is well known to every corps that has had to perform garrison duty on the Rock. This monotony falls much more heavily on the men than on the officers of a regiment; the former, although they may leave the garrison gate under certain restrictions, cannot pass the lines which separate the neutral ground from Spanish territory.

A few of the more gifted, therefore, of the 79th, during its seven years' sojourn at Gibraltar, tried from time to time to enliven the community by such means as were at their command, which were slender enough, but went a long way when properly utilised and duly encouraged. Among these, the most popular, perhaps, was the performance of private theatricals by a small company selected from more or less qualified volunteers; and in truth the way in which they contrived to put small pieces of a broad farcical nature on their improvised stage, did no small credit to their natural histrionic abilities. These performances at first took place in the schoolroom, or such other well-sized apartments as could be made available, and "the house" was at all times crammed with a most appreciative audience, comprising all ranks, and representing every corps in the garrison. [2]

At a later period the amateurs of the 79th having discovered their strength, and the real merits of one or two stars (of whom more presently), engaged the town theatre, and gave one or two performances of the national drama " Rob Roy," in a manner which would not have disgraced the boards of many a provincial theatre at home. The one " bright particular star " of the company undoubtedly was a bandsman of the regiment, named C———. His rôle was broad comedy, and the Liston-like gravity of his immovable features gave irresistible point to the humour of such parts as he was accustomed to fill. But the one special character with which he became identified in his limited circle, nearly as completely as the late Mr Mackay was with the Edinburgh public, was "Bailie Nicol Jarvie." Dignity of position, bluntness of perception, dyspepsia itself, were not proof against his quaint delineation of this well-known character.

In 1849 or '50 the dramatic corps had been playing " Rob Roy" with much acceptance in an improvised theatre at Quebec, being a large room used for public meetings and so forth in the principal hotel there. The city is, or was, full of Scotchmen, most of them enthusiastically national, and the performances had been a great success. Unfortunately certain festivities, which were scarcely included in the programme submitted to the commanding officer, followed in connection with these entertainments, and poor C———, among others, was not entirely proof against their seductions. The members of the dramatic corps showed symptoms of falling into habits which could not but be detrimental both to their own welfare and the discipline of the regiment; and the performances after a while had to be stopped.

Shortly after this, one fine morning, as the commanding officer, accompanied by the adjutant and one or two other officers, was crossing the barrack square on his way from the orderly-room, the party encountered the unfortunate quondam Thespian in a state of considerable elevation, between two men of the guard, who were conveying him to durance vile. As his dim eye fell on the form of the commanding

[2] For these and other personal anecdotes relating to the history of the 79th during the last forty years, we are indebted to the kindness of Lt.-Colonel Clephane.

officer, a gleam of tipsy humour for a moment lighted up his somewhat grotesque lineaments; John Barleycorn had, for the time, extinguished all terrors of the august presence. "Hang a bailie!" hiccuped poor C—— as he passed the group, who were carefully ignoring his vicinity: "Hang a bailie! ma conscience!" It is scarcely necessary to say that, when brought up for judgment some four-and-twenty hours afterwards, the unfortunate magistrate was dealt with as lightly as the code of military discipline permitted. C—— was discharged soon afterwards, having served his time; and his subsequent career was never, we believe, traced by his former comrades of the 79th."

On leaving Gibraltar, in June 1848, the regiment proceeded to Canada, but before embarking, the officers and men erected by voluntary subscription a handsome marble tablet, in the Wesleyan Chapel at Gibraltar (where divine service was held for the Presbyterian soldiers of the garrison), to the memory of those non-commissioned officers and soldiers who died during their period of service on the Rock. The regiment arrived at Quebec on the 27th of July 1848, and remained in Canada till August 1851, when it embarked for England, arriving in Leith Roads at the end of the month. On disembarking the headquarters proceeded to Stirling Castle and formed a junction with the dépôt, while three companies were detached to Perth and three to Dundee.

Previous to embarking for England, a highly complimentary letter was addressed to Lieutenant-Colonel the Honourable Lauderdale Maule, by the magistrates and council of Quebec. "It is," says this letter, "with great pleasure that the magistrates bear testimony to the excellent conduct of the men of your regiment during their sojourn in Quebec, where they will be long and favourably remembered." Here also did the officers and men of the 79th erect, in the Scotch Presbyterian Church of St Andrew's, a handsome marble tablet to the memory of the non-commissioned officers and soldiers who died during the period of service in Canada.

In February 1849, Major-General James Hay, C.B., was appointed Colonel in succession to Lt.-General Sir James Macdonell, appointed to the Colonelcy of the 71st Regiment; and in December 1852, Major Edmund James Elliot succeeded to the command of the regiment as Lt.-Colonel by the retirement of the Hon. Lauderdale Maule on half-pay.

In February 1852 the regiment removed to Edinburgh Castle, where it remained till April 1853, and after spending some time at Bury, Preston, and Weedon, it joined the encampment at Chobham in July, where it was brigaded with the 19th and 97th regiments, under the command of Colonel Lockyer, K.H. Here the regiment remained till the 20th of August, when the encampment was broken up, and the 79th proceeded to Portsmouth.

II.

1853—1874.

War with Russia—New Colours—the 79th parts with some of its best men to the 93rd—ordered to the Crimea—the Highland Brigade—The Alma—Sebastopol—Balaklava—Valley of Death—Kertch—Yenikali—Sir Colin Campbell—Dr Mackenzie—Home—Madras—Allahabad—Lucknow—Boodaoon—End of the Indian Mutiny—Meeanmeer—Peshawur—Rawul Pindee—Earl of Mayo—Jubbulpoor—the —93rd Highlanders—Nagpoor—Kamptee—Bombay—Home—Isle of Wight—the Queen's attentions and honours—Colonel Hodgson—Colonel Miller—Ashantee—Coomassie.

The Cameron Highlanders had had a long rest from active service since those two glorious days at Quatre Bras and Waterloo, in the events of which it bore such a prominent and gallant part and lost so many of its braves; now once again the declaration of war with Russia, on the 1st of March 1854, was to afford its untried men a chance to show what stuff they were made of. The 79th was destined to form part of that famous "Highland Brigade," which, under Sir Colin Campbell, did its duty so gallantly with the allied army in the Crimea.

Previous to its embarkation for the East, Lt.-General W. H. Sewell, C.B., was in March appointed colonel in succession to the deceased Lt.-General James Hay; and on April 21st, new colours were, without ceremony, committed to its keeping by Lt.-Col. Edmund James Elliot.

The 79th embarked for active service under rather disheartening circumstances. Only a few weeks before, while it remained uncertain whether it would form part of the expedition, the regiment had been called upon to furnish volunteers to the 93rd regiment, which had received its orders, and was short of its complement. That strange feeling of restlessness which at all times characterises soldiers, added to the natural and praiseworthy wish to be where hot work was expected, had its result in depriving the 79th of some of its best soldiers. Many of the finest flank-company men took the opportunity of changing their tartan, and the officers of the grenadiers and light company were to be seen one fine morning, like Achilles, "arming, weeping, cursing," to attend the parade which was to see their "best and bravest" handed over to a rival corps. Then speedily came similar orders for the 79th, and volunteers for *it* were hastily summoned. In obedience to the above natural laws forth they came as fast as they were wanted, but not exactly the sort of men to replace those who had gone. However, they did their duty well and bravely throughout the hard days that were in store for them, and it would be wronging them deeply to say a slighting word.

The regiment embarked at Portsmouth in H.M. ship "Simoom" on the 4th of May, and arrived at Scutari on the 20th. Here it was encamped on the plain of Scutari, and was brigaded with the 93rd regiment, the two being joined on June 7th by the 42nd Royal Highlanders; the three regiments, as we have indicated, forming the Highland Brigade under Brigadier General Sir Colin Campbell, and along with the brigade of Guards the 1st division of our army in the East. The regiment remained at Scutari till June 13th, when along with the other regiments of the division it was removed to Varna, where it encamped on the plain overlooking Lake Devnoe, about a mile south of the town. While stationed here, it had the misfortune to lose its two senior field-officers, Lt.-Col. E. J. Elliot, and Brevet Lt.-Col. James Ferguson, from fever. About the same time also died Colonel the Hon. L. Maule, who for many years commanded the regiment, and who was now Assistant Adjutant-General to the second division.

Lt.-Col. Elliot was on August 13th succeeded by Major John Douglas. The regiment remained in the district about Varna till the end of August, the strength of many of the men being very much reduced by fever

On the 29th of August the 79th embarked at Varna, and along with the rest of the allied army arrived at Kalamita Bay on Sept. 14th, disembarking on the same day. Along with the other regiments of its division it marched four miles inland, and bivouacked for the night near Lake Tuzla.

On the 19th, the army was put in motion along the coast towards Sebastopol. For details as to the order of march and incidents by the way, including the slight skirmish near the Bulganak River, we must refer the reader to our

Major-General Sir John Douglas, K.C.B.
From a photograph.

account of the 42nd. This regiment, along with the rest of the army, bivouacked near the Bulganak on the night of the 19th, and on the morning of the 20th advanced towards the River Alma, on the heights forming the left bank of which the Russians had taken up what they thought an impregnable position, and were awaiting the arrival of the invading army, never doubting but that, ere night, it should be utterly routed, if not extinguished.

About half past one o'clock the action commenced by the Russians opening fire from the redoubt on the left upon the French, who were attempting to assail their position in that direction. The British forces then formed in line, and proceeded to cross the river about the village of Burliuk. The light and second divisions led the way preceded by the skirmishers of the Rifle Brigade, who advanced through the vineyards beyond the village, and spreading themselves along the margin of the river, engaged the Russian riflemen on the opposite bank.

The first division, which formed the left of the allied army, advancing in support, traversed the vineyard and crossed the river, protected by its overhanging banks. On reaching the slope of the hill, the three Highland regiments formed line in échelon, and, "with the precision of a field-day advanced to the attack, the 42nd Royal Highlanders on the right, and the 79th Cameron Highlanders on the left, the extreme left of the allied army." [1]

From its position, the 79th was the last of the Highland regiments to mount the slope on the Russian side of the river, and its appearance on the crest of the slope was opportune; it came in time to relieve the mind of Sir Colin, who trembled for the left flank of the 93rd, down upon which was bearing a heavy column of the enemy—the left Sousdal column. "Above the crest or swell of the ground," Kinglake tells, "on the left rear of the 93rd, yet another array of the tall bending plumes began to rise up in a long ceaseless line, stretching far into the east, and presently, with all the grace and beauty that marks a Highland regiment when it springs up the side of a hill, the 79th came bounding forward. Without a halt, or with only the halt that was needed for dressing the ranks, it sprang at the flank of the right Sousdal column, and caught it in its sin—caught it daring to march across the front of a battalion advancing in line. Wrapped in the fire thus poured upon its flank, the hapless column could not march, could not live. It broke, and began to fall back in great confusion; and the left Sousdal column being almost at the same time overthrown by the 93rd, and the two columns which had engaged the Black Watch being now in full retreat, the spurs of the hill and the winding dale beyond became thronged with the enemy's disordered masses." [2]

The three Highland regiments were now once more abreast, and as Kinglake eloquently puts it, the men "could not but see that this, the revoir of the Highlanders, had chanced in a moment of glory. A cheer burst from the reunited Highlanders, and the "hillsides were made to resound with that joyous, assuring cry, which is the natural utterance of a northern people so long as it is warlike and free."

There were still a few battalions of the enemy, about 3000 men, on the rise of a hill separated from the Highland regiments by a hollow; on these the Highland Brigade opened fire, and the Ouglitz column, as it was called, was forced to turn.

The loss in the battle of the Alma of the Cameron Highlanders, who, although they performed most important and trying service, had no chance of being in the thick of the fray, was 2 men killed and 7 wounded.

On account of the conduct of the regiment, a Companionship of the Bath was conferred upon Lt.-Col. John Douglas, and Captain Andrew Hunt was promoted by brevet to be major in the army. [3]

After clearing the Russians out of the way the allied army marched onwards, and on the 26th took up its position before Sebastopol, Balaklava being taken possession of as a base of operations. On the 1st of October the first division encamped on the right of the light division to assist in the duties of the siege; and the 79th afterwards furnished a number of volunteers, to act as sharpshooters in picking off

---

[1] "The magnificent mile of line," says Captain Jameson, "displayed by the Guards and Highlanders, the prominent bear-skin, the undulating waves of the clan-tartans, the stalwart frames, steady and confident bearing of these young and eager soldiers advancing under fire, can never be forgotten by those who witnessed it, whilst it contributed materially to the discouragement of the enemy, whose columns perceptibly wavered as they approached. His masses of four-and-twenty deep, absolutely reeled and staggered to and fro under the murderous fire of the Scottish line, which was delivered with great effect at a distance of 2 0 yards."

[2] *Invasion of the Crimea*, vol. ii. p. 487.

[3] For the episode of Sir Colin Campbell's Scotch bonnet, and other incidents connected with the Highland Brigade generally, we must again refer the reader to our account of the 42nd.

the enemy's gunners and engage his riflemen. On the 8th of October, Sir Colin Campbell was appointed to the command of the troops and position of Balaklava, and was succeeded in command of the Highland Brigade by Colonel Sir D. A. Cameron, K.C.B., of the 42nd, whose portrait we have given on the steel-plate of colonels of that regiment.

After the battle of Balaklava, on October 25th, the 79th along with the 42nd, was moved to a new position on the heights of the north side of the valley of Balaklava, where it continued till May 1855. "Although the Highland Brigade," says Captain Jameson,[4] "was thus at an early period of the campaign unavoidably withdrawn from the siege operations before Sebastopol, it had all-important duties to perform besides those inseparable from the unremitting vigilance imperatively called for in the defence of the base of operations of the army; for in the months of December 1854, and January and February 1855, all the available duty men of the Highland brigade were usually employed at daylight every morning in the severe fatigue of conveying to the army before Sebastopol round shot, shell, and provisions, the load assigned to each man being generally a 32 lb. shot, carried in a sack, or 56 lbs. of biscuit. The preparation of gabions and fascines for the work of the siege, numerous public fatigue duties in the harbour of Balaklava and elsewhere, as well as the labour required for strengthening the entrenchments, likewise devolved upon the brigade."

During the first four months of 1855, low fever and dysentery prevailed in the regiment to such an extent that it was found necessary to put the 79th under canvass in a position about 300 yards higher up the slope, exposed to the sea breezes from the south-west. Very soon after this move the health of the regiment underwent much improvement.

In connection with what we have just stated, we shall introduce here a striking and intensely pathetic reminiscence of the campaign, which has been furnished us by Lt.-Col. Clephane. It shows how these comparatively raw soldiers of the Cameron Highlanders displayed a gallant

[4] *H'stof'l Ecord*, p. 100.

devotion to their duty under the most trying circumstances which would have reflected credit upon veterans of a dozen campaigns.

"Shortly after the opening of the bombardment of Sebastopol, the 79th Highlanders furnished a party for trench duty, consisting of about 150 men, under command of a field officer, and accompanied by a similar number detailed from the brigade of Guards. They marched for the post of duty shortly before daybreak, taking the well-known route through the "Valley of Death," as it was called. At that time a foe more dreaded than the Russians had persistently dogged the footsteps of the army, never attacking in force, but picking out a victim here and there, with such unerring certainty that to be sensible of his approach was to feel doomed. The glimmering light was at first insufficient for making out aught more than the dark body of men that moved silently along the above gloomy locality in column of march four deep; but as the sun approached nearer the horizon, and the eye became accustomed to the glimmer, it was seen that one man was suffering under pain of no ordinary nature, and was far from being fit to go on duty that morning. Indeed, on being closely inspected, it became evident that the destroyer had set his seal on the unfortunate fellow's brow, and how he had mustered the determination to equip himself and march out with the rest was almost inconceivable. Upon being questioned, however, he persisted that there was not much the matter, though he owned to spasms in his inside and cramps in his legs, and he steadily refused to return to camp without positive orders to that effect, maintaining that he would be better as soon as he could get time to "lie down a bit." All this time the colour of the poor fellow's face was positively and intensely blue, and the damps of death were standing unmistakeably on his forehead. He staggered as he walked, groaning with clenched teeth, but keeping step, and shifting his rifle with the rest in obedience to each word of command. He ought probably to have been at once despatched to the rear, but the party was now close to the scene of action (Gordon's battery), the firing would immediately commence, and somehow he was for the moment forgotten. The men took their places lining the breastwork, the troops whom they relieved marched off, and the firing began, and was kept up with great fury on both sides. All at once a figure staggered out from the hollow beneath the earthen rampart where the men were lying, and fell groaning upon the earth a few paces to the rear. It was the unfortunate man whose case we have just noticed. He was now in the last extremity, and there was not the ghost of a chance for him in this world; but three or four of his comrades instantly left their place of comparative safety, and surrounded him with a view of doing what they could to alleviate his sufferings. It was not much; they raised him up and rubbed his legs, which were knotted with cramps, and brandy from an officer's flask was administered without stint. All in vain, of course; but, curiously enough, even then the dying man did not lose heart, or show any weakness under sufferings which must have been frightful. He was grateful to the men who were busy rubbing his agonised limbs, and expressed satisfaction with their efforts, after a fashion that had even some show of piteous humour about it. "Aye," groaned he, as they came upon a knot of sinews as large as a pigeon's egg, "that's the *reynabone!*" It became evident now that the best thing that could be done would be to get him home to camp, so that he might at least di b l go and th r h of sh t and a ll. The open ground to the rear of the battery was swept by a perfect storm of these missiles; but volunteers at once came forward, and placed upon one of the bloodstained litters the dying man, who, now nearly insensible, was carried back to his tent. This was effected without casualty to the bearers, who forthwith returned to their post, leaving their unfortunate comrade at the point of breathing his last."

Such were the men who upheld the honour of the Scottish name in those days, and such, alas! were those who furnished a royal banquet to the destroyer, Death, throughout that melancholy campaign.

The 79th, in the end of May and beginning of June, formed part of the expedition to Kertch, described in the history of the 42nd. This expedition came quite as a little pleasant pic-nic to those regiments who were lucky enough to be told off as part of the force, and the 79th, along with the other regiments of the Highland brigade, had the good fortune to be so. Yenikali had been very hastily evacuated, all its guns being left in perfect order, and signs everywhere of little domestic establishments broken up in what must have been excessive dismay—expensive articles of furniture, ladies' dresses, little articles of the same sort appertaining to children, all left standing as the owners had left them, fleeing, as they imagined, for their lives. Truth to tell, they would not have been far wrong, but for the presence of the British.[*]

On its return in the middle of June, the Highland brigade took up its old position beside the Guards before Sebastopol, the command of the re-united division being assumed by Sir Colin Campbell. After this the division was regularly employed in the siege operations, it having been drawn up in reserve

[*] The British showed a curious contrast to their allies in this respect. Their complete subordination and obedience to orders were no less remarkable than praiseworthy. This, however, was of no real benefit to the owners, for our free and easy allies had no such scruples. As is usual with them, the comic element soon began largely to intermingle with the thirst for "loot," and grim-looking Zouaves and Sappers were to be seen parading with absurd airs and paces about the streets dressed in ladies' garments, with little silk parasols held over smart bonnets perched on the top of their own appropriate head-dresses, and accompanied by groups of quasi-admirers, demeaning themselves after what they doubtless considered to be the most approved Champs Elysées fashion, to the no small wonder and amusement of their less mercurial allies of Scotland, who stood about looking on with broad grins at "Francais makin' a fule o' a m'l."

during the unsuccessful attack on the Malakoff and Redan on the 18th of June.

In August, on account of the formation of an additional division to the army, the old Highland Brigade was separated from the Guards, and joined to the 1st and 2nd battalion Royals, and the 72nd Highlanders, these now forming the Highland division under Sir Colin Campbell.

On the 8th of September, the 79th, along with the other regiments of the brigade, was marched down to the front to take part in the contemplated assault upon the enemy's fortifications. About four in the afternoon, the 79th, under command of Lt.-Col. C. H. Taylor, reached the fifth or most advanced parallel, in front of the great Redan, the 72nd being in line on its left. Before this, however, the Redan had been attacked by the right and second divisions, who, "after exhibiting a devotion and courage yet to be surpassed," were compelled to retire with severe loss; the French attack on the Malakoff had at the same time been successful.

The brigade continued to occupy its advanced position during the remainder of the day exposed to a heavy fire, it being appointed to make another assault on the Redan next morning. Such a deadly enterprise, however, fortunately proved unnecessary, as early next morning it was ascertained that the enemy, after having blown up their magazines and other works, were in full retreat across the harbour by the bridge of boats. The only duty devolving upon the 79th was to send two companies to take possession of the Redan and its works.

The loss of the regiment on the day of the assault, and in the various operations during the siege, was 17 rank and file killed, Lt. D. H. M'Barnet, Assistant-Surgeon Edward Louis Lundy, 3 sergeants, 1 drummer, and 39 rank and file wounded. While recording the losses of the regiment, honourable mention ought to be made of Dr Richard James Mackenzie, who gave up a lucrative practice in Edinburgh in order to join the British army in the east. He was appointed to the 79th while the regiment was stationed at Varna, and until his death on September 25th 1854, shortly after [illegible] he rendered to the regiment and the army generally services of the highest importance. He followed the army on foot, undergoing much fatigue and many privations, which, with the arduous labours he took upon himself after the battle, no doubt hastened his much lamented death. After the battle of the Alma, it is said, he performed no fewer than twenty-seven capital operations with his own hand. "So highly were his services appreciated by the 79th, that, after the battle of the Alma, on his coming up to the regiment from attendance on the wounded, several of the men called out, 'Three cheers for Dr Mackenzie!' which was promptly and warmly responded to." The regiment, after the notification of peace, erected to his memory a neat tombstone, with an appropriate inscription, fenced in by a stone wall, on the heights of Belbek, near his resting-place.

His heroic and humane deeds on the battle-field of the Alma were thoroughly appreciated by the 79th, and have been recorded by others. We may, however, faintly gather something of them from his letter to his brother Kenneth—the last he ever wrote. It was written on the day after the battle. In this letter he says : " We " (Dr Scott and himself) " were shaking hands with all our friends, when, to my no small surprise and gratification, as you may believe, a voice shouted out from the column as they stood in the ranks— ' Three cheers for Mr Mackenzie,' and enough I say it who shouldn't I never heard three better cheers. You will *laugh*, my dear fellow, when you read this, but I can tell you I could scarcely refrain from doing t'other thing. All I could do was to wave my Glengarry in thanks." As to Dr Mackenzie's coolness under fire, the quartermaster of the 79th wrote : "During the height of the action I was in conversation with him when a round shot struck the ground, and rebounding over our regiment, flew over our heads and killed an artillery horse a few yards in our rear." Mackenzie quietly remarked, "That is a narrow escape."

The regiment continued in the Crimea till June 1856, on the 15th of which month it embarked at Balaklava, and disembarked at Portsmouth on the 5th of July, proceeding immediately by rail to the camp at Aldershot.[7]

After being stationed for a short time at Shorncliffe, and for some months at Canterbury, and having been present at the distribution of the Victoria Cross by Her Majesty in Hyde Park on June 26th 1857, the 79th proceeded to Dublin, where it landed on the 28th. Here, however, it remained but a short

Richard James Mackenzie, M.D., F.R.C.S. From photograph in 1854, in possession of Kenneth Mackenzie, Esq.

time, as on account of the Sepoy revolt in India, it was again ordered to prepare for active service. The regiment was rapidly completed to 1000 rank and file, and set sail in the beginning of August, arriving at Madras Roads early in November, when it received *orders* to proceed to Calcutta, where it disembarked on the 28th of

[7] The two addresses delivered to the Highland brigade in the Crimea by Sir Colin Campbell—the first on Sept. 21st, 1855, in connection with the distribution of medals and clasps, and the second on May 9th, 1856, on his leaving the Crimea for England will be found in the account of the 42nd.

November and occupied Fort-William. After remaining there for a few days, the 79th, on Dec. 2nd, proceeded by rail to Raneegunge, under the command of Lt.-Colonel John Douglas. Towards the end of the month the regiment left Raneegunge for Allahabad, where it halted till the 5th of Jan. 1858, a day memorable in the history of the 79th for its having marched upwards of 48 miles, and gained its first victory in the East, viz., that of Secundragunge, in which happily it had no casualties.

The regiment left Allahabad for Lucknow on the 18th of Jan., and on the 28th of Feb. it joined the force under Sir Colin Campbell at Camp Bunterah. The regiment was then commanded by Lt.-Colonel Taylor, Lt.-Colonel Douglas having been appointed to the command of the 5th Infantry Brigade. After passing the Goomtee, the 79th joined the force under Sir James Outram, and was brigaded with the 1st battalion of the 23rd Fusiliers and the 1st Bengal Fusiliers, under the command of Brigadier General Douglas. The regiment was present, and performed its part bravely during the siege and capture of Lucknow, from the 2nd to the 16th of March 1858, its loss being 7 non-commissioned officers and privates killed, and 2 officers, Brevet-Major Miller and Ensign Haine, and 21 non-commissioned officers and privates wounded.[a]

After the capture of Lucknow the 79th joined the division under the command of Major-General Walpole, in the advance towards Allahgunge, Shahjehanpoor, and Bareilly. Its next engagement was the action of Boodaoon, where the regiment had only 1 man wounded, who afterwards died of his wounds. On the 22nd of April the 79th was present at the action of Allahgunge, where it had no casualties. On the 27th, Sir Colin Campbell assumed command of the force and marched on Bareilly, the 79th, along with the 42nd and 93rd, forming the Highland brigade. On the 5th of May the 79th was formed in line of battle before Bareilly, when it helped to gain

another glorious victory, with a loss of only 2 men killed and 2 wounded. The regiment received the special thanks of Sir Colin Campbell.

The 79th next made a forced march to the relief of Shahjehanpoor, under the command of Brigadier-General John Jones, and on the 21st of May was again under fire at the attack of that place. Thence it went to Mohoomdee, in the attack on which it took part on the 24th and 25th; here it had 2 men wounded, and, according to the Record-Book, upwards of 100 men suffered from sunstroke.

After this last action the regiment once more found itself in quarters at Futtehgurh and Cawnpoor, one wing being detached to Allahabad; this, however, was only for a short time, as on the 21st of October an order was received for the 79th to join the brigade in Oudh, under Brigadier-General Wetherall, C.B. On the 3rd of November the 79th was present at the storm and capture of Rampoor Kosilab, the regiment losing only 2 men killed, and 1 sergeant and 6 privates wounded. For its conduct on this occasion the 79th was complimented in General Orders by His Excellency the Commander-in-Chief.

Brig.-Gen. Wetherall having left the force, was succeeded in command by Sir Hope Grant, K.C.B., who appointed Lt.-Col. Taylor, 79th, to command the brigade, Major Butt succeeding the latter in command of the 79th.

The 79th proceeded by forced marches to Fyzabad to commence the trans-Ghogra operations, and was present at the action of the passage of the Ghogra on the 25th of November, the skirmish at Muchligan on the 6th of Dec., and the skirmish at Bundwa Kotee on the 3rd of Jan. 1859. After the last-mentioned engagement the 79th received orders to proceed to Meean Meer in the Punjab, under the command of Lt.-Col. Taylor.

Thus ended the Indian Mutiny, during which the casualties to the 79th Highlanders amounted to 2 officers wounded, and 158[b] of all ranks killed. For its gallant conduct during the Indian campaign the 79th received the thanks of both Houses of Parliament, and

---

[a] We regret that the Record-Book of the 79th is extremely meagre in its account of the part taken by the regiment in the Indian campaign, and we have been unable to obtain details elsewhere. This, however, is the less to be regretted, as the details given in the history of the 42nd, 78th, and 93rd are so full that our readers will be able to form a tolerably good idea of what the 79th had to do.

[b] So in the Record-Book, and if correct, must include a very large number who died from sunstroke, some of whom

was authorised to bear on its colours the inscription "Capture of Lucknow." Lt.-Col. Douglas was appointed a K.C.B., and Lt.-Col. Taylor a C.B.

The regiment arrived at Meean Meer on the 8th of April 1859, and on the 15th the command passed into the hands of Lt.-Col. Butt, Colonel Taylor having proceeded to Europe on leave. Lt.-Col. Butt continued in command till the 2nd of April 1860, when he was appointed Chief Inspector of Musketry for Bengal, and was succeeded in command of the regiment by Lt.-Col. Hodgson. On the 16th of March, Lt.-Col. Douglas had retired on half-pay, and Lt.-Col. Taylor did the same on the 10th of May following.

The 79th remained in India till Sept. 1871. On the 5th of Nov. 1860, the right wing, consisting of 287 of all ranks, proceeded to Amritzir under the command of Major M'Barnet. Headquarters left Meean Meer on the 19th of Jan. 1861 for Ferozepoor, where it was joined by the wing from Amritzir in April.

The 79th left Ferozepoor in Feb. 1862 for Nowshera, where it remained till the following November, on the 23rd of which the regiment proceeded to Peshawur, on the frontiers of Afghanistan. In the previous March the regiment lost by death its colonel, General W. A. Sewell, who was succeeded by General the Honourable Hugh Arbuthnott, C.B.

During the stay of the regiment in Peshawur it lost two of its officers. A frontier war having broken out, Lts. Dougal and Jones volunteered their services, and were permitted to proceed with the expedition against the Sitana fanatics, under the command of Brigadier-General Sir M. Chamberlain, K.C.B.; the former was killed when on picquet duty on the 6th of Nov. 1863, and the latter in action on the 18th of the same month.

The 79th remained in Peshawur till Jan. 1864, when it removed to Rawul Pindee, where it remained till 1866. During its stay it furnished a volunteer working party on the Murree and Abbattabad road, and also during 1864 a detachment of 300 of all ranks, under the command of Captain C. Gordon, to the Camp Durrgaw Gully.

In October 1864 the 79th lost by exchange its senior Lt.-Colonel, Colonel Butt having exchanged with Colonel Best of H.M.'s 86th Regiment. By this exchange Lt.-Colonel Hodgson became senior Lt.-Colonel.

For some time after its arrival at Rawul Pindee the regiment continued to suffer from Peshawur fever, a considerable number of men having had to be invalided to England. On the 8th of May 1865 the headquarters and 650 of all ranks proceeded as a working party to the Murree Hills, where the regiment remained till October, much to the benefit of the men's health, as in a fortnight after its arrival all traces of Peshawur fever had disappeared. A similar working party, but not so large, was sent to the Murree Hills at the same time in the following year.

On the 10th of July of this year (1865) Lt.-Colonel Hodgson received his promotion by brevet to full Colonel in the army.

On the 1st of November 1866, the headquarters and left wing marched from Rawul Pindee for Roorkee, and the right wing under command of Major Maitland for Delhi, the former reaching Roorkee on the 15th and the latter Delhi on Dec. 27th. During the regiment's stay at these places the two wings exchanged and re-exchanged quarters, both suffering considerably from fever during the spring of 1867. Both wings in the end of March proceeded to Umballah, to take part in the ceremonial attending the meeting between Earl Mayo, Governor-General of India, and Shere Ali Khan, the Ameer of Cabul; the Cameron Highlanders had been appointed part of His Excellency's personal escort.

On Dec. 7th the headquarters, under the command of Colonel W. C. Hodgson, left Roorkee en route to Kamptee, and on the 15th it was joined by the right wing from Delhi, at Camp Jubbulpoor. Here the regiment remained until the 24th, when it commenced to move by companies towards Kamptee, at which station the headquarters arrived on the 1st of January 1870. Shortly before leaving Roorkee a highly complimentary farewell letter was sent to Colonel Hodgson from Major-General Colin Troup, C.B., commanding the Meerut Division.

During January 1870 the 93d Sutherland Highlanders passed through Kamptee en route for home, when a very pleasing exchange of civilities took place between that distinguished regiment and their old comrades of the 79th. At a mess meeting held at Nagpoor on the 30th by the officers of the 93d, it was proposed and carried unanimously that a letter be written to the officers of the 79th, proposing that, in consideration of the friendship and cordiality which had so long existed between the two regiments, the officers of the two corps be perpetual honorary members of their respective messes. The compliment was, of course, willingly returned by the 79th, and the officers of the 93rd Highlanders were constituted thenceforth perpetual honorary members of the 79th mess.

The regiment remained at Kamptee for nearly two years, furnishing a detachment to the fort at Nagpoor. A very sad event occurred in the regiment during its stay at Kamptee: on Aug. 28th, 1871, Captain Donald Macdonald when at great gun drill at the artillery barracks, dropped down on parade, died instantaneously, and was buried the same evening. Captain Macdonald was by birth and habit a Highlander, and was most warmly attached to his regiment, in which he had served for seventeen years. Great regret was felt by all ranks in the regiment on account of his premature and unexpected death. He was only 34 years of age, and a monument was erected by his brother officers over his grave at Kamptee.

On the 2nd of August 1871 Colonel Best was appointed to the command of the Nagpoor field force, with the rank of brigadier-general.

In the same month the 79th received orders to be in readiness to proceed to England, and the non-commissioned officers and men were permitted to volunteer into regiments remaining in India. About 177 of all ranks availed themselves of this offer, a considerable number of whom were married men. The regiment left Kamptee in two detachments on Sept. 22nd and 23rd, and proceeded by Nagpoor and Deolallee to Bombay, where it embarked on board H.M.'s India troop-ship "Jumna" on the 29th and 30th. The "Jumna" sailed for England on the 1st of October, and after a prosperous voyage by way of the Suez Canal arrived at Spithead on the evening of the 6th of November. Next day the regiment was transferred to three ships, and conveyed to West Cowes, Isle of Wight, where it disembarked the same evening, and marched to the Albany Barracks, Parkhurst.

During the fourteen years that the 79th was stationed in India it was inspected by many distinguished general officers, including Sir Colin Campbell (Lord Clyde), Sir William Mansfield (Lord Sandhurst), Sir Hugh Rose, (Lord Strathnairn), Sir Hope Grant, &c., all of whom expressed themselves highly satisfied with the appearance, conduct, and discipline of the regiment.

During its sojourn in the Isle of Wight the 79th was highly honoured on more than one occasion by the very particular notice of Her Majesty Queen Victoria. In Feb. 1872, Her Majesty being at Osborne, was pleased to express her desire to see the 79th Highlanders in marching order. The regiment accordingly paraded at 10 o'clock on the morning of the 16th, and proceeded towards Osborne. When the 79th was within a short distance of the approach to the house, Her Majesty, with several members of the Royal Family, appeared at an angle of the road, and watched the marching past of the regiment with great interest. The regiment, after making a detour towards East Cowes, was returning to Parkhurst by way of Newport, when Her Majesty reappeared, paying particular attention to the dress and appearance of the men as they marched past her for the second time.

This was the last occasion on which Colonel Hodgson was destined to command the 79th. On the 1st of March the regiment sustained an irreparable loss in his death, which took place, after a very short illness. Colonel Hodgson was 49 years of age, had served in the 79th for 32 years, and commanded it for 12, and by his invariable kindness and urbanity had endeared himself to all ranks. His sad and unexpected death spread a deep gloom over the whole regiment. Colonel Maitland, in announcing Colonel Hodgson's death in regimental orders said,—

" The officers have to lament the loss of one who was always to them a kind and considerate commanding officer; and the non-commissioned officers and men have been deprived of a true friend, who was ever zealous in guarding their interests and promoting their welfare."

Colonel Hodgson was buried in Carisbrooke Cemetery, and over his grave a handsome monument of Aberdeen granite has been erected by his brother officers and friends.

By Colonel Hodgson's death Colonel Maitland succeeded to the command of the regiment; he, however, retired on half-pay on the 19th of October following, and Lt.-Colonel Miller was selected to succeed him.

On the 17th of Sept. the 79th had the honour of being reviewed by the late ex-Emperor of the French, Napoleon III., and his son, the Prince Imperial, who lunched with the officers. The Emperor made a minute inspection of the men, and watched the various manœuvres with evident interest, expressing at the conclusion his admiration of the splendid appearance and physique of the men, the high state of discipline of the corps, and the magnificent manner in which the drill was performed.

During Her Majesty's stay at Osborne the 79th always furnished a guard of honour at East Cowes at each of her visits. On the 17th of April 1873 Her Majesty bestowed one of the highest honours in her power on the regiment, when on that day she attended at Parkhurst Barracks to present it with new colours. The presentation took place in the drill-field, and was witnessed by a large number of spectators, who were favoured with a bright sky.

At 11 o'clock A.M. the 79th marched into the field under command of Colonel Miller. The ground was kept by the 102nd Fusiliers, the same regiment also furnishing a guard of honour to Her Majesty. General Viscount Templeton, K.C.B., commanding the district, was present, and also Sir John Douglas, K.C.B., commanding in North Britain, with his A.D.C., Lieutenant Boswell Gordon, of the 79th. The Mayor and Corporation of Newport attended officially, in their robes of office. At 11.45 A.M. Her Majesty arrived, attended by their Royal Highnesses Prince Leopold and Princess Beatrice, the Countess of Errol and other ladies, besides the Equerries in

Waiting. The royal party having driven along the line, the band and pipers playing, the usual order of presentation was proceeded with.

The old colours were in front of the left of the line, in charge of a colour party and double sentries. The new colours, cased, were in the rear of the centre, in charge of the two senior colour-sergeants, Taylor and Mackie. The old colours having been trooped, these honoured and cherished standards, around which the Cameron Highlanders had so often victoriously rallied, were borne to the rear by Lts. Annesley

Lieutenant-Colonel W. C. Hodgson.
From a Miniature in possession of Mrs Hudson, North Petherton, Devonshire, sister of Colonel Hodgson.

and Money to the strains of "Auld Lang Syne." The regiment was then formed into three sides of a square, the drums were piled in the centre, the new colours were brought from the rear, and having been uncased by the Majors, were placed against the pile. Then prayer was offered by the Rev. Charles Morrison, formerly chaplain to the 79th in India, who had come from Aberdeen expressly to perform this duty. This being concluded, Major Cumming handed the Queen's colour and

Major Percival the regimental colour to Her Majesty, who presented the former to Lt. Campbell and the latter to Lt. Methven, at the same time addressing them thus:—" It gives me great pleasure to present these new colours to you. In thus entrusting you with this honourable charge, I have the fullest confidence that you will, with the true loyalty and well-known devotion of Highlanders, preserve the honour and reputation of your regiment, which have been so brilliantly earned and so nobly maintained by the 79th Cameron Highlanders."

Colonel Miller then replied as follows :—

" I beg permission, in the name of all ranks of the 79th Cameron Highlanders, to present our loyal and most grateful acknowledgments of the very high honour it has pleased your Majesty this day to confer on the regiment. The incident will ever remain fresh in the memories of all on parade, and of those also who are unable to have the honour of being present on this occasion, and of others who have formerly served with the 79th; and I beg to assure your Majesty that, wherever the course of events may require these colours to be borne, the remembrance that they were received from the hands of our Most Gracious Queen, will render them doubly precious, and that in future years, as at present, the circumstance of this presentation will be regarded as one of the proudest episodes in the records of the Cameron Highlanders."

After Colonel Miller's address the regiment re-formed line, and the colours were received with a general salute, after which they were marched to their place in the line in slow time, the band playing " God save the Queen." The ranks having been closed, the regiment broke into column, and marched past Her Majesty in quick and double time. Line was then re-formed, and Lt.-Gen. Viscount Templetown, K.C.B., called for three cheers for Her Majesty, a request which was responded to by the regiment in true Highland style. The ranks having been opened, the line advanced in review order, and gave a royal salute, after which the royal carriage withdrew.

After the parade was dismissed, the old colours, carried by Lts. Annesley and Money, escorted by all the sergeants, were played round the barracks, and afterwards taken to the officers' mess. On the 30th of the month the officers gave a splendid ball at the Town-hall, Ryde, at which about 500 guests were present, the new colours being placed in the centre of the ball-room, guarded on each side by a Highlander in full uniform. To mark the occasion also, Colonel Miller remitted

all punishments awarded to the men, and the sergeants entertained their friends at a luncheon and a dance in the drill field.

At the unanimous request of the officers, Colonel Miller offered the old colours to Her Majesty, and she having been graciously pleased to accept them, they were taken to Osborne on the 22nd of April. At 12 o'clock noon of that day the regiment paraded in review order and formed a line along the barracks for the colours to pass, each man presenting arms as they passed him, the band playing "Auld Lang Syne." The colours were then taken by train from Newport to Cowes. At Osborne the East Cowes guard of honour, under command of Captain Allen, with Lts. Bucknell and Smith, was drawn up at each side of the hall door. The old colours, carried by Lts. Annesley and Money, escorted by Quartermaster-Sergeant Knight, Colour-Sergeant Clark, two other sergeants, and four privates, preceded by the pipers, were marched to the door by Colonel Miller, the guard of honour presenting arms. The officers then advanced, and, kneeling, placed the colours at Her Majesty's feet, when Colonel Miller read a statement, giving a history of the old colours from the time of their presentation at Portsmouth, in the month of April 1854, by Mrs Elliot (the wife of the officer at that time colonel of the regiment), a few days before the regiment embarked for the Crimea.

Colonel Miller then said.—

" It having graciously pleased your Majesty to accept these colours from the Cameron Highlanders, I beg permission to express the gratification which all ranks of the 79th feel in consequence, and to convey most respectfully our highest appreciation of this kind act of condescension on the part of your Majesty."

The Queen replied,—

" I accept these colours with much pleasure, and shall ever value them in remembrance of the gallant services of the 79th Cameron Highlanders I will take them to Scotland, and place them in my dear Highland home at Balmoral."

The guard then presented arms, and the colour party withdrew. Her Majesty afterwards addressed a few words to each of the colour-sergeants.

On the 24th of April, Colonel Miller received orders for the troops of the Parkhurst garrison to march towards Osborne on the following day, for Her Majesty's inspection, and the troops accordingly paraded at 10 o'clock A.M. in review order. On arriving near Osborne the brigade was drawn up in line on the road, the 79th on the right, and the 102nd on the left. Her Majesty was received with a royal salute, and having driven down the line, the royal carriage took up its position at the cross-roads, and the regiments passed in fours; the royal carriage then drove round by a bye-road, and the regiment again passed in fours, after which the troops returned to Parkhurst.

We may state here that on the day on which Her Majesty presented the new colours to the regiment, Colonel Ponsonby, by Her Majesty's desire, wrote to the Field-Marshal Commanding in Chief that "Her Majesty was extremely pleased with the appearance of the men and with the manner in which they moved," and hoped that His Royal Highness might think it right to communicate the Queen's opinion to Lt.-Colonel Miller. The letter was sent to Colonel Miller.

The Queen still further showed her regard for the 79th by presenting to the regiment four copies of her book, "Leaves from our Journal in the Highlands,"—one to Colonel Miller, one for the officers, one for the non-commissioned officers, and one for the privates.

To crown all these signal marks of Her Majesty's attachment to the Cameron Highlanders, she was graciously pleased to let them bear her own name as part of the style and title of the regiment, as will be seen by the following letter, dated—

"*Horseguards*, 10*th July* 1873.

SIR,—By direction of the Field-Marshal Commanding in Chief, I have the honour to acquaint you that Her Majesty has been pleased to command that the 79th Regiment be in future styled "the 79th Queen's Own Cameron Highlanders," that the facings be accordingly changed from green to blue, and that the regiment be also permitted to bear in the centre of the second colour, as a regimental badge, *the Thistle ensigned with the Imperial Crown*, being the badge of Scotland as sanctioned by Queen Anne in 1707, after the confirmation of the Act of Union of the kingdoms.—I have, &c. &c.

(Signed) " J. W. ARMSTRONG,
" *Deputy Adjutant-General.*
" Lieutenant-Colonel Miller,
"Commanding 79th Regiment."

In acknowledgment of this gracious mark of Her Majesty's regard, Colonel Miller despatched a letter to Major-General Ponsonby, at Osborne, on the 12th of July, in which he requests that officer

"To convey to the Queen, in the name of all ranks of the 79th, our most respectful and grateful acknowledgments for so distinguished a mark of royal condescension, and I beg that you will assure Her Majesty of the gratification felt throughout the regiment in consequence of the above announcement."

Finally, on the 13th of August Colonel Miller received a notification that Her Majesty had expressed a wish that the regiment should be drawn up at East Cowes to form a guard of honour on her departure from the island on the following day. The regiment accordingly marched to East Cowes on the following afternoon, and presented arms as Her Majesty embarked on her way to Balmoral.

On 18th of September of the same year the 79th left Parkhurst for Aldershot, where it arrived on the same afternoon, and was quartered in A and B lines, South Camp, being attached to the 1st or Major-General Parkes' brigade.

The Black Watch has received great and well-merited praise for its conduct during the Ashantee War, in the march from the Gold Coast to Coomassie. It ought, however, to be borne in mind that a fair share of the glory which the 42nd gained on that dangerous coast, under the able command of Major-General Sir Garnet J. Wolseley, really belongs to the Cameron Highlanders. When the 42nd, at the end of December 1873, was ordered to embark for the Gold Coast, 135 volunteers were asked for from the 79th, to make up its strength, when there at once stepped out 170 fine fellows, most of them over ten years' service, from whom the requisite number was taken. Lieutenants R. C. Annesley and James M'Callum accompanied these volunteers. Although they wore the badge and uniform of the glorious Black Watch, as much credit is due to the 79th on account of their conduct as if they had fought under the name of the famous Cameron Highlanders, in which regiment they received all that training without which personal bravery is of little avail.

Monument in the Dean Cemetery, Edinburgh, erected in 1857.
The monument is of sandstone, but the inscription is cut in a block of granite
inserted below the shaft.

In Memory of
Colonel the Honourable Lauderdale Maule;
Lieut.-Colonel E. J. Elliot, Lieut.-Colonel James Ferguson;
Captain Adam Maitland;
Lieutenant F. J. Grant, Lieutenant J. J. Harrison;
and
Dr A. J. Mackenzie.
also
369 Non-Commissioned Officers and Men of the 79th Highlanders, who died in Bulgaria and the
Crimea, or fell in action during the Campaign of 1854–55.

Lieut. Colonel Clephane, who for many years was connected with the Cameron Highlanders, has been good enough to furnish us with a number of anecdotes illustrative of the inner life of the regiment and of the characteristics of the men in his time. Some of these we have already given in their chronological place in the text, and we propose to conclude our narrative with one or two others, regretting that space does not permit our making use of all the material Colonel Clephane has been so obliging as to put into our hands.

It may probably be affirmed, as a rule, that there exists in the regiments of the British army an amount of harmony and cordial reciprocation of interest in individual concerns, which cannot be looked for in other professional bodies. From the nature of the circumstances under which soldiers spend the best years of their lives, thrown almost entirely together, sometimes exclusively so, and moving, as fate and the War Office may determine, from one point to another of Her Majesty's dominions on their country's concerns, it naturally arises that an amount of familiar knowledge of each other's characteristics is arrived at which in the world at large is rarely attainable. We should state that the period of the following reminiscences is comprehended between the year 1835 and the suppression of the Indian mutiny.

In the 79th Highlanders the harmony that existed among the officers, and the completeness of the chain of fellow-feeling which bound together all ranks from highest to lowest, was very remarkable. It used to be said among the officers themselves that, no matter how often petty bickerings might arise in the fraternity, anything like a serious quarrel was impossible; and this from the very reason that it was a *fraternity*, in the best and fullest sense of the word.

And now a temptation arises to notice one or two of those individual members of the regiment whose demeanour and eccentricities of expression furnished a daily supply of amusement:—There was a non-commissioned officer, occupying the position of drill-sergeant about five-and-thirty or forty years ago, whose contributions in this way were much appreciated. "I think I see him now," writes Colonel Clephane, "sternly surveying with one grey eye, the other being firmly closed for the time being, some unlucky batch of recruits which had unfavourably attracted his attention; his smooth-shaven lip and chin, a brown curl brought forward over each cheek-bone, and the whole surmounted by the high white-banded sergeant's forage cap of that day set at the regulation military angle over the right ear. He was a Waterloo man, and must have been verging on middle age at the time of which I write, but there was no sign of any falling off in the attributes of youth, if we except the slight rotundity beneath the waistbelt." No one could be more punctiliously respectful to his superior officers than 'the sergeant, but when he had young gentlemen newly joined under his charge at recruit drill, he would display an assumption of authority as occasion offered which was sometimes ludicrous enough. On one of these occasions, when a squad of recruits, comprising two newly-fledged ensigns, was at drill in the barrack square, the sound of voices (a heinous offence as we all know) was heard in the ranks. The sergeant stopped opposite the offending squad. There was "silence deep as death"— "Ah—m—m!" said he, clearing his throat after a well-known fashion of his, and tapping the ground with the end of his cane—"Ah—m—m! if I hear any man talkin' in the ranks, I'll put him in the guard 'ouse" there he looked with stern significance at each of the officers in turn)—"*I don't care who he is!*" Having thus, as he thought, impressed all present with a due sense of ... ...

a parting "Ah—m—m!" tapped the ground once or twice more, keeping his eye firmly fixed to the last on the more suspected of the two ensigns, and moved stiffly off to the next batch of recruits. No one ever dreamed of being offended with old "Squid," as he was called, after his pronunciation of the word squad, and those who had, as he expressed it, "passed through his hands" would never consider themselves as unduly unbending in holding serious or mirthful colloquy with their veteran preceptor. Thus, on another occasion of considerably later date than the above, some slight practical joking had been going on at the officers' mess, a practice which would have been dangerous but for the real cordiality which existed among its members, and a group of these conversed gleefully on the subject next morning after the dismissal of parade. The peculiar form assumed by their jocularity had been that of placing half a newspaper or so upon the hoof of a slumbering comrade, and setting it on fire, as a gentle hint that slumber at the mess-table was objectionable. One officer was inclined to deprecate the practice. "If he had not awoke at once," said he, "he might have found it no joke." "Ah—m—m!" uttered the well-known voice close behind the group, where the sergeant, now dépôt sergeant-major, had, unnoticed, been a listener to the colloquy, "I always grease the paper." This was literally throwing a new light on the subject, and was the worthy man's method of testifying contempt for all undue squeamishness on occasions of broken etiquette.

One or two subordinates in the same department were not without their own distinguishing characteristics. Colonel Clephane writes—"I remember one of our drill corporals, whose crude ideas of humour were not unamusing when all were in the vein, which we generally were in those days. He was quite a young man, and his sallies came, as it were, in spite of himself, and with a certain grimness of delivery which was meant to obviate any tendency therein to relaxation of discipline. I can relate a slight episode connected with this personage, showing how the memory of small things lingers in the hearts of such men in a way we would little expect from the multifarious nature of their occupations, and the constant change to them of scenes and features. A young officer was being drilled by a lance-corporal after the usual recruit fashion, and being a tall slip of a youth he was placed on the flank of the squad. They were being marched to a flank in what was called Indian or single file, the said officer being in front as right hand man. When the word 'halt' was given by the instructor from a great distance off—a favourite plan of his, as testing the power of his word of command—the officer did not hear it, and, while the rest of the squad came to a stand still, he went marching on. He was aroused from a partial reverie by the sound of the well-known broad accent close at his ear, 'Hae ye far to gang the nicht?' and, wheeling about in some discomfiture, had to rejoin the squad amid the unconcealed mirth of its members. Well, nearly thirty years afterwards, when probably not one of them, officer, corporal, or recruits, continued to wear the uniform of the regiment, the former, in passing through one of the streets of Edinburgh, came upon his old instructor in the uniform of a conducting sergeant (one whose duty it was to accompany recruits from their place of enlistment to the head-quarters of their regiments). There was an immediate cordial recognition, and, after a few inquiries and reminiscences on both sides, the quondam officer said jestingly, "You must acknowledge I was the best recruit you had in those days." The sergeant hesitated, smiled grimly, and then replied, "Yes, you were a good enough recruit; but you were a bad right hand man!"

The ... of the ... ... furnishes an

apt illustration of the cupidity of feeling wherewith his officer is almost invariably regarded by the fairly dealt with and courteously treated British soldier. A few years subsequent to the period of the above episode, Colonel Cleghorn received a visit at his house, quite unexpectedly, from his old instructor. The latter had been forced by this time, through failure of health, to retire from the active duties of his profession, and it was, indeed, evident at once, from his haggard lineaments and the irrepressible wearing cough, which from time to time shook his frame, that he had "received the route" for a better world. He had no request to make, craved no assistance, and could with difficulty be persuaded to accept some refreshment. The conversation flowed in the usual channel of reminiscences, in the course of which the officer learned that matters which he had imagined quite private, at least to his own circle, were no secret to the rank and file. The sergeant also adverted to an offer which had been made to him, on his retirement from the 79th, of an appointment in the police force. "A policeman!" said he, describing his interview with the patron who proposed the scheme; "for Godsake, afore ye mak a policeman o' me, just tie a stane round my neck and fling me into the sea!" After some time, he got up to retire, and was followed to the door by his quondam pupil, who, himself almost a cripple, was much affected by the still more distressing infirmity of his old comrade. The officer, after shaking hands, expressed a hope, by way of saying something cheering at parting, that he should yet see the veteran restored to comparative health. The latter made no reply, but after taking a step on his way, turned round, and said, in a tone which the other has not forgotten, "I've seen you once again any way;" and so they parted, never to meet again in this world.

These are small matters, but they furnish traits of a class, the free expenditure of whose blood has made Great Britain what she is.

There is in all regiments a class which, very far remote as it is from the possession of the higher, or, at all events, the more dignified range of attributes, yet, as a curious study, is not undeserving of a few notes. It is pretty well known that each officer of a regiment has attached to his special service a man selected from the ranks, and in most cases from the company to which he himself belongs. Now, it is not to be supposed that the captain of a company will sanction the employment in this way of his smartest men, nor, indeed, would the commanding officer be likely to ratify the appointment if he did; still, I have seen smart young fellows occasionally filling the position of officer's servant, though they rarely continued long in it, but reverted, as a rule, sooner or later, to their places in the ranks, under the influence of a soldier's proper ambition, which pointed to the acquisition of at least a non-commission officer's stripes; not to speak of the difference between Her Majesty's livery and that of any intermediate master, however much in his own person deserving of respect. The young ensign, however, in joining will rarely find himself accommodated with a servant of this class. He will have presented to him, in that capacity, some steady (we had almost said "ober," but that we should have been compelled forthwith to retract), grave, and experienced old stager, much, probably, the worse of wear from the lapse of time and from subsidiary influences, and serving out his time for a pension (I speak of days when such things were), after such fashion as military regulations and an indulgent captain permitted. This sort of man was generally held available for the newly joined ensign, upon much the same prin-

recruit on the back of some stiff-jointed steed of supernatural sagacity and vast experience of a recruit's weak points in the way of security of seat, which last, however, he only puts to use when he sees a way of doing so with benefit to his position, uncompanied with danger to his hide; in other words, while regarding with much indifference the feelings of the shaky individual who bestrides him, he has a salutary dread of the observant rough-rider. A soldier servant of the above class will devote himself to making what he can, within the limits of strict integrity, out of a juvenile master; but woe betide the adventurous wight whom he detects poaching on his preserve! On the whole, therefore, the ensign is not badly off, for the veteran is, after all, really honest, and money to almost any amount may be trusted to his supervision; as for tobacco and spirits, he looks upon them, I am afraid, as contraband of war, a fair and legitimate forfeit if left within the scope of his privateering ingenuity.

Many years ago, while the 79th Highlanders formed the garrison of Edinburgh Castle, Her Majesty the Queen, who had very lately ascended the throne of Great Britain, paid a visit to the metropolis of her Scottish dominions, and a guard of honour from the above regiment was despatched down to Holyrood to keep watch and ward over the royal person. It was late in the season, or early, I forget which, Colonel Cleghorn writes, and when the shades of evening closed round, the officers of the guard were sensible, in their large, gloomy chamber, of a chilly feeling which the regulated allowance of coals failed to counteract. In other words, the fuel ran short, and they were cold, so it was resolved to despatch one of their servants, a type of the class just alluded to, for a fresh supply. Half-a-crown was handed to him for this purpose—a sum which represented the value of more than a couple of hundredweights in those days,—and Donald was instructed to procure a scuttlefull, and bring back the change. Time went on, the few embers in the old grate waxed dimmer and dimmer, and no Donald made his appearance. At last, when the temper of the expectant officers had reached boiling point, increasing in an inverse ratio to their bodily caloric, the door opened, and Donald gravely entered the apartment. The chamber was vast and the light was dim, and the uncertain gait of the approaching domestic was at first unnoticed. Calmly disregarding a howl of indignant remonstrance on the score of his dilatory proceedings, the latter silently approached the end of the room where the two officers were cowering over the dying embers. It was now seen that he carried in one hand a piece of coal, or some substance like it, about the size of a sixpounder shot. "Where have you been, confound you! and why have you not brought the coals?" roared his master. Donald halted, steadied himself, and glanced solemnly, first at the "thing" which he carefully bore in his palm, then at the speaker's angry lineaments, and in strangely husky accents thus delivered himself :— "Not another—hic—bit of coal in Edinburgh; coalsh—hic—'sh very dear just now, Mr Johnstone!" The delinquent's master was nearly beside himself with fury when he saw how the matter stood, but he could not for the life of him help, after a moment or two, joining in the merriment which shook the very frame of his comrade. Donald, in the meantime, stood regarding both with an air of tipsy gravity, and was apparently quite bewildered when ordered to retire with a view to being placed in duresse vile. This incident naturally ended the connection between him and his aggrieved master. It is but fair to state that the hero of the above little anecdote, though I

SUCCESSION LIST OF COLONELS AND LIEUTENANT-COLONELS OF THE 79th, THE QUEEN'S OWN CAMERON HIGHLANDERS.

COLONELS.

Names.	Date of Appointment.	Remarks.
Major Alan Cameron	August 17, 1793	Died Lieut.-General, March 9, 1828.
Lieut.-General R. C. Ferguson, G.C.B.	March 24, 1828	Died, April 10, 1841.
Major-General the Hon. J. Ramsay	April 27, 1841	Died, June 28, 1842.
Lt.-General Sir James Macdonell, K.C.B.	July 14, 1842	To 71st Foot, February 8, 1849.
Major-General James Hay, C.B.	February 8, 1849	Died, February 25, 1854.
Lieut.-General W. H. Sewell, C.B.	March 24, 1854	Died, 1862.
Hugh Arbuthnot, C.B.	March 14, 1862	Vice Sewell, deceased.
J. F. Glencairn Campbell	July 12, 1868	Vice Arbuthnot, deceased.
Henry Cooper, C.B.	August 21, 1870	Vice Campbell, deceased.

LIEUTENANT-COLONELS.

Batt.	Names.	Date.	Remarks.
1.	Alan Cameron, Major-Com.	Lt.-Col. Feb. 19, 1794	Major-General, July 25, 1810.
1.	The Hon. A. C. Johnstone	May 2, 1794	Promoted to colonel of a regiment, Jan. 26, 1797.
1.	William Ashton	September 13, 1794	Died, September 1796.
1.	Patrick Macdowall	November 1, 1796	Died of wounds, August 1801.
1.	William Eden	August 13, 1798	To 84th Foot, December 11, 1806.
1.	Archibald Maclean	September 3, 1801	Retired, May 28, 1807.
2.	Philip Cameron	April 19, 1804	To 1st Battalion, December 11, 1806.
2.	John Murray	December 11, 1806	To 1st Battalion, May 28, 1807.
1.	Philip Cameron	December 11, 1806	From 2nd Battalion. Died of wounds, May 13, 1811.
1.	John Murray	May 29, 1807	To Malta Regiment, February 22, 1808.
2.	Robert Fulton	May 28, 1807	To 1st Battalion, May 13, 1811.
1.	Robert Fulton	May 13, 1811	Retired, December 3, 1812.
2.	Wm. M. Harvey	May 30, 1811	To 1st Battalion, December 3, 1812.
1.	Wm. M. Harvey	December 3, 1812	Died at sea, June 10, 1813.
2.	Neil Douglas	December 3, 1812	To 1st Battalion, February 20, 1813.
1.	Neil Douglas	February 20, 1813	To Half-pay, August 16, 1833.
2.	Nathaniel Cameron	June 24, 1813	Reduced with 2nd Battalion, Dec 25, 1815.

Only one Battalion in Regiment.

Batt.	Names.	Date.	Remarks.
1.	Duncan Macdougal	September 6, 1833	Retired, March 13, 1835.
1.	Robert Ferguson	March 13, 1835	Retired, June 8, 1841.
1.	Andrew Brown	June 8, 1841	To 1st Battalion Royals, October 29, 1841.
1.	John Carter, K.H.	October 29, 1841	Retired June 14, 1842.
1.	The Hon. Lauderdale Maule	June 14, 1842	To Half-pay unattached, December 24, 1852.
1.	Edmund James Elliot	December 24, 1852	Died, August 12, 1854.
1.	John Douglas, K.C.B.	August 13, 1854	
1.	R. C. H. Taylor, C.B.	December 12, 1854	To Depôt Battalion, October 1, 1856.
1.	R. C. H. Taylor, C.B.	August 1, 1857	
1.	T. B. Batt	April 15, 1859	Chief Inspector of Musketry, Bengal, 1860. Exchanged to 85th Regiment, Sept. 13, 1864.
1.	W. C. Hodgson	July 10, 1860	Died at Parkhurst, Isle of Wight, March 1, 1872.
1.	R. M. Best	September 13, 1864	Brigadier-General, India, May 24, 1870. Exchanged from 85th Regiment, Sept. 13, 1864.
1.	K. R. Maitland	March 2, 1872	To Half-pay, October 19, 1872.
1.	G. M. Miller	October 19, 1872	

THE 91st PRINCESS LOUISE ARGYLL SHIRE HIGHLANDERS.

I.

1794-1848.

Raising of the Regiment—At first the 98th—South Africa — Wynberg — Saldanha Bay — Number changed to 91st—Faithfulness of the Regiment — Returns to England — Germany — Ireland — The Peninsula — Obidos —Vimeiro—Corunna—The detached company — Talavera — Walcheren — Peninsula again—Vittoria—Pamplona—Nivelle—Nive— Bayonne — Orthes — Toulouse — Ireland — Quatre Bras — Waterloo — France — Ireland — 91st loses Highland dress—Jamaica—England—Ireland—St Helena—Cape of Good Hope—The Reserve Battalion formed and sails for S. Africa — Wreck of the "Abercrombie Robinson"—Insurrection of Dutch farmers—Frontier service—The Boers again—New colours—The Kaffir War—Amatola Mountains— Attack on Fort Peddie — Buffalo Spruits — 1st Battalion goes home.

XCI

NE OBLIVISCARIS.

ROLEIA.	NIVELLE.
VIMEIRO.	NIVE.
CORUNNA.	ORTHES.
PYRENEES.	TOULOUSE.

PENINSULA.

THIS regiment was raised, in accordance with a desire expressed by His Majesty George III., by the Duke of Argyll, to whom a letter of service was granted, dated the 10th of February 1794. In March it was decided that the establishment of the regiment should consist of 1112 officers and men, including 2 lieutenant-colonels. Duncan Campbell of Lochnell, who was a captain in the Foot Guards, was appointed Lieutenant-colonel commandant of the regiment, and assumed the command at Stirling on the 15th of April, 1794.

The regiment was inspected for the first time, on the 26th of May, when it had reached a strength of 738 officers and men, by General Lord Adam Gordon, who particularly noticed the attention and good appearance of the men. The regiment remained at Stirling for a month after this inspection, marching about the middle of June to Leith, at which port, on the 17th and 18th of that month, it embarked en *route* for Netley, where it went into encampment. On the 9th of July the king approved of the list of officers, and the regiment was numbered the 98th.

The 98th, which had meantime removed to Chippenham, marched to Gosport about the end of April, 1795, and on the 5th of May it embarked at Spithead as part of the joint expedition to South Africa, against the Dutch, under Major-General Alured Clark. It arrived in Simon's Bay on the 3rd, landing at Simon's Town, on the 9th of September, and encamped at Muysenberg.[1]

After the army under Major-General Clark arrived at the Cape, it advanced on the 14th of September and carried Wynberg, the battalion companies of the regiment, under Colonel Campbell, forming the centre of the line. On this occasion the 98th had 4 privates wounded. On September 16th the regiment entered Cape Town Castle, and relieved the Dutch garrison by capitulation, all the forts and batteries of Cape Town and its dependencies having been given over to the possession of the British. About a year afterwards, however, an expedition was sent from Holland for the purpose of winning back the Cape of Good Hope to that country, and in the action which took place at Saldanha Bay on the 17th of August 1796, and in which the British were

[1] Here we cannot help expressing our regret at the meagreness of the regimental Record Book, which, especially the earlier part of it, consists of the barest possible statement of the movements of the regiment, no details whatever being given of the important part it took in the various actions in which it was engaged. This we do not believe arose from any commendable modesty on the part of the regimental authorities, but, to judge from the preface to the present handsome and beautifully kept Record Book, was the result of pure carelessness. In the case of the 91st, as in the case of most of the other regiments, we have found the present officers and all who have been connected with the regiment eager to lend us all the help in their power; but we fear it will be difficult to supply the deficiencies of the Record Book, which, as an example, dismisses Toulouse in about six lines.

Exl 2

completely victorious, the grenadier and light companies of the 98th took part. The regiment remained in South Africa till the year 1802, during which time little occurred to require special notice.

In October 1798, while the regiment was at Cape Town, its number was changed from the 98th to the 91st.

In May 1799 a regimental school was established for the first time for the non-commissioned officers and men.

In the beginning of 1799 a strong attempt was made by a number of the soldiers in the garrison at Cape Town to organise a mutiny, their purpose being to destroy the principal officers, and to establish themselves in the colony. Not only did the 91st not take any part in this diabolical attempt, but the papers containing the names of the mutineers and their plans were discovered and seized by the aid of private Malcolm M'Culloch and other soldiers of the regiment, who had been urged by the mutineers to enter into the conspiracy. Lt.-Col. Crawford in a regimental order specially commended the conduct of M'Culloch, and declared that he considered himself fortunate in being the commander of such a regiment.

In November 1802 the first division of the 91st embarked at Table Bay for England, arriving at Portsmouth in February 1803. On the 28th of the latter month the second division had the honour of delivering over the Cape of Good Hope to the Dutch, to whom it had been secured at the peace of Amiens. After performing this duty the division embarked at Table Bay, arriving at Portsmouth in May, and joining the first division at their quarters in Bexhill during the next month.

During the next few years the Record Book contains nothing but an enumeration of the various places to which the regiment marched for the purpose of encamping or acting as garrison. A slight, and no doubt welcome interruption of this routine was experienced in December 1805, at the end of which month it embarked for Hanover, and was brigaded along with the 26th and 28th regiments, under the command of Major-General Mackenzie Fraser.[2] After the regiment had been about

a month in Germany the British army was recalled, and the 91st consequently returned to England in the end of January 1806, taking up its quarters at Faversham.

In August 1804, in accordance with the recent Act of Parliament known as the Defence Act, means were taken to add a second battalion to the 91st, by raising men in the counties of Perth, Argyll, and Bute.

The regiment remained in England until the end of 1806, when it embarked at Dover for Ireland, disembarking at the Cove of Cork on Jan. 7th, 1807, and marching into Fermoy. It remained in Ireland, sending detachments to various places, till the middle of 1808, embarking at Monkstown on the 15th of June, to form part of the Peninsular expedition under Lieutenant-General Sir Arthur Wellesley. The 91st was brigaded with the 40th and 71st regiments under Brigadier-General Crawford, the three regiments afterwards forming the 5th Brigade.[3] The 91st was engaged in most of the actions during the Peninsular war, and did its part bravely and satisfactorily.

On August 9th 1808, the 91st advanced with the rest of the army, and, on the 17th, in the affair at Obidos the light company of the regiment, with those of the brigade under the command of Major Douglas of the 91st, were engaged, when the advanced posts of the enemy were driven from their positions. On August 21st, the regiment was present at the battle of Vimeiro, forming part of the reserve under General C. Crawford, which turned the enemy's right,—a movement which was specially mentioned in the official despatch concerning this important battle.

In the beginning of September, by a new distribution of the army, the 91st was placed in Major-General Beresford's brigade with the 6th and 45th regiments, and in the 4th division, that of Lieutenant-General Sir Arthur Wellesley. On Sept. 20th, however, it seems to have been attached, with its brigade, to the 3rd division.

On Oct. 19th the regiment advanced into Spain, with the rest of the army under Lt.-Gen.

---

[2] See his portrait on p. 642, vol. ii.

[3] The account we are able to give here may be supplemented by what has been said regarding the Peninsular war in connection with some of the other regiments.

Sir John Moore, proceeding by Abrantes, Covilhão, Belmonte, Morilhão, Ciudad Rodrigo, and Salamanca, arriving at the last-mentioned place on Nov. 18th. On the 28th the regiment was formed into a brigade with the 20th, 28th, 52nd, and 95th regiments, to compose a part of the reserve army under Major-General the Hon. Edward Paget, in which important capacity it served during the whole of Sir John Moore's memorable retreat to Corunna. On Jan. 11th, 1809, the 91st, along with the rest of the army, took up its position on the heights of Corunna, the reserve brigade on the 16th—the day of battle—being behind the left of the British army. The 91st does not appear to have been actively engaged in this disastrous battle,—disastrous in that it involved the loss of one of England's greatest generals, the brave Sir John Moore. On the evening of the 16th the 91st embarked, and arrived in Plymouth Sound on the 28th.

The officers, non-commissioned officers, and men who were left sick in Portugal on the advance of the regiment with Sir John Moore, were formed into a company under Captain Walsh, and placed as such in the first battalion of detachments. This battalion was commanded by Lt.-Col. Bunbury, and composed part of the army in Portugal under Lt.-General Sir Arthur Wellesley. This company was actively employed in the affairs of May 10th, 11th, and 12th, which led to the capture of Oporto. It afterwards advanced with the army which drove the enemy into Spain.

The company was engaged on July 27th and 28th in the battle of Talavera, in which, out of a total strength of 93 officers and men, it lost 1 officer, Lieutenant Macdougal, and 9 rank and file killed, 1 sergeant and 30 rank and file wounded, and 1 officer, Captain James Walsh, and 19 men missing; in all, 61 officers and men. Captain Walsh was taken prisoner by the enemy in a charge, and with many other officers was marched, under a strong escort, towards France. He, however, effected his escape at Vittoria on the night of August 20th, and after suffering the greatest privation and hardship, he rejoined the army in Portugal, and reported himself personally to Lord Wellington. Captain Thomas Hunter, of the 91st, who was

acting as major of brigade, was also wounded and taken prisoner in this action.

Meantime, the main body of the 91st, after being garrisoned in England for a few months, was brigaded with the 6th and 50th Foot, under Major-General Dyott, and placed in the 2nd division, under Lieut.-General the Marquis of Huntly, preparatory to its embarkation in the expedition to Walcheren, under Lieut.-General the Earl of Chatham. The regiment disembarked at South Beveland on August 9th, and entered Middelburg, in the island of Walcheren, on Sept. 2nd. Here it seems to have remained till Dec. 23rd, when it re-embarked at Flushing, arriving at Deal on the 26th, and marched to Shorncliffe barracks. In this expedition to Walcheren the 91st must have suffered severely from the Walcheren fever, as in the casualty table of the Record Book for the year 1809 we find, for the months of Sept. and Oct. respectively, the unusually high numbers of 37 and 42 deaths.

The 91st remained in England till the month of Sept. 1812, on the 18th and 19th of which it again embarked to take its share in the Peninsular war, arriving at Corunna between the 6th and the 12th of October. On October 14th the regiment set out to join the army under the Duke of Wellington, arriving on Nov. 1st at Villafranca, about 12 miles from Benavente. After taking part in a movement in the direction of Bragança, on the frontiers of Portugal, the 91st, which had been placed in the Highland or General Pack's brigade, then under the command of Colonel Stirling of the 42nd Regiment, in the 6th division,—finally removed to San Roma, where it remained during the winter.

In April 1813, the 91st left its winter quarters, and on May 14th advanced with the combined army to attack the enemy. At the battle of Vittoria, on June 21st, the 6th division, to which the 91st belonged, was ordered to defile to the right to watch the movements of a division of the enemy during this important action, and on the 22nd it marched through Vittoria, and took charge of the guns and other warlike stores abandoned by the enemy.

On June 27th the 91st, along with the rest of the army, commenced the march towards Pamplona, and on July 6th the 6th division, in conjunction with the 5th, invested that fortress. But the blockade of Pamplona having been left to the 5th division and the Spanish legion, the 6th division advanced to San Estevan on July 15th. On the 26th of the same month, the enemy having made some movements to raise the siege of Pamplona, the 6th division moved from San Estevan on that day, and, in conjunction with the 4th and 7th divisions, on July 28th attacked the head of the French column at the small village of Sorauren, near Pamplona, and completely checked its progress. On the 30th, at daybreak, the action recommenced on the right of the division by an attack from the enemy's left wing. The action continued hotly until about noon, when the light companies of the Highland brigade, under the direction of Major Macneil of the 91st Regiment, stormed and carried the village of Sorauren, causing the enemy to flee in all directions, pursued by the division.

On the 28th the regiment lost 1 sergeant and 11 rank and file killed, and 6 officers— Captain Robert Lowrie, Lts. Allan Maclean, John Marshall, and S. N. Ormerod, and Ensigns J. A. Ormiston and Peter M'Farlane— and 97 rank and file wounded; on the 30th, 1 private was killed, and Major Macneil and 8 rank and file wounded. At least about 40 of the wounded afterwards died of their wounds.

The 91st continued to take part in the pursuit of the enemy, and on the night of August 1st bivouacked on the heights of Roncésvalles; on August 8th it encamped on the heights of Maya. The regiment remained in this quarter till the 9th of Nov., on the evening of which the army marched forward to attack the whole of the enemy's positions within their own frontier; and on the next day, the 10th of Nov., the battle of Nivelle was fought, the British attacking and carrying all the French positions, putting the enemy to a total rout. The 91st lost in this action, Captain David M'Intyre and 3 men killed, and 2 sergeants and 4 men wounded.

On November 11th the British continued to pursue the enemy towards Bayonne, but the weather being extremely wet the troops were ordered into cantonments. The British were in motion again, however, in the beginning of Dec., early on the morning of the 9th of which

the 6th division crossed the Nive on pontoon bridges, and attacked and drove in the enemy's outposts. As the 6th division had to retire out of the range of the fire of the 2nd division, it became during the remainder of the day merely an army of observation. The only casualties of the 91st at the battle of the Nive were 5 men wounded.

Marshal Soult, finding himself thus shut up in Bayonne, and thinking that most of the British troops had crossed the Nive, made, on the 10th, a desperate sally on the left of the British army, which for a moment gave way, but soon succeeded in regaining its position, and in driving the enemy within the walls of Bayonne. During the action the 6th division recrossed the Nive, and occupied quarters at Ustaritz.

At Bayonne, on Dec. 13th, Sir Rowland Hill declined the proffered assistance of the 6th division, which therefore lay on its arms in view of the dreadful conflict, that was terminated only by darkness. The enemy were completely driven within the walls of Bayonne.

During December and January the British army was cantoned in the environs of Bayonne, but was again in motion on Feb. 5th, 1814, when, with the exception of the 5th division and a few Spaniards left to besiege Bayonne, it proceeded into France. On Feb. 26th the 6th division arrived on the left bank of the Adour, opposite Orthes; and on the morning of the 27th the 3d, 4th, 6th, and 7th divisions crossed on pontoons and drew up on the plain on the right bank of the river. The French thought themselves secure in their fortified heights in front of the British position. About 9 o'clock in the morning the divisions moved down the main road towards Orthes; each division, as it came abreast of the enemy's position, broke off the road and attacked and carried the position in its front. About noon the enemy fled, pursued by the British, who were stopped only by the darkness of night. In the battle of Orthes the 91st had Captain William Gunn and Lts. Alexander Campbell, John Marshall, and John Taylor, and 12 rank and file wounded. At the Aire, on March 2nd, the 91st had 1 man killed, and Captain William Douglas, Ensign Colin Macdougal, 1 sergeant, and 14 men wounded.

The 91st continued with its division to advance towards Toulouse, where the great Peninsular struggle was to culminate. On March 26th, the 6th division arrived at the village of Constantine, opposite to and commanding a full view of Toulouse, and on the 8th it moved to the right, and occupied the village of Tournefeuille. Early on the morning of April 4th the division moved a few miles down the Garonne, and a little after daybreak crossed.[4] On the morning of April 10th the army left its tents at an early hour, and at daybreak came in sight of the fortified heights in front of Toulouse. The 6th division was ordered to storm these heights, supported by the Spaniards on the right and the 4th division on the left. About ten o'clock the Highland brigade attacked and carried all the fortified redoubts and entrenchments along the heights, close to the walls of Toulouse. Night alone put an end to the contest. We are sorry that we have been unable to obtain any details of the conduct of the 91st; but it may be gathered from what has been said in connection with the 42nd and 79th, as well as from the long list of casualties in the regiment, that it had a full share of the work which did so much honour to the Highland brigade.

At Toulouse the 91st had 1 sergeant and 17 men killed, and 7 officers—viz., Col. Sir William Douglas,[5] who commanded the brigade after Sir Dennis Pack was wounded, Major A. Meade, Captains James Walsh and A. J. Callender, Lts. J. M. Macdougal, James Hood, and Colin Campbell—1 sergeant, and 93 rank and file wounded; a good many of the latter afterwards dying of their wounds.

As is well known, on the day after the battle of Toulouse news of the abdication of Napoleon, and the restoration of the Bourbons, was re-ceived, and hostilities were therefore suspended. On April 20th the 6th division marched for Auch, and on the 24th of June the first detachment of the regiment sailed for home, the second following on July 1st, both arriving at Cork towards the end of the latter month.

Lt.-Colonel Macneil was presented with a gold medal, and promoted to the rank of lt.-colonel in the army, for his services in the Peninsula, and especially for his gallant conduct in command of the light companies of the light brigade of the 6th division at Sorauren. Captain Walsh was also promoted to the rank of brevet lt.-colonel.

On March 17th the 91st, accompanied by the 42nd, 71st, and 79th regiments, sailed for Carlingford Bay, in the north of Ireland, and from thence to the Downs, where it was transhipped into small crafts and sailed for Ostend, where it arrived on the night of the 17th of April.

Although at Quatre Bras and Waterloo,[6] the 91st had no opportunity of coming to close quarters with the enemy, yet its service in these days was so efficient as to gain for it all the honours, grants, and privileges which were bestowed on the army for that memorable occasion. The 91st did good service on the morning of the 18th of June by helping to cover the road to Brussels, which was threatened by a column of the French. On the 19th the 91st took part in the pursuit of the flying enemy, and on the 24th it sat down before Cambray, which, having refused to capitulate, was carried by assault. On this occasion the 91st had Lt. Andrew Cathcart and 6 men wounded; and at Antel de Dieu, on June 26th, a private was killed on this post by some of the French picquets. On July 7th the 91st encamped in the Bois de Boulogne, where it remained till Oct. 31st, when it went into cantonments.

The 91st remained in France till Nov. 2nd, 1818, when it embarked at Calais for Dover; sailed again on Dec. 17th from Gosport for Cork, where it disembarked on the 24th; finally, marching in two divisions, on Dec. 27th and

---

[4] In connection with the 42nd and 79th Regiments, which with the 91st formed the Highland brigade, many details of the battle of Toulouse have already been given, which need not be repeated here.

[5] Shortly after Sir William Douglas assumed the command, the Duke of Wellington came up and asked who had the command of the brigade. Colonel Douglas replied that he had the honour to command it just then; when Wellington said, "No man could do better," adding, "take the command, and keep it," which Colonel Douglas did until the brigade reached home. Lt.-Colonel Douglas was presented with a gold medal for his services in the Peninsula, and subsequently created K.C.B.

[6] At Waterloo Captain Thomas Hunter Blair of the 91st was doing duty as major of brigade to the 3rd brigade of British Infantry, and for his meritorious conduct on that occasion was promoted Lt.-Col. of the army.

28th, for Dublin, which it reached on the 6th and 7th Jan. 1819.

By this time the 91st had ceased to wear both kilt and tartan, lost its Highland designation, and had gradually become an ordinary regiment of the line. From the statement of John Campbell, who was living at Aberdeen in 1871, and who served in the 91st throughout the Peninsular war, we learn that in 1809, just before embarking for Walcheren, the tartan for the kilts and plaids reached the regiment; but an order shortly came to make it up into trews. Along with the trews, a low flat bonnet with a feather on one side was ordered to be worn. About a year after, in 1810, even the tartan trews were taken from the 91st, a kind of grey trousers being ordered to be worn instead ; the feathered bonnet was taken away at the same time, and the black cap then worn by ordinary line regiments was substituted.

The 91st remained in Dublin till July 22nd, 1820, eliciting the marked approbation of the various superior officers appointed to inspect it. On July 22nd it proceeded to Enniskillen, furnishing detachments to the counties of Cavan, Leitrim, and Donegal. Orders having been received in June 1821 that the regiment should prepare to proceed for Jamaica from the Clyde, the 91st embarked on the 18th at Donaghadee for Portpatrick, and marched to Glasgow, where it arrived on the 27th and 28th.

The regiment embarked at Greenock in two divisions in Nov. 1821 and Jan. 1822, arriving at Kingston, Jamaica, in Feb. and March respectively.

The 91st was stationed in the West Indies till the year 1831, during which time nothing notable seems to have occurred. The regiment, which lost an unusually large number of men by death in the West Indies, left Jamaica in three divisions in March and April 1831, arriving at Portsmouth in May and June following. The reserve companies having come south from Scotland, the entire regiment was once more united at Portsmouth in the beginning of August. In October the 91st was sent to the north, detachments being stationed at various towns in Lancashire and Yorkshire till the 10th of July 1832, when the detachments reunited at Liverpool, where the regiment embarked for Ireland, landing at Dublin on the following day. The 91st was immediately sent to Mullingar, where headquarters was stationed, detachments being sent out to various towns. From this time till the end of 1835 the regiment was kept constantly moving about in detachments among various stations in the centre, southern, and western Irish counties, engaged in duties often of the most trying and harassing kind, doing excellent and necessary service, but from which little glory could be gained. One of the most trying duties which the 91st had to perform during its stay in Ireland at this time, was lending assistance to the civil power on the occasion of Parliamentary elections. On such occasions the troops were subjected to treatment trying to their temper in the highest degree ; but to the great credit of the officers and men belonging to the 91st, when employed on this duty, they behaved in a manner deserving of all praise.

The 91st having been ordered to proceed to St Helena, embarked in two detachments in November, and sailed from the Cove of Cork on the 1st of Dec. 1835, disembarking at St Helena on the 26th of Feb. 1836. The companies were distributed among the various stations in the lonely island, and during the stay of the regiment there nothing occurred which calls for particular notice. At the various inspections the 91st received nothing but praise for its discipline, appearance, and interior economy.

On the 4th of June 1839, headquarters, grenadiers, No. 2, and the light infantry companies, left St Helena for the Cape of Good Hope, disembarking at Algoa Bay on the 3d of July, and reaching Grahamstown on the 8th.

Nothing of note occurred in connection with the regiment for the first two years of its stay at the Cape. It was regularly employed in detachments in the performance of duty at the various outposts on the Fish river, the Kat river, the Koonap river, Blinkwater, Double Drift, Fort Peddie, and other places, the detachments being relieved at regular intervals.

Government having decided upon the formation of reserve battalions, for the purpose of facilitating the relief of regiments abroad, and shortening their periods of foreign service, early in the month of April 1842, the establishment of the four company dépôts of certain regiments was changed, and formed into battalions of six skeleton companies by volunteers from other corps. The 91st, the depôt companies of which were then stationed at Naas, was selected in March 1842 as one of the regiments to be thus augmented. When complete the numbers and distribution of the rank and file stood as follows:—1st battalion, 540; reserve battalion, 540; depôt, 120; total, 1200.

The Lt.-Colonel, whose post was to be with the 1st battalion, had the general charge and superintendence of the whole regiment, assisted by an additional major. The reserved battalion had the usual proportion of officers and non-commissioned officers appointed to it, but had no flank companies. The senior major had the immediate command of the reserve battalion.

The reserve battalion having been reported fit for service, was directed to hold itself in readiness to proceed to the Cape of Good Hope.

The wing under Capt. Bertie Gordon—who had joined the regiment about nine years previously, and who was so long and honourably connected with the 91st—joined the head-quarters of the regiment at Naas on May 26th 1842, where the six companies were united under his command, both the lt.-col. and the major being on leave. On the 27th of May the battalion, under Capt. Gordon, proceeded from Naas to Kingstown, and embarked on board the transport "Abercrombie Robinson." On the 2d of June the transport sailed for the Cape of Good Hope, the strength of the regiment on board being 17 officers and 460 men, Lt.-Col. Lindsay being in command. The ship also contained drafts of the 27th regiment and the Cape Mounted Rifles. The transport having touched at Madeira, arrived in Table Bay on the 25th of August 1842. Here the battalion was warned for service on the north-eastern frontier of the colony, relieving the 1st battalion of the regiment, which was to be stationed at Cape Town. In consequence of this arrangement Lt.-Col. Lindsay and Major Ducat disembarked on the 27th, for the purpose of joining the 1st battalion, to which they belonged. All the other officers, not on duty, obtained permission to go ashore, and all landed except six, the command of the troops on board devolving on Capt. Bertie Gordon.

An event now took place which can only be paralleled by the famous wreck of the "Birkenhead" ten years afterwards, the narrative of which we have recorded in our history of the 74th.

At 11 o'clock P.M., on the night of the 27th, it was blowing a strong gale, and the sea was rolling heavily into the bay. The ship was pitching much and began to feel the ground, but she rode by two anchors, and a considerable length of cable had been served out the night before. Captain Gordon made such arrangements as he could, warning the officers, the sergeant-major, and the orderly non-commissioned officers to be in readiness.

From sunset on the 27th the gale had continued to increase, until at length it blew a tremendous hurricane, and at a little after 3 o'clock on the morning of the 28th the starboard cable snapped in two. The other cable parted a few minutes afterwards, and away went the ship before the storm, her hull striking with heavy crashes against the ground as she drove towards the beach, three miles distant under her lee. About the same time the fury of the gale, which had never lessened, was rendered more terrible by one of the most awful storms of thunder and lightning that had ever been witnessed in Table Bay.

While the force of the wind and sea was driving the ship into shoaler water, she rolled incessantly and heaved over fearfully with the back set of the surf. While in this position the heavy seas broke over her side and poured down the hatchways, the decks were opening in every direction, and the strong framework of the hull seemed compressed together, the beams starting from their places. The ship had been driven with her starboard bow towards the beach, exposing her stern to the sea, which rushed through the stern-posts and tore up the cabin floors of the orlop deck. The thunder and lightning ceased towards morning, and the ship seemed to have worked a bed for herself on the sand; for the rolling had greatly diminished, and there then arose the hope that all on board might get safe ashore.

At daybreak, about 7 o'clock, the troops, who had been kept below, were now allowed to come on deck in small numbers. After vain attempts to send a rope ashore, one of the cutters was carefully lowered on the lee side of the ship, and her crew succeeded in reaching the shore with a hauling line. The large surf-boats were shortly afterwards conveyed in waggons to the place where the ship was stranded, and the following orders were given by Captain Gordon for the disembarkation of the troops:—1. The women and children to disembark first; of these there were above 90. 2. The sick to disembark after the women and children. 3. The disembarkation of the troops to take place by the companies of the 91st Regiment drawing lots; the detachment of the 27th Regiment and the Cape Mounted Rifles to take the precedence. 4. The men to fall in on the upper deck, fully armed and accoutred, carrying their knapsacks and their greatcoats. 5. Each officer to be allowed to take a carpet-bag or small portmanteau.

The disembarkation of the women and children and of the sick continued from half-past 8 until 10 o'clock A.M. The detachments of the 27th Regiment and the Cape Mounted Rifles followed. The disembarkation of the 91st was arranged by, first, the wings drawing lots, and then the companies of each wing.

At half-past 10 one of the surf boats, which had been employed up to this time in taking the people off the wreck, was required to assist in saving the lives of those on board the "Waterloo" convict ship, which was in still more imminent peril about a quarter of a mile from the "Abercrombie Robinson." There was now but one boat to disembark 450 men, the wind and sea beginning again to rise, and the captain was apprehensive that the ship might go to pieces before sunset.

The disembarkation of the six companies went on regularly but slowly from 11 A.M. until 3.30 P.M., the boat being able to hold only 30 men at a time. At half-past 3 the last boat-load left the ship's side. It contained those of the officers and crew who had remained to the last, Captain Gordon of the 91st, Lt. Black, R.N., agent of transports, the sergeant-major of the reserve battalion of the 91st, and one or two non-commissioned officers who had requested permission to remain.

Nearly 700 souls thus completed their disembarkation after a night of great peril, and through a raging surf, without the occurrence of a single casualty. Among them were many women and children, and several sick men, two of whom were supposed to be dying. Although it had been deemed prudent to abandon the men's knapsacks and the officer's baggage, the reserve battalion of the 91st went down the side of that shattered wreck fully armed and accoutred, and ready for instant service.

It would be difficult to praise sufficiently the steady discipline of that young battalion, thus severely tested during nearly seventeen hours of danger, above eight of which were hours of darkness and imminent peril. That discipline failed not when the apparent hopelessness of the situation might have led to scenes of confusion and crime. The double guard and sentries which had at first been posted over the wine and spirit stores were found unnecessary, and these stores were ultimately left to the protection of the ordinary single sentries. Although the ship was straining in every timber, and the heavy seas were making a fair breach over her, the companies of that young battalion fell in on the weather side of the wreck as their lots were drawn, and waited for their turn to muster at the lee gangway; and so perfect were their confidence, their patience, and their gallantry, that although another vessel was going to pieces within a quarter of a mile of the transport ship, and a crowd of soldiers, sailors, and convicts were perishing before the eyes of those on board, not a murmur arose from their ranks, when Captain Gordon directed that the lot should not be applied to the detachment of the 27th regiment and Cape Mounted Riflemen, but that the 91st should give the precedence in disembarking from the wreck.

The narrative of the wreck was submitted to Field-Marshal the Duke of Wellington, who wrote upon it words of the highest commendation on the conduct of officers and men. "I have never," the Duke wrote, "read anything so satisfactory as this report. It is highly creditable, not only to Captain Bertie Gordon and the officers and troops concerned, but to the service in which such an instance has occurred, of discretion and of firmness in an officer in command, and of confidence, good order, discipline, and obedience in all under his direction, even to the women and children." The Duke did not forget the conduct of those concerned in this affair; it was mainly owing to the way in which Sergeant-major Murphy performed his duty on this occasion, that in 1846, through the Duke of Wellington's influence, he was appointed to a wardership of the Tower.

In consequence of this unfortunate disaster the 91st remained stationed at Cape Town until Feb. 1843. In Oct. 1842 Lt.-Col. Lindsay

took command of the 1st battalion at Grahamstown, and Major Ducat assumed command of the reserve.

As the histories of the two battalions of the 91st during their existence are to a great extent separate, and as the 1st battalion did not remain nearly so long at the Cape as the 2nd reserve, nor had so much fighting to do, it will, we think, be better to see the 1st battalion safely home before commencing the history of the 2nd.

During the remainder of its stay at the Cape, till 1848, the 1st battalion continued as before to furnish detachments to the numerous outposts which guarded the colony from the ravages and ferocity of the surrounding natives. Such names as Fort Peddie, Fort Armstrong, Trompeter's Drift, Commity Drift, Eland's River, Bothas Post, &c., are continually occurring in the Record Book of the regiment.

The three companies that were left at St Helena in June 1839 joined the headquarters of the 1st battalion on Dec. 6th, 1842.

In the beginning of Dec. 1842 a force, consisting of 800 men, of whom 400 belonged to the 1st battalion of the 91st, was ordered to proceed from the eastern frontier to the northern boundary, an insurrection of the Dutch farmers having been expected in that quarter. This force, commanded by Colonel Hare, the Lieutenant-Governor, arrived at Colesberg, a village near the Orange river, about the end of the month. No active operations were, however, found necessary, and the troops were ordered to return to their quarters, after leaving 300 men of the 91st in cantonment at Colesberg. Previous to the force breaking up, Colonel Hare issued a frontier order, dated Feb. 1st, 1843, in which he expressed his admiration of the conduct of officers and men.

In the beginning of June 1843 nearly all the disposable troops on the eastern frontier were ordered on a special service to Kaffirland. The 1st and reserve battalions of the 91st furnished detachments for this service. The object of the expedition was to drive a refractory Kaffir chief, named Tola, from the neutral territory, and to dispossess him of a number of cattle stolen from the colony. The third division, commanded by Lt.-Col. Lindsay of the 91st Regiment, in the performance of this day encountered some opposition from a body of armed Kaffirs, in a skirmish with whom one man of the battalion was severely wounded. The force returned to the colony in the beginning of the following July, having captured a considerable number of cattle.

The emigrant farmers beyond the Orange river, or N.E. boundary of the colony, having early in the year 1845 committed aggressions on the Griquas or Bastards, by attacking their villages and kraals, and carrying off their cattle, &c., the Griquas claimed the protection of the British Government, the Boers having assembled in large bodies. Accordingly, the detachment of the 91st stationed at Colesberg, consisting of the grenadiers No. 2 and light companies, under the command of Major J. F. G. Campbell, was ordered to the Orange river, about fifteen miles from Colesberg. The detachment, along with a company of the Cape Mounted Riflemen, crossed the river on the night of April 22nd, and marched to Philippolis, a village of the Griquas.

Information having been received that the Boers were encamped in force at Touw Fontein, about thirty-five miles from Philippolis, the detachment marched on the night of the 23rd of April for the camp, within four miles of which camp the Boers and Griquas were found skirmishing, the former, 500 strong, being mounted. Dispositions were made to attack the camp, but the troops of the 7th Dragoon Guards and the company of the Cape Rifles pushed forward, and the Boers fled in all directions, after offering a very slight resistance. The detachment of the 91st remained encamped until the 30th of June, when it was ordered to Grahamstown.

On Nov. 25th of this year the 1st battalion was inspected by Colonel Hare, who, at the same time, presented the regiment with new colours, and expressed in a few words his entire approval of the battalion.

At the commencement of the Kaffir war, in March 1846, the battalion proceeded to Fort Peddie, in the ceded territory,[7] and shortly afterwards it was joined by detachments of the corps from various outposts. The grenadier company

at the commencement of the war was attached to the field force under Colonel Somerset, K.H., and was engaged in the Amatola Mountains with the enemy on the 16th, 17th, and 18th of April, when Lt. J. D. Cochrane was severely wounded. What details we have been able to collect concerning the part taken by the 91st in this long and arduous engagement we shall record in speaking of the reserve battalion, which was also largely engaged during these three days.

After this the grenadier company was attached to the reserve battalion, with the exception of a few men, who accompanied Captain Hogg's Hottentot levy to Makassa's Country.

The headquarters of the battalion was engaged in protecting the Fingoe settlement at Fort Peddie, being stationed there when the post was attacked, on the 28th of May 1846, by upwards of 8000 Kaffirs. The strength of the battalion consisted of 254 officers and men; there was also a weak troop of cavalry at the post. The details of this attack will be best told in the words of a writer quoted by Mrs Ward:—[8]

"Finding their scheme of drawing the troops out did not succeed, small parties advanced in skirmishing order, and then the two divisions of Pàto and the Gaikas moved towards each other, as if intending a combined attack on some given point. Colonel Lindsay was superintending the working of the gun himself, and, as soon as a body of the Gaikas came within range, a shot was sent into the midst of them, which knocked over several, disconcerted them a little, and threw them into confusion; rapid discharges of shot and shell followed. The Kaffirs now extended themselves in a line six miles in length. These advancing at the same time, so filled the valley that it seemed a mass of moving Kaffirs; rockets and shells were poured rapidly on them, and presently a tremendous fire of musketry was poured, happily, over our heads. The enemy, however, did not come near enough for the infantry to play upon them, and only a few shots were fired from the infantry barracks.

"The dragoons were ordered out, and, though rather late, followed up some of Pàto's men, who fled at their approach, Sir Harry Darell galloping after them with his troop. The daring Fingoes followed the Kaffirs to the Gwanga river, four miles off.

"Upwards of 200 of the enemy fell, and more were afterwards ascertained to be dead and dying, but they carried off the greater part of the cattle."

Towards the end of June the battalion furnished to the second division of the army, under Colonel Somerset, three companies under a field officer, which proceeded with the division as far as the Buffalo affluents in Kaffraria, and rejoined headquarters, when the division

---

[7] The ceded territory was occupied by certain Kaffir tribes only conditionally; by their depredations they had long forfeited all right to remain there.

[8] The Cape and the Kaffirs, p. 191.

fell back for supplies, on Waterloo Bay in September. The whole force was under the command of Sir Peregrine Maitland, and, after encountering many difficulties, hardships, and privations, successfully effected the object of the expedition.

Soon after this the battalion furnished detachments for the Fish River line, from Trompeter's Drift to Fort-Brown ; and, after the second advance of the 2nd division into the enemy's country, performed a very considerable amount of escort duty in guarding convoys of supplies for the Kei river and other camps.

During the remainder of the stay of the 1st battalion at the Cape, we have no record of its being engaged in any expedition. On January 12th, 1848, it marched from Grahamstown to Algoa Bay, and thence proceeded to Cape Town, where headquarters and three companies embarked for home on the 23rd of February, followed on the 10th of March by the other three companies, arriving at Gosport on the 28th of April and 11th of May respectively. The dépôt was consolidated with the battalion on the 1st of May.

By a memorandum, dated " Horse Guards, 5th May 1846," a second lieut.-colonel was appointed to the 91st, as well as to all the regiments having reserve battalions; he was to have the command of the reserve battalion.

II.

1842–1857.

The reserve battalion—Captain Bertie Gordon cures desertion—Grahamstown—Fort Beaufort—Kaffir War—Amatola Mountains—The Tynnie River—A daring deed—Trompeter's Hill—Amatola and Tabindoda Mountains—"Weel done, Sodger!"—The Kei River—The Rebel Boers—Grahamstown—The Second Kaffir War—Fort Hare—The Yellow Woods—Amatola Mountains—Fort Hare attacked—Kumnegana Heights—The Waterkloof—The Kumnegana again—Amatola Mountains and the Tynmie—The Waterkloof—The Waterkloof again—Patrol work—The Waterkloof again—Eland's Post—The Kei—The Waterkloof again—Blinkwater and other posts—From Beaufort to Port Elizabeth—The battalion receives an ovation—Home—Redistribution of regiment—Aldershot—The Queen visits the lines of the 91st—"The Queen's Hut "—Duke of Cambridge compliments the regiment—Second visit of the Queen—Berwick—Preston—Final absorption of the second battalion.

To return to the reserve battalion. During Oct. and Nov. 1842 desertions had taken place among the young soldiers of the reserve battalion, then at Cape Town, to an unusual extent. At length, when eighteen soldiers had deserted in less than six weeks, and every night was adding to the number, Captain Bertie Gordon volunteered his services to the Major commanding, offering to set off on the same day on a patrolling expedition, to endeavour to apprehend and bring the deserters back. Captain Gordon only stipulated to be allowed the help of one brother officer and of a Cape Corps soldier as an interpreter, with a Colonial Office Order addressed to all field-coronets, directing them to give him such assistance, in the way of furnishing horses for his party and conveyances for his prisoners, as he might require. Captain Gordon's offer was accepted.

Captain Gordon had not the slightest trace or information of the track of a single deserter to guide his course over the wide districts through which his duty might lead his patrol. In taking leave of his commanding officer before riding off, Major Ducat said to him,— " Gordon, if you do not bring them back we are a ruined battalion." The patrol was absent from headquarters for eight days, during which Captain Gordon rode over 600 miles ; and when, on the evening of the 16th of Nov., his tired party rode into the barracks of Cape Town, just before sunset, after a ride of 80 miles in 13 hours, 16 out of 18 deserters had been already lodged in the regimental guard-room as the result of his exertions. Two more deserters, hearing that Captain Gordon was out, had come in of their own accord, and thus all were satisfactorily accounted for. The desertions in the reserve battalion from that period ceased.

The battalion embarked on the morning of Feb. 22nd, 1842, for Algoa Bay, but the ship did not sail till the 27th, anchoring in Algoa Bay on March 4th, the battalion disembarking at Port Elizabeth on the 5th. On the 7th the reserve battalion set out for Grahamstown, which it reached on the 13th, and took up quarters at Fort England with the 1st battalion of the regiment.

In the beginning of Jan. 1844 the reserve battalion left Grahamstown for Fort Beaufort, which became it headquarters for the next four years, detachments being constantly sent out to occupy the many posts which were established, and keep the turbulent Kaffirs in check.

In the early part of 1846 the Kaffir war was commenced, and on April 11th the headquarters of the reserve battalion, augmented to 200 rank and file by the grenadier company of the 1st battalion, marched from Fort Beaufort into Kaffirland with the division, under command of Col. Richardson of the 7th Dragoon Guards; and, on the 14th, the detachment joined Col. Somerset's division near the Debe Flats. The object of this expedition was to chastise the Kaffirs for some outrages which they had committed on white settlers,—one of which was the murder of a German missionary in cold blood, in open day, by some of the people of the chief named Páto.

The attack on the Kaffirs in the Amatola mountains having been ordered for an early hour on April 16th, and the rendezvous having been fixed at the source of the Amatola River, the 91st, of the strength already given, under command of Major Campbell, with about an equal number of Hottentot Burghers, crossed the Keiskamma river, and ascended the Amatola valley. During the greater part of the way the march was through dense bush, with precipitous and craggy mountains on each hand. On reaching the head of the valley the Kaffirs, estimated at from 2000 to 3000, were seen on the surrounding heights, closing in upon the force. The ascent to the place of rendezvous was by a narrow rugged path, with rocks and bush on both sides, and, when the party had got about halfway up the hill, it was attacked on each flank, and was soon exposed to a cross-fire from three sides of a square, the enemy having closed on the rear. The height was gained, however, and the party then kept its ground until joined by Colonel Somerset with the rest of the force shortly afterwards; while waiting for the latter the party was repeatedly attacked. In the performance of this service the 91st had 3 privates killed, and several wounded, 3 severely.

During the night of the 16th a division, under Major Gibsone of the 7th Dragoon Guards, which had been left in charge of the baggage at Burns' Hill, was attacked and the

recklessly brave Captain Bambrick of the same regiment killed.

"Major Gibsone's despatch states further—'About seven o'clock, just as I had diminished the size of my camp, we were attacked by a considerable body of Kaffirs, whom we beat off in six or seven minutes, I am sorry to say, with the loss of 4 men of the 91st killed, and 4 wounded.'

"On the 17th, Major Gibsone, in compliance with Colonel Somerset's instructions, moved from Burns' Hill at half-past ten A.M. From the number of waggons (125), and the necessity of giving a support to the guns, Major Gibsone was only enabled to form a front and rear baggage-guard, and could not detach any men along the line of waggons. After proceeding about a mile, shots issued from a kloof by the side of the road; Lieut. Stokes, R.E., ran the gun up to a point some 300 yards in advance, and raked the kloof with a shell. When half the waggons had passed, the Kaffirs made a dash upon one of them, firing at the drivers and some officers' servants, who were obliged to fly; then took out the oxen, and wheeled the waggon across the river. An overpowering force then rushed down from the hills in all directions, keeping up an incessant fire, which was returned by the 7th Dragoon Guards and the 91st with great spirit. The gun was also served with much skill; but, owing to the Kaffirs' immense superiority in numbers, Major Gibsone, to prevent his men from being cut off, was obliged to return to Burn's Hill, where he again put the troops in position. A short time after this, a company of the 91st, under Major Scott, advanced in skirmishing order, keeping up a heavy fire; but the waggons completely blocking up the road, the troops were obliged to make a détour, and, after considerable difficulty, succeeded in getting the ammunition-waggons into a proper line, but found it quite impracticable to save the baggage-waggons, the Kaffirs having driven away the oxen. One of the ammunition-waggons broke down, but the ammunition was removed to another; the troops then fought their way, inch by inch, to the Tyumie camp, where they were met by Colonel Somerset's division, and where they again encamped for the night."[2]

On the 18th the camp, with captured cattle, was moved to Block Drift; the guard on the large train of waggons consisted of a detachment of the 91st regiment, under Captain Scott. The rear of the retiring column was brought up by Captain Rawstorne of the 91st and his company, assisted by Lieut. Howard of the 1st battalion. The enemy vigorously attacked the waggons and the division whenever they found cover from the dense bush, which extended the greater part of the distance to Block Drift. Captain Rawstorne was wounded in the stomach by a musket ball, and 1 man of the 91st was killed and 1 mortally wounded.

On approaching the Tyumie river, the ammunition of Captain Rawstorne's company being all expended, it was relieved from pro-

Mr Wolf [...] and C. X [...] t, p. 86.

tooting the rear by the grenadier company of the 91st. The waggons crossed the river, the drift being held by the reserve battalion of the 91st and a few dismounted dragoons, the guns of the royal artillery firing from the higher ground on the opposite side of the river. Again to quote Mrs Ward—[1]

"Thus, scarcely 1500 men, not all regular troops, encumbered with 125 waggons, made their way into the fastnesses of these savages, who were many thousands in number; and although unable to follow up the enemy, of whom they killed at least 300, succeeded in saving all their ammunition, captured 1800

head of cattle, and finally fought their way to the original ground of dispute.

"Among the slain was afterwards discovered a soldier of the 91st, who had probably been burned to death by the savages, as his remains were found bound to the pole of a waggon, and horribly defaced by fire."

The headquarters of the reserve battalion remained at Block Drift until the July following. On the 12th of May it was attacked by the Kaffirs, who were repulsed, with the loss of a chief and 60 men killed; the 91st had 1 man mortally wounded.[2]

Crossing the Tyumie or Chumie River.
From a drawing by Major Ward, 91st.

Lieut. Dickson of the reserve battalion of the 91st, while commanding at Trompeter's

[1] Page 87.
[2] When the reserve battalion was holding Block Drift, a very daring act was performed by two private soldiers of the regiment. A despatch arrived for the Governor, Sir Peregrine Maitland, escorted by 18 mounted burghers, with a request from the commandant at Fort Beaufort, that it should be sent on as soon as possible. The communication between Block Drift and Fort Cox, where the Governor was, was completely cut off; and accordingly volunteers were called for to carry the despatch. Two men immediately came forward, Robert Welsh and Thomas Reilly, and to them the despatch was entrusted. They left Block Drift shortly after dark, and proceeded on their perilous journey—dressed in uniform and with their muskets. All went well for the first six miles, although they found themselves in the vicinity of the Kaffirs. Suddenly, on entering a wooded valley at the

Drift, frequently obtained the approbation of Sir Peregrine Maitland and Lt.-Col. Johnston

foot of the Amatola mountains, they came right upon a Kaffir encampment, and had hardly time to throw themselves on the ground in the thick underwood, when they found to their horror that the natives had heard their footsteps, as the latter rushed into the thicket in all directions to look for the intruders. Fortunately a porcupine was sighted, and the Kaffirs evidently satisfied, returned to their camp, muttering that it was an "Easterforke," Anglice porcupine, that had alarmed them. Walsh and Reilly, holding their breath, saw the Kaffirs prepare to eat their supper, after which they began to post their sentries! One was put within six yards of the gallant fellows, who, not quite discouraged, still kept quiet. The remaining Kaffirs rolled themselves up in their blankets, and went to sleep. The sentry stood for a few minutes,—looked round, then sat down for a few more minutes, looked round again, and then wrapped for his great zeal and activity, and on the 21st of May, when a convoy of waggons, proceeding from Grahamstown and Fort Peddie, was attacked and captured by the enemy on Trompeter's Hill, the gallant conduct of Lt Dickson, who had voluntarily joined the escort, was highly commended by his Excellency the commander-in-chief, in general orders In reference to this incident, Mrs Ward writes as follows —

"On this occasion Lieut Dickson, 91st Regiment, who had been ordered to assist in escorting the waggons a certain distance, till the other escort was met, nobly volunteered to proceed further, and led the advance, nor did he retire till his ammunition was expended On reaching the rear, he found the commanding officer of the party retreating, by the advice of some civilians, who considered the defile impassable for so many waggons, under such a fire Lieut Dickson's coolness, courage, and energy, in not only leading the men, but literally 'putting his shoulder to the wheel' of a waggon, to clear the line, were spoken of by all as worthy of the highest praise His horse, and that of Ensign Aitchison, were shot under their riders"

On July 27th, the battalion proceeded with Colonel Hare's division to the Amatola mountains, and was present in the different operations undertaken against the Kaffirs between that time and the end of December, when the battalion returned to Block Drift and thence proceeded to Fort Beaufort, where it remained stationary until the renewal of hostilities against the Kaffirs in the following year

The head quarters and two companies entered Kaffirland with Col Campbell's column, and were present in the operations undertaken in the Amatola and Tabindoda mountains during the months of Sept and Oct [3] As a

himself in his blanket, and slept peacefully too Walsh and Reilly, is may be imagined, did not give him the chance of waking, but made off They then made a wide circuit, and after numerous escapes from detection, once having been challenged by a Kaffir sentinel (who was not asleep), they came to the Keiskama river, and knowing that all the fords were guarded by the kaffirs, they had to cross by swimming, finally reaching Fort Cox shortly before daylight Here their dangers were not over, for the sentries, not expecting anything but Kaffirs, treated them to some rapid file firing Again they lay down in shelter until daybreak, when, being recognised as British soldiers, they were warmly welcomed and delivered their important despatches Poor Walsh was afterwards killed in action, and Reilly was discharged with a pension after 21 years' service, though it is to be regretted that neither received at the time any public reward of their gallant night's work, which in these days would certainly have been rewarded with the Victoria Cross

[3] During the advance of the enemy on Block Drift, at t'   ', ... the p ...
com   1 ,   ... an Cap B,

result of these operations the Kaffir chief, Sandilli, surrendered, the 91st having had only 3 men wounded Lt -Col Campbell and the above column received the warmest approbation of Lt Gen Sir George Berkeley in Orders of Dec 17th, 1847, at the close of the war

At the end of Oct. the two companies above mentioned, under the command of Capt. Scott, marched to King-Williamstown to join the force about to proceed to the Kei river, under the commander-in-chief, Lt -Gen Sir George Berkeley They were attached to Col Somerset's division, and served therewith until the end of December, when peace was concluded, and the detachment of the 91st returned to Fort Beaufort.

We regret that we have been unable to obtain more details of the part taken by the 91st during the Kaffir War of 1846-47, in which it was prominently employed Among those who were honourably mentioned by Sir Peregrine Maitland, in general orders, for their conduct in defending their respective posts when attacked, were Lts Metcalfe and Thom, and Sergeants Snodgrass and Clark of the 91st

The reserve battalion removed from Fort Beaufort to Grahamstown in Jan 1848, nothing of note occurring until the month of July In that month two companies under the command of Capt Rawstorne marched from Grahamstown to Colesberg, to co-operate with a force under the immediate command of the Governor, Lt Gen Sir Harry Smith, against the rebel Boers in the N E district After an arduous and protracted march, owing to the inclement season, and swollen state of the rivers the companies reached the Governor's camp on the Orange river, on August 24th Detachments under Lt. Owgan, from Fort Beaufort, and under Ensign Crampton, from Fort England, here joined, so that the strength

he took up a position on the top of the school house, rifle in hand , four men were employed in loading his arms for him, and he brought down two of the enemy successively in a few minutes When a third fell dead, a soldier of the reserve battalion 91st Regiment could restrain himself no longer, forgetting Col Campbell's rank as an officer, in his delight at his prowess as a soldier, the man slapped his commanding officer on the back with a shout of delight, and the exclamation, "Well done, Sodger '" Was not such a compliment worth all the praise of an elaborate   th H (, ... ' K ' p 198 of the party of the 91st amounted to 178 officers and men.

After the troops had crossed, Captain Rawstorne remained at Bothas Drift, on the Orange river, with a party of 40 men of the 91st, to guard the Drift, and keep open the communication with the colony. The remainder of the party, furnished by the reserve battalion, under Lt. Pennington, proceeded with the Governor's force in pursuit of the rebels, and was engaged in a most severe and spirited skirmish with the enemy at Boem Plaats on Aug. 29th, when Ensign Crampton, Lt. Owen, and 5 privates were wounded. The enemy held a very strong position, occupying a series of koppies on the right of the road, from which they kept up a heavy fire, against which the Rifle Brigade advanced, supported by the 45th Regiment and artillery. The 91st remained with the guns till the enemy appeared among the ridges on the left, when they were immediately ordered to fix bayonets and charge, which they did in the most gallant manner, causing the enemy to retreat in the greatest confusion, and driving them from every successive hill on which they took up a position, until nightfall. The pursuit was continued with untiring energy, and severe loss to the enemy. Lt. Pennington's name was mentioned by the Commander-in-Chief in his despatch as commanding on that occasion a detachment of the reserve battalion of the 91st, which shared in the praise bestowed by His Excellency on the troops.

The companies returned to Grahamstown on the 15th of October, and from this date the headquarters of the battalion remained at Fort England and Drostdy's Barracks, Grahamstown, for upwards of two years, sending out detachments to perform the ordinary outpost duties of the frontier.

At the outbreak of the second Kaffir war, at the end of 1850, every available man was required for active operations in the field, and the reserve battalion of the 91st marched en route to Fort Hare on Dec. 12th. On the 26th a small detachment of the regiment, under Lt. Mainwaring, marched from Fort Hare to patrol the vicinity of the "military villages,"[4]

about six miles distant. As Kaffirs were observed to be assembling in force, a reinforcement from Fort Hare was sent for; on the arrival of this, the patrol proceeded across the country to the Tyumie (or Chumie) Missionary Station, where it halted for a short time. On the patrol leaving the missionary station, a fire was opened on its rear, which was kept up until the party got in sight of Fort Hare, when a company was sent out to assist.

On Dec. 29th a detachment of the 91st, led by Colonel Yarborough, marched towards Fort Cox, under Colonel Somerset, for the purpose of opening a communication with the Commander of the Forces, who was surrounded by the enemy, and of throwing in a supply of cattle for the troops. When nearing the Kamka or Yellow-Woods river, the Kaffirs opened a heavy fire upon this force, when two companies were thrown out in extended order, and advanced till they reached the base of the hill which surmounts the Umnassie (or Peel's) Valley, where a formidable force of the enemy had taken up a position behind rocks which skirt the summit of the hill. It was then found necessary to retire, the Kaffirs endeavouring to outflank and cut off the retreat. A reinforcement was sent from Fort Hare to the assistance of the patrol, which enabled it to return to the fort after a severe struggle, in which Lts. Melvin and Gordon, and 20 men were killed, and Lt. Borthwick, 2 sergeants, and 16 men were wounded; 2 of the latter dying of their wounds.

On the 7th of January 1851, Fort Beaufort, in which was a small detachment of the 91st, under Captain Pennington, was attacked by a numerous force of Kaffirs, under the Chief Hermanes, when the latter was killed in the square of the fort.

On Feb. 24th, the Kaffirs in force, from 5000 to 7000, surrounded Fort Hare, and endeavoured to capture the Fingoes' cattle, but were repulsed by 100 men of the 91st, under Ensign Squirl.

For the next few months the regiment furnished frequent detachments for the perform-

<hr/>

[4] Among the arrangement for the protection of the colony a for· w·· organised in 1850, by placing soldiers discharged from various regiments, including th 91st, on settlements of land in British Kaffraria, and the forming military villages.

ance of patrol duty, which required considerable tact, and was attended with considerable
danger. On one of these occasions, June
27th, when a detachment of the 91st was with
Colonel Eyre's division, Ensign Pickwick and
1 private were wounded.

On the 24th of June, a detachment of 180
men of the 91st, under Major Forbes, proceeded to the Amatola mountains, under command of Major-General Somerset, and was
engaged with the enemy on the 26th, 27th,
and 28th of June, and the 2nd of July. A
General Order was issued on July 3rd, in
which the Commander-in-Chief spoke in high
terms of the conduct of the troops on this
occasion, when the operations were crowned
with signal success and the complete discomfiture of the enemy; 2200 head of cattle and
50 horses fell into the hands of the troops,
while the enemy were driven with considerable
loss from every one of the strong and almost
insurmountable passes they attempted to
defend.

"The accuracy and energy," the Order says, "with
which Major-General Somerset carried into effect with
the 1st division [to which the 91st Regiment be-
longed], the part assigned to him in the complicated
and combined movements, deserve the Commander-
in-Chief's highest praise. His column sustained the
chief opposition of the enemy, principally composed
of rebel Hottentots, who resisted our troops with great
determination."

Previous to this, on June 6th, Captain
Cahill of the 91st, with a small detachment,
joined a patrol under Lt.-Col. Michell, which
was attacked by a body of the enemy at Fort
Wiltshire. It joined Colonel M'Kinnon's
division on the Debè, captured a number of
cattle and horses, and patrolled Seyolo's
country, returning to Fort Peddie on the
12th.

On the 14th of June the enemy, taking
advantage of Major-General Somerset's absence
from Fort Hare, assembled their bands in the
neighbourhood, with the intention of carrying
off the Fingoe's cattle. Lt.-Col. Yarborough
promptly despatched all the Fingoes, supported by 160 men of the 91st, under Lt.
Mainwaring, for the protection of the herds.
The Fingoes gallantly attacked the Kaffirs,
completely routing them, killing 14 of their
number, and re-capturing the whole of the
cattle.

On the 8th of August a detachment of the
91st, under Lt. Rae, proceeded from Fort
Peddie to escort cattle and waggons to Gentleman's Bush, and after handing them over returned and joined a patrol under Lt.-Col.
Michell. The patrol on the following morning marched to Kamnegana Heights, and on
arriving there lay concealed till 9 A.M., and
afterwards descending to reconnoitre were
nearly surrounded by the enemy, when Major
Wilmot's life was saved by Sergeant Ewen Ferguson of the 91st. The patrol retired, and
attacked the enemy again on the following
morning, returning to Fort Peddie on the
11th.

From October 13th to the 23rd a detachment
of the 91st, consisting of 318 of all ranks under
Lt.-Col. Yarborough, was engaged with the
enemy in a series of combined movements at
the Waterkloof, as also on the 6th and 7th of
November. An idea of the nature of the work
which the regiment had to perform may be
obtained from the following extract from the
"Precis," transmitted to the Commander-in-
Chief by Major-General Somerset, who commanded the expedition. On the night of the
13th the force had encamped on one of the
spruits of the Kaal Hoek river, and on the
14th Major-General Somerset writes:—

"Marched at 1 A.M.; very thick fog. Gained the
ascent above Bush Nek by 5 A.M. At 7 A.M. moved
to the bush at the head of the Waterkloof; observed
the enemy in force along the whole face of the ridge.
At half-past 7 I observed Lt.-Col. Fordyce's brigade
on the opposite ridge; moved up Lt. Field's guns, and
opened on the enemy, who showed at the head of the
Blinkwater. Ordered Lt.-Col. Michel's brigade forward, and sent a squadron of Cape Mounted Rifles and
two battalions forward, directing a strong body of
skirmishers to be thrown into and line the forest.
These were immediately received by a smart fire from
the enemy at several points. This sharp attack drove
the enemy from their position, which they evacuated,
and retired into Blinkwater and Waterkloof. The
enemy continued to show themselves. I reinforced
the skirmishers with two companies of the 91st, dismounted a troop of the Cape Mounted Rifles, and
ordered the whole to push through the ravine, and to
communicate with Lt.-Col. Fordyce's brigade, and to
order them through. This movement was well effected.
In the meantime the enemy continued their efforts to
annoy us. Having brought the brigade through, and
the enemy being beaten, and all the troops having
been under arms from 1 A.M., I retired to form camp
at Mandell's Farm, leaving one squadron, one
battalion, and two guns of the Royal Artillery to cover
the movement. On commencing our move the enemy
came out in force and opened a smart fire, following
the rear-guard. The enemy were driven off. The
troops encamped at Mandell's at 5 o'clock, after being
under arms for eighteen hours."

So in all the operations of the succeeding days, in and around the almost inaccessible Waterkloof, the 91st, to judge from the merest hints in Major-General Somerset's despatches, must have performed important services, especially when acting as skirmishers. The fighting continued almost without intermission up to the 7th of November, the loss to the regiment being 1 private killed, and Ensign Ricketts and 8 privates wounded; the ensign afterwards died of his wound, and was buried in the little group of graves at Post Retief.

The next operations in which the 91st seems to have been engaged was on the 30th of December, when Lt. Mackenzie and a small detachment joined a patrol under Major Wilmot, which proceeded from Fort Peddie to the Goga, where it arrived at daylight on the following morning. The patrol lay concealed in the bush until the morning of the 1st of January 1852, and then proceeded to the Kamnegana, scouring the bush and destroying a number of huts. On entering a path lined on both sides with huts the patrol commenced to destroy them, and was vigorously opposed by the Kaffirs, who commenced a heavy fire on its advance, when Major Wilmot was killed by a musket ball fired from one of the huts. Lt. Mackenzie immediately assumed command of the patrol, which was between three camps occupied by the enemy, when he found it necessary to retreat to Fort Peddie, carrying Major Wilmot's body with him.

On the 26th of Jan. a detachment of 416 of all ranks of the 91st under Lt.-Col. Yarborough marched from Fort Hare, and was employed in destroying the enemy's crops on the Amatola mountains and Tyumie until the end of Feb., when it proceeded to Haddon. On the 4th of March the force proceeded to the Waterkloof, and was engaged in a combined movement [5] against the Kaffirs from daylight on that morning until evening, the casualties to the regiment being 1 sergeant and 3 privates killed, and Lt.-Col. Yarborough, Ensign Hibbert, 3 sergeants, and 12 privates wounded, 1 of the sergeants and 1 private ultimately dying of their wounds. [6] Sir Harry Smith in

writing to Earl Grey said, "Lt.-Col. Yarborough of the 91st is a steady officer, and greatly distinguished himself on the day he was wounded;" and in reference to this occasion a Division Order, dated March 5th, was issued by Major-General Somerset, from which the following is an extract:—

"The movement was most ably and gallantly conducted by Lt.-Col. Yarborough. . . . . He attributes the comparatively small loss to the manner in which the enemy was charged, checked, and driven back when pressing on in great force, although with every advantage of ground."

We may mention here that on board the "Birkenhead" when she was wrecked on the morning of Feb. 26, 1852, [7] were Captain Wright and 41 privates of the 91st.

On the 10th of March a force of 375 of all ranks of the 91st, under Major Forbes, was again engaged at the Waterkloof in a combined movement, [8] in which 11 rank and file of the regiment were wounded. The Commander-in-Chief, in writing of these operations, said:—

"Lt.-Col. Napier moved on the 10th up the Waterkloof Valley, and on entering the narrow and difficult ground towards its head, it was evident that the enemy meditated an attack upon the rear, and Colonel Napier accordingly placed the 91st regiment, under Major Forbes, in a position to resist it. This was most effectually done after a short fight, and Colonel Napier gained and maintained his position."

On the 17th of March the battalion, under Major Forbes, proceeded from Blinkwater en route to Thorn river with Colonel Napier's division, patrolling the country, capturing the enemy's cattle, and destroying the crops. The following extracts from a report of Colonel Napier, dated "Camp, Quantie River, 8th

skirmishing order, that of the 91st was under Lt. Bond. This officer was very short-sighted, and by some means or other was separated from his men, and was nearer the enemy than his skirmishers. Suddenly he was attacked by two Kaffirs, armed, one of whom seized him by the coat. At that time men wearing only side arms were always told off to carry stretchers for the wounded. One of these men, John Sharkie by name, suddenly saw Lt. Bond in the clutches of the savages. He rushed up, struck one of them on the head with his stretcher, killed him dead, and drawing a butcher's knife which he carried in a sheath, plunged it into the throat of the other. Lt. Bond, who then realised the extent of his escape, coolly adjusted his eyeglass, which he always carried, looked steadily at Sharkie, then at the Kaffirs, and said, "By God, Sharkie, you're a devilish plucky fellow; I will see you are properly rewarded for your bravery;" and he kept his word.

---

[5] See vol. ii. p. 599.
[6] When the force was retiring in the direction of their camp, each regiment covered by a company in
[7] See vol. ii. p. 604.
[8] Ibid. p. 599.

April 1852," gives some details of the work done by the force, of which the 91st formed part:—

"I marched from the camp at the Thomas river at 9 A.M. on the 5th instant, and encamped at the Quantic river at 4 P.M. Next morning I sent Captain Tylden's force, the whole of the mounted Burghers and Fingoes, before daylight to scour the country between the Thomas river and the Kei, while I followed in support with the Cape Mounted Rifles, 80 of the 74th regiment, 200 of the 91st regiment, and the Kat River levy, leaving Captain Robinson, R.A., with the gun and 100 of the line to take charge of the camp. At noon I perceived Captain Tylden on a hill to my front, and the Burghers on another to my left, who made a signal (previously agreed upon) that they saw cattle and wanted support."

The cattle, however, were too far off to attempt to capture them that afternoon, and

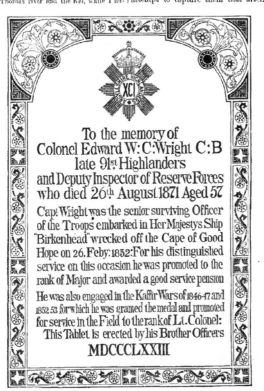

To the memory of
Colonel Edward W: C: Wright C: B
late 91st Highlanders
and Deputy Inspector of Reserve Forces
who died 26th August 1871 Aged 57

Capt Wright was the senior surviving Officer of the Troops embarked in Her Majestys Ship "Birkenhead" wrecked off the Cape of Good Hope on 26. Feby: 1852: For his distinguished service on this occasion he was promoted to the rank of Major and awarded a good service pension

He was also engaged in the Kaffir Wars of 1846-47 and 1852-53 for which he was granted the medal and promoted for service in the Field to the rank of Lt. Colonel:
This Tablet is erected by his Brother Officers

MDCCCLXXIII

Brass Tablet erected in Chelsea Hospital.

the infantry remained on the heights. The attack was resumed next day, when the Kaffirs were made to retreat, and a great quantity of cattle, horses, and goats were captured.

"The infantry, under Major Forbes, 91st regiment," the report adds, "were not engaged with the enemy; but, from the judicious position the Major took up, were of great use in preventing the cattle escaping from Captain Tylden."

The battalion returned to Blinkwater on the 16th of May. During the greater part of July operations were carried on against the enemy in the Waterkloof region, in which a detachment of the 91st formed a part of the force engaged. It was probably during these operations that an attack by a body of rebels upon Eland's Post was gallantly repulsed by a small detachment of the 91st stationed there under Captain Wright (the survivor of the "Birkenhead.") The enemy appeared in considerable force, and manœuvred with all the skill of disciplined troops, extending, advancing, and retiring by sound of bugle. After endeavouring, almost successfully, to draw the little garrison into an ambuscade, they sounded the "close" and the "advance," and moved on to the fort. Captain Wright, with only 23 men of the 91st, then marched out to meet them, and, being joined by a party of the Kat River levy, drove them off with loss.

On the 30th of July the battalion marched from Blinkwater, under Major Forbes, on an expedition which lasted during a great part of August, across the Kei, to capture cattle from the chief Kreli. The expedition was very successful, having captured many thousand head of cattle.

On the 14th of September the battalion, under Major Forbes, marched from Blinkwater to unite with a force under His Excellency General Cathcart to expell the Kaffirs and rebel Hottentots from the Waterkloof. The troops having been concentrated in the neighbourhood of the Waterkloof, were so posted as to command every accessible outlet from the scene of the intended operations, which consisted of an irregular hollow of several miles in extent, nearly surrounded by precipitous mountains, the bases of which, as well as the greater part of the interior basin, were densely wooded. The arduous nature of the duty imposed upon the troops of dislodging such an enemy from such a position may thus be faintly imagined. Four companies of the 91st and Cape Mounted Rifles were posted on the northern heights of the Waterkloof, while another detachment of the regiment and some irregulars from Blinkwater were to move up the Fuller's Hoek ridge; other troops were judiciously posted all around the central position of the enemy. The dispositions having been completed, the several columns moved upon

the fastnesses they were to clear at daylight on the 15th.

"The operations of that and the following day," to quote General Cathcart's order, "were conducted with unabated vigour and great judgment on the part of the officers in command. The troops bivouacked each night on the ground of their operations, and pursued on the following day, with an alacrity which cannot be too highly commended, the arduous task of searching for and clearing the forest and kraantzes of the enemy. These appeared to be panic-stricken, offering little resistance, but endeavouring to conceal themselves in the caverns and crevices of the wooded hills, where many of them were killed. The results of the three days' operations have been, the evacuation of the Waterkloof and other fastnesses by the Tambookie chief Quashe and the Guika chief Macomo and his adherents, and the expulsion and destruction of the Hottentot marauders."

Among those specially mentioned by the Commander-in-chief was Major Forbes of the 91st.

The battalion returned to Blinkwater on the 20th of September, where it stayed till the 29th, when it proceeded to Fort Fordyce, sending out detachments to the Waterkloof, Post Retief, and various other posts. The headquarters of the battalion remained at Fort Fordyce till the 10th of November 1853, when it marched to garrison Fort Beaufort, where it remained till July 1855, sending out detachments regularly to occupy various frontier posts.

On July 6th 1855 the battalion marched, under command of Major Wright, from Fort Beaufort en route for embarkation at Port Elizabeth, having been ordered home, after a stay of thirteen years in the colony. Previous to its march, the Commander of the forces issued a General Order highly complimentary to the battalion; and the inhabitants of Fort Beaufort presented an address to the officers and men, which spoke in the highest terms of the conduct of the regiment during the Kaffir wars.

In marching through Grahamstown the battalion received a perfect ovation from the inhabitants and from the other regiments stationed there. About the middle of the pass which leads out of the town a sumptuous luncheon had been prepared for officers and men by the inhabitants; before partaking of which, however, the regiment was presented with an address, in the name of the inhabitants, expressive of their high regard and admiration for the officers and men of the 91st.

A very large crowd of the men remained

behind as settlers, as the battalion, when it embarked at Port Elizabeth on the 30th of July, numbered only 5 captains, 7 lieutenants, 4 staff, 21 sergeants, 14 corporals, 9 drummers, and 340 privates. Nothing of importance occurred during the voyage, the battalion disembarking at Chatham on the 29th of September.

On the 10th of Nov., a letter was received from the Horse-Guards, directing a redistribution of the regiment into 6 service and 6 dépôt companies, each of 60 rank and file,

Lieutenant-Colonel Bertie Edward Murray Gordon.
From a Photograph.

besides officers and non-commissioned officers, the term "reserve battalion" being thenceforth discontinued, though, practically, the battalion seems to have lasted till 1857, when the dépôt companies of the two battalions were incorporated. We shall briefly carry the history of this battalion up to that time.

On the 4th of April 1856, the dépôt companies, as the reserve battalion was now called, left Chatham for Aldershot, under command of Lt.-Col. Gordon, and took up their quarters in the North Camp (Letter M).

On the 19th and 20th of April the troops in camp, including the 91st, were reviewed by Her Majesty, and on July the 16th the Queen visited the lines of the 91st. The royal carriage stopped in the centre of the 91st lines, where Her Majesty alighted, and entered one of the soldiers' huts. The Queen walked quite through the hut, and asked questions of Lt.-Col. Gordon, and made observations indicating Her Majesty's Gracious satisfaction. After leaving this hut, which belonged to No. 2 company (Capt. Lane's), the Queen signified her desire to see the soldiers' cook-house, which she entered, expressing her praise of its cleanliness and order, and of the excellence of the soup. The Queen then re-entered her carriage and proceeded at a foot pace through the other portions of the lines, Lt.-Col. Gordon walking by the side of Her Majesty, and pointing out various other excellent arrangements. After the Queen had departed the soldiers visited the hut which had received the royal visit, and surveyed it with a sort of wondering and reverential interest.

The following inscriptions were afterwards placed on the doors at each end of the hut (No. 6 hut, M lines, North Camp), which had been honoured by Her Majesty's visit. On the front door:—

"Her Most Gracious Majesty, the Princess Royal, and the Princess Alice, visited the lines of Her Majesty's faithful soldiers of the 91st Argyll Regiment, and deigned to enter this hut. 16th June 1856."

On the door in the private street :—

"Henceforth this hut shall be a sacred place,
    And its rude floor an altar, for 'twas trod
By footsteps which her soldiers fain would trace,—
    Pressed as if the rude planking were a sod,
By England's monarch; none these marks efface,
    They tell of Queenly trust, and loyalty approved
        of God."

Orders were afterwards issued to the troops in camp at Aldershot, by direction of H.R.H. the Duke of Cambridge, calling attention to the manner in which the lines of the 91st camp were kept, and desiring that the same order and the same efforts to procure occupation and amusement for the soldiers might be

made by the other regiments. The strictest
orders were also issued to the barrack department to maintain the inscription on the
" Queen's Hut," as it is called.

On the 7th of July, the lieutenant-general
commanding made an unexpected visit of inspection of the lines of the regiment. Lt.-Gene-
ral Knollys expressed himself satisfied in the
highest degree with the order of the lines,
and with the companies' huts, as also with the
works completed by the dépôt to give amusement to the men.

On the same day Lt.-Col. Gordon received
orders to be ready to proceed to Berwick-on-
Tweed early on the following morning, and on
the same evening the Queen, without warning, again passed down through the lines of
the 91st, the royal carriage stopping opposite
the door of the hut previously visited by Her
Majesty, who read the inscription which had
been placed over the door.

On the morning of July 8th the companies
of the 91st left Aldershot by train for Berwick, stopping at Peterborough and York, and
reaching Berwick on the 10th.

On Jan. 20th, 1857, Lt.-General Sir Harry
Smith inspected the dépôt companies, and addressed Lt.-Col. Gordon and the battalion in a
speech which was highly complimentary, afterwards assuring Lt.-Col. Gordon in a private
note, that his words of praise " were as fully
merited as they were freely bestowed."

The dépôt companies remained in Berwick
till the 3rd of March, when they proceeded by
train to Preston, almost the entire population
of Berwick accompanying the dépôt to the
railway station. The Mayor and Sheriff had
previously expressed to Lt.-Col. Rawstorne the
general respect with which the conduct of all
ranks had inspired the citizens, and the general
regret which was felt at the removal of the
91st. At Preston, on the 30th of March 1857,
the remains of the dépôt companies were incorporated with the dépôt battalion at Preston, commanded by Lt.-Col. Smith, C.B., while under
the command of Brevet Lt.-Col. Rawstorne.

Thus ends the somewhat chequered history
of the reserve battalion of the 91st; and now
we shall return to the point at which we left
off the history of the 1st battalion of the
regiment.

II.

III.

1857–1874.

We left the 1st battalion at Gosport in May
1848, and on Oct. the 13th of the same year
Lt.-Col. Lindsay retired from the service, when
the command of the battalion devolved upon
Lt.-Col. Yarborough. The regiment remained
at Gosport till April 1850, during which time
there is nothing remarkable to record.

The 91st proceeded to Dover in three divisions, on the 4th, 6th, and 9th of April;
headquarters, under the command of Lt.-Col.
Campbell, occupying the Heights' Barracks,
other companies being located in the Castle.

After the arrival of the regiment at Dover
it was inspected by Major-General G. Brown,
C.B., K.H., Adjutant-General to the Forces,
who, for some inscrutable reason, ordered the
immediate abolition of the bagpipes, which
had been fondly clung to as the last relic that
remained of the origin, the history, and the
nationality of the corps. To the unofficial mind
this must appear an exceedingly harsh, and
quite uncalled for measure, though, as will be
seen, ample amends was in the end made to the
regiment for this " unkindest cut of all." In
the meantime the 91st lost its bagpipers.

The 91st did not stay long at Dover; having
received orders to move to the northern district, it proceeded by detachments, in the end
of Dec. 1850 and beginning of Jan. 1851, to
Preston, Liverpool, and Manchester, moving
about among these three towns for the next
few months, the grenadier company, under
Captain Bayly, being sent to the Isle of Man.
After about six months' duty in the northern

district, the regiment proceeded to Fleetwood, and embarked in detachments on the 22nd and 24th of July for Belfast, whence a draft of 1 sergeant and 60 rank and file, under Captain Wright, proceeded to Cork on the 26th Dec., and embarked on board the ill-fated "Birkenhead," on Jan. 7th, 1852, to join the the reserve battalion at the Cape of Good Hope.

The stay of the regiment in Belfast was comparatively short; but during that time officers and men won the respect and attachment of the inhabitants for their excellent behaviour, their

Major-General John Francis Glencairn Campbell.
From a Photograph.

kindliness, and their liberality to charitable institutions. On the occasion of the regiment's leaving Belfast, an address, signed by the Mayor, the Earl of Belfast, and about 200 of the leading citizens, was presented to Lt.-Col. Campbell and the other officers, expressive of their gratitude and esteem for the "high-toned gentlemanly conduct" of the officers, and the soldierlike and exemplary conduct of the men.

Between the 26th of April and the 3rd of May the regiment marched in detachments to

Enniskillen, where it was next to be stationed. On several occasions, during its stay at Enniskillen, the 91st had to perform the delicate, and not very agreeable duty of aiding the civil power to maintain order at elections as well as on other occasions. This duty the regiment always performed with admirable promptness, great tact, and excellent effect.

The 91st remained at Enniskillen until the month of March 1853, when, between the 19th and 30th of that month, it marched in detachments to Dublin, and was there quartered in Richmond Barracks. The 91st was, of course, regularly inspected while in Ireland, the reports of the inspecting officers being invariably of the most favourable kind.

After a year's stay in Dublin the 91st left that city by railway, in detachments, for Cork, and outstations, between the 25th of April and the 1st of May 1854, detachments being sent from headquarters to Spike Island, Haulbowline Island, and Carlisle Fort. The regiment, although as a body it did not take part in the Crimean war, liberally furnished volunteers to the three Highland regiments that bore so distinguished a part in that contest; and also to the 50th Regiment. In this way it parted with about 250 of its best men.

On the 23rd of June Lt.-Col. J. F. G. Campbell was promoted to the rank of Colonel.[9]

The 91st made but a short stay at Cork, as on the 15th of December it embarked, under command of Col. Campbell, on board H.M.S. "Saint George," *en route* for Malta, and this heavy old-fashioned three-decker did not cast anchor in the harbour of Valetta till Jan. 11th 1855. Besides 26 officers and staff, the strength of the regiment, as it landed at Malta, was 649 non-commissioned officers and privates, 39 women, and 51 children.

After a stay of about two months at Malta the 91st embarked on the 20th of March for

[9] On Nov. 12, 1860, Colonel Campbell became Major-General.

the Piræus, in Greece, which it reached on the 23rd. The regiment took up its quarters in the miserable warehouses that formed the barracks of the British soldiery. Colonel Straubenzee of the 3rd Regiment handed over the command of the British Force in Greece to Colonel Campbell, who also retained the command of the regiment; but he was ordered by the general commanding-in-chief to hand it over, on the 3rd of June, to Major Bertie Gordon.

The 91st was located in Greece for about two years, during which time it was engaged in operations which were of the highest benefit, not only to the men, but also to the district in which they were stationed. We regret that space prevents us from giving a detailed account of the various ways in which the regiment rendered itself useful, and staved off the *ennui* and consequent demoralisation which always attend the idle soldier. The presiding genius of the regiment during its stay in Greece, and, indeed, during the whole time that he had any important connection with it, was Major Bertie Gordon.

The relations of the 91st with the French force stationed in Greece, officers and men, were particularly cordial, both as regards work and enjoyment.

The accommodations allotted to the regiment were very defective in every detail that is deemed necessary for the permanent barrack occupation of British soldiers, while, owing to a peculiar arrangement with the commissariat department, the evil could not be remedied. It was, no doubt, the thoughtful ingenuity of Major Gordon that discerned a happy remedy for the evil, by selecting a spot at Salamis Bay, about three miles from the Piræus, on a slope close to the sea, for the construction of a camp in which a detachment of the regiment might take up its quarters, and thus remedy to some extent the stinted accommodation provided in the town. To this place the grenadiers and No. 1 company marched on the 4th of April, under the command of Major Gordon, who commenced at once a system of road-making, throwing up field-works, the construction of a small landing place, and other works, which employed and interested both officers and men; thus the little camp soon became a cheerful and accessible spot. The only difficulty

that they had to encounter was the want of tools, of which the supply from headquarters was very stinted indeed; it consisted of three spades and three pickaxes. But by dint of persistent applications, Major Gordon obtained an additional supply from the Greek authorities. An ancient well, which may have watered part of the fleet of Xerxes, was at the bottom of the hill, and furnished excellent water.

To this delightful little encampment detachments were sent in rotation at intervals during the stay of the regiment in the Piræus; and it was no doubt greatly owing to this and to the other exertions of Major Gordon for the good of his men, that the regiment was in such excellent condition, notwithstanding its miserable quarters in the town.

Another excellent service of Major Gordon, one which both benefited the health of the men and trained them to the practical duties of the soldier, was to take a detachment occasionally to a considerable distance from camp where it bivouacked as best it could, and sometimes slept out all night on extemporised couches of heath and branches, arranged round the bivouac fires.

On the 15th of June, another encampment was formed at a spot selected near the monastery of Pentelicus, on Mount Pentelicus, nine miles from Athens, and fifteen miles from the Piræus, the ground having been previously selected by Major Gordon. To this camp also detachments were sent in regular rotation.

In September 1855 Major Gordon was very deservedly promoted to the rank of Brevet Lieutenant-Colonel.

We should have stated before, that, on the 29th of June, a reading-room for the soldiers was established for the first time in the regiment. A sergeant and his wife were placed in charge, a roll of members was prepared, and a subscription of 6d. a month was charged from each member. Periodicals and newspapers were procured, and coffee and light drinks were prepared by the sergeant's wife for those who cared to pay for them.

Lt.-Col. Gordon, after repeatedly urging it upon those in authority, at length gained permission to commence the reconstruction and elevation of the whole surface-level of the wide projecting quay which formed the parade of the battalion; also to raise, drain, and level the roadways of the streets, in which the barracks of the battalion were situated. These useful works were commenced on the 18th of December, and ten days later, Lt.-Col. Gordon went home to take command of the six dépôt companies, when the command of the service companies devolved on Major W. T. L. Patterson, who had recently been promoted from captain.

The 91st embarked in two divisions on the 28th of Feb. 1857 for the Ionian Islands, where it was stationed for the next eighteen months, detachments being located in Corfu, Vido, Zante, and latterly, Cephalonia. Here, also, the regiment was employed in the construction of useful works. Among these was an approach from the esplanade at Argostoli, in Cephalonia, in the shape of steps upon a large scale, formed from the materials of a useless five-gun battery, which work was described by the Resident of Cephalonia as a "great public improvement," and, with his authority, obtained the appellation of "The Argyll Steps."

Lt.-Col. Bertie Gordon arrived at Corfu in April 1857, and assumed command of the regiment, Colonel Campbell having obtained leave of absence in the previous March.

In taking leave of the headquarters companies on the 17th of August, they having been ordered from Corfu to the Southern Islands, Major-General Sir George Buller, C.B., told them " he had selected the 91st for the service of the Southern Islands, partly because it was a more formed regiment, a finer body of men, and better drilled than the others."

The 91st, having received orders to proceed to India by the overland route, embarked at Corfu, and sailed on the 5th of Sept. 1858, arriving at Alexandria on the 8th; but it seems to have remained on board H.M.S. "Perseverance" until the 18th. On that day headquarters, with 5½ companies, disembarked at 1.30 P.M., and at once entered railway carriages prepared for their conveyance, and proceeded towards Suez. The left wing disembarked on the following day. Partly by railway, and partly on donkeys, the two wings were conveyed to Suez, where they embarked on board two vessels, which arrived at Bombay on the 7th and 9th of October respectively. Both detachments were reunited at Poonah on the 11th.

On Oct. 28th Colonel Campbell, C.B., having been appointed to the command of a brigade at Toogoo, in Burmah, Major Patterson assumed command of the regiment.

On Nov. 3rd the 91st commenced its march to Kamptee, where it did not arrive till the 11th of the following month. On its march, while at Jafferabad, on Nov. 20th, an order was received by telegraph from the Commander-in-Chief of the Madras army to leave a wing at Jaulnah. The left wing, under command of Major Savage, accordingly returned to that place, and did not arrive at headquarters until the 25th of Feb. 1859. It had been employed during the latter part of January and the beginning of February in operations against insurgent Rohillas, to the south of Jaulnah, and had made long marches, without, however, being engaged with the enemy.

On the 7th of March Lt.-Colonel Bertie Gordon arrived from England and assumed the command, and on the 9th a small detachment, under Lieut. Gurney, proceeded to Chindwarrah, a village about 84 miles north of Kamptee. On the same day No. 5 company, under Captain Battiscombe, marched as part of a field-force directed on Mooltye and Baitool. On the 27th Major Patterson joined and took command of the field-force, which remained out till the 18th of April. A similar field-force was sent out on April 22nd for a short time to the same districts.[1]

It was about this time that Colonel Bertie Gordon inaugurated his new system of promotion in the non-commissioned ranks of the regiment. Competitive examinations of lance and full corporals, under a strictly organised system, were the basis of this plan. During the period extending from Sept. 1860 to Jan. 1861, seventy corporals and lance-corporals were examined, twenty-five of whom obtained

---

[1] We must mention here that on the 1st of Nov. of this year Quartermaster Paterson took his final leave of the regiment, which, as a private, he joined in 1832, and from which he had never been absent since joining it. He was with it in St Helena, Africa, Greece, the Ionian Islands, and India, from which last place he now left the regiment as an invalid. In his long and varied service he always proved himself a worthy soldier.

promotion out of their regular turn, owing to their position on the merit roll.

The 91st remained in India till the year 1868, and we can note only in the briefest possible manner the principal occurrences in connection with the regiment during that period.

An event of very great interest to the regiment occurred on the 27th of Aug. 1871; this was the discovery of the old Waterloo roll of the regiment among the orderly-room papers. It had been saved from destruction by Sergeant Hirst in 1848, when a quantity of old books and papers had been ordered to be burned. The interesting document was now sent to London, where it was so handsomely bound as to ensure, we hope, its preservation in all time coming.

On the 16th of Oct. of the same year, Col. Gordon received from the daughters of the late Lt.-Col. Lindsay an offer of the old colours of the 91st. Col. Gordon gladly accepted this graceful offer, and sent the colours, which had seen many a hard-fought field, to Ellon Castle, Aberdeenshire, there to find a permanent home, and to be preserved as an heirloom in his family.

In Aug. 1861, Lt.-Col. Gordon was promoted to be colonel by brevet. He had succeeded to the command of the regiment in Nov. 1860, on the promotion of Lt.-Colonel Campbell to the rank of Major-General. There had been for some time, in accordance with the regulations for the augmentation of the Indian establishment, two Lt.-Cols. to the 91st, Major W. T. L. Patterson having been raised to that rank on the retirement of Col. Campbell.[2]

On the 24th of April 1862, Col. Gordon proceeded on leave to England. During his absence, in Feb. 1863, the 91st left Kamptee for Jubbulpoor, which it reached on the 19th, after a march of fifteen days. The regiment was now in the Bengal Presidency, and under the command of Gen. Sir Hugh Rose, G.C.B. then Commander-in-Chief in India.

One of the most notable and gratifying events in the history of the 91st during the *régime* of Col. Bertie Gordon was the restoration to it of its original Highland designation, along with the Highland dress, the tartan trews, however, taking the place of the more airy kilt. So far back as 1833, an ineffectual effort had been made to have its nationality restored to the regiment. Col. Gordon resumed the attempt shortly after he obtained command of the regiment at Kamptee in 1859, and with the most determined perseverance, amid discouragements that would have daunted any ordinary man, he did not cease his solicitations until they resulted in complete success in the year 1864. Col. Gordon found a powerful and willing supporter in his Grace the Duke of Argyll, who was naturally anxious to have the regiment raised by his ancestors once more recognised by its original name, "the Argyllshire Highlanders." The voluminous correspondence carried on between Col. Gordon, the War Office authorities, and the Duke of Argyll, we cannot reproduce here. The letters of Col. Gordon show clearly his ability, his enthusiasm, his perseverance, and his intense

[2] This, we think, is the proper place to give a few personal details of Col. Bertie Gordon, who was in many respects a very remarkable man—a man imbued with the most chivalrous notions of a soldier's vocation, and at the same time one of the most practical men that ever held command of a regiment. He was a strict disciplinarian, and yet no officer could take more care than he of the personal comfort and best welfare of his men. He loved his regiment dearly, and it is greatly owing to him that the 91st has attained its present position. He has found a successor in every respect worthy of him in the present commander, Lt.-Col. Sprot.

Bertie Edward Murray was born at Auchlunies, Aberdeenshire, on the 17th of Dec. 1813. He was the son of Alexander Gordon, Esq., of Auchlunies, afterwards of Ellon Castle, Aberdeenshire, and Albinia Louisa Cumberland, daughter of Lady Albinia Cumberland. He was educated at Ruinham, Kent, the Edinburgh Academy, and the Edinburgh Royal Military Academy. He obtained his first commission in the 91st Regiment in the year 1832, and joined in 1833. At school Bertie Gordon showed abilities much beyond average. Reserved, and sometimes proud, Bertie Gordon was slow to form intimate friendships, but he was warm-hearted and generous, ever ready to assist a companion, or to prevent the oppression of a younger boy. Always strictly honourable and truthful, he was fearless of danger, and if, in boyish pranks, there was anything to be done which required nerve and courage, Bertie Gordon was sure to be found in the front ranks. The chief incidents in his military career have been already told. Did space permit, we could fill pages concerning the institutions he founded in the regiment—gymnasia for non-commissioned officers and men, reading-rooms, refreshment-rooms, dancing-rooms, children's homes, &c. His name is worthy of remembrance as one who had the loftiest ideas of the duties of his position, and who spared no pains to carry out his ideas by the wisest action. A regiment commanded by such a man could not fail to attain the highest degree of efficiency.

nationality and love for his regiment. We can only say that, after a long correspondence, Col. Gordon's efforts resulted in triumph, as will be seen in the following War Office memorandum, notifying the restoration to the 91st of its Highland designation and dress, of which it had been deprived fifty years before:—

"WAR OFFICE, PALL MALL, *May* 3, 1864.

"Her Majesty has been graciously pleased to approve of the 91st Foot resuming the appellation of the 91st Argyllshire Highlanders, and being clothed and equipped as a non-kilted Highland corps, as follows:—TUNIC, as worn in all Highland regiments; TREWS, of the Campbell tartan; CHACO, blue cloth, with diced band and black braid; FORAGE CAP, Kilmarnock, with diced band. The officers to wear plaids and claymores. The alteration of the dress is to take place from 1st April 1865. The white waistcoat with sleeves, issued to other Highland regiments, will not be worn by the 91st Foot."

In Jan. 1866 Col. Gordon arrived at Jubbulpoor, and assumed command of the regiment. In Dec. of the same year the 91st left its quarters at Jubbulpoor and proceeded partly on foot and partly by train to Dumdum, which it reached on the 11th. While at Dumdum Col. Gordon's health broke down, and on the recommendation of a medical board, he left India for Europe in Oct. 1866, handing over the command of the regiment to Major Battiscombe.

After staying a year at Dumdum, the 91st was removed in Jan. 1867 to Hazareebagh. Here the 91st remained until the end of the year, setting out on Dec. 1st for Kamptee again, which it reached after a long and tedious journey, partly on foot and partly by train, on the 26th of January 1868.

After a stay of a few months at Kamptee, the 91st got the welcome route for home, setting out in two detachments on the 7th and 8th of Oct. for Bombay, where it embarked on the 12th. The regiment proceeded by Suez, and arrived at Portsmouth on Nov. 13th, disembarking on the 15th, and proceeding by rail to Dover, where Col. Bertie Gordon resumed command. The 91st had been on foreign service for the long period of fourteen years, and it is very remarkable that during all that time there were only ten desertions. The dépôt companies removed from Fort George and were amalgamated at Dover with the service companies on Nov. 25th.

In August of this year Her Majesty was pleased to place the name of Col. Bertie Gordon on the list of officers receiving the reward of £100 a year for distinguished service.

The 91st remained at Dover until June 1870, during which time two events occurred of some importance in its domestic history. The first of these was the presentation of new colours on the 24th of Aug. 1869, on the glacis of the Western Heights, Dover. As the Duke and Duchess of Argyll were unable to be present, the colours were presented to the regiment by Mrs Bertie Gordon, as her Grace's representative. The Archbishop of Canterbury consecrated the colours, being assisted by five other clergymen in full canonicals. After an impressive prayer by his Grace the Archbishop, the colours were received by Mrs Gordon at the hands of Major Penton and Major Sprot, and by her given to Ensigns Lloyd and Gurney, with these words:—

"Colonel Gordon, officers, non-commissioned officers, and soldiers of the 91st Argyllshire Highlanders,—Proud as I am this day to present to you your new colours, I would fain have had my place better filled by her Grace the Duchess of Argyll. Soldiers, your colours have been well earned, not alone in the protracted struggle of three Kaffir campaigns, but also by long service in tropical climes under a burning sun. I know you will receive them as a sacred trust. Guard them carefully. Fight manfully around them when called upon. Be foremost, as you have always been, in serving your Queen and country; and be the pride, as you are at this moment, of your commanding officer."

After a fervent address by Col. Gordon, thanking Mrs Gordon for the service she had performed, which was only one of "many acts of unobtrusive kindness" by which she showed her interest in the welfare of the regiment.

The old colours having been gladly accepted by the Duke of Argyll, were, in the month of October, taken by an escort to Inverary Castle, in the great hall of which they now occupy a conspicuous position.

The other important event in the history of the regiment while it was stationed at Dover, was the retirement of Colonel Bertie Gordon. This was indeed an event of very great moment in the career of the 91st, and we therefore must find space for the pathetic order in which Colonel Gordon bade farewell to the regiment he loved so dearly. He had left on leave on the 11th of Nov. 1869, handing over the command of the regiment to Major Sprot, and his farewell order is dated "Ellon Castle, Ellon, 29th January 1870 :"——

"His Royal Highness the Field Marshal Commanding-in-Chief having been pleased to grant compliance with the request preferred by Colonel Bertie Gordon, to be permitted to retire on the half-pay of the army, Colonel Gordon bids farewell to the noble regiment in which he has served for more than seven and thirty years, and in which he has held command ever since April 1855. Colonel Gordon's service in the 91st Highlanders comprises exactly one-half the period of its existence as a corps, and he has held command in his regiment during a fifth part of its history. Years have gone by since every officer, non-commissioned officer, and private soldier with whom he stood in these noble ranks, when he commenced his career in the army, have passed away. For twelve years Colonel Gordon has been the very last of the 800 who formed the Argyllshire regiment in 1832, and in its ranks of the present day he leaves behind him but one soldier (Lt. Grant) who shared with him those hours of impending death, when he commanded the Reserve Battalion of the regiment in 1842, cast away on the shores of Africa in that dark night of tempest, when its discipline and devotion came forth from the shattered wreck unbroken and undiminished by that sorest trial. Colonel Gordon calls to mind that he has served under three stands of colours presented to the regiment, and that at the recommendation of His Royal Highness the Field Marshal Commanding-in-Chief, he was permitted, by the favour of Her Most Gracious Majesty, to announce to his old regiment, seven years ago, the restoration of that nationality in its designation and uniform, under which it was embodied by its ducal chieftain in the last century.

"Colonel Gordon believes that the time has come to retire from the regiment he has loved, and to leave its fortunes in younger and stronger hands. But, although severed from its noble ranks, Colonel Gordon will still feel that the words of his regimental order of 1863 must ever prove true—'The Argyllshire regiment has ever served their sovereign and their country steadily;' while he calls upon all ranks to remember those that the late Lieut.-General Sir George Napier addressed to the Reserve Battalion in 1842—'Ninety-first, I have known you in camp and quarters, and I have seen you in action, and I have never known or seen a better.'"

In such words did this brave, noble-minded, and accomplished soldier bid farewell to his dear old regiment. He survived the "farewell" only a few months, having died at Ellon Castle on the 27th of July of the same year, at the comparatively early age of 57 years. So long as the name of the 91st Argyllshire Highlanders remains on the roll of the British Army, the memory of Colonel Bertie Gordon ought to be cherished in its ranks.

As we have already said, Colonel Gordon found a successor in every way worthy of him in Major Sprot, who succeeded to the lieutenant-colonelcy of the regiment on the 29th of January 1870. Captain Wood succeeded to the vacant majority, Lieutenant Alison to the company, and Ensign Chater to the lieutenancy

and adjutancy, in which latter capacity he had acted for one year.[3]

On succeeding to the command of the regiment Colonel Sprot issued an order, dated "Dover, 29th January 1870," in which he said——

"With two exceptions I have seen the troops of all the states of Europe. Full half my service was spent with our armies in India. I have become intimate with the greater portion of our regiments, and I have seen no body of soldiers of whom I have formed a higher opinion than that of the Argyllshire Highlanders. . . . . I have now under my care a regiment in the highest state of discipline and efficiency. . . . . Let us then join together in one continued effort to attain this end, that the 91st Argyllshire Highlanders may ever be second to none."

The remainder of the distinctive history of the 91st may be very briefly told. The regiment left Dover on the 18th of June 1870 and proceeded to Aldershot, marching the greater part of the way, and reaching the camp on the morning of the 25th. Notwithstanding the excessive heat of the weather, and that the men marched fully accoutred, the column came in each day to its halting-place with the

[3] We very much regret that space does not permit our giving a detailed account of the many and varied services of Colonel Sprot since he joined the army in 1848. Colonel Sprot, we may here mention, belongs to one of the oldest and best known Edinburgh families. He is son of Mark Sprot, Esq. of Riddell, Roxburghshire, and has connections among many old and well-known Scottish families, both Highland and Lowland. It would be difficult to find an officer in any branch of Her Majesty's service who has taken more pains to attain a thorough knowledge of every branch of science that in any way bears upon the duties which an officer may, under any circumstances, be called upon to perform. His preparations for a military career did not cease when he obtained his commission, but by persevering study he so mastered the arts of engineering, surveying, and similar branches of applied science, that while still a lieutenant he was employed by Government in the superintendence of works of the highest importance in India. From 1849 Colonel Sprot spent about twelve years in India, during the greater part of which he occupied positions, both civil and military, of the greatest responsibility. As captain he served continuously throughout the whole of the Indian Mutiny from May 1857 until May 1860; was present in one action, and received the Indian war medal for his services. Colonel Sprot joined the 91st as a major from the 83rd regiment in the year 1868, and since he assumed command he has set himself heart and soul to raise the 91st Highlanders to the highest possible pitch of efficiency. Every man in the regiment is carefully trained in all the practical duties of a soldier; and, indeed, to a great deal more than a soldier is bound to know, and that in such a manner, that were the regiment to be suddenly engaged in an active campaign, it would likely have less difficulty than most regiments in adapting itself to the emergencies of the occasion.

greatest regularity, a compact body of men without a single straggler.

As soon as it was announced that a marriage was to take place between the Princess Louise and the Marquis of Lorne, Lt.-Col. Sprot wrote to the Duke of Argyll, offering to send a detachment of the regiment to form a guard of honour at the wedding. The Duke replied very graciously, and only a few days before the wedding was to take place, Colonel Sprot learned that Her Majesty had been graciously pleased to order that a detachment of the 91st

INSCRIPTION.—From the Soldiers of the 91st Argyllshire Highlanders presented by the kind permission of Her Majesty to HER ROYAL HIGHNESS THE PRINCESS LOUISE, on her Marriage, 21st March 1871.

should attend at Windsor on the day of the marriage, March 21st, 1871.

On Saturday morning, the 17th of March, a body of 100 picked men, with band, pipers, and full complement of officers, after having been inspected by Colonel Sprot, marched off to the tune of "Haste to the Wedding," amidst the encouraging cheers of their less fortunate comrades. The guard was commanded by Captain Gregg, and marched by Bagshot and Ascot Heath, reaching Windsor at 4 P.M. When the detachment arrived at

Windsor it found that everything had been prepared for it by the Grenadier Guards; the officers of the latter corps invited the officers of the 91st to be their guests, and the soldiers had not only drawn rations and fitted beds, but had even cooked dinner for the Highlanders.

On Monday the 20th, Lt.-Col. Sprot rode over from Aldershot to Windsor, and on arriving at the Castle received Her Majesty's command to meet her at 3 o'clock P.M., in the private apartments, where she would be prepared to receive the wedding present for her daughter, which the officers and men of the 91st intended to give. The gift of the officers consisted of a BROOCH, the fac-simile of that worn by them to fasten their plaids, but in pure gold, and with a very handsome cairngorm pebble, set transparently, together with a copy in miniature of the regimental dirk, in Scotch pebble, suited for a shawl pin. On the back of the brooch were engraved the names of all the officers then serving. The gift from the soldiers, to which they unanimously subscribed, was a SILVER BISCUIT-BOX, in the shape of one of their own drums, with the honours of the regiment engraved on the side, and an appropriate inscription on the head. It was mounted on a stand of Scotch bog oak, with silver corners and feet.

Colonel Sprot, in his audience with the Queen, was accompanied by Captain Gregg, Lt. Grant, Sergeant-Major Fasinidge, and Pipe-Major M'Dougal. Her Majesty was accompanied by the Princess Louise, Prince Arthur, Prince Christian, and others. Lt.-Col. Sprot, in a few appropriate and well-chosen words, presented the officers' present, which the Princess graciously accepted, and desired

Colonel Sprot to convey to the officers "her sincere thanks for their very pretty present." Colonel Sprot then intimated to Her Majesty the wish of the non-commissioned officers and men to offer the present above mentioned, at which Her Majesty expressed much gratification.

On the day of the ceremony the guard of Highlanders was drawn up at the entrance to St George's Chapel, Windsor, Colonel Sprot having command of the troops at the chapel. After the ceremony, the officers of the guard had the honour of being present at the déjeuner, the bagpipes and drums of the 91st playing alternately with the band of the Grenadier Guards.

The guard of the 91st returned to Aldershot on the 22nd by the way it came. During its stay at Aldershot it went through the usual routine of field-days, inspections, and other duties, invariably winning the genuine approbation of every officer that had the opportunity of witnessing its training. On the 10th of July, when the Queen reviewed the troops at Aldershot, the 91st marched past by double companies of 70 file, and marched so well, that Her Majesty sent a complimentary message to the regiment by the General commanding the brigade.

In August, while the festivities consequent on the wedding of the Marquis of Lorne were going on at Inverary,[4] the soldiers' present was sent to the Princess Louise, who, as well as the Marquis, cordially accepted and acknowledged it. On the application of the Duke of Argyll, three pipers of the regiment, with the Pipe-Major, attended these rejoicings, and were much admired both for their soldier-like appearance and good playing.

In September 1871 the 91st formed part of the force which was called out for field manœuvres, immediately after the conclusion of which, the regiment received orders to proceed to Aberdeen and Fort George.

On the 27th and 30th the regiment left Aldershot in two detachments for London, and embarked the same day at Wapping, and reached Aberdeen on the 29th of September and the 4th of October respectively; the second detachment was delayed by stormy weather.

The former detachment, headquarters, reached Fort George on the day of its arrival at Aberdeen, but the second detachment, of four companies, remained at Aberdeen.

Shortly after the marriage of the Princess Louise, Her Majesty expressed a desire to confer some distinguishing mark on the 91st Argyllshire Highlanders to commemorate the event, and desired Lt.-Col. Sprot to be communicated with as to what the regiment would like. Colonel Sprot, after consulting with his oldest officer, suggested the kilt, to which Her Majesty readily agreed, but to which the military authorities objected. Colonel Sprot then intimated that the regiment would like to be designated "the Princess Louise Argyllshire Highlanders," and bear on its colour the boar's head, with the motto "Ne Obliviscaris" (crest and motto of the Argyll family). To this there could be no objection, and a War-Office memorandum, of April 2nd, 1872, authorised the regiment to indulge its wish, the Princess Louise's coronet and cypher to be also placed on the three corners of the regimental colour.

After staying about eighteen months at Fort George, the 91st proceeded to Edinburgh in May 1873. The regiment arrived at Granton on the morning of May the 12th, and after landing in the most orderly manner, commenced its march under Colonel Sprot up the hill to the old castle on the rock. On the route the 91st passed the 93rd Sutherland Highlanders, who were marching out of the castle, and were on their way to embark at Granton; each corps shouldered arms to the other, and the pipers struck up a merry greeting. The large crowds of people who had collected along the route to witness the departure of the 93rd, waited to give a hearty welcome to the Princess Louise Highlanders.

During its stay in Edinburgh the regiment gained the respect and admiration of the inhabitants for their steady conduct and soldierly bearing. The efforts made by Colonel Sprot to keep his troops up to the highest state of efficiency won the praise both of the press and the citizens.[5]

---

[4] Lt.-Col. Sprot was invited to the castle on the occasion, but by a severe illness was prevented from being able to accept the invitation.

[5] Colonel Sprot, we may mention here, is the author of a little manual of outpost duty, written in a concise and clear manner, and giving a reason for everything. This manual will be found useful to all ranks, from the field-officer to the private.

For the first time in Edinburgh the military stationed in the Castle had a field-day in the prosecution of drill in outpost duty, which excited a deal of interest and curiosity on the part of the citizens, who had not been made aware of the arrangements. Col. Sprot of the 91st so highly appreciates this method of training, which is frequently practised at Aldershot and other large military stations, that at Fort George he had frequent recourse to it. A variety of exciting movements took place, ranging from Duddingston and Arthur Seat all along the route to the Castle Esplanade. The crowd attracted by the firing in the streets gradually augmented both in numbers and excitement. The whole proceedings lasted over seven hours, and the troops being drawn up in square, were complimented on their conduct throughout the engagement.

During the time that the 91st were in Edinburgh they had repeatedly been out on field-days, and besides such strategic movements as above, have also been systematically exercised in throwing up trenches, tent-pitching, flag-signalling, &c.

After remaining in Edinburgh for about a year only, to the great regret of the inhabitants, the 91st left for Newry in Ireland on the 29th of June 1874.

In conclusion, we should mention, that belonging to the officer's mess of the Argyllshire Highlanders is quite a little museum of precious and artistic curiosities. One of the most valuable and interesting of these is a tontine snuff-box of silver gilt, casket-shape, 8¼ inches long, 6 inches wide, and 3 inches deep. This very handsome box was originated by the officers who were in the regiment in the year 1810, on the condition that it could be claimed by the last survivor, if replaced by a similar box. It was claimed in 1841 by Colonel Anderson, who replaced it by a similar box, the original box being now in Edinburgh, in possession of General Anderson, late R.A., the nephew of the late Colonel Anderson. In 1870 Colonel Bertie Gordon was the last survivor of those whose names were inscribed on the box of 1841, and as it was not claimed by him, it became the property of the officers then serving in the regiment, whose names are inscribed on the inner lids of the box. On the outside of the lid is the arms of the regiment, surmounted by the crown, and on the oval the names of the victories up to the Peninsula. On the bottom of the box, underneath the Rose, Shamrock, and Thistle, and the date 1810, are the names of those who started the original box, headed by Lt.-Col. William Douglas. There are 50 names in all, and of these 11 are Campbells, and 17 others belong to various Highland clans; of the remainder, 11 seem distinctly Scotch. On the inside of the lid are the names of the officers of the regiment in 1841, when the new box was presented, headed by Colonel Gabriel Gordon and Lt.-Col. R. Anderson. Here there are in all 41 names, only 2 of them being Campbells, although 15 seem certainly Scotch, 3 being Gordons. On the inner lids of the box, as we have said, are the names of the officers who were in the regiment in 1870, when Colonel Bertie Gordon, failing to claim it, it became the property of the officers. The list is headed by Lt.-Col. Sprot, and there are 37 in all. Let us hope that it will be long before there will be a last survivor to claim it.

Among the mess plate there are several other articles of beautiful characteristic and artistic design. Of these we may mention the following:—

A large punch-bowl, of repoussé work, silver; height, 9 inches, diameter, 13¼ inches., presented by General Duncan Campbell of Lochnell. It is handsomely embossed with a design of flowers, grapes, and other fruits, and is supposed to have been originally taken by the French from a Spanish convent during the Peninsular war, and to have afterwards fallen into the hands of General Campbell. The ladle belonging to the bowl is of very ancient and peculiar design, having a Spanish coin, date 1758, at the bottom.

A silver snuff-box in two divisions, the gift of Lt.-Col. Catlin Crawfurd, who commanded the 91st in the Peninsula. Several silver mounted horn snuffmulls, presented at different periods, including a very large and handsome ram's head, mounted with silver, studded with cairngorms, as a snuff and cigar box, the joint gift of Lieutenants W. Grant and C. L. Harvey in the year 1864, bearing the names of the officers then serving in the regiment. The width across the horns is 17 inches.

A cigar-lighter in the form of a boar's head, the regimental crest in silver, mounted on an oval ebony stand with wheels. The upper part of the head forms a receptacle for spirits of wine. The tushes are removable and tipped with asbestos. This is the joint gift of Captain C. G. Alison and Lieutenant and Adjutant Verner Chater, date 1870.

Lastly, we shall mention a large silver quaich, 4½ inches in diameter, with straight projecting handles, with the boar's head engraved on them. It is of ancient Highland pattern, and has engraved round the upper portion a tracing taken from one of the remarkable stones of Argyll. It bears this inscription in Gaelic,—"From the Officers of the Highland Rifle Regiment (Militia) to the Officers of the 91st Princess Louise's Highlanders, Fort George, May 1872."

A fine example of the spirit of friendly rivalry and mutual good feeling subsisting between the line and the volunteers was shown on the 23rd of May and the 6th of June 1874, in a competition between ten sergeants of the 91st (Princess Louise Argyllshire Highlanders) and an equal number of the 1st Mid-Lothian Rifle Volunteers, which took place at the Seafield Ranges. At the conclusion of the first match the volunteers entertained their military friends and competitors at dinner; and at the conclusion of the second match, which came off at the ranges in Hunter's Bog, when there was only one point of difference in the scores, the Mid-Lothian team were invited by their military friends to the castle, where they were entertained at dinner in a very handsome and cordial manner. Before separating, the Leith men presented the team of the 91st with a beautiful gold cross, to be competed for by those who had shot in both matches, the conditions to be arranged by themselves. It was much regretted that the early departure of the 91st prevented a third trial of skill, the more especially as the competitors were so equally matched.

A portrait of General Duncan Campbell of Lochnell, after the painting by Sir Henry Raeburn, R.A., is given on the plate of Colonels of the 91st, 92nd, and 93rd Regiments.

SUCCESSION LIST OF COLONELS AND LIEUTENANT-COLONELS OF THE 91st PRINCESS LOUISE ARGYLLSHIRE HIGHLANDERS.

COLONELS.

Names.	Date of Appointment.	Age when appointed	Of what Country.	Date of First Commission in the Army.	By whose vacancy, and by what means.	Remarks.
General Duncan Campbell	May 3, 1796	...	Scotland	Not known.	New appointment.	Promoted to Major-General, April 29, 1802; Lt.-General, April 25, 1808; General, August 12, 1819.
General G. Gordon.	April 10, 1837	...	Do.	Jan. 6, 1781	Vice General D. Campbell deceased.	Died Aug. 7, 1855.
Lieut.-General C. Gore	Aug. 8, 1855	...	Ireland	...	Vice General Gordon deceased, Aug. 7, 1855.	Transferred to 6th Regiment, March 9, 1861.
Major-General C. Murray Hay.	March 9, 1861	...	Scotland	...	Vice Lt.-General Sir Charles Gore removed.	Promoted Lt.-General, Aug. 24, 1861.
Lieut.-General C. G. J. Arbuthnot	July 15, 1864	...	...	...	Vice Lt.-General C. Murray Hay deceased.	Transferred from 88th, July 15, 1864.
General James R. Craufurd	Aug. 27, 1870	...	...	...	Vice Lt.-General C. G. J. Arbuthnot transferred to 72nd.	

LIEUTENANT-COLONELS.

Names.	Date of Appointment.	Age when appointed	Of what Country.	Date of First Commission in the Army.	By whose vacancy, and by what means.	Remarks.
D. Macneil	Aug. 23, 1818	41	Scotland	April 17, 1794	Vice Douglas deceased.	Removed Sept. 23, 1824.
J. M'Donald	Sept. 23, 1824	36	Do.	Dec. 17, 1803	Vice Macneil retired.	Army rank, Sept. 4, 1817; retired on Half-pay.
J. M. Sutherland	Sept. 16, 1827	44	Do.	Nov. 27, 1794	Vice Dalyell.	Army rank, May 1825; retired Dec. 2, 1831.
R. Anderson	Dec. 2, 1831	42	Do.	July 9, 1803	Vice Sutherland retired.	Retired July 2, 1841.
C. Burne	July 2, 1841	46	Ireland	Oct. 4, 1810	Vice Anderson retired.	Exchanged to Half-pay, July 16, 1841.
R. Macneil	July 16, 1841	...	...	Never joined.	Vice Burne to Half-pay.	Exchanged to 78th Regiment, April 15, 1842.
M. G. T. Lindsay	April 15, 1842	46	England	Dec. 16, 1813	Vice Macneil, 78th Regiment.	Retired Oct. 13, 1848.
J. F. G. Campbell	April 14, 1746	36	Scotland	Oct. 25, 1827	Without purchase.	Colonel, June 20, 1854, Augmentation Reserve Battalion; promoted Major-General, Nov. 12, 1860.
C. C. Yarborough	Oct. 13, 1848	40	England	June 9, 1825	With purchase; vice Lindsay retired.	Reduced to Half-pay, 1855; Colonel, Nov. 28, 1853.
Bertie Gordon	Aug. 31, 1858	42	Scotland	Oct. 26, 1832	Augmentation to the Indian Establishment.	Retired by sale, Jan. 29, 1870.
W. T. L. Patterson.	Nov. 12, 1860	38	Do.	Feb. 22, 1859	Without purchase; vice Campbell promoted.	Seconded April 1, 1861: to Half-pay on reduction.
J. Sprot	Jan. 29, 1870	39	Do.	Oct. 17, 1851	With purchase; vice Gordon retired on Half-pay.	

THE 92ND GORDON HIGHLANDERS.

I.

1794–1816.

Raising the regiment—The Duchess of Gordon's bounty—The Lochaber men and Captain John Cameron—First list of officers—Thoroughly Highland character of the Gordon Highlanders—M'Kinnon the bard—First five years of service—Ireland—Holland—Egmont-op-Zee—Sir John Moore's regard for the regiment—Egypt—Severe losses of the regiment—M'Kinnon's poem on the battle of Alexandria—Ireland—Glasgow—Wesley—Copenhagen—Sweden—Portugal—Walcheren—Peninsula—Fuentes d'Onor—Arroyo de Molinos—Almaraz—Alba de Tormes—Vittoria—Pyrenees—Maya—92nd disregards orders—Nive—Orthes—Aire—Ireland—2nd battalion disbanded—Brussels—Quatre Bras—Colonel John Cameron—Waterloo—Paris—Home.

EGMONT-OP-ZEE.	VITTORIA.
MANDORA.	PYRENEES.
EGYPT WITH SPHINX.	NIVE.
CORUNNA.	ORTHES.
FUENTES D'ONOR.	PENINSULA.
ALMARAIH.	WATERLOO.

THE Marquis of Huntly,[1] whilst a captain in the 3rd Foot Guards, having offered to raise a regiment for general service, letters were granted to him for this purpose on the 10th of February 1794. In his zeal for the service the marquis was backed by his father and mother, the Duke and Duchess of Gordon, both of whom, along with the marquis himself, took an active share in the recruiting. It is quite a true story that the beautiful Duchess of Gordon recruited in person on horseback at markets, wearing a regimental jacket and bonnet, and offering for recruits the irresistible

[1] His portrait is on the plate of colonels of the 91st, 92nd, and 93rd regiments.

bounty of a kiss and a guinea. The result was, that, within the short space of four months, the requisite number of men was raised, and on the 24th of June the corps was inspected at Aberdeen[2] by Major-General Sir Hector Munro, and embodied under the denomination of the "Gordon Highlanders." The officers appointed were :—

Lieutenant-Colonel Commandant.
George, Marquis of Huntly.

Majors.
Charles Erskine of Cardross, killed in Egypt in 1801.
Donald Macdonald of Boisdale, died in 1795.

Captains.
Alexander Napier of Blackstone, killed at Corunna in 1809.
John Cameron of Fassifern, killed at Quatre Bras, 16th June, 1815.
Honourable John Ramsay, son of Lord Dalhousie.
Andrew Paton.
William Mackintosh of Aberarder, killed in Holland in 1799.
Alexander Gordon, son of Lord Rockville, killed at Talavera in 1802, Lieutenant-Colonel 83rd regiment.
Simon Macdonald of Morar.

Captain-Lieutenant.
John Gordon, retired as Major.

Lieutenants.
Peter Grant, died in 1817, Major on half-pay
Archibald Macdonell, died in 1813, Lieutenant-Colonel of veterans.
Alexander Stewart.
Sir John Maclean, Major-General, K.C.B., 1825.
Peter Gordon, died 1806.
Thomas Forbes, killed at Toulouse in 1814, Lieutenant-Colonel of the 45th regiment.
Ewan Macpherson.
George H. Gordon.

[2] "Here the Lochaber men (raised by Captain Cameron) showed at once the influence of that clan-feeling under which they had consented to go to war. When it was proposed to draft them into the separate divisions of grenadiers and light troops, they at once declared that they would neither be separated from each other, nor serve under any captain except Cameron, that they had followed him as their leader, and him only they would serve. It required all his persuasion to induce them to submit to the rules of the service; but, assisted by his relative, Major Campbell of Auch,—a man of weight and experience,—and promising that he himself would always watch over their interests in whatever division they were ranked, he prevailed on them to submit; and as we shall subsequently see, none of them ever had cause to reproach him with forgetting his pledge." Memoir of Colonel Cameron, by Rev. A. Clerk.—When Huntly first resolved to raise the regiment, he called on old Fassifern, and offered to his son John a captain's commission in it. Fassifern, however, declined the gratifying offer on the ground that he was unable to raise the number of men necessary to entitle his son to such a rank; whereupon the marquis offered the captaincy without any stipulation or condition, saying he would be glad to have John Cameron as a captain in his regiment, though he brought not a single recruit.

Ensigns.
Charles Dowle, died of wounds in Egypt in 1801.
George Davidson, killed at Quatre Bras in 1815, then Captain in the 42nd regiment.
Archibald Macdonald.
Alexander Fraser, killed 2nd October 1799.
William Tod.
James Mitchell, Lieutenant-Colonel in 1815, retired in 1819.

Staff.
Chaplain.—William Gordon.
Adjutant.—James Henderson, died in 1796.
Quarter-master.—Peter Wilkie, died in 1806.
Surgeon.—William Findlay, died in Egypt in 1801.

It is apt to be supposed that because the Gordon estates now lie only in Aberdeen and Banff, and because the regiment was first collected at Aberdeen, that it belongs particularly to that district; but this is quite a mistake. The 92nd was raised principally in the highland districts of the Gordon estates, and from the estates of the officers or their relations; but it should be remembered that these estates then extended, or the Duke had seignorities over the lands, as far west as Ballachulish and Lochiel, taking in Strathspey, and Lochaber, and it was from these highland districts, of which Fort-William is the centre, that it was mostly raised and for a long time after recruited. It also drew very many of its men from Argyll and the Western Isles. The 92nd along with the 79th should be classed with the Inverness-shire, &c., Militia, and, in conjunction with the 91st and 74th, along with the Argyllshire; the 92nd being connected with North Argyll and Isles, the 91st with Lorn, and the 74th with Cowal and Kintyre. It has always been particular in its recruiting; even after giving nearly all its men as volunteers to regiments going to the Crimea, and stress being laid upon it to fill up quickly, the commanding officers determined to enlist, as usual, only Scotchmen, and hence the great popularity of the corps in Scotland. Although the men (with the exception of volunteers from other regiments), are still all Scotch, they are not so entirely from the Highlands as formerly; yet the regiment is quite an example in spirit and feeling of the old Highland clan, and M'Donald is still the most common name in its ranks. Several Gaelic poets or "bards" have worn its tartan, the most distinguished being Corporal Alexander M'Kinnon, a native of Arasaig, in Inverness-shire, whose descriptions of the battles of Bergen-op-Zoom and the war in Egypt are among the most spirited modern Gaelic poems. The officers have all along been mostly taken from among good Scottish families; and so highly were its non-commissioned officers thought of in the army, that it was, and is, no uncommon thing for them to be promoted as sergeant-majors and as adjutants into other corps, and to be selected as adjutants of militia and volunteers.

The regiment embarked at Fort-George on the 9th of July 1794, and joined the camp on Netley Common in August, when it was put on the list of numbered corps as the 100th regiment. The first five years of its service were spent at Gibraltar, Corsica, Elba, and Ireland, in which latter place it had most arduous and trying duties to perform; these, however, it performed with the best results to the country.

The Gordon Highlanders left Ireland in June 1799 for England, to join an armament then preparing for the coast of Holland. The number of the regiment was changed about this time to the 92nd, the former regiment of that number, and others, having been reduced.

The first division of the army, of which the 92nd formed part, landed on the Dutch coast, near the Helder, on the morning of the 27th of August, without opposition; but the troops had scarcely formed on a ridge of sand hills, at a little distance from the beach, when they were attacked by the enemy, who were however driven back, after a sharp contest of some hours' duration. The 92nd, which formed a part of General Moore's brigade, was not engaged in this affair; but in the battle which took place between Bergen and Egmont on the 2nd of October it took a very distinguished share. General Moore was so well pleased with the heroic conduct of the corps on this occasion, that, when he was made a knight of the Bath, and obtained a grant of supporters for his armorial bearings, he took a soldier of the Gordon Highlanders in full uniform as one of them.[2]

[2] Stewart.—The following extract from a letter from Moore to Lt.-Col. Napier will explain the reason of this:—

"RICHMOND, 17th Nov. 1804.

"MY DEAR NAPIER,——. . . . . My reason for troubling you for a drawing is that, as a knight, I am entitled to supporters. - I have chosen a light infantry soldier for one, and a Highland soldier for the other, in gratitude to and commemoration of two soldiers of

In the action alluded to, the 92nd had Captain William Mackintosh, Lts. Alexander Fraser, Gordon M'Hardy, 3 sergeants, and 54 rank and file, killed; and Colonel, the Marquis of Huntly, Captains John Cameron, Alexander Gordon, Peter Grant, John Maclean, Lieutenants George Fraser, Charles Chadd, Norman Macleod, Donald Macdonald, Ensigns Charles Cameron, John Macpherson, James Bent, G. W. Holmes, 6 sergeants, 1 drummer, and 175 rank and file, wounded.

After returning to England, the regiment

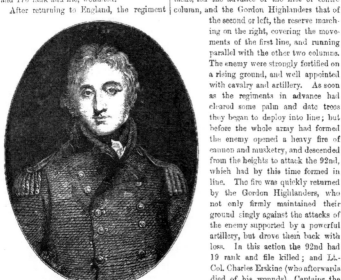

General Sir John Moore.
(From a painting by Sir Thomas Lawrence.)

again embarked on the 27th of May 1800, and sailed for the coast of France; but no landing

the 92nd, who, in action of the 2nd October, raised me from the ground when I was lying on my face wounded and stunned (they must have thought me dead), and helped me out of the field. As my senses were returning I heard one of them say, 'Here is the General, let us take him away,' upon which they stooped, and raised me by the arm. I never could discover who they were; and, therefore, concluded they must have been killed. I hope the 92nd will not have any objection—as I commanded them, and as they rendered me such a service—to my taking one of the corps as a supporter . . . . . believe me, &c.,
"JOHN MOORE."

took place, and the fleet proceeded to Minorca, where the 92nd disembarked on the 20th of July. It formed part of the expedition against Egypt, details of which will be found in the account of the service of the 42nd regiment. The Gordon Highlanders particularly distinguished themselves in the battle of the 13th of March 1801. The British army moved forward to the attack in three columns of regiments; the 90th, or Perthshire regiment, led the advance of the first or centre column, and the Gordon Highlanders that of the second or left, the reserve marching on the right, covering the movements of the first line, and running parallel with the other two columns. The enemy were strongly fortified on a rising ground, and well appointed with cavalry and artillery. As soon as the regiments in advance had cleared some palm and date trees they began to deploy into line; but before the whole army had formed the enemy opened a heavy fire of cannon and musketry, and descended from the heights to attack the 92nd, which had by this time formed in line. The fire was quickly returned by the Gordon Highlanders, who not only firmly maintained their ground singly against the attacks of the enemy supported by a powerful artillery, but drove them back with loss. In this action the 92nd had 19 rank and file killed; and Lt.-Col. Charles Erskine (who afterwards died of his wounds), Captains the Honourable John Ramsay, Archibald Macdonald, Lts. Norman Macleod, Charles Dowle (both of whom also died of their wounds), Donald Macdonald, Tomlin Campbell, Alexander Clarke (the two last died of their wounds), Ronald Macdonald, Alexander Cameron, Ensign Peter Wilson, 10 sergeants, and 100 rank and file wounded.

The regiment had suffered much from sickness during the voyage from Minorca to Egypt, and with this and its recent loss in battle it was so reduced in numbers that General Abercromby ordered it to the rear on the night of the 20th of March, in order to take post upon the shore at Aboukir. Major Napier, on whom the command of the 92nd had devolved in consequence of the death of Col. Erskine, did not, however, remain long in this position, but hurried back as soon as he heard the firing, and assumed his former place in the line. The regiment lost 3 rank and file killed, and Captain John Cameron, Lt. Stewart Matheson, and 37 rank and file wounded.

At the battle of Alexandria, Corporal M'Kinnon, the Gaelic poet already alluded to, was severely wounded, and was nearly buried for dead, when his friend, Sergeant M'Lean, saved him. He composed a Gaelic poem, full of spirit, on the battle, part of which we give in a translation by the Rev. Dr Maclauchlan:—

A SONG ON THE BATTLE IN EGYPT.

It was not heard in the course of history,
In the conflict or strife of arms,
That fifteen thousand men so famous as you
Drew swords under their King.
Glorious was the Scottish champion
Who had that matter entrusted to him;
They were not clowns who were chosen with him,
To bring their deeds of arms to an issue.

  *   *   *   *

The brave heroes were drawn
Into a heavy, fierce body;
Powerful, strong were the hands,
The fine spark going off;
Seeking a place where they might kneel,
If any enemy were to meet them,
The ground would be left bloody
With steel that pierces men's bodies.

There were hearty, vigorous lads there,
Who never yielded in fear,
Following them as best they might.
Fifty horse were turned by their exploits.
It was a vain thought for the horsemen
That they could not find men to contend with them;
And the heroes, who could not be shaken,
Chasing them out on the hill.

  *   *   *   *

We were ready on our legs,
To pursue with all speed,
On the thirteenth morning which they fixed,
With our noble fearless commander.
The two youngest of our regiments—
The Grahams and the Gordons—
Running swiftly to meet them
Pouring down from the hill.

  *   *   *   *

Heavy was the flight for them,
Hard as ever was heard of;
Abercromby was up with them,
With his men who were ready at hand.
Were it not for the town which they reached
With cannon all surrounded,
More of them were in their graves,
And had got cold upon the hill.

In a short time the regiment recovered its health, and shared in all the movements of the army in Egypt till the termination of hostilities, when it embarked for Ireland, and landed at Cork on the 30th of January 1802.

For their services in Egypt, King George III. conferred upon the 92nd and other regiments the honour of bearing on their colours and appointments the "Sphinx," and the word "Egypt." The Grand Seignior established the order of the Knighthood of the Crescent, of which the general officers were made members; and gold medals were presented to the field-officers, captains, and subalterns.

The regiment was removed from Ireland to Glasgow, where it arrived on June 6th, and remained until the renewal of hostilities in 1803, when it was marched to Leith, and embarked for the camp which was then forming at Weeley. At this time was embodied a second battalion of 1000 men, raised under the Army of Reserve Act, in the counties of Nairn, Inverness, Moray, Banff, and Aberdeen. This corps served as a nursery for the regiment during the war.

In January 1806 Major-General the Honourable John Hume was made colonel, in room of the Marquis of Huntly removed to the 42nd.

The regiment formed part of the expedition sent against Copenhagen in 1807, and served in Sir Arthur Wellesley's brigade. The only instance which offered on this occasion to the regiment to distinguish itself was a spirited and successful charge with the bayonet, when it drove back a greatly superior number of the enemy.

In the year 1808 the regiment embarked for Sweden under Sir John Moore, but its services were not made use of; and immediately upon the return of the expedition to England the troops employed were ordered to Portugal under the same commander, landing on the 27th of August. The 92nd accompanied all the movements of General Moore's army, and had the misfortune to lose its commanding officer, Col. Napier of Blackstone, who was killed at Corunna, where the first battalion was posted towards the left of the army on the road leading to Betanzos, "and throughout the day supported its former reputation." Col. Napier was adored by the regiment, to which he was more like a father than a commanding officer. The regiment had only 3 rank and file killed, and 12 wounded; among the latter was Lt. Archibald Macdonald, who afterwards died of his wounds.

On its return to England the regiment was quartered at Weeley, where it received a reinforcement of recruits, which increased the strength of the corps to rather more than 1000 men. This number was, however, greatly reduced in the Walcheren expedition, only 300 out of the 1000 returning fit for duty; but the loss was speedily supplied by recruits from the second battalion. The regiment embarked for Portugal on the 21st of September 1810, and joined the British army under Lord Wellington at the lines of Torres Vedras, in the following month.

The service of the 92nd in the Spanish Peninsula and the south of France is so blended with the operations of Lord Wellington's army that, to give a complete idea of it, it would be necessary to enter into details which the limited space allotted to this division of the history will not admit of, and the most important of which have been given in our notices of the other Highland regiments, especially the 42nd and 71st. In all the actions in which they were engaged, the Gordon Highlanders upheld the high military reputation which they had acquired in Egypt, and supported the honour of their native country in a manner worthy of Highlanders.

The 92nd was brigaded with the 50th and 71st under the command of Sir William Erskine at Fuentes d'Onor, May 5th, 1811. The first battalion of the 92nd was stationed to the right of the town, covering a brigade of nine pounders, and was exposed to a very heavy cannonade. The regiment had 7 rank and file killed, and 2 officers, Major Peter Grant and Lt. Allan M'Nab, and 35 rank and file wounded. Lt.-General Rowland Hill having driven the French from their post at Caceres, the latter, on the approach of the British, retired, halting at Arroyo de Molinos. After a very fatiguing march from Portalegre, the first battalion of the 92nd arrived close to Arroyo on the 27th of October 1811, and next day took part in a well fought battle. The 92nd was placed in the centre of its brigade, and was ordered to proceed to the market-square, and, if possible, to the other side of the town. As the regiment was proceeding along one of the streets, the French, taken by surprise, came out to see what was the matter, and the Prince D'Aremberg was taken prisoner in a half-naked state by a sergeant of the 92nd. The French, however, soon assembled, threw themselves across the head of the street, and commenced firing upon the advancing regiment, the shot taking deadly effect, owing to the narrowness of the street. By this time great confusion and uproar prevailed in the town. The 71st moved down to the assistance of the 92nd, while the 50th secured all the passages to the town, and captured the French artillery. The 92nd thus reinforced now pushed its way through the suburbs, and cleared the town of the enemy. The latter, however, afterwards formed in a field, and fired down a lane upon the advancing regiment. The 92nd had 3 men killed, and Col. Cameron, Brevet-Major Dunbar, and Captains M'Donald and M'Pherson, and 7 rank and file wounded.

At Almaraz, on May 19th, 1812, the 92nd again did good service in assisting materially to destroy the bridge and fortifications. This point was of great importance to the enemy, as it secured the only direct communication between his two armies, which were now in effect placed several days more distant. The 92nd had only 2 rank and file wounded.

At Alba de Tormes, on November 10th and 11th, the 92nd had 8 rank and file killed, and 1 officer and 33 rank and file wounded.

At the battle of Vittoria, fought on June 21st, 1813, the 92nd distinguished itself by seizing the height occupied by the village of Puebla, holding it against a most determined resistance, and, after a fierce struggle, put the enemy to flight. Its casualties were 4 rank and file killed, and 16 wounded. A medal was conferred on Lt.-Col. John Cameron of the 92nd.

In the various actions connected with the passage of the Pyrenees the 92nd took a prominent part, behaving itself in its usual valorous manner; in the words of Sir William Napier, "the stern valour of the 92nd would have graced Thermopylæ."

On the 25th of July 1813, the 92nd was stationed in the Maya Pass, on the right of the road leading from Urdax, and the 71st still farther to the left. The enemy collected a force of about 15,000 men behind some rocky ground in front of the British right, and with this overwhelming force drove in the light companies of the second brigade, gaining the high rock on the right of the allied position before the arrival of the second brigade from Maya, which was therefore compelled to retrace its steps towards the village, instead of falling back to its left on the first brigade. Lt.-Col. Cameron detached the 50th to the right the moment the action commenced. That regiment was severely engaged, and was forced to retire along the ridge. The right wing of the 92nd, under Major John M'Pherson, was sent to its support, and for some time had to stand the whole brunt of the enemy's column. The right wing of the 71st regiment was also brought up, but such was the advantage of the position the enemy had gained by separating the two brigades, and in a manner descending upon the Pass of Maya, while a fresh division was pushing up to it from the direction of Urdax, that the small body of troops received orders to retire to a high rock on the left of the position. This movement was covered by the left wings of the 71st and 92nd regiments, which, relieving each other with the utmost order and regularity, and disputing every inch of ground, left nothing for the enemy to boast of. The brigade continued to hold the rock until the arrival of Major-General Edward Barnes' brigade, when a general charge was made, and every inch of ground recovered as far as the Maya Pass.

On this occasion the 92nd was ordered by Lt.-General the Honourable Sir William Stewart not to charge, the battalion having been hotly engaged for ten successive hours, and in want of ammunition. The 92nd, however, for the first time disregarded an order, and not only charged, but led the charge.[3]

The 92nd behaved with equal bravery on July 30th and 31st and August 1st, its casualties altogether during the passage of the Pyrenees being 53 rank and file killed, 26 officers and 363 rank and file wounded.

In the passage of the Nive the 92nd had its full share of the fighting. On the 13th of December, besides being exposed during the day to a continued fire of musketry and artillery, the battalion made four distinct charges with the bayonet, each time driving the enemy to his original position in front of his entrenchments. At one time the 92nd while pressing onwards was arrested by a fearful storm of artillery. Of one of these charges Sergeant Robertson writes:—

"The order was given to charge with the left wing of the 92nd, while the right should act as riflemen in the fields to the left of the road. The left wing went down the road in a dashing manner, led by Col. Cameron, who had his horse shot under him, and was obliged to walk on foot. As soon as we came up to the French many of them called out for quarter, and were made prisoners. After the enemy had maintained their ground for a short time, they saw that it was impossible for them to stand against us. The road was soon covered with the dead and dying. The French now broke off to their own right, and got into the fields and between the hedges, where they kept up the contest until night. Although the action ended thus in our favour, we did not gain any new ground. After the battle was over, we were formed on a piece of rising ground about a mile to our own rear, when Lord Wellington came in person to thank the 92nd for their gallant conduct and manly bearing during the action, and ordered a double allowance of rum, and that we should go into quarters on the following day."[4]

On this occasion Lts. Duncan M'Pherson, Thomas Mitchell, and Alan M'Donald were killed. Major John M'Pherson (mortally), Captains George W. Holmes, Ronald M'Donald, and Donald M'Pherson; Lts. John Catenaugh, Ronald M'Donald, James John Chisholm, Robert Winchester, and George Mitchell, and Ensign William Fraser were wounded. 28 rank and file were killed, and 143 wounded.

In commemoration of this action an honorary badge was conferred by His Majesty on Lt.-Col. Cameron, bearing the word "Nive," and the senior captain of the regiment (Captain James Seaton) was promoted to the brevet rank of major. The royal authority was also granted for the 92nd to bear the word "Nive" on its regimental colour and appointments.

On the morning of the 15th of Feb., the 92nd marched in pursuit of the enemy, who was discovered late in the evening, strongly posted on the heights in front of Garris, which the division attacked and carried in gallant style. The French obstinately disputed their ground, and made several attempts to recover it after dark, but finding the British troops

---

immovable, they retreated with considerable loss through St Palais. On this occasion Major James Seaton was mortally wounded, and expired on the 22nd of the following month. The other casualties were 3 rank and file wounded.

During the night the enemy destroyed the bridge at St Palais, and every exertion was made to repair it. On the 16th of Feb., the 92nd crossed in the afternoon, and occupied a position in advance.

On the 17th of Feb., the enemy was discovered in the village of Arriverete, on the right bank of the Gave de Mauléon, endeavouring to destroy the bridge over it. A ford was discovered a little higher up, which the 92nd crossed under cover of the British artil-

Colonel John Cameron's Coat of Arms.

lery, and immediately attacking the troops in the village with its usual success, drove the enemy out of it, and secured the bridge by which the troops were enabled to cross. The enemy retired across the Gave d'Oléron, and the battalion, which had 10 rank and file wounded in this enterprise, was cantoned in Arriverete and the neighbouring villages.

In honour of this occasion, it was granted by royal warrant, that Lt.-Col. Cameron should bear for his crest a Highlander of the 92nd regiment, up to the middle in water, grasping in his right hand a broad sword, and in his left a banner inscribed 92nd, within a wreath of laurel; and as a motto over it the word "Arriverete."

At Orthes the 42nd, 79th, and 92nd met for the first time in the Peninsula, and a joyful meeting it was, as the men of the three regiments were almost all Scotchmen, many of whom were old friends. Lord Wellington was so much pleased with the scene at the meeting of these regiments that he ordered them to encamp beside each other for the night.

In the affair at Aire there were 3 rank and file killed, and 3 officers and 29 men wounded. His Majesty granted permission to Lt.-Col. Cameron to bear upon his shield a view of the town, with the word "Aire." Both in Division and General Orders the 92nd was specially mentioned, along with the 50th, as deserving to have "the good fortune of yesterday's action decidedly attributed to it." Moreover, a special letter from the Mayor of Aire warmly thanked Col. Cameron for the conduct of his men, and for having preserved the town from pillage and destruction. The losses of the regiment in these actions were not great, being altogether, according to General Stewart, 2 rank and file killed, and 5 officers and 55 rank and file wounded.

On the 10th of April the 92nd advanced by the Muret road to the vicinity of Toulouse, and drove Marshal Soult's outposts into his entrenchments on that side. The services of the battalion were not again required during this day; it however witnessed the gallant conduct of its comrades on the opposite bank of the river, driving the enemy from his redoubts above the town, and gaining a complete victory.

During the 11th of April nothing particular occurred beyond a skirmish, and confining the enemy to the suburbs. The French evacuated Toulouse during the night, and the white flag was hoisted. On the 12th of April the Marquis of Wellington entered the city amidst the acclamations of the inhabitants. The 92nd followed the enemy on the Villa Franche road, and encamped in advance of that town.

In the course of the afternoon of the 12th of April, intelligence was received of the abdication of Napoleon: had not the express been delayed on the journey by the French police, the sacrifice of many valuable lives would have been prevented.

A disbelief in the truth of this intelligence occasioned much unnecessary bloodshed at

Bayonne, the garrison of which made a desperate sortie on the 14th of April, and Lt.-General Sir John Hope (afterwards Earl of Hopetoun), the colonel of the 92nd regiment, was taken prisoner. Major-General Andrew Hay was killed, and Major-General Stopford was wounded. This was the last action of the Peninsular war.

On April 20, 1814, the 92nd marched into Villa Franche; on the 24th to Beziège; and on the 25th occupied quarters in Toulouse.

After peace had been established between Britain and France, the 92nd returned home, disembarking at Monkstown, Ireland, on the 29th of July, and proceeding to Fermoy Barracks, at which the thanks of Parliament were communicated to the regiment for " the meritorious and eminent services it had rendered to the King and country during the course of the war."

On the 24th of October 1814, the second battalion was disbanded at Edinburgh, and 12 sergeants, 13 drummers, and 161 rank and file were transferred to the first battalion.

The 92nd, however, had not long to rest at home, being called again into active service, to take part in the grand concluding act of the drama enacted by Napoleon for so many years on the theatre of Europe. The regiment sailed from the Cove of Cork on the 1st May 1815, and arrived at Ostend on the 9th. On the 11th the regiment went to Ghent, where it stayed till the 28th, when it removed to Brussels, the men being billeted throughout the city. Here they were served with four days' bread, and supplied with camp-kettles, bill-hooks, and everything necessary for a campaign, which, according to all accounts, was fast approaching. The inhabitants of Brussels like those of Ghent treated the Highlanders with great kindness, the latter, by their civility and good behaviour, making themselves great favourites.

On the evening of the 15th of June the alarm was sounded in Brussels, and hasty preparations were made to go out to meet the enemy. Col. Cameron, who had that day been invested with the order of the Bath, and who was present at the famous ball given by the Duke of Wellington when the alarm was given, was quickly at the head of the regi-

ment. The march was commenced at daybreak on the 16th by the Namur gate. Lt.-General Sir Thomas Picton's division, to which the 92nd belonged, came under fire about two o'clock in front of Genappe, at Quatre Bras, where the main road from Charleroi to Brussels is crossed by another from Nivelles to Namur, and which served as the British communication with the Prussians on the left. The 92nd was formed in front of Quatre Bras farm-house on the road, lining a ditch, with its rear to the walls of the building and garden, its right resting on the cross-roads, and its left extending down the front. Shortly after the 92nd was thus formed, the Duke of Wellington and his staff came and dismounted in the rear of the centre of the regiment. The enemy poured a very hot fire of artillery on this post, and his cavalry charged it, but was received by a well-directed volley from the regiment, and forced to retire with great loss of men and horses. Immediately after this the French infantry attacked the position on the right and in front, and the Gordon Highlanders, who had been standing impatiently eager for action, were now ordered to charge the advancing enemy: " 92nd, you must charge these fellows," the Duke said, and with one bound the regiment was over the ditch advancing at full speed, and making the French give way on all sides. The 92nd continued to pursue the enemy, and was hotly engaged till nightfall, when the action ceased. It was very much cut up both in officers and men, as it was among the first to go into action, and, along with the other Highland regiments, had for a long time to resist the attack of the entire French army. Undoubtedly its greatest loss on this hot day was the brave and high-minded Col. Cameron, concerning whom we give a few details below.[5]

[5] John Cameron was son of Ewen Cameron of Fassifern, a nephew of the "Gentle Lochiel." As we have seen, he entered the regiment at its formation, and took part in most of its hard services. He was universally beloved and respected, especially by the Highland soldiers, in each man of whom he took the interest of a father, and felt himself responsible for their welfare and good conduct. The following account of his death is taken from his biography, written by the Rev. Dr Archibald Clerk of Kilmallie :—" The regiment lined a ditch in front of the Namur road. The Duke of Wellington happened to be stationed among them. Colonel Cameron seeing the French advance asked permission to charge them. The Duke replied,

Besides their colonel, the 92nd lost in the action Captain William Little, Lt. J. J. Chisholm, Ensigns Abel Becker and John M. R. Macpherson, 2 sergeants, and 33 rank and file. The wounded officers were Major James Mitchell (afterwards lieutenant-colonel); Captains G. W. Holmes, Dugald Campbell, W. C. Grant (who died of his wounds); Lts. Thomas Hobbs, Thomas Mackintosh, Robert Winchester, Ronald Macdonnell, James Kerr Ross,

Colonel John Cameron.
From Original Painting in possession of Mrs Cameron Campbell of Monzie.

George Logan, John Mackinlay, George Mackie, Alexander Macpherson, Ewen Ross, Hector M'Innes; Ensigns John Barnwell, Robert Logan, Angus Macdonald, Robert Hewit, and Assistant-Surgeon John Stewart; also 13 sergeants, 1 drummer, and 212 rank and file.

On the morning of the 17th Lord Wellington had collected the whole of his army in the position of Waterloo, and was combining his measures to attack the enemy; but having received information that Marshal Blucher had been obliged, after the battle of Ligny, to abandon his position at Sombref, and to fall back upon Wavre, his lordship found it necessary to make a corresponding movement. He accordingly retired upon Genappe, and thence upon Waterloo. Although the march took place in the middle of the day the enemy made no attempt to molest the rear, except by following, with a large body of cavalry brought from his right, the cavalry under the Earl of Uxbridge. On the former debouching from the village of Genappe, the earl made a gallant charge with the Life Guards, and repulsed the enemy's cavalry.

Lord Wellington took up a position in front of Waterloo. The rain fell in torrents during the night, and the morning of the 18th was ushered in by a dreadful thunder-storm; a prelude which superstition might have regarded as ominous of the events of that memorable and decisive day. The allied army was drawn up across the high roads from Charleroi and Nivelles, with its right thrown back to a ravine near Merke Braine,

'Have patience, you will have plenty of work by and by.' As they took possession of the farm-house Cameron again asked leave to charge, which was again refused. At length, as they began to push on the Charleroi road, the Duke exclaimed, 'Now, Cameron, is your time, take care of the road.' He instantly gave the spur to his horse, the regiment cleared the ditch at a bound, charged, and rapidly drove back the French; but, while doing so, their leader was mortally wounded. A shot fired from the upper storey of the farm-house passed through his body, and his horse, pierced by several bullets, fell under him. His men raised a wild shout, rushed madly on the fated house, and, according to all accounts, inflicted dread vengeance on its doomed occu-

pants. Ewen Macmillan (Cameron's foster brother), who was ever near his master and his friend, speedily gave such aid as he could. Carrying him with the aid of another private beyond reach of the firing, he procured a cart, whereon he laid him, carefully and tenderly propping his head on a breast than which none was more faithful." He was carried to the village of Waterloo, and laid in a deserted house by the roadside, stretched upon the floor. "He anxiously inquired how the day had gone, and how his beloved Highlanders had acquitted themselves. Hearing that, as usual, they had been victorious, he said, 'I die happy, and I trust my dear country will believe that I have served her faithfully.' . . . . Thus he met with a warrior's death, and more, with a Highland which was occupied, and its left extended to a height above the hamlet Ter-la-Haye, which was also occupied. In front of the right centre, and near the Nivelles road, the allies occupied the house and farm of Hougoumont, and in front of the left centre they possessed the farm of La Haye Sainte. The Gordon Highlanders, who were commanded by Major Donald Macdonald, in consequence of the wound of Lt.-Col. Mitchell, who had succeeded Col. Cameron in the command, were in the ninth brigade with the Royal Scots, the Royal Highlanders, and the 44th regiment. This brigade was stationed on the left wing upon the crest of a small eminence, forming one side of the hollow, or low valley, which divided the two hostile armies. A hedge ran along this crest for nearly two-thirds its whole length. A brigade of Belgians, another of Hanoverians, and General Ponsonby's brigade of the 1st or Royal Dragoons, Scotch Greys, and Inniskillings, were posted in front of this hedge. Bonaparte drew up his army on a range of heights in front of the allies, and about ten o'clock in the morning he commenced a furious attack upon the post at Hougoumont. This he accompanied with a very heavy cannonade upon the whole line of the allies; but it was not till about two o'clock that the brigades already mentioned were attacked. At that time the enemy, covered by a heavy fire of artillery, advanced in a solid column of 3000 infantry of the guard, with drums beating, and all the accompaniments of military array, towards the position of the Belgians. The enemy received a temporary check from the fire of the Belgians and from some artillery; but the troops of Nassau gave way, and, retiring behind the crest of the eminence, left a large space open to the enemy. To prevent the enemy from entering by this gap, the third battalion of the Royal Scots, and the second battalion of the 44th, were ordered up to occupy the ground so abandoned; and here a warm conflict of some duration took place, in which the two regiments lost many men and expended their ammunition. The enemy's columns continuing to press forward, General Pack ordered up the Highlanders, calling out, "Ninety-second, now is your time; charge." This order being repeated by Major Macdonald, the soldiers answered it by a shout. Though then reduced to less than 250 men, the regiment instantly formed two men deep, and rushed to the front, against a column ten or twelve men deep, and equal in length to their whole line. The enemy, as if appalled by the advance of the Highlanders, stood motionless, and upon a nearer approach they became panic-stricken, and, wheeling to the rear, fled in the most disorderly manner, throwing away their arms and every thing that incumbered them. So rapid was their flight, that the Highlanders, notwithstanding their nimbleness of foot, were unable to overtake them; but General Ponsonby pursued them with the cavalry at full speed, and cutting into the centre of the column, killed numbers and took nearly 1800 prisoners. The animating sentiment, "Scotland for ever!" received a mutual cheer as the Greys galloped past the Highlanders, and the former felt the effect of the appeal so powerfully, that, not content with the destruction or surrender of the flying column, they passed it, and charged up to the line of the French position. "Les braves Ecossais; qu'ils sont terribles ces Chevaux Gris!" Napoleon is said to have exclaimed, when, in succession, he saw the small body of Highlanders forcing one of his chosen columns to fly, and the Greys charging almost into his very line.

During the remainder of the day the 92nd

warrior's death. His remains were hastily interred in a green alley—*Allée verte*—on the Ghent road, under the terrific storm of the 17th." In the April of the following year his remains were removed to Scotland, and from Leith conveyed in a King's ship to Lochaber, and committed to their final resting-place in the churchyard of Kilmallie, where lie many chiefs of the Cameron clan. His age was only 44 years. In honour of Cameron's distinguished service his father was created Baronet of Fassifern. A handsome monument—an obelisk—was afterwards erected to Cameron at Kilmallie, for which an inscription was written by Sir Walter Scott, who seems to have had an intense admiration for the brave and chivalrous Highland hero, and who, in his *Dance of Death*, speaks of him thus :—

"Through battle, rout, and reel,
Through storm of shot, and hedge of steel,
Led the grandson of Lochiel,
    The valiant Fassifern.

Through steel and shot he leads no more,
Low laid 'mid friend's and foemen's gore;
But long his native lake's wild shore,
And Suuart rough, and wild Ardgour,
    And Morven long shall tell;

And proud Ben Nevis hear with awe,
How, at the bloody Quatre Bras,
Brave Cameron heard the wild hurrah
    Of conquest as he fell."

regiment remained at the post assigned it, but no opportunity afterwards occurred of giving another proof of its prowess. The important service it rendered at a critical moment, by charging and routing the élite of the French infantry, entitle the 92nd to share largely in the honours of the victory.

"A column of such strength, composed of veteran troops, filled with the usual confidence of the soldiers of France, thus giving way to so inferior a force, and by their retreat exposing themselves to certain destruction from the charges of cavalry ready to pour in and overwhelm them, can only be accounted for by the manner in which the attack was made, and is one of the numerous advantages of that mode of attack I have had so often occasion to notice. Had the Highlanders, with their inferior numbers, hesitated and remained at a distance, exposed to the fire of the enemy, half an hour would have been sufficient to annihilate them, whereas in their bold and rapid advance they *lost only four men.* The two regiments, which for some time resisted the attacks of the same column, were unable to force them back. They remained stationary to receive the enemy, who were thus allowed time and opportunity to take a cool and steady aim; encouraged by a prospect of success, the latter doubled their efforts; indeed, so confident were they, that when they reached the plain upon the summit of the ascent, they ordered their arms, as if to rest after their victory. But the handful of Highlanders soon proved on which side the victory lay. Their bold and rapid charge struck their confident opponents with terror, paralysed their sight and aim, and deprived both of point and object. The consequence was, as it will always be in nine cases out of ten in similar circumstances, that the loss of the 92nd regiment was, as I have just stated, only 4 men, whilst the other corps in the stationary position lost eight times that number." [*]

At Waterloo the 92nd had 14 rank and file killed, and Captains Peter Wilkie and Archibald Ferrier, Lts. Robert Winchester, Donald Macdonald, James Kerr Ross, and James Hope, 3 sergeants, and 96 rank and file wounded.

After Waterloo, the 92nd, along with the rest of the army, proceeded to Paris, in the neighbourhood of which it encamped on the 3rd of July. Shortly after leaving Waterloo, while halting near a small village for the night, the Duke of Wellington in person came up and thanked the 92nd for the manner in which the men had conducted themselves during the engagement, and lavished upon them the highest eulogiums for their exertions to uphold the reputation of the British army. The Highland Society of Scotland unanimously passed a vote of thanks "for the determined valour and exertions displayed by the regiment, and for the

[*] Stewart.

credit which it did its country in the memorable battles of the 16th and 18th of June 1815."

The 92nd stayed at Paris till the end of November, when it was marched to Boulogne, and on December 17th it embarked at Calais, landing at Margate on the 19th. After staying at various places in England, it marched from Berwick-on-Tweed to Edinburgh on the 7th of September 1816, and took up its quarters in Edinburgh Castle on the 12th, this being the second visit to its native country since its embodiment. Like the 42nd in similar circumstances, the men of the 92nd were treated with the greatest kindness, and entertained with profuse hospitality at almost every place on the way. On their entry into Edinburgh, a vast crowd assembled in the roads and streets. The 42nd, between which and the 92nd there has always been a friendly rivalry, had been there shortly before, and a man of that regiment standing among the crowd cried in banter to a passing company of the 92nd, "This is nothing to what it was when we came home; we could hardly make our way through the crowd." A 92nd man quickly retorted, "You should have sent for us to clear the way for you, as we have often done before."

II.

1816—1874.

The regiment was quartered in Edinburgh till April 1817, when it was sent to Ireland, where it remained till 1819, performing duties somewhat similar to those already recorded of the 42nd. On the 16th April the 92nd sailed for Jamaica, where it arrived on June 2nd. On its march to Up-Park Camp, it was followed by the whole population of Kingston and vicinity, who crowded from all quarters to witness so novel a sight as a Highland regiment in Jamaica. Shortly after its arrival in Jamaica the regiment suffered fearfully from yellow fever in its most virulent form. Indeed, such was the sickness and mortality, that the regiment was, in August, in a manner ordered to be dispersed. On the 28th of that month, a strong detachment, chiefly composed of convalescents, embarked on board the "Serapis" guard-ship, then at anchor off Port-Royal.

The total loss sustained by the regiment from the 25th of June to the 24th of December 1819, consisted of 10 officers,—namely, Majors Archibald Ferrier, and John Blainey (Brevet Lt.-Col.), Lts. Andrew Will, Thomas Gordon, Hector Innes, George Logan, Richard M'Donnell, and George Mackie (Adjutant), Ensign Francis Reynolds, and Assistant-Surgeon David Thomas; 13 sergeants, 8 drummers, and 254 rank and file. This considerably exceeds the total number of men of the regiment killed in all the engagements, from the time of its formation in 1794 down to Waterloo in 1815.

In January 1820, Lt.-Gen. John Hope succeeded the Earl of Hopetoun as Colonel of the 92nd; the latter being removed to the 42nd. General Hope continued to be Colonel till 1823, when he was removed to the 72nd, and was succeeded in the colonelcy of the 92nd by Lt.-Gen. the Hon. Alexander Duff.

The regiment remained in Jamaica till 1827, and from the exemplary conduct and orderly demeanour of the officers and men, gained the respect and good wishes of the inhabitants wherever it was stationed. In the summer of 1825 it had again been attacked with fever, and lost in the course of two months Major Charlton, Captain Donaldson, Lt. Deans, and 60 men. The gaps then made in the regiment were, however, regularly filled up by considerable detachments of recruits from England, so that the strength of the 92nd was never far below the proper mark.

Owing to the terrible death-rate in the West Indies and other causes, Lt.-Col. Gardyne writes, as the 92nd had fallen into comparatively bad order for a time, and on its return home, Lt.-Col. John M'Donald, of Dalchoshnie, afterwards General Sir John M'Donald, K.C.B., was appointed to the command; an officer who had served with great distinction in Spain, a thorough soldier, and a true Highlander, he soon brought the 92nd back to its natural condition of perfect discipline, and remained in command till he was promoted Major-General.

In February and March 1827, the regiment embarked in detachments at Kingston for England, on reaching which it was sent to Scotland, the whole of the regiment, depôt and service companies, joining at Edinburgh in the end of May. In the beginning of 1828 the 92nd was removed to Glasgow, from which it sailed to Ireland in July, landing at Dublin August 4th. It remained in Ireland till 1834.

In 1829, orders having been received directing that steel-mounted swords should be adopted by Highland regiments, the officers of the 92nd immediately supplied themselves with the claymore, a sword similar to that originally used in the regiment. In 1830, the regiment was authorised to adopt trousers of the regimental tartan for all occasions when the kilt was not worn. While in Jamaica, white trousers alone were allowed to be used.

At all the inspections that took place while in Ireland, the 92nd, like the other Highland regiments, received the unqualified praise of the inspecting officers. It also gained for itself the respect and esteem of all classes of the inhabitants in performing the disagreeable duty of assisting the civil power in suppressing the "White Boy" outrages, to which we have referred in our account of the 42nd. Once only were the men compelled to resort to the last military extremity.

On the 13th of December 1830, the anniversary of the battle of the Nive, a new stand of colours was presented to the regiment in Dublin by His Excellency Lt.-Gen. the Right Hon. Sir John Byng, who complimented the regiment on its brilliant and distinguished conduct in all its engagements.

In July 1831 Lt.-Gen. Duff was succeeded in the colonelcy of the regiment by Lt.-Gen.

Sir John Hamilton Dalrymple (afterwards Earl of Stair).

In August 1833 the regiment was divided into six service and four depôt companies, preparatory to the embarkation of the former for Gibraltar. The depôt companies proceeded to Scotland in October, where they remained till 1836, when they returned to Ireland.

The service companies embarked at Cork in February 1834 for Gibraltar, where they arrived on the 10th of March. Here they remained

Sir John M'Donald, C.B.
From Original Painting at Dunalastair.

till January 1836, when the regiment removed to Malta, where it was stationed till 1841.

In May 1840 the depôt companies were again removed from Ireland to Scotland. In January 1841, the service companies left Malta for Barbadoes, where they arrived in April. In May 1843 the headquarters and one company removed to Trinidad, while detachments were stationed at Grenada and Tobago. In the same month, Lt.-Gen. Sir William Maclean succeeded the Earl of Stair as colonel of the regiment, the former being removed to the 46th.

The service companies embarked in Decem-

ber 1843 for Scotland, arriving in February 1844 at Aberdeen, where they were joined by the depôt companies from Dundee. From Aberdeen the 92nd went to Glasgow, and in July 1845 to Edinburgh, where it remained till April 1846, when it removed to Ireland, where it remained till March 5th, 1851, when headquarters and 4 companies under command of Lt.-Col. Atherley sailed from Queenstown for the Ionian Islands. A complimentary address was received from the mayor and citizens of Kilkenny, on the 92nd quitting that city, expressive of the regret they experienced in parting with the regiment, the conduct of which had gained the esteem of all classes.

The regiment disembarked at Corfu on March 29th, and on May 17th was joined by the other two service companies under command of Major Lockhart.

While in the Ionian Islands, the 92nd received notice that kilted regiments were to use the Glengarry bonnet as a forage cap, with the regimental band or border similar to that on the feather bonnet.

The 92nd remained in the Ionian Islands until March 1853, embarking in three detachments for Gibraltar on the 21st, 23rd, and 28th of that month, respectively. During its stay in the Ionian Islands it was regularly inspected, and was invariably complimented, we need scarcely say, by the inspecting officer, on its high state of efficiency in all respects.

While the regiment was in Gibraltar, the war between this country and Russia broke out, and in consequence the 92nd was augmented to 1120 of all ranks, and subsequently to 1344. This increase, however, was soon destined to be considerably reduced, not by the casualties of war,—for the 92nd was not fortunate enough to be in the thick of the fray,—but by the large numbers who volunteered into other regiments destined for the Crimea. So large a number of men volunteered into those regiments about to proceed to the scene of the struggle that little more than the officers' colours and band remained of what was the day before one of the finest, best drilled, and best disciplined regiments in the army. The depôt companies, stationed at the time at Galway, volunteered almost to a man into the 42nd and 79th. The men of the service companies entered English regiments, and on their arrival at Varna asked to be allowed to enter Highland corps. This, however, could not be done, and on the conclusion of the war many of those that were left unscathed petitioned to be allowed to rejoin their old corps, saying they had volunteered for active service, and not to leave their regiment. Their request was not granted; but so strong was their *esprit de corps*, that at the expiration of their first period of service many of them re-enlisted in the 92nd, two of their number bringing back the Victoria cross on their breasts. Such a loss to the regiment as these volunteers occasioned almost broke the spirit of the officers and of the soldiers left; but by unsparing exertions the regiment was recruited in an incredibly short time with a very superior class of men, mostly from the Highland counties, but all from Scotland.

On the 25th of June 1855 Lt.-General John M'Donald, C.B., was appointed to the colonelcy of the regiment, in room of the deceased Sir William M'Bean, K.C.B.

The 92nd was, after all, sent to the Crimea, but too late to take any part in active operations. At the request of Lord Clyde the regiment was sent out to join his division before Sebastopol, and about 600 officers and men left Gibraltar during September 1855, landing at Balaklava just after the taking of Sebastopol. Though the 92nd was actually under fire in the Crimea, it did not obtain any addition to the numerous names on its colours. It remained in the Crimea till May 1856, on the 23rd of which month it embarked at Balaklava for Gibraltar, where it remained for eighteen months longer before embarking for India, previous to which the establishment of the regiment was considerably augmented, the service companies alone numbering upwards of 1100 officers and men. The 92nd embarked on the 26th of January 1858, to take part in quelling the Indian Mutiny; and before leaving, both in general orders and in

brigade orders, Lt.-Col. Lockhart and the officers and men were eulogised in the highest terms for the splendid character of the regiment.

The light companies of the 92nd disembarked at Bombay on the 6th of March, under the command of Col. Atherley; the other two companies, under the command of Lt.-Col. Mackenzie, joined head-quarters at Bombay on the 30th of March. The 92nd, during its stay in India, was employed in the Central Provinces, under Sir Hugh Rose, formerly a 92nd officer, and distinguished itself by the rapidity of its forced marches and steadiness under fire; but although it took part in many combats, skirmishes, and pursuits, doing good and important service to its country, it had not the good fortune to be in any great victory such as to be thought worthy of being recorded on the colours beside such glorious names as Egypt and Waterloo. Lt.-Col. Lockhart was made a C.B. for his services while commanding the 92nd in this campaign. We shall endeavour briefly to indicate some of the services performed by the regiment while taking its share in the suppression of the mutiny.

On the 30th of March a detachment, under the command of Major Sutherland, proceeded to Surát on field-service, rejoining head-quarters on the 8th of June. Four days after, the right wing of head-quarters, under command of Lt.-Col. Archibald Inglis Lockhart, proceeded to Mhow on field-service, but must have returned before the 22nd of August, on which day head-quarters, consisting of Nos. 1, 3, 7, and 10 companies, marched upon Oojein, to the north of Indore, having received sudden orders to that effect on the afternoon of the 21st. The companies formed part of a field-force column, which was required to put down some rebellious symptoms that had shown themselves near Oojein. The column was placed under the command of Lt.-Col. Lockhart, and reached Oojein on the 25th. Here all was found quiet, and the column was directed toward Mundesoor, but on its march intelligence was received that the rebels had crossed to the right bank of the Chumbul river, and in consequence the march of the column was directed upon Agoor, which place it reached on the 28th, having marched 50 miles through a most difficult country in 38 hours. After remaining here for three days the column advanced to Soosneer, 16 miles to the northward; and intelligence having been received that a force of 15,000 rebels, with 38 guns, had taken possession of the fortified town of Jhalra Patun, it was resolved to wait at Soosneer until support arrived. On the 9th of Sept. a squadron of H.M.'s Lancers and 2 guns of the Bengal Artillery joined the camp; on the morning of the 10th, a change in the enemy's movements having meantime taken place, the reinforced column marched to Zeera-

Colonel (now Major-General) Lockhart, C.B.
From a Photograph.

poor, about 10 miles south of Machilpoor, to which the enemy had moved, both towns being on the right bank of the Kallee Sind. At Zeera-poor the column was joined by another force under the command of Lt.-Col. Hope of the 71st Highland Light Infantry, which was also under Col. Lockhart's orders. On the same night, the 10th, Major-General Michel, C.B., commanding the Malwah division, joined and assumed command, entirely approving of the arrangements which had been made. The united column set out in pursuit of the rebels

on the 12th, and marching by Hullwatrah and Rajghur, on the 15th came upon the enemy's camp at a short distance from the latter town, but found it had been quite recently abandoned, the rebels having evidently beat a precipitate retreat. The European infantry was left here to breakfast and grog, and the Major-General, with the cavalry, native infantry, and artillery, pushed on and brought the enemy to a stand in a jungly country. The latter opened a well-sustained fire upon their pursuers, which, however, proved nearly harmless. On the European infantry coming up, the 92nd, under Captain Bethune, and the 4th Bombay Rifles deployed into line and advanced, covered by their own skirmishers, and supported by the 71st Highlanders and the 19th Bombay Native Infantry. According to orders not a shot was fired until the jungle thinned so much as to enable the skirmishers to see the enemy. After a few rounds from the guns, the infantry again advanced, and the rebels abandoned their position and fled, pursued by the cavalry. The infantry proceeded to Bhowra, where they encamped, having marched 20 miles in the course of the day under a burning sun, by which many of the men were struck down. The only casualties of the 92nd in the above action were 2 men wounded.

The force halted at Bhowra until the 18th of Sept., the whole being formed into one brigade under Lt.-Col. Lockhart. Setting out on that day, the force marching by Seronj reached Mungrowlee on the 9th of Oct., when just as the tents had been pitched, it was reported that the rebels were advancing in force, and were within half a mile of the camp. The squadron of the 17th Lancers was immediately pushed forward, rapidly followed by the artillery and infantry, the 92nd being commanded by Captain Bethune. The enemy, taken by surprise, retreated, and took up position on an eminence 3 miles distant from Mungrowlee, and crowned by the ruins of a village. The rebels covered their front with guns placed in a strip of jungle, which was filled with cavalry and infantry. The British infantry deployed into line, and, covered by skirmishers, advanced upon the enemy's position. The guns of the latter at once opened, and there was also a well-sustained but not very effective fire of small arms kept up from the jungle. The skirmishers directing their fire on the enemy's guns (whose position could only be ascertained from their smoke), steadily advanced. After an ineffectual attempt to turn the left wing of the British by the enemy's cavalry, the latter gave way, leaving their infantry to be severely handled by the Lancers. The line continued to advance, and six guns were taken by a rush of the skirmishers, many of the gunners being shot and bayoneted when endeavouring to escape. The guns being now brought up, the rebels soon were in rapid retreat. There appears to have been no casualties to the 92nd in this well-fought action.

It having been ascertained that the rebels had crossed the Betwa, and were now located on the right bank of that river, Major-General Michel arranged with Brigadier Smith, commanding a field column in the Chundaree district, that the two forces should make a combined movement, and for this purpose they were divided into three columns. The left column, consisting of the infantry of his brigade, under Brigadier Smith, was to move down the left bank of the river towards the Chundaree, prepared to cross to the right bank if necessary. The cavalry and horse artillery of both brigades, forming the centre column, under the immediate command of Major-General Michel, was to cross at the ford by which the enemy had retreated. The right column, consisting of the infantry and artillery of Lt.-Col. Lockhart's brigade, under that officer, was to cross the river by the Khunjea Ghaut and proceed to Nurat. This place it reached on the 17th of October, and on the 18th was joined by the centre column, which had been unable to penetrate the very dense jungle.

On the morning of the 19th, the 92nd being led by Captain A. W. Cameron, the two combined columns marched upon the village of Sindwaho, about 12 miles distant, and where the enemy were reported to be in strength. The force halted within half a mile of the vil-

lage, to the right of which the enemy were discovered drawn up in order of battle. The cavalry and horse artillery advanced to the attack, and the infantry, who were to advance upon the village, under Lt.-Col. Lockhart, were deployed into line, covered by skirmishers. The 71st passed to the right of the village, the 92nd through the village and thick enclosures on the left, and the 19th Bombay Native Infantry were on more open ground to the left of the 92nd. The enemy were found to have abandoned the village, but many were shot down in the advance of the skirmishers through the enclosures. When clear of the village, the infantry advanced in echelon of battalions from the right. While the 71st took ground to the right, and the 19th Bengal Native Infantry went to the help of the Bombay Artillery, the 92nd, under Captain Cameron, advanced in the face of a large body of cavalry, who had posted themselves under a large tope of trees on a rising ground and frequently threatened to charge. By this time the 92nd was quite separated from the rest of the force. A battery of artillery having been sent to join the 92nd, and as the enemy still threatened to charge, the skirmishers were recalled, and fire opened from right to left; as shot and shell were at the same time thrown into the tope, the enemy retired, and were soon in rapid retreat, pursued by the cavalry.

During the 20th the force halted at Tehree and on this as on previous occasions the Major-General issued an order congratulating the troops on their success, and justly praising the exertions and bravery of officers and men. On this last occasion, Col. Lockhart's ability in handling his brigade elicited the Major-General's warmest approbation.

The force set out again on the 21st, and marching each day reached Dujorial on the 24th. The Major-General having heard that the enemy were at Kimlasa, moved on Kurnya at 2 A.M. on the 25th, and at dawn the whole of the rebel army was discovered crossing in front just beyond Kuraya. When the cavalry, which had started an hour later than the infantry, came up, they found that the infantry under Col. Lockhart, having cut through the enemy's line of march, had just wheeled to the right and part advanced skirmishing.

The infantry had indeed dispersed the enemy when the cavalry arrived; the latter therefore set out in rapid pursuit, the infantry following for about five miles and clearing the villages of the rebels.

The force remained at Kuraya till the 27th, when it proceeded south, and reached Bhilsa on the 2nd of November. On the 4th the Major-General proceeded with the cavalry in pursuit of the rebels, who had crossed the Nerbudda, leaving the infantry and Le Marchant's battery of artillery to watch Bhilsa and Bhopal, both being threatened by bodies of local rebels. The infantry remained at Bhilsa until the 9th, when, proceeding by Goolgong, they reached Bhopal on the 17th, leaving it on the 23rd for Sehore.

The rebels, in the meantime, after crossing the Nerbudda, had been again repulsed by the troops in Candeish. One hundred men of the 92nd, part of a small column under Major Sutherland, proceeded on the 20th of November to cross the Nerbudda, and on the 24th reached Jeolwana, where they were joined by another 50 men of the 92nd and a like number of the 71st mounted on camels. On the morning of the 24th Major Sutherland proceeded with 120 Highlanders and 80 sepoys, partly on camels, and soon ascertaining that the rebels, under Tantéa Topee, with two guns, were on the road to Rajpoor, pushed on in pursuit. On approaching Rajpoor, the rebel force was perceived passing through it, and the Highlanders, on camels, pushing rapidly forward, came on the enemy in half an hour. Before the men, however, could dismount for the attack, the rebels again retired. By this time the men following on foot, both Europeans and natives, having marched at a very rapid pace in rear, overtook the men on camels. The whole now advanced together direct upon the enemy, who had taken up a strong position, in order of battle, on a rocky and wooded ridge, their two guns on the road commanding the only approach. The Highlanders, supported by the native troops, at once advanced, and rushing up the road under a shower of grape, in a very short time captured the guns, on which the rebels precipitately abandoned their position. In this attack, Lt. and Adjutant Humfrey was wounded.

Major Sutherland's force remained in the neighbourhood of Kooksee until the 27th of December, when it was ordered to join headquarters at Mhow.

Lt.-Col. Lockhart's column left Sehore and marched upon Indore on the 29th of November, that town being considered in danger of an attack by the rebels. Indore was reached on December 4th, and the column halted there until the 6th, when it returned to quarters at Mhow, having detached No. 10 and part of No. 3 companies under Captain Bethune to join a small force proceeding towards Rutlâm. These companies were subsequently attached to Brigadier Somerset's column, and mounted on camels, they underwent great privations and severe fatigue during the rapid pursuit in the Banswarra country. On the morning of the 1st of January 1859, the column came up with the rebels at daylight at Baroda, but the men had scarcely dismounted ere the rebels had, as usual, commenced a rapid retreat; this, however, they did not effect before being considerably cut up by the cavalry and guns attached to the force. These companies did not rejoin headquarters until the 24th of May 1859.

On the 2nd of March, headquarters, numbering about 1000 officers and men, marched from Mhow to Jhansi, there to be quartered; but, on reaching Bursud, they were directed by Brigadier-General Sir R. Napier to assist in clearing that neighbourhood of some rebels said to be located in the jungles. For this purpose all the heavy baggage was left at Bursud in charge of a company, and the remainder proceeded in light order to Ummeerghur and subsequently to Karadev. The jungles were in vain searched for any rebels, and on the 25th the force again got on to the main road at Goona and proceeded towards Jhansi, which it reached on the 7th of April. Nos. 8 and 9 companies proceeded direct to Lullutpoor, where they were stationed on detached duty under Major Sutherland. Remnants of rebels who had, after being broken up into small parties, reunited under Feroze Shah, and taken refuge in the dense jungles, were by the junction of forces from Lullutpoor and other places driven from their refuge, without, however, their having been actually come in contact with. The duty was, nevertheless, of a harassing nature, and was rendered more so by the sickness which had latterly prevailed at Lullutpoor and reduced the men stationed there to a weak condition.

On the 1st of June 1859, No. 7 company was detached to Seepree, and on the evening of the 30th, 40 men of that company under Ensign Emmet, mounted on elephants, proceeded with a mixed native force, the whole under the command of Major Meade, to surprise a numerous party of rebels who had located themselves in a village about 28 miles distant. The village, which was situated on an eminence and surrounded by thick jungle, was reached by 5.30 A.M. on the 1st of July, and the attack immediately commenced. The rebels in considerable numbers took refuge in a large house well loop-holed, and kept up a warm fire of musketry on their assailants; they were not finally subdued until the house caught fire. Of the 92nd, 4 rank and file were wounded, and Major Meade, in reporting the affair to the commanding officer, said:—"I cannot speak too highly of Ensign Emmet and your men; their coolness and steadiness was most conspicuous."

On the 14th of October, Nos. 1 and 2 companies proceeded, mounted on camels, as part of a small force ordered from Jhansi under command of Col. Lockhart, in conjunction with 6 other columns, to clear the Bundelcund jungles of rebels. The force continued in the field until the 14th of December. Some difficult and harassing marches were performed in the course of these operations, but the rebels having broken through the circle to the north-east, the Jhansi column, being stationed on the west, did not come in contact with them.

Thus it will be seen that the 92nd performed important and harassing duties during the suppression of the great Indian Mutiny, and certainly seem to have deserved some outward mark of the services they then rendered to their country. Brigadier-General Sir Robert Napier, in bidding farewell to the officers and men of the Gwalior division on the 11th of January 1860, specially acknowledged the important assistance he had received from Col. Lockhart and the men under his command. Notwithstanding the fatiguing work the 92nd had to undergo, both Sir Robert Napier and Lord Clyde, in reporting on their inspection, spoke in the highest terms of the condition of the regiment.

The various detachments having joined headquarters at Jhansi, the regiment, numbering about 960 officers and men, under command of Col. Lockhart, C.B., left Jhansi on the 15th of March for Dugshai, there to be quartered.

The 92nd remained in India for nearly three years longer, during which little occurred in connection with the regiment calling for special notice. Besides the places already mentioned, it was stationed at Umballa, Benares, Rajghaut, and Calcutta, and, on its half-yearly inspection, invariably elicited the unqualified commendation of the inspecting officers and the War Office authorities; the regimental school gained the special praise of the latter.

While stationed at Dugshai, in September 1861, the regiment received the gratifying intelligence that Her Majesty had been graciously pleased to authorise the 92nd being designated "The Gordon Highlanders," by which name it was popularly known at the period of its being raised and for some time afterwards; indeed we suspect it had never ceased to be popularly known by this title.

The Gordon Highlanders embarked at Calcutta for England in two detachments on the 24th and 28th of January 1863, respectively, and rejoined at Gosport on the 20th of May. This was the first time the regiment had been quartered in England since the 22nd of August 1816. Before the 92nd left India, 396 men volunteered into regiments remaining in the country; the deficiency was, however, soon filled up, as, on its being made known, Scotchmen serving in English regiments gladly availed themselves of the opportunity of serving in so distinguished a corps.

The 92nd did not remain long at Gosport. It embarked at Portsmouth on the 10th of July for Edinburgh, arriving off Granton Pier on the 13th, and marching to the Castle through an enthusiastic crowd. It was 17 years since the Gordon Highlanders had last been in Edinburgh. Shortly after its arrival the regiment was inspected by its Colonel, General Sir John M'Donald, K.C.B., who had formerly commanded the 92nd for the long period of 18 years.

The regiment remained scarcely a year in Edinburgh, during which time only one event occurred to mark the "even tenor of its way;" this was the presentation of new colours on the 13th of April 1864. The Highlanders, on that day, were formed in review-order on the Castle Esplanade, shortly after which Major-General Walker, C.B., commanding in Scotland, arrived on the ground accompanied by his staff. General Sir John M'Donald, K.C.B., the veteran colonel of the regiment, was also present, along with Lady M'Donald and other members of his family. After the usual ceremony had been gone through with the old colours, and after the Rev. James Millar, Chaplain of Edinburgh Castle, had offered up an appropriate prayer, the Major-General placed the new colours in the hands of Lady M'Donald, who addressed the regiment in a few most appropriate words :—

"It would be, I believe," she said, "according to established custom, that, in placing these colours in your hands, I should remind you of the duty you owe to them, your Queen, and your country; but, to the Gordon Highlanders, any such counsel would, I feel, be superfluous; their glorious deeds of the past are sufficient guarantee for the future, that wherever and whenever these colours are borne into action, it will be but to add new badges to them and fresh honour to the regiment. I cannot let this opportunity pass without touching on the many happy years I spent among you, without assuring you of the pleasure it gives me to see you again, and of my warmest wishes for your welfare and prosperity."

On the 25th of May 1864, the 92nd left Edinburgh for Glasgow under the command of Col. A. I. Lockhart, C.B. Detachments were also sent to Paisley and Ayr. The 92nd remained in Glasgow till March 1865, during which time it took part in a large sham fight in Renfrewshire, and was present at the inauguration by the Queen of a statue of Prince Albert at Perth, the first erected in the kingdom. On the 25th of January 1865, the depôt joined headquarters from Stirling. It is unnecessary to say that in all its public appearances, and at all inspections while in Scotland, as elsewhere, the Gordon Highlanders received, and that deservedly, the highest encomiums on their appearance, discipline, and conduct.

On the 6th of March 1865, the 92nd, consisting of 1033 officers, men, women, and children, embarked on the Clyde for Portsmouth, en route for Aldershot, arriving at the Camp on the 10th of the same month. While at Aldershot, Major C. M. Hamilton was promoted to Lieutenant-Colonel, and succeeded to the command of the regiment in place of Col. Lockhart, C.B.

The 92nd after remaining a year at Aldershot, during which nothing of note occurred, left for Portsmouth on the 1st of March 1866, and embarked on the same day for Ireland, Lt.-Col. Hamilton commanding. The regiment disembarked at Kingstown on the 5th, and proceeded to the Curragh Camp, where it remained till the 9th, when it removed to Dublin, with the exception of A and C companies, which were left at the Curragh to go through a course of musketry instruction. On the regiment leaving Aldershot, a most gratifying report concerning it was sent to headquarters; the 92nd Highlanders, the Brigade General reported,—

"Are well drilled, their conduct sober, orderly, and soldierlike; discipline good, and all one could desire in a well regulated corps."

During its stay in Ireland the 92nd had a taste of the unpleasant duty of aiding the civil power. On the 31st of December 1867, two detachments were sent out for this purpose from the Curragh Camp, where the whole regiment was then stationed, one, under command of Major A. W. Cameron, to Cork; and the other, under command of Captain A. Forbes Mackay, to Tipperary. These detachments seem to have performed their duty effectively and without the sad necessity of resorting to extreme measures;[1] they did not return to Dublin, the former remaining at Cork and the latter proceeding to that place on the 18th of January 1868. Here these detachments were joined by the rest of the regiment on the 25th of January, on which day it embarked at Queenstown for India, sailing next day under command of Lt.-Col. Hamilton. The regiment proceeded by the overland route, and landed at Bombay Harbour on the 26th of February. Here the 92nd was transhipped into three vessels to be

[1] The regiment had arranged a grand New Year's entertainment, and the unfortunate men of these detachments, who had to march on two hours' notice, had to leave the dinner cooking. They turned out as cheerfully as circumstances would permit, there being just enough of grumbling to have made it very hot work for the Fenians had they showed fight.

taken to Kurrachee, where headquarters arrived on the 8th of March. From Kurrachee this detachment made its way partly by river (the Indus), partly by rail, and partly by road, to Julinder, in the Punjaub, which it reached on the 30th of March, and was joined by the remaining portion of the regiment on the 7th of April. During its stay at Julinder the 92nd furnished detachments regularly to garrison Fort Goviudghur, Umritsur, and had the honour, in February 1870, to take part in the reception at Meean Meer of H.R.H. the Duke of Edinburgh; on this occasion the regiment was commanded by Lt.-Col. M'Bean, who had been promoted to the command of the 92nd in room of Lt.-Col. Hamilton. Detachments, consisting mostly of young and sickly men, were also sent occasionally to Dalhousie to be employed in road-making in the Chumba Hills.

The 92nd remained quartered at Julinder until the 18th of December 1871, on which day headquarters and three companies under command of Major G. H. Parker, proceeded by rail to Delhi to form part of the force collected there at the Camp of Exercise. Here it was posted to the 1st brigade (Col. N. Walker, C.B., 1st Buffs) of the 2nd division commanded by Major-General M'Murdo, C.B. The remaining three companies joined headquarters on the following day. The camp of exercise was broken up on the 1st of February 1872, and in the brigade order issued on the occasion by Col. Walker, he stated that—

"The last six weeks have added to the interest I have for many years taken in the career of my old friends the 92nd Highlanders;"

he also specially mentioned the name of Captain Chalmer of the 92nd, for the valuable services which the latter invariably rendered him.

On the 2nd of February the regiment set out on its march to Chukrata, which it reached on the 2nd of March.

We have much pleasure in referring our readers to the plate of Colonels of the 91st, 92nd, and 93rd regiments, on which we give a portrait of the Marquis of Huntly, who raised the regiment, and was afterwards the last Duke of Gordon, from a painting by A. Robertson, miniature painter to H.R.H. the late Duke of Sussex, and kindly lent us by the Duke of Richmond for our engraving. The portrait was painted in 1806 A.D., and exhibited the same year at the Royal Academy.

The Duke of Gordon's statue stands in Castle Street, Aberdeen, with the inscription "First Colonel 92nd Gordon Highlanders" at the foot of the granite pedestal. His familiar name in his own district was "The Cock of the North."

The 92nd uniform is the full Highland costume of Gordon tartan. The officers have a black worm through their lace, as a token of mourning for Sir John Moore.

SUCCESSION LISTS OF COLONELS AND LIEUTENANT-COLONELS OF THE 92ND GORDON HIGHLANDERS.

COLONELS.

GEORGE, MARQUIS OF HUNTLY,   .   May 3, 1796
Served as Brigadier-General in Ireland in . 1798
Went to Holland, ...   1799
Wounded at Egmont-op-Zee,   .   Oct. 2, 1799
Major-General, ...   Jan. 1, 1801
Colonel of the 42nd,   .   .   .   Jan. 3, 1806
Lieut.-General, ...   April 1808
General, ...   Aug. 1809
To the 1st (Royal Foot),   .   .   .   1820
K.G.C.B., Duke of Gordon,   .   .   .   1827
Governor of Edinburgh Castle and Keeper of
  the Great Seal of Scotland,   .   .   .   1834
Removed to the Scots Fusilier Guards,   .   1834
Died, ...   May 28, 1836
JOHN, EARL OF HOPETOUN, G.C.B.,   Jan. 3, 1806
Cornet Light Dragoons,   .   .   May 28, 1784
Lieutenant in 27th Foot,   .   .   .   1786
Captain 17th Light Dragoons,   .   .   1789
Major in 1st Foot, ...   1792
Lieut.-Col. 25th, ...   1793
M.P. for Linlithgowshire,   .   .   .   1796
Deputy Adjutant-General in Holland,   .   1799
Adjutant-General to the Army in the Medi-
  terranean, ...   1800
Served in Egypt, ...   1801
Colonel of the Lowland Fencible Infantry
  and Major-General, ...   1802
Deputy Governor of Portsmouth,   .   .   1805
Lieut.-General,   .   .   .   April 25, 1808
Commanded under Moore in Spain,   .   1809
Succeeded in command on Moore's death,   ,,
Last on board the fleet at Corunna; K.C.B.,   ,,
Commander-in-Chief in Ireland,   .   .   1813
At Nivelle, Nive, Bayonne,   .   .   .   1813
Baron Niddry and Earl of Hopetoun,   .   .   1814
General, ...   1819

Colonel of the 42nd, ...   1820
Died at Paris, ...   Aug. 27, 1823
SIR JOHN HOPE, G.C.H.,   .   .   Jan. 29, 1820
Cadet in Houston's Brigade,   .   .   .   1778
Ensign, ...   1779
Captain, ...   1782
Captain 60th Foot, ...   1787
Captain 13th Light Dragoons,   .   June 30, 1788
Aide-de-Camp to Sir Wm. Erskine, 1793 and 1794
Major 28th Light Dragoons,   .   .   .   1795
Lieut.-Colonel, ...   1796
Served at the Cape,   .   .   .   1796–1799
To 32nd Foot, ...   1799
In the West Indies,   .   .   .   1800–1804
Assistant Adjutant-General in Scotland,   .   1805
Deputy Adjutant-General to Copenhagen,   .   1807
Brigadier-General to the Staff, N. Britain,   .   1808
And then Deputy Adjutant-General there,   .   1809
Major-General, ...   1810
On the Peninsular Staff,   .   .   .   1812
For Salamanca, a medal.
On the Staff in Ireland and N. Britain till
  1819; made Lieut.-General and G.C.H.,   .   1819
Colonel of the 92nd,   .   .   .   Jan. 29, 1820
To the 72nd Highlanders,   .   .   Sept. 6, 1823
Died, ...   Aug. 1, 1836
HON. SIR ALEXANDER DUFF, G.C.H., Sept. 6, 1823
Removed to the 37th Regiment,   .   July 20, 1831
JOHN, EARL OF STAIR, K.T.,   .   July 20, 1831
Removed to the 46th Regiment,   .   May 31, 1843
SIR WM. M'BEAN, K.C.B.,   .   .   May 31, 1843
SIR JOHN MACDONALD, K.C.B.,   .   June 25, 1855
LORD STRATHNAIRN, G.C.B., G.C.S.I., June 25, 1866
SIR JOHN CAMPBELL,   .   .   .   March 1869
Lieut.-General. Died,   .   .   Dec. 28, 1871
LIEUT.-GENERAL GEORGE STAUNTON, Dec. 29, 1871

LIEUTENANT-COLONELS.

Names.	Date of Appointment.	Date of Removal.	Remarks.
The Marquis of Huntly, Lieut.-Col. Commandant	Feb. 10, 1794	May 3, 1796	Promoted Colonel 92nd, May 3, 1796.
Charles Erskine	May 1, 1795	March 13, 1807	Died of wounds received in action near Alexandria, March 13, 1801.
James Robertson	Oct. 11, 1798	Aug. 3, 1804	Retired on Half-pay.
Alexander Napier	April 5, 1801	Jan. 16, 1809	Killed at Corunna, Jan. 16, 1809.
James Willoughby Gordon	Aug. 4, 1804	June 13, 1808	Quarter-Master General of the Forces, and promoted Lieut.-Col. Commandant of the Royal African Corps.
John Cameron	June 23, 1808	June 16, 1815	Killed at Quatre Bras.
John Lamont	Mar. 30, 1809	Dec. 25, 1814	Retired on Half-pay.
James Mitchell	June 13, 1815	Sept. 1, 1819	Retired.
Sir Frederick Stovin	Sept. 2, 1819	Aug. 8, 1821	Removed to the 90th Foot.
William Brydges Neynoe	Aug. 9, 1821	Oct. 3, 1821	Exchanged to H. P. of the 4th Foot.
David Williamson	Oct. 4, 1821	Nov. 20, 1828	Retired.
John Macdonald	Nov. 21, 1828	Nov. 8, 1846	Promoted Major-General, Nov. 9, 1846.
John Alex. Forbes	Nov. 9, 1846	Nov. 22, 1849	Retired.
Mark Kerr Atherley	Nov. 23, 1849	Sept. 25, 1855	
Geo. Edward Thorold	Sept. 25, 1855	Nov. 16, 1856	Retired on Half-pay; 42nd, July 23, 1857; retired on full-pay, March 16, 1858. See 42nd R. H.
Archibald Inglis Lockhart	Dec. 26, 1857	March 1865	Retired.
E. E. Haines	Mar. 4, 1865	Sept. 1, 1865	Retired.
Christian Monteith Hamilton	Sept. 1, 1865	Dec. 14, 1865	Retired.
Forbes M'Bean	Dec. 15, 1869	Dec. 23, 1873	Retired.
Arthur Wellington Cameron	Dec. 24, 1873		

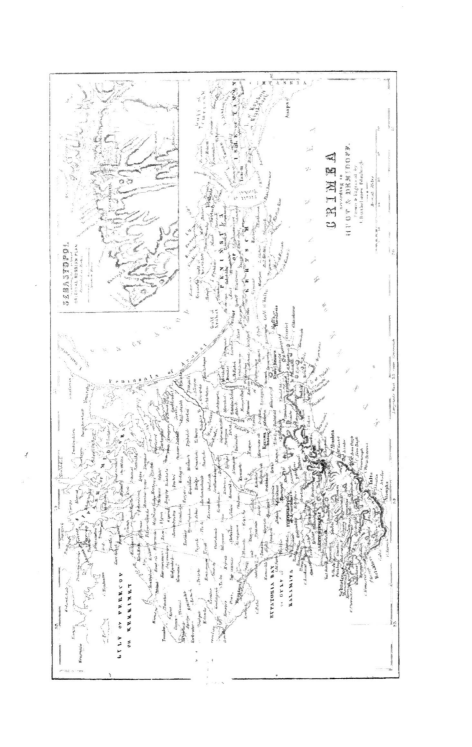

CRIMEA

according to
HUOT & DEMIDOFF,
General English Map
by
J. Bartholomew, Edinburgh.

THE 93RD SUTHERLAND HIGHLANDERS.

I.

1800–1854.

Curious method of raising the regiment—Character of the men—Guernsey—Ireland—Cape of Good Hope—Battle of Blauw-berg—High character of the regiment—A regimental church formed—Its benevolence — England — America — New Orleans — Dreadful carnage—Ireland—West Indies—Canterbury—Presentation of New Colours by the Duke of Wellington—Weedon—The northern district—Ireland—Canada—Stirling—Edinburgh—Glasgow—Aberdeen—Portsmouth—Chobham—Devonport—War with Russia.

CAPE OF GOOD HOPE.   BALAKLAVA.
ALMA.   SEVASTOPOL.
LUCKNOW.

THIS, perhaps the most Highland of the Highland regiments, was raised in the year 1800, letters of service having been granted for that purpose to Major-General Wemyss of Wemyss,[1] who had previously raised the Sutherland Fencibles, many of the men from which joined the new regiment. The strength at first fixed upon was 600 men, which number was in a short time raised, 460 being obtained from Sutherland, and the remainder from Ross shire and the adjoining counties. The regiment was however, soon augmented to 1000 men, with officers in proportion; and in 1811 it numbered 1049 officers and men, of whom 1014

[1] His portrait will be found on the Plate of Colonels of the 91st, 92nd, and 93rd regiments.

II.

were Highlanders and Lowlanders, 17 Irish. and 18 English.

One striking peculiarity in the constitution of the 93rd consists in its having probably furnished the last instance of the exercise of the clan influence on a large scale in the Highlands. The original levy was completed not by the ordinary modes of recruiting, but by a process of conscription. A census having been made of the disposable population on the extensive estates of the Countess of Sutherland, her agents lost no time in requesting a certain proportion of the able-bodied sons of the numerous tenantry to join the ranks of the Sutherland regiment, as a test at once of duty to their chief and their sovereign. The appeal was well responded to; and though there was a little grumbling among the parents, the young men themselves seem never to have questioned the right thus assumed over their military services by their chief. In a very few months the regiment was completed to its establishment.

As a crucial proof of the high character of the first levy for the 93rd it may be stated, that until the final inspection of the corps the recruits were never collected together. They were freely permitted, after enrolling their names, to pursue their callings at home, until it was announced in the various parish churches that their presence was required, when a body of 600 men was assembled, and marched, without a single absentee, to Inverness, where the regiment was inspected by Major-General Leith Hay in August 1800.

During the sojourn of the regiment at Inverness there was no place of confinement in connection with it, nor were any guards mounted, the usual precautions necessary with soldiers being quite inapplicable to the high-principled, self-respecting men of Sutherland. Many of the non-commissioned officers and men were the children of respectable farmers, and almost all of them of reputable parentage, the officers being mostly well-known gentlemen connected with Ross and Sutherland. Indeed, the regiment might be regarded as one large family, and a healthy rivalry, and stimulus to the best behaviour was introduced by classifying the different companies according to parishes. While the characteristics referred to seem to have strongly marked the Sutherland Highlanders,

5 F

our readers will have seen that to a greater or less degree they belonged to the original levies of all the Highland regiments.

In Sept. 1800 the 93rd embarked at Fort George for Guernsey, where it was for the first time armed and fully equipped, and where it made rapid progress in military training.[2]

In February 1803 the 93rd was removed to Ireland, where it continued till July 1805. While in Dublin, like most of the other Highland regiments at one time or another in Ireland, it had to assist in quelling an attempted insurrection, performing the disagreeable duty kindly, but firmly and effectually.

In July 1805 the 93rd joined the armament against the Cape of Good Hope, under Major-General Sir David Baird, referred to already in connection with the 71st and 72nd, which took part in the expedition.

The expedition sailed early in August, and, after a boisterous voyage, arrived and anchored in Table Bay on Jan. 4th, 1806. The troops formed two brigades, one of which, consisting of the 24th, 38th, and 83rd regiments, was under the command of Brigadier-General Beresford; the other, called the Highland brigade, comprehending the 71st, 72nd, and 93rd regiments, was commanded by Brigadier-General Ronald C. Ferguson. On the 5th, General Beresford, who had been detached to Saldanha Bay, in consequence of the violence of the surf in Table Bay, effected a landing there without opposition; and on the 6th the Highland brigade landed in Lospard Bay, after a slight resistance from a small body of light troops stationed on the adjoining heights. In landing, 35 men of the 93rd were drowned by the upsetting of a boat in the surf. and Lt.-Colonel Pack of the 71st, and a few men, were wounded.

Having landed his stores on the 7th, General

---

[2] At Guernsey, on May 6, 1802, died at the age of 40, Sergeant Sam. M'Donald, well known at the time by the appellation of "Big Sam." He served in the American War, was afterwards fugleman to the Royals, and subsequently lodge porter at Carlton House. In 1793 he was appointed sergeant in the Sutherland Fencibles, joining the 93rd when it was raised. He measured 6 ft. 10 in. in height, 4 feet round the chest, was strongly built, muscular, and well-proportioned. His strength was prodigious, but he was never known to abuse it. His tomb was restored by the non-commissioned officers of the 79th Cameron Highlanders in 1820, and in 1870 by the officers of the 93rd.

Baird moved forward the following day, and ascending the summit of the Blauw-Berg (Blue Mountain), he found the enemy, to the number of about 5000 men. drawn up in two lines on a plain, with twenty-three pieces of cannon. Forming his troops quickly in two columns, he thereupon directed Lt.-Colonel Joseph Baird, who commanded the first brigade, to move with that brigade towards the right, while the Highland brigade, which was thrown forward upon the high road, advanced against the enemy. Apparently resolved to retain their position, the enemy opened a heavy fire of grape, round shot, and musketry, which was kept up warmly as the British approached, till General Ferguson gave the word to charge. This order was obeyed with the accustomed alacrity of the Highlanders, who rushed upon the enemy with such impetuosity as at once to strike them with terror. After discharging the last volley without aim or effect, the enemy turned and fled in great confusion, leaving upwards of 600 men killed and wounded. The loss of the British was only 16 men killed and 191 wounded. The 93rd had only 2 soldiers killed, and Lt.-Col. Honyman, Lts. Scobie and Strachan, Ensigns Hedderick and Craig, 1 sergeant, 1 drummer, and 51 rank and file wounded. After this victory the colony surrendered.

The Sutherland Highlanders remained in garrison at the Cape till 1814, when they embarked for England. During this long period nothing occurred to vary the quiet and regular life of the regiment. This life was, indeed, remarkably regular, even for a Scottish regiment, and, we fear, would find no parallel in any corps of the present time. The men, who were mostly actuated by genuine religious principle, such principle as is the result of being brought up in a pious Scottish family, conducted themselves in so sedate and orderly a fashion, that during their stay at the Cape severe punishments in their case were unnecessary, and so rare was the commission of crime, that twelve and even fifteen months have been known to elapse without a single court-martial being assembled for the trial of any soldier of the 93rd. Moreover, as an emphatic compliment to the steadiness of the men, their presence was generally dispensed with when the other troops of the garrison were commanded to witness the infliction of corporal punishment.

But the most remarkable proof of the intensity and genuineness of the religious feeling in the regiment, as well as of its love of all that was peculiar to their native land, remains to be told. There being no divine service in the garrison except the customary one of reading prayers to the troops on parade, these Sutherland men, in addition to their stated meetings for reading the Bible and for prayer, in 1808 formed a church among themselves, appointed elders and other office-bearers, engaged and paid a stipend to a minister of the Church of Scotland, and had divine service regularly performed according to the forms of the Presbyterian Church. As a memorial of this institution there still remains in possession of the sergeants' mess the plate used in the communion service, and until recently there existed among the regimental records the regulations intended for the government of its members. This establishment had an excellent effect, not only on its immediate members, who numbered several hundreds, but also upon those who made no pretence of being guided by religious principle.

Such men were not likely to forget the claims of relationship and benevolence, and indeed such was their frugality, that in addition to their contributing to the support of their minister and to the charitable funds formed in the regiment, the men were in the habit of lodging in a trusted officer's hands savings amounting to from £5 to £50, until an opportunity occurred of forwarding the money to their relatives at home; upon one occasion, in particular, £500 were remitted to Sutherland, exclusive of many minor sums sent home through the post-office.

In the month of April 1814, the 93rd embarked for Europe, amid, as may easily be believed, the general regret of the colony; it landed at Plymouth on August 15th of the same year. Of the 1018 non-commissioned officers and men who disembarked, 977 were Scotch.

The regiment had not been many weeks at home when it was again ordered on foreign service, this time, alas, of a much more disastrous kind than that which it performed during its long stay at the Cape. Although it had not the good fortune to take part in the stormy events which were shortly to take place on the field of Europe, and share in the glory accruing therefrom, yet the work it was called upon to perform, so far as bravery, endurance, and suffering are concerned, deserved as great a meed of praise as if it had been performed on the field of Quatre Bras or Waterloo.

Early in September 1814,[2] the 93rd had received orders to hold itself in readiness for immediate embarkation, and on the 16th it embarked in three divisions as part of the armament under Major-General Sir John Keane, destined to operate in North America; for at this time, unfortunately, Britain was at war with the United States. The fleet sailed on the 18th, and on November 23rd, joined, at Jamaica, the squadron under Vice-Admiral the Honourable Alexander Cochrane.

The united forces, the command of which was now assumed by General Keane, amounted to 5400 men. With this force he sailed from Jamaica on the 27th of November, and on December 13th landed near Cat Island, at the entrance of a chain of lakes leading to New Orleans. On the 23rd the troops landed without opposition at the head of the Bayonne; but were attacked on the following night by a large body of infantry, supported by a strong corps of artillery. After a spirited contest the enemy were repulsed with loss. On the 27th, Major-General the Honourable Sir Edward Pakenham, who had arrived and assumed the command of the army on the 25th, moved the troops forward in two columns, and took up a position within six miles of New Orleans, in front of the enemy's lines. The position of the Americans was particularly favourable, having a morass and a thick wood on their left, the Mississippi on their right, and a deep and broad ditch in front, bounded by a parapet and breast-works, extending in a direct line about a thousand yards, and mounted

---

[2] In 1813 a second battalion was added to the regiment. It was formed at Inverness, and after some instructions in discipline, was destined to join the army under the Duke of Wellington in France; but owing to the peace of 1814 this destination was changed to North America. This battalion was embarked, and landed in Newfoundland, where it was stationed sixteen months, and then returning to Europe in 1815, was reduced soon after landing.

with artillery, and a flanking battery on the right bank of the river.

For several hours on the 28th, the force was kept in front of these works, under insufficient shelter, and, allowed neither to advance nor retire, suffered considerable loss from the storm of shot and shell poured upon it; the 93rd lost 3 men killed and several were wounded. On the three following days, the 93rd, as did every other corps, lost several men in their encampment, from the guns of the enemy, which were placed in battery on the right bank of the Mississippi. We shall give the rest of this narrative in the words of the well-kept Record-Book of the regiment, which, we believe, quotes from the journal kept by Captain Charles Gordon, one of the early officers of the 93rd.

On the 1st of January 1815, long before daybreak, the army was in motion, and placed in position similar, but closer to the American lines than on the 28th of December. Forming in close column of regiments, the troops were ordered to lie down and wait for the favourable issue of the British batteries against the enemy's works, the former opening with a brisk fire at daylight, but unfortunately all in vain. After a cannonade of several hours, the greater part of the guns were silenced and dismounted, and after a harassing day, the army was ordered to retire to its former bivouac. The 93rd lost 1 subaltern, 1 sergeant, and 6 rank and file killed, and several wounded.

Nothing was done for the next few days, though the army underwent great fatigue in the carriage of guns, stores, &c., and were continually annoyed by the batteries of the enemy on the opposite side of the Mississippi. On the afternoon of the 7th, the army had its hopes again raised by the orders issued for a general attack on the following morning, but, in the words of Captain Gordon, "as this expedition commenced, so did it terminate, in disappointment—utter disappointment and calamity."

On the 8th of January the main body of the 93rd, flushed with the hope of measuring bayonets with their hitherto concealed opponents, advanced in compact close column towards the centre of the American lines, from which poured a tremendous fire of grape and musketry (including buckshot); but its patience and discipline were again put to the test when within about 80 yards of the enemy's breastworks, by an order to halt. In this unenviable position, without permission or even power to fire with any effect whatever, with nothing visible but the murderous muzzles of thousands of American rifles, only the tops of the men's caps being seen as they loaded and fired resting upon their parapets, a staff-officer was heard to exclaim as he hurriedly came up and rode away,—"93rd, have a little patience and you shall have your revenge." But, alas! it was decreed otherwise; the regiment continued in its fatal position without receiving any further orders, officers and men being mowed down in all directions, until Sir John Lambert, the senior surviving general officer, thought it advisable to order the army to retire. In this most disastrous affair, action it could not well be termed, the regiment was dreadfully cut up.

The following is a list of the killed and wounded in this sadly mismanaged affair, in which the gallant 93rd probably lost more officers and men in a few hours than it did throughout the whole of the Indian Mutiny campaign, in which, as will be seen, it had perhaps hotter work to do than ever fell to the lot of any single regiment. The killed were Lt.-Col. Dale, commanding the 93rd, Captains Hitchins and Muirhead, Lieutenants Munro and Phaup (both prisoners, who died of their wounds), Volunteer Johnston, 4 sergeants, 1 drummer, and 115 rank and file, including those who died next day of their wounds. There were wounded, Captains Ryan, Boulger, M'Kenzie, and Ellis; Lieuts. John M'Donald, Gordon, Hay, Graves, M'Lean, Spark, and D. M'Pherson, Volunteer John Wilson, 17 sergeants, 3 drummers, and 348 rank and file. It is sad to think that neither gain nor glory resulted from this dreadful carnage.

The army having re-embarked, the fleet weighed anchor again on the 7th of February, and made for the mouth of the Bay of Mobile, where the greater part of the army disembarked on the Dauphin Isle. Preparations were here being made to attack the fortified town of Mobile, when news arrived that preliminaries of peace had been signed between Great Britain and the United States. After being encamped about six weeks, the army was ordered to embark for Europe. The 93rd, at least the fragment left of it, arrived at Spithead on the 15th of May 1815, and being in too weak a state to take part in the stirring events taking place on the Continent, it was ordered to Ireland, disembarking at Cork on the 28th of May, and proceeding to Birr Barracks.

The second battalion having been disbanded at Sunderland, the ranks of the first battalion were filled up by a large draft of non-commissioned officers and privates from the former. As the history of the regiment is comparatively uneventful up to the time of the Crimean War and Indian Mutiny, we shall rapidly run over its movements previous to these stirring periods.

The 93rd appears to have moved about successively from Birr to Athlone, Nenagh, and Limerick, sending out numerous detachments, and in June 1818, to have proceeded to Dublin, where it remained till the following

May (1819). On leaving Dublin, it was again detached to the southern counties, where it was frequently called upon to perform the most delicate and harassing duties.

Between the 3rd and 8th of November 1823, the regiment embarked at the Cove of Cork in four transports for the West Indies, without having lost a single man by desertion. It may be taken as a proof of the continued good conduct of the regiment during the eight years it was stationed in Ireland, that Lieutenant-General Lord Combermere, in his general order issued on its departure, stated that

"No regiment in the service stands in greater estimation, or has been more conspicuous for its discipline and soldier-like conduct, than the 93rd."

Only one detachment proceeded to Demerara, the others being landed at Barbados in December 1823; the former, however, shortly afterwards joined the latter. The regiment remained in garrison at Barbados till the month of February 1826, when it was removed to Antigua and St Christopher, sending a detachment from the former island to Montserrat. These stations the 93rd occupied till February 1830, when it was removed to St Lucia and Dominica, where it remained till January 1832, when all the service companies were again collected together at Barbados, where they were stationed for upwards of two years longer. After having spent ten and a half years in the Windward and Leeward Island, the regiment embarked for England in two detachments on the 26th of March and the 3rd of April 1834, leaving behind it 117 of its men as volunteers to other regiments. On its arrival at Spithead on the 6th of May, the strength of the regiment was only 371, having been thus reduced by death, the discharge of invalids, and volunteers to other corps. The proportions of deaths in the regiment, however, while stationed in the West Indies, was considerably below that of other regiments.

It was originally intended that the regiment should proceed at once to Scotland, where it had not been quartered since its first formation; but on account of the serious demonstrations that were made by the populace in London about the period of the regiment's return to England, it was deemed expedient to draw as many troops as possible around the capital. The 93rd was consequently sent to Canterbury, where it arrived on the 8th of May 1834, and where it was shortly afterwards joined by the depôt companies from Scotland.

During the stay of the Sutherland Highlanders in Canterbury, the most notable incident in its history was the presentation of new colours to the regiment by his Grace the Duke of Wellington, an event which seems even now to be looked back upon as marking a red-letter day in the calendar of the 93rd. The presentation took place on the 7th of October 1834, and immense preparations were made for the ceremony. The day fortunately turned out particularly favourable, and not fewer than 10,000 persons must have turned out to witness the presentation, including many of the nobility and gentry of the county. We regret that space forbids us entering into details, or giving at length the wise and stirring address of the "Great Duke." Suffice it to say, that after referring to the past achievements of the 93rd, and of the soldier-like appearance and orderly conduct of individuals of the regiment who had attracted his attention in passing through the town, he urged upon officers and men, as the result of his long and valuable experience, the inestimable value of discipline in maintaining the efficiency of a regiment, without which no amount of personal valour would be of avail.

"I have passed," the Duke said, "the best years of my life in the barracks and the camps of the troops. The necessities of the service and my duty have compelled me to study the dispositions and the wants of the soldiers, and to provide for them. And again I repeat to you, enforce the observance of the rules of discipline, subordination, and good order, if you mean to be efficient, to render service to the public, to be respectable in the eyes of the military world as a military body, to be respected by the community, to be comfortable and happy among yourselves, and, above all, if you mean to defend to the last your colours which I have presented to you, the person of your sovereign, and the institutions, dominions, and rights of your country, and to promote its glory (as your predecessors have in this same regiment), by your actions."

Lt.-Col. M'Gregor having replied in feeling and most appropriate terms, the regiment performed several evolutions before the Duke, who expressed his approbation of the soldier-like appearance of the men, and of their steadiness under arms. The rest of the day, both by officers and men, was given up to festivity and rejoicing. The officers entertained the Duke and upwards of 200 guests at a magnificent banquet in the mess-room, which had been ingeniously enlarged for the occasion. On the opposite side of the barrack-yard tables were laid for nearly 700, including the non-commissioned officers, privates, their wives and children, who enjoyed an excellent dinner of roast beef and plum-pudding, with an allowance of beer, given by the amiable and benevolent lady of Col. M'Gregor. It was altogether a proud day for the Sutherland High-

Lieutenant-Colonel (now General) Sir Duncan M'Gregor, K.C.B.
From a painting in possession of the 93rd.

landers. The whole terminated with the greatest good humour and conviviality. The soldiers continued to enjoy themselves to a late hour, dancing their native dances to their national music.

A few days after this memorable occasion, the regiment left Canterbury for Weedon, in Northamptonshire, where it was stationed till the spring of the following year (1835), detaching three companies to Newcastle-under-Lyme. In the end of May 1835, the 93rd left Weedon for the northern district of England, head-

quarters being stationed at Blackburn, and detachments at Bolton, Rochdale, Burnley, and Nottingham. In the following September headquarters was removed to Liverpool, and the other companies to Haydock Lodge, Wigan, and Chester Castle. The whole regiment was collected at Liverpool in October, on the 27th and 29th of which month it embarked in two detachments for Dublin. Here the 93rd remained till October 1836, when it was removed to Newry; after being stationed at which town for upwards of a year, it was removed, in the end of November and beginning of December 1837, to Cork, preparatory to its embarkation for Canada, to quell the serious insurrection which was threatening the British power in that colony.

The 93rd in two divisions, under Lt.-Col. M'Gregor and Major Arthur, sailed from Cork on the 6th and 23d of January 1838 respectively. The division under Major Arthur reached Halifax on the 29th of January; but that under Lt.-Col. M'Gregor met with so boisterous a passage, that it did not reach its destination till the 5th of March. On the following day the two divisions were reunited at Halifax. It is unnecessary to follow the various and complicated movements of the regiment during the suppression of the Canadian rebellion, more especially as it never had a chance of coming into contact with the rebels, except at Prescott, on the 16th of November 1838, when it was present at the attack and capture of the brigands in the Windmill, in which affair it suffered no casualties. The 93rd, in the performance of its duties at this period, was often much divided, and frequently had to endure great hardships in its movements about the country. No. 4 company was, throughout the whole rebellion, in the Lower Provinces, attached to the 71st Highland Light Infantry.

The regiment was re-united at Toronto on the 28th of November, and the women, children, and baggage arrived on the 13th of December, just before the closing of the navigation. On the 4th of the latter month Lt.-Col. Spark arrived at Toronto, and assumed the command of the regiment, in succession to Lt.-Col. M'Gregor.

The 93d remained at Toronto till the 17th of June 1843, with the exception of one year —from May 1840 till May 1841—when it was stationed at Drummondsville, Falls of Niagara. It is scarcely necessary to say that, during this time, as always indeed, the Sutherland Highlanders received the unqualified approbation of the officers whose duty it was to inspect it.

"This fine regiment still continues," to use the words of an order issuing from the Horse Guards, in December 1842, "to maintain its character for comparative sobriety and good order amidst the dissipation with which it appears to be surrounded; and that it is as remarkable for its splendid appearance in the field, and the correctness of its evolutions, as for the quiet and orderly habits of its men in their quarters."

On leaving Toronto, in May 1845, the 93rd went to Montreal, a wing which was sent to Kingston in the previous June joining headquarters there. On this wing leaving Canada West, Major-General Sir Richard Armstrong issued an order, in which he spoke of the appearance ("superb," he called it) and conduct of the regiment in the highest possible terms.

The 93rd continued for other four years in Canada, leaving Montreal in July 1846—the same month that the regiment received its first supply of percussion muskets—for Quebec, where it remained till August 1, 1848, when it embarked for home, after an absence of more than ten years. On the arrival of the "Resistance" at Portsmouth, it was ordered to proceed to Leith, where it arrived on the 30th of August. The regiment disembarked next day, and proceeded to Stirling Castle, where, in a few weeks, it was joined by the depôt companies. During its stay at Stirling detachments were sent to Perth and Dundee, and the regiment was twice selected to furnish a guard of honour for her Majesty the Queen,— in the summer of 1849, during her stay at Balmoral, and in August of the same year, when Her Majesty paid a visit to Glasgow.

The 93rd remained at Stirling till April 5, 1850, when it was removed to Edinburgh, where it was stationed for only one year, during which it again furnished a guard of honour to Ballater, as well as to Holy-

rood, during her Majesty's stay at that historical palace. From Edinburgh the regiment went to Glasgow, on the 15th of April 1851, and on the 23rd of the following February removed to Weedon. The 93rd remained at Weedon for only six months, proceeding, on the 11th of August and two following days, to Portsmouth, where it occupied the Anglesea Barracks. After a stay at Portsmouth of about ten months, the 93rd, on June 14, 1853, proceeded to Chobham Common, to form part of a force which was encamped there under the command of General Lord Seaton, C.B., for the purpose of manœuvring. On leaving Cobham, on July 15, the regiment proceeded to Devonport, part of it being stationed at Dartmoor Prison, and another part at Millbay, Plymouth.

We should mention here that, on Nov. 30, 1852, died Lt.-General William Wemyss, who for two years had been colonel of the regiment, and who from infancy had been associated with it, his father having been Major-General Wemyss, who raised the Sutherland Highlanders. Lt.-General Wemyss had all along taken an intense interest in the regiment, in which he had been almost born. He was succeeded in the colonelcy by Major-General Edward Parkinson, C.B.

Once more had the war-trumpet sounded, calling the nations of Europe to take sides and do battle with each other, after a long, long rest. The Sutherland Highlanders were destined to have their own share in the struggle, being one of the first Highland regiments selected to meet the Russians in the East. In connection with the 42nd and 79th, the other two regiments of the famous Highland Brigade, we have given some general details of the movements of the army in the East, and especially in the Crimea, that we shall confine ourselves here strictly to the work of the 93rd, more especially so as, before it could again lay down its arms and take breath, it had harder, if not bloodier, work to perform than has fallen to its lot since it was first embodied. In the Indian mutiny the Sutherland Highlanders had a magnificent opportunity (perhaps their first real one) of showing what sort of stuff they were made of. How gloriously they came out of their trial will be seen in the sequel.

II.

1854–1857.

Embarks for the East—Gallipoli—Scutari—Varna—Sickness and cholera—Crimea—Battle of the Alma—Sebastopol—Balaklava—Battle of Balaclava—The "Thin Red Streak"—Heavy duties—Discomforts—Terrible hurricane—Disease—Kertch—First assault on Sebastopol—Second assault—Evacuation of Sebastopol—Exploit of Lt. M'Bean—Return home—Aldershot—Visited by the Queen—Dover—Presentation of Colours by H.R.H. the Duke of Cambridge—Embarkation for China—Destination changed for India—The Indian Mutiny—Lands at Calcutta.

On the 12th of February 1854, orders were received to prepare for embarkation on active service; and as the establishment of the regiment was on the peace footing, it received 170 volunteers from the 42nd and 79th, including a few men from the dépôt battalion. On the 27th of February, when the regiment embarked at Plymouth, it consisted of 1 lieut.-colonel (Ainslie), 2 majors, 8 captains, 9 lieutenants, 7 ensigns, and 6 staff officers, 41 sergeants, 20 drummers, and 850 rank and file. After it had been in the East for a few months, this establishment was considerably increased. After staying at Malta for a few weeks, the regiment, on the 6th of April, sailed for Gallipoli, where it encamped, and where it had the first taste of official mismanagement in the shape of miserably inadequate rations. The 93rd stayed at Gallipoli, part of the time engaged in throwing up entrenchments, till May 6th, when it was removed to Scutari, where it had the misfortune to lose Lieut. M'Nish, who was drowned in a swollen stream.

After a few weeks' stay at Scutari, the 93rd was sent, on the 13th of June, to Varna, in the neighbourhood of which it remained till it embarked for the Crimea, along with the rest of the allied army, and where, in common with many other regiments, it suffered severely from sickness, cholera here first making its appearance. From this cause the regiment lost, while at Varna, 21 men and 1 officer (Lieut. Turner). From this and other causes, a general depression of spirits prevailed in the brigade; for the 93rd had been joined by the 42nd and 79th. This temporary feeling, however, rapidly disappeared when it became certainly known, towards the end of August, that active operations were about to take place in the Crimea.

When, on the 31st of August, the 93rd was transferred to the transports in which it was to be taken to the Crimea, it numbered 792 officers and men; 102 non-commissioned officers and men, and 20 soldiers' wives being left behind at Varna, with most of the baggage, under Ensign M°Bean. The landing of the armies at Old Fort, Kalamita Bay, has been already described in connection with the 42nd,[1] as well as what happened until the allied army came face to face with the Russians entrenched on the left bank of the Alma.

We should mention here, that at the time of landing in the Crimea the general health of the regiment was much impaired by the sickness and exposure it had been subjected to while in Bulgaria: on the passage to the Crimea it lost several men from cholera. Its first night in the Crimea gave the 93rd a taste of the hardships and privations which it, like other British regiments, was destined to undergo. It passed the night, a very tempestuous and wet one, without shelter of any kind.

On the 19th of Sept. the allied armies commenced their march towards Sebastopol, over an undulating plain, the English being on the left, the post of danger, as Kinglake so forcibly points out, the French in the centre, and the Turks on the right, close to the sea. As our readers know, the 93rd, along with the 42nd and 79th, formed the Highland brigade, under Sir Colin Campbell, which, with the Guards, constituted the First Division under H.R.H. the Duke of Cambridge. After bivouacking near the small stream Boolganak, where the first brush with the enemy occurred, the 93rd, with the rest of the army, advanced, about mid-day on the 20th, towards the river Alma, on the left bank of which the Russians had already been descried, entrenched on formidable-looking and strongly-fortified heights. On coming to within a short distance of the river, the English army deployed into line successively of divisions. The First Division thus became the second line, the Light Division forming the first. The Highland brigade formed the extreme left of the allied army, and was thus opposed to the Russian right, the

[1] Vol. ii. p. 410.

93rd being in the centre of the brigade, having the 42nd on the right, and the 79th on the left. Full general details of the advance will be found in the history of the 42nd,[2] and here we shall confine ourselves to the work of the 93rd.

The battle commenced about half-past one P.M. After the Light and Second Divisions had crossed the river, the First Division advanced, the Guards in front, and the three Highland regiments on the left in échelon. The latter, after advancing a short distance under heavy fire, were ordered to lie down in rear of the wall of a vineyard. After remaining there for a few minutes, the order to advance was again given, and was promptly complied with, the Highland regiments, led by their brigadier, the gallant and much-beloved Sir Colin Campbell, pushing through a vineyard into and across the river, the water in many places coming up to the men's waists. After a momentary delay in reforming, the three regiments advanced up the hill, in échelon, the 42nd leading on the right, the 93rd close behind on the left. The hill was steep, and the fire from the battery in front of the enemy's battalions very severe. Yet the Highlanders continued to advance for nearly a mile without firing a shot, though numerous gaps in their ranks showed that that of the enemy was doing its work. A short distance above the river, the 93rd passed the 77th regiment, part of the Light Division, halted in line, and thus found itself immediately opposed to the enemy. Having nearly gained the summit of the heights, the regiment opened a brisk fire upon the battalions immediately in its front, accompanied by a hearty Highland cheer as it still advanced. After a hesitating delay of a few minutes the enemy fell back, and commenced their retreat in great confusion, suffering fearfully from the destructive volleys of the newly-tried Minié. The command was then given to halt, a brisk fire being kept up until the enemy had fled out of range; and in less than an hour from this time no vestige of the Russian army remained in sight but the dead and wounded.

The 93rd in this battle lost 1 officer (Lieut. Abercromby), 1 sergeant, and 4 rank and file killed; 2 sergeants and 40 rank and file wounded.

[2] Vol. ii. p. 412.

After a halt to bury the dead and look after the wounded, the army continued its march in the direction of Sebastopol, reaching Balaklava on the 26th, where it bivouacked for the night. The 93rd was at first posted before the village of Kadikoi, at the entrance of the gorge leading to Balaklava, partly to protect the position, but principally for the purpose of being employed in fatigue duty. It was only on the 3rd of Oct. that a few tents, barely sufficient to hold the half of the men, were issued to the regiment. On the 6th of the same month the 93rd had to deplore the loss from cholera of Major Robert Murray Banner, an officer universally beloved and respected.

On the 13th of October a large force of the enemy having concentrated in the valleys of Baidar and the Tchernaya, and threatening Balaklava, Sir Colin Campbell was sent down by Lord Raglan to assume command of the troops in Balaklava. He immediately ordered a force of 331 officers and men of the 93rd, under Major Charles Henry Gordon, to proceed to the heights eastward of Balaklava to assist in intrenching and strengthening the position there already occupied by the marines. Below these heights, eastward of Balaklava, and on the western heights, a number of intrenched batteries had been raised, to command the approaches to Balaklava. Each of these was manned by a force of about 250 Turks, and they formed a sort of semicircle, being numbered from the eastward from No. 1 to 6.

About 7 o'clock on the morning of Oct. 25th, a large force of the enemy debouched from the direction of the Tchernaya and Baidar valleys, and attacked the Turkish redoubts with a large body of skirmishers and artillery. The British force, which had been under arms since before daylight, consisted of about 800 marines on the heights, with the detachment of the 93rd under Major Gordon. The main body of the regiment under Lt.-Col. Ainslie, was drawn up in line on a small hill in front of its encampment, covering the approach to Balaklava from the plain, having some Turkish regiments on the right and left; and on the left front the brigades of light and heavy cavalry were drawn up in columns. The action commenced by the Russians concentrating a severe fire of artillery upon No. 1, the eastward redoubt, from which, after a short resistance, the Turks were dislodged, and the redoubt, containing three guns, was captured by the enemy. In obedience to an order previously received in case of such a casualty, Major Gordon with his detachment at once proceeded to join Lt.-Col. Ainslie in the plain, a distance of about two miles. The capture of No. 1 redoubt was speedily followed by that of Nos. 2 and 3, when the Russians commenced a severe fire upon the flying Turks. The 93rd, now joined by the detachment from the heights, was directed to advance, covered by the light company, and throwing forward the left. The enemy then opened upon the regiment with round shot and shell from the redoubts from which they had driven the Turks. This caused some casualties, and the 93rd was ordered by Sir Colin Campbell—who at the moment may be said to have commanded in person—to retire under cover of a small rising ground immediately in the rear, where the regiment remained for a short time lying down under a fire of artillery, till a large body of cavalry appeared on the opposite side of the plain, about 1000 yards in front. The order was then given to the regiment, which was in line, to advance a short distance to the summit of the rising ground in front, and to commence firing upon the cavalry, which were bearing down upon it at a rapidly increasing gallop. To quote the words of Dr Russell, the well-known *Times'* correspondent, who witnessed the action :—

"The Russians in one grand line charged in towards Balaklava. The ground flies beneath their horses' feet; gathering speed at every stride, they dash on towards that thin red streak tipped with a line of steel. The Turks fire a volley at 800 yards and miss; as the Russians came within 600 yards, down goes that line of steel in front, and out rings a volley of Minie musketry. The distance is too great, the Russians are not checked, but still sweep onwards through the smoke with the whole force of horse and man, here and there knocked over by the shot of our batteries alone. With breathless suspense every one awaits the bursting of the wave upon the line of Gaelic rock; but ere they came within 200 yards, another deadly volley flashes from the levelled rifle, and carries terror into the Russians. They wheel about, open files right and left, and fly back faster than they came. 'Brave Highlanders! Well done,' about the spectators. But events thicken, the Highlanders and their splendid front are soon forgotten. Men scarcely have a moment to think of this fact, that the 93rd never altered their formation to receive that tide of horsemen. 'No,' said Sir Colin Campbell, 'I did not think it worth while to form them even four deep.' The ordinary British line, two deep, was quite sufficient to repel the attack of these Muscovite cavaliers."

Another attack by the Russians was gallantly repulsed by the heavy cavalry, and about 10 o'clock A.M. the Guards, along with the 42nd and 79th Highlanders, came up under H.R.H. the Duke of Cambridge. It was about this time that the heroic but disastrous charge of the light cavalry under Lord Cardigan took place, after which the First and Fourth Divisions advanced, the enemy retiring and concentrating on Nos. 1 and 3 redoubts. At nightfall the First and Fourth Divisions returned to their position before Sebastopol, the 42nd and 79th remaining behind at Balaklava. In this engagement the 93rd had only 2 privates wounded. The Russian force was estimated at about 18 battalions of infantry, with from 30 to 40 guns, and a large body of cavalry.

Sir Colin Campbell in his despatch drew Lord Raglan's special attention to the gallantry and eagerness of the 93rd under Lt.-Col. Ainslie, and Lord Raglan in his despatch to the Duke of Newcastle spoke in high terms of the conduct of "that distinguished regiment."

After this the 93rd, along with the rest of the Highland brigade, had heavy duties to perform in intrenching the position at Balaklava; and now that the weather began to break, and the clothes of the men were in tatters, and the accommodation afforded by the tents miserably insufficient, their condition was wretched indeed. The climax came on the 14th of Nov., when the ever-memorable hurricane swept almost every kind of shelter off the face of the ground, and tore the tents to rags, leaving the poor soldiers completely exposed to its violence. All this, combined with the wretched and insufficient food, soon told sadly on the health of the soldiers. It was only in the spring of 1855 that anything was done to remedy this state of matters. With the erection of huts, and the arrival of good weather, the health of the regiment began to improve. Meantime, from Oct. 1854 to March 1855, nearly the whole regiment must have, at one time or other, been on the sick list, and nearly 100 died from disease. Among the latter was Lt. Kirby, who arrived in the Crimea on Dec. 2nd, and died on Feb. 15th following. We may also mention here the deaths of Lt. James Wemyss, of cholera, on June 13, and that of Lt. Ball, of fever, on June 18.

It is unnecessary to enter into the details of the siege of Sebastopol, in which the 93rd, like all the other regiments in the Crimea, had to do its share of harassing and dangerous duty. The regiment took part in the expedition by the Straits of Yenikale to Kertch in the end of May and beginning of June, returning to Balaklava on the 14th of the latter month. In the first assault on Sebastopol on June 18th, 1855, the 93rd, with the rest of its division under Sir Colin Campbell, held a position close to the Woronzoff Road, in rear of the 21 gun battery, ready to act as circumstances might require. This attack, as is known, was unsuccessful; and from the 18th of June to the 22nd of August, the duties in the trenches of the right attack were entirely performed by the First, Second, and Light Divisions alternately, and during this period the 93rd sustained a loss of 6 killed and 57 wounded, several of the latter dying of their wounds. On the night of the 6th of August Bt.-Major J. Anstruther M'Gowan of the 93rd was unfortunately severely wounded and taken prisoner, while visiting some sentries posted in front of the advanced trench right attack. It was a considerable time after his capture that it was ascertained that Major M'Gowan had died of his wounds on August 14th at Simpheropol.

Lt.-Col. Ainslie was compelled twice to proceed on sick leave; first on the 28th of June, when Major Ewart assumed command of the regiment, and again on August 17th, when Lt.-Col. Leith Hay occupied his place. We may state here that Lt.-Col. Ainslie did not return to the regiment, retiring on Jan. 25th, 1856, when he was succeeded by Lt.-Col. Leith Hay.

On the 8th of Sept. the second grand assault upon Sebastopol took place, and early in the morning of that day the whole of the Highland brigade marched from Kamara to their old encampment on the heights before Sebastopol, where the knapsacks were deposited. The brigade then proceeded at once to the trenches of the right attack, remaining in support during the attack, in which, however, the Highlanders took no part. The assault on the Redan having again failed, the Highland brigade was pushed on to occupy the advanced trenches of the right attack, remaining there during the night, ready to repel any sortie that might be made. On the 9th it was the intention again to assault the Redan, the four Highland regiments to form the storming party; but on the night of the 8th

the Russians evacuated the south side of Sebastopol, and the brigade in consequence returned to Kamara on the evening of the 9th.

A circumstance connected with the evacuation of Sebastopol should be mentioned. About midnight on the 8th, the Russian fire having previously ceased, and everything appearing unusually quiet, Lt. W. M'Bean, the adjutant of the 93rd, left the advanced trench and approaching the Redan, was struck with the idea that it was deserted by the Russians. He accordingly gallantly volunteered to enter it, which he did with a party of 10 volunteers of the light company, under Lt. Fenwick, and a like number of the 72nd, under Capt. Rice; they found no one in the Redan but the dead and wounded left after the assault. The party, however, had a narrow escape, as an explosion took place in the Redan shortly after.

The loss of the 93rd on the 8th of Sept. was 2 rank and file killed and 7 wounded.

During the winter of 1855–56, the regiment was employed in erecting huts, making roads, draining camps, and latterly in brigade drill and target practice with the Enfield rifle, which had been issued to the regiment in Sept. 1855; the health of the battalion was very good.

During its stay in the Crimea, 158 non-commissioned officers and privates were invalided to England; 11 officers and 323 non-commissioned officers and privates were either killed in action or died of wounds or disease; and 92 non-commissioned officers and privates were wounded.

The 93rd left the Crimea on June 16th, 1856, and arrived at Portsmouth on July 15th, proceeding to Aldershot on the same day. Next day the regiment was inspected by The Queen, who walked down the line accompanied by Prince Albert and a numerous staff, minutely noticing everything, and asking many questions regarding the welfare of the corps. Again, on the 18th, Her Majesty, attended by the Princess Royal, visited the huts of the regiment, several of which she was pleased to enter; she also tasted the rations prepared for the dinners of the men.

As the next episode in the history of the Sutherland Highlanders is the most important in its career, as they had, in the Indian Mutiny, an opportunity of showing what mettle they were made of, such as they never had since their embodiment, we feel bound to give it considerable prominence, and must therefore pass briefly over events both before and after.

On the 23rd of July the regiment left Aldershot for Dover, where shortly after it was joined by the depôts from Malta (under Bt. Lt.-Col. Gordon), and from Dundee, under Captain Middleton. On Jan. 31st, 1857, orders were received for the 93rd to hold itself in readiness for immediate embarkation for India, on which occasion it received 201 volunteers

Lieutenant-Colonel the Hon. Adrian Hope.
From a photograph.

from the 42nd, 72nd, 79th, and 92nd. On the 6th of March, however, orders were received that the 93rd hold itself in immediate readiness for embarkation for China, and a few days after, Lt.-Col. the Hon. Adrian Hope was brought in from half-pay as second lieutenant-colonel.

On the 22nd May, H.R.H. the Duke of Cambridge was graciously pleased to present new colours to the 93rd, in lieu of the now tattered ensigns that, twenty-three years before, had been presented at Canterbury by the Duke of Wellington. After the usual cere-

mony, H.R.H. made an appropriate address, in which he expressed his confidence that, should the services of the 93rd be required, it would guard the new colours with the same zealous feeling of honour and nobleness of conduct as it displayed in the late campaign.

By the 25th of May all the service companies were collected at Portsmouth, one depôt company being left behind at Dover, under Captain Brown. On the 1st of June, Nos. 3, 7, and 8 companies, under Lt.-Col. Hope, proceeded to Plymouth, and embarked on board H.M.'s ship "Belleisle" for China, sailing on the 3rd of June.

On the 4th of June the remaining service companies, under Lt.-Col. Leith Hay, proceeded to the Clarence dockyard, Gosport, where, drawn up in line, they received Her Majesty on her landing from the Isle of Wight. After a royal salute, Her Majesty was pleased to walk down the whole line, minutely inspecting every man. The regiment then marched in slow and quick time past the Queen, who expressed to Lt.-Col. Leith Hay how much pleased she was with its appearance.

On the 16th of June, the grenadiers, Nos. 1, 2, 4, and 6, and light companies, with part of No. 5, embarked on board the s.s. "Mauritius," and sailed the following morning for China, under Lt.-Col. Leith Hay. The remainder of No. 5 company followed with the next transport. The strength of the regiment on embarkation for China was 52 officers and 1069 non-commissioned officers and men. The "Mauritius" entered Simon's Bay, Cape of Good Hope, where she found the "Belleisle" at anchor. Here Lt.-Col. Hope conveyed to the detachment on board the "Mauritius" the startling intelligence of the mutiny of the Bengal Native Army, and that orders had been received for the 93rd to proceed with all possible despatch to Calcutta, instead of China. The "Mauritius" anchored in the Hooghly, opposite Fort William, on the 20th of Sept. 1857, the anniversary of the battle of the Alma, and the

93rd was welcomed by its old brigadier, the newly appointed Commander-in-Chief, Sir Colin Campbell. The detachment under Lt.-Col. Adrian Hope did not arrive until the 26th.

III.

1857–1875.

On the road to Cawnpoor—Engagement near Futteh-poor—Attack on Buntara—Force assembled on the Plain of the Alum Bagh—Sir Colin Campbell's address to 93rd—Disposition of the force—on the road to Lucknow—Lucknow—The Dilkoosha—The Martinière—Banks's Bungalow — The Secunder Bagh—A terrible fight—Capt. Stewart—The Shah Nujaef—Adrian Hope's last effort—Sergeant Paton—Meeting of Campbell, Outram, and Havelock—Back to Cawnpoor—Dispersion of the rebel army—Second attack upon Lucknow—93rd in Lucknow—The Dilkoosha taken—The Martinière taken—The Begum Kotee — Terrible slaughter — Individual bravery—The 93rd at Rohileund—Death of Adrian Hope—At Bareilly—March into Oude—Rebel hunt-ing—End of the Mutiny—Losses—Peshawur—Cholera—Conduct of the men—Medical officers—Sealkote — The Umbeyla Campaign — Jhansi — Surgeon-major Munro — Bombay — 93rd sails for home—New colours- Duke and Duchess of Suther-land—Ball at Holyrood—The Queen's interest in the regiment—Honours to officers—The Autumn Manœuvres—Strength of the regiment.

No time was lost in sending the 93rd up the river to Chinsurah, and by the 10th of October, the whole regiment in detachments was hurrying along the grand trunk road towards Cawnpoor, distant about 600 miles. By October 31st, the main body of the regiment, with Cols. Hay and Hope, had reached Cawnpoor, and in a day or two had crossed the Ganges and joined the column under Brigadier Hope Grant, assembling in Oude, for operations against Lucknow; the force was encamped between Bunnee Bridge and the Alum Bagh, about 10 miles in rear of the latter place. At Futtehpoor, three companies, under Brevet Lt.-Col. Gordon, were left to garrison that place, and to hold in check a considerable force of rebels, known to be in the neighbourhood. On the 1st of Nov. one of these companies, under Captain Cornwall, formed part of a small force which had a severe but successful engagement with a considerable body of the rebels at Khaga, near Futtehpoor. This was a severely contested affair, and the men were exhausted by a long march before reaching the enemy's position, but neverthe-less fought with such spirit and gallantry

as to excite the admiration of Captain Peel, R.N., who had command of the force. The casualties of the 93rd company (No. 3) in this action were severe, being 3 men killed, and Ensign Cunningham and 15 men wounded.

On the following day, Nov. 2nd, the detach-ment under Lt.-Col. Adrian Hope, consisting of the grenadiers, Nos. 1, 2, and 4 companies, was also engaged in an attack on a fortified village in Oude, Buntara, and drove the enemy from the position, killing a number of them, and destroying the village. The casualties of the 93rd were 1 man killed and 3 wounded.

By Nov. 13th the detachment under Brevet Lt.-Col. Gordon had come up, and the whole of the regiment was thus once more together. On the 11th of Nov. the entire force assembled in the plain of the Alum Bagh, divided into brigades, and was reviewed by the commander-in-chief. The brigade to which the 93rd was posted consisted of headquarters of the 53rd, the 93rd, and the 4th Punjab Rifles, and was com-manded by Lt.-Col. the Hon. Adrian Hope of the 93rd, appointed brigadier of the 2nd class. The little army, numbering about 4200 men, was drawn up in quarter distance column facing Lucknow. The 93rd stood in the centre of the brigade, on the extreme left, and after passing in front of the other regiments and detachments, Sir Colin Campbell approached the regiment, and thus addressed it :—

"93d, we are about to advance to relieve our countrymen and countrywomen besieged in the Resi-dency of Lucknow by the rebel army. It will be a duty of danger and difficulty, but I rely upon you."

This short and pointed address was re-ceived by the regiment with such a burst of enthusiasm that the gallant old chieftain must have felt assured of its loyalty and devotion, and confident that wherever he led, the 93rd would follow, and if need be, die with him to the last man. The 93rd was the first regiment on that occasion that made any out-ward display of confidence in their leader, but as the veteran commander returned along the line, the example was taken up by others, and cheer upon cheer from every corps followed him as he rode back to the camp.

All the sick and wounded having been sent into the Alum Bagh on the 13th, preparations were made for the advance, which commenced next day. The army marched in three columns, viz., the advance, the main column, and the rear guard. The 93rd, along with the 53rd, 84th, 90th, 1st Madras Fusiliers, and 4th Punjab Rifles, constituted the 4th Infantry Brigade forming part of the main column, and was under command of Brigadier Adrian Hope. The regiment had already lost, of sick, wounded, and killed, about 140 men, so that its strength as it entered the desperate struggle was 934 men. A detachment of 200 men of the 93rd formed part of the rear guard, which also contained 200 of the 5th Brigade under Lt Col. Ewart of the 93d.[1]

Instead of approaching by the direct Cawnpoor road to Lucknow, Sir Colin determined to make a flank march to the right, get possession of the Dilkoosha and Martinière, on south side of the city, which the enemy occupied as outposts, push on thence to attack the large fortified buildings Secunder Bagh, Shah Nujeef, &c., lying between the former and the Residency, and thus clear a path by which the beleaguered garrison might retire.

As the narrative of the advance and succeeding operations is so well told in the Record Book of the regiment, we shall transcribe it almost verbatim, space, however, compelling us to cut it down somewhat.[2]

At nine o'clock A.M. of November 14, 1857, the flank march commenced. As the head of the advance column neared the Dilkoosha, a heavy musketry fire was opened on it from the left, and the enemy made some attempt to dispute the advance, but were soon driven over the crest of the hill sloping down to the Martinière, from the enclosures of which a heavy fire of artillery and musketry opened upon the advancing force. This was soon silenced, and the infantry skirmishers rushed down the hill, supported by the 4th Infantry Brigade, and drove the enemy beyond the line of the canal.

During the early part of the day two companies of the 93rd were detached, viz., the Grenadiers, under Capt. Middleton, close to the Cawnpoor road, to command it, while the baggage, ammunition, &c., were filing past; and No. 1, under Capt. Somerset Clarke, was pushed on to the left to seize and keep possession of a village so as to prevent the enemy from annoying the column in that quarter.

While the leading brigade, in skirmishing order, was gradually pushing the enemy beyond the Dilkoosha, the 4th Brigade followed in support, at first in open column, and while doing so, the 93rd lost 1 man killed and 7 wounded. After the enemy had been driven down the hill towards the Martinière, the 93rd was allowed to rest under cover of some old mud walls to the left rear of the Dilkoosha, until the order

[1] For details and illustrated plan as to previous operations, see vol. ii. p. 667 and 677.

[2] See vol. ii. p. 677, where a plan is given, illustrative of the operations for the Relief of Lucknow.

was given for the brigade to advance upon the Martinière itself. Then the 4th Punjab Rifles moved first in skirmishing order, supported by the 93rd, the Naval Brigade keeping up a heavy fire on the left, the result being that the enemy were driven back upon their supports beyond the canal. The Punjab Rifles pushed on and occupied part of a village on the other side of the canal, while the 93rd, with the Madras Fusiliers occupied the wood and enclosures between the Martinière and the canal. Immediately on taking up this position, three companies of the regiment under Capt. Cornwall were sent to an open space on the left of the Martinière, close to the Cawnpoor road, for the purpose of protecting the Naval Brigade guns, while the headquarters, reduced to three companies under Col. Hay, remained within the enclosure. Towards evening the enemy from the other side of the canal opened a sharp artillery and musketry fire on the whole position, part of it coming from Banks's Bungalow. This continued till nearly seven P.M., when the Commander-in-Chief rode up and called out the Light Company and part of No. 8, and desired them to endeavour to seize Banks's Bungalow. As soon as the Naval Brigade guns were fired, this party under Col. Hay, in skirmishing order, made a rush towards the canal, which, however, was found too deep to ford. As the night was closing in, the Light Company remained extended in skirmishing order behind the bank of the canal, while Col. Hay with the remainder returned to the Martinière compound. Capt. Cornwall with the three detached companies also returned; but the Grenadiers and No. 1 company remained, holding detached positions to the left of the army.

During the day the rear-guard (of which 200 of the 93rd formed part), under Lt.-Col. Ewart, was several times hotly engaged with the enemy, but drove them back on each occasion, with no loss and few casualties on our side. The casualties of the regiment throughout the day's operations amounted to 1 man killed and 11 men wounded.

On the 15th, the 93rd was not actively engaged; but in its position behind the Martinière compound was exposed to a constant fire, by which only 1 man was killed and 2 men were wounded. By this time headquarters was joined by the 200 who formed part of the rear-guard. Late in the evening all the detached parties were called in, and the regiment bivouacked for the night in a position close under the Martinière.

At six o'clock A.M. on the 16th the force was under arms, and formed in the dry bed of the canal en masse, at quarter-distance column, and about nine o'clock advanced, close along the western bank of the Goomtee, for about two miles, when the head of the column encountered the enemy in a wood, close to a large village, on the southern outskirts of the city, and drove them in on their own supports. The 93rd —nearly every available officer and man being present—was the leading regiment of the main column, and, in consequence of the press in the narrow lanes, it was some time before it could be got up to support the skirmishers of the 53rd that were struggling with the enemy among the enclosures. Having driven the enemy back in this quarter, the 93rd emerged from the tortuous lanes of the village into an open space, directly opposite the Secunder Bagh, a high-walled enclosure, about 160 yards square, with towers at the angles, and loopholed all round. Here the regiment deployed into line, exposed to a biting musketry fire from the loopholed building, to avoid which Col. Hay was ordered to move the regiment under cover of a low mud wall about 30 yards from the southern face of the Secunder Bagh, while some guns were being placed in position in an open space between the Secunder Bagh and another building opposite on the west side, for the purpose of breaching the south-western angle of the former.

As the last company of the 93rd—the 8th, under Capt. Dalzell—was moving into its place in line, the Commander-in-Chief called upon it to drag up a heavy gun to assist in breaching the wall; and gallantly and willingly was the difficult and dangerous duty performed, and the huge gun wheeled into position under a most withering fire. When the breach was being made, two companies, under Col. Leith Hay, took possession of a large serai or mud enclosure opposite the Secunder Bagh, driving the enemy out before them. In the meantime, the breach having been considered practicable, the assault was given by the 4th Punjab Rifles and the 93rd, supported by part of the 53rd and the battalion of detachments.

It was a glorious and exciting rush. On went, side by side in generous rivalry, the Sikh and the Highlander—the 93rd straining every nerve in the race, led gallantly by the officers. The colours, so lately confided to the regiment by H.R.H. the Duke of Cambridge, were opened to the breeze, and carried proudly by Ensigns Robertson and Taylor.

The greater part of the regiment dashed at the breach, and among the first to enter were Lt.-Col. Ewart and Capt. Burroughs. At the same time, three companies advanced between the Secunder Bagh and the serai on the left, so as to keep down the artillery fire opened on the British flank by the enemy from the direction of the European barracks. The opening in the wall of the Secunder Bagh was so small that only one man could enter at a time; but a few having gained an entrance, they kept the enemy at bay, until a considerable number of the Highlanders and Sikhs had pushed in, when in a body they emerged into the open square, where commenced what was probably the sternest and bloodiest struggle of the whole campaign.

Shortly after the breach had been entered, and while the men were struggling hand to hand against

The Secunder Bagh.

From a photograph in possession of the Regiment.

unequal numbers, that portion of the 93rd which had driven the enemy out of the serai, under Col. Hay, succeeded in blowing open the main gate, killing a number of the enemy in two large recesses on each side; and pressing their way in, rushed to the support of those who had passed through the breach. Away on the right also of the building, the 53rd had forced an entrance through a window. Still, with desperate courage and frightful carnage, the defence went on, and for hours the sepoys defended themselves with musket and tulwar against the bayonets and fire of the Highlanders, and 53rd, and the Punjab Rifles; but there was no escape for them, and the men, roused to the highest pitch of excitement, and burning to revenge the butchery of Cawnpoor, dashed furiously on, gave no quarter, and did not stay their hands while one single enemy stood to oppose them. No, not until, at the close of the day, the building formed one mighty charnel house—for upwards of 2000 dead sepoys, dressed in their old uniforms, lay piled in heaps, and on almost all was apparent either the small but deadly bayonet wound, or the deep gash of the Sikh tulwar.

As might be guessed, the regiment did not pass scatheless through this fiery contest; not a few were killed, and many wounded. The sergeant-major, Donald Murray, was one of the first to fall; he was shot dead as he advanced in his place in the regiment. Then fell Capt. Lumsden, of the H.E.I.C.S., attached to the 93rd as interpreter. Within the building, Capt. Dalzell was killed by a shot from a window above. Lts. Welch and Cooper were severely wounded; and Lt.-Col. Ewart, Capt. Burroughs, and Ensign Macnamara bore away with them bloody reminiscences of the dreadful fray.

A large number of officers and men were recommended for the Victoria Cross, though few of the former obtained it; for although all richly deserved the honour, it is well known that mere personal adventure is discouraged on the part of those who are in command. Of the men of the regiment the coveted honour was conferred on Lance-Corporal John Dunley, Private David Mackay, and Private Peter Grant, each of whom performed a feat of bravery which contributed not a little to the success of the day. They were elected for the honour by the vote of the private soldiers. No doubt many others deserved a similar honour, and it seems almost invidious to mention any names, when every one doubtless did his best and bravest.

During the desperate struggle within, one of the boldest feats of arms of the day was performed by Capt. Stewart of the 93rd, son of the late Sir W. Drummond Stewart of Murthly. Of the three companies which had moved out between the Serai and the Secunder Bagh, to keep down the flank fire of the enemy while the breaching was going on, two, with a few of the 53rd, led on by Capt. Stewart, in the most gallant style, dashed forward, seized two of the enemy's guns, which were raking the road, and immediately after effected a lodgment in the European barracks, thus securing the position on the left. For this splendid and useful feat of bravery he was elected by the officers of the regiment for the honour of the Victoria Cross, which was most deservedly conferred on him.

All this was effected by three o'clock P.M.

The regimental hospital had been established early in the day beneath the walls of the Secunder Bagh, and throughout the desperate struggle, in the midst of the hottest fire, the Assistant-Surgeons Sinclair, Menzies, and Bell, were constantly to be seen exposing themselves fearlessly in attendance on the wounded.

Almost immediately after the above operations, the 4th Brigade was withdrawn by Brigadier Adrian Hope, with the exception of the two companies of the 93rd occupying the barracks; and after a short rest, was sent to clear a village on the right of the road leading to the Residency, and between the Secunder Bagh and the Shah Nujeef. This was easily effected, and the brigade remained under cover in the village, while preparations were being made to take the Shah Nujeef. It having been found impossible to subdue the enemy's musketry fire from the latter building by artillery, the Commander-in-Chief collected the 93rd around him and said, "I had no intention of employing you again to-day, but the Shah Nujeef must be taken; the artillery cannot drive the enemy out, so you must, with the bayonet." Giving the regiment some plain directions as to how they were to proceed, he said he would accompany them himself.

At this moment the Naval Brigade redoubled its fire, and Middleton's troop of Horse Artillery poured a continuous stream of grape-shot into the brushwood and enclosures around the building. Under this iron storm the 93rd, under Col. Hay, all excited to the highest degree, with flashing eye and nervous tread, rolled on in one vast wave, the greyhaired warrior of many fights, with drawn sword, riding at its head surrounded by his staff, and accompanied by Brigadier Adrian Hope. As the regiment approached the nearest angle of the building, the men began to drop under the enemy's fire, poured forth from behind the loopholed walls; but still not a man wavered, and on went the regiment without a check, until it stood at the foot of the wall, which towered above it 20 feet, quite uninjured by the artillery fire.

There was no breach and no scaling-ladders; and unable to advance, but unwilling to retire, the men halted and commenced a musketry battle with the garrison, but of course at great disadvantage, for the Sepoys poured in their deadly volleys securely from behind their cover, while the 93rd was without shelter or protection of any kind, and therefore many fell.

By this time nearly all the mounted officers were either wounded or dismounted. Brigadier Hope, his A.D.C. and Brigade Major, had their horses shot under them; Lt.-Col. Hay's horse was disabled by a musket shot; and two of the Commander-in-Chief's staff were dangerously wounded. As there was no visible means of effecting an entrance on this side, a party of the regiment pushed round the angle to the front gate, but found it was so well covered and protected by a strong work of masonry as to be perfectly unassailable. One more desperate effort was therefore made by artillery, and two of Peel's guns were brought up under cover of the fire of the regiment, dragged along by a number of men of the 93rd, Brigadier Hope, Colonel Hay, and Sir David Baird heartily lending a hand. Still, though the guns hurled their shot in rapid succession at only a few yards distance, no impression could be made.

Success seemed impossible, the guns were withdrawn, and the wounded collected, in which last duty Lt. Wood and Ensign Macnamara rendered good service under a galling fire at considerable risk to themselves. Evening was fast closing in, and the assault must necessarily soon be given up, but Brigadier Hope resolved to make one last effort. He collected about fifty men of the 93rd, and crept cautiously through some brushwood, guided by Sergeant Paton, to a part of the wall in which the sergeant had discovered a spot so injured that he thought an entrance might be effected. The small party reached this unperceived, and found a narrow rent, up which a single man was pushed with some difficulty. He reported that no enemy was to be seen near the spot, and immediately Brigadier Hope, accompanied by Colonel Hay and several of the men, scrambled up and stood upon the inside of the wall. The sappers were immediately sent for to enlarge the opening, when more of the 93rd followed, and Brigadier Hope with his small party gained, almost unopposed, the main gate, threw it open, and in rushed the 93rd, just in time to see the enemy in their white dresses gliding away into the darkness of the night. Sergeant Paton for the above daring service deservedly received the Victoria Cross. Thus ended the desperate struggle of the day, and the relief of the Residency was all but secured. Lts. Wood and Goldsmith were here severely wounded, and a number of men killed and wounded. A deep silence now reigned over the entire position, and the little army, weary and exhausted by its mighty efforts, lay down upon the hard-won battle-ground to rest, and if possible to sleep.

The casualties throughout the day to the 93rd were very great. Two officers and 23 men killed, and 7 officers and 61 men wounded. As many of the latter died of their wounds, and most of the survivors were permanently disabled, they may be regarded as almost a dead loss to the regiment.

Early on the following morning, as soon as daylight had sufficiently set in to enable anything to be seen, the regimental colour of the 93rd was hoisted on the highest pinnacle of the Shah Nujeef, to inform the garrison of the Residency of the previous day's success. The signal was seen and replied to. This act was performed by Lt. and Adjt. M'Bean, assisted by Sergeant Hutchinson, and it was by no means unattended with danger, for the enemy, on perceiving their intention, immediately opened fire, but fortunately without injury to either.

The 93rd was not employed on the 17th further than in holding the different positions taken on the previous day. The 53rd and 90th captured the Messhouse, Hospital, and Motee Mahal. The communication with the Residency was now opened, and there was great joy among the relieving force when Generals

Outram and Havelock came out to meet the Commander-in-Chief.

On the evening of Nov. 18th, 1857, the distribution of the 93rd, which was now completely broken up, was as follows:—Head-quarters under Col. Hay, consisting of 120 men, occupied the Serai in rear of the European barracks; three companies under Lt.-Col. Ewart held the barracks; one company under Capt. Clarke held the Motee Mahul, while part of the garrison of the Residency held the Hern Khanah and Engine-house. These two latter positions secured the exit of the garrison. One company and part of the light company, under Capt. Dawson, held the Shah Nujeef, and kept in check the enemy's batteries placed close down on the eastern bank of the Goomtee. All these parties were constantly on the alert, and exposed night and day to the fire of the enemy's artillery and musketry. On the 18th only 1 man was wounded.

During the 19th, 20th, and 21st the evacuation of the Residency was carried on, and by the night of the 22d all was ready for the garrison to retire. The whole was successfully accomplished, the retirement taking place through the lane by which the relieving force had approached the Secunder Bagh on the 16th. The brigade to which the 93rd belonged had the honour of covering the retreat as it had led the advance of the main body on the 16th;[3] and, early on the morning of the 23d, the whole regiment was once more together in the grounds round the Martinière, but retired and bivouacked behind the Dilkoosha during the afternoon. From the 19th to the 23rd the 93rd had 6 men wounded and 1 man killed. Two unfortunate accidents occurred on the 23d: a corporal and 3 men were blown up by the explosion of some gunpowder, and Colour-Sergeant Knox, who answered to his name at daylight, did not appear again; it is supposed that in the uncertain light he had fallen into one of the many deep wells around Lucknow.

Thus was accomplished one of the most difficult and daring feats of arms ever attempted, in which, as will have been seen, the 93rd won immortal laurels. But its work was by no means done.

On the 24th the army continued its retrograde movement towards Cawnpoor, staying three days at the Alum Bagh, removing the baggage and the sick, to enable preparations to be made for the defence of that position. On the 27th the march was resumed by the Bunnee bridge, the army encumbered with women, children, sick, and baggage, which, however, after a little confusion, the main column got clear of. Next day, as the march went on, the sound of heavy firing was heard; and when the troops were told that it was the Gwalior rebel contingent attacking Cawnpoor, they, fatigued as they were, braced themselves for renewed exertions. About ten o'clock on that night (the 28th) the main column arrived at within a short distance of the bridge of boats at Cawnpoor. Between heat, and dust, and hunger, and exhaustion the march was a dreadfully trying one, yet not a man was missing by twelve o'clock that night. A short but welcome sleep came to renew the strength of the brave and determined men.

At daylight on the 29th the enemy commenced a heavy fire on the entrenched camp and bridge of boats. Peel's guns immediately opened fire, under cover of which the 53rd and 93rd approached the bridge, and, under a perfect storm of shot, shell, and bullets, succeeded in crossing it, and in gaining the open plain close to the artillery barracks, taking up a position between this and the old sepoy lines in front of the city of Cawnpoor, and near that sacred spot where General Wheeler had defended himself so long and

nobly against the whole power of Nana Sahib. By this movement the communication with Allahabad was reopened, the only casualty to the 93rd being Ensign Hay slightly wounded. All the convoy of women, wounded, &c., was got over, and by December 3rd the greater portion were safely on their way to Allahabad, and everything nearly ready for an attack on the rebel army.

On the morning of December 1, as the 93rd was turning out for muster, the enemy opened fire upon it with shrapnel, by which Captain Cornwall, Sergeant M'Intyre, and 5 privates were severely wounded. The regiment, therefore, took shelter under cover of the old lines, returning, except the picquet, at night to the tents, and continuing so to do until the morning of the 6th.

On the morning of the 6th the 93rd paraded behind the old sepoy lines, afterwards moving to the left and keeping under cover until the whole disposable force of the army was formed in mass on the left, under cover of the new barracks and some ruins behind them. Brigadier Greathead kept the line of the canal, extending from the fort; Walpole crossed the canal on Greathead's left, so as to secure all the passes from the city. While these operations were being carried out, Hope's brigade, consisting of the 42nd, 53rd, and 93rd, supported by Brigadier Inglis, moved away to the left, towards the open plain where the enemy's right rested, while the cavalry and horse artillery, making a wide sweep, were to turn the enemy's right flank, and unite their attack with that of Hope. On debouching into the plain, the enemy opened fire, when the 53rd and Sikhs were immediately thrown to the front in skirmishing order, and pressed eagerly forward, while the 93rd and 42nd, in successive lines, followed rapidly up. Notwithstanding the unceasingly hot fire of the enemy, which began to tell upon the men, still onward in majestic line moved the Highlanders, for a time headed by the Commander-in-Chief himself, who rode in front of the 93rd.

On approaching the broken ground near the bridge, it was found necessary to alter the formation somewhat. The enemy disputed the passage of the bridge by a heavy shower of grape, which, however, caused little loss. As the regiment cleared the bridge, the enemy retired, and at the same time Peel's heavy guns came limbering up, and as they passed along the left of the 93rd, a number of the men seized the drags, pulled them to the front, and helped to place them for action. They opened, and caused the enemy to retire still further, when the 93rd again formed into line, as also did the 42nd, and both continued to advance still under a heavy fire, for the enemy's artillery disputed every inch of ground. But gradually, steadily, and surely the Highlanders pressed on, urging the enemy back, until at last the standing camp of the Gwalior contingent opened to view, when the Commander-in-Chief ordered Nos. 7 and 8 companies to advance at a run and take possession. It was empty, but no preparations had been made to carry off anything. The hospital tents alone were tenanted by the sick and wounded, who, as the soldiers passed, held up their hands and begged for mercy; but the men turned from them in disgust, unable to pity, but unwilling to strike a wounded foe.

After passing through the camp, the 93rd formed line again to the right and advanced, still annoyed by a galling fire of round shot and shrapnell. During a momentary halt, Lieut. Stirling was struck down by a round shot, and General Mansfield, who was with the regiment at the time, was struck by a shrapnell bullet. The advance continued, and the enemy drew back, disputing every foot of ground. General Mansfield with some guns, the rifles, and 93rd secured the Subadar's Tank in rear of the enemy's left, while Sir

[3] For the details of the retreat see the history of the 78th, vol. ii. p. 679.

II.   5 F

Colin Campbell with a small force, including two companies of the 93rd, pressed the pursuit of the routed Gwalior contingent along the Calpee road. By sunset the rebels in the city, and on the left beyond it, had retired by the Bithoor road.

The casualties to the 93rd were 2 officers and 10 men wounded. That night the regiment bivouacked in a large grove of trees which had been occupied in the morning by the enemy, who, unwittingly, had prepared an evening meal for their opponents, for beside the many little fires which were still burning were found half-baked cakes, and brazen vessels full of boiled rice.

The centre and left of the rebel army retreated during the night by the Bithoor road, but were followed on the 8th by General Hope Grant with the cavalry, light artillery, and Hope's brigade, and carry on the morning of the 9th, after a long march of twenty hours, they were overtaken at the Serai Ghat on the Ganges, attacked, dispersed, and all their guns, 15 in number, and ammunition taken.

Thus was defeated and dispersed the whole of the rebel army which but a few days before had exultingly laid siege to the entrenched camp at Cawnpoor; broken, defeated, pursued, and scattered, it no longer held together or presented the semblance of an organised body. That evening the force encamped close to the river, and next day fell back on Bithoor, where it remained till the end of the month.

The next few days were occupied in clearing the rebels from the whole district around Lucknow, the British force advancing as far as Futtehgurh. Here it was encamped till the 1st of February 1858, when the camp was broken up. The Commander-in-Chief returned to Cawnpoor, and the troops commenced to move by different routes towards Lucknow, now become the centre of the rebel power. Hope's brigade marched to Cawnpoor, and on arriving there was broken up, the 53d being removed from it. This was a source of great disappointment both to that corps and the 93rd. The two regiments having been together in so many dangers and difficulties, and having shared in the glorious relief of the Residency of Lucknow, a feeling of attachment and esteem had sprung up between them, which was thoroughly manifested when the 93rd left Cawnpoor and passed into Oude on the 10th of February; the band of the 53rd played it to the bridge of boats, by which the 93rd crossed the Ganges, and both officers and men of the former lined the road in honour of their old comrades.

From the middle to the end of February, the army destined to attack the city of Lucknow was collecting from all quarters, and stationed by regiments along the road leading thither from Cawnpoor, to protect the siege train in its transit. By the end of the month the largest and best equipped British army ever seen in India, led by the Commander-in-Chief in person, was collected in the Alum Bagh plains, prepared for the attack. A new organisation of the army now took place, new brigades and divisions were formed, and new brigadiers and generals appointed to each.

On February 28, 1858, the 93rd arrived at the Alum Bagh, and on the following morning, March 1, moved, with two troops of horse artillery, the 9th Lancers, and 42nd Highlanders, round Major-General Outram's rear and right flank, behind the fort of Jelalabad, and, making a sweep of some miles, came suddenly upon an outlying picquet of the enemy about a mile to the south of the Dilkoosha. The enemy, taken by surprise, fell back fighting, but in the end fled in disorder to the Martinière, leaving the Dilkoosha and the villages and enclosures on both sides to be occupied by their pursuers. Towards the afternoon other brigades and regiments followed, and took up positions on the left, extending so as to communicate with Major-General Outram's right. In this position the

whole force bivouacked for the night; and in a day or two the regimental camp was formed close to the river Goomtee, where it remained till March 11. From March 2nd the regiment was employed every other day as one large outlying picquet, and posted in a dense tope of trees surrounded by a high wall. A constant fire was kept up on this position by the enemy, happily with no loss to the 93rd. The regiment was also kept constantly employed in other duties. On the 9th, along with its brigade, the 93rd took part in the storming of the Martinière, which was given up by the enemy after a very slight resistance, only a few of the 93rd being wounded. The enemy were pursued by the 42nd and 93rd, the latter pushing on beyond Banks's bungalow, and taking possession of a large garden close to the enemy's second chain of works, which was formed by the Begum's Palace, the Mess House, the Motee Mahul, the old Barracks, the Shah Nujeef, and the Secunder Bagh. While this was being effected, the 53rd, which had been allowed to rejoin their comrades of the 93rd, made a dash at the Secunder Bagh and took possession, just as a large body of the enemy was approaching to garrison it. The 93rd bivouacked in the garden for the night. During the day the enemy had been driven close up to the city by other sections of the army, and the next day was employed in making breaches in the Begum Kotee or Palace, a large pile of buildings and enclosures in front of and covering the celebrated Kaiser Bagh, known to be strongly garrisoned, and fortified and protected, as the enemy considered it to be the key of the whole position.

At 3 o'clock P.M., on the 11th, it was announced to the 93rd that the honour of assaulting the position was allotted to them by the Commander-in-Chief. The regiment formed up in a patch of thick wood close to road leading directly to the front of the Begum Kotee, and thence to the Kaiser Bagh. It was told off by Brigadier Adrian Hope into two divisions,—the right wing, under Col. Leith Hay, consisting of the grenadiers, Nos. 1, 2, 3, and 4 companies, and the left wing, under Bt. Lt.-Col. Gordon, consisting of Nos. 5, 6, 8, and light companies; the former to assault and enter by the front breach, and the latter by that on the right flank of the position made by the battery from Banks's bungalow. No. 7 company was left to guard the camp. At 4 P.M. the large guns became silent, and at the same time the enemy's musketry fire slackened. At this moment the 93rd wound out of the enclosures, advanced up the road, and, without a shot fired at it, got under cover of some ruined buildings,—Col. Hay's division almost in front of the gate, and Col. Gordon's to the right flank.

At a signal given by Brigadier Adrian Hope, both storming parties emerged from their cover, and each dashed at headlong speed, and with a deafening cheer, right at its respective breach. The enemy were taken by surprise, but quickly manning the walls and loopholes, poured a perfect storm of musketry on the advancing columns. Not a man fell, for the enemy fired too high; not a man wavered, and, under a storm of bullets hissing over and around them, the gallant stormers came close up to the breaches, but were suddenly, though only for a moment, checked by a broad ditch, the existence of which was not known before. A moment of surprise, not hesitation, ensued, when a few of the grenadiers, headed by Capt. Middleton, leapt into the ditch, and were immediately followed by the whole. Colonel Hay, Capt. Middleton, and a few more having gained the other side of the ditch, dragged the others up, and then, one by one, they commenced to enter the narrow breach. At the same time the left wing storming party, with equal rapidity and daring, had gained the breach on the right, and the leading files, headed by Capt. Clarke, effected an entrance.

Every obstacle that could be opposed to the stormers had been prepared by the enemy; every room, door, gallery, or gateway was so obstructed and barricaded that only one man could pass at a time. Every door, every window, every crevice that could afford the slightest shelter, was occupied by an enemy; and thus, in threading their way through the narrow passages and doorways, the men were exposed to unseen enemies. However, one barrier after another was passed, and the men in little parties, headed by officers, emerged into the first square of the building, where the enemy in large numbers stood ready for the struggle.

No thought of unequal numbers, no hesitation for a moment, withheld the men of the 93rd, who, seeing their enemy in front, rushed to the encounter; and for two hours the rifle and the bayonet were unceasingly employed. From room to room, from courtyard to courtyard, from terrace to terrace, the enemy disputed the advance; at one moment rushing out and fighting hand to hand, at another gliding rapidly away, and taking advantage of every available shelter. No one thought of giving or asking quarter; and useless would any appeal for mercy have been, for the Highlanders, roused to the highest state of excitement, were alike regardless of personal danger, and deaf to everything but the orders of the officers. There were two wickets by which the enemy could escape, and to these points they crowded, many of them only to meet destruction from parties of the regiment stationed outside. One wicket was to the right rear, and the other was to the left front, both opening to roads that led to the Kaiser Bagh. The left wing, on gaining an entrance through the right breach, drove the enemy with great slaughter across to the wicket on the left flank of the buildings, and followed hard in pursuit up the road leading along this flank of the Begum Kotee to the Kaiser Bagh; then retired, and taking up positions along the side of this road, kept in check the enemy's supports that attempted to come down this road, and destroyed such of the garrison as attempted to escape. As the leading companies of the right wing were effecting their entrance at the front breach, Capt. Stewart led his company, No. 2, along the ditch round to the right flank of the position, seeking another entrance. He failed in finding one, however, but met a small party of the 93rd belonging to the left wing, supported by the 42nd, engaged with a large body of Sepoys. The enemy had been driven back by a rush, and a large brass gun taken from them and turned upon themselves in their retreat. The enemy, reinforced, returned to the attack, and obliged their opponents to retire slowly. A party of the regiment under Capt. Middleton arriving, the enemy again retired, leaving their brass gun in possession of the 93rd. At this moment, and at this point, numbers of the enemy were shot down or blown up in attempting to escape by the wicket on this side of the buildings. At last, about 7 o'clock P.M., as darkness was closing in, the masses of the enemy had disappeared, the fire had slackened, the position was won, and the regiment rested from its struggle.

The wounded were all collected and taken by Dr Munro to the regimental camp. All the medical officers were present throughout the day, the assistant-surgeons Sinclair and Bell with the right wing, and Menzies with the left, accompanied the stormers; Dr Munro remained outside to receive the wounded.

The casualties amounted to 2 officers (Capt. C. W. M'Donald and Lt. Sergison) and 13 men killed; 2 officers (Lt. Grimstone and Ensign Hastie), and 45 men wounded. The losses of the enemy must have been enormous, as next day 866 dead bodies were buried, all found within the different enclosures;

many must have escaped wounded. It was afterwards known that the garrison consisted of eight picked Sepoy regiments, altogether amounting to nearly 5000 men, who had sworn to die in defence of this position of the city. The 93rd numbered about 800 men.

Several individual acts of bravery, performed both by officers and men, are well worthy of being recorded. Lt. and Adjt. M'Bean encountered eleven of the enemy in succession, and after a hand-to-hand fight killed them all; for this he received the Victoria Cross. Young Captain M'Donald had been wounded severely in the early part of the day by a splinter of a shell in his sword arm, but refused to retire to hospital. On entering the breach at the head of his company, cheering them on, he was shot through the thigh, and in this disabled state, was being carried to the surgeon, when a bullet passed through his neck and killed him. Lt. Sergison, in attempting to break open a door, behind which a number of the enemy were concealed, was shot dead. Lt. Grimstone received a wound while in hot and deadly pursuit of an enemy, whom he overtook and killed. Capt. Clarke, several paces in front of his company, was the first man of his party to enter the breach. Indeed, almost all the officers had hand-to-hand encounters with single enemies. The pipe-major, John M'Leod, was the first to force his way in at the front breach, and no sooner was he in than he began and continued throughout the whole of the fighting, in places perfectly exposed, to cheer and encourage the men with the wild notes of his bagpipes. No words can suffice to express the gallantry and devotion and fearless intrepedity displayed by every man in the regiment; and well deserved indeed was the meed of high praise contained in the general orders of Major-General Lingard and the Commander-in-chief. All the operations connected with the storming of the place were conducted by Brigadier Adrian Hope, and the position was carried by the 93rd Highlanders exclusively, supported at first by part of the 42nd, and the 4th Punjab Rifles.

The Commander-in-Chief, Sir Colin Campbell, colonel of the regiment, was sitting in Durbar with Jung Bahadoor,[a] when an aide-de-camp hastily entered his presence, with the intelligence that the Begum Kotee was taken after a hard struggle and severe loss. The gallant chief sprang from his seat, and exclaimed, "I knew they would do it."

On the afternoon of the 13th the regiment was relieved and returned to camp, where it remained till the evening of the 20th, when, with the exception of No. 7 company, it returned and took up a position around the Imambarah, preparatory to an attack which was to be made next day on the last position held by the enemy on the north side of the city. During the interval between the 13th and the 20th, the Kaiser Bagh, Imambarah, and other positions had been taken from the enemy; the regiment, however, had no share in these operations.

On the 21st the 93rd, supported by the 4th Punjab Rifles, after some severe skirmishing and street fighting, succeeded in expelling the enemy from several large mosques and enclosures, situated at the north end of the city. Only 11 of the 93rd were wounded. This terminated the fighting within the city, which was now completely in possession of the British. The 93rd returned to the Dilkoosha, and remained in camp till April 7th, when it was ordered to prepare to form part of a force destined for Rohilcund, under Brigadier-General Walpole.

It will have been seen that no regiment was more

[a] This loyal chief, when Nepaulese ambassador in England, saw the 93rd at Edinburgh, and expressed a wish to *buy* the regiment!

frequently employed than the 93rd in all the operations against Lucknow, under the Commander-in-Chief, who intrusted to this trustworthy regiment some of the most difficult duties.

At daylight on April 7th, the regiment moved from the Dilkoosha, and joined the rest of the force about five miles on the north-west side of Lucknow. This force consisted of the old Crimean Highland brigade, the 42nd, 79th, and 93rd, two troops of horse artillery, some heavy siege guns, the 9th Lancers, some Native Infantry, Sappers, and Native Cavalry, all under Brigadier-General Walpole. The strength of the 93rd was 41 officers and 833 men.

The "Old Highland Brigade" thus reunited, was commanded by Brigadier the Hon. Adrian Hope. The force continued to march in a north-west direction till April 16th, a day which can never be forgotten by the 93rd, for with every certainty of success, energy, ability, and desire to fight, the force was entirely mismanaged.

Before the regiment marched from Lucknow, Bt. Lt.-Col. Charles Gordon, C.B., the senior major, an officer who had served many years in the 93rd, took leave, having effected an exchange with Bt. Lt.-Col. Ross, commanding a depôt battalion in Scotland.

Long before daylight on the 16th of April 1858 the force was under arms, and moved cautiously a few miles across country, when a halt was called, the baggage collected, and a strong guard told off to protect it; this guard consisted of two guns and detachments from every corps. About 10 o'clock A.M., the whole force cautiously advanced through some thick wood, and came suddenly on a native mud fort, the garrison of which immediately opened fire with guns and musketry. The 42nd was in advance, supported by the 93rd, the 79th being in reserve. The guns were quickly placed in position, and opened a rapid fire on the fort, while the 42nd and two companies of the 93rd and 4th Punjab Rifles were pushed forward close to the walls, under cover of some low banks, and commenced a brisk fire on the garrison. The 42nd occupied the cover in front, the 93rd on the left flank, and the Punjab Rifles on the right flank of the fort. During the whole day things remained in this state; the guns played on the fort without the least effect, and the skirmishers exchanged shots with the garrison, with but little loss to the enemy, while that of the 93rd and the rest of the force was severe and irreparable.

Brigadier the Hon. Adrian Hope, a leader not only admired but beloved by his brigade, and by the 93rd especially, fell while endeavouring to find out the arrangements of the fort, and see if there was any means of entering; not that any order had been given to assault, but it is more than probable that had he lived a few hours longer, an assault would have taken place. For an hour or two the guns played upon the fort, but after the death of Hope nothing was done, and the force outside only continued to get the worst of it. While the other regiments suffered severely in officers and men, the 93rd thus lost their much-beloved brigadier, while 6 men were wounded.

At sunset the force was withdrawn, and to the amazement of all (the enemy firing at the force as it retired), the camp was formed within a mile of the fort. Next morning the fort was empty, the enemy having vacated it during the night, evidently at leisure, for nothing was left except the ashes of their dead and a broken gun-carriage. The force having taken possession of the place, measures were at once taken to destroy it. Originally it had been a square enclosure, but had fallen into decay; it was so open and unprotected by any work behind, that a regiment of cavalry might have ridden in. And before this paltry place was lost the brave Adrian Hope, who had passed unscathed through the fierce fires of Lucknow and Cawnpoor. In the evening his remains were buried with military honours, along with two officers of the 42nd.

On the death of Brigadier Hope, Col. Hay, C.B., of the 93rd assumed command of the Highland Brigade, and Major Middleton that of the 93rd. Next day, April 17th, the force resumed its march, and in three days afterwards, at the village of Allahgunge, the enemy in force were again encountered, attacked, and dispersed, with a very large loss to them, but none to their assailants. Here Bt. Lt.-Col. Ross took command of the 93rd.

The force stayed at Allahgunge for three days, during which it was strongly reinforced, and the Commander-in-Chief himself took command of the entire army. On the 27th of April the largely augmented force moved *en route* for Bareilly and Shahjehanpoor, where it arrived on the 30th of April. The army moved again next day, and on the 4th of May was joined by another brigade. On the 5th it encountered a rebel army on the plains east of Bareilly, which after an engagement of some hours retired. This was a most trying day, for the heat was tremendous; the 93rd was the only regiment that did not lose men from the effects of the heat, neither had it any casualties during the engagement. On the 7th the city of Bareilly was taken possession of. On that day a wing of the regiment, under Lt.-Col. Ross, was employed to dislodge a body of the enemy which had occupied some buildings in the city. After a struggle of some hours the enemy were all dislodged and killed, the casualties of the 93rd being only 3 men wounded.

The regiment had now a rest of five months, during which it remained at Bareilly, where, however, the men suffered extremely from fever; and there were also a good many cases of sunstroke, a few of which were fatal.

On October 17th, the 93rd marched to Shahjehanpoor to form a brigade along with the 60th Royal Rifles and 66th Ghoorkas; along with this were some guns, cavalry, and regular troops, all under command of Brigadier Colin Troup. Two days after the junction of the regiments the whole column entered Oude, and in the second day's march encountered a large body of rebels at a village called Poosgawah, in which they had entrenched themselves. From this position they were quickly expelled, and the force breaking up into small columns followed in pursuit. No sooner had the bulk of the force passed through the village than a body of rebel cavalry appeared in the rear, and attacked the baggage as it was struggling through the narrow entrance into the village. The main body of the baggage guard was far in the rear, and the enemy was at first mistaken for the irregulars of the force, until they began to cut up the camp followers. At this moment, the sick of the 93rd, 12 in number, who at Surgeon Munro's request had been armed the night before, turned out of their dhoolies, and kept up a sharp fire, which held the enemy in check until the arrival of the Mooltanee Cavalry, which had been sent from the front, and which immediately dispersed the enemy's cavalry. The regiment lost 1 man killed.

The force remained in the vicinity of the village for a few days. At daylight on October 24th it was under arms, and the enemy was found in position at a village called Russallpoor, on the opposite side of a deep nullah, flanked on one side by a large village, and on the other by some rising ground. The guns and the 6th Rifles attacked, the main body of the 93rd being held in reserve; one company, under Captain M'Bean, supported the heavy guns. The enemy were driven from their position and put to flight, with considerable loss to themselves, particularly on the right, where Captain M'Bean's company was engaged.

Next day the force moved on to Noorungabad, where it remained till Nov. 8, 1858, and where the Royal proclamation was read, transferring the government of India to H.M. the Queen. On the 8th, at midnight, the force got under arms and marched towards Meethoolee, a strong mud fort belonging to one of the Rajahs of Oude, who had refused to surrender. By a circuitous route, the force felt its way towards the fort, upon which it suddenly came about mid-day on the 10th. Firing immediately commenced on both sides, and active preparations were made for an assault next day; but it was found that the enemy had slipped off during the night.

After this the 93rd, until the beginning of February 1859, was constantly employed under General Troup, sometimes united and sometimes detached, hunting the rebels out of their hiding-places, ultimately driving them beyond the Gogra (or Sarúj). Thus ended the work of the SUTHERLAND HIGHLANDERS in the suppression of the Indian Mutiny, in which it took, at least, as prominent a part as did any other regiment, and in which it won for itself never-dying fame. Not, however, did it gain its glory cheaply; between Sept. 30, 1857, and Dec. 31, 1859, the 93rd lost in killed, died of disease, wounded, accidents, and missing, 180 men, besides 58 who were invalided to England. The remainder of its history we must run over with the utmost brevity.

After its great exertions and sufferings, the 93rd stood much in need of rest, and means of restoration for the jaded constitutions of officers and men. Therefore, the route to Subhatoo, a hill station near Simla, was welcomed by the regiment, which set out for its new quarters on Feb. 27th, 1859, and arrived on April 13th. Here it remained till the beginning of November, when it was ordered to Umballah for drill and musketry instruction.

The 93rd was destined to make an unusually long stay in India, as not till 1870 did it again set foot on its native shores. During this time it was kept constantly moving from place to place, but these movements we need not, even if we had space, follow minutely. The two main events which marked this period of the regiment's history, were a most severe attack of cholera while at Peshawur, and a short campaign against the Mussulman fanatics of the Mahaban hills.

The regiment left Umballah in January 1860, its next station being Rawul Pindee,

where it arrived on March 9th, leaving it again on November 14, 1861, for Peshawur, which it reached on the 22nd. The health of the regiment here was at first particularly good, but in May 1862 rumours of the approach of cholera began to circulate. The rumours turned out to be too true, as an undoubted case of cholera occurred in the regiment on the 7th of July; and between this and the beginning of November, it was attacked four separate times, so that there was scarcely a man, woman, or child who did not suffer to a greater or less extent. Among the men there were 60 deaths, among the women 13, and among the children 12. Nor did the officers escape; several of them were attacked, of whom 4 succumbed,—Col. Macdonald, Major Middleton, Ensign Drysdale, and Dr Hope—making 89 in all. It was only by moving out and encamping at a distance from the pestilential town that the epidemic was got rid of, though for a long time after it the regiment was in a very feeble condition.

On the death of Col. Macdonald, Major Burroughs took command of the regiment, till the arrival shortly after of Col. Stisted.

The Record-Book pays a high and well-merited tribute to the admirable conduct of the men during this terrible and long continued attack from a mysterious and deadly foe, far more trying than the bloodiest struggle "i' the imminent deadly breach." There was scarcely a man who did not feel the workings of the cholera poison in his system; yet, notwithstanding, there was never any approach to panic, no murmuring or shrinking from duties of the most trying and irksome kind. At one time the same men would be on hospital fatigue duty almost every day, rubbing the cramped limbs of groaning, dying men. Yet no one ever complained or tried to hold back. So long as their strength held out, they not only performed the duties assigned to them willingly, but with a kindness, tenderness, and devotion which can never be forgotten by those who witnessed it.

It is only simple justice, also, to enter upon record a statement of the distinguished services rendered during this trying period to the regiment, by the surgeon, Dr Munro, and the assistant-surgeons, Bouchier, Hope, and Baxter. No man could have worked more faithfully than did Dr Munro. Night and day his thoughts were with the men, his zeal never flagged, his resources never failed, and he seemed never to think he had done enough. Even when his own strength gave way, and he was reduced to a shadow, he still clung to his post. None who witnessed his energy, skill, and love for the men will ever forget it.

On Nov. 3rd the regiment had reached Kuneh Khúl, from which it proceeded to Sealkote by Hattee on the Grand Trunk road, where the detachments from Peshawur, Chumkunah, and Cherat were waiting to receive it. Seal-kote was reached on December 30, 1862.

Into the details of the Umbeyla campaign against the Mussulman fanatics we need not enter, as the 93rd had really no fighting to do. The 93rd, under command of Col. Stisted, set out to join Sir Neville Chamberlain's force in the Umbeyla Pass, on November 3rd, reaching Permowli, in the Yuzufzai country, on November 25th. Thence a long detachment of the regiment with some artillery, by means of elephants, camels, mules, and ponies, under command of Major Dawson of the 93rd, set out on December 9th to join the force in the Umbeyla Pass, which was reached after a most fatiguing march.

The 93rd remained at the camp in the Umbeyla Pass until December 20th, taking its share in the camp and picquet duties. On December 15th, General Garvock, who had succeeded to the command, advanced with half his force against the enemy, leaving the other half behind to guard the camp. Among the latter half was the 93rd. After General Garvock's advance, the enemy attacked the camp, with a very trifling loss on the side of the British. General Garvock was completely successful, and the 93rd detachment joined the rest of the regiment at Nowakilla. From this, on December 23rd, under Col. Stisted, the regiment set out for Durbund, where it remained encamped till the end of January 1864. It again set out on February 1st, and after a long march reached Sealkote once more on the 27th.

At all the official inspections of the regiment the reports of the inspecting-officers were perfectly satisfactory.

The 93rd made a long stay at Sealkote, during which it sent detachments to garrison various forts in the surrounding district. It quitted Sealkote on Nov. 1st, 1866, and, under command of Col. Burroughs, proceeded to Jhansi, which, after a long march and many encampments, it reached on January 18, 1867.

During its stay at Jhansi, the regiment sustained a great loss, in the promotion, in March 1867, of Surgeon-Major William Munro, M.D., C.B., to be a Deputy Inspector-General of Hospitals. Dr Munro had been surgeon of the Sutherland Highlanders since 1854, when he joined the regiment whilst on its march

from Old Fort to the River Alma. He was present with the regiment throughout the Crimean and Indian campaigns, and we have already referred to his conduct during the attack of cholera at Peshawur. By his zeal, ability, and heroic devotion to duty, Dr Munro had endeared himself to every officer and man of the regiment, by all of whom, whilst rejoicing at his well-earned promotion, his departure was sincerely deplored. At his departure he expressed a wish to be enrolled as an honorary member of the officer's mess, a request that was acceded to with acclamation.

While at Jhansi, the colonel, General Alex. Fisher M'Intosh, K.H., died, Aug. 28, 1868. He had formerly been a major in the regiment, and was succeeded in the colonelcy by Lt.-General Charles Craufurd Hay.

In August 1869, the regiment was again scourged with cholera, a very large number being attacked, both at Jhansi and among the detachment at Sepree; the deaths, however, were only 11. During the latter part of September, moreover, and throughout October, the regiment was prostrated by a fever, which though not deadly, was very weakening. On October 20th, 50 per cent. of the soldiers at headquarters were on the sick list.

The 93rd, under Col. Burroughs, left Jhansi on December 27, 1869, en route for Bombay, to embark for home, after an absence of 12½ years. Partly by road and partly by rail, it proceeded leisurely by Cawnpoor, so full of sad memories, Allahabad, Jubbulpoor, Nagpoor, and Deolalee, to Bombay, which it did not reach till February 14, 1870.[5] On the same evening, officers, men, wives, and children, 681 in all, were safely on board the troop-ship "Jumna," which steamed out of the harbour on the following morning. By Suez, Alexandria (where the 93rd was transferred to the "Himalaya"), and Gibraltar, the regiment arrived off Portsmouth on March 21, sailing again next day for Leith, which it reached on the 25th, but did not disembark till the 28th. One detachment, under Col. Dawson, and another, under Bt. Lt.-Col. Brown, disembarked at Burntisland, the

---

[5] For an account of the very pleasant interchange of civilities between the officers of the 93rd and 79th, when both met at Nazpoor, see vol. ii. p. 718.

former proceeding to Stirling, and the latter to Perth. Headquarters, under Col. Burroughs, disembarked in the afternoon, and proceeded by rail to Aberdeen, and, after an absence of 19 years, was welcomed home to Scotland with unbounded enthusiasm by the citizens. Before leaving India, 117 non-commissioned officers and men had volunteered into other regiments remaining in the country.

After a stay of upwards of a year at Aberdeen, the 93rd was removed to Edinburgh, where on its arrival on June 15, 1871, notwithstanding the miserable state of the weather, it met with a warm welcome. One company was left at Ballater, as a guard of honour to the Queen, one at Aberdeen, one at Fort George, and another was sent to Greenlaw.

On Aug. 4, 1871, while the regiment was stationed at Edinburgh, it was presented with new colours by Her Grace the Duchess of Sutherland. The ceremony in the Queen's Park was witnessed by about 10,000 spectators. Accompanying the Duchess were the Duke of Sutherland and the Marquis of Stafford. After the old colours, worn and tattered by service in India, had been trooped, and the usual ceremonies gone through, Ensigns Cunliffe and Hannay advanced, and kneeling, were presented with the new colours by the Duchess, who addressed the regiment in a few appropriate and touching words. Colonel Burroughs made an exceedingly appropriate reply, in which he offered for Her Grace's acceptance the old colours of the regiment, which had waved over so many deadly struggles. The Duchess accepted the colours, returning the Queen's colour, however, to be placed over the memorial erected in St. Giles' Cathedral to the officers and soldiers who fell in the Crimea. Shortly after, however, it was decided that, owing to the little care taken of the colours at St Giles, they should be removed and sent to Dunrobin, to be placed beside the others. The Duke of Sutherland, in January 1873, was elected an honorary member of the officer's mess of the 93rd.

The Duke and Duchess, and a large party of ladies and gentlemen, were entertained at luncheon by the officers in the Picture Gallery of Holyrood. After a number of appropriate toasts had been drunk, the tables were cleared

away, and reel dancing commenced, and entered into enthusiastically. It is said that till then, no dancing had taken place in Holyrood since the days of Bonnie Prince Charlie; according to some even, not since the days of the "braw gallant" Charles II. The Duke and Duchess of Sutherland afterwards went to the Castle, and visited the non-commissioned officers and soldiers, and their wives and families, by all of whom they were enthusiastically received. A few days after, the sergeants gave a very successful ball to their friends to celebrate the occasion.

In the autumn of 1870, we may mention here, Her Majesty the Queen, having noticed that a detachment of the regiment, under, Capt. M. W. Hyslop, H.M.'s guard of honour at Ballater, wore kilts and plaids of hard tartan, and that after a march in wind and rain the men's knees were much scratched and cut by the sharp edge of this tartan, the Queen was graciously pleased to direct that soft instead of hard tartan be in future supplied to Highland regiments. Accordingly, as soon as the hard tartan in store was used up soft tartan kilts and plaids were issued to the non-commissioned officers and men of the 93rd; this took place in April 1872.

Another instance of Her Majesty's womanly disposition, and of her thoughtfulness and care for all about her, we shall mention. During her stay at Holyrood in August 1872, a captain's guard of the 93rd Highlanders was stationed at the palace. Her Majesty walked across from the palace to the guard-room, and satisfied herself that the guard was comfortably housed and properly taken care of, entering into conversation with the soldiers cooking the day's rations.

On Monday May 12, 1873, the 93rd left Edinburgh for Aldershot. On the previous Saturday, the Lord Provost (the Right Hon. James Cowan) and magistrates of Edinburgh publicly bade farewell in the name of the citizens to the regiment, the Lord Provost addressing officers and men in the courtyard of the Council Chambers, in a few appropriate and highly complimentary words, to which Col. Burroughs made a brief but feeling reply. The officers were then invited to a banquet in the Council Chambers, and the soldiers were also liberally regaled with refreshments.

On their way to Granton, on the 12th December, to embark on board the "Himalaya," the 93rd marched through crowds of admiring spectators, and passed the 91st Argyllshire Highlanders on the way to take their place.

It reached Aldershot on the 15th, and occupied D, G, and H lines of the North Camp.

Among the list of recipients of Her Majesty's favour on her 54th birthday (1873), Col. Burroughs' name appeared as nominated a C.B., making the ninth officer of the regiment who had been thus honoured.

Lieutenant-Colonel William M'Bean, V.C.
From a Photograph.

In July and August 1873, the 93rd, commanded by Colonel Burroughs, took part in the "Autumn Manœuvres" in Dartmoor, and received great praise from the generals under whom it served, as well as special notice from H.R.H. the Field Marshal, Commanding-in-Chief, for its smart appearance on parade, and the excellency of its skirmishing.

On August 8th Lt.-Col. J. M. Brown retired on full pay, after a service of 45 years in the regiment.

On Sept. 28th, Lt.-General Sir H. W. Stisted, K.C.B., was appointed honorary colonel, vice Lt.-General C. C. Hay deceased.

On Oct. 29th, Col. Burroughs, C.B., retired on half-pay, and was succeeded in command by Lt.-Col. M'Bean, V.C., who has well earned the honourable position he now fills.

Lieut.-Col. M'Bean commanded the 93rd during the manœuvres of 1874 at Aldershot, where it remained till the 2nd of July, when it removed to Cambridge Barracks, Woolwich.

The strength of the 93rd, one of the finest Highland regiments, at the present time (1875) is 31 officers, and 642 non-commissioned officers and men, including the depôt.

On the next page we give an engraving of the splendid Centre-Piece of plate belonging to the officer's mess, which was designed by one of the officers of the regiment. The sculpture on one side is supposed to represent the shot-riven wall of an outwork at Sebastopol, where an officer of the 93rd contemplates the dead body of a Russian soldier lying near a private of the regiment, who reclines severely wounded, the regimental pipe-major, in a commanding position above the group, playing "the gathering." The other side (which we engrave) has an exact reproduction from a photograph of one of the gateway towers of the Secunder Bagh at Lucknow, for an account of the storming of which place in November 1857, see pages 790, 791. An officer and private of the 93rd, and a dead Sepoy, emblematise that terrible Indian struggle and its result. Ornamental silver shields on each side of the ebony pedestal bear on one side the badge of the regiment, and on the other the presentation inscription, describing it as a memorial from some of the officers (whose names run round a silver rim on the top of the pedestal) of the part taken by the regiment in the Crimean war of 1854, and suppression of the Indian Mutiny in 1857.

This splendid work of art was inspected by Her Majesty the Queen at Windsor Castle in July 1870, when she was graciously pleased to express her approval both of the design and workmanship. It cost the subscribers nearly £500; and when we consider that it exactly reproduces the dresses, &c., of the regiment at the period represented, time will greatly enhance its present value. The uniform and accoutrements of the Russian soldier are of one of the regiments overthrown by the 93rd at the Alma, and those of the Sepoy the dress of one of those rebel corps entirely annihilated in the Secunder Bagh.

We have the pleasure of giving, on the Plate of Colonels of the 91st, 92nd, and 93rd regiments, the portrait of Major-General Wm. Wemyss of Wemyss, from a painting by Raeburn, at Wemyss Castle, Fife; and that of Sir Henry W. Stisted, K.C.B., from a photograph.

CENTRE-PIECE OF OFFICERS' PLATE.
Described on page 800

SUCCESSION LIST OF COLONELS AND LIEUTENANT-COLONELS OF THE 93RD SUTHERLAND HIGHLANDERS.

COLONELS.*

Names and Titles.	Date of Appointment.	Date of Retirement.	Remarks.
William Wemyss of Wemyss	Aug. 25, 1800	1822	Died.
Sir Thomas Hislop, Bart., G.C.B.	Feb. 8, 1822	June 4, 1822	Removed to 51st Foot.
Sir Hudson Lowe, K.C.B.	June 4, 1822		
Sir John Cameron, K.C.B.	July 23, 1832	May 31, 1833	Removed to 9th Foot.
Sir Jasper Nicolls, K.C.B.	May 31, 1833	July 15, 1840	Removed to 38th Foot.
Sir James Douglas, K.C.B.	June 15, 1840	April 10, 1850	Removed to 42nd Royal Highlanders.
William Wemyss...............	Mar. 10, 1850	Nov. 30, 1852	Died Colonel.
Lt.-General Edward Parkinson, C.B.	Dec. 10, 1852	1858	Died Colonel.
Lord Clyde (Sir Colin Campbell), G.C.B., K.S.I., D.C.L........	Jan. 15, 1858	June 22, 1860	Removed to Coldstream Guards. Raised to the Peerage, Aug. 16, 1858. Died Aug. 14, 1863.
Lt.-General William Sutherland,	June 4, 1860	1862	Died Colonel.
Lt.-General Alex. Fisher Macintosh, K.H.	June 3, 1862	Aug. 28, 1868	Died Colonel.
Lt.-General Charles Cranfurd Hay	Aug. 29, 1868		Died Colonel.
Lt.-General Sir Henry William Stisted, K.C.B.	Sept. 28, 1873		

LIEUTENANT-COLONELS.

Alexander Halket	Aug. 25, 1800	May 3, 1810	To 104th Foot.
George Johnstone....	May 3, 1810		
Andrew Creagh	Sept. 29, 1814	Mar. 7, 1822	Removed to 51st Foot.
William Wemyss......	Mar. 16, 1815		
Henry Milling.....................	Mar. 7, 1822	Dec. 26, 1822	From 51st Foot. Retired without joining the regiment.
The Hon. Sir Charles Gordon	Dec. 26, 1822		Retired on Half-pay. Died in command of 42nd in 1835.
Duncan M'Gregor	Mar. 23, 1826		
Robert Spark	July 28, 1838		
Lorenzo Rothe....................	Feb. 21, 1852		
William Bernard Ainslie, C.B.....	Oct. 21, 1853	Jan. 25, 1856	Retired.
Alex. Sebastian Leith Hay	April 16, 1855		
The Hon. Adrian Hope.............	Jan. 25, 1856	April 16, 1858	Retired on Half-pay, Nov. 10, 1856, and in March 1857 brought in from Half-pay as second Lt.-Col. Killed in action, April 16, 1858.
John A. Ewart, C.B.	April 16, 1858	Sept. 30, 1859	Exchanged to 78th.
Henry William Stisted, C.B.......	Sept. 30, 1859		Exchanged from 78th.
Robert Lockhart Ross...............	Dec. 21, 1860		
Frederick William Traill Burroughs, C.B.	Aug. 10, 1864	Oct. 29, 1873	Retired on Half-pay.
Erskine Scott Francis G. Dawson	Nov. 29, 1864		
William M'Bean, V.C.	Oct. 29, 1873		

* We are sorry that the dates are so defective; but, after making every exertion to obtain them, we have not been able to fill up all the blanks.

APPENDIX TO THE 42ND ROYAL HIGHLAND REGIMENT, THE BLACK WATCH.

1873–1875.

The Ashantee Campaign—Malta.

WE left the Black Watch at Devonport in the beginning of 1873, with no likelihood then of its being called upon to engage in actual service. On the Gold Coast of Africa, however, mischief had been brewing for many years, and during the course of 1873 the conduct of Coffee Calcallee, king of the barbarous country of Ashantee, had been such that unless a decisive blow were immediately struck, Britain would be compelled to resign possession of her territory in that part of the African coast; and, as our readers no doubt know, that territory had been considerably increased by the cession to Britain, in 1872, of the Dutch possessions on the Gold Coast. Thus in 1873 the coast for many miles, both east and west of Cape Coast Castle, the seat of government, was under the British protection. The principal native population of the territory are the Fantees, who from years of oppression had been reduced to a state of abject cowardice, as was but too well shown in the brief campaign against their inland enemy, the King of Ashantee. The Ashantee territory extends northwards from the Gold Coast to a distance of about 300 miles, its middle being traversed by the River Prah, which flows in the upper part of its course from east to west, but turns at Prah-su towards the south, and reaches the sea at Chamah, to the west of Cape Coast Castle. The capital of the Ashantee territory is Coomassie, about 100 miles directly north from Cape Coast Castle, and about half that distance north of the bend of the Prah, at the town of Prah-su. The population of Coomassie had been very much exaggerated. At the commencement of the campaign it was probably between

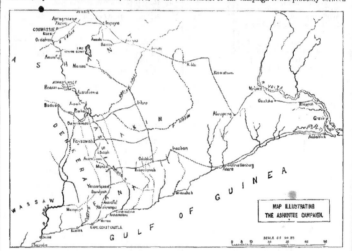

MAP ILLUSTRATING THE ASHANTEE CAMPAIGN.

20,000 and 30,000. Here the despotic King of Ashantee lived in great state, and in the indulgence of the superstitions and terribly cruel practices known as the Ashantee "Customs." It is hoped that the lesson which has been read him by a handful of British soldiers will ultimately lead to the abolition of these "Customs," and to a general amelioration of the miserable lot of the peoples in that part of Africa.

We need not enter upon the very complicated event which led to the British Government sending out an expedition, under the determined, clear-headed, and accomplished Sir Garnet Wolseley, C.B., to let this barbarous despot know the strength of the British arm. The measures hitherto taken to keep the Ashantees in their place had been so inadequate, that their kings had become intolerably bold and confident, and had indeed acquired an utter contempt of the British power as exhibited on the Gold Coast. King Coffee Calcallee resolved, about the end of 1872, to strike such a blow as would utterly stamp out the British

rule on that coast. And in January 1873 an army of 60,000 warriors—and the Ashantees though cruel are brave and warlike—was in full march upon Cape Coast Castle. The whole force at the disposal of Colonel Harley, in whom the administration was vested, was about 1000 men, mainly West India troops and Houssa police, with some marines. It was estimated that a contingent of about 60,000 would be raised from the friendly tribes, but this number figured only on paper. By April the Ashantees were within a few miles of Cape Coast Castle. Things were getting desperate, when a small force of marines, under Lt.-Col. Festing, arrived from England in the beginning of June. With this and other small reinforcements, the English managed to keep the barbarians at bay until the arrival, on October 2nd, on the Gold Coast of Major-General Sir Garnet J. Wolseley, who had been selected to command a force which was being organised in England to sweep back the threatening horde. He was accompanied only by his staff.

and immediately on landing set about clearing the Ashantees out of several towns in the neighbourhood of Cape Coast Castle. Sir Garnet's clear-headedness and admirable power of organisation soon inspired the few troops at his command with perfect confidence; and by the time the force of which the 42nd formed part arrived at the Gold Coast, everything was prepared for an advance towards the capital of the Ashantee kingdom. We cannot linger over the preliminary work in which Lord Gifford, Colonel Festing, the unfortunate Lieut. Eardley-Wilmot, and other officers whose names are now familiar to the British public, played a prominent part. By the end of November the Ashantee force was in full retreat on Coomassie, and by the end of December General Wolseley with his staff and some 500 sailors and marines was at Prah-su

Major-General Sir Garnet J. Wolseley, K.C.M.G., C.B.
From a photograph taken Oct. 22, 1874.

Meantime the small force which had been organising in England was on its way to the scene of operations. The 42nd was the principal regiment of the line, as a large part of the 23rd Welsh Fusileers had to re-embark, owing to the desertion of some thousands of native carriers who had been engaged to carry the necessary baggage through the unwholesome country. As we said at the conclusion of the history of the 79th, a considerable number of volunteers from that regiment accompanied the Black Watch, which left Portsmouth on the 4th of December 1873, and arrived off Cape Coast Castle on the 17th, disembarking on the 3rd and 4th of January 1874. Besides the 23rd, 42nd, and 2nd battalion Rifle Brigade, there were detachments of Royal Artillery, Royal Engineers, and Royal Marines, which, with the force already on the ground, formed the army with which Sir

Garnet Wolseley was to pierce into the very heart of the Ashantee kingdom, through a country of marshes and matted forests, the growth of centuries, and forming an almost impenetrable ambush for the enemy, who knew how to take advantage of it. As Lord Derby remarked, this was to be "an engineers' and doctors' war." The engineers worked admirably in the construction of roads, bridges, telegraphs, and camps; and it became simply a question whether the British soldiers would be able to hold out against the pestiferous climate long enough to enable them to reach Coomassie and return to the Gold Coast ere the heavy rains set in in the early spring. Happily the energy, skill, and knowledge of General Wolseley were quite equal to the emergency; and backed by an able and determined staff, and his small force of brave and willing soldiers, he accomplished his mission with complete success. All possible preparations were made on the road to Prah-su, previous to the commencement of the march of the main body, in order that not a moment of the precious time might be lost,—the white troops must be back and ready to embark by the end of February.

We have said that at starting there was considerable difficulty in procuring a sufficient number of native carriers for the baggage of the small force. This caused some delay after the landing of the force at Mansu, some distance to the north of Cape Coast Castle,—which delay, a 42nd officer said with truth, "did more harm to our men than all the hard work in Ashantee." To Europeans idleness in such a climate is utterly prostrating. In the dearth of carriers, the 42nd men themselves, greatly to their honour, volunteered to act as porters. On the 23rd of January General Wolseley with the advanced guard had crossed the Adansi Hills, and fixed his headquarters at Fomannah, the palace of the Adansi king. On the 26th Colonel M'Leod of the 42nd, who commanded the advanced guard, took Borborassie. After this service the 23rd Fusileers, 42nd, Rifle Brigade, the 2nd West India Regiment, and the Naval Brigade, which by this time had reached Prahsu, were brought forward, resting on Insarfu. They encamped on the night of the 30th about that place, and about two miles north of it, towards the enemy's main position at Amoaful. The advanced guard, under Colonel M'Leod, was at Quarman, within a mile or two of the enemy's position.

The entire country hereabout is one dense mass of brush, penetrated by a few narrow lanes, "where the ground, hollowed by rains, is so uneven and steep at the sides as to give scanty footing. A passenger," to quote the *London News* narrative, "between the two walls of foliage, may wander for hours before he finds that he has mistaken his path. To cross the country from one narrow clearing to another, axes or knives must be used at every step. There is no looking over the hedge in this oppressive and bewildering maze. Such was the battlefield of January 31st. The enemy's army was never seen, but its numbers are reported by Ashantees to have been 15,000 or 20,000. Its chief commander was Amanquatia, the Ashantee general. The Ashantees were generally armed with muskets, firing slugs; but some had rifles. As they were entirely concealed in the bush, while our countrymen stood in the lane or in the newly-cut spaces, precision of aim was no advantage to our side."

The main body of the enemy was encamped on the hill rising towards the town of Amoaful; but thousands of them also must have been skulking in the bush through which the small British force had to march before reaching the encampment. At early dawn on the 31st the British force moved upon the village of Egginassie, where the first shots were fired from an Ashantee ambush. The force was carefully arranged to suit the nature of the ground, with a front column, a left column, a right column, and a rear column, all so disposed that when they closed up they would form a square, the columns taking in spaces to the right and left of the central line of advance, so as to prevent any attack on the advancing front centre.

The front column was commanded by Brigadier-General Sir Archibald Alison, Bart., C.B. It consisted of the 42nd, under Major Baird, Major Duncan Macpherson, and Major Scott, a detachment of the 23rd Fusileers, Captain Rait's Artillery, manned by Houssas, and a detachment of the Royal Engineers. The left column was commanded by Brigadier-Colonel M'Leod of the 42nd, and the right column by Lt.-Col. Evelyn Wood, 90th Light Infantry; part of the right column consisted of miscellaneous native African levies, under Captain Furze of the 42nd. The paths through the jungle were cut for each column of troops by large parties of native labourers.

Thus clearing their way through the jungle, and often scarcely able to obtain foothold from the slippery state of the marshy ground, the force advanced against the enemy. When the front of the small force had got a few hundred yards beyond the village of Egginassie, it was assailed by a tremendous fire of musketry from an unseen foe, very trying to the nerves even of an experienced and well-trained soldier. By this time five companies of the 42nd were in skirmishing order. The slugs were dropping thick and fast; had they been bullets, scarcely a man of the Black Watch would have lived to tell the tale. As it was, there were few of the officers who did not receive a scratch, and nearly 100 of the men were wounded. Major Macpherson was shot in the leg, but limped on with a stick, and kept the command for some time, when he was compelled to give it up to Major Scott. It was at this critical moment that Capt. Rait's gun—there was no room for two—came into action at 50 yards from the enemy, on the direct line of advance. The shells fired at that short distance, with deadly effect, soon forced the enemy to clear the road. In a moment, as they gave way upon their own left upon the road, the 42nd pushed them in thence along the whole line, and they began to yield another 50 yards or more, and Rait's gun again came into action against the enemy, who had at once taken up a fresh position, as the bush prevented the Black Watch from forming quickly.

Again the enemy per force gave way before the shells along the road. Again the 42nd took instant advantage of it, and the enemy rolled back. The men were now in such high spirits, according to the account of one who was present, that the terrors of the bush were no more. Sir Archibald Alison saw that the moment had come. He ordered the pipers to play. Down together, with a ringing cheer, went the splendid regiment under his orders, straight at the concealed foe. Away rolled every Ashantee in front of them; away

down one hill and up another, on which stood the village of Amoaful itself. By half-past eleven the village was in the hands of the British force. It was not, however, till after two that the fighting was over, as the flank parties, the left as we have said, commanded by the Colonel of the 42nd, had much more trouble and numerous casualties in fighting and clearing their way through the bush. By the time mentioned, however, the last Ashantee had shown his heels in full retreat. Of the 42nd Bt.-Major Baird was severely wounded, from which he died at Sierra Leone on the 6th of March. Major Macpherson, Captains Creagh and Whitehead, Lts. Berwick, Stevenson, Cumberland, and Mowbray, and 104 men wounded.

On Feb. 1st, the day after this signal victory, the adjacent village of Becquch was captured and destroyed by Col. M'Leod, with the naval brigade and several

Sir John M'Leod, K.C.B

From a photograph.

detachments, supported by portions of the 42nd and 23rd. On the 2nd, the army was at Agemanu, six miles beyond Amoaful, every inch of the ground between the two places being disputed by the enemy. On this day Lt. Wauchope of the 42nd was slightly wounded. On the 3rd, Sir Garnet moved by the westerly road, branching off to the left from Agemanu, through Adwabin and Detchiasa to the river Dah or Ordah, the enemy again opposing the advance and hanging round the flanks of the force. King Coffee Calcallee had tried to stop the advance of the British by offering to pay an indemnity, but in vain, as no reliance whatever could be put in any of his promises; the King therefore resolved to dispute the passage of the river. The battle of Ordah-su, as it is called, was fought on Feb. 4th, and lasted seven hours. When the ... reached the Dah on the evening of the 3rd, it was a tremendous downpour of rain, and it was not till next morning that the engineers managed to complete their bridge over the river. By this bridge, on the morning of the 4th, the advanced guard, the rifle brigade and some native troops under Colonel M'Leod, crossed the bridge, and soon found itself fiercely engaged with very large numbers of the enemy, who had crowded into the villages on each side of the road, from which it was found exceedingly difficult to dislodge them. The first shots were fired about 7 A M, and Sir Garnet Wolseley in his official despatch, dated Coomassie, Feb 5th, thus describes the rest :—

"The advanced guard, under the command of Col M'Lead, 42nd Highlanders, was brought to a stand still shortly after the advance began, and a general action soon developed itself, lasting for more than six hours. The enemy did not, however, fight with the same courage as at Amoaful, for although their resistance was most determined, their fire was wild, and they did not generally attack us at such close quarters as in the former action

"The village of Ordahsu having been carried by the rifle brigade at nine o'clock, I massed all my force there, having previously passed all the reserve ammunition, field hospitals, and supplies through the troops, who held the road between the river and the village, a distance of about a mile. The enemy then attacked the village with large numbers from all sides, and for some hours we could make no progress, but steadily held our ground. The 42nd Highlanders being then sent to the front, advanced with pipes playing, and carried the enemy's position to the north of the village in the most gallant style, Captain Rait's artillery doing most effective service in covering the attack, which was led by Col M'Leod.

"After some further fighting on the front line, a panic seems to have seized the enemy, who fled along the road to Coomassie in complete rout. Although the columns they had detailed to assault our flanks and rear continued for some time afterwards to make partial attacks upon the village, we followed close upon the enemy's heels into Coomassie. The town was still occupied by large numbers of armed men, who did not attempt to resist. The King had fled no one knew whither. Our troops had undergone a most fatiguing day's work, no water fit for drinking having been obtained during the action or the subsequent advance, and the previous night's rest having been broken by a tornado, which drenched our bivouac. It was nearly six o'clock when the troops formed up in the main street of Coomassie, and gave three cheers for the Queen."

The 42nd was the first to enter the capital, the pipers playing at its head, about half past four in the afternoon, by half past seven the whole force was inside Coomassie, and the discomfiture of the Ashantees was complete, the king himself having fled.

Mr H M Stanley, the well known correspondent of the *New York Herald*, in describing the advance on Coomassie, wrote as follows of the bravery of the Black Watch :—

'The conduct of the 42nd Highlanders on many fields has been considerably belauded, but mere laudation is not enough for the gallantry which has distinguished this regiment when in action. Its bearing has been beyond praise as a model regiment, exceedingly disciplined, and individually nothing could surpass the standing and gallantry which distinguished each member of the 42nd or the Black Watch. They proceeded along the well ambushed road as if on parade, by twos. 'The Forty second will fire by companies, front rank to the right, rear rank to the left,' shouted Col Macleod. 'A company, front rank fire' 'rear rank fire!' and so on, and thus vomiting out twoscore of bullets to the right and twoscore to

the left, the companies volleyed and thundered as they marched past the ambuscades, the bagpipes playing the cheers rising from the throats of the lusty Scots until the forest rang again with discordant medley of musketry, bagpipe music, and vocal sounds. It was the audacious spirit and true military bearing on the part of the Highlanders, as they moved down the road toward Coomassie, which challenged admiration this day. Very many were borne back frightfully disfigured and seriously wounded, but the regiment never halted nor wavered, on it went, until the Ashantees, perceiving it useless to fight against men who would advance heedless of ambuscades, rose from their coverts, and fled panic stricken towards Coomassie, being perforated by balls when ever they showed themselves to the hawk eyed Scots. Indeed, I only wish I had enough time given me to frame in fit words the unqualified admiration which the conduct of the 42nd kindled in all who saw or heard of it. One man exhibited himself eminently brave among brave men. His name was Thomas Adams. It is said that he led the way to Coomassie, and kept himself about ten yards ahead of his regiment, the target for many hundred guns, but that, despite the annoying noise of iron and leaden slugs, the man bounded on the road like a well trained hound on a hot scent. This example, together with the cool, calm commands of Col Macleod, had a marvellous effect upon the Highland battalion.'

In the action on the 4th, Capt Moore and Lts Grogan and Wauchope of the 42nd were wounded, the latter severely this time, 14 men were also wounded.

Thus, in the space of about a month, by the decision and energy of the leader of the expedition, and the willingness of his officers and troops, was the great object of the campaign accomplished in the most masterly manner, and the Ashantees humbled as they had never been before, and taught a lesson they are not likely soon to forget. As during the 5th there seemed no hope of the treacherous king coming to terms, and as it was absolutely necessary for the safety of the troops that the return march should be immediately commenced, Sir Garnet resolved to destroy Coomassie, and set out at once. Having, therefore sent off all the wounded, he issued orders for an advance on the morning of the 6th. Early on that morning the homeward movements commenced, headed by the naval brigade, and covered by a rear guard of the 42nd, which did not retire till the town had been set on fire in every quarter, and the mines which had been placed under the palace fired. A tornado had raged during the previous night, but the destruction of the town by fire was complete.

Thus the campaign was virtually at an end, and Gen Wolseley made all possible haste to bring his little army back to Cape Coast Castle, which, notwithstanding the swollen state of the rivers, he accomplished by February 19th. While on his way back Gen Wolseley received the unqualified submission of the humbled king. No time was lost in getting the troops out of the influence of the deadly climate. Without delay, therefore, the embarkation took place. The 42nd embarked in the "Nebraska" on the 23rd, and sailed on the 27th in the "Sarmatian," the steamer which brought them from England. It arrived at Portsmouth on March 23rd, where it was received with tremendous enthusiasm. All had suffered more or less from the effects of the climate, but what with good constitutions and care, the 42nd in course of time regained its "wonted health and strength." Previous to its embarkation for Ashantee the 42nd, like the other regiments, was provided with suits of dark grey (retaining in the head dress their red feathers), as being much more appropriate for the work to be done than the usual regimental costume. The men's kits were, however, on board the "Sarmatian," and the national garb was therefore donned before landing, so that the regiment came ashore in all the glory of its national garb.

Among the officers specially mentioned by Sir Garnet Wolseley for having performed prominent services during the campaign were Col. Macleod, C.B., who was afterwards made a K.C.B.; Majors Macpherson and Scott; Capts. Farquharson, V.C., Furze, and Kidston; and Lt. Wauchope. The special thanks of Parliament were awarded to the troops, and honours were showered upon the Commander by the Queen and country. Major Macpherson and Scott were made Lieutenant-Colonels and C.B.'s., and had the brevet of lieutenant-colonel conferred on them. Captains Bayly, Farquharson, V.C., and Furze, were made Bt.-Majors. The Victoria Cross was conferred on Sergt. Samuel M'Gaw. The non-commissioned officers and men selected to have medals "for distinguished conduct in the field" at the hand of the Sovereign—and had them presented by Her Majesty the Queen at Windsor Castle on the 18th of May 1874, in presence of Colonel Sir John M'Leod, K.C.B., commanding the regiment, were— Wm. Street, sergt.-instructor of musketry; sergt. Henry Barton; privates John White, George Ritchie, George Cameron, and William Bell; piper James Wetherspoon; privates Henry Jones, Wm. Nichol, and Thomas Adams. Also, Sergeant-Major Barclay was awarded the medal for "meritorious services" for distinguished conduct during the campaign.

In conclusion, we think the following is worth recording; it is told in a letter from a soldier of the 42nd, which appeared in the *Inverness Advertiser*:—

"We were the objects of great curiosity on the part of the Fantees (natives of this bit of the country), who hung round the camp all day in crowds, and numbers of whom had followed us from a large village through which we passed just as the sun was rising,

our pipes making the whole street ring with the tune of 'Hey, Johnnie Cope,' which they struck up just as we entered the village; the whole place was in an uproar at once, the people rushing out of their huts in the utmost consternation, evidently thinking the Ashantees were on them. The pipes were something new; bugles they had heard something of, but bagpipes were unknown instruments of warfare to them. As soon as they realised that it was not their dreaded foes who were present, they began to approach cautiously, but catching sight of the pipers, who still adhere to the garb of old Gaul in defiance of War-Office regulations, a fresh stampede took place, to the intense amusement of our men; nor did the boldest of them venture to come near until the rear of the detachment was clear of the village. By the time, however, that we reached our halting-place, we were surrounded by a considerable crowd, the pipers still forming the attraction, the natives evidently looking on these as officers or dignitaries of the very highest importance, and the pipes themselves as some kind of mysterious instrument by which the enemy is to be vanquished. So far, indeed, did their respect for these personages carry them, that a war-dance in their honour was got up, and carried on with great vigour, to the evident disgust of big Duncan, our pipe-major, who wanted to know what he was made a peep show of for, and if they had never seen a kiltie before."

The regiment remained at Portsmouth until Nov. 15th, when it embarked for Malta under command of Sir John Macleod, K.C.B. Its strength on embarkation was 26 officers, 43 sergeants, 21 drummers and pipers, and 630 rank and file. It arrived at Malta, after calling at Queenstown, on the 27th, and, after being a few days under canvas, went into Isola barracks, &c., the same that was occupied by the regiment in 1832, and again in 1844.

FENCIBLE CORPS.

The plan of raising Fencible corps in the Highlands was first proposed and carried into effect by Mr Pitt (afterwards Earl of Chatham), in the year 1759. During the three preceding years both the fleets and armies of Great Britain had suffered reverses, and to retrieve the national character great efforts were necessary. In England county militia regiments were raised for internal defence in the absence of the regular army; but it was not deemed prudent to extend the system to Scotland, the inhabitants of which, it was supposed, could not yet be safely entrusted with arms. Groundless as the reasons for this caution undoubtedly were in regard to the Lowlands, it would certainly have been hazardous at a time when the Stuarts and their adherents were still plotting a restoration to have armed the clans. An exception, however, was made in favour of the people of Argyll and Sutherland, and accordingly letters of service were issued to the Duke of Argyll, then the most influential and powerful nobleman in Scotland, and the Earl of Sutherland to raise, each of them, a Fencible regiment within his district. Unlike the militia regiments which were raised by ballot, the Fencibles were to be raised by the ordinary mode of recruiting, and like the regiments of the line, the officers were to be appointed and their commissions signed by the king. The same system was followed at different periods down to the year 1799, the last of the Fencible regiments having been raised in that year.

The following is a list of the Highland Fencible regiments according to the chronological order of the

commissions, with the date of their embodiment and reduction:—

1. The Argyll Fencibles (No. 1), 1759–1763.
2. The Sutherland Fencibles (No. 1), 1759–1763.
3. The Argyll or Western Fencibles (No. 2), 1778–1783.
4. The Gordon Fencibles, 1778–1783.
5. The Sutherland Fencibles (No. 2), 1779–1783.
6. The Grant or Strathspey Fencibles, 1793–1799.
7. The Breadalbane Fencibles (three battalions), 1793 and 1794–1799 and 1802.
8. The Sutherland Fencibles (No. 3), 1793–1797.
9. The Gordon Fencibles (No. 2), 1793–1799.
10. The Argyll Fencibles (No. 3), 1793–1799.
11. The Rothesay and Caithness Fencibles (two battalions), 1794 and 1795–1802.
12. The Dumbarton Fencibles, 1794–1802.
13. The Reay Fencibles, 1794–1802.
14. The Inverness-shire Fencibles, 1794–1802.
15. The Fraser Fencibles, 1794–1802.
16. The Glengarry Fencibles, 1794–1802.
17. The Caithness Legion, 1794–1802.
18. The Perthshire Fencibles, 1794–1802.
19. Argyll Fencibles (No. 4), 1794–1802.
20. Lochaber Fencibles, 1799–1802.
21. The Clan-Alpine Fencibles, 1799–1802.
22. The Ross-shire Fencibles, 1796–1802.
23. Regiment of the Isles, or Macdonald Fencibles, 1798.
24. Argyll Fencibles (No. 5), 1798–1802.
25. The Ross and Cromarty Rangers, 1799–1802.
26. The Macleod Fencibles, 1799–1802.

INDEX.